ROTH FAMILY FOUNDATION

Music in America Imprint

Michael P. Roth
and Sukey Garcetti
have endowed this
imprint to honor the
memory of their parents,
Julia and Harry Roth,
whose deep love of music
they wish to share
with others.

The publisher gratefully acknowledges the generous support
of the Music in America Endowment Fund of the University
of California Press Foundation, which was established by a major
gift from Sukey and Gil Garcetti, Michael P. Roth, and the
Roth Family Foundation.

Beyond Reason

The publisher gratefully acknowledges the Joseph Kerman
Endowment of the American Musicological Society, funded in
part by the National Endowment for the Humanities and the
Andrew W. Mellon Foundation.

Beyond Reason

Wagner contra Nietzsche

Karol Berger

UNIVERSITY OF CALIFORNIA PRESS

University of California Press, one of the most distinguished university presses in the United States, enriches lives around the world by advancing scholarship in the humanities, social sciences, and natural sciences. Its activities are supported by the UC Press Foundation and by philanthropic contributions from individuals and institutions. For more information, visit www.ucpress.edu.

University of California Press
Oakland, California

© 2017 by Karol Berger
First paperback printing 2024

Library of Congress Cataloging-in-Publication Data

Names: Berger, Karol, 1947– author.
Title: Beyond reason : Wagner contra Nietzsche / Karol Berger.
Description: Oakland, California : University of California Press, [2016] | Includes bibliographical references and index.
Identifiers: LCCN 2016015325 | ISBN 9780520292758 (cloth) | ISBN 9780520966130 (ebook) | ISBN 9780520409255 (pb)
 Subjects: LCSH: Wagner, Richard, 1813–1883. Operas. | Wagner, Richard, 1813–1883—Philosophy. | Nietzsche, Friedrich Wilhelm, 1844–1900— Criticism and interpretation. | Operas—Philosophy and aesthetics.
Classifica tion: LCC ML410.W13 B45 2016 | DDC 782.1092—dc23
LC record available at https://lccn.loc.gov/2016015325

25 24
10 9 8 7 6 5 4 3 2 1

For Anna, Trine, Matthew, and Zuzia

There are questions in which man is not entitled to a decision about truth and untruth; all the highest questions, all the highest value problems, lie beyond human reason. To comprehend the limits of reason—that alone is truly philosophy.

FRIEDRICH NIETZSCHE, *THE ANTICHRIST*,
TRANS. WALTER KAUFMANN

Thinking begins only when we have come to know that reason, glorified for centuries, is the most stiff-necked adversary of thought.

MARTIN HEIDEGGER, "THE WORD OF NIETZSCHE:
'GOD IS DEAD,'" TRANS. WILLIAM LOVITT

CONTENTS

Preface   xi

Prologue: Beyond Autonomy   1
The Uncanny Grace: A Gloss on Kleist's Marionettes   1
Reason   10
Beyond Reason   22
   History   22
   Nation   25
   Will   34
Religion, the Enlightenment, the Counter-Enlightenment: The New Configuration   44

PART ONE

1. The Secret of Music-Dramatic Form: Music Drama as Opera   49
2. *Der Ring des Nibelungen*: The Anarchist Utopia   62
   Das Rheingold: *The Fall*   65
   Die Walküre: *How One Becomes Human*   78
      Act 1: Becoming Wagner   78
      Act 2: Becoming Brünnhilde   99
      Act 3: Waiting for the Hero   113
   Siegfried: *How One Becomes a Hero*   118
      Act 1: Getting the Sword   119

Act 2: Using It	124
Act 3: The Awakening	129
Götterdämmerung: *The Apocalypse*	140
Prologue: The Past and the Future	140
Act 1: The Entrapment 1	147
Act 2: The Entrapment 2	157
Act 3: Death and Transfiguration	164
The Myth of Revolution	178

PART TWO

3. *Tristan und Isolde:* The Erotic Utopia — 193
   - The Lyrical Axis — 194
   - The Narrative Axis — 203
   - The Orchestral Strand — 217
   - The Music-Dramatic Form — 220
   - The Myth of Will — 226
   - Postscript — 234

4. *Die Meistersinger von Nürnberg*: Politics after *Tristan* — 242
   - Act 1: The Knight's Failure — 242
   - Act 2: The Clerk's Failure — 249
   - Act 3, Part 1: A Lesson in Poetics — 257
   - Act 3, Part 2: The Shoemaker's Triumph — 267
   - The Myth of Nation — 279

5. *Parsifal*: Ethics after *Tristan* — 293
   - The Communion Sequences of Acts 1 and 3 — 293
   - The Monologues of Acts 1 and 3 — 308
   - Act 2: The Kiss of Self-Knowledge — 329
   - The Music-Dramatic Form — 335
   - Eros and Agape — 339
   - The Myth of Redemption — 345

Epilogue: Wagner contra Nietzsche — 359
- Wagner and Nietzsche: A History of the Relationship — 363
- Becoming Nietzsche — 376
- Nietzsche contra Wagner, Wagner contra Nietzsche — 393

Appendix 1. Das Rheingold: The Music-Dramatic Plan	*413*
Appendix 2. Die Walküre: The Music-Dramatic Plan	*417*
Appendix 3. Siegfried: The Music-Dramatic Plan	*423*
Appendix 4. Götterdämmerung: The Music-Dramatic Plan	*427*
Appendix 5. Tristan und Isolde: The Music-Dramatic Plan	*431*
Appendix 6. Die Meistersinger von Nürnberg: The Music-Dramatic Plan	*437*
Appendix 7. Parsifal: The Music-Dramatic Plan	*445*
Acknowledgments	*449*
Abbreviations Used in Notes	*453*
Notes	*455*
Works Consulted	*501*
Index	*517*

PREFACE

The story has often been told and will be known to anyone likely to open this book. In May 1849, Richard Wagner, the *Kapellmeister* of the Royal Saxon Court Opera in Dresden and already the author of three operas (*Der fliegende Holländer, Tannhäuser,* and *Lohengrin*) destined to be recognized as the core of the German romantic repertoire, took an active part in the uprising against the government of Saxony. A few weeks later, the revolution having failed, he found himself an exile in Switzerland, without employment or access to the German opera houses on which his professional life depended, and he took the opportunity of the enforced leisure to rethink his operatic theory and practice so radically that the eventual fruits of this reinvention (*Der Ring des Nibelungen, Tristan und Isolde, Die Meistersinger von Nürnberg,* and *Parsifal*) deserve a new generic label of music dramas. These four works of the second half of the composer's career (four or seven, if one wants to count the four component evenings of the *Ring* tetralogy separately) are the subject of the present book.

In writing it, I had two aims in mind. First, I wanted to penetrate the "secret" (to use Alfred Lorenz's locution) of large-scale form in Wagner's music dramas, to understand how the composer shaped each act and each work as a whole. At the same time I also wanted to find out whether, and to what extent, his large forms provide clues as to how he wanted his dramas to be heard and understood. From early on, the originality and novelty of Wagner's formal principles and solutions provoked skeptics. Friedrich Nietzsche, in many ways (but not in this one) the most perceptive of Wagner's critics, quipped that the composer was "our greatest *miniaturist* in music," thus at once praising Wagner's uncanny ability to capture the most subtle stirrings of his characters' souls in small but eloquently expressive gestures and blaming him for his inability to weld such gestures into larger wholes.[1] I am not the first, of course, to answer such accusations (and neither was Lorenz, though his answer was delivered at the most doggedly systematic length),[2] and I shall have to leave it to my readers to decide whether the answer I propose here is at all persuasive. I can only note that the answer has been something of a surprise, in that it turned out to be different from what I had expected as I began the project. Like so many of my predecessors (Lorenz included), I began under the influence of Wagner's own theories (those of *Oper und Drama*, in particular), and these naturally emphasized the distance between the composer's proposed innovations and the current operatic practice. Turning from the theories to the works themselves, I gradually discovered just how deeply indebted to traditional operatic procedures Wagner remained also in the music dramas. As I take leave of this book, my admiration for Wagner's control over unprecedentedly long spans of time, as well as for the originality, novelty, and variety of his specific formal solutions, is greater than ever, but my understanding of this control and these solutions has been transformed.

But Wagner was not only a great composer; he was also a significant dramatic poet and a restless thinker. The second aim that guided me here has been to see the ideological import of Wagner's dramas against the background of the worldviews that were current in his lifetime and, in particular, to confront his works with Nietzsche's critique. What connects the two aims is my conviction that a grasp of Wagner's large forms affords insights into the dramatic and philosophical implications of his works. As I shall argue, the music dramas of Wagner's later years registered and reacted to every major component in the complex ideological landscape that emerged during his century—a landscape which, I believe, is still the one we inhabit today. Like a number of artists of his time, in his later years Wagner understood himself to be something more than just an artist; he saw himself as a cultural prophet announcing and preparing better, more desirable forms of life for humanity. The specific content of his message never ceased to evolve, but his self-understanding as someone with a message to deliver remained constant. My aim has been to capture with some precision the specific place each of the music dramas occupies on the ideological map of its time. The confrontation with Nietzsche, a rival cultural prophet, takes on a particular urgency in this context, since what was at stake in the philosopher's objections to the artist was precisely the ideological import of Wagner's works.

Also here the direction my project took surprised me. Like so many people today, I had begun loving the music, but suspecting the message. Having finished the project, I still love the music and still find some aspects of the message disturbing, but disturbing for somewhat different reasons and in different works. For instance, I no longer consider *Parsifal* to be as guilty as some of its critics would have us believe; I have also learned better to appreciate the full extent of the ambiguity of *Die Meistersinger*. My understanding of the Wagner-Nietzsche relationship has been transformed, too. I started out convinced that Nietzsche's objections to Wagner were by and large well taken, and that the study of their encounter would likely illuminate Wagner's dramas, but not Nietzsche's books. Today I still admire Nietzsche's critical acumen, but I see as well not only that Wagner's works can defend themselves surprisingly effectively against some of the philosopher's central strictures, but also that these works implicitly offer an unexpectedly perceptive critique of a number of Nietzsche's most cherished doctrines. This is why I felt the need to amplify *Nietzsche contra Wagner* with *Wagner contra Nietzsche*.

The music-dramatic core of this book begins with an exposition and explanation of the analytical approach I shall be taking in it (chapter 1) and continues with individual discussions of each of the four music dramas (chapters 2 through 5). The order in which the works are discussed is significant and deliberate. The problem, of course, is what to do with the *Ring* on which Wagner started to work earliest, but which he finished only after the completion of *Die Meistersinger*. The Wagner literature offers examples of every imaginable solution to this problem. I have decided not to break the cycle into its individual components (it is important to understand the tetralogy as a single whole) and to place it at the beginning of the story I want to tell here. Both Wagner's discovery of how one might give a single form to a whole act (in the first act of *Die Walküre*) and his decision regarding what he wanted to say in the *Ring* predated his work on *Tristan*.

The *Ring*, though many years in gestation (1848–74), was essentially the fruit of Wagner's politically most radical anarchist period, concurrent with and immediately following the midcentury revolts. The nineteenth century was obsessed with the myth of revolution, the myth that was one of that century's two most baleful legacies to the one that followed (the other one was the myth of nation). In Wagner's tetralogy this obsession found its arguably grandest artistic expression. Inspired by Ludwig Feuerbach, Pierre-Joseph Proudhon, and Mikhail Bakunin, it is a poem intoxicated by the orgy of destruction of the old world in which humans compete for power and riches and by the hopeful anticipation of the world to come, the world of spontaneous solidarity and love—an anarchist utopia. *Tristan* (1857–59), however, put this revolutionary optimism of the *Ring* into question. Prompted in part by his disillusionment with the failed revolution and in part by his enthusiastic reading of Arthur Schopenhauer, Wagner now realized that the erotic love that was supposed to provide the foundations of the new postrevolutionary society was singularly unsuited for this role. Eros turned out to be a cruel deity inexorably driving its devotees to transcend the finite daily realm of customary social rights and obligations and ecstatically enter the infinite metaphysical night of nothingness. For those unwilling to follow the erotic utopia of *Tristan*, a new answer had to be found to the political and ethical questions raised in the *Ring*. And this is precisely what Wagner provided in his last two projects. I read

Die Meistersinger (1861–67) as an attempt, partly inspired by the nationalism of Johann Gottlieb Fichte, to see whether something of the political optimism of the *Ring* might still be salvageable after the pessimistic discoveries of *Tristan*. The answer the opera gives to this question is affirmative, but the specific content of this answer is profoundly disturbing, a utopia of post-political aestheticized metapolitics pregnant with sinister implications for the future. *Parsifal* (1877–81), finally, offers a vision of ethics that might be viable in the wake of *Tristan*, a vision derived from Schopenhauerian, Buddhist, and Christian inspirations that suggested a turning away from the nihilistic self-obsessed eros toward the other-directed agape.

The music-dramatic core of my book is framed by sections designed to place Wagner's late works within the context of the political and ethical ideas of his time. The prologue provides the broadest philosophical and ideological canvass, a background against which the music dramas will eventually appear. I have attempted there to provide a genealogy of the principal worldviews available to Wagner and his contemporaries, describe how they arose, and sketch a map that will show how they related to one another. The options I describe are of diverse age, some with roots going as far back as antiquity (the Judeo-Christian religious outlook), some characteristic of the modern age (the Enlightenment), some arising even more recently in the late eighteenth and nineteenth centuries (the main currents of the Counter-Enlightenment that proceed under the banners of history, nation, and will). I do not see these options as successively replacing one another. Rather, I would prefer to compare them to geological layers, deposited at different times, but all actively shaping the landscape in which Wagner found himself, and in which we still find ourselves today. Wagner's work, I argue in the core of this book, exists in the field of tensions created by all of these principal worldview options; they all left traces on his music dramas. The epilogue returns then to the philosophical issues raised in the prologue, but narrows the focus to a single relationship, that of Richard Wagner with his most important critic, Friedrich Nietzsche.

I imagine two kinds of readers for this book. There will be those, I hope, who simply want to get acquainted with Wagner's music dramas, or to get to know them better; these readers will give most attention to chapters 2 through 5, reading chapter 1 as a background to these. They would profit most if they read the chapters devoted to individual works with score in hand, or, if they do not read music, a recording at the ready, examining critically each of my claims. I have attempted to facilitate this kind of reading by indicating precisely the discussed passage so that the reader will have no difficulty finding it. If you are going to use the scores of the new Schott *Sämtliche Werke*, or the new Eulenburg study scores derived from those, scores in which measures are numbered, I identify each discussed passage by Roman numerals for acts and Arabic numerals for measure numbers. (Thus, I.23–45 refers to act I, measures 23 through 45.) Please note that I start counting always from the first downbeat of the passage, even if an upbeat precedes it. (Thus it will be I.23, even if there is an upbeat in I.22.) The available vocal scores unfortunately do not provide measure numbers. To facilitate their use, I provide the initial words of the libretto that are placed as close as possible after the beginning of the passage in question. This method, however, cannot be precise when the passage begins without words, and it cannot be used at all when it is wordless. For those who prefer to use recordings, the passages in numerous figures and the appendices that summarize the music-dramatic plan of each work are identified by Roman numerals for the CD in a given set and Arabic numerals for the track number; the numbers that follow indicate the minutes and seconds on the track where the passage in question begins and ends. Thus, CDI.2.0:12–3:45 refers to the first CD of the set, second track, with the passage starting at 12 seconds and ending 3 minutes and 45 seconds after the beginning of the track. I have chosen recordings that are sufficiently well known and admired to warrant confidence that they will be widely available, as follows:

Der Ring des Nibelungen: cond. Georg Solti, 1958–65, Decca 455 555
Tristan und Isolde: cond. Wilhelm Furtwängler, 1952, EMI 56254
Die Meistersinger von Nürnberg: cond. Herbert von Karajan, 1970, EMI 7243 5 67152 2 6
Parsifal: cond. Hans Knappertsbusch, 1962, Philips 289 464 756-2

But I expect that the book will also find readers who are already familiar with these works and whose main interest is to understand the philosophical-ideological significance of the Wagner phenomenon. These readers will want to concentrate on the final sections of chapters 2 through 5 and the epilogue, reading the prologue for the background it provides. If they resemble the author at all, they are likely to be conflicted about Wagner's achievement, loving and admiring it and at the same time being disturbed and even revolted by it. I do not intend to help them resolve such conflicts; rather, I aim to shift the components within this unstable mixture and hope that, like myself, they will close this book equally, but differently, conflicted. Like many of the Wagner critics since 1945, I too am convinced that to understand him is to gain insight into some of the sources of the multiple disasters that befell Europe in the twentieth century. But also here, the work on this project has transformed my understanding of where Wagner fits in the prehistory of these catastrophes. I began my research convinced that Wagner's anti-Semitism would play the central role in this story. I end it as revolted as ever by the composer's prejudice, but convinced that this is a symptom of something even more fundamental and sinister, something that the debate over the putative presence of anti-Semitism in Wagner's operas has managed to obscure rather than illuminate: the brew compounded of the revolutionary radicalism of the *Ring* and the aestheticized utopian post-political politics of *Die Meistersinger*. The history of the debate over the Wagnerian roots of Nazi ideology has been succinctly characterized by Hans Rudolf Vaget: "In their examination of the Hitler-Wagner nexus, Mann, Adorno, Viereck, and others highlighted a whole range of ideological affinities, among them nationalism, megalomania, the substitution of myth and fairy tale for history, the totalitarian mind-set, demagoguery, self-praise, love of pomp, the rejection of liberalism, the espousal of revolutionary dynamism for its own sake, and the obsession with racial purity. Today, however, it seems fair to say, that the topic of anti-Semitism virtually monopolizes the debate about the historical legacy of Richard Wagner."[3] In a sense I would like to return to this earlier, and richer, stage in the debate.

The ethical vision of *Parsifal*, Wagner's "last card," might have provided an antidote to the radical proposals embodied in the preceding music dramas, but the twisted history of this opera's reception does little to inspire confidence in the antidote's efficacy. For the foreseeable future we shall have to live with the ambiguous legacy of this great and endlessly thought-provoking artist. His work remains what it was for Thomas Mann in 1933, "one of the most splendidly questionable, ambivalent and fascinating phenomena in all artistic creation."[4]

Prologue
Beyond Autonomy

The spiritual landscape that confronted Richard Wagner at midcentury and Friedrich Nietzsche a generation later has taken a long time to emerge. Below I shall indicate its most prominent features and tell the story of its emergence. I begin with a snapshot of the situation around the time of Wagner's birth as perceived by one of the more sensitive observers of the age (section 1) and then outline the main stages of my story: the slow withdrawal of God to make room for the Reason of the Enlightenment (section 2); the principal challenges mounted by those Counter-Enlightenment figures who perceived Reason's insufficiency (section 3); and the resulting complex cultural configuration in which both Wagner and Nietzsche had to find their ways (section 4).

THE UNCANNY GRACE: A GLOSS ON KLEIST'S MARIONETTES

The grand piano has by now disappeared from the living rooms of the educated, but during the long nineteenth century it was an indispensable piece of equipment, as indispensable as the gramophone record player was during the short twentieth, or the portable media player has become since the early twenty-first—by far the most important musical tool.

In retrospect, the piano's climb to the dominant position in the kingdom of music seems inevitable. Already by the sixteenth century, if not earlier, the keyboard, perspicuously separating the basic seven white diatonic keys from the subordinated five black chromatic ones within each octave, and replicating such octaves up and down almost the whole audible range, provided musicians with their most important image of all the usable tones as well as the relationships obtaining among them—the image of the abstract order of music itself. And not just the image: the mechanism attached to the keyboard made music incarnate, putting the complete universe of tones under the fingertips of a single musician, and making it possible for him to sound even the most complex polyphony. All that remained for the universal musical instrument to be perfected was Bartolomeo Cristofori's invention that allowed the musician to control the dynamics. In an inventory of 1700, the new invention is described as making "soft and loud" sounds and all earliest references to the instrument mention this essential feature.[1] A single musician could now not only call up with his fingers all the tones, but could also make them sing; the orderly but abstract tonal universe has been ensouled. By the last quarter of the eighteenth century, in the middle movements of Wolfgang Amadé Mozart's concertos, the fortepiano has become the channel of the most intimate self-expression, as if an immediate and uninterrupted conduit linked the inmost recesses of the musician's soul with his fingers and the sounds they summoned.

This immediacy, however, is an illusion. Unlike in the even more intimate clavichord, not to mention the violin or that supreme maker of the ensouled sound, the human voice, in the piano the link between the body and the sound is in fact broken. The pianist controls the velocity and force with which he strikes the key, but this is all he controls. Once the key is struck, the finger can no longer shape the produced sound, bend its pitch, make it vibrate or swell. A multiple lever transmits and amplifies the motion of the key to the hammer, releasing it before the string is reached. For the last portion of its voyage the hammer travels freely, beyond the control of the pianist's will and subject only to the same blind forces that control the motions of all medium-size and large objects described by classical Newtonian mechanics. Uncannily, behind the warm illusion of the self-conscious and free human soul expressing itself there stands the cold reality of the blindly ticking and determined mechanism.

Of the two sides of the piano, the animate and the mechanical, the musicians of the long nineteenth-century age of raptures preferred to emphasize the illusion of the singing soul; the disabused short twentieth century brought the reality of the ticking mechanism to the surface. And nowhere more so than in the player piano, a piano that dispensed with a live player altogether, activating its mechanism instead by means of electrically propelled pneumatic switches controlled by a prerecorded perforated paper roll. In the first quarter of the twentieth century, this provided the intermediate link in the musical evolution of the middle-class parlor between the piano and the record player. To see (and not just hear) this instrument in operation is to come face to face with the uncanny: the keys seem to be moving on their own, as if struck by ghostly fingers. The sense of the uncanny intensifies when one learns that the fingers belong to a long-departed musician: the reproducing player piano was the perfect musical instrument of the era of Spiritualist séances. The illusion of a living human presence in the music is broken; the sounds are made by an automaton. What was implicit in the operation of the piano—the mechanism that runs independently of an immediate human control—has been made explicit.

The musician who realized the artistic potential of the player piano most fully was Conlon Nancarrow. An American Communist living since 1940 in self-imposed exile and isolation in Mexico, without easy access to performers, Nancarrow chose to bypass live players altogether and write directly for the ghostly player piano. Like the blacklisted Hollywood scriptwriters of the 1950s, he in effect invented his own form of ghostwriting. Punching piano rolls manually, he encoded music of often formidable rhythmic and contrapuntal complexity and breathtaking speed—far in excess of anything a live pianist would be capable of playing. To hear one of his *Studies* is an exhilarating and somewhat scary experience, even if one does not see the instrument in operation—as if Art Tatum has grown additional hands.

This imaginative body of work, in turn, provided a central inspiration for one of the great masterpieces of late twentieth-century music—György Ligeti's three books of piano *Études*, arguably the most significant extension of the piano repertoire since Claude Debussy. It is the music of the sorcerer's apprentice; indeed, one of the *Études* is entitled "Der Zauberlehrling," and some of Ligeti's other characteristically Lisztian titles—"Désordre," "Vertige," "L'escalier du diable"—are similarly suggestive. Having emerged from the twilight zone of the player piano without forgetting its lessons, Ligeti's live pianist conjures poems at once hilarious and frightening, blending anarchic slapstick with the terror of a mechanism running wildly out of control.

The notion of the uncanny invokes that of the double—the going back and forth between the familiar and the strange, between the embodied and the ghostly. Music that elides the distinction between the animate and the mechanical is uncanny. The early nineteenth-century German writer Heinrich von Kleist may be our best guide to such slippery aesthetic phenomena.

A marionette, recall, is a puppet suspended by one or more strings attached to its body—usually to the head, back, hands, and legs—and controlled from above by a manipulator. The marionette Kleist has in mind in his 1810 essay "On the Marionette Theater" is most likely a single-string puppet, one with limbs left free, which the manipulator operates relying on gravity and pendular motion.[2] In explaining the "mechanism" of such puppetry, he has Herr C. tell the narrator not to imagine that it was "as if every limb were individually . . . placed and pulled by the machinist."[3] Each puppet, he further explains, each moving mass, has an internal point of gravity: "It would be enough to control this . . . ; the limbs, which were nothing but pendulums, would follow . . . in a mechanical way of themselves."[4]

The fingers of the puppeteer set the marionette in motion and then the puppet's limbs continue to move on their own, relying on the laws of Isaac Newton's mechanics. Similarly, the finger of the pianist sets the hammer in motion and then the hammer flies on its own, subject to the same laws. And similarly, God sets the celestial bodies in motion and then allows them to move mechanically on their own. But I should not get ahead of myself.

Herr C., himself a successful first dancer of the local opera, is fascinated by the dancing marionettes and believes he might learn from them, since he finds their motions "most graceful."[5] This is a major provocation that dwarfs the minor one of preferring a lowly entertainment set up in the marketplace for the amusement of the "rabble" to a high art involving live performers and polite society.[6] Normally we attribute grace only to animate beings, seeing in a graceful gesture a bodily expression of a soul unconstrained and at peace with itself.

One swallows this provocation, since one assumes that the soul that expresses itself through a graceful motion of a marionette is ultimately that of the manipulating puppeteer, just as one assumes that it is the pianist's, and not the hammer's, soul that sings in the music. And, indeed, Herr C. confirms: the line of motion that the point of gravity in the puppet should make is nothing less than "the *path of the soul of the dancer*" and it could be found only if "the machinist puts himself into the point of gravity of the marionette, that is, . . . *dances*."[7]

But just when we think that we have found a way of neutralizing the provocation, Herr C. springs another, much graver, one. Like those later inventors of the completely mechanical player piano, Herr C. dreams of a completely mechanical marionette, one that dances without the manipulator's fingers, moved by means of a "crank," similarly to a barrel organ.[8] He would like to break the last link between the marionettes and the living human "spirit" and thus move "their dance entirely into the realm of mechanical forces."[9] The dancing of such a marionette would surpass anything achievable by even the most skillful live dancer. Herr C. dreams of becoming the Conlon Nancarrow of dancing.

And now his provocation can no longer be evaded: grace, a moral quality and hence normally attributable to an animate being only, inheres in a purely mechanical puppet. More: it is only in the motions of such an improved, completely mechanical marionette that grace will reach perfection.

To justify this seemingly paradoxical claim, Herr C. offers a philosophy of history. A graceful motion, he believes, has to be instinctive, involuntary. Anyone who has attempted to perform, whether as a dancer, musician, or actor, will recognize at least an aspect of what Herr C. is driving at. A performance has to be to a considerable extent mechanical, automatic; the performer cannot consciously control every motion he makes. Constant practice transforms what might initially have been conscious motions into something like "second nature." In fact, in a closely related "Paradox" published a few days earlier, "On Reflection," Kleist argued that *all* action, and not only a graceful one, has to precede reflection if it is to be effective: "Know that reflection is far more appropriate *after* than *before* the act."[10] The main cause of imperfections in the motions of a live dancer is "consciousness," which puts his point of gravity and his soul, the "moving force," out of sync with one another and contaminates grace with "affectation."[11] Consciousness is also self-consciousness, the ability to see oneself as if from the outside, hence the distance it introduces between the moved body and the moving soul. Eliminate self-consciousness, not only that of the dancer, but even that of the puppeteer, and the problem disappears. With live dancers, however, such elimination is impossible. Perfect grace can be an attribute of a mechanical puppet, or of a god, but not of a human being. It "appears at its purest in that human frame that has either no consciousness whatsoever or an infinite one, that is, in a puppet or god."[12] Inanimate matter or god, total absence of consciousness or completely conscious self-presence—"here is the point where the two ends of the round world interlock."[13]

And here Herr C. recommends to the narrator that he read Genesis 3 with attention: "With someone who does not know this first period of the whole human development one could not speak conveniently about the following ones, let alone about the last one."[14] We have eaten from the Tree of Knowledge and have thus acquired consciousness, including self-consciousness. We have been expelled from Paradise, thereby losing the original oneness with nature, and there is for us no way back, only forward: "The Paradise is locked up and the Cherub behind us; we have to travel around the world and see whether it is perhaps open again somewhere in the back."[15] Such a return through the back door would constitute "the last chapter of the history of the world."[16] At the end of time, the infinite linear progress of consciousness and knowledge in human history would turn out to have been a cycle.

It is obvious that Herr C. has read not only Genesis, but also Jean-Jacques Rousseau. We cannot simply go back to the lost original state of nature. The only way out of our present civilized alienation from nature and from ourselves is forward—toward the utopia of the perfected civilization and complete knowledge that would bring consciousness and nature together again. Seen from a distance, Herr C.'s philosophy of history appears Rousseauist and derivative.

But seen from up close, a difference is visible, and it is this difference that makes Kleist's text so intriguing. When Rousseau wants to capture the original state of nature, in the second *Discourse* and elsewhere he reaches for organic images and metaphors. His pre-alienated man resembles an animal—*is* an animal. Herr C., by contrast, is drawn by the mechanical. His prelapsarian humans resemble, or *are*, marionettes. To see a soul in an animal, or to expect that it might acquire one as it evolves, is one thing; to suspect that an ensouled being is a machine is something else again. It is precisely this difference that accounts for Kleist's peculiar aesthetic sensibility, allowing him to formulate thoughts that speak directly to the aesthetic phenomena with which I have begun—to the uncanny cohabitations of the animate and the mechanical.

Moreover, we do not need to wait for the arrival of the player piano to find use for Herr C.'s aesthetics. Relevant musical phenomena can be found also closer to Kleist's own time. Music-playing automata have been constructed since the early modern age and the century preceding Kleist's own witnessed the invention of such celebrated examples as the 1737 flute player of Jacques de Vaucanson and the Jaquet-Droz female organist of 1768–74. Kleist himself mentions the most widespread of such devices, the barrel organ. In 1816, just a few years after Kleist's text appeared, E. T. A. Hoffmann immortalized the figure of an artistic automaton in Olympia, the harpsichord-playing, singing, and dancing doll in "The Sandman," a short story that, in turn, was to be the subject of Sigmund Freud's interpretation in the 1919 essay on "The Uncanny." (Hoffmann seems to have been about the only reader to have noticed Kleist's essay in the nineteenth century.)[17] In Hoffmann's story, the protagonist comes to see his living fiancée, Clara, as an inanimate automaton and the actual automaton, Olympia, as a living love object. Regardless of whether the story involves castration anxieties, as Freud claims, it surely concerns itself also with the anxiety raised by the uncertainty as to whether we are confronted by a living being or a mechanism.

But when I think of music from Kleist's time that would deserve Herr C.'s attention most, I think of Gioachino Rossini. In a thought-provoking essay on the "transcendental character of the Rossinian comic theater," a text whose very title, "To Die of Laughter," announces the subtlety of its argument, Alessandro Baricco proposed a brief philosophical history of *opera buffa*.[18] The genre was born, Baricco reminds us, as an alternative to *opera seria*, replacing its premodern dualistic picture of the world whereby the actual was wholly dependent upon the transcendent both for its development and for its sense with the modern picture that eliminated all transcendence and released the immanent worth and dynamism of the actual. *Opera buffa* replaced heroes driven by divine destiny with autonomous subjects driven by desires. It tested the Enlightenment hypothesis that the actual world has its own developmental dynamics in the desires of individual autonomous subjects and that a salvation is possible without any interference from a deus ex machina, that mutually satisfactory outcomes may be negotiated among subjects communicating in dialogue.

Its zenith was reached with *Le nozze di Figaro* and its limit with *Don Giovanni*. In the protagonist of the latter the autonomy is radicalized and the desires intensified to such a degree that the subject itself dissolves. For Baricco as for Søren Kierkegaard, Don Giovanni is not a person, that is, the hypothetical origin of desires; he is desire itself. The autonomous subject, the master of desires and the source of authority in dialogue, is replaced by the uncontrollable force of desire and the equally uncontrollable mechanism of communication. The Enlightenment dream of autonomous rational subjects individually and collectively in charge of their future evaporates as the actual is revealed to be governed by irrational instincts and impersonal social mechanisms.

But if Mozart and Lorenzo Da Ponte reach the outer limit of the Enlightenment experiment, they also stop at this limit: with the figure of the stone guest, the old-regime deus ex machina is brought back to reestablish the vertical authority of transcendence and provide the destiny of the otherwise incomprehensible non-hero with tragic significance. It was left to Rossini to leap beyond this limit. What Mozart still feared—the submergence of subjective autonomy in a sea of objective biological instincts and social mechanisms—Rossini embraced with full confidence in the possibility of human felicity. "The porcelain figurines preferred a hundred years earlier to the world of heroes and gradually elevated by the spirit of the Enlightenment to the status of pure and proper subjects, allow themselves, finally, to go crazy . . . of happiness."[19]

It is Rossini himself, rather than his librettists, who "stages the overcoming of the concept of the subject"[20] by applying to it the solvent of his extraordinarily abundant and florid vocal ornamentation, otherwise uncommon in *opera buffa*. By his ornamentation Rossini overwhelms and neutralizes both the subjective expressivity of the melody and the significance of the sung words with the objective coloratura mechanism. While his predecessors have long endeavored to mimic in music the cadences of the speaking subject, it was "the fundamental tendency of Rossini's music to liberate the musical language from the pre-forming logic of human language," to replace both the rationality and the emotion of the subject with music's own internal abstract logic. Rossini's "is no longer the music made in man's image; rather, it is man . . . who transforms himself into a pure musical fact." In Rossini's comic operas, especially in their finales, "the personages do not dominate the situations any more, but rather are possessed by them." They take leave of conscious subjectivity and sing "like machines or like lunatics."[21]

Craziness, folly, insanity, madness—the specter of chaos sensibly feared by the Enlightenment is accepted by the "organized and complete lunacy" (Stendhal's brilliant phrase quoted by Baricco) of the Rossinian comedy.[22] Organized lunacy—the formula for a world no longer controlled by the autonomous subject, but nevertheless orderly after its own objective fashion and accepted by Rossini as offering a possibility of human happiness. The Rossinian subject achieves happiness by dissolving herself in folly, her coloraturas scurrying up and down the silken ladder of felicity. "Cenerentola," concludes Baricco, "is the last heroine to get crazy of happiness. All the others after her, if it will be their lot to lose reason, it will be on account of suffering."[23] Thus, "what Kleist imagined . . . occurred in fact in Rossini"—a theater of marionettes, their individual psychological characterization and subjective autonomy severely reduced, their involuntary grace and beauty, that promise of happiness, all the greater.[24]

Baricco's characterization of Rossini's art as leaning away from the mimesis of individual psychology toward a purely musical abstraction is not unprecedented, of course. Already Richard Wagner saw Rossini in this light. According to *Opera and Drama* (1852), the "monstrous" nature of all opera consisted precisely in its application of "absolute music" to drama (music is "absolute" when it can exist independently of words and follows its own laws), but Rossini pushed this general anti-mimetic tendency toward musical abstraction to its most radical and "frivolous" extremes.[25] What is uncommon, then, is not the characterization itself, but its positive valuation. One can only guess that a reading of Kleist's essay helped Baricco to arrive at his position.

In the past two centuries, it was more usual for non-mimetic, nonhuman, abstract, mechanical music to give rise to, or accompany, anxiety. No less than Rossini, Wagner was capable of showing a whole society in the grip of folly, as he did in the finale of the second act of *Die Meistersinger*; but the Wagnerian *Wahn* is something altogether more threatening and sinister than the happy abandon of Rossini's *follia*. And when Rossini's contemporary admirer, Franz Schubert, reached for a mechanical instrument, it was not to celebrate the prospect of human liberation from excessive rational control in a delirious self-abandonment of ecstatic happiness. The static, repetitive, monotonous droning of the hurdy-gurdy (an instrument that relies on the use of a crank, like a barrel organ, or like Herr C.'s completely mechanized marionette) emerges at the end of the era's darkest musical vision, *Winterreise* (1827). It is the sound of the inhospitable universe slowly freezing over, a world offering neither exit nor consolation.

Images of a mechanism turning in circular motion appear relatively rarely in Schubert's work, but they do appear, and in strategically exposed places: in addition to the ending of *Winterreise*, also at the beginning of *Die schöne Müllerin* (1823) and of course in his Op. 2, "Gretchen am Spinnrade" (1814). But to Schubert such images do not suggest a promise of happiness and abandon in a self-forgetting ecstasy; quite the contrary. The spinning wheel that accompanies Gretchen's reverie is emblematic of the hypnotic power at once enchanting and terrifying in the grip of which she finds herself and over which she has no control, a power about to destroy her. And while at the outset the incessantly turning wheels and the cheerful dance of the heavy millstones seem emblematic to the journeyman of *Die schöne Müllerin* of his joy in wandering, at the end he will perish in the waters of the brook that moves these wheels and stones.

It is not that Kleist's and Rossini's exhilaration at the mechanical is wholly untroubled. Rossini's even greater admirer, Stendhal, famously defined beauty as "nothing but the *promise* of happiness."[26] I am inclined to believe him. But if happiness needs to be promised, it means it is not here, not now. Beauty is an absence of happiness, Stendhal's formula implies, something we hope for and perhaps remember, but not something we presently possess—a home we have left behind and long to recover. ("She dwells with Beauty—Beauty that must die," says John Keats of melancholy.) Pleasure and pain, past and future bliss but present suffering, are all intertwined and inseparable in the experience of beauty. Paradise, when contemplated from the perspective of the Fall, is beautiful. All the same, the distance between Rossini and Schubert is unbridgeable. Schubert promises nothing; his deadly winter, unlike that of Caspar David Friedrich, knows no hope whatever, no early sprouts of future growth.

Who is closer to truth, then, Rossini or Schubert? How should the uncanny mechanical music produced by the spherically turning crank be heard: with hope or with dread? Is it with hope or with dread that we should encounter the spectacle of the soul emerging from the motions of a mechanical puppet, or the as yet unfathomable mystery of consciousness being produced by a network of firing neurons? Our uncertainty in this regard began when Newton and his colleagues announced that the universe itself is a mechanism. When describing the operation of his marionettes, Kleist reaches with telling frequency for terms such as *mechanisch, Mechanismus,* and *Maschinist,* as well as the whole telltale language of *mechanische Kräfte* (mechanical forces), *Schwerpunkt* (point of gravity), *Gesetz der Schwere* (law of gravity). The universe, on the surface so varied, unruly, protean, chaotic, and incomprehensible, turned out to be at bottom a machine regularly functioning according to a small number of immutable laws expressed in mathematical equations. Moreover, it functioned automatically: God might have been needed to wind up the clockwork mechanism at the beginning, but once wound up, the mechanism ticked on indefinitely on its own, like the independently flying piano hammer, or the pendulous limb of a puppet. ("I had no need of that hypothesis," as Pierre-Simon Laplace was said to tell Napoleon when asked why he had never mentioned God in his *Celestial Mechanics.*) It was a vision at once consoling and chilling: the universe was perspicuously comprehensible and endowed with the beauty of a well-functioning clockwork, but it was a soulless universe, one in which the spirit of the prime mover left an unforgettable trace, but from which it then permanently withdrew. Without the transcendent machinist striking keys and pulling strings, what hope was there that music and dance will make sense, or that they will not grind to a halt in frozen immobility? Not for nothing is "Erstarrung" (Freezing) the title of one of the songs in *Winterreise* and the cycle's central image.

For a time, that hope was provided by the invention of human autonomy, by Rousseau and Immanuel Kant. Kleist's language and images certainly suggest a memory of the Newtonian shock and perhaps also an early awareness that a further, even more troubling, shock to worry about has appeared on the horizon: the suspicion that the autonomous human subject, God's spiritual successor, rests on unstable foundations, that it too might evaporate under the combined pressure of uncontrollable instinctual forces within and equally uncontrollable social mechanisms without. Herr C.'s philosophy of history suggests that the Enlightenment with the notion of autonomy at its center might be radicalized to the point of self-elimination. His is a vision of the linear progress of knowledge bending into a cycle in the end to allow us reenter the Paradise of second nature through the back door. Some sixty years later, Friedrich Nietzsche too will suggest this historical geometry in his image of the linear progress of Socratic scientific optimism—"that thought, using the thread of logic, can penetrate the deepest abysses of being," encountering impenetrable limits (presumably at the Kantian distinction between the phenomenal and the noumenal) where "logic coils up . . . and finally bites its own tail" and thus transforming itself into a cycle.[27] It is a tribute to Kleist's independence of mind (independence from the idealist climate that prevailed in Germany of the time), to something that might be called a proto-Nietzschean instinct for freedom, that he did not panic in the face of this two-stage withdrawal of spiritual authority, that he saw in it also an opportunity and a promise. It is a tribute to his skeptical sense of reality that he did not forget about the utopian nature of all such promises. A perfectly mechanical marionette has yet to be constructed; meanwhile, our art remains an index of our fallen state.

REASON

But by 1810 the slow process of undermining the authority of Reason was far from having been completed. In spite of the powerful Counter-Enlightenment, or Romantic, currents, the Reason of the Enlightenment maintained much of its ground until the mid-century revolutions. How did we get from Reason to Beyond Reason? Let me trace the main stages of this development.

Reason itself, recall, has been the modern replacement for the premodern God. In an earlier book I described the development that led to that replacement.[28] The development involved a change in the way one anchored the idea of human dignity and a correlated change in the way one located the ultimate source of our deepest, most absolute values (the unshakable foundation of what we consider to be true, good, and beautiful), and in particular the centrally important distinction between good and evil. The traditional Christian worldview grounded the notion of human dignity in the attribution to humans, alone among earthly beings, of moral responsibility, and it grounded values in God. It envisaged the imperfect and contingent (the fallen and mortal) but morally responsible human (morally responsible, because endowed with the knowledge of good and evil and the capability freely to will one or the other) as radically dependent on his perfect and absolute, omnipotent and benevolent Creator and Judge. Man was understood to crave a reconciliation with Him, a return from the exile of the fallen state and time to the original home of perfection and union with the divine source of all values at the end of time.

Inherent in this outlook was an insoluble contradiction between God's omnipotence and man's freedom, a contradiction that became apparent when one reflected on human prospects of salvation. Should my salvation depend on my own moral choices and actions, then the significance of my freedom and moral responsibility, as well as God's reputation for justice, were safeguarded, but His omnipotence seemed limited. Should my salvation depend solely on God's grace, His omnipotence was safeguarded, but not His reputation for justice and, worse, there seemed to be little point to human freedom and responsibility. The contradiction was likely one of the main sources of the intellectual fertility and dynamism of the Christian tradition, its various branches leaning toward one or the other pole: Saint Paul, Saint Augustine, and Martin Luther chose to emphasize God's omnipotence; Pelagius stressed man's freedom; the Roman Church navigated a middle course, trying to stitch together the requirements of divine grace and human responsibility. A perfect balance and reconciliation, however, was beyond reach.

One way to understand the transition from the premodern age to the modern one is to see that it tipped the balance in the Pelagian direction, emphasizing human freedom and playing down divine omnipotence. Regardless of whether one continued or not to be concerned with the prospects of salvation in the beyond, one paid greater attention to the prospects of improving one's earthly lot and recognized that this was something humans were capable of doing on their own, without supernatural assistance. The transition involved both a transformation in our conception of freedom and a correlated change in our understanding of how the values of truth, goodness, and beauty are grounded.

In the traditional conception, man's moral status depended in part on his being endowed with free will. The theory of the undetermined free will, however, seems to involve a contradiction: If I am to be morally responsible, my actions cannot be externally determined, but neither can they be irrational and arbitrary. They must follow rational choices determined by antecedent norms. The contradiction can be avoided only if one distinguishes between an action determined by causes and one motivated by reasons: I am morally responsible for my action when this has not been causally determined *and* when it has been motivated (determined) by my own reasons—self-determined, in other words, when I am both free and autonomous. Thus the modern notion of autonomy (or rational self-determination of the will) came to supplement and enrich the traditional notion of freedom (or absence of causal determination of the will) as the central component of the modern self-image of man.

But if the will is to be rationally determined, where do its reasons come from, and what is the ultimate ground or authority that allows us to judge that something is true, or good, or beautiful? In the traditional conception, the ultimate authority was God, who in divinely inspired scriptures revealed the general norms, and the moral norms in particular, in the light of which we are to judge each particular case. This, however, seems to have left a residuum of arbitrariness at the heart of the whole picture. Could God, in His omnipotence, suspend the logical laws of identity, contradiction, and excluded middle, or decide that two plus two equals five, or that torturing innocent children is a good thing?

Already the premoderns (Thomas Aquinas) argued that He could not, but that this in no way limited His omnipotence: God, "without being in any way limited, cannot do what is logically impossible or morally wrong because the corresponding rules are identical with Himself."[29] What this argument may suggest is the thought that God is the name we give to absolutely binding norms rather than the source or ground of such norms. Following a suggestion of this sort, Kant will argue that the norms are not the result of God's fiat, but rather are grounded in the very constitution of the eternal and universal rationality shared by every rational being, God and humans alike; in effect he proposed to exchange one name for another, to rename God as Reason. The norms of truth and goodness are fundamental components of the rational constitution of cosmos, indispensable ways for rational beings to orient themselves in the world. It is our duty to obey such norms because we are rational and free, and in obeying them we obey ourselves; to say that God commands them would be superfluous. In any case it would be incompatible with the dignity of a free being to obey the norms because a more powerful being so commands. We obey them because they are the command of our own rational nature. In this sense we are autonomous, self-governed. It belongs to the essence of Reason to set the ends we may freely accept or reject. It is on this ability to set rational ends (autonomy) and to follow them (freedom) that human dignity now depends.

The construction of the modern autonomy-centered idea of human dignity was largely completed by Rousseau and given its fully elaborated form by Immanuel Kant (1724–1804). Kant's critical philosophy was one of the Enlightenment's two most thoroughgoing and profoundly meditated attempts to replace God with Reason, to ground our norms in our own rational nature rather than in divine Revelation (the other such attempt was by Georg Wilhelm Friedrich Hegel). (In an essay of 1784, "What Is Enlightenment?," Kant explained: "Enlightenment is man's release from his self-incurred tutelage. Tutelage is man's inability to make use of his understanding without direction from another. Self-incurred is this tutelage when its cause lies not in lack of reason but in lack of resolution and courage to use it without direction from another. *Sapere aude!* 'Have courage to use your own reason!'—that is the motto of enlightenment.")[30] The attempt involved mapping out Reason's complete and eternal architecture, the necessary structure of the self-conscious mind from which these norms were to be derived. The transcendental argument of each of the three *Critiques* (published, respectively, in 1781 [rev. ed. 1787], 1788, and 1790) was designed to show what this architecture had to look like, if universally valid knowing of objects (objective experience with a claim to truth rather than mere effectiveness), universally valid willing of actions (moral experience with a claim to goodness rather than mere utility), and universally valid feeling of pleasure (aesthetic experience with a claim to beauty rather than mere agreeableness) were to be possible.

It would be hard to overestimate the importance of this epoch-defining enterprise. Kant's attempt to ground the universal validity of our norms in Reason appears to be the only alternative to grounding them in divine Revelation, and we need some such grounding if we are to continue to make claims to truth, goodness, and beauty. In the practical domain, in particular, it would appear that, unless we can claim that there is a genuine distinction to be made between what is good and what is merely useful, we shall not be able to differentiate what should be from what is. Without a strong conception of good and evil as distinct from what is useful or harmful, how shall we find the limits beyond which no action can possibly be considered morally acceptable? How shall we know which individual and collective actions suggested by the putative dictates of biology, anthropology, or history to follow and which to resist? Similarly, without some notion of natural law, how shall we criticize a tyrannical positive legislation? How shall we be able, in short, to criticize what is from the standpoint of what should be?

But if the importance and nobility of Kant's enterprise are hard to doubt, its success has been doubted almost from the start.

Universally valid empirical knowledge was possible, Kant claimed, because the sensible world that is the object of such knowledge is in part constituted by the structuring activities of the mind (the passively received perceptual matter is actively shaped by the a priori, independent of experience, forms provided by our own cognitive powers), and all subjects of knowledge are endowed with the same cognitive capacities. Kant's "transcendental deduction" purported to prove that it was the necessary condition of self-consciousness that objective empirical knowledge depended on the mental activities of perceiving (in which sense was provided with variable data of perception, subjecting them to its own invariant forms of space and time), synthesizing (in which imagination collected the manifold of presentations given in perception into a single image), and judging (in which understanding applied its universal concepts—including a priori concepts Kant called "categories" that were the necessary conditions of experience, categories such as substance and cause—to the particular image provided by imagination). It was possible to reach secure a priori knowledge concerning those elements of cognition that were the mind's own contribution, that is, concerning the necessary conditions of all possible experience—space, time, and categories such as substance and cause. And it was possible to reach secure empirical knowledge of the sensible world, the spatiotemporal world of substances that interact in accordance with causal laws.

But where do the data of perception come from in the first place? They arise when our senses are affected by something the existence of which Kant's account implies but about which we can otherwise know nothing, the intelligible world behind the sensible one, the noumenon or "thing-in-itself"—"in itself," that is, independent of the contribution made by our mental powers. Once this something is subjected to the forms provided by these powers (space and time, as well as concepts and categories), it is transformed into the plural phenomena of the sensible world, the only reality we can actually know. Critics (specifically Friedrich Heinrich Jacobi in "David Hume on Faith or Idealism and Realism: A Dialogue," 1787) objected almost immediately: How can Kant claim both that the category of causality (along with other categories of understanding) applies only to phenomena and not to the noumenon *and* that it is the thing-in-itself that causes the appearance of the perceptual data? Kant's picture of the structure of objective knowledge was fundamentally flawed and self-contradictory. Accordingly, Kant's successors either gave up on the notion of the unknowable noumenon entirely, seeing that it was empty, or, like Arthur Schopenhauer, retained it, but claimed that something could be known about it after all.

This line of criticism had troubling implications not only for Kant's account of objective experience, but also, and more crucially, for his account of moral experience, of the possibility of universally valid willing of what ought to be, which he developed in the second *Critique*. The ultimate goal of critical philosophy, after all, was to defend the possibility of human freedom and autonomy on which the idea of human dignity depended, the possibility that was undermined by the determinism of modern science. Kant's "transcendental idealism," involving the distinction between the noumenal and phenomenal worlds, was the key component of the defense. Human knowledge, including science, pertains only to the world of appearances; of the intelligible world we can know nothing more than that it must exist. Hence the universal determinism of science applies only to the world of phenomena. Yet it is the intelligible world that makes freedom possible. It is not that we can know that freedom exists: we do not know anything about the noumenon. But we do know that we cannot deny the possibility of freedom's existence. If the self-conscious mind is rooted not only in the realm of phenomena, but also in the noumenon, then faith in human freedom is not impossible. In this way Kant could claim that his first *Critique* made room for faith in freedom. But if we give up on the notion of noumenon, that room disappears and with it the very foundation of human moral responsibility and dignity.

This line of criticism, however, does not need to doom the whole enterprise. Kant could, and did, claim that every human being has an inescapable awareness of moral law and responsibility, even if they disagree about the ultimate source of the law's authority, or about its specific demands. This awareness, he thought, implies that freedom must be possible, even if we did not know how it is possible, because freedom is the necessary condition of moral law (there can be no moral responsibility without it). It would seem that this argument stands even if one rejects transcendental idealism.

But while one may thus go around the problems raised by Kant's defense of the possibility of freedom, the problems raised by his defense of the possibility of autonomy are more difficult to overcome. Kant's *Groundwork of the Metaphysics of Morals* (1785) as well as his second *Critique* claimed that it was possible to ground specific moral norms, specific principles for moral conduct, in the dictates of Reason itself—in other words, that in morality we are our own lawgivers and that the law we give ourselves is the same for everyone, since we all share the same rationality. This claim, the basis for belief in the possibility of human autonomy, was also soon found wanting.

Specifically the claim took the following form: Since I am a rational being, whenever I act I can always describe my particular action in a general "maxim" that specifies the action's end as my reason for acting, the circumstances under which the action is undertaken, and the means to achieve the end. A maxim, that is, will typically state that "given these sorts of circumstances, I shall perform this kind of action in order to achieve this type of end." (Kant's example of such a maxim involves my end to increase wealth by every safe means applied to a situation in which someone made a deposit with me and then died without leaving a record of the deposit, so that I may safely keep it rather than returning it to his heirs: "Given that someone made an unrecorded deposit with me, I shall deny it and keep it in order to increase my wealth by every safe means.") In order to find out whether my maxim is morally allowed, I need to test its validity by means of the "categorical imperative" (the ultimate principle of morals) and ask whether it would be possible to will it as a universal law, possible in the sense that the resulting law would not be self-contradictory. (In Kant's example, such law would state that "everyone may deny a deposit which no one can prove has been made," and such a law fails the test of the categorical imperative, since it would self-destruct when, as its result, no one would be making deposits.)

In this way, Kant thought, Reason itself tells us what is and what is not morally allowed. This suggests a morality ideally suited to the needs of a liberal society, a morality that sets its intransgressible limits by the categorical imperative, but otherwise provides no substantive guidance and leaves each individual to pursue his or her own aims. Critics, most prominently Hegel, pointed out that the test of the categorical imperative was empty and useless in practice. With a minimum of ingenuity one would be able to universalize most maxims without generating contradictions: I just had to describe what I wanted to do in a maxim that would allow me to do it and at the same time prohibit others from undertaking actions that would render the universalized maxim self-contradictory. (Thus, instead of describing my action by the maxim "I may deny a deposit which no one can prove has been made," I might tell myself that an undocumented deposit is not a deposit at all, but a gift, and describe my action in the maxim "I may keep gifts.")

Kant's defenders point out that the categorical imperative exists in several equivalent formulations and that the formula better suited to test my maxims is the one that enjoins me never to use humanity, whether in my person or that of another, merely as a means to an end, but always also as an end in itself.[31] By "humanity" Kant means the rational capacities that distinguish us from other animals, in particular our ability to resist instinctual drives, posit rational ends for ourselves, and give ourselves laws. Humanity, that is, rationality, the capacity of positing ends, is the highest value, Kant claims, because it is the ground or condition of our having any values at all: something can have a value for us only if we can posit it as an end for ourselves.[32] It follows that every rational being deserves unconditional and equal respect as an end in itself, that our dignity is grounded in our autonomy. Moreover, it also follows that morally bad actions are those that fail to respect humanity (rationality) in me and in others. Autonomy grounds not only our dignity, but also the specific content of our moral norms.

Kant's way of using Reason to ratify Reason itself as the highest value is undoubtedly ingenious (and perhaps can escape the charge of being circular). Moreover, the test provided by the humanity formula of the categorical imperative does indeed seem to work better than the one provided by the universal law formula. It does not offer an unfailing and automatic solution to every moral dilemma, to be sure, but it does offer guidance to a rational deliberation over the moral evaluation of our actions, prompting us to search for solutions that favor truthfulness and persuasion over deception and violent coercion.

More, it also offers a clue as to the meaning of human history. We have history at all because, unlike other animals, we are not imprisoned by instincts, and can posit ends for ourselves: the possibility of history, too, is rooted in our rationality and autonomy. While as animals existing in nature we are subject to mechanical laws, as rational beings existing in culture (or what Kant dubs the "realm of ends") we are, or can be, united by a harmonious system of self-imposed and mutually compatible moral laws and we can make sense of history when we interpret it as a long, halting, tortuous, and gradual search for, and development of, such a system. "The history of mankind can be seen, in the large, as the realization of nature's secret plan to bring forth a perfectly constituted state as the only condition in which the capacities of mankind can be fully developed, and also bring forth that external relation among states which is perfectly adequate to this end," Kant wrote in his 1784 essay on the "Idea for a Universal History from a Cosmopolitan Point of View."[33] As Kant explained earlier in the same essay, a perfectly constituted state, one allowing human capacities their full development, would be a "society with the greatest freedom. Such a society is one in which there is mutual opposition among the members, together with the most exact definition of freedom and fixing of its limits so that it may be consistent with the freedom of others."[34] Similarly, perfectly adequate relations among states would be ones based on law securing "the external safety of each state."[35] To be sure, the complete solution of this task "is impossible, for from such crooked wood as man is made of, nothing perfectly straight can be built."[36] A progress toward this desirable state of affairs is by no means guaranteed. But the "idea" offers guidance for action (it tells us that we should strive to bring reality ever closer to this state of affairs) and for interpretation of the past (it tells us which events in our history helped us to get closer to our goal and which hindered our progress). A guarded optimism with regard to the prospects of progress is justified, since what has once been attained cannot be completely reversed: "For such a phenomenon in human history [as the French Revolution] *is not to be forgotten*," Kant wrote in an essay of 1798, and hence he concluded, "The human race has always been in progress toward the better and will continue to be so henceforth."[37]

This "idea for a universal history," too, is rooted in Reason. Driven by our radical propensity to evil (Kant is no more sentimental about human nature than Augustine; his doctrine of radical evil is a secularized or demythologized version of the doctrine of the original sin), we frequently make choices that satisfy our self-regard (*amour-propre*), the desire to be recognized as superior by our fellows, rather than the moral law. This mechanism inevitably breeds unhappiness, as not everyone can be superior and no one can be superior all the time. But the very same mechanism also spurs humanity to develop its capacities and powers to the fullest through competitive efforts. Thus it affords us the prospect, though by no means the assurance, that we may gradually and increasingly replace natural inclinations with the moral law that would govern pacific and just relations between free citizens within each republic as well as pacific and just relations between free republics, creating in this way an enlightened cosmopolitan (today we would say global) community. It is noteworthy that, in the age of revolutions, Kant, for all his sympathy for the French Revolution, put his long-run hopes in slow and gradual progress, not in an instantly transforming apocalypse.

Kant's Reason clearly does have a social and historical dimension. Kant knew that one can think only in a community and that human capacities develop over time. Nevertheless the impression conveyed by his central works, the *Critiques* above all, is of a Reason that is fundamentally individualistic and ahistorical: each rational being is endowed with the same basic and unchanging rational capacities, and the structure of each self-consciousness is at bottom the same. A theory of history was suggested in a series of essays that remained on the margins of the philosopher's oeuvre. It was the role of Georg Wilhelm Friedrich Hegel (1770–1831) to develop the social-historical conception of Reason to the fullest and to place this conception at the center of his vision (most influentially in the *Phenomenology of Spirit* of 1807, *Elements of the Philosophy of Right* of 1821, and *Lectures on the*

Philosophy of History published posthumously in 1837). For most readers, Kant's Reason is fundamentally individual and eternal, and Hegel's Reason is social and historical. To be sure, Kant also acknowledged that since the time of life allotted to each individual is limited, "in man (as the only rational creature on earth) those natural capacities which are directed to the use of his reason are to be fully developed only in the race, not in the individual."[38] But this tendency to emphasize the species is much more pronounced in Hegel. Kant's model individuals are "independent thinkers, who, after throwing off the yoke of tutelage from their own shoulders, will disseminate the spirit of the rational appreciation of both their own worth and every man's vocation for thinking for himself."[39] Hegel's model individuals participate imperfectly and incompletely in a supra-individual social and historical rationality of the communal spirit (*Geist*), or, as we would say today, culture. The difference is one of emphasis, but it is a difference all the same. While both Kant and Hegel understand that ideal rational principles need to be actualized in real social institutions and that such institutions take time to develop, for Kant the principles are discoverable by individual reason and, it seems, independently of the social-historical context. By contrast, for Hegel they can emerge only in the process of the historical development of humanity's culture. This shift toward a social-historical conception of Reason as well as the positing of a specific mechanism, the dialectic, that drives the process of Reason's development was arguably Hegel's most important contribution.

Hegel, we have seen, concluded that Kant's project of discovering the principles of morality in Reason failed, that the deliveries of isolated individual reason were empty. But from this perceived failure of Kant's project Hegel did not draw the conclusion that the project of rational autonomy as such was doomed, only that one needed to do better than Kant. His is the most heroic attempt yet to deliver a conception of Reason adequate to the task of underwriting human autonomy and hence also human dignity, as well as providing us with specific values.

Concerning Kant's categorical imperative, Hegel concluded that "it is possible to justify any wrong or immoral mode of action by this means."[40] He explained: "The fact that *no property* is present is in itself no more contradictory than is the non-existence of this or that individual people, family, etc., or the complete *absence of human life*. But if it is already established and presupposed that property and human life should exist and be respected, then it is a contradiction to commit theft or murder; a contradiction must be a contradiction with something, that is, with a content which is already fundamentally present as an established principle."[41] Hegel may have exaggerated. Assuming that Kant's self-ratification of Reason as the highest value stands and is not circular, the humanity formula of the categorical imperative offers a test that makes it possible to evaluate moral principles, a test that would prompt us to favor truthfulness and persuasion over deception and coercion. But even so, Kantian Reason seems capable at most of evaluating the principles we already have, not of providing us with such principles, of telling us what not to do rather than what to do.

From where, then, do we get our principles? They arise, Hegel thought, in the historical development of the communal collective culture or spirit. (In Hegel's terminology, the communal spirit is "objective" when it is embodied, made objective, in the community's ongoing social practices and in the social institutions that enable and sustain such practices; it is "absolute" when it becomes self-aware, that is, embodied in the sensuous intuitions of the community's art, and in the imaginative representations—myths and doctrines—and ritual practices of its religion, and reflected upon in the conceptual thinking of its philosophy. Philosophy finally renders explicit what was implicitly experienced in art and lived in religion. All these embodiments are absolute because the community recognizes nothing of normative significance beyond the norms captured by its art, religion, and philosophy.) If Reason was to deliver specific values, we needed a richer conception of what Reason was; we needed to reconceive it as spirit.

Hegel follows Kant in believing that consciousness requires self-consciousness, that if I am to be aware of an object of knowledge as distinct from myself, I need also to be aware of myself as the subject of this knowledge. But he goes beyond Kant in believing that self-consciousness is not enough. I do not begin to think in isolation. To be a self means to desire a sense of self-worth. To obtain this sense, self-consciousness requires further that I recognize and acknowledge the existence of other self-conscious subjects as self-conscious and, reciprocally, that they recognize my existence as a self-conscious subject. In other words, objective knowledge presupposes self-consciousness (Kant) and self-consciousness presupposes mutual recognition of self-conscious subjects (Hegel). We can be self-conscious subjects only within a community of self-conscious subjects who mutually acknowledge one another as such; it is only within such a community that rational thought becomes possible. Such a community is not a derived secondary whole constituted of antecedent independently existing individuals; it is the primary antecedent condition for the existence of any individual.[42]

A community's objective spirit is the specific distinct shape the mutual recognition takes within it, the shape objectified in the community's particular social practices and institutions. It is here, within the customary practices and forms of life of his community, that an individual finds his principles of action. This occurs when he joins in a given practice trying to pursue its aims and even, through his achievements, to extend the practice's self-understanding of what these aims might be. If Kant's individualistic *Moralität* (morality) could do no better than to tell us what not to do, Hegel's communal *Sittlichkeit* (ethical life) can tell us what to do with ourselves; it can offer specific, shareable forms of life we might choose to follow. Hegel does not repudiate Kantian morality. He recognizes that it enjoins us to respect ourselves and other members of our community as free persons and subjects and provides us with an indispensable premise of any moral deliberation (my actions have to follow principles that could be universal), but he claims that this premise by itself will not tell us what such actions might be. For this we need a thicker social-historical web of the practices and institutions of our community's ethical life. For us moderns these are: the institutions of the family, which are held together by the bonds of mutual love, and which provide a refuge from the competitive individualism of the civil society; the institutions of the market, which include estates and corporations as well as the legal order of the civil society, which together protect each individual's freedom to pursue his private interests; and the institutions of the state, which are concerned with the protection of collective freedom.

Like Rousseau and Kant before him, Hegel understands history as the story of our gradual achievement of full rational autonomy, the story of how we got to realize that in principle each human being is equally free (the modern moral ideal contributed by Christianity to replace the ancient self-conception according to which only some men were free), and how we made sure that this equal freedom of all became reality (and not only a professed norm) by developing appropriate practices and institutions in a long and laborious process marked by such signposts as the Renaissance, the Protestant Reformation, the Enlightenment, and the French Revolution. (As Hegel put it, "This *application* of the principle to secular affairs, the penetration and transformation of secular life by the principle of freedom, is the long process of which history itself [is made up].")[43] "The aim of world history," Hegel claimed, "is that the spirit should attain knowledge of its own true nature [which is freedom],[44] that it should objectivize this knowledge and transform it into a real world, and give itself an objective existence."[45] The same pattern governs the development of an individual biography: I begin by being socialized and educated into the practices and norms of my society; sooner or later, however, I begin to subject these practices and norms to rational scrutiny with the aim of satisfying myself that they pass the test of rationality and hence deserve my allegiance.

But, just like Rousseau and Kant, Hegel did not consider this aim preordained, nor did he think that the actual course history took was inevitable. Rather, he thought of this aim as an assumption, a heuristic norm that would allow us to decide what is desirable for the future and what brought us closer to (or further from) our aim in the past: "That world history is governed by an ultimate design, that it is a rational process ... this is a proposition whose truth we must assume; its proof lies in the study of world history itself, which is the image and enactment of reason."[46] Once again, just like Kant and despite his sympathy for the French Revolution, Hegel did not believe that future progress would require another revolutionary breakthrough. Rather, he put his hope in gradual, piecemeal reforms.

Hegel's position emphatically does not imply that we are condemned to be social conservatives and conformists; above all, it does not mean that we have no standpoint from which to criticize the practices and forms of life of our community. Historical progress, Hegel thought, was driven by a mechanism he dubbed "dialectic," in essence an effort to synchronize the objective with the absolute spirit, to bring harmony between the self-understandings and norms we profess, on the one hand, and our actual social practices and institutions, on the other. Most fundamentally, as just described, progress involves precisely the series of attempts to develop practices and institutions that would actualize rather than contradict the moral ideal of equal freedom introduced by Christianity. There is no absolute starting point: we are always already located somewhere, within some web of moral-political norms and practices. Once we discover contradictions between the norms we profess and the forms of life we actually follow, sooner or later we want to eliminate these contradictions in order to make our world less irrational and less unfree. This is how progress is made.

There also seems to be no absolute point of arrival, although here Hegel may seem ambiguous. On the one hand, philosophy is "*its own time comprehended in thoughts.* It is just as foolish to imagine that any philosophy can transcend its contemporary world as that an individual can overleap his own time."[47] We can think about and evaluate our past and present norms and practices only from the place we have reached so far, from our own level of rationality and freedom. We shall never have anything more than our own fallible Reason. This suggests that our standpoint may be surpassed in the future, that our norms and practices are subject to criticism and may be improved: the historicity of Reason is inescapable. But, on the other hand, Reason is not only historical, it is also a self-criticizing affair, and the standpoint we moderns have reached, the standpoint of the Enlightenment, is, for the first time in history, one where we no longer put trust in revealed myths, no matter how venerable, and will accept nothing but rational arguments. We are the first people who can dispense with all revealed norms, all dogmatic foundations. And thus the ambiguity disappears. We shall continue to reinvent ourselves, to be sure, but from now on we should reinvent ourselves under the guidance of the interpersonal, communal, self-criticizing and self-grounding Reason embodied in a variety of our social, scientific, legal, and political practices. Hegel's vision of the desirable future for humanity is no less "cosmopolitan" than Kant's. He too rejects a world of many equally valid cultures, each worshiping its own traditional gods, in favor of a single modern culture grounded in universal Reason.

On this interpretation—and this is only one of the possible interpretations of his thought—Hegel not so much repudiates Kant as supplements him, adding *Sittlichkeit* to *Moralität* and stressing the social and historical nature of Reason reconceived as spirit or culture (Jürgen Habermas will talk of "communicative reason").[48] They both agree that freedom belongs to the spirit's, or Reason's, essence. And they are probably both right, Hegel when he claims that we respect rationality and equal moral worth of each human being not because abstract Reason compels us to do so, but because we belong to a cultural tradition on which the teachings of Socrates and Jesus (and Plato and Saint Paul) left their indelible imprints; and Kant when he answers that the reason why the imprints of Socrates and Jesus have been indelible was that they discovered something essential about human rational nature. For both, the self-ratifying and self-criticizing Reason retains the position previously occupied by God, grounding our most fundamental norms. The difference between them is the difference between those who say that the principles of Reason, while discovered by us only gradually, are in themselves eternal, and those who say that no principles are eternal, that they can all be changed, but add that if societies are to survive and have some stability, they can change these principles only gradually and very few at any given time.

BEYOND REASON

History

Almost from the start, the Enlightenment did not go unchallenged, but generated various reactive forms of the Counter-Enlightenment or Romanticism, forms that shook the foundations of our modern self-understanding as autonomous, free, morally responsible, rational beings.[49] Three of these forms found particular resonance in subsequent political and cultural history and, as it happens, all three provide an indispensable background to any understanding of Wagner's intellectual development.

One of these forms, the latest to appear but the earliest to impinge on Wagner's mature outlook, took its point of departure directly from Hegel. In Central Europe in the period between the revolutions of 1830 and 1848, Hegel was the philosopher to follow, to struggle with, and to overcome. The most influential fruit of this overcoming was the theory of history formulated by Karl Marx (1818–1883) in a series of texts among which *The Communist Manifesto* (1848, written together with his collaborator, Friedrich Engels) and especially the preface to *A Critique of Political Economy* (1859) enjoyed particular resonance.[50] (I shall discuss the extent as well as the limits of Marx's relevance to Wagner's work in the chapter on *Der Ring des Nibelungen*.) No less than Kant and Hegel before him, Marx inherited and developed further the philosophical dream formulated a century earlier by Rousseau. The dream involved the abolition of the hostile and painful separation between humans and their world, also between man and his fellows; it foresaw a return on a higher level, under the conditions of a fully developed civilization, to the primeval harmony among humans and between humans and nature. To realize this dream, one needed first to locate the causes of man's alienation from his world. Hegel identified these causes in the self-developmental activity of the supra-individual social-cultural spirit, in the internal dialectical dynamic of culture, and specifically in our common efforts to harmonize our actual practices and institutions with our professed norms and aspirations. Unlike Hegel, Marx agreed with the leaders of the Young Hegelians, such as Ludwig Feuerbach (1804–1872), that the causes of alienation lie in the empirical this-worldly situation of man, though he rejected Feuerbach's specific claim that the alienation was the result of our mythologizing displacement of our own values onto the other, divine, world. (For a brief moment in the early 1840s, Feuerbach's books, especially *The Essence of Christianity* of 1841 and *Principles of the Philosophy of the Future* of 1843, enjoyed considerable influence; years later, Engels would testify that Feuerbach's writings helped him and Marx turn away from Hegelian idealism toward a more materialist mode of thinking.)[51] Instead, Marx proposed to seek the external material causes of alienation, to see alienation as the inevitable result of technological progress that led to the division of labor and the resultant alienation of labor—the situation in which, instead of recognizing ourselves in our own products when using them, we are enslaved by them, because we treat them as tradable commodities whose value lies not in the use we make of them, but in the possibility of exchange by means of the abstract medium of money. The social process of exchange, functioning without any human control as if it were an impersonal law of nature, inevitably leads to the accumulation of capital in the hands of a few and the enslavement of the dispossessed many. In this way, alienation of labor results in the institution of private property and the political and legal arrangements that defend it. (In other words, Marx formulated one version of what Theodor Adorno and Max Horkheimer would later dub the "dialectic of enlightenment": our very success in subjugating nature to our will leads to our enslavement.)[52] Once one has identified the causes of alienation, one can work toward its elimination by removing these causes. Hence Marx's political program: the abolition of private property, and, presumably, of its source in the division of labor. But since the owners of capital are unlikely to give it up of their own free will, a violent revolution is the only way in which this program might be realized.

Thus, taking his point of departure from Hegel, Marx ended up on the philosopher's antipodes. For Marx, the abolition of private property is the prerequisite for the abolition of alienation and hence the emancipation of humankind. For Hegel, the right to property is the barest minimum of what is required if an individual's freedom is to be safeguarded. If a person is to be able to exercise free choice (not just to know that he is free, but actually to be free), he must have available to him an inviolable sphere around him within which he can make his arbitrary choices. This sphere is, precisely, property, which for Hegel includes my right to my life and body.[53] Had he been able to read Marx's prescriptions, Hegel would have likely concluded that they were a recipe for despotism.

But Marx's theory does more than undermine the "negative" and "bourgeois" freedom of individuals to be, within limits, free of interference with their arbitrary choices. It also undermines the most essential component of the modern self-image, our autonomy. Marx's historical materialism puts forward a highly determinist picture of human history. Technological progress is inevitable, and so are its consequences, from the division of labor, through its alienation (the commodification of its products, trade, private property), the accumulation of the capital in the hands of the bourgeoisie and the enslavement of the proletariat, all the way to the inevitably resulting proletarian revolution and the final Communist emancipation of humankind. A picture like this empties autonomy, our ability to rationally guide ourselves, of all meaning. History is going to march forward regardless of what we do. Our best course of action is to hasten this march (for instance by philosophically guiding the proletarians as their intellectual avant-garde), even if such acceleration would involve violence and coercion. While Kant and Hegel located the ultimate authority for our inescapable moral obligations— the distinction between good and evil as well as the sense of responsibility for them—in Reason, Marx and his followers located it in History. In so doing they implied that History's victors were not merely factually victorious, but also morally right no matter how much blood they had on their hands.

Already Kant had talked of "a history with a definite natural plan for creatures who have no plan of their own," thus giving the impression that the course of history may be governed by a predetermined law of nature.[54] Similarly, there are statements in the introduction to Hegel's *Lectures on the Philosophy of World History* (his single most widely read and influential text and one that Wagner also chose as his introduction to the philosopher in the revolutionary winter of 1848–49)[55] that, taken out of context, might give the impression that his theory of history, too, is determinist, statements such as that "the history of the world is a rational process, the rational and necessary evolution of the world spirit."[56] But this impression would be as incorrect for Hegel as it is for Kant. Both would consider the search for laws of history to be fundamentally misguided: one should not confuse culture, the domain of freedom, with nature, the realm of determinism. Hegel did not claim that humanity was predetermined to become increasingly free, only that one way to interpret history was to see in it a series of attempts, growing out of Greek and Judeo-Christian roots, to give our collective aspiration to equal freedom for all an embodiment of adequate practices and institutions. Marx, on the other hand, does seem to believe that he is discovering genuine laws of history. What he offers in his historical materialism is not a hermeneutic device for interpreting the past or a norm that helps us to distinguish desirable future developments from undesirable ones (as Kant and Hegel do), but a "scientific" theory presumably capable of explaining the past and, more importantly, predicting the future. A theory of this sort, if widely believed (as it has been for about a century), is bound to undermine the very foundations of the autonomy-centered self-image of man that Kant and Hegel had articulated and perfected with so much effort.

Nation

But History was only one of the three main rivals of the autonomous Reason or God for the role of the ultimate authority grounding our inescapable moral obligations that competed with one another during Wagner's lifetime. Another potent idea, and one that emerged the earliest of the three, was that of Nation. (The extent and the limits of the relevance of this idea to Wagner's work will be discussed in the chapter on *Die Meistersinger von Nürnberg*.)

Nationalism became a significant component of the political-ideological landscape in Europe only during the early years of the nineteenth century, but its intellectual roots go back to two seminal eighteenth-century thinkers.[57] One of these was, once again, the ubiquitous Jean-Jacques Rousseau (1712–1778). In *The Social Contract* (1762), Rousseau proposed the principle of popular sovereignty according to which if the sovereign authority in the state was to be legitimate, it had to emanate not from the will of God, or a God-anointed prince, but from the "general will" (*volonté générale*) of the people, the whole collectivity of equal and free citizens, rather than the prince's subjects. The French Revolution made popular sovereignty its guiding principle and gave the people, the collective of all the citizens of the country, the name of "the nation" (*la nation*). Thus Rousseau may be considered the intellectual architect of what is often referred to as democratic or "civic" nationalism, the ideology that sees all legitimate sovereign power in a country as emanating from the united general will of the nation.

Nineteenth-century nationalism, however, is not just "civic." It is also "cultural" or even "ethnic." For the modern nationalist ideology to be born, more was needed than Rousseau's principle of popular sovereignty. The other, in this respect much more seminal, eighteenth-century figure presiding over the birth of nationalism was Kant's erstwhile student and later opponent, Johann Gottfried von Herder (1744–1803). It was Herder who provided the nationalist ideology with its most characteristic ingredient, the idea of the essential rather than merely accidental differences between nations. In a series of writings that culminated in his voluminous *Ideas for the Philosophy of History of Humanity* (1784–91), Herder articulated the principles of what might be called cultural nationalism, and what much later was to be called multiculturalism.[58]

For all their disagreements with one another, Rousseau, Kant, and Hegel shared a belief in the essential similarity of all humans. Herder, by contrast, was fascinated by human diversity. He insisted on radical differences between cultures and celebrated, rather than deplored, these differences. Humanity, he thought, is naturally divided into nations (which he termed "the people"—*das Volk*), societies united by common cultures consisting of shared practices and institutions, traditions and memories. Each culture is unique—it embodies a unique way of experiencing the world, a unique attitude to life, a unique set of likes and dislikes and values. His

Enlightenment predecessors and contemporaries thought of "culture" primarily in opposition to "nature" and tended to emphasize its universalizing tendency, arguing that it was the function of culture to lead us to a more universal point of view, raising us above our natural instincts and drives as well as our tribal traditions and prejudices. Herder on the other hand preferred to think of a culture as in opposition to other cultures and tended to emphasize and cherish its original particularity and authenticity.

The main vehicle of a culture and the carrier of its uniqueness from one generation to the next is language. Humans are inescapably linguistic creatures. Their whole mental life finds a necessary embodiment and expression in language, and language is not something we create; it is something we inherit. We become who we are by learning to speak and think in this inherited medium that transmits the collective and intergenerational experience and attitude to life of our people. Thus we acquire an individual identity simultaneously with a collective one. In his understanding of language, too, Herder characteristically differs from his contemporaries. When Rousseau thinks about language in his *Essay on the Origin of Languages* (1754–61), he is interested in language as such and pays little attention to linguistic diversity; by contrast, Herder, in his *Essay on the Origin of Language* (1772), is particularly struck precisely by the fact that there are so many languages and that they are so different from one another. One imagines that, had Rousseau reminded him that one can translate from one language to another, Herder would retort that such translations are never completely successful.

It is because we are inescapably linguistic that we are inescapably social, necessarily belonging. Like later Hegel, whom he certainly influenced, and unlike Kant, Herder insisted on seeing individuals as essentially social and historical, as belonging to a social group. Unlike most thinkers of the Enlightenment, but like many Romantics after him, Herder does not see individuals as primary and groups as derived. Quite the contrary. A society is not something that preexisting isolated individuals contract to establish; rather, individuals are formed and determined by the communal culture that both precedes and survives them. My most essential identity is that of a group member: my people and their culture determine who I am. "Determine" is the key word here. Whether I want it or not, whether I am aware of it or not, all that I do, think, and say expresses not just me, the individual person, but my group, its values and its aspirations.

Herder's most essential beliefs, in sum, are these:

- that humanity is naturally divided into a plurality of peoples, each united by its own individual culture, its practices, institutions, traditions, memories, and above all language (cultural pluralism);
- that cultures are not only plural and different from one another, but also embody and express values that are incommensurable and hence cannot be

compared with, or hierarchically related to, one another; which is to say, there are no higher universal rational standards that would allow us to step outside and evaluate a given culture (cultural relativism);
- that cultures are primary and the identities and values of individuals are derived from, and determined by, them (cultural determinism).

It should be obvious that these beliefs run against some of the most fundamental, at once universalizing and individualizing, tenets of the Enlightenment: that all humans are essentially similar; that, for all the local surface variations, the universal human nature always and everywhere is basically the same; that humankind as a whole steadily progresses with higher, more universal civilizations replacing lower, more parochial ones; that individuals are autonomous, their most fundamental principles grounded in their own universal Reason.

The debate between the Kantian Enlightenment and the Herderian Counter-Enlightenment continues unabated. In particular, the cosmopolitan Kantians worry—with good grounds—that their opponents have no way of explaining what, if anything, is wrong with such cultural practices as, say, female circumcision or chopping off thieves' hands. For their part, the multiculturalist Herderians fear that their adversaries would make the world bleakly uniform and homogeneous. Kantians respond that their minimalist universal standards leave plenty of room for cultural diversity and that a world without some cultural practices they find particularly repugnant is preferable to a world with them, and while they persuade *me*, they leave a thoroughgoing Herderian unmoved. It is a debate with no resolution in sight, because the insights offered by each side have become indispensable, but difficult to reconcile. We moderns have come to believe both that our individual identity is powerfully shaped by the group or groups to which we belong *and* that some notion of universal human rights is an essential component of this identity. The precise balancing of these insights will remain a never-ending task.

The central issue in this debate is whether or not we have a standpoint from which to criticize our culture as well as the cultures of others. Herder's insight that we are profoundly formed by our culture is incontestable; what is contested is the extent of this forming. A conclusion that we are completely determined by our group identity would render any notion of autonomy null and void and carry with it morally and politically catastrophic consequences. If humanity is not a moral but merely a biological and cultural concept, if our notion of what constitutes good and what evil is wholly determined by the values of our group, it would follow that anything we want is ipso facto good, good because *we* want it, and hence that we can and should climb over the dead bodies of those who would stand in our way. Consistent followers of Herder are in an analogous position to the followers of Marx: if the ultimate authority for our fundamental rights and obligations is located in *our* nation rather than in God or in the universal Reason, then the victors in any struggle between nations can feel not merely factually victorious, but also morally justified, no matter what crimes they committed to achieve their victory. To be sure, Herder himself expressly avoided this consequence and tried to combine his cultural pluralism, relativism, and determinism with some notion of a universal "humanity," but he did not succeed in synthesizing his cosmopolitanism and his multiculturalism in an entirely coherent way. In any case, it was his multiculturalism that made the lasting impression.

Herder's views differ in one important respect from those professed by the fullfledged nineteenth-century nationalists. His nationalism is cultural rather than political. Unlike the *nation* born of Rousseau and the French Revolution, Herder's *Volk* is not a political collectivity of all the citizens of a state. Rather, it is a cultural collectivity of all the people who share a common language, customs, and memories. This distinction between a (Herderian) *Kulturnation* and a (Rousseauist) *Staatsnation* will retain particular resonance in nineteenth-century Germany, where numerous intellectuals from Goethe on will express a preference for the former. This group includes Wagner, at least in some periods of his life. The final words of *Die Meistersinger*, "Even if the Holy Roman Empire goes up in smoke, we would still have the holy German art!" ("zerging' in Dunst das heil'ge römsche Reich, uns bliebe gleich die heil'ge deutsche Kunst!"), have a distinctly Herderian ring to them. For the modern political ideology of nationalism to be born, a synthesis of Rousseau and Herder was necessary, as modern nationalism is political and cultural at once. Moreover, Herder's conviction that cultural variety need not breed conflict was much easier to maintain as long as one imagined a world consisting of apolitical cultural entities. In the world of distinct political nations, it was hard not to replace a pacific patriotism by a defensive-aggressive nationalism. These signal developments—the Rousseau-Herder synthesis and the recognition that such a synthesis implies international conflict—are particularly associated with the theories of Johann Gottlieb Fichte (1762–1814).

Fichte's *Addresses to the German Nation*, delivered in Berlin in 1807–8 and published in 1808, is the founding document of full-fledged modern nationalism. The philosopher's defense of the German particularity against the universalizing pretentions of the victorious French Empire was undoubtedly a reaction to the shock of Napoleon's dissolution in 1806 of the Holy Roman Empire of the German Nation, the empire with a supposedly thousand-year-old history initiated by Charlemagne. But the anti-French animus had roots going back far into the eighteenth century. For at least a hundred years before Fichte, French culture was widely seen in Europe as cosmopolitan and aristocratic. As such, it attracted resentment among the increasingly assertive middle classes in the Protestant northern European countries, in particular England, Holland, and Germany. Against the perceived aristocratic cosmopolitanism, artificial vanity, and immorality of the French-based culture of the courts, the Protestant middle classes raised the banner of patriotism, natural authentic values, and virtue, articulating their ideals in the emerging Habermasian "public sphere" of city media such as the press, and city spaces such as the theater.[59] Attempts at establishing a national German theater, first in Hamburg by Gotthold Ephraim Lessing and then in Weimar by Johann Wolfgang von Goethe and Friedrich Schiller—theater centered on the new genre of bourgeois tragedy and independent of French models—were a characteristic outcome of this trend. Wagner's Festival Theater in Bayreuth will be a distant echo, or, as he would more likely put it, a culmination of these attempts.

Herder's defense of the cultural particularity of each nation, a particularity rooted especially in the traditions and customs of its lower classes, was of course also directed against the universalist pretensions of French classicism, just as Rousseau's defense of the sovereignty of the people was directed against the power of the princes and their courts. Thus, in synthesizing the claims of Herder with those of Rousseau, Fichte was tapping into cultural and intellectual currents that were alive long before the Napoleonic invasion, although there can be no doubt that the crisis produced by Napoleon served as the immediate catalyst of the synthesis. The result was the fully developed modern nationalist ideology, the claim that an authentic, culturally rooted nation such as the Germans had the right to be politically sovereign.

Like Herder, Fichte sees the nation as a family writ large. It is not the artificial product of a coldly pragmatic social contract between isolated and calculating individuals arranging to limit their freedom in order to gain security. Rather, it is a moral community held together over many generations by profound emotional ties of common culture—namely, commonly held and deeply loved practices and institutions, traditions, customs, memories, and above all a common language. For Fichte, a national community of this sort takes the place of the transcendent realm once occupied by God. The nation answers our need for transcendence and immortality, as it is by making contributions to our national community that we survive our deaths: "The belief of the noble man in the eternal continuance of his activity even on this earth is accordingly based on the hope for the eternal continuance of the people from which he has sprung and on the particularity of that same people as given by the hidden law we have mentioned, without admixture of and corruption by some alien element.... This particularity is the eternal element to which he entrusts the eternity of his self."[60] Unlike Herder, Fichte prefers to call such a moral community *Nation* rather than *Volk*, a possibly deliberate choice. In the opinion of a recent historian of nationalism, "Fichte's implication is that, although the empire [*Heilige Römische Reich deutscher Nation*] no longer exists, its constituent *Nation* still does."[61] This too resonates with the last words of *Die Meistersinger* quoted above, as does Fichte's insistence that there is a difference between the nation and the state and that the state is there for the sake of the nation: "From all this it follows that the state ... is not something primary, existing for itself, but is merely the means to a higher end, that of the ever-uniform and continuing development of the purely human in this nation."⁶² In this respect, the Germans resemble the ancient Greeks: "As was the case only among the ancient Greeks before them, among the Germans the state and the nation were actually separate from each other."⁶³ As in ancient Greece, so in Germany, the plurality of states was conducive to "the greatest freedom of inquiry and expression that ever a people possessed," since what was suppressed in one territory would be allowed elsewhere.⁶⁴

Fichte also differs from Herder by centering his vision on the opposition between the Germanic and Latinate "halves" of Europe, between the peoples speaking Germanic languages and occupying the largely Protestant center and north of the continent, and the peoples speaking Romance languages in the continent's Catholic west and south. More specifically he focuses on the opposition between Germany and France. The Slavic peoples—and, with the exception of the Greeks, other, smaller groups—remained beyond the philosopher's horizon.

The image that will dominate the thinking of German intellectuals through the nineteenth century and until well after the First World War was born here: Germany as the realm of *Kultur*, intuitive, alive, creative, and philosophical, above all deep, versus France as the realm of *Zivilisation*, rational, dead, imitative, practical, and above all shallow. The image would certainly be recognized by Wagner of the period of *Die Meistersinger* with its centrally important opposition between what is "German" (*deutsch*) and hence "genuine" (*echt*) and what is "romance" (*wälsch*) and hence full of "pretense" (*Dunst*) and "trumpery" (*Tand*), and it would still organize Thomas Mann's thoughts on the significance of the First World War in *Reflections of a Nonpolitical Man* of 1918. Indeed, Wagner's dependence on Fichtean categories in both *Die Meistersinger* and in his writings of the 1860s is striking. It is not surprising to learn that "the centenary of Fichte's birth in 1862 . . . witnessed a remarkable explosion of popular and scholarly interest in the man and his work."⁶⁵ With the rise of the political and racist anti-Semitism in the later nineteenth century, for some thinkers, Wagner early on among them, the qualities ascribed to the French will be ascribed even more emphatically to the Jews, and the German-Jewish or Aryan-Jewish opposition will supplement or supplant the German-French one as the chief engine driving history.⁶⁶

But where Fichte moves most decisively beyond Herder is in his conviction that the Germans are not only different and opposed to the French, but also superior to them and to other nations. Unlike other Germanic tribes who, in abandoning their native realm and moving beyond the Rhine (the Franks and the Burgundians), the Alps (the Ostrogoths and the Longobards), and the Pyrenees (the Visigoths), abandoned also their native language and adopted the language of the Roman Empire, the Germans stayed put and remained true to their own language, traditions, and customs:

The first difference between the fate of the Germans and that of the other [Teutonic] tribes produced from the same stock to present itself directly to our notice is this: the former remained in the original homelands of the ancestral race, whereas the latter migrated to other territories; the former retained and developed the original language of the ancestral race, whereas the latter adopted a foreign language and gradually modified it after their own fashion. This earliest difference explains those which came later—for example, in the original fatherland, in conformity with ancient Teutonic custom, there continued to exist a confederation of states under a ruler with limited powers, whereas in foreign lands, more in keeping with the hitherto prevailing Roman system, the form of government passed over into monarchies.[67]

Fichte continues: "More significant ... is the second change, that of language, which, I believe, establishes a complete contrast between the Germans and the other peoples of Teutonic descent. And here the issue ... is ... that in the former case something peculiar [*Eigenes*] to them has been retained and in the latter something foreign adopted; ... for men are formed by language far more than language is by men."[68] Hence the conclusion: "The difference [between the Germans and the other peoples of Teutonic descent] ... consists in this, that the Germans still speak a living language and have done so ever since it first streamed forth from nature, whereas the other Teutonic tribes speak a language that stirs only on the surface yet is dead at the root."[69] The only other equally original language as German that Fichte mentions is Greek. (The longevity of these ideas is remarkable. As late as 1966, in the notorious interview published posthumously in *Der Spiegel* in 1976, Martin Heidegger will say: "I have in mind especially the inner relationship of the German language with the language of the Greeks and with their thought. This has been confirmed for me today again by the French. When they begin to think, they speak in German, being sure that they could not make it with their own language.")[70]

The superiority of the Germans over the French rests on this loyalty, integrity, and authenticity, above all on loyalty to the language that, for all its historical evolution, they have spoken since its origins. Fichte summarizes:

> (1) With a people who speak a living language spiritual culture intervenes in life; with its opposite spiritual culture and life each go their separate ways. (2) For the same reason a people of the first kind takes all spiritual culture very seriously ... ; conversely, for a people of the second kind spiritual culture is rather an ingenious game ... (3) ... A people of the first kind are honestly diligent and serious in all things, and are assiduous, whereas the second kind allow themselves to be guided by their happy nature. (4) ... In a nation that speaks a living language the great mass of people can be educated ... ; conversely, in a nation of the second type, the cultivated classes divorce themselves from the people.[71]

The fickle French lost their soul when they abandoned their language and adopted a dead one, and their culture is as dead as their language. They are actually not a nation at all. By contrast, the Germans are a true nation:

> All who either live creatively, bringing forth the new themselves, or . . . at least decisively abandon things of vanity and keep watch to see whether somewhere they will be caught by the stream of original life, or . . . at least have an inkling of freedom and do not hate or fear it, but love it: all these are original men; they are, when viewed as a people, an original people, the people as such: Germans. All who resign themselves to being secondary and derivative . . . ; . . . they are, viewed as a people, outside the original people and strangers and foreigners unto it.[72]

And finally: "From this it is clear that men who, following our earlier description of foreignism, do not believe at all in something original and in its continued development, . . . are not a people in the higher sense; and, since they do not, strictly speaking, actually exist, they are equally incapable of possessing a national character."[73]

Herder's nationalism was cultural rather than ethnic or racial. A *Volk* is held together by its evolving historical practices and traditions, not by ties of blood. In fact, Herder expressly rejected the notion of race: "I see no reason for employing this term [race]," he stated; "in spite of the vast realm of change and diversity, *all mankind is one and the same species upon earth.*"[74] Fichte's nationalism was certainly cultural, too, centered as it was on language and the worldview it embodied. It is hard to decide whether it was also ethnic, whether it depended also on biological descent. On the one hand, one can find in the *Addresses* this pronouncement: "Those who believe in spirituality and in the freedom of this spirituality, who desire the eternal progress of this spirituality through freedom—wherever they were born and whichever language they speak—are of our race."[75] On the other, one also reads: "A people is this: the totality of men living together in society and continually producing themselves out of themselves both *naturally* and spiritually" (emphasis mine).[76] But no doubt, the cultural component is the dominant one.

All the same, one can see why the distinction between cultural and ethnic nationalisms can be blurry, why language and ethnicity might blend. In 1786 a British philologist active in India, Sir William Jones (1746–1794), proposed the common derivation of Sanskrit as well as the classical Greek and Latin languages from a no longer extant source that linguists would eventually call Proto-Indo-European. By 1822, in the second edition of the first part of his *German Grammar*, the German philologist Jacob Grimm (1785–1863) systematized the relationships between various linguistic branches and individual languages within the Indo-European family on the basis of consonant shifts among them (Grimm's law), establishing comparative linguistics as a serious and prestigious science in the eyes of the educated public. (Grimm's *German Mythology* of 1835 would become an important point of reference for Wagner.) But once language was recognized as providing the foundation of national identity, a science of language could not remain ideologically and politically neutral and innocent: in Grimm's writings, language and ethnicity blend into one. "Philology, Grimm-style, from its early days had always shown an ambition to become a type of national anthropology," writes Joep Leersen.[77] Like Fichte, Grimm divides the Teutonic tribes inhabiting Europe into those who maintained their original language and those who abandoned it and thus abandoned their very selves. As the nineteenth century progressed, the ethnic and eventually racial conception of nationality grew stronger. Leersen estimates that "the link between race and language was not just Grimm's, it prevailed everywhere in Europe by the mid-century."[78] Gradually, nations came to be defined primarily not in cultural, but in genetic-biological, terms.

But it is only in the later nineteenth century that the ideology of nationalism will be fatefully infected by racism. Herder, we have seen, still believed in the essential unity of the human species. Nineteenth-century thinkers, by contrast, were increasingly inclined to stress racial differences. The cultural originality and authenticity for which Fichte and Grimm praised the Germans was acquiring a biological-racial basis among their successors. The key role in this development was played by Wagner's friend, the French aristocrat Arthur de Gobineau (1816–1882).[79] (The question of the relevance of racism to Wagner's work will be discussed in the chapter on *Parsifal.*) Gobineau was an early proponent of "scientific" racism (like Grimm's linguistics, Gobineau's racism too was for a time taken to be a science) and of racial interpretation of history. He argued for the superiority of the "white" race—the only race that has historically been able to generate true cultures—and especially of its Indo-European "Aryan" component, the progenitor of European aristocracies, over the "yellow" and "black" races. He also argued against the mixing of races, which, he thought, can only lead to cultural degeneration.

Wagner's friendship with the author and his enthusiasm for Gobineau's theories helped to spread their subsequent influence in Germany. A German translation of Gobineau's main work, *An Essay on the Inequality of the Human Races* (1853–55), prepared by a member of the Bayreuth circle, Ludwig Schemann, appeared in 1897. The book made an impression on the circle's most influential intellectual, Houston Stewart Chamberlain (1855–1927), the English friend and son-in-law of Cosima Wagner, the composer's widow. In his widely admired *The Foundations of the Nineteenth Century* (1899), Chamberlain moved beyond Gobineau, however, by making the materialistic Jews into the main historical rivals of the spiritual Aryans (Gobineau was not notably anti-Semitic). A synthesis of the Wagners' and Chamberlain's anti-Semitism with Gobineau's racism, the book was Bayreuth's main contribution to the origins of Nazi ideology. About its general importance Reinhold Brinkmann correctly observed: "The significance of the Bayreuth circle for the propagation and carrying out of the national-socialist thinking and politics in Germany cannot be overestimated."[80] More specifically, Saul Friedländer concluded: "The Bayreuth circle placed the struggle against the Jews in the center of world history and thus made a decisive contribution to the apocalyptic vision of the redemption through the elimination of the Jewish enemy.

To be sure, the redemption still meant for Wagner and even for the Bayreuth circle the elimination of the 'Jewish spirit.'"[81] The transition from the elimination of the "spirit" to the elimination of the people was the Nazis' own contribution. True, racism need not become an indispensable component of the nationalist ideology: both logically and factually, it has been, and remains, possible to be a nationalist without being a racist. Nevertheless, it was the Nazi nationalist-racist synthesis, the marriage of the Fichtean cult of German purity and authenticity with the Gobineau-style cult of racial purity and fear of miscegenation, that revealed the murderous potential of nationalism in the most radical and devastating fashion.

But regardless of whether it is cultural-anthropological or ethnic-biological, nationalism is clearly incompatible with the ideal of self-governing rationality. National determinism, the belief that our individual identity and collective fate are inscribed in the cultural or ethnic blueprint of our people, undermines the notion of the autonomous Reason no less fundamentally than historical determinism. Neither ideology gives us access to a standpoint from which the putative dictates of History or Nation might be examined and criticized.

Will

The notions of History and Nation proved to be the nineteenth century's most fatal ideological legacy to the century that followed. They provided justification for the twin totalitarian systems that were made possible by the avoidable catastrophe of the First World War and the unavoidable arrival of mass societies and thus contributed to Europe's economic, cultural, and moral ruin, threatening for a time to erase from the political map of the continent the last vestiges of the liberal-conservative constitutional order. Ever since, the political mass murders of civilians committed in the European "bloodlands" in the name of these two notions have decisively shaped our moral imagination.[82] By contrast, the third great nineteenth-century rival of the autonomous Reason or God to emerge in Wagner's lifetime, the notion of Will as our ultimate authority, differed from either History or Nation in that it did not provide the basis for a political ideology. It was, in fact, thoroughly antipolitical. Nevertheless it too challenged autonomy-centered human self-understanding, undermining its very foundations. (The idea affected all of Wagner's late music dramas, but its relevance to his work will be discussed in particular in the chapters on *Tristan und Isolde* and *Parsifal*.)

The central figure in the development of this strand of nineteenth-century thought was Arthur Schopenhauer (1788–1860). With a rather grotesque arrogance, Schopenhauer dismissed the philosophy of his much more successful Berlin academic rival Hegel as "absurd" and "senseless," "charlatanism" and "nonsense,"[83] but he worshipped Kant and considered his own work as drawing ultimate consequences from the premises of the critical philosophy. In his magnum opus, *The World as Will and Representation* (1819, with a second, enlarged edition produced in 1844), he accepted, unlike most of Kant's successors, the distinction between the noumenal and phenomenal realms—the former, Kant thought, implied by our exercise of freedom, but otherwise unknown. Not so, Schopenhauer claimed: something can actually be known about the noumenon. For Kant, my inescapable awareness of moral law and responsibility implied the possibility that I may be free, and my freedom implied in turn that the self-conscious mind may be rooted in the noumenal realm. From this carefully drawn chain of inferences, and from the fact that I exercise freedom only when I will something, Schopenhauer somewhat rashly concluded that my will must be identical with the noumenon. But not only *my* will: since the forms of space and time as well as the category of causality are not operative in the noumenal realm, this precedes any phenomenal individuation, and hence the thing-in-itself must be identical not just with my will, but with the undifferentiated will in general (in which my individual will somehow participates). At bottom, everything that is, is constituted of the will-to-be; will is the ultimate ground of all being. And far from unknown, will is something I know immediately, without the mediation of the intellect and its forms and categories. I need these to know the representations of the phenomenal realm; I do not need them, however, to know that I am willing or acting.

But it is misleading to talk of two realms here, as Schopenhauer is not really a dualist. It might be better to talk of two points of view. The world is one, but it can be seen as either will or representation: "This world is, on the one side, entirely *representation*, just as, on the other, it is entirely *will*."[84] Viewed in itself, the world is unitary, unindividuated will. Viewed as the object of the subject's knowledge, through the prism of the subject-provided forms of space, time, and causality, the world is representation, or, rather, a plurality of representations. Thus Schopenhauer avoids Jacobi's charge against Kant that he applied the category of causality to the noumenon. For Schopenhauer, the will does not cause the phenomena, "but that which in itself is will, exists on the other hand as representation."[85]

Representations can be intuitive (perceptions) or abstract (concepts). "The capacity for these [concepts] which distinguishes him [man] from all animals has at all times been called *reason* [*Vernunft*]."[86] Reason endows human existence with a dimension animals lack. "It is therefore worth noting, and indeed wonderful to see, how man, besides his life in the concrete, always lives a second life in the abstract. In the former . . . he must struggle, suffer, and die like the animal. But his life in the abstract . . . is the calm reflection of his life in the concrete. . . . From this double life proceeds that composure in man, so very different from the thoughtlessness of the animal."[87] In addition, Schopenhauer thinks that the will objectifies at different "grades," as individual objects, but also as Platonic Ideas or eternal forms of things. Ideas differ from concepts: "The *concept* is abstract, discursive, wholly undetermined within its sphere, determined only by its limits, attainable and intelligible only to him who has the faculty of reason, communicable by words without further assistance, entirely exhausted by its definition. The *Idea*, on the other hand, definable perhaps as the adequate representative of the concept, is absolutely perceptive, and, although representing an infinite number of individual things, is yet thoroughly definite."[88]

But representations are merely objectifications of what the world is in itself and what "we shall [call] . . . 'will' after the most immediate of its objectifications."[89] It is my own will that provides a clue as to the inmost nature of the world. I am aware of my body as a representation among representations, but I am also aware of it immediately in every act of my will and every action of my body. "The act of will and the action of the body are not two different states objectively known, connected by the bond of causality; they . . . are one and the same thing, though given in two entirely different ways, first quite directly, and then in perception for the understanding. The action of the body is nothing but the act of will objectified, i.e., translated into perception. . . . The whole body is nothing but the objectified will, i.e., will that has become representation."[90] "It is just this double knowledge of our own body which gives us information . . . about what it is, not as representation, but as something over and above this, and hence what it is *in itself*."[91] And this gives us

> a key to the inner being of every phenomenon in nature. We shall judge all objects . . . according to the analogy of this body. We shall therefore assume that as, on the one hand, they are representation . . . , so on the other hand, if we set aside their existence as the subject's representation, what still remains over must be . . . the same as what in ourselves we call *will*. For what other kind of existence or reality could we attribute to the rest of the material world? From what source could we take the elements out of which we construct such a world? Besides the will and the representation, there is absolutely nothing known or conceivable for us. . . . If, therefore, the material world is to be something more than our mere representation, we must say that, besides being the representation, and hence in itself . . . , it is what we find immediately in ourselves as will.[92]

And hence the conclusion: "Only the *will* is *thing-in-itself*. . . . It is that of which all representation . . . is the phenomenon. . . . It is the innermost essence . . . of every particular thing and also of the whole."[93]

To will is to strive: "Universal conflict . . . is essential to the phenomenon of the will."[94] This is because "every grade of the will's objectification fights for the matter, the space, and the time of another."[95] It is a striving that lacks an ultimate purpose.[96] "Absence of all aim, of all limits, belongs to the essential nature of the will in itself, which is an endless striving. . . . Every attained end is at the same time the beginning of a new course, and so on *ad infinitum*."[97] Elsewhere Schopenhauer adds: "No satisfaction . . . is lasting; . . . it is always merely the starting-point of a fresh striving."[98] Therefore, "so long as we are the subject of willing, we never obtain lasting happiness or peace."[99] Schopenhauer's conclusion could not be more pessimistic: "Life swings like a pendulum to and fro between pain and boredom, and these two are in fact its ultimate constituents."[100] (Or, as the Duke in William Shakespeare's *Measure for Measure* put it, "Happy thou art not; / For what thou hast not, still thou striv'st to get, / And what thou hast, forget'st" [III.1.21–23].) And he rejected all optimism explicitly: "I cannot here withhold the statement that *optimism* ... seems to me to be not merely an absurd, but also a really *wicked*, way of thinking, a bitter mockery of the unspeakable sufferings of mankind."[101]

A remedy available only to some is art. Most knowledge is merely instrumental, helping the will to achieve its aims. Knowledge can, however, "free from all the aims of the will, exist purely for itself, simply as a clear mirror of the world; and this is the source of art."[102] As individuals we can know only particular things. We can raise ourselves to the knowledge of Ideas, however, when "knowledge tears itself free from the service of the will precisely by the subject's ceasing to be merely individual, and being now a pure will-less subject of knowledge."[103] The subject now "rests in fixed contemplation of the object ... out of its connexion with any other. ... We do not let abstract thought, the concepts of reason, take possession of our consciousness, but, instead of all this, devote the whole power of our mind to perception ... and let our whole consciousness be filled by the calm contemplation of the natural object actually present. ... We *lose* ourselves entirely in this object ... ; in other words, we forget our individuality, our will."[104] "If, therefore, the object has to such an extent passed out of all relation to something outside it, and the subject has passed out of all relation to the will, what is thus known is no longer the individual thing as such, but the *Idea*. ... Thus at the same time, the person who is involved in this perception is no longer an individual ... ; he is *pure will-less, painless, timeless subject of knowledge.*"[105] This is precisely what art, "the work of genius," does. Unlike everyday experience and science, art "repeats the eternal Ideas apprehended through pure contemplation, the essential and abiding element in all the phenomena of the world. ... Its only source is the knowledge of Ideas; its sole aim is communication of this knowledge."[106] In aesthetic contemplation, "the perceived individual thing is raised to the Idea of its species, and the knowing individual to the pure subject of will-less knowing."[107] This is how we can step "out of the endless stream of willing."[108]

It is clear that Schopenhauer's analysis of what goes on in aesthetic experience runs a variation on Kant's analysis of the judgment of the beautiful in the third *Critique*. In conformity with his critical project, Kant's transcendental argument is designed to unveil the necessary structure of the self-conscious subject that makes aesthetic experience (a universally valid feeling of pleasure) possible. The essential point about esthetic pleasure, Kant argues, is that it is "disinterested." It is not the sort of pleasure we feel when we satisfy a desire; in fact, it is independent of all desiring. It follows that it is also independent of all conceptual thought. When I am interested in an object because I want to use it to satisfy a desire, I need to bring this object under a concept (I must know what it is, what purpose it serves), but I need not have any concept of it when all I want is to contemplate it for its own sake. When, hungry, I eye an apple, I must identify it as an apple and, moreover, a real one, before I can know it as a suitable object of my appetite. But there are other occasions when I am not hungry and can contemplate the apple for the sheer pleasure its play of forms and colors gives me. On such occasions, I do not need to bring the contemplated object under a concept (it is enough to identify it as an "it") and I do not need even to know if it is real. A painted apple will serve just as well, if not better. (Even when I know that what I see is an apple, I put such knowledge in brackets, so to speak.) It is precisely because aesthetic pleasure is disinterested that, even though aesthetic judgment is subjective rather than objective (refers not to the object, but to the subject's feeling of pleasure), it is universal. Since the pleasure I feel in the contemplated object does not depend on my particular condition (say, my being hungry right now) but only on the cognitive capacities I share with all rational beings, I can claim that it is universal. I find the apple that satisfies my hunger *agreeable* to me, but I have no reason to claim that it needs to be agreeable to you (you may, for instance, not be hungry right now). But when I judge an apple, whether painted or real, *beautiful*, I say something more than merely "I like it"; I say, rather, "I like it and you should like it, too." I cannot argue the point since my judgment is non-conceptual, but I can make the claim.

One might object that, as a theory of artistic experience, Kant's analysis is incomplete. We expect more of art than that it merely gives us pleasure in the play of its materials and forms; we expect also that this play embodies a significant spiritual content. We expect, in short, not only beauty, but also truth—truth about ourselves and our world. It was, however, not Kant's intention to provide us with a complete theory of art (his primary interest, in fact, was not the experience of art at all, but rather the experience of nature), but only with a theory of its aesthetic side. And about the specifically aesthetic component of experience, whether of nature or of art, he did say something essential and definitive. It is easy to see why Schopenhauer found Kant's analysis of the judgment of beauty so compelling: for someone who would like to step out of the "endless stream of willing," the idea that the aesthetic experience is "disinterested," free of all desiring and all conceptual thought, would have to be appealing. Thanks to Kant, Schopenhauer found a respite from the curse of individuality and will in aesthetic experience, and specifically in the experience of art (his interest in the experience of nature was relatively limited).

But Schopenhauer did not limit his interest in art to beauty only. Truth mattered, too, as his remarks on tragedy show: "Tragedy is to be regarded . . . as the summit of poetic art. . . . The purpose of this highest poetical achievement is the description of the terrible side of life. . . . It is the antagonism of the will with itself which is here most completely unfolded at the highest grade of its objectivity."[109] One gets the impression that the truth of tragedy is akin to that discovered by philosophy: "The true sense of the tragedy is the deeper insight that what the hero atones for is not his own particular sin, but original sin, in other words, the guilt of existence itself."[110] The beauty of tragedy, then, would be designed as an antidote for its truth. As Nietzsche will put it in a note of 1888, "*We have art*, so that we do not perish of the truth."[111] But the ethical significance of the revelation of tragic truth is that it leads to resignation: "What gives to everything tragic . . . the characteristic tendency to the sublime, is the dawning of the knowledge that the world and life can afford us no true satisfaction, and are therefore not worth our attachment to them. In this the tragic spirit consists; accordingly, it leads to resignation."[112]

If much of Schopenhauer's theory of aesthetic experience repeated the teachings of Kant, his theory of music was highly original (though, as I have argued elsewhere, anticipated to a certain extent by E. T. A. Hoffmann)[113] and destined to enjoy tremendous resonance among musicians, and not only musicians, of the late nineteenth and early twentieth centuries. Music, the philosopher argued, "stands quite apart from all the others [other arts]. In it we do not recognize the copy . . . of any Idea."[114] And yet "we must attribute to music a far more serious and profound significance that refers to the innermost being of the world and of our own self."[115] Music, he concluded, "is as *immediate* an objectification and copy of the whole *will* as the world itself is, indeed as the Ideas are."[116] To be sure, Schopenhauer honestly recognized "that it is essentially impossible to demonstrate this explanation [of the inner essence of music], for it assumes and establishes a relation of music as a representation to that which of its essence can never be representation, and claims to regard music as the copy of an original that can itself never be directly represented."[117] But he thought that his theory plausibly explained why "the effect of music is so very much more powerful and penetrating than is that of the other arts," namely, "these others speak only of the shadow [the Ideas], but music of the essence [the Will]."[118]

Musicians were understandably flattered by a theory that told them that their art alone "reveals the innermost nature of the world."[119] But, as Carl Dahlhaus correctly observed, given the terrible nature of the truth it revealed, the metaphysical dignity of music was a rather equivocal gift.[120] Here is why:

In addition to the innumerable fragments of the real world that we perceive with our senses, we can imagine also the transcendent totality that gives these fragments their place and sense. "Cosmos" was one name the ancients gave such a vision—the harmonious, rational and beautiful, natural order of things against which one transgresses at one's peril. The name premodern Jews and Christians gave transcendence was God—the omnipotent and benevolent author of creation and guarantor of its essential goodness, against whom we have rebelled at the beginning of history and with whom we hope to be reconciled in the posthistorical beyond. The moderns might call it "spirit" (*Geist*)—the totality of human culture in its historical development as we pursue power to set us free of various yokes imposed on us by nature and by ourselves.

What all these visions have in common is their underlying confidence in the fundamental hospitality of the world—its beauty, or goodness, or amenity to our purposes. A Christian, to be sure, sensibly does not expect the return of earthly paradise and knows that his redemption—reconciliation with God—will occur in the other world, if at all, but at least he is confident that redemption is possible. A modern, if he is moderate, is confident that even this world can be gradually improved and turned into a more comfortable and less cruel place, if not quite the paradise on earth imagined by some of his radically utopian (and murderous) brethren. Admittedly, for the premoderns and moderns alike, no positive outcomes are ever guaranteed. Tragedy, or damnation, or failure—slipping back from civilization to barbarism—remain possible, even likely. But all the same, positive outcomes, however imagined, are not out of the question, and hence the pursuits of beauty or goodness or power are not completely pointless. The enlightened moderns in particular, guided by the ideal of rational autonomy or self-governance, were confident that emancipated, mature humans were capable, though by no means certain, of creating for themselves a better, freer, less cruel future. While their religious predecessors and contemporaries put their trust in God, they believed they could have some confidence in Reason.

This, painted with the broadest of brushes, was the picture that prevailed until about the middle of the nineteenth century. After the middle of the century, however, the picture began to darken. What was characteristic of the era that started to emerge then was that for the first time large numbers of educated people began to suspect that the world is not only not underwritten by an omnipotent and benevolent God, but that it is also a world in which even Reason does not amount to much. The prophet of this new era was Schopenhauer. Until quite recently the totality stood for being, harmonious order, logos and sense, beauty and goodness. The importance of Schopenhauer is that he inaugurates the suspicion that the totality stands for nothingness, chaos, senselessness, ugliness, and evil.

In other words, from Plato through Kant, the central tradition of philosophical insight suggested that if you dig sufficiently deeply, to the very foundations of things, what you will discover is a harmonious cosmic order of some sort, the Idea of the Good, or God, or Reason. Schopenhauer challenged this tradition, suggesting that if you dig sufficiently deeply you will discover a discordant chaos, the endless and pointless striving. And art could offer no more than temporary respite from this striving, in transient moments of aesthetic contemplation. "The consolation afforded by art ... is due to the fact that ... the in-itself of life, the will, existence itself, is a constant suffering.... The same thing, on the other hand, as representation alone, purely contemplated, ... presents us with a significant spectacle."[121]

A permanent respite from the will to live is available not to the artist or aesthete, but to an even rarer creature, the saint, someone who "can bring about the will's self-elimination, in other worlds, resignation. This is the ultimate goal, and indeed the innermost nature of all virtue and holiness, and is salvation from the world."[122] Such ascetic surrender should not be confused with suicide: "Far from being denial of the will, suicide is a phenomenon of the will's strong affirmation."[123] Schopenhauer's ethics derives from his view that "essentially *all life is suffering*."[124] Accordingly, "the suffering of another is a direct pleasure for the wicked, and a welcome means to their own well-being for the unjust. The merely just person is content not to cause it."[125] It is otherwise, however, with the noble person: "The suffering he sees in others touches him almost as closely as does his own. He therefore tries to strike a balance between the two, denies himself pleasures, undergoes privations, in order to alleviate another's suffering.... In fact, he recognizes that this extends even to the animals and to the whole of nature; he will therefore not cause suffering even to an animal."[126] He is guided, in short, by love of neighbor (*agape, caritas*), compassion, "whose origin and nature we know to be seeing through the *principium individuationis* [seeing that my individuality and difference from my neighbor is an illusion]." This is what "leads to salvation, that is, to the entire surrender of the will-to-live."[127] The virtue of compassion is the stepping stone on the way to ascetic surrender, to resignation.

For more than thirty years Schopenhauer was largely ignored by the reading public, while the philosophical youth flocked to his despised rival, Hegel, and his followers. The failing revolutions of 1848–49 coincided with, and perhaps partially caused, a diametric reversal in the fortunes of the two philosophers. Hegel's star was temporarily eclipsed as the disappointed revolutionary disciples of the Young Hegelians searched for new philosophical guides and found an explanation for their disappointment in Schopenhauer's pessimism. (It is telling that when Wagner learned of Schopenhauer's existence in 1854, it was from the revolutionary poet and fellow exile in Zurich, Georg Herwegh.) In 1853, an enthusiastic essay on Schopenhauer and his doctrines appeared in *Westminster Review* and transformed the philosopher into an international intellectual celebrity overnight.[128] At long last, the time was ripe and the public was ready.

The single most important thing the public learned from the philosopher was the doctrine of the metaphysical primacy of Will over Reason. Reason, worshiped by the Enlightenment, by Kant, by Hegel, turned out to be a mere instrument in the service of something more primordial and fundamental. To be sure, also Schopenhauer thought that reason, the capacity for abstract conceptual thought, was what distinguished humans from other animals. But this distinction mattered little to him—much less than it did to other philosophers. "Essentially and in the main, we are the same as the animals," he asserted.[129] Intellect, not will, distinguishes us from other animals, but it is will that is primary and intellect is merely its tool. "In our own consciousness the *will* always appears as the primary and fundamental thing, and throughout asserts its preeminence over the intellect."[130] And further: "In all animal beings the *will* is the primary and substantial thing; the *intellect*, on the other hand, is something secondary and additional, in fact a mere tool in the service of the will."[131] Unlike Kant's, Schopenhauer's reason merely helps will to get what it wants; it does not set aims for it. In other words, it is will, not reason, that is the ultimate authority for us, the source of our values.

It should be obvious that the doctrine of the metaphysical primacy of the irrational Will was just as incompatible with the image of man centered on the notion of the autonomous Reason as were the doctrines of historical or national determinism, and that also in this case humans were deprived of a standpoint from which the desires of will might be subjected to examination and critique. More: Schopenhauer's teaching undermined human autonomy at a more fundamental, metaphysical, level than the apparently more empirical, "scientific" theories of historical materialists, nationalists, or racists. (Almost a century will pass until Freud's attempt to provide a scientific theory of the instinctual forces that Schopenhauer would consider to be the phenomenal expression of the noumenal will.)

One would expect that the enthusiastic reception of this teaching was destined for a short life, given that Schopenhauer's metaphysics rested on a rather flimsy analogy, that his identification of the *noumenon* as will is far from compelling. In fact, however, the thinker's vision has had tremendous staying power. Ignored or dismissed by professional philosophers, he continues to resonate with artists from Wagner through Marcel Proust all the way to Samuel Beckett and beyond (Thomas Bernhard). One reason for this staying power, I suspect, is that it proved possible to divorce Schopenhauer's worldview from his metaphysics—that it proved possible to naturalize him, so to speak. Within the same decade in which the philosopher came to public notice, the image of the human condition he propagated was powerfully and unexpectedly reinforced by the theories of Charles Darwin (1809–1882).

In a number of ways, the picture of the world and of humanity's place in it suggested by Darwin's *The Origin of Species* (1859) is strikingly similar to that offered by Schopenhauer, though, of course, unlike Schopenhauer's, it is thoroughly naturalistic. Nature, for Darwin, is a crowded realm of limited resources where plants and animals struggle with one another for existence and where might is the only right there is, where the strong devour the weak. Only those species that carry the best traits (best adapted to their environment) survive. Random variants of these traits arise by chance (eventually Gregor Mendel will elucidate the specific mechanism of heredity producing such variants through mutations of genes) and nature selects from among such chance variants the best ones, allowing those species that carry them to go on living. The adaptive evolution of life, the process of random variation and natural selection, is completely blind and purposeless. If nature can be metaphorically said to "care" for anything, it is surely not any individual organism, but only the species: no individual survives, only species do. Humankind is neither the aim of evolution nor the pinnacle of creation, merely a species among others, though singularly adept at using intellectual tools (tools of social cooperation, such as language and culture in general) in the service of survival.

There is, of course, nothing in Schopenhauer that even remotely approaches Darwin's theory of natural selection. I also do not mean to suggest that the philosopher influenced the biologist in any way. It is, rather, a matter of an affinity of vision. For both, the world is at bottom driven by the will to live and the arena of a pitiless and amoral struggle for survival in which the strong overpower and destroy the weak. ("This world is the battle-ground of tormented and agonized beings who continue to exist only by each devouring the other," Schopenhauer wrote.)[132] For both, it is a struggle lacking an overall ultimate purpose. And for both, it is a struggle in which individuals are doomed to perish no matter what; only the species to which they belong may survive. Schopenhauer makes this last point as emphatically as Darwin will: "It is not the individual that nature cares for, but only the species; and in all seriousness she urges the preservation of the species.... The individual, on the contrary, has no value for nature."[133] Elsewhere he makes this point specifically about organic nature: "From the grade of organic life upwards, she [nature] has only *one* purpose, namely that of *maintaining all the species*.... On the other hand, the individual has for nature only an indirect value, in so far as it is a means for maintaining the species."[134]

Schopenhauer attributes to this fundamental will to live a metaphysical, noumenal, status and sees it operating behind all phenomena, also those of inorganic nature. Less sweepingly, but by the same token also more plausibly, Darwin limits its operation to the phenomenal world (the only one that exists for a scientist) and, moreover, to organic nature only (the only kind that interests a biologist). And it is the tremendous explanatory power of the theory of natural selection that made so compelling the underlying vision of an amoral and pitiless nature that cares not a bit for each one of us. Retrospectively, it lent plausibility, I believe, also to those aspects of Schopenhauer's worldview that might be considered proto-Darwinian even in the eyes of those who might be inclined to doubt the philosopher's metaphysical claims: they saw that the worldview could be naturalized. Thus it is the triumph of Darwinism that accounts, at least in part, for the unexpected staying power of Schopenhauer's theories among artists. They can read in these theories an early version of what has become, since the late nineteenth century, one of the dominant views of the world.

In short, Darwinism, with its vision of the universal and purposeless will to live as the ultimate reality, of nature as completely amoral and indifferent to human fate and offering us no guidance whatsoever, could be read as a naturalized version of Schopenhauerism. And so, in any case, was it interpreted by Wagner. On June 29, 1872, Cosima noted in her *Diary* that her husband was reading now Darwin's

The Origin of Species.¹³⁵ On July 1, 1872, she added: "R. is reading Darwin with enjoyment, only regretting that he [Darwin] did not know Schopenhauer, which would have made so many things easier for him."¹³⁶ On February 10, 1873, she wrote further: "In the evening we begin Darwin's *Origin of Species*, and R. observes that between Schopenhauer and Darwin the same thing has happened as between Kant and Laplace: the *idea* came from Schopenhauer and Darwin developed it, perhaps even without having known Schopenhauer, just as Laplace certainly did not know Kant."¹³⁷ It is evident that, for Wagner, Darwin accomplished a scientific translation of Schopenhauer's essential insights into the very nature of the world.

RELIGION, THE ENLIGHTENMENT, THE COUNTER-ENLIGHTENMENT: THE NEW CONFIGURATION

The story sketched above bears some resemblance to the history of the evolution of the Western worldview repeatedly told by Heidegger.¹³⁸ The essentially Platonic metaphysics of the West describing "the fundamental structure of that which is, as a whole, insofar as that whole is differentiated into the sensory and the suprasensory world and the former is supported and determined by the latter" underlies both Christian religion and European philosophy through Kant.¹³⁹ Subsequently, the suprasensory normative realm (whether the Judeo-Christian God or the autonomous Reason of the Enlightenment) has been abolished. The story I have just told suggests that in the nineteenth century into the void thus created stepped in History (Marx), Nation (Fichte), or Will (Schopenhauer and Darwin).

But the rough chronology of this evolution, from Religion, to the Enlightenment, on to the Counter-Enlightenment in its three principal varieties, is potentially misleading. Heidegger (or, for that matter, Nietzsche before him, and Hegel before Nietzsche) tends to see later developments as replacing earlier stages in the evolution, each philosopher presenting himself as not just the latest one but the last one, the one who offers the last view of the world we will ever need. Unlike the philosophers, a cultural historian would prefer to use a different metaphor and see the successive stages as akin to geological layers, deposited at different times, but not abolishing or replacing one another. In this view, the evolution of culture is not a relay race (to change the metaphor yet again). Rather, it results in layered configurations in which successively introduced worldviews coexist in uneasy and unstable tension. It is one of the characteristic features of the modern age that it is not subject to a single, monolithic world description.

The Enlightenment has never replaced Religion. Rather, the configuration that emerged in the late eighteenth century continued to play the two against each other. Similarly, the Counter-Enlightenment has had several strands, none of which has ever been completely victorious. Rather, the new configuration that emerged in the middle of the nineteenth century and that is still ours complicated the old one further by adding yet another layer to the unstable, conflicted mix. For more than a century and a half now, the inhabitants of the West and, increasingly, other portions of the globe exist in a cultural landscape in which God, Reason, History, Nation, and Will, whether singly or in a variety of alliances, engage in a never-ending competition for their allegiance. This is the grid of tensions that anyone in search of self-understanding has had to navigate. Just as after, roughly, the middle of the eighteenth century it was no longer possible for a thinking and informed person on either side of the Atlantic to maintain an allegiance to God completely untroubled by the notion of autonomous Reason, so after roughly the middle of the nineteenth century it has been no longer possible for such a person to maintain an allegiance to the ideals of the Enlightenment completely untroubled by the disturbing discoveries of the Counter-Enlightenment.

Throughout this period the Western-style liberal-democratic constitutional order that had slowly and haltingly emerged in the wake of the American and French Revolutions of the late eighteenth century has been underpinned by a human self-image that centers on the notion of rational autonomy—our modern self-understanding as autonomous, free, morally responsible, and rational beings—the self-understanding that gave legitimacy and plausibility to our hope that we should be able to govern ourselves successfully. And throughout this period this self-image has had to define and defend itself against competing views, against the tradition that saw humans as radically dependent on a transcendent and eternal divine order on the one hand, and, on the other, the new suggestions that undermined our faith in the autonomous subject by seeing it overwhelmed externally by uncontrollable social forces of historical or national determinism and internally by equally uncontrollable irrational instinctual-biological mechanisms.

Richard Wagner (1813–1883) and Friedrich Nietzsche (1844–1900, though it needs to be remembered that Nietzsche's creative life was effectively over with his mental collapse in the early days of 1889) were among the earliest major figures to react creatively but in different ways to this new cultural configuration, our own post-Enlightenment paradigm that emerged in a fully articulated form by the 1850s. They are among the earliest of our contemporaries. Nietzsche was too young to have played a significant role in shaping Wagner's outlook; quite the contrary, it was Wagner whose impact on Nietzsche's development was decisive. Their fateful encounter, and Nietzsche's role in articulating an important strand in the reception of Wagner's work, will be the subject of this book's epilogue. But their relationship cannot be fully understood without considering the context in which they developed their contrasting reactions to the new cultural constellation. These are worth seeing side by side, as they mutually illuminate one another and allow us to grasp more fully the implications of the current paradigm. These too will be the subject of the epilogue. More specifically, both Wagner and Nietzsche felt the need to confront the way Schopenhauer and Darwin undermined the very foundations of the modern autonomy-centered human self-understanding. Neither was willing or able to make his way back to the most fully developed form the theory of autonomy ever took—to Hegel's interpersonal, communal, self-criticizing and self-grounding "communicative" Reason—though late Wagner did grope in that direction. Having flirted with some of the most radical forms the critique of autonomy took, he was making his way back toward a revitalization of ancient communal traditions. Nietzsche, by contrast, chose to press forward toward the unknown individual projects of self-creation ex nihilo. Their dialogue, explicit and implicit, still goes on.

PART ONE

1

The Secret of Music-Dramatic Form

Music Drama as Opera

1.

The "secret of form" in the music dramas of Richard Wagner, a secret whose existence was announced and solution promised in the title of Alfred Lorenz's tetralogy that appeared between 1924 and 1933, remains unsolved.[1] But if we rightly feel to be closer today to its solution than Lorenz ever got, this is surely due to Carl Dahlhaus's voluminous writings on the subject. Not that Dahlhaus himself ever offered a solution; he was far too brilliant and impatient to be interested in answering questions. His strength lay elsewhere—in an uncanny ability to identify interesting questions and in knowing how to ask them. The working out of answers he left for the most part to others. But to ask a question in the right way is to go far toward providing an answer.

A central concern in this book will be with Wagner's large-scale music-dramatic form, the shaping of complete acts and works in the post-1848 music dramas. To the best of my knowledge, Dahlhaus himself never presented a comprehensive analysis of a complete music drama or even of a complete act; his analytical observations remained focused on smaller music-dramatic units, on "poetic-musical periods" and scenes. All the same, his reconstruction of Wagner's operatic dramaturgy, I believe, offers an indispensable starting point for anyone who might want to attempt a large-scale analysis today.

The most comprehensive statement of these insights can be found in the 1971 book *Wagners Konzeption des musikalischen Dramas*.[2] The ideas presented there were repeated and further developed on a number of occasions, the most important of which are another book of 1971, *Richard Wagners Musikdramen*, and two late statements: "The Dramaturgy of Italian Opera," first published in Italian in 1988, and "What Is a Musical Drama?," first published in English a year later.[3] My reconstruction of Dahlhaus's thought will be based primarily on these four texts, and on the first one in particular. And it will be a reconstruction rather than a straightforward summary. Dahlhaus's thinking is too nimble-footed and mercurial, too ready to digress and follow its quarry along some obscure but promising byway, to allow for a simple summary. But there is a systematic structure hidden beneath the luxuriant overgrowth, and I shall try to bring it out into the open.

2.

What Dahlhaus calls "dramaturgy" is not (as an English-speaking person might expect) the theory of dramatic production and performance, but something more inclusive, the theory of drama, a part of what Aristotle called "poetics": "'Dramaturgy' is to drama what 'poetics' is to poetry: it denotes the essential nature of the categories that form the basis of a drama and can be reconstructed in a dramatic theory."[4] At a minimum, it seems to me, such a theory has to answer two questions. First, what is drama, which is to say, what are its aims? And second, what are its means and how do they serve the aims? It is by following these questions that we should be able to enter the thickets of Dahlhausian thinking without losing our way in them.

"The common definition of drama as a series of events represented onstage" is dismissed right away as "unexceptionable" but also "so banal as to be useless as a starting-point in the search for the basic difference between an ordinary play and a drama in which music is essential."[5] Perhaps the most characteristic feature of Dahlhaus's method as he develops his conception of the Wagnerian post-1848 dramaturgy is that he proceeds by comparing and contrasting this dramaturgy with that of earlier opera (a common move) and by comparing and contrasting the dramaturgy of earlier opera with that of spoken drama (a move that is not common at all, and that may reflect Dahlhaus's eight years of experience as the dramaturg at the Deutsches Theater in Göttingen). Like Wagner, and indeed like Aristotle, Dahlhaus accepts that drama is an onstage representation of an action (a series of events) involving acting and suffering characters. But he also understands that, if he is to capture the essential differences between spoken drama and opera, on the one hand, and between both of these and music drama, on the other, he must consider the means employed by each.

That the main means employed by spoken drama is language, and that that employed by opera is music, is obvious. Less obvious, and crucial, is Dahlhaus's next step. The main discursive form of modern spoken drama, he claims (taking his clue primarily from Peter Szondi's 1956 *Theorie des modernen Dramas*),[6] is dialogue: "The medium of modern drama, as it developed since the sixteenth century, is the dialogue. And dialogue, as the carrier of form, tends to be exclusive. Epic and contemplative moments, which were constitutive for the ancient and medieval theater . . . , were eliminated from drama."[7] And similarly: "The medium and the sole formal principle of modern drama since the Renaissance is dialogue. . . . The goal of dramatic dialogue is a moment of decision when a character becomes aware of his moral autonomy and acts according to his inner motivation."[8] Since the late sixteenth century, modern spoken drama develops its action, a series of events in each of which one situation is changed into another, primarily by means of a dialogue in which the participating characters come to decisions concerning how they will act. Other discursive forms, such as the monologue or the chorus, forms that might introduce contemplative or epic components, are either absent or marginal; in any case more often than not monologues are in effect interior dialogues designed to allow the character to arrive at a decision.

In opera, a dramatic type that developed simultaneously with modern spoken drama ("opera came into the existence at the same time as the drama of the modern era—the drama of Shakespeare and Racine"),[9] the principal means are both language and music and Dahlhaus never tires to remind us that, contrary to popular misrepresentations, the Wagnerian reform of the early 1850s did not envisage putting the music in the service of the words, but rather putting it, along with the words, in the service of the drama: "The text, the poem, is—just like the music—understood by Wagner as a means of the drama, not as its essence."[10] But if in theory both the language and the music are to serve the drama, in operatic practice, in singing, the music overwhelms the language and becomes the opera's principal and defining means. "When, therefore, we speak of 'musical dramaturgy'—dramaturgy that makes use of musical means—we should refer only to the function of music in the creation of a drama. . . . Music does not alight from somewhere outside upon a drama that already has an independent existence, but rather . . . the music alone creates the drama, which is that drama of a special kind."[11] Moreover, the main discursive form of opera is not one that would correspond to the dialogue of the spoken drama, that is, recitative dialogue, but rather one corresponding to the spoken monologue, the aria. What is central in the spoken drama is marginal in the opera, and vice versa. The predominant forms of operatic discourse are the "closed" forms of "melody" (primarily the aria but also others, such as the duet and the ensemble), not the "open" form of "declamation" (the recitative). Conflict between characters is expressed in a configuration of arias, not in dialogue:

> The emphasis has shifted from dialogue, where it lies in a play (which expresses conflict in arguments), to a configuration of monologues in which the affects, as the underlying structure of the drama taking place among the characters, are made musically manifest. . . . If modern European spoken drama . . . rests on the premise that everything important which happens between people can be expressed through

speech, then opera ... has at its core a profound distrust of language. It is not arguments exchanged in recitatives, but affects expressed in arias—i.e., in soliloquies—that reveal the true substance of relationships between characters in a musical drama.... Presenting a configuration of characters in a drama of affects is the stylistic principle opera imposes on the action represented, just as expressing human conflicts in dialogue is the stylistic principle of a play.[12]

The different means and discursive forms emphasized, respectively, by the spoken drama (speaking, dialogue) and opera (singing, aria) are correlated with the difference of the essential features of what gets represented in them—correlated, since it would be hard, and perhaps unnecessary, to decide what is the cause and what the effect in this case. Speaking is a medium of reflection that allows the characters to connect the experienced present with the recollected past and anticipated future, and a dialogue involves at least two such reflective characters. Hence a spoken play emphasizes external action (what happens between individual characters) and its protagonists are reflective in the sense that they relate the present moment to the past and the future: one acts on motives deriving from the remembered past, attempting to change the presently experienced situation into an anticipated future one. Singing, on the other hand, and in particular the solo aria, is a medium of self-expression that allows the character to vent his presently experienced affect without connecting it to the past or the future. Hence an opera emphasizes internal passion, what happens not between individual characters but within this individual character who remains unreflective, that is, imprisoned in the present, and passive, that is, interested not in acting but in passionate self-expression. Thus, Dahlhaus argues:

> [In opera] the stress falls on the scenic-musical moment which is fulfilled by itself and therefore encloses a lyrical aspect. Any given situation is unreflectively experienced in its presence, rather than interpreted on the basis of the relationships that link it with the past and the future. And it seems that the difference with drama is rooted in the nature of music....: The musical tone, just as the affect that it expresses, is "fettered to the sensuous present," so that what went on before and what is still to come pale in significance. Paradoxically speaking, the decisive moments of the action in opera are those when the action stops and is suspended.... The musical-scenic present is not a function of the dramatic aim-directed process that transcends them, but the reverse, the process is a function of the self-sufficient present.[13]

The correlation of the difference in the way time is handled in drama and in opera with the difference between the dominant medium of each is repeatedly emphasized by Dahlhaus: "If, in a play, emphasis lies less on what is happening at the present moment than on the relations to past and future that generate the dialectics of the moment, it is because of the primacy of speech over scenic elements.... In opera, conversely, the focus on the present moment has to do with music's affinity to the scenic."[14] And again:

THE SECRET OF MUSIC-DRAMATIC FORM 53

TABLE 1 Ideal Types I: Drama versus Opera

Aims
Represented object: action versus passion
Temporality: the present related to the past and future versus the present isolated

Means
Kind of discourse: speaking versus singing
Form of discourse: dialogue versus aria

In spoken drama, ... a large ... part of the action is usually unseen. The language of the dialogue adds other meanings to what is shown onstage and these may be remote in both space and time. Music, by contrast, is tied to the place in which it occurs and relates to the moment in which it belongs.... Singing is the essence of operatic music, expressing as it does the present moment ...; and the musical present manifested in it is simultaneously the scenic present. Melodic expression, unlike verbal expression, does not reach beyond the present moment but exists entirely in the given situation; it isolates that situation and lifts it out of its context, so that what has gone before recedes into oblivion with no thought given to the consequences which will follow the particular moment.[15]

In short (table 1), the spoken drama centers on action (dynamic change of situation), and opera on passion (static expression of affects released by the situation). The protagonist of the former relates his present to the past and future, and the protagonist of the latter remains imprisoned in the present. This contrast is correlated with (that is, it is either the cause or the effect of) the contrast between the means and discursive forms emphasized in each type of drama—spoken dialogue and sung aria, respectively. While Dahlhaus's view of opera as centering on passion and aria rather than on action and recitative is something of a commonplace, the second component of his analysis—the observation that opera, unlike spoken drama, emphasizes the present moment at the expense of its connections with the past and future—is highly original. As we shall see, it is crucially important for his understanding of Wagner's dramaturgy.

3.

"The name 'music drama,'" writes Dahlhaus, "seems to have established itself in the 1860s as a designation for what was specific to Wagner's works that one ... did not want to classify as operas."[16] The Wagnerian music drama, Dahlhaus implies, can be understood only with reference to the contrast between spoken drama and opera: it is a new dramatic type that falls somewhere in between the two older ones. The music drama aspires to the condition of the spoken drama, without wanting or being able to give up entirely on its operatic heritage and musical means—that is, on being, precisely, a *music* drama:

> Wagner proceeds in an ambiguous fashion. While the intention to realize drama musically as a dialogue-drama is unmistakable, the subterranean operatic tradition remains paramount.... On the one hand, music drama confers on dialogue the rights that were reserved for it in the modern spoken drama, but not in opera; and the epic-contemplative parts, chorus and monologue, are pushed back.... On the other hand, however, the dialogic structure of music drama that was Wagner's aim is not infrequently endangered by relicts of compositional technique deriving from operatic tradition from which he did not emancipate himself as completely as he believed.[17]

The aspiration to the condition of spoken drama means that an attempt had to be made to shift the point of gravity from monologues to dialogue, that is, from arias to recitative. But for this shift of the point of gravity to be effective, it was not enough simply to phase out or attenuate the arias; rather, the recitative dialogue had to become musically more emphatic, more substantial and interesting, more weighty. Moreover, and this is a crucial point, it would not do simply to make the recitative more like aria, to transform the recitative dialogue into something akin to a duet. The closed forms of vocal melody—the aria, the duet—tend to isolate the present from the past and future, and this isolation was precisely what the music drama wanted to overcome. Thus, what was needed was a new way to compose the recitative, a way that would preserve its "open" declamatory character and yet make it musically more substantial, and, most important, put these new musical means at the service of the drama: it is on them primarily that the burden of binding the present with its past and future was to rest. Indeed, in an entry in her *Diary* on January 12, 1873, Cosima Wagner noted her husband's remark: "'That is my real innovation: that I have incorporated dialogue into opera, and not just as recitative.'"[18]

This new way of composing recitative dialogue Wagner found by examining and adapting the developmental discourse of the Beethovenian symphony. In a nutshell, his solution was to leave the style of the vocal lines in principle intact (the declamation was pushed in the arioso direction already in the Romantic operas of the 1840s) and to concentrate the musical and dramatic interest on the developing variation of the accompanying orchestral discourse based on motives of reminiscence and anticipation—on the *Leitmotivtechnik* that provided a present moment with a recollected past and expected future. Wagner's aim, says Dahlhaus, was "to create a rapprochement between the arioso-declamatory style of vocal melody and the expressive and allegorical motivic writing for orchestra."[19] And the main point of the latter was not merely to provide the orchestral discourse with melodic substance and interest, but to accomplish by musical means what in a spoken drama was accomplished by means of language:

TABLE 2 Ideal Types II: Open versus Closed Composition

Syntax: irregular prose versus regular poetry
Tonality: floating versus stable
Motivic relationships: developing variation versus patterns based on contrast and repetition
Texture: contrapuntal versus homophonic
Form: logical versus architectonic

> The symphonic style in Wagner is the foundation of a leitmotivic technique which forms a counter-instance to the predominance . . . of the musical and scenic present. Leitmotifs, which dramaturgically nearly always function as reminiscence motifs, link the present moment, the visible event, with earlier events or with ideas whose origins lie in the pre-history. However, the delineation of a second, unseen action . . . belongs . . . to the dramaturgy of the spoken genre.[20]

In short, "the symphonic style of orchestral composition, as Wagner recognized, assists the dialogizing of music and the musicalizing of dialogue, and dialogue in turn constitutes the primary medium of a drama whose poetics reflects that of the spoken genre."[21]

Here, too, Dahlhaus relies on an implied contrast between two ideal types, two ways of composing (table 2)—implied, since, admittedly, I am systematizing his thoughts on the subject perhaps beyond the limits he himself would find comfortable. Taking his cue at least in part from Jacques Handschin, who in his 1948 book *Musikgeschichte im Überblick* distinguished the "architectonic" and the "logical" form, Dahlhaus contrasts two compositional systems—systems in the sense that the individual components of each strongly imply, though do not absolutely require, one another.[22] The open system favors prose-like syntax of irregular phrase-lengths, floating or modulating tonality, developing variation of motives, and contrapuntal texture with the main melodic line freely circulating among the inner and outer voices. Its overall result is the open logical form based primarily on a web of motivic relationships spun over the entire length of the musical discourse, relationships that ensure that every present moment of the discourse is connected to moments in the past and future. (Dahlhaus has a weakness for Schoenbergian terminology: "musical prose," "floating tonality," and "developing variation" are all Arnold Schoenberg's locutions.) The closed system, by contrast, favors a "poetic" (or "quadratic") syntax of regular phrase-lengths that do not merely follow one another but form hierarchical patterns (such as the antecedent and consequent phrases in a period), stable tonality, patterns of phrases based on contrast and repetition (such as ABA or AAB), and homophonic texture with the main melodic line staying in one voice. Its overall result is the closed architectonic form that, instead of emphasizing the passage of time, tends to isolate and, so to speak, "absolutize" the present moment so that the discourse as a whole is an extended *nunc stans*.

The individual components of each system are correlated. Thus, for instance, since musical comprehensibility depends on both the regularity of phrasing and the motivic connections, Wagner, "who always aimed at musical innovation, but on the other hand wanted to be immediately and precisely understood,"[23] compensates for the irregular syntax with the increased interconnectedness of leitmotifs: "To make a rough contrast, *Lohengrin* is regular in the musical syntax and difficult to grasp—poor in melodic connections—in its form.... *Ring*, on the other hand, is rich in form-creating pregnant motivic connections ..., but complicated and irregular in the musical syntax."[24] In general, "Between symphonic style, emphasis on dialogue, dissolution of 'quadratic' syntax in 'musical prose' ... , leitmotivic technique, and the delineation of an unseen action beyond the seen, there exists in Wagner a nexus, the individual elements of which can be derived as consequences of each other."[25] In short: "The compositional technique of the *Ring* tetralogy constitutes a 'system' and was described as such by Wagner himself. The 'musical prose,' the 'floating' tonality, and the constitutive leitmotivic technique are just as correlated or complementary as are the 'quadratic' rhythmic syntax, the stable tonality, and the accidental leitmotivic or reminiscence technique."[26]

When conceived at their most abstract, the two systems are clearly independent of the distinction between vocal and instrumental genres. In opera, elements of the open system can be adapted to serve the purpose of "declamation" in recitative, while the closed system serves "melody" in arias, duets, and ensembles. In symphony the themes are articulated in the closed system, while the open system serves to formulate the transitions and developments. Accordingly, one might claim that throughout the long nineteenth century open and closed systems of composition coexisted and that their interplay defined the large-scale form in both opera and instrumental music. Dahlhaus's own claim that "in the evolution of the sonata allegro from the late eighteenth century to the early twentieth, the focus shifted progressively from architecture to logic" is certainly correct and can be extended to embrace opera, too, provided one does not take this shift of focus to signify a complete replacement.[27] In both symphony and opera, for Wagner and his contemporaries the overall form remained based on the interplay of the two principles. Dahlhaus would probably not deny all this, but he might persuasively argue that a natural affinity of some sort exists between the open system of composition and the dynamic developmental temporal logic of the symphony, on the one hand, and the closed system of composition and static atemporal architecture of the aria, on the other. Wagner's post-1848 reform, then, would consist of importing into the composition of recitative dialogue the full resources of the symphonic open system, in particular the developing motivic variation and contrapuntal texture, and thus providing the vocal dialogue with the orchestral substance and weight it required, while ensuring that these resources (the resources of the *Leitmotivtechnik*) serve the drama by connecting the present with the past and future.

The unprecedented density of the motivic content in the orchestral part had one further far-reaching consequence: it gave the orchestra an independent dramatic voice. In addition to its usual functions of providing a privileged direct insight into the mind of the currently speaking and acting character and every now and then a touch of local color, the orchestra now could also allow the composer to step forward occasionally to speak in his own name as a narrator. Thus the music drama not only approached the condition of the spoken drama, but also approximated the poetics of the main literary genre of the nineteenth century—the novel:

> Accordingly, if in the "closed" form of drama the speech is exclusively the expression of the acting personages and not of the dramatist who remains as it were aesthetically anonymous, in music drama, the prototype of which is the *Ring* tetralogy, the author intervenes with his comments in the proceedings, and he does so as a composer, not as a poet. In the musical speech of the leitmotifs, the "orchestral melody," it is Wagner himself who speaks and reaches an understanding with the listeners above the head of the acting personage, so long as the listeners are able to comprehend the musical metaphors.[28]

In his later writings, Dahlhaus expressed himself less categorically, without fundamentally changing his opinion:

> It is unmistakable and was never doubted that what is being expressed musically in the motives is sometimes the conscious and not infrequently the unconscious remembrance of the speaking personage. But a significant number of motives express . . . a sense or a meaningful connection implied in the text or in the stage situation, about which the composer reaches an understanding with the public. . . . Thus, in those leitmotifs that are not grounded in psychology, it is the author—as the narrator in a novel or epic—who is aesthetically present.[29]

4.

What are the analytical consequences of this picture? That is, how can it guide us in an effort to understand Wagner's long-range forms, his way of giving shape to a complete act or even a complete music drama?

One finds in Dahlhaus's writings two separate answers to this question, answers that neither support nor contradict one another, but rather run along parallel and independent lines. The first answer, and the one to which he devotes the most space and attention, centers on Wagner's notion of the "poetic-musical period," which Dahlhaus wants to save from Lorenz's misinterpretations, but in which he, like Lorenz, sees the key to the secret of the Wagnerian form. Lorenz, Dahlhaus argues, misunderstood the nature of the poetic-musical period, but he was right to see in it the principal formal unit of the music drama, articulating the flow of "endless melody" and giving shape and formal coherence to what otherwise would be merely a stream of events. Correctly understood, all poetic-musical periods would be of roughly comparable size of some twenty to thirty measures, similar to the size of a normal nineteenth-century period, and each would be defined by its distinctive poetic and musical contents—its specific configuration of characters and events, on the one hand, and its specific configuration of the constitutive principal motives and the inessential secondary motives, on the other.[30] The form these periods articulated was hierarchical. Motives were grouped into configurations; these constituted periods; these in turn combined into scenes; and finally the whole drama was a series of such scenes: "Musical form, in so far as it is intended, is realized hierarchically as it were: motives are combined into motivic complexes or groups, groups into 'poetic-musical periods,' periods into scenes or parts of scenes . . . , and scenes into the whole drama."[31]

"In so far as it is intended" is the key clause here. The tidy picture is disturbed by Dahlhaus's admission that not everything in the music dramas can be accommodated by it. In addition, the dramas contain sections that are, quite simply, formless. "The Wagnerian exegesis," writes Dahlhaus, "should not presuppose the existence of form throughout, and then assume a failure when the discovery or construction of what was presupposed does not succeed; rather, it must try to decide whether or not it at all makes sense to analyze a complex of motives, a 'poetic-musical period,' or a scene as a form."[32] Accordingly, in an act, individual hierarchically organized units (scenes divided into periods) could swim in a shapeless stream of events. Moreover, Dahlhaus refrained from investigating the shapes of whole acts and dramas and limited his analyses to a few selected scenes. It is a measure of his impact on subsequent research in this area that so did his most interesting successors in Wagnerian analysis.[33]

However, even if this vision of large-scale form in Wagner's music dramas were to be proven correct (and the matter is by no means closed at this point), one problem with it would remain: it offers no clues as to how these individual formal units suspended in the shapeless stream are related to one another. Do they simply follow one another, or do they configure themselves into larger shapes? Dahlhaus's vision does not offer even a suggestion as to how a question of this sort might be investigated.

But twice in *Richard Wagner's Music Dramas*, Dahlhaus offers glimpses of another vision, one that seems to me much more promising. He writes: "The theory that the distinction between recitative and aria or arioso is completely annulled in Wagner's 'endless melody' is one of those dogmas which by over-insistence turn insight into error; the difference is certainly diminished in music drama but not wiped out, and far from being a tiresome relic of traditional form, it plays a structural role."[34] And further: "To ignore the presence of degrees that to some extent recall the division of a scene in opera into recitatives, ariosos and arias would merely be to exchange one kind of simplistic listening—the search for lyrical passages—for another—the immersion in an undifferentiated stream of music.... The differentiation within endless melody must be recognized before the form can be understood."[35]

These are no more than glimpses, as they are never developed or analytically substantiated. But they do suggest how one might move forward in an effort to understand Wagner's long-range forms. They imply a three-step analytical procedure. First, accepting the idea that the Wagnerian recitative dialogue based on the open system of composition constitutes the discursive norm of the music drama, one should proceed to identify all those sections that depart from this norm, whether because they employ some or all of the elements of the closed system of composition, or because what they set is not a dialogue. Second, one should see whether these individual abnormal sections suspended in the sea of discursive normality are or are not related to one another in such a way as to form families and create larger patterns. And third, one should ask whether different kinds of discourse that depart from the norm are coordinated with different kinds of dramatic aims. These ideas will guide the analyses of the music dramas to be undertaken in this book.

Why then did Dahlhaus himself not take this particular road?

The answer surely had something to do with his desire to correct Lorenz. It was Lorenz who offered an understanding of the Wagnerian music-dramatic form that was still authoritative when Dahlhaus began his own Wagner studies, and it was this understanding that had to be addressed at the time. More fundamentally, however, it was probably the result of his desire to capture what was specific and new to Wagner's post-1848 reforms, to emphasize the way the music drama differed from the romantic opera. And there can be little doubt that Dahlhaus's understanding of what was new in later Wagner corresponded to the composer's own understanding of his reforms. In a "Prologue to a Reading of the 'Götterdämmerung' before a Select Audience in Berlin," published in 1873, Wagner wrote:

> People talk of innovations made by me in Opera: for my own part I am conscious of having, if not achieved, at least deliberately striven for this one advantage, the raising of the dramatic dialogue itself to the main subject of musical treatment; whereas in Opera proper the moments of lyrical delay, and mostly violent arrest of the action, had hitherto been deemed the only ones of possible service to the musical composition. The longing to raise the Opera to the dignity of genuine Drama could never wake and wax in the musician, before great masters had enlarged the province of his art in that spirit which now has made our German music acknowledgedly victorious over all its rivals.[36]

Specifically new was Wagner's extraordinary ability to create long stretches of recitative dialogue capable of holding the listener's interest as much for dramatic as for musical reasons. And hence this was what Dahlhaus and his followers concentrated on, singling out for particular attention Wagner's own famous comment on one such stretch in a letter of October 29, 1859, to Mathilde Wesendonck:

> I recognize now that the characteristic fabric of my music . . . , which my friends now regard as so new and so significant, owes its construction above all to the extreme sensitivity which guides me in the direction of mediating and providing an intimate bond between all the different moments of transition that separate the extremes of mood. I should now like to call my most delicate and profound art the art of transition, for the whole fabric of my art is made up of such transitions. . . . My greatest masterpiece in the art of the most delicate and gradual transition is without doubt the great scene in the second act of *Tristan and Isolde*. The opening of this scene presents a life overflowing with all the most violent emotions,—its ending the most solemn and heartfelt longing for death. These are the pillars: and now you see, child, how I have joined these pillars together, and how the one of them leads over into the other. This, after all, is the secret of my musical form, which, in its unity and clarity over an expanse that encompasses every detail, I may be bold enough to claim has never before been dreamt of.[37]

But—even though Wagner's pride here was completely justified, even though the musical-dramatic density, richness, and interest of his dialogue goes far beyond anything attempted by his predecessors and contemporaries—the conjunction of the dialogue and the open system of composition is the discursive norm not only of music drama, but of opera in general. To investigate the large-scale structural implications of the distinction between open and closed sections of an act would deemphasize the specificity of the music drama, treat it as in principle no different from opera. By concentrating on what was new about the music drama, Dahlhaus opened fruitful ways of investigating individual sections of Wagnerian dialogue, but may have obscured access to a comprehensive vision of complete acts and dramas. And the reverse: by turning to the question of large-scale form, I am proposing to treat the music drama as opera.

One implication of such a turn (let the reader be forewarned) is that the analyses that follow will refer relatively rarely to this central staple of the Wagnerian music-dramatic commentary since the days of Hans von Wolzogen's "thematic guidebooks" (the publication of the earliest one, devoted to the *Ring*, coincided with the first Bayreuth Festival; guidebooks to *Tristan* and *Parsifal* followed in 1880 and 1882, respectively), the leitmotif.[38] I do not wish to suggest that leitmotifs are unimportant. Far from it: they are likely to continue to engage the attention of Wagner critics for the foreseeable future and I too will need to invoke them every now and then.[39] But they will not be central to my enterprise. Instead I propose to make liberal use of the vocabulary more at home since the days of Abramo Basevi (whose book on Verdi's operas appeared in 1859) in the world of (*horribile dictu*) the Verdi commentary, the vocabulary associated with the *solita forma* (the usual form) of a multipartite "closed" number in Italian and French operas—terms such as *tempo d'attacco* (an optional "open" introductory section of a duet, ensemble, or aria), *cantabile* (the obligatory "closed" slow opening section), *tempo di mezzo* (an optional "open" middle section motivating a change of mood), and *cabaletta* (the obligatory "closed" fast closing section, usually repeated).[40] My aim throughout is not to provoke traditional Wagnerites (should they still be surviving anywhere) with this distinctively *welsch* terminology and certainly not to diminish our appreciation for the originality of the composer's achievement. Quite the contrary: the originality is likely to stand out even more impressively when we realize that the music dramas are not completely unrelated to the operatic traditions from which they sprang.

When he reconsidered "Wagner's Relevance for Today" in 1963, Theodor Adorno particularly stressed the individuality of Wagner's forms:

> Wagner is the first case of uncompromising musical nominalism . . . : his work is the first in which the primacy of the individual work of art and, within the work, the primacy of the figure in its concrete, elaborated reality, are established fundamentally over any kind of scheme or externally imposed form. He was the first to draw the consequences from the contradiction between traditional forms . . . and the concrete artistic tasks at hand. The contradiction had already made itself felt, rumblingly, in Beethoven, and in essential ways generated his late style. Wagner, then, realized without reservation that the binding, truly general character of musical works of art is to be found, if at all, only through the medium of their particularity and concretion, and not by recourse to any kind of general types.[41]

The claim is correct, as is the postulate Adorno drew from it: "The task of the Wagner interpretation that is needed would be to describe . . . how his forms, without borrowing, express, develop, and create themselves with compelling necessity from within."[42] In proposing to treat the music drama as opera, I intend to deny neither the profound gulf that separates Wagner's dramaturgy from that of Verdi, nor the uniqueness of each of his individual formal solutions. But I do want to suggest that, in creating his unique forms, Wagner reached not only for devices of Beethovenian symphonic development, but also, and centrally, for traditional operatic distinctions and methods.

2

Der Ring des Nibelungen
The Anarchist Utopia

The genius of the loud Steam Age,
Loud WAGNER put it on the stage
W. H. AUDEN, NEW YEAR LETTER, JANUARY 1, 1940

Humanity's youth: troglodyte, anthropopithecus. Total liberation: cage.
LESZEK KOŁAKOWSKI, "REVOLUTION AS A BEAUTIFUL ILLNESS"

Many details of the allegory that is Wagner's *Der Ring des Nibelungen* are unclear and are likely always to remain subject to diverse interpretations, none more so than the ending. But the most general outline of the allegory is neither opaque nor particularly controversial: this is a story of "the twilight of the gods," the end of the old regime that has ruled the world until now, so that it might be replaced by something better.

The old regime has locked two competing powers in a life-and-death struggle. On one side is the traditional political power of the aristocratic pleasure- and beauty-loving elite of mountain-heights gods led by Wotan. His rule rests on legal and constitutional arrangements that have been accumulating since the beginning of history and that limit his freedom of action—constraining, for instance, the freedom of action to deal with the giants who are the gods' providers of paid labor. On the other side is the more recent, modern economic power of the capital accumulated by the new financial elite of plutocrats such as the subterranean dwarf Alberich, who forswears the sensuous beauty and pleasure of love for the sake of single-minded acquisition of wealth. Alberich's rule rests on nothing more than naked economic domination that allows him to enslave and ruthlessly exploit the toiling proletariat of his Nibelung brethren. There can be little doubt that Wagner thought of the myth of *Der Ring des Nibelungen* as capturing the essential features of the contemporary world. An entry in his wife's *Diary* (May 25, 1877) quotes the composer's impressions after a visit to London's docklands: "This is Alberich's dream come true—Nibelheim, world dominion, activity, work, everywhere the oppressive feeling of steam and fog."[1]

This part of Wagner's allegory captured well the essential tension within the public realm in European and North American societies of the mid-nineteenth century, and it has lost little of its diagnostic force even for the liberal democracies of our own day. Power exercised on the basis of traditional legal and constitutional arrangements can be experienced by the members of the society as legitimate, even if these arrangements are seen as highly imperfect and unjust; such power is political, subject to at least a certain degree of public scrutiny and control, and hence it can be exercised openly. Power exercised by a plutocrat simply because he has at his disposal vastly larger sums of money than his fellows will necessarily lack legitimacy in the eyes of the society's members. This applies even if they accept, as most of Wagner's contemporaries did, that only property owners have political rights such as the right to vote, let alone if they are egalitarians, as most of us are now. The more recent and vast the fortune in question, the more tenuous the legitimacy. Such power is economic rather than political, subject to no public scrutiny or control, and hence has to be exercised surreptitiously, remain hidden. The aristocracies that, in spite of all the revolutions, had continued to dominate much of European politics until at least the First World War have long since disappeared, but the potential of privately owned money to influence, undermine, and corrupt publicly debated and arrived at political decisions remains as alive in the mass liberal democracies of today as it was circa 1850; it is one of the central unresolved issues destabilizing our public world.

Indeed, this inescapable instability of liberal democracy might be seen as the tension between its democratic and liberal components, between the public good and private selfishness. For the last two and a half centuries a debate has raged on the respective claims of democratic politics and liberal markets, pitting those who, from Jean-Jacques Rousseau through Karl Marx and beyond, fear the power of privately owned capital to undermine and corrupt the public good against those who, from Adam Smith on, fear that the public suppression of private self-interest would stifle the main engine of economic growth and hence both enslave and impoverish all. This debate is unlikely to abate anytime soon, since we shall continue to have to balance the need to protect the wealth-producing innovation that goes with free markets with the need to defend public-good-producing democratic politics from contamination by private money. The struggle between Wotan and Alberich goes on.

To continue with Wagner's allegory, the "something better" with which this unsatisfactory old regime should be replaced is the world of free and loving humans, Siegfried and Brünnhilde, humans liberated both from the burdens of history and its accumulating obligations and from the lust to dominate others. They are guided instead by mutual love. The background to this apocalyptic-revolutionary regime change is provided by the natural world that predates history and its struggles for power. This is the prelapsarian eternal world of the earth-goddess Erda, whose three daughters, the Norns, spin the threads of destiny to which even the gods are subject, and of the river Rhine and his three daughters, who guard natural resources such as gold, the exploitation of which is the basis of Alberich's claim to power. The regime change involves wiping the slate of nature clean of all history and culture, burning down the gods' luxury residence of Valhalla, returning the Ring fashioned from the stolen Rhine gold to its rightful owners, and beginning from the beginning.

As with the allegory, so too with the music-dramatic form of the tetralogy: many details remain unclear and will be subject to conflicting interpretations, but the general outline of the shape Wagner gave to his gigantic sequence of four operas is not particularly mysterious. Even if we did not know that he had originally (1848) written the text of the last of the four operas (eventually to be called *Götterdämmerung*) and only subsequently decided to provide it first (1851) with one prequel (eventually to be called *Siegfried*) and then (1851–52) with two additional ones (*Das Rheingold* and *Die Walküre*), it would not escape our notice that the main events of the story all take place in *Götterdämmerung*. The two preceding evenings serve to introduce, respectively, the two main human protagonists, Brünnhilde and Siegfried, and show how they became ready for the world-historical roles assigned to them in the drama, the former by becoming a human (*Die Walküre*) and the latter by becoming a hero (*Siegfried*). The first evening, *Das Rheingold*, in turn, a somewhat shorter single act (the remaining three operas are each divided into three acts), is an introduction to the following two introductory evenings as well as the main evening at the end. It serves to present the divine premises of the human tragedy that follows—the main nonhuman protagonists, Wotan and Alberich, and the origin of their historical conflict, as well as the natural forces, the Rhine and Earth, in the background. The whole *Ring*, then, has its main focus in the final evening. This is preceded by two preparatory evenings as well as the first evening that in turn prepares these two—surely the longest throat clearing in the whole history of European drama. Wagner himself explicitly designated the cycle as "a stage festival for three days and a preceding evening" ("Ein Bühnenfestspiel für drei Tage und einen Vorabend"). Unlike the text, the music was composed in the proper order, making it easier for Wagner to control and project this overall music-dramatic shape: 1853–54 *Das Rheingold*; 1854–56 *Die Walküre*; 1856–57 *Siegfried* through the second complete draft of act 2; after an interlude taken by *Tristan und Isolde* (text 1857, music 1857–59) and *Die Meistersinger von Nürnberg* (text 1861–62, music 1862–67), 1864–65 and 1869–71 the rest of *Siegfried*; and 1869–74 *Götterdämmerung*. Only the work on the last music drama, *Parsifal* (text 1877, music 1877–81) did not in the main overlap with the *Ring* project.

DAS RHEINGOLD: THE FALL

The introductory evening of the cycle is Wagner's most doctrinaire work in the sense that it follows most closely (though far from perfectly) the doctrines expounded in *Opera and Drama* (1851), being dominated for particularly long stretches by the composer's most characteristic invention: the arioso recitative dialogue with an orchestral accompaniment saturated with symbolically pregnant motives. But, perhaps precisely because they are relatively rare, the sections of non-recitative, closed-composition discourse stand out with particular clarity and help to shape the whole.

The most important sections of this sort, and the only ones whose significance transcends the limits of a single scene, occur at the beginning of scene 2 and at the end of scene 4, and they are closely related to one another: being related, they provide a unifying frame for scenes 2–4. Dramatically the whole opera is divided into four scenes that take place, respectively, at the bottom of the Rhine (the playground of the Rhinedaughters), on a mountain height near the Rhine where Wotan and other gods dwell, in the subterranean Nibelheim (the abode of Alberich and other Nibelungs), and again on a mountain height near the Rhine. This in itself suggests an introduction (scene 1) followed by the ABA plan (scenes 2–4). The suggestion is strengthened by the corresponding sections of closed-form music at the beginning of scene 2 and the end of scene 4. And it is strengthened further by the tonal plan of the whole: the music of scene 1 is in E-flat/c, and the music framing scenes 2–4 is in D-flat (as will be seen in appendix 1). This, again, suggests an introduction (in E-flat/c) followed by the main body of the opera (in D-flat). The key of D-flat, not incidentally, is also where the whole cycle will end. As if the *Ring* did not have enough introductions already, *Das Rheingold*, the introduction to the two introductory evenings, gets an introduction of its own in scene 1.

And this introduction, in turn, gets its own introduction, the last (or rather first) and most primordial one, the *ur*-introduction of the Prelude that depicts the very beginning, the unchanging natural world before culture and history, the eternally flowing Rhine. According to an entry in Cosima's *Diary* (July 17, 1869), Wagner thought of it as "the world's lullaby."[2] This famously audacious gesture of musical scenery painting (audacious in the unprecedented minimalism of its 136 measures of unadulterated E-flat major chord) announces at once the colossal scale of the whole project and its artistic radicalism—the project of the pursued exile who, having nothing more to lose, can afford to take exorbitant risks. Here the birth of the world, the birth of music from a single tone unfolding into a single consonant harmony, and the birth of modernism are one.

The primal scene that follows seems more intricately structured than any other in *Das Rheingold*. It consists of two sub-scenes separated by an internal, mostly orchestral pantomime interlude, with the first sub-scene ending and second beginning with a brief ensemble Song of the Rhinedaughters (see appendix 1: scene 1). Throughout, the streaming Rhine music of the Prelude is periodically reappearing in the background, unifying the whole scene.

Since the Rhinedaughters' Song is framed in the orchestra (421–27 and 441–47) by the motive one of the daughters had introduced vocally at the beginning of the scene (137–43), the three sections of the first sub-scene suggest an ABA' shape. The second subsection, in turn, gives this shape to the Rhinegold Song itself: an orchestral introduction with superimposed voices (514–35) is here followed by another simple ensemble song of the daughters, the two corresponding statements of which (536–68 and 643–62) frame the Rhinedaughters' recitative dialogue with Alberich (569–642). But both songs are too short and too simple to have much significance for the formal organization of scene 1 as a whole: instead, this is essentially shaped by the orchestral segments—the framing Prelude and Interlude as well as the internal interlude that divides the whole into two halves. (Orchestral interludes that accompany the changes of scenery by a raised curtain will also separate the remaining scenes of the opera, serving as its most obvious articulating signposts.)

Accordingly the most important dramatic event of the scene takes place not within the songs, but within its last open-form section of recitative dialogue. In the first half of the scene, the Rhinedaughters had spurned Alberich's amorous advances, teasing and mocking him mercilessly. Subsequently, during the conversation within the Rhinegold Song, they had provided him with crucial information concerning the gold of their father: "The world's wealth would be won by him who forged from the Rhinegold the ring that would grant him limitless power," sings one of the daughters somewhat tautologically, her vocal line twisting the diatonic triadic fanfare that had announced the radiant appearance of the gold at the beginning of the song into the chromatic shape creeping down and up a minor triad with a minor third added below.[3] From now on it will be associated with the fatal eponymous Ring. "Only the man who forswears the love's sway, only he who disdains love's delights can master the magic spell that rounds a ring from the gold," explains another, she too twisting the ending of her line into the shape of the Ring.[4]

This line, providing as it does the crucial information that the prerequisite for the forging of the wealth- and power-giving Ring is the renunciation of love, must count as the most memorable in *Das Rheingold*: we shall see that not only will it be recalled shortly by the orchestral narrator in the first interlude, it will also reappear, rather enigmatically but significantly, in the first act of *Die Walküre*. Indeed, Wagner is right to see the link between the renunciation of love and the ability to amass money as essential. It is not simply a matter of delayed gratification, the need to postpone expenditure on pleasure in order to be able to accumulate. It is, rather, that the expenditure on pleasure is completely out of place here. Among things we value, love is perhaps the most important example of something that cannot have a monetary price without getting corrupted.

From the Rhinedaughters' hints, Alberich now draws the conclusion of the practical syllogism: since the girls are not to be had, the Rhinedaughters' words on his mind (as the orchestra, fulfilling its usual role of providing a window into a character's thoughts and feelings, makes clear in 671–72), he goes for the pursuit of unlimited wealth and power, curses love and steals the gold.

In the essentially Rousseauist vision that Wagner shared with virtually all of his Young Hegelian generation, thus begins the history of the world—with the fall from the original unchanging and harmonious unity with nature into man's alienation from, and suppression of, his natural instincts and drives so that he may concentrate on the world-changing accumulation of wealth and power. (Hence it was one of the rare missteps in Patrice Chéreau's otherwise perceptive centennial 1976 staging of the *Ring* at Bayreuth to set the opening scene at the foot of a dam controlling the flow of the Rhine's waters: industrial projects taming the forces of nature cannot precede Alberich's fatal deed, since they are precisely what only the rape of the Rhine gold will make possible. To be sure, as we shall find out much later, by the time of the first scene nature had already been long violated by Wotan's original sin of hewing a branch from the world ash tree. But it is Alberich's money, not Wotan's Spear alone, that makes grand industrial projects such as dams possible.) Scene 1 sets the stage for everything that will follow, and proximately for the main story of *Das Rheingold*—the story, told in scenes 2 through 4, of how the luxurious abode of the gods, Valhalla, was paid for with the Nibelung's Ring: the history-initiating Alberich's fall is the price of civilization.

The connection between the Ring and Valhalla is made explicit in the Interlude that separates scenes 1 and 2 (example 1): at 744–50, the Rhinedaughter's crucial line of 617–24 is evoked, again ending with the motive of the Ring, and the motive is then repeated several times (753–54, 757–58, 761–68) to emerge at the beginning of scene 2 (in 769) transformed into the straightened and diatonic motive associated with Valhalla. The orchestra's dual role here deserves attention. As usual in all the interludes of *Das Rheingold*, it accompanies and paints the change of scenery (which takes place with the curtain raised). But in addition, the motivic transformation from Ring to Valhalla also outlines a thought process, an argument, pointing out that there is a connection between Alberich's Ring and Wotan's home. And since there is no one onstage, the interlude seems one of those rare moments in later Wagner where the orchestra gives voice to the narrator, rather than sticking to its normal operatic role of telling us what is on a character's mind. Once the second scene gets under way, however, we realize our mistake: the Ring motive accompanies the moment of Wotan's awakening (791–94) and the god's opening words make clear that his dream was of Valhalla, the splendid residence that would be the seat of his power and fame. It was not the narrator's, but Wotan's, thoughts we have been witnessing all along.

EXAMPLE 1. *Das Rheingold*, 761–70

But was it a mistake? The question cannot be decided: the thinking may be either Wotan's or the narrator's. At this point the god knows nothing about the Ring yet. If the orchestra really conveys his thoughts, it must be his subconscious that is creating the link between the Ring and the dream residence. Regardless, Wagner's orchestra does not want us to miss this crucially important connection between the Ring and the castle; if we miss it, we shall never understand why the damage Alberich wrought cannot be repaired by simply returning the golden Ring to its rightful owners, the Rhine and his daughters, why it requires also that Valhalla be burned down—and this is the question that any interpretation of the *Ring* must answer. Wagner's orchestra obliges by providing an answer. The institutions of the luxurious civilization that the fall made possible must be destroyed if a different and better, unalienated world is to emerge.

The Valhalla music with which scene 2 begins reappears, we already know, toward the end of the last scene, providing a formal frame for the main portion of the opera (table 3). At the beginning of scene 2 the music takes the simple ABA' shape: the initial, purely orchestral presentation of Valhalla (769–88) is repeated at the end with Wotan's voice superimposed (804–26); between these two statements there is a brief section of recitative dialogue (789–803) dominated by the Ring motive in the orchestra (791–94). Wotan and his wife, Fricka, awaken on a mountain height near the Rhine and contemplate the just-completed castle visible on a cliff on the other side of the river, he with delight since for him the castle is the site of "boundless might," but delight tinged with subconscious unease (this orchestral

TABLE 3 *Das Rheingold*, Valhalla Frame of Scenes 2–4

Form	Key	Text incipit	Measures	CD.track.time
Valhalla Orchestral (with superimposed voices)	D-flat		769–826	I.7.0:00–3:51
A	D-flat		769–88	I.7.0:00–1:19
B		Wotan, Gemahl! Erwache!	789–803	I.7.1:19–2:22
A′	D-flat	Vollendet das ewige Werk!	804–26	I.7.2:22–3:51
Gods' entry into Valhalla	D-flat		3666–897	II.13–15
Orchestral, except for an ensemble song (with superimposed voices)				
The thunderstorm	B-flat	Schwüles Gedünst schwebt in der Luft	3666–712	II.13.0:00–2:17
Introduction	G-flat	Zur Burg führt die Brücke	3713–33	II.13.2:17–3:11
A	D-flat	Abendlich strahlt der Sonne Auge	3733–62	II.14.0:00–1:47
B		Von Morgen bis Abend, in Müh' und Angst	3763–93	II.14.1:47–3:35
A′	D-flat	Was deutet der Name?	3793–806	II.14.3:35–4:16
B′		Ihrem Ende eilen sie zu	3807–22	II.14.4:16–4:50
A″	A-flat		3823–26	II.15.0:00–0:13
The Rhinegold Song	A-flat	Rheingold! Rheingold! Reines Gold!	3827–42	II.15.0:13–0:56
"A"	→D-flat	Wehre ihrem Geneck'!	3842–57	II.15.0:56–1:34
The Rhinegold Song	D-flat	Rheingold! Rheingold! Reines Gold!	3858–73	II.15.1:34–2:14
Coda	D-flat		3873–97	II.15.2:14–3:41

Ring motive!), she with foreboding since she knows that the mortgage needs to be paid, but does not know where the money will come from.[5]

Indeed, if one were to summarize the plot of *Das Rheingold* in one sentence, one would have to say that this is a story of how Valhalla was paid for: with the Ring Wotan had stolen from Alberich. By the end, the mortgage has been paid off and the gods can enter the castle. This second part of the frame is formally considerably more complex than the first one was. What in scene 2 was a simple ABA′ pattern is expanded in scene 4 to accommodate not only a recapitulation of the beginning of scene 2, but also a glance back to scene 1 and a proleptic vision of what will be coming in the following evenings. Nevertheless, the main melodic substance is again in the orchestra, and the periodically returning Valhalla music remains the single most important unifying factor also here, just as it was at the beginning of scene 2.

The whole is preceded by music (essentially orchestral, though with a voice declaiming over much of it) that depicts a thunderstorm clearing away the mists that until now had veiled the view of the castle. Its function is to separate the final Valhalla music from the rest of the scene and thus set it into additional relief. The sequence of the gods' entry into Valhalla proper begins with the appearance, onstage and in the orchestra, of the rainbow bridge that extends over the Rhine valley and that will allow the gods to enter the castle on the other side of the river (3713–33). There follows an expanded version of the beginning of scene 2: what before was just ABA′ becomes now ABA′B′A″. As before, the beginnings of B sections are marked by the prominently displayed Ring motive. But, in addition, the first of these presents also something new: a triumphant triadic trumpet fanfare (3779–87; in C), the content of which is specified only most vaguely in the stage direction that describes Wotan "as though seized by a grandiose idea."[6] Wotan's words indicate further that this "grandiose idea" allows him to greet the castle without "dread and dismay."[7] It is only the next evening that we shall find out what the great liberating thought was about: the fanfare stands for the Sword to be wielded by a human hero who, in an as yet unspecified way (unspecified not only for us, but most likely also for Wotan), would secure the gods' rule.

This close succession of the Ring (3763–70) and Sword motives (3779–87) in the first B section (3763–93) is again a significant orchestral representation of a thought process, and this time there is no doubt that the thinking is done by Wotan. In the corresponding spot in scene 2 (789–803), we had to attribute the thought of the Ring to Wotan's subconscious, since he had not yet learned about the Ring's existence. But already then, if only subconsciously, the thought tinged Wotan's dream of Valhalla with foreboding. Now Wotan knows of the Ring and much else, and his dread is fully conscious and justified: the existence of the Ring (the private capital accumulating without any public scrutiny) threatens the stability of the castle (the legitimate if not perfectly just political rule of the traditional elites). He cannot, as before, move directly from the idea of the Ring (at 3763) to that of the castle (at 3793). The "grandiose idea" of the defending Sword (at 3779) needs to intervene and dispel the "anguish" first.[8] And it makes sense that at this point the thought is articulated by the orchestra only: like that of the Ring at the beginning of scene 2, Wotan's thought of the Sword is not yet entirely conscious, an expression of vague hope rather than a fully worked-out plan of action.

Note how the relationship between the idea of the Ring and that of the castle has been enriched between the beginning of scene 2 and the ending of scene 4. At the beginning, the orchestral juxtaposition of the two motives suggested the close relationship, almost equivalence, of these two symbols of power, one economic or financial, the other political, and it also anticipated one of the central insights of *Das Rheingold*: that the luxurious civilization of the gods will have to be paid for with the gold amassed by the Nibelungs toiling for Alberich. At the end of the opera, however, what is emphasized is not the equivalence but the opposition of the two ideas, since it is now clear why the thought of the Ring overshadows with anxiety any pleasure one might feel at the sight of Valhalla. More is at stake, it turns out, than simply uncertainty as to how the castle will be paid for. The Ring and the money it stands for is a threat to the castle and the politics it represents even after the payment has been made. The significance of not only individual motives, but also the relationships among them, is gradually enriched over the course of the drama.

The triumphant fanfare of the Sword in the first B section is likely the reason why scene 4, unlike scene 2, needs the second such section (3807–22): Wotan's hope in the Sword may well be a case of self-delusion. As the gods walk toward the bridge, Loge, the god of fire (an intellectual, more intelligent and crafty than the rest of the lot and hence not much liked by them, but protected by Wotan on account of his usefulness), makes an ironic comment, with the ominous orchestral strains of the Ring motive again in the background: "They're hurrying on towards their end, though they think they will last for ever."[9] Loge's status is ambivalent: a god, he is also fire, a natural element, like the Rhine or Erda, and hence not threatened with extinction as the remaining gods are. It is to his fire that Valhalla will eventually succumb, and even now he is tempted to burn them all down: "To burn them up . . . , instead of feebly fading away with the blind . . . that seems to me not so foolish!"[10] But for now he decides to play along.

Meanwhile, the song of the three daughters of the Rhine is heard from the valley below—the only section in the whole final sequence of events in which voices carry essential melodic material, but only the offstage voices of the Rhinedaughters; those of the onstage characters remain superimposed here as throughout. It is the same Rhinegold Song with which they had joyfully greeted the appearance of the radiant gold in scene 1, but now dimmed and sad as they bewail their loss and plead for the return of the stolen treasure. As in scene 1, also here the Song takes the ABA form, its two statements framing now a brief development of the Valhalla music during which Loge cynically suggests to the daughters that they should rejoice not in the radiance of the gold, but in that of the gods, a suggestion that meets with the gods' equally cynical and derisive laughter. But the last words of the opera belong to the Rhinedaughters, just as the first ones had: "Trusty and true is it here in the depths alone: false and fated is all that rejoices above!"[11] The gold is radiant and beautiful, and provides pure pleasure and joy, only in nature. In culture, transformed into money, it pays for a counterfeit, base civilization.

The final peroration, however, belongs to the orchestra. While the gods cross the rainbow bridge to the castle, a march rhythm of the Valhalla music is heard as the background first to the Sword motive (3873–83) and then to the motive of the rainbow bridge with which the whole sequence began and with which it now ends (3883–97). The saving Sword, as yet only a hope, dispels yet again all anxieties and doubts, allowing the gods to take possession of their residence in the spirit of unbearably pompous and fatuous self-satisfaction.

The sections framing scenes 2 through 4 are the sole bits of closed-form composition in those scenes. The only other formal signposts articulating the otherwise continuous recitative dialogue are the orchestral interludes between the scenes and, within each scene, primarily the entrances and exits of personages that mark the sub-scenes. One might add to these the few monologues that emerge from within the dialogue (appendix 1: scenes 2–4).

Frankly descriptive and endowed with little of the psychological interest of the interlude between scenes 1 and 2, the orchestral passages that link the remaining scenes are Wagner's closest approximation of cinematic music. Since the curtain never goes down and the changes of the scenery are meant to be seen by the audience, the orchestral music goes beyond the normal operatic practice of depicting a static locale and accompanies the changes—something that is easier to convey in the cinema than in the theater. Wotan's and Loge's descent from the mountain height of scene 2 to the subterranean caves of Nibelheim in scene 3, and their ascent back, this time dragging imprisoned Alberich with them, to the same mountain height of scene 4, the scenery transforming itself in reverse order, is tracked both visually and aurally, underscoring what is obvious in any case—the ABA symmetry of scenes 2 through 4.

The plot of this main part of *Das Rheingold* consists of just two essential events: first, in scenes 3 and 4, Wotan, aided by Loge, takes the Ring away from Alberich by force (evidently Wotan's rule of law has its limitations), and second, in scene 4, he reluctantly uses the Ring to pay the builders of the castle, the two brother giants, Fasolt and Fafner. Otherwise, everything that happens serves to prepare for these two events, mainly by providing the characters with information that would motivate them to act in this way. The function of the monologues is either to speed up the delivery of the information or to give the words of the speaker special emphasis and thus commend them to the listeners' attention; otherwise, the monologues differ little from the surrounding dialogue, either dramatically or musically. Loge's monologue, for instance, contains a songlike portion in a single key, D major, at its center, complete with an intimation of an antecedent and consequent (1340–60 plus 1361–73), but such brief lyrical precipitations are not uncommon also within the recitatives (see for instance the earliest such gesture in the direction of songlike diction in the conversation between Wotan and Fricka, at 865–96, or the little D major song of one of the giants, Fafner, about the virtues of Freia's golden apples at 1111–27). Similarly, Mime's monologue in scene 3, which is prompted now and then with brief questions from Loge, begins with a lyrical closed phrase in g (2084–99) but loosens up into a recitative-like open discourse afterward, the whole kept together by a single persistent accompanimental rhythm and periodically returning g minor cadences (at 2136 and 2201).

The payment the giants had been promised for their toils is Freia, the lovely goddess who dispenses the golden apples that keep the gods young and vigorous. Since the gods obviously cannot do without Freia and her apples, a substitute acceptable to the giants has to be found, and Wotan counts on Loge to find one. Loge delivers. Scene 2 centers on his narrative of Alberich's theft of the Rhine gold and its aftermath: having renounced the love of women, the dwarf was able to forge the gold into the Ring that gives its owner unlimited power. Loge's revelations seduce his listeners. Even the dimmer of the gods understand the danger that the Ring represents as long as it remains in Alberich's hands. Donner, otherwise noted mostly for his ability to hammer opponents with thunder, observes that "the dwarf would enslave us all were the Ring not wrested from him" (1521–25), and Wotan immediately agrees: "I must have the ring!"[12] The giants, too, are seduced. The gold, Fafner thinks, is worth more than Freia; with it one might buy even eternal youth. Like many a fool then and now, Fasolt reluctantly consents. (Throughout, it is Fasolt who desires Freia more; Fafner's interest is power.) Once the giants agree to accept Alberich's gold in exchange for Freia, whom they treat as security, Wotan has no choice but to attempt to rob the dwarf.

This is precisely how money corrupts. The fact that we can assign a monetary price to anything does not mean that we should. There are goods that get corrupted once we assign a price to them. Love is the supreme example of such a good, because it belongs to its essence that it be freely given and received, not traded. The corruption was hidden in the giants' bargain with Wotan from the beginning: the loveworthy Freia should not have been treated as a suitable payment for labor. Exchanging her now for money, the giants bring the latent corruption into the open. Alberich was the first to trade love for gold. The giants are his worthy successors. One can disagree with Wagner's and his fellow left-wingers' total condemnation of financial capitalism, one can acknowledge the tremendous benefits financial institutions bestow on us, and yet still recognize that the critics of these institutions make a valid point. The problem with money is that it seems to be capable of replacing all other kinds of value and hence makes everything seem interchangeable. While we need the convenience and benefits of trade, we also need to recognize the value of things that cannot be replaced. Some things are not instrumentally, but intrinsically, valuable—and none more so than human beings.

If scene 2 makes clear why Wotan had to decide to rob Alberich, scene 3 and the beginning of scene 4 show how he did it. The only additional information conveyed in scene 3 is what we learn from the narrative monologue of Alberich's subjugated and rebellious brother, Mime. We Nibelungs, he tells Wotan and Loge, used to be carefree smiths who forged decorative trinkets for our women, but Alberich has used the Ring's power to force us to prospect for gold and amass a hoard for him. (Thus money incessantly breeds more money, enslaving the whole society in the process.) But Mime quickly shows himself no better than his brother, just weaker. Alberich has ordered me to forge him a magic helmet that can make one invisible, he continues. I had hoped to use it to wrest the Ring away from him and thus to enslave him in turn. Alas, I could not guess the spell that would make it work.

Alberich could. The second monologue of scene 3, Alberich's Warning, makes the dwarf's intentions explicit. Already in the dialogue that precedes his monologue he explains to Wotan and Loge that he is amassing the golden hoard with a goal in mind: "The whole of the world I'll win with it as my own."[13] And then he delivers a warning: "You who live, laugh and love up there in the breath of gentle breezes: in my golden grasp I'll capture all you gods! As love has been forsworn by me, so all that lives shall also forswear it: lured by gold, you'll lust after gold alone."[14] For the time being, he tells the god, "you . . . scorn the black elf."[15] Soon, however, "when your menfolk yield to my power, your pretty women, who spurned my wooing, shall forcibly sate the lust of the dwarf."[16]

Has Alberich in this last sentence for a moment forgotten that he speaks to a god? In talking to "men" and "women" he seems to be addressing the whole of humanity. Or is it Wagner who is addressing us? Alberich's warning is easy to read as the composer's prediction of our common fate. All the usual elements of the leftist critique of capitalist society are here, as familiar in the mid-nineteenth as they are in the early twenty-first century, above all the class resentment of the excluded from the luxurious pleasure-and-beauty-loving culture of the ruling elites and the prediction that uncontrolled capital accumulation in private hands will lead to the total subordination of politics to money and the general enslavement of all to the pursuit of money. In Alberich's empire, power will belong to those who have gold and everything, even love, will have a price. Marx could not have said it better.

Alberich believes that in the Tarnhelm—a helmet that allows him to assume any shape and even become invisible—he has a weapon that makes him invulnerable to the theft of the Ring. The crafty Loge proves him wrong: he tricks Alberich into transforming himself into a toad so that the gods can capture and drag him, roped, back to their mountain height. Thus is Alberich hoisted with his own petard. All the same, the Tarnhelm, even if ultimately ineffective, is a perfectly appropriate weapon to defend a financial potentate, sharing its two most characteristic properties with money itself: it belongs to the essence of money that it can be exchanged into anything; and we have already argued that the power money gives its owner tends to be invisible. It acts behind the scenes, bending public political processes and society itself to the financier's will, very much as Alberich, made invisible by his helmet, whips his Nibelung slaves into submission. The musical shape Wagner gives this magic weapon is a minor trick of harmonic sorcery in itself (example 2). The penultimate dominant apart, he uses only consonant diatonic triads of the minor tonic, mediant, and submediant. Yet the flattening of the third in the submediant chord subtly disturbs and destabilizes

EXAMPLE 2. *Das Rheingold*, 1953–68

this consonant ambience, chromatically bending the tonic note itself, so that one cannot be completely sure of the solidity of the harmonic ground on which one treads.

The Tarnhelm is as appropriate a weapon for Alberich as the Spear is for Wotan. Indeed, if the Ring and Valhalla are fitting symbols of what the Nibelung and the god stand for (roughly, the unlimited and hidden private power of money versus the legally limited and open public politics and culture of the traditional elites), the Tarnhelm and the Spear are weapons well suited to defend these different value systems. The Spear is first introduced in scene 2, when Fasolt gives Wotan a civics lesson: "The runes of well-considered contract, safeguarded by your spear, are they no more than sport to you?"[17] And he reminds him: "What you are you are through contracts alone."[18] Wotan himself is fully aware of this, as he makes clear when he stops a potential outbreak of violence between the giants and the gods. Inserting his Spear between them, he tells Donner to hold his thunder: "Stop, you firebrand! Nothing by force! My spearshaft safeguards contracts: spare your hammer's haft."[19] The Spear is the visible public weapon that defends the legal agreements engraved on its shaft. It is as different from the Tarnhelm as Wotan is from Alberich and Valhalla from the Ring.

The two central events of the main part of *Das Rheingold* occur in scene 4. First, the imprisoned Alberich is forced to buy his freedom by yielding to Wotan one by one the golden hoard, the Tarnhelm, and finally the Ring. Second, Wotan, entangled by his contract with the giants, is forced to pay them off by yielding the very same objects. The parallelism is impossible to miss: living in the social space of legal contracts Wotan may feel and be superior to Alberich, who recognizes only the twin logic of violence and money, but otherwise the two competitors for world domination are not all that different from each other.

Perhaps the clearest indication of Wotan's superiority is that he experiences shame, or at least discomfort, at his inappropriate bargain with the giants. He seems to know that love should be freely given, not bought. But Fasolt, marginally less crude than his brother, is susceptible to Freia's charm and will yield her only if the ransom hides her entirely from his sight. Love and gold are incommensurable, but now they need to be measured with the same yardstick. Poles are stuck in the ground on the goddess's two sides to measure her height and breadth and the hoard must fill the same amount of space that she does, or else. Wotan cringes: "Make haste with the work: it irks me greatly!"[20] A little later, he adds: "Deep in my breast the shame of it sears me."[21] But the full measure of shame is yet to be taken. Fasolt can still glimpse Freia's hair; this has to be covered with the Tarnhelm. Yet Fasolt remains dissatisfied: "Her glance still gleams on me here. . . . While I still see this lovely eye, I'll not give up the woman."[22] Freia's eye, the window of her soul, is the last remaining thread that links Fasolt to his vague dream of a higher, freer sort of existence. His brutish brother knows how to cut the thread: Wotan needs to yield the Ring, too. But Wotan also dreams, of world domination, and the Ring is the one thing he is reluctant to yield.

The two monologues of the scene provide, as monologues usually do, information to which both the characters and the audience need to pay particular attention. In this case, there are two of them precisely because Wotan, absorbed in the contemplation of the Ring he had just violently wrested from Alberich, does not pay attention during the first one. Together, the monologues explain why Wotan changes his mind and gives up the Ring as well as the immediate aftermath of his decision—Fasolt's murder of Fafner so that he might be the Ring's sole proprietor.

The essential content of the Curse Alberich pronounces on the forfeited Ring, the content that Wotan initially ignores, is simple: "So shall its [the Ring's] spell now deal death to whoever shall wear it!"[23] Alberich's declamation is held together musically by a single key and an orchestral support dominated by (though not limited to) a single motive, usually identified as the motive of hate. The rest of the Curse reads like an analysis of the effect money has on the human soul. The Ring will bring joy to no one: "May he who owns it be wracked by care, and he who does not be ravaged by greed! Each man shall covet its acquisition, but none shall enjoy it to lasting gain."[24] The lord of the Ring is in reality its slave, deriving no pleasure from its possession and fearing death from him who would have it next. Money enslaves equally all. Those who have it live in fear of losing it, and those who do not have it envy those who do.

Since Wotan is oblivious to the danger, the earth goddess Erda needs to deliver her Warning: "Yield, Wotan! Yield! Flee the curse on the ring!"[25] Erda's impressive statement, like that of Alberich held together by a unifying key and a dominating orchestral motive, finally manages to get the message across: the Ring is better avoided. But Erda's revelations are not completely redundant, since in addition to advising Wotan to shun the Ring she also delivers herself of this dark prophesy (she claims to know the future): "All things that are—end. A day of darkness dawns for the gods."[26] More she will not say, and she leaves Wotan understandably worried. No matter what he does, the twilight of the gods is inevitable. The yielding of the Ring can at best postpone, but not prevent, the final catastrophe.

Erda's prophesy casts a long shadow over the triumphant ending of *Das Rheingold*. Clearly there is something desperate and self-deluding in Wotan's hope in the saving hero and his Sword. As the curtain falls on the introductory evening of the *Ring*, we are left acquainted with the principal powers that govern the world and the conflicts between them. What we do not know is whether, and how, these conflicts can be reconciled. The most fundamental opposition is between the eternal forces of nature and the transitory but still divine (or superhuman) forces of culture. The forces of nature are symbolized principally by the river Rhine and its unsullied natural resource, the gold, while those of culture are represented both by Alberich and his Ring fashioned from the stolen gold and by Wotan and his luxurious abode Valhalla, which needs to be paid for with the stolen Ring. The question this opposition raises is whether culture and nature can be reconciled, whether it is possible, or even desirable, to return the stolen gold to its rightful owner.

But there is a second opposition that arises within culture. This is the conflict between Wotan's often unjust but public and law-based politics defended by his Spear and the corrupting influence of Alberich's private money shielded from public scrutiny by the Tarnhelm. Here too the question arises as to whether reconciliation between these two forces is possible and desirable. Can the conflicting claims of politics and money (to use a tendentious formula of the democrats) or of equality and liberty (to use an equally tendentious formula of the liberals) be balanced? If the answer is yes, then how? If the answer is no, then what next? What can, or should, replace the unstable and hence unsatisfactory disorder of the present world? Wotan's final "grandiose idea" of the saving Sword suggests that he still hopes to find a solution that would perpetuate his rule. Erda's dark but unmistakable prophesy that the rule of the gods is coming to an end suggests that this hope is deluded, but leaves us without a clue as to what might follow this rule—the empire of Alberich, a return to the natural, pre-cultural order, or an as yet unimaginable something else again?

If the world of *Das Rheingold* seems hopelessly entangled, devoid of any viable perspectives, it is because it is not complete: it is a world without humans. The next two evenings of the *Ring* are designed to introduce the two humans whose role it will be to open a different, more hopeful, future: Siegfried, who will yield the dream Sword, and, more importantly still, Brünnhilde, who will be the only protagonist of the cycle without her own weapon and hence perhaps the only one capable of coming up with a solution. The story of *Die Walküre* is basically the story of how Brünnhilde became human and defenseless.

DIE WALKÜRE: HOW ONE BECOMES HUMAN
Act 1: Becoming Wagner

Der Ring des Nibelungen is a myth, and it is the function of a myth to tell the story of an encounter between the human and the divine, to elucidate the human condition by showing how it is inscribed into a larger context, one that transcends the merely human. So far, however, we have met only the eternal forces of nature and the mutable but still superhuman forces of culture. We have not yet met any humans. The introduction of human protagonists in *Die Walküre* raises the emotional and, frankly, the artistic stakes. *Das Rheingold* is an impressive achievement, but in its almost exclusive reliance on recitative dialogue, it is also rather doctrinaire and theory dependent; both artistically and dramatically, it lays out the premises for what is to follow. If *Die Walküre* is Wagner's first masterpiece in his new post-1848 style (and arguably the *Ring*'s most sustained artistic triumph), it is at least in part because in act 1 the composer came up for the first time with a persuasive answer to the question of how to provide an act with unity and formal shape without limiting one's resources to a continuous recitative. Having to work with human protagonists, and more specifically with a soprano and tenor doing what operatic sopranos and tenors have long learned to do best—falling in, and making, love—must have helped him find this answer.

The solution Wagner came up with was simple, though not easy to execute in a convincing fashion: apply the most general formal principle that governs a normal operatic *scena* to the organization of a whole act. The principle relies on the distinction between the open recitative-like discourse and the closed songlike discourse, placing the former at the beginning and the latter at the end of a scene. This provides the scene with a forward thrust and overall shape, moving from a tentative open beginning to a forceful close. Additionally—to introduce categories from an operatic tradition Wagner knew well—a division of the lyrical portion of the scene into an opening slow cantabile and the closing fast cabaletta may help to reinforce this general formal sense. The first act of *Die Walküre* demonstrates in a relatively simple and straightforward fashion how these ideas may be applied. Subsequently Wagner will apply them in various more complex ways and will experiment with other solutions as well, but to the end of his career he will hold on to the thought that he might shape his acts as other composers have shaped their scenes.

Thus, in spite of its nominal division into three scenes, the first act of *Die Walküre* is an operatic *scena* writ large. Taking place inside the forest dwelling of the brutish tribesman, Hunding, it involves primarily Hunding's unloved and unloving young trophy wife, Sieglinde, Wotan's daughter by a no-longer-living mortal woman, and her twin brother, Siegmund, who stumbles into the place accidentally, fleeing his enemies. Hunding himself makes an appearance only in scene 2 of the act; his entrance and exit are the reasons why the act is divided into the three scenes. The twins had been separated early in life, do not know their respective sibling's subsequent fate, and, at first, do not recognize one another. They both know their father under the name of Wälse and thus know themselves to be the Wälsungs, but they do not seem to be aware of Wälse's true identity. Their gradual recognition that they are related and that they are in love is the essential content of the act. It determines the music-dramatic form of the whole. As a first approximation, one might say that the first half of the act (scenes 1 and 2) consists of preparatory recitative dialogues, while the second (scene 3) is an elaborate culminating love duet.

But this is an approximation only. The forms of both halves of the act deserve closer scrutiny. The first one, we already know, is divided by Hunding's entrance into two sections, each articulated further (appendix 2: act 1, scenes 1 and 2). In the first section, the articulation is deliberately attenuated: the Prelude flows directly into scene 1 with no caesura in between, thus assuring that we experience the Prelude, at least in retrospect, as an integral part of the scene and not a mere introduction to it or to the opera. A division, such as it is, results from the fact that at some point after the curtain has been raised and Siegmund appears onstage the d minor music of the Prelude subsides and gives way to the tonally less stable recitative dialogue. In the second section, the internal articulation arises because the centerpiece of the section is a monologue framed by two shorter sections of dialogue, an introduction and a coda of sorts.

Thus Siegmund's monologue is the only section that stands out from the recitative dialogues that surround it in the first half of the act. This too will from now on become Wagner's common procedure. In musical terms, placing a substantial monologue within the recitative dialogues that dominate the first half of the act provides this half with some variety and a focal point. Moreover, it does so without detracting from the sense of the overall formal direction and end-oriented emphasis that the act is given by the use of closed discourse in the second half. In dramatic terms, a narrative monologue at this relatively early point delivers most efficiently the background information that both the characters and the audience need in order to understand what is going on, and it does this emphatically enough so that the listeners pay attention.

While in principle a monologue uses the same kind of open-composition discourse as a recitative dialogue, it may be marked as somewhat different from its surroundings by some elements of closed-composition discourse placed especially at, or near, the beginning. It may also be given some rudimentary formal articulation by interruptions, usually from the listeners prompting the narrator with questions. Thus, Siegmund's narrative is articulated into three parts by brief dialogues involving his listeners (table 4). And it begins with a gesture that suggests that here perhaps we might get an aria at long last: an introductory orchestral phrase (I.476–81), an introductory vocal phrase (I.482–89), both setting up the stable key of g

TABLE 4 *Die Walküre*, Act 1, Siegmund's Monologue

Form	Key	Text incipit	Measures	CD.track.time
Part 1	g	Friedmund darf ich nicht heißen	476–530	I.5.0:00–2:47
Interruption		Wunder und wilde Märe	530–40	I.5.2:47–3:18
Part 2	a	Ein starkes Jagen auf uns	541–94	I.5.3:18–6.2:00
Interruption		Die so leidig Los dir beschied	594–607	I.6.2:00–2:37
Part 3	c	Ein trauriges Kind rief mich zum Trutz	608–74	I.6.2:37–6:02

minor, and something that promises to become the opening phrase of a lyrical statement (I.490–94; example 3). But no sooner is it intimated than the closed discourse is abandoned for an open, free-flowing recitation or arioso: the intimation was all that was needed to mark the beginning of the monologue.

Only two traces of closed discourse remain. One is the relative tonal stability of each of the three parts of the monologue. The other is more important: both verbally and musically, each part gets a similar ending, creating a kind of large-scale rhyme and thus providing additional articulation not only internally, but also for the monologue as a whole (example 4). Moreover, since this element is clearly related to the introductory vocal phrase of the monologue (compare example 4 with I.482–89 in example 3), and since at its last appearance it is introduced by the orchestra similarly to the way that introductory vocal phrase was itself orchestrally introduced (compare I.654–57 in example 4 with I.476–81 in example 3), the whole monologue gets an articulating frame. Thus, in spite of its predominant use of open-composition discourse, the monologue is not deprived of some formal organization that allows it to stand out somewhat from the remaining music of the first two scenes of the act.

The information conveyed by Siegmund's narration is indeed essential. His hosts, Hunding and Sieglinde, want to know who their intruding guest is. Human identity has necessarily a narrative character: we are our life stories. Appropriately, Siegmund answers with a brief autobiography. He barely knew his mother and twin sister: the one was murdered by the numerous enemies of his warlike father, the latter disappeared without a trace. He himself spent many years with his father in the forest pursued by the enemies until one day the father disappeared, too. Ever since, unable to make friends or find a female companion, completely alienated from all humanity, he has roamed the forest. What happened to him most recently is particularly telling, as it shows a characteristic pattern of behavior and previews the rest of his brief existence. A maid whom relatives wanted to force into a loveless marriage called for his help, and help her he did, killing her brothers in the process, causing indirectly her own death, losing his weapons as he fended off the avengers, and ultimately finding himself yet again in flight. Now we know who Siegmund is: a tragic figure, the kind of youth with no chance to succeed in life,

EXAMPLE 3. *Die Walküre*, I.476–94

EXAMPLE 4. *Die Walküre*

a. I.526–30

b. I.581–87

EXAMPLE 4. *(continued)*

c. I.654–66

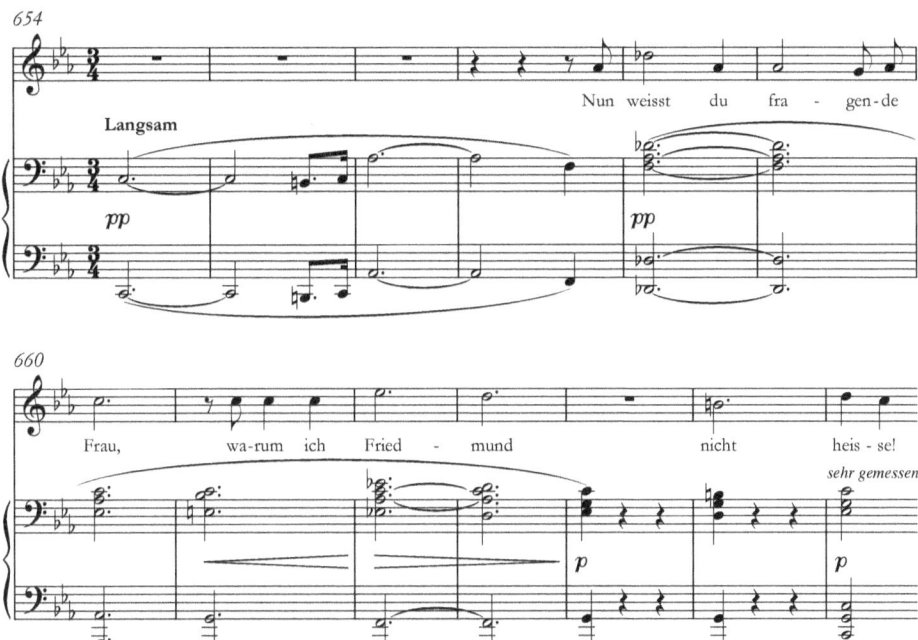

alienated and persecuted, the very image (or, rather, self-image) of the modern nineteenth-century artist. Most essentially he is someone always in flight from death, which is likely to catch up with him soon enough. Indeed, in flight from death is how we see him from the moment he enters the stage all the way to his end. The *Ring* will present no more sympathetic and tragic human characters than he and his sister—their brief love the only flash of lightning illuminating their otherwise bleak and violent existence.

Telling your life story is one way of establishing your identity; another is simply telling your name, especially if this name is telling—if, that is, it encapsulates who you are. But Siegmund is still young, still in search of an answer to the question of who he is, still in search of his true name. The rhyme-like phrases that frame and punctuate his narrative all center on the question of the right name for him, rehearsing various ones in the process (see again examples 3 and 4 above). Thus, Siegmund begins his tale: "Friedmund I may not call myself [*Friede* is "peace"];

Frohwalt fain would I be [*froh* is "glad"]: but Wehwalt I must name myself [*wehe* is "woe"]."[27] Is he right about this? Finding the proper name will be one of his central aims in act 1. The others will be finding the right weapon and the right woman—all three, name, weapon, and woman, definitive of his identity.

There is yet another, third way to answer the question of who you are: this is to talk about your parents. About these, however, Siegmund does not seem to know much, even about the father whom, unlike the mother, he remembers well. At the point in his narrative when he recalls his father's disappearance, the orchestra intervenes with the Valhalla motive we know from *Das Rheingold* (I.556–58). Siegmund may not be aware of his father's real identity, but the orchestral narrator knows whose son he is and shares this information with the audience—another of the rare moments in the *Ring* (and in Wagner's operas in general) where we are compelled to attribute the orchestral voice to the narrator or author speaking directly to the audience above the heads of the characters onstage.

The normal role of the operatic orchestra, we already know, whether with Wagner or anyone else, is to give voice not to some external, third party, such as the narrator, but to what is hidden in the depth of the stage character's soul (a mood, an emotion, a thought). In one of the Zurich reform essays, "The Art-Work of the Future" (written in 1849 and published in 1850), Wagner wrote: "But the inner man can only find *direct* communication through the ear, and that by means of *his voice's* Tone."[28] It is the main job of the orchestra to amplify this tone. In the first two scenes of act 1, the orchestra fulfills this role in a particularly interesting and innovative fashion. Siegmund's monologue aside, this part of the act is entirely given to recitative dialogue. But there is something truly remarkable about this dialogue: from the beginning through the end of scene 2, it is regularly punctuated by sections when the characters are silent and merely perform various actions, pantomime-like, accompanied by the orchestra. Wagner will use pantomime elsewhere, often to great effect—for instance in the first act of *Tristan und Isolde*—but never again at such length. Siegmund and Sieglinde are young, inexperienced, and relatively un-self-reflective. At first they scarcely comprehend what is happening to them—the sudden, immediate birth of mutual sympathy, erotic attraction, passion. They are not yet ready, or able, to verbalize their feelings. But they do feel them, and the orchestra provides us with an insight into what they feel.

The actual pantomime begins right with Siegmund's entrance at I.122. But in a way it begins even earlier, with the first measure of the Prelude (and we already know that no caesura separates the Prelude from scene 1). The "stormy" ("Stürmisch" is the only tempo indication we get) music depicts Siegmund's flight from the pursuing enemies, the flight that will lead him, exhausted, to Hunding's dwelling—the pantomime is implied from the start. It is hard to decide whether the remarkable similarity of the music's main gesture to the accompaniment of Franz Schubert's "Erlkönig" is accidental or not.[29] If the allusion was intended, it is apt: the

Schubert-Goethe ballad, too, is the image of humans in desperate flight from death. The essence of Siegmund's fate is revealed to us even before he enters the stage.

I have indicated that the music surrounding Siegmund's monologue consists of recitative dialogues interspersed with orchestrally accompanied pantomime. This is true enough, but there is a more accurate way to characterize this music. The Prelude and the first scene of the act, in particular, provide an almost uninterrupted, continuous, self-sufficient orchestral discourse, with alternating sections of dialogue and sections of wordless pantomime superimposed over it. (The only, brief and insignificant, interruptions of this continuous orchestral discourse occur in I.142–44, 158–61, 169, 182–84, 237–61, 312–24, 340–49, and 361–64.) It is the striking continuity of this music, the fact that it would make satisfactory sense even if heard without the voices, that (in addition to the pantomime sections, of course) makes it differ from the normal recitative dialogue in which the orchestral part, even when richly saturated with significant motives, is rarely continuous and self-sufficient in this way. As a result, even when Siegmund and Sieglinde do converse, it is the orchestra that is heard to provide most of the content to their dialogue, not the voices, and certainly not the words. From the start the orchestra unites them, makes them in a way single-minded, shows them to be twins and intertwined.

Dramatically, what is perhaps most striking about this remarkable scene is the contrast between the visible and audible surface and the imperceptible depth. The words and actions we hear and observe are tepid and conventional—they belong to any first visit among as yet unacquainted country neighbors. The music, intense and passionate, fraught with suffering and longing from the start, belies this placid surface: these neighbors find one another more than conventionally interesting.

This is particularly so in the three longer passages of wordless pantomime once Sieglinde joins Siegmund onstage (I.185–221—with only a brief splash of superimposed recitative in 200–203; 269–311—again, with a brief superimposed dialogue in 280–86; and 349–80—again, with a brief recitative in 361–65). Even before the first of these passages, the orchestra begins to link Siegmund and Sieglinde by intertwining their characteristic motives in the lower and higher strings as "she bends over him and listens" while he lies motionless and exhausted on the ground (example 5a).[30] Such brief moments of carefully choreographed pantomime are interspersed even within the sections of dialogue, as here. In the first longer pantomime passage (example 5b), this intertwining is developed toward a *forte* culmination (at I.193), the warmth of which seems hardly justified by the simple action we see performed onstage: a hostess bringing a thirsty guest some water to drink. The continuation (I.204–21) is even more striking—a passionate cello solo in which Siegmund's motive unfolds into full-fledged love music, seemingly hardly appropriate as an accompaniment to the simple gesture of thanks from the thirsty guest, even if he begins to eye his hostess with some interest (or "his gaze fixes on her features with growing interest," as the stage direction would have it).[31]

EXAMPLE 5. *Die Walküre*

a. I.170–74

b. I.185–221

EXAMPLE 5. *(continued)*

The second pantomime passage is similar in musical and dramatic content to the first one, and still warmer, with I.269–86 corresponding to I.185–203, and I.287–311 corresponding to I.204–21 (compare example 6 with example 5b). As before, the passage begins with Sieglinde's music accompanying her action of bringing her guest another drink (this time it is mead), and continues with Siegmund's passionate love music as he expresses his gratitude "while fixing his eyes on her with growing warmth."[32] But this time they share the drink and the love music: hers is the first sip and the first love-music phrase (I.287–89); he takes over at I.290.

The third and final pantomime passage is related, consisting of the same ideas (Siegmund, Sieglinde, love) but no longer distributing them into two consecutive phases, even though the passage is again divided into two parts (I.349–61 and 365–80), the latter serving as a major-mode coda to the whole scene (example 7). Siegmund has just expressed his intention to leave: he does not want to bring his new acquaintance the misfortune that pursues him wherever he goes. "Then tarry here!" she replies. "Ill-luck you cannot bring to a house where ill-luck lives!"[33] This *cri de coeur* is the first moment in the dialogue where the vocal line surpasses in its pained eloquence the expressive weight of the orchestral melody, and it is certainly the first moment that shatters the glass ceiling of conventional propriety. The outcry decides Siegmund. The wife is unhappy, and hence he will stay and await the husband. Like the previous two passages of pantomime, the orchestral music that closes scene 1 develops from the duet of the Siegmund and Sieglinde motives (compare examples 7 and 5a) and goes on to add the love music to the mix (by I.373), but the intertwined motives of the unfortunate siblings dominate the discourse. The emphasis is now on the suffering that unites them.

EXAMPLE 6. *Die Walküre*, I.269–311

EXAMPLE 6. *(continued)*

The expressive eloquence of this beautiful first scene is truly remarkable, especially since ostensibly it is no more than a simple recitative dialogue. The continuous orchestral discourse and, above all, the three longer passages of similarly constructed pantomime provide the scene at once with a subtle formal design and with its essential dramatic content—a bond, sympathetic and erotic, begins to unite the protagonists. That it is left to the orchestra to convey this content is testimony to the psychological subtlety of the Wagnerian dramaturgy at this point. He needs and wants to show characters who feel more than they are able to comprehend or express in words. It is also a testimony to the composer's ability to develop the orchestra's traditional operatic role (as the amplifier of the characters' interiorities) far beyond anything attempted in this area until now. In this scene the orchestra provides us with insight into the essence of things, and the words of the protagonists do not penetrate beyond the phenomenal surface.

This corresponds remarkably well to Arthur Schopenhauer's understanding of the relationship between music and language and, by the same token, to Friedrich Nietzsche's understanding of this relationship in *The Birth of Tragedy*, since at this early stage Nietzsche assumed the Schopenhauerian theory of music without reservations. (Subsequently, he would, of course, emancipate himself from Schopenhauer no less profoundly, though with less bitterness, than he would emancipate himself from Wagner. In fact, the two emancipations will be closely intertwined:

EXAMPLE 7. *Die Walküre*, I.349–80

the very distinction between surface and depth, or appearance and essence, on which the Schopenhauerian theory of music relies will be something later Nietzsche asks us to leave behind.) This correspondence between Wagner's practice and Schopenhauer's theory is so close that one is tempted to attribute the composer's newly found psychological insightfulness and artistic courage to an acquaintance with the philosopher's theories. This, however, will not do. The composition of the continuity draft of the first act of *Die Walküre* took place between June 28 and September 1, 1854—that is, it preceded the composer's first reading of Schopenhauer in the fall of 1854.

In any case, as Carl Dahlhaus correctly observed, Wagner's early reception of Schopenhauer concentrated on the philosopher's metaphysical-ethical doctrines, not on his music aesthetics. At this early stage, Wagner would claim that Schopenhauer helped him understand better Wotan's resignation in act 2, not his own artistic practice. (Recalling his first encounter with the philosopher's works in his autobiography, the composer wrote: "Only now did I understand my own Wotan myself and, greatly shaken, I went on to a closer study of Schopenhauer's book.")[34] Schopenhauer's music aesthetics were assimilated by the composer only gradually (an assimilation articulated publicly only in the Beethoven essay of 1870) and incompletely. Instead of a wholesale conversion from the empirical doctrine of *Opera and Drama* (1851), according to which music needs the text or scenic action to achieve semantic definition, to the metaphysics of music as a medium disclosing the deepest ground of being, Wagner attempted a synthesis between the two theories, converting the empirical semantic deficiency of music into the source of its metaphysical dignity: empirically, music needed drama so that its gestures might be semantically defined, but metaphysically, drama needed music to express its deepest significance. Thus, when compared with language, music came short, but this very shortcoming allowed it to jump over language directly into the deep waters of the will.[35]

One might want to argue, then, that in elevating the orchestra far above the scenic word and action, in letting the former voice the deepest truth of the erotic will driving the protagonists and allowing the latter to glide on the trivial surface, Wagner was a Schopenhauerian *avant la lettre* (or, in any case, before the *lettre* became known to him). But in fact such a convoluted and ultimately mysterious explanation of his musical dramaturgy in the first scene of *Die Walküre* is unnecessary. A simpler and more likely explanation lies nearer to hand, and it is twofold. First, in *Die Walküre*, for the first time in the *Ring* cycle, Wagner deals with human protagonists, and his humans have much deeper interior lives than the allegorical natural and divine powers that populate *Das Rheingold*. Second, and more important, he was in fact doing nothing more than following the normal operatic practice of using the orchestra to reveal the unspoken interiority of the characters. He was just doing it more thoroughly, more radically, than it was ever done before, whether by him or by his predecessors and contemporaries.

But the orchestral pantomime that is so central to scene 1 does not end with it. Scene 2 contains a number of pantomime passages, too, both before and after Siegmund's monologue. There are three such passages alone in the short time before Siegmund begins his story (I.381–95, 412–35, 459–70—with brief superimposed recitatives at 415–16 and 428–31). But the longest section of orchestral pantomime occurs within the coda that follows the monologue (I.716–73). Carefully annotated with precisely placed stage directions, it is a ballet of glances solicited, exchanged, and averted. Having heard Siegmund's story, Hunding reveals that it was his kinsmen whom Siegmund most recently offended. This night, he tells Siegmund, you are my guest, but tomorrow I shall fight you—a craven threat, since he knows his guest to be weaponless. And he orders Sieglinde out of the hall. In the pantomime that follows, Sieglinde attempts to meet Siegmund's gaze and to direct it toward a particular spot in the stem of an ash tree that stands in the center of the hall—all of this without calling Hunding's attention—before she and her husband leave (the orchestra informs us that the Sword that was the subject of Wotan's hope at the end of *Das Rheingold* must be hidden in the ash tree, I.764–67 and 770–72). The general character of the pantomime passages in scene 2 is different from that of the ones in scene 1. There the characters could not have verbalized their feelings even if they had wanted to. Now they cannot do this, because they are being watched by the hostile husband. Nevertheless the very existence of such passages significantly links the two scenes: this whole first part of the act is dominated and unified by them.

What could not be said in scenes 1 and 2 will gradually come to full verbal consciousness in scene 3. In terms of the music-dramatic form, if the first two scenes consisted of preparatory recitative dialogues, the last scene of the act is a fully developed closed lyrical number, a love duet; thus together, the three scenes make up a large operatic *scena*. But just as the recitative dialogues were hardly straightforward, permeated as they were by long passages of continuous orchestral discourse and sections of pantomime, so also the duet is not straightforward. First, Wagner is too committed to his theoretical doctrines (which advocate in effect that opera approximate as closely as possible spoken drama) to allow the two protagonists ever to sing simultaneously. If they nevertheless convey the sense that what they sing is a duet rather than two separate arias, this is because their musical and verbal utterances share common substance. Second, and more important, the duet proper (from I.1087 on) is preceded by a quasi-duet stylistically halfway between the predominantly open discourse of the first two scenes and the predominantly closed discourse of the final duet. This creates a smooth transition between the recitative and the duet portions of the act—the avoidance of sharp articulations between sections being of course one of the most characteristic features of Wagner's style (see appendix 2: act 1, scene 3).

The whole first part of the scene (I.790–1087) occupies a stylistic halfway house, suggesting here and there closed discourse and then withdrawing from the suggestion. Thus, by I.880 Siegmund's opening arioso (I.790–879) can contain its lyrical tendency no longer and flowers into a full-fledged tonally unified C major aria dominated by fairly regular cantabile vocal phrases (8 + 7 + 9 = I.882–89 + 893–99 + 902–10) with the streaming orchestral accompaniment discreetly receding into the background and emerging with significant motives only when the singer pauses for breath between the phrases (I.880–81, 889–92, 899–901, 910–11). By I.912, however, this lyrical outpouring runs out of steam and disintegrates back into a recitative.

The motive that punctuates Siegmund's quasi-cantabile is that of Wotan's "grandiose idea" from the ending of *Das Rheingold*—the thought of the saving Sword. Indeed, the motive completely dominates the whole section. It is first heard even before Siegmund begins his arioso at I.806–7, and emerges in its full blazing C major glory when the arioso culminates at I.849–79; thereafter it reappears regularly between the phrases of the cantabile (at I.880–81, 889–90, 900–901, and 910–11). It is hardly surprising that Siegmund is obsessed by this idea. He needs to fight Hunding the next morning and has no weapon, yet his father promised that he would find a sword when in highest need. What is perhaps surprising is the extent to which in Siegmund's mind the thought of the Sword is intertwined with the recollection of Sieglinde's enchanting glances. As a beam of light strikes the spot in the stem of the ash tree where the Sword is hidden, making its hilt visible, he remembers the glance with which she had pointed out to him this very spot and cannot separate her glance then from the gleam he notices now. But how surprising is this? Siegmund needs the Sword not only to defend himself, but also to win Sieglinde by freeing her from Hunding's slavery—the sexual significance of the weapon cannot be missed. Wagner may have been a pre-Freudian, but he clearly already knew that sometimes a sword is more than just a sword.

The corresponding quasi-cantabile of Sieglinde, too, occupies a stylistic halfway house between the open and closed discourses. (Sieglinde reenters the hall to tell Siegmund of the weapon that awaits him there—she has put a sleeping drug into Hunding's night cup so that the two can now talk undisturbed.) What I am calling Sieglinde's quasi-cantabile is in fact simply a narrative monologue, but it departs from the recitative style by more than just the fact that it is not a dialogue: it is tonally unified and formally shaped (table 5). At its center lies a modulating section of continuous orchestral music that develops the Sword motive. The motive is then also prominently featured in the following two sections (I.1009–10 and 1022–25). It is clearly the main subject of Sieglinde's discourse, just as it had been the main topic of Siegmund's meditation before. It is precisely because the two discourses share this topic and motive that they are perceived as related, as belonging to a common duet rather than two independent cantabiles. The central section of Sieglinde's monologue is similarly framed on both sides, so that the monologue as a whole acquires an ABA shape. The frame consists, first, of a section of music in what I would like to refer to as the narrative tone (the sparest

TABLE 5 *Die Walküre*, Act 1, Sieglinde's Monologue

Form	Key	Text incipit	Measures	CD.track.time
Narrative tone	e	Der Männer Sippe sass hier im Saal	955–63	I.9.0:52–1:30
Valhalla music	E	ein Greis in grauem Gewand	963–86	I.9.1:30–2:40
Sword music	→	Auf mich blickt' er	986–1003	I.9.2:40–3:34
Narrative tone	e	Der Männer Alle, so kühn sei sich mühten	1004–12	I.9.3:34–4:05
Valhalla music	E→	Da wusst' ich wer der war	1012–25	I.9.4:05–4:33

sort of recitation, frequently staying on a single pitch supported by a chordal accompaniment reduced to a bare minimum), since Wagner will employ it often to signal the beginning of a narrative monologue; and then of a recitative supported by continuous orchestral music presenting and developing the Valhalla motive.

The use of the Valhalla motive here recalls its earlier use in Siegmund's monologue (at I.556–58). Sieglinde tells Siegmund how during her wedding a stranger entered the hall and—looking with tenderness at her, the unwilling bride, while glaring threateningly at Hunding's kinsmen—he swung a sword, burying it to the hilt in the stem of the ash tree: "The steel would rightly belong to him, who could draw it forth from the trunk."[36] They had all tried, but so far without success: "I knew then who he was who greeted me in my grief: I also knew for whom alone he destined the sword in the tree."[37] The sexual significance of the Sword is again quite transparent: Hunding and his kin are not man enough for this particular bride. Still unclear is what precisely Sieglinde thinks she knew and knows. Most likely she realized then that the stranger was her father, and she realizes now that the weapon is intended for her brother—both remembered, but not so distinctly that she could recognize them. It is also unclear whether she really knows who her father is. We learn later that, just like her brother, she knows him as Wälse; most likely, like Siegmund, she does not realize that Wälse is Wotan. But the orchestral narrator knows this and, at I.963–76 and 1012–21, conveys this information to the audience, just as he did during Siegmund's monologue—another one of these rare occasions when it makes sense to attribute the orchestra's utterance to the narrator or author communicating with us above the heads of the characters onstage.

Then follows immediately what I am calling the quasi-cabaletta of the duet: two roughly parallel and tonally unified arioso statements in G major from Sieglinde and Siegmund respectively, appropriately enthusiastic and lively ("Sehr lebhaft" is the tempo indication at I.1022), with the orchestra relegated to an accompanying role, as Sieglinde expresses the hope that her savior from the humiliating wedlock has finally arrived and Siegmund confidently confirms that he is "that friend . . . to whom both weapon and wife [mark the conjunction!] were destined!"[38]

But all of this has been just a warm up for the true duet that now begins. In a beautifully conceived, simple, and symbolically pregnant *coup de théâtre*, at the final beat of the quasi-cabaletta (I.1087) the great entrance door at the back of the hall opens, letting in a breath of fresh spring air (the storm had long subsided) and the light of the full moon "so that they can suddenly see each other in total clarity."[39] The door of their roughly civilized tribal prison has sprung open, they are on the threshold of natural freedom and, no longer deceived by the false, conventional social identities of a "wife" or a "stranger," can see clearly who they truly, authentically are—two young people irresistibly drawn to each other.

Siegmund's and Sieglinde's successive, slow cantabiles ("Mäßig bewegt" is the tempo indication at I.1099) that now follow deploy all the characteristic features of closed lyrical discourse. This is no longer a mere suggestion of an operatic duet, but the real thing (except, of course, that they do not sing simultaneously). The closed discourse is emphasized, in particular, at the very beginning, where, apart from a lovely clarinet counterpoint, the orchestra is reduced to providing a discreetly shimmering background figuration to Siegmund's opening antecedent-consequent period (12 + 8 = I.1107–18 + 1119–26). Thereafter the vocal phrasing abandons the antecedent-consequent construction and the orchestra becomes more active motivically, but the domination of the cantabile vocal lines, his in B-flat major, her modulating to D-flat, is never in doubt. However, it is the orchestra rather than the voices that links his and her statements, making sure we understand that they belong together, that this is a duet, and a love duet at that, not two successive arias. The love motive that appeared first in the pantomime at the beginning of the act (I.216) is now introduced again (I.1135) and from that point on is never long absent from either Siegmund's or Sieglinde's orchestral background (I.1135–39, 1144–51, 1157–60, 1163–64, 1178–81, 1194–99, 1210–13).

What additionally links the two statements is, of course, the text. Sieglinde responds to Siegmund, picking up his images and ideas just as he picks up on what has just happened to the world around them. Winter storm has given way to mild spring, he tells her. Spring has come to liberate his "sister-bride" Love from Winter's slavery and to be united with her—it helps that in German "spring" (*der Lenz*) is a masculine and "love" (*die Liebe*) a feminine noun.[40] Siegmund unconsciously anticipates: at this point the two lovers do not know yet that they are siblings. But then in Wagner's proto-Freudian world it is in the subconscious that the more profound sorts of truths lie hidden.[41] Sieglinde dots the "i": "You are the Spring for which I longed in frosty wintertime."[42] They no longer merely love one another; their mutual love has now been fully avowed and accepted.

The arioso character of the vocal lines continues for the most part through the tempo di mezzo section of the duet, but now the music gets to be more modulatory and developmental, and the lovers' utterances are shorter—they engage in a genuine dialogue again, exchanging information and learning new things about themselves. It is, after all, the traditional job of a tempo di mezzo to introduce new information that would justify the change from the slow cantabile to the fast cabaletta. The beginning of the section, from I.1221 to I.1268, is marked and dominated by the new motive of "delight" made up of the first three notes of Siegmund's line (I.1221).[43] Thereafter the discourse occasionally begins to approach again the level of recitative dialogue and the motivic content of the orchestral accompaniment gets more varied as it shadows the course of the conversation.

Perhaps the most prominent moments in this accompaniment are the three statements of the Valhalla music, at I.1269–78, 1327–42, and 1362–65, all in E major just as they were when this music had appeared within the monologues of Siegmund (I.556–58) and Sieglinde (I.963–86), where it referred to their common father. Running through the whole act, all these E major statements of the Valhalla music belong together. Siegmund and Sieglinde know at this point that they love one another, but they do not know who they are. The recognition that they are siblings is the essential business of the tempo di mezzo—an important component in Siegmund's discovery of his identity that is the subject of act 1. To recognize this, they need to discover that they have a father in common. Hence the prominence of the Valhalla music, which stands for their father, even if they do not know this father's full identity. They begin by taking a closer look at one another. At the first appearance of the Valhalla music, Sieglinde states that from the beginning Siegmund reminded her of someone. The music reveals who this someone was, even though Sieglinde may not be fully aware of this yet. She thinks he reminded her of herself, which, of course, is also the case—they are siblings. Is this another case of the narrator talking to us directly, above Sieglinde's head? Not necessarily. In the first place, it is Sieglinde's subconscious that is talking and telling us who is on her mind even though she is not fully aware of this and does not know this person's full identity. But, as before, the narrator is additionally whispering Wotan's name.

At the second sounding of the Valhalla music, Sieglinde is already aware that Siegmund's gaze reminds her of the gaze of the mysterious stranger and additionally reveals that she had then recognized the stranger as her father: "By his glance his child knew who he was."[44] All that remains for the full recognition is that Siegmund is discovered to have the same father, perhaps by revealing his true name. But Siegmund does not have a real name yet: "Name me yourself as you'd like me called: I'll take my name from you."[45] (Note the allusion to the Valhalla music in the last three measures, I.1357–59, of Siegmund's declaration: the identity of the father is the key to the identity of the son.) It is only at this point that Siegmund, accompanied by the third statement of the Valhalla music, reveals the true name of his father, Wälse. Hearing this, Sieglinde is "beside herself"[46] and the music of these final measures of the tempo di mezzo becomes "more lively."[47]

What this excitement unmistakably suggests, although she does not explicitly say so, is that Wälse must also have been the name under which she had known her own father, and hence that she must realize now that her lover is also her brother. The incestuous nature of their relationship does not bother her for a moment and neither will it bother Siegmund when he becomes aware of it. They are both votaries of natural instinct and know civilization and its discontents only for the suffering they bring. To be sure, it was bound to provoke and bother Wagner's audience. Why then did he insist on making Siegmund and Sieglinde siblings? Perhaps he too wanted to proclaim his allegiance to a love free of all traditional constraints. Perhaps also because the new humanity that was to replace the existing society and its order was to be as different from the old one as possible—different from the brutish Germanic tribes like Hunding's Neidings or the Gibichungs we shall encounter in Götterdämmerung. But at the moment of discovery, Sieglinde is convinced that Wälse must have destined the Sword for his son and she gives this son his true name: neither Wehwalt, nor Friedmund, but Siegmund (*Sieg* is "victory"). At the beginning of the cabaletta that immediately follows, Siegmund confirms that the name and the essential identity are one: "Siegmund I am called and Siegmund I am."[48]

It is, in short, Sieglinde who helps Siegmund find out who he is. It is from her that he receives all three components that define his true identity: the love, the name, and the Sword. All that remains for Siegmund is to perform this identity, to be a victor not just in name, but in actuality, to possess both the Sword and the woman. These essential actions are the subject of the concluding "very fast" G major cabaletta.[49] Musically, what is perhaps most striking here is the pervasive use of the Sword motive. It completely dominates the orchestral discourse at the beginning (I.1378–96); it is heard again at the fortissimo climactic moment when "with a violent effort he draws the sword from the tree and shows it to Sieglinde, who is seized by astonishment and ecstasy," as the faintly comical, proto-Freudian stage direction would have it; and finally it opens the orchestral coda as the last distinct motive heard in the act (I.1498–501).[50] Recall the prominent use of the motive in the quasi-cavatinas that opened scene 3. Its equally prominent presence now ensures that the whole third scene of the act is heard as a single unit, rather than a succession of two unrelated duets. In addition, at one point the cabaletta significantly refers also to the music of the true cavatinas (I.1460–77), thereby confirming even more forcefully the essential unity of the whole love duet.

But what may well be the most interesting moment in the cabaletta occurs just before the Sword is drawn (I.1397–436). As Siegmund grasps the hilt of the Sword, he solemnly announces: "Highest need of holiest love . . . burns brightly within my breast, urging me on to deed and death!—Nothung! . . . So I name you, sword!"[51] It is love that gives him the strength to perform the deeds he is about to perform. That he associates these deeds with death is noteworthy and again proto-Freudian, as well as, alas, prophetic. It is even more noteworthy that he quotes at this point the music of the announcement one of the Rhinedaughters had made in the opening scene of *Das Rheingold*: "Only the man who forswears love's sway . . . can master the magic spell that rounds a ring from the gold" (*Das Rheingold*, 617–24; compare especially *Die Walküre* I.1400–1408 with *Das Rheingold* 617–21). The music is the same, but not its significance. Wagner wants to draw our attention to the fact that the actions of Alberich (the taking of the Rhine gold) and of Siegmund (the taking of the Sword) may look similar, but their implications are symmetrically opposed. The Nibelung forswears the divinity to which the Wälsung submits himself; the former thus acquires the ability to amass sterile wealth and power, the latter to perform his life- and death-giving deeds. For Siegmund, as for Wagner, life and death belong together. Since Siegmund could not have possibly heard the Rhinedaughter, it is undoubtedly Wagner or his narrator who offers this contrast as a subject for our reflection.

The Sword is drawn and the consummation of love quickly follows, but not before they both explicitly confirm that they are aware of being siblings. The consummation coincides with the final sounding of the Sword motive and the mercifully swift falling of the curtain: "He draws her towards him with furious passion. The curtain falls quickly," Wagner's stage direction orders, leaving it to the orchestra alone to provide the triple-forte tonic release.[52] Much later we shall realize that we have just (nearly) witnessed the conceiving of Siegfried.

The first act of *Die Walküre* is a miracle of double self-discovery, one represented, another actual. It tells the story of how its hero found out, and became, who he authentically was—how love, spurned by Alberich, liberated him to "deed and death," gave him his name, his weapon, and his woman. But perhaps its true hero is Wagner himself, who for the first time discovers here who he can, and is going to, be in the second half of his life, discovers that he is able to control time on an unprecedented scale, creating a single gigantic *scena* of about one hour in length and thus giving real time a single music-dramatic shape that, from tentative, open-discourse beginnings inexorably drives forward through increasingly more and more closed-discourse forms toward its joyfully inevitable erotic conclusion. It is here that Siegmund became Siegmund and Wagner became Wagner, the master of what he would eventually call his "art of transition," an art that relied on making the distinction between the open and closed discourses a matter of "more or less" rather than of "either or" and that thus made it possible for him to control and shape hugely long timespans, including complete acts.

In a general sort of way at least, Wagner must have been planning his music-dramatic forms already at the stage at which he was writing his poems. His repeated claims that he was thinking musically already at this pre-compositional stage are entirely plausible.[53] We have seen, for instance, how in the Love Duet the cantabiles of Siegmund and Sieglinde were linked not only by the use of the same motivic content in the orchestra (the love motive), but also by the same verbal imagery (the enslaving winter followed by the liberating spring); it is clear that Wagner planned to relate the two sections already at the time when he was writing the poem. In what follows, I shall note a number of such instances where features of the music-dramatic form are prepared already in the poem. While a systematic study of how Wagner's poems adumbrate and prepare his dramatic-musical forms would expand the size of the present book beyond manageable proportions and hence cannot be undertaken here, my hope is that someone will take up this topic in the future. The analyses presented here provide a proper springboard for a study of this sort.

But of course the music needed to be composed before Wagner could know for sure that what he had planned would actually work; the success of the first act of *Die Walküre* must have been tremendously encouraging. On February 16 [?], 1855, the composer reported to Franz Liszt: "The score of the first act of *Die Walküre* will be soon ready: it is extraordinarily beautiful; I have never yet done anything even remotely like this."[54] Wagner's pride in what he has achieved is palpable and justified. Similarly palpable and justified will be his pride when he finishes the whole opera and reports to Anton Pusinelli on April 28, 1856: "It is more beautiful than anything I have ever written."[55]

Act 2: Becoming Brünnhilde

The haste with which the lovers embrace one another at the end of act 1 is part of what makes them so touching. They are like so many young people living in a world torn apart by war: they know they are unlikely to have much time while "the world has taken up arms" against them.[56] And indeed, time and the world catch up with them almost as soon as they begin their flight from Hunding's dwelling. Their flight is the subject depicted in the Prelude to the second act, just as Siegmund's flight shaped the Prelude to the first. Nothing much has changed. He, and now they both, remain the kind of creatures who are always in flight, while their fate is decided elsewhere. In act 2, the ray of hope that in act 1 had illuminated their tragic existence for a brief moment is quickly extinguished.

The music-dramatic form of the second act is somewhat more involved than that of the first one, if only because the number of characters appearing onstage is larger. This is no longer what it was in act 1—essentially a duet. But the formal lessons of act 1, in particular the idea of focusing an entire act on a single large "closed number," have not been forgotten. Also act 2 divides into two parts (scenes 1–2 and 3–5, respectively), with the first part dominated by recitative dialogues and one monologue, and the second part culminating in, though this time not ending with, the only large-scale piece of closed discourse of the act—the duet between Brünnhilde and Siegmund (see appendix 2: act 2). For all their differences, the parallel construction of the two acts is unmistakable.

Even though the act completes the story of Siegmund and Sieglinde, they are no longer its main protagonists. Instead the focus now shifts back from humans to gods, respectively, to Wotan in the first part and Brünnhilde in the second. The first

TABLE 6 *Die Walküre*, Act 2, Scene 1, Fricka's Arietta

Form	Text incipit	Measures	CD.track.time
A	O, was klag' ich um Ehe und Eid	281–98	II.4.0:54–1:26
A'	Trauernden Sinnes mußt' ich's ertragen	298–314	II.4.1:26–1:58
B	Doch jetzt, da dir neue Namen gefielen	314–39	II.4.1:58–2:45
Postlude		339–44	II.4.2:45–2:58

part divides additionally into two sections, the first showing Wotan with Fricka, the second showing him with Brünnhilde. At bottom, this is a story of two conversions. First, Wotan (I emphasize: Wotan, not Wagner) converts from a left-Hegelian optimism to Schopenhauerian pessimism and begins to acquire the virtue of resignation. Second, Brünnhilde converts from divine to human values and begins to acquire the virtue of compassion for human suffering; above all, she learns to appreciate the transcendent power and value of human love. Thus she makes the first step toward becoming human herself, that is, toward becoming capable of performing the world-historical role for which she is destined in the *Ring*.

The recitative dialogues that dominate the first part of the act are not completely shapeless. They are punctuated by brief pieces of closed discourse that are too short to be of formal consequence for the act as a whole, but sufficient to shape their immediate context. Thus, Brünnhilde's first speech in the introductory conversation between her and Wotan (II.74–153) is framed by her two exuberant though inarticulate calls (II.94–112 and 131–48)—the sort of mock-Norse yodeling that parodists find irresistible. Between the end of *Das Rheingold* and now, Wotan has not wasted time. In addition to the human Wälsung twins, he sired with Erda nine divine girls, the Valkyries, of whom Brünnhilde is the preferred one. Theirs is a war-loving brood, unquestioningly obedient to their father, and their job is to collect from human battlefields fallen heroes and bring them to Valhalla, where they serve as Wotan's standing army in his cold war with Alberich and have a jolly good time. Like her sisters, Brünnhilde is loud, rather brainless, and overflowing with animal spirits—hence the inarticulate calls she emits. At this point she is singularly inauspicious material for the world-transforming heroine she is to become.

Similarly, the following encounter between Wotan and Fricka (II.154–588) is punctuated and thus shaped by the latter's three brief ariosos, each of which ends one of the dialogue's three sections. The first arioso is actually a full-fledged g-sharp minor arietta in AA'B (or Bar) form (table 6), with the orchestral motive that twice opens the A sections returning toward the end of the B section (at II.330–33 and again at II.339–41) and with the orchestral postlude echoing Fricka's opening phrase (at II.342–44). While Fricka's other two ariosos do not attain this level of formal definition, they still employ sufficiently elevated diction to provide the dialogue with strong points of articulation. The last one, in E-flat major, embeds a brief but decisive recitative exchange in which Wotan swears to his wife that he will sacrifice Siegmund to her (II.556–65) and ends with an orchestral postlude that evokes the motives of Alberich's Curse and Wotan's discouragement (II.581–88).

Wotan has good reason to feel discouraged. His confrontation with Fricka reminds us just how similar Wagner's Norse divinities are to the Homeric gods. The *Ring* was surely intended to provide the Germans with a national epic and revive Aeschylean tragedy all at once. But, given the extent to which German elites since at least the times of Johann Joachim Winckelmann have been mesmerized by the culture of ancient Greece and aspired to make Germany into a new Athens, there was nothing objectionable in finding that Wotan and Fricka were just like Zeus and Hera. Quite the contrary. Like Zeus, Wotan philanders; like Hera, Fricka finds this regrettable and offensive. And like Hera, as a guardian of marriages and traditional sexual conventions she confronts her husband, demanding that Siegmund's and Sieglinde's adultery and incest be punished and Hunding avenged.

It is to Wagner's credit that, unlike Wotan, he treats Fricka seriously and does not reduce her to a caricature of a nagging housewife. Fricka's utterances, and in particular her three ariosos, are full of genuine nobility and dignity. In the first section of their dialogue (II.154–344) Wotan shrugs off her moral qualms. For him, the rival claims of love override the inviolability of marriage, especially a loveless one, or the prohibition of incest. The values the two gods defend are genuine and incompatible; humans need both, and in this sense Wotan and Fricka make a good couple. But while she rigidly insists on the absolute and eternal validity of her claims, he is wiser in recognizing that genuine values can come into conflict and that such conflicts are to be encouraged, since they are the source of moral innovation and growth: "Wherever forces are boldly stirring, I openly council war," he tells her.[57] A little later he adds, encapsulating their difference: "Age-old custom is all you can grasp: but *my* thoughts seek to encompass what's never yet come to pass."[58] He is more modern and forward looking than she and thus, in front of a modern jury, he easily wins the first part of their argument.

But if he wins a battle, he loses the war, and this not because Fricka is able to convince him, or us, of the eternal validity of her claims, but because she is able to show up the self-deluding character of his hopes. At the end of *Das Rheingold* we left Wotan optimistically entertaining the "grandiose idea" of the sword that will somehow assure the gods' future. Now, in the second part of his confrontation with Fricka (II.345–478), we learn the specific content of this thought. The danger the gods face is that the Ring might fall back into Alberich's hands; hence it is imperative that Wotan gets the Ring first. But, bound by the contract it is his role to protect, he cannot simply take the Ring away from Fafner by force. He needs someone who will do this for him, unbidden and unprompted, of his own free will—someone like Siegmund, who would use the Sword to kill Fafner. Or, as

Wotan explains to Fricka, "A hero is needed who, lacking godly protection, breaks loose from the law of the gods: thus alone is he fit to perform that feat which, needful though it is to the gods, the god is forbidden to do."[59]

Fricka has no trouble seeing through and demolishing this "grandiose idea." Siegmund has indeed disentangled himself from the divine laws and is capable of killing Fafner, but, armed with the Sword as he is, he can hardly be considered "lacking godly protection." If you want to be consistent, she tells her husband, take back the magically potent Sword you gave your son. Wotan has to recognize the devastating force of this argument. All that remains for Fricka is to extract from her dejected husband an oath that he will not protect Siegmund in his upcoming battle with Hunding, neither directly, nor through his Valkyrie "handdaughter," nor by means of the Sword's magic. This, we have already seen, she does in the third and last section of their dialogue (II.479–588).

The confrontation leaves us, and Wotan, with a clear understanding of the god's predicament. The following scene, with Wotan's monologue at its center, gives us insight into his state of mind now that he understands his situation. Just like the dialogue of the preceding scene, the monumental monologue is divided into three sections (II.688–769, 777–869, 873–989), this time by brief recitative interruptions from Brünnhilde (at II.770–76, 870–73), to whom Wotan's self-revelation is addressed. This punctuation is additionally reinforced by brief passages of discourse that depart from strict recitative: a short arietta (II.742–69) placed at the end of the first section, and a passage of recitation held together by continuous, single-motive-based music of the orchestra (II.815–69) at the end of the second one. The beginning of the monologue is marked by the same characteristically narrative style of hushed monotone recitation over a pedal point that marked the opening of Sieglinde's narration in act 1.

Wotan recapitulates all the important events of the story thus far, much of it redundantly, since we already know most of the relevant facts. But what matters here is not so much the story itself as his own perspective on it. This is an act of self-revelation, one of the few such acts from him in the *Ring*. We learn that he understands that his main motivation has been power and that he sees Alberich as his adversary in the struggle for world domination. The way Wotan understands his present situation will not surprise us. The only danger to the continued rule of gods is that Alberich might recover his Ring from Fafner, which is why Wotan needs to get it first; but, bound by the contract, he cannot. And Fricka has just convincingly demonstrated the self-contradictory nature of his plan to use a surrogate hero who would be at once independent of, and dependent on, the god's will and protection, "for the free man has to fashion himself."[60]

Hence the utter desperation to which Wotan gives vent in the last part of the monologue. He must sacrifice his beloved son to Fricka. Worse, he must give up all hope of preserving the rule of the gods: "One thing alone do I want: the end . . . !"[61]

This is his Schopenhauerian moment. He now recalls Erda's prediction that the end of the gods will be at hand when Alberich begets a son; indeed, the latest rumor has it that the Nibelung used gold to buy himself a woman who is now with his child. (This, by the way, would make Alberich's son, Hagen, and Wotan's grandson, Siegfried, the main antagonists of *Götterdämmerung*, roughly contemporaries.) He ends the monologue bitterly blessing this child as his own heir.

Wotan's monologue leaves Brünnhilde confused. Simple girl that she is, she feels she should protect her half brother, the son Wotan loves, in the upcoming duel with Hunding. Wotan angrily sets her straight: fight for Fricka, or else! Their lively dialogue—"Somewhat livelier" ("Etwas lebhafter") is the tempo indication at II.989—provides the scene with a cabaletta-like closure. After Wotan's exit, the Valkyrie's own heavy-hearted departure serves as a brief postlude, her parting words making clear that she has understood her father's orders.

If the first part of the act dealt with Wotan and his conversion to a resigned pessimism, the second part now beginning will be focused on Brünnhilde and her conversion in the opposite direction—from Wotan's obedient tool without a will of her own to an independent agent, the first step on her road to becoming a compassionate human. Appropriately, both conversion scenes take place during sections that are the music-dramatic points of gravity in their parts of the act: respectively, Wotan's monologue in the first part, and the Brünnhilde-Siegmund Duet in the second. And appropriately again, the second of these music-dramatic points of gravity is the more weighty of the two: the monologue is characterized by fewer closed-discourse features than the duet. Wotan and his development matter a lot, but in the perspective of the whole *Ring*, the evolution of Brünnhilde matters even more because it is she, together with her partner, Siegfried, who are destined to transcend the world run by the Wotan-Alberich competition. She is the main protagonist of *Die Walküre* and, as it will eventually turn out, of the whole cycle—she, and not, as is commonly claimed, her father, who does not even make an appearance in the main, final, evening of the tetralogy.

The Duet dialogue between Brünnhilde and Siegmund (needless to say, they never sing simultaneously), scene 4 of act 2, is one of the artistic high points of the cycle, one of those scenes that compel us to take seriously Wagner's pretentions to be the reviver of Attic tragedy. For the first time in the *Ring* we witness directly the devastating mythic encounter between a human and a divine power, an encounter of momentous consequences to both, since it brings death to the human and transforms the divine. It is this latter transformation that defines the modernity of the *Ring*: ancient divine powers were eternal and immutable.

While the "Very solemn and grave" (II.1462)[62] tempo is maintained with the usual momentary fluctuations until almost the end of the scene (only at II.1777 does a molto accelerando set in, leading to a "Very lively" tempo at II.1785),[63] the introductions of nervous accompanimental figuration at II.1619 and then of steady

EXAMPLE 8. *Die Walküre*, II.1462–73

pulsation dividing each beat into triplets at II.1716 divide the scene into three distinct phases, each more agitated than the preceding one. The last one includes a still more frantic final stretto and an orchestral postlude that first brings the accumulated energy to a climax and then gradually dissipates it (see appendix 2: act 2, Duet of Brünnhilde and Siegmund).

Just as in the Love Duet of act 1, here too the lyrical closed discourse sets in gradually: it is fully in place only in the cabaletta. The sections that precede it are halfway between the open and closed forms, with the orchestra rather than the voices providing their formal shape. In the cantabile the voices engage in free declamation of great nobility, leaving the musical action to the orchestra, which cycles hypnotically through patterns created by various arrangements of essentially only three distinct motives. Two are heard for the first time, the third is the Valhalla music well known to us since the second scene of *Das Rheingold*. Additional motives make occasional appearance when called for by the dialogue, but these three dominate the discourse.

The two new ideas are traditionally labeled the Fate motive (presented here twice, at II.1462–65 and 1466–69) and the Death Lamentation motive (II.1470–73). Example 8 shows their appearance at the beginning of the scene. The first of these labels is well chosen (it being understood, of course, that such names are convenient, but inherently unsatisfactory, since the significance of each motive is gradually enriched with each new context in which it appears throughout the *Ring*). It accompanies the moment when Siegmund first casts his eyes on Brünnhilde, and

Fate is as good a name as any for the encounter between a mortal and an eternal power. The second label, on the other hand, is less persuasive. The initial portion of the dialogue takes the form of Siegmund asking questions and Brünnhilde answering them, and the motive is used to accompany the questions (the Valhalla music accompanies the answers). Something like Questioning Fate would be more appropriate, though admittedly not particularly elegant. The Fate motive, incidentally, bears uncanny resemblance to the Grave opening of the finale of Beethoven's last String Quartet in F major, Op. 135, which the composer famously accompanied with the words "Must it be?" ("Muss es sein?"), only to answer in the immediately following Allegro "It must be!" ("Es muss sein!"). Given how appropriate the Beethovenian allusion is to the present situation of a mortal encountering fate (and given Wagner's close involvement with the late quartets), the likelihood that the motivic resemblance is accidental is not particularly great.[64]

Even before Brünnhilde addresses Siegmund and thus makes him notice her presence, the motivic pattern of example 8 (Fate, Fate, Question; II.1462–73) is sequentially repeated (II.1474–85) and followed by the Valhalla music (II.1486–90). Once the dialogue begins, the orchestra repeats this whole sequence almost literally, except that the second question is omitted and the Valhalla music transposed (so that it is now Fate, Fate, Question, Fate, Fate, Valhalla; II.1491–516). It is precisely this presentation of the motivic sequence first by the orchestra alone (II.1462–90) and then by the orchestra with superimposed declamation (II.1491–516) that allows us to assign conceptual content to the motives. This is suggested by the dramatic situation (Fate as Siegmund notices Brünnhilde, Questioning Fate as he asks her who she is) and by the words (Valhalla as she answers that she appears to noble warriors on the battlefield, and that those who see her have to die and follow her—the already familiar music identifying the destination).

The remaining portion of the cantabile (II.1517–619) consists essentially of Siegmund's questions over the Question motive and Brünnhilde's answers over the Valhalla motive. The Fate motive plays a role only at the beginning (II.1517–30), before the questioning starts, as Siegmund looks at the fateful visitor. Siegmund asks the Valkyrie where she would lead him and whom he would meet there; she tells him of Wotan's Valhalla populated by fallen heroes and the god's daughters (the Valkyries) serving them drinks. The systematic deployment of motives breaks down only with Brünnhilde's last answer. When Siegmund asks whether he would also meet Sieglinde in Valhalla, the Valkyrie answers in the negative and the Valhalla music is not heard. All of a sudden the prospects of future bliss she has been painting for Siegmund appear much less enticing. Instead, it is Siegmund who now picks up the Valhalla motive as, for the first time, he does not ask questions but provides an answer of his own: greet Valhalla and its inhabitants for me, "to them I follow you not."[65]

This polite but firm turning down of the invitation changes the dynamic of the encounter and occasions the beginning of the tempo di mezzo. The static, though

TABLE 7 *Die Walküre*, Act 2, Scene 4, Duet of Brünnhilde and Siegmund, the Beginning of the Cabaletta

Form: motifs	Number of measures	Measures
Introduction: B	3	1716–18
Antecedent: A + B	4 + 4 = (2 + 2) + (2 + 2)	1719–26
Consequent: A + B	4 + 5 = (2 + 2) + (2 + 3)	1727–35

flexible, ostinato is now replaced by music of a more developmental character, with a more extensive participation of motives external to the basic thematic content of the scene. But traces of the ostinato remain in evidence, in particular at first: the Fate-Fate-Question sequence of motives accompanies the two initial statements from Brünnhilde (II.1618–26, 1636–43). With the Valkyrie's two subsequent statements the pattern is abbreviated to one or two appearances of the Fate motive (II.1650–51, 1657–60). And the Fate motive reappears twice again with Brünnhilde's last statement of the section (II.1704–9).

The tempo di mezzo ends just as the cantabile did, with Siegmund's refusal to follow the Valkyrie to Valhalla. Something, however, has changed since the end of the cantabile. Siegmund now understands that he must die and that the magic power of the Sword on which he had counted has been withdrawn, and he is so incensed by the betrayal that he would rather go to hell than to Valhalla (he may not know that Wälse is Wotan, but he somehow understands that the Sword's power originates in Valhalla): "Ha, shame upon him who sent me the sword . . . ! If I must fall, I'll not go to Valhalla—Hella shall hold me fast!"[66] This decision weakens Brünnhilde's resolve. She is "shaken," says the stage direction.[67] She finds it difficult to comprehend that anyone might give up on the "bliss everlasting"[68] out of loving loyalty to "this pitiful woman who, tired and sorrowful, lies there, faint, in your lap,"[69] but she is visibly moved by the spectacle. A chink has been found in her steely, divine armor; the imperturbable goddess has been perturbed. The ending of the tempo di mezzo marks the beginning of the most decisive turning point in the drama: the encounter of the human with the divine is about to humanize and thus transform the Valkyrie.

The process is rapidly completed in the cabaletta. Here, for the first time in the Duet, a fully closed lyrical discourse emerges. Siegmund's opening statement in particular is shaped as a strikingly four-square antecedent-consequent period (example 9 and table 7). To see just how regular the construction of this period is, one needs to pay attention to the placement of the main melodic line here. The first two measures of Siegmund's statement (II.1719–20) may give the impression that the melodic substance of the music has now shifted decisively from the orchestra to the voice (this too signals a shift toward the lyrical discourse). The domination of the vocal line, however, quickly proves illusory. From the start, the voice is doubled by the orchestra and

EXAMPLE 9. *Die Walküre*, II.1716–36

(continued)

EXAMPLE 9. *(continued)*

EXAMPLE 9. *(continued)*

after the initial two measures one realizes that, throughout the whole period, it is the orchestra that carries the main melodic line, the voice providing a counterpoint. And the construction projected by the orchestra is strikingly rigid: a three-measure introduction, an eight-measure antecedent consisting of two four-measure incises (each of which divided in turn into two two-measure units), and a nine-measure consequent (consisting of two incises of four and five measures respectively, the first one divided into two two-measure units and the second into a two- and a three-measure unit). Only the last three measures, as well as the three measures of the orchestral introduction, escape the otherwise strictly quadratic construction. It would be hard to signal more emphatically the onset of the closed discourse. Only the harmonic plan of the period escapes this rigidity and conveys the mounting tension. Instead of keeping it all in the cabaletta's f-sharp minor key, Wagner proceeds by a chain of rising fourths—from f-sharp to b for the antecedent, and from b to e for the consequent. And since the main motive here (marked "A" in table 7) is a variant of the Question phrase, he makes sure that we hear the cabaletta as flowing from the music that preceded it.

Brünnhilde's answer to Siegmund begins by mirroring closely his statement—a standard cabaletta procedure (example 10). Once again a three-measure orchestral

EXAMPLE 10. *Die Walküre*, II.1736–48

EXAMPLE 10. *(continued)*

introduction similar to the original one (II.1736–38 corresponding to II.1716–18) is followed by a similar first incise (II.1739–42 corresponding to II.1719–22). But this time an imitation at an upper fifth, starting at II.1742, prolongs the incise by one measure and Brünnhilde's second incise (II.1744–47) frees itself from Siegmund's model. Having firmly established the cabaletta character of the section (nothing is more characteristic of a cabaletta than such a presentation of the same material twice), Wagner can afford to proceed from now on in a more flexibly developmental manner. The chain of the ascending fourths continues from where it was left at the end of Siegmund's statement, the orchestral introduction to Brünnhilde's statement moving from e to a, and the statement itself continuing from a to D. The key of F-sharp, the major variant of the main key of the Duet, will be reestablished only at the climactic moment of Brünnhilde's decision in her stretto (II.1789).

We saw Brünnhilde "shaken" already at the end of the tempo di mezzo. In the cabaletta Siegmund breaks her defenses down completely. When Brünnhilde informs him that Sieglinde is pregnant with his child and asks that he commit the woman and the child to her protection, he draws his Sword and, embittered by the gods' betrayal, threatens to kill his beloved rather than allow them to take care of her. This is too much even for the "cold and hard"—as she seems to him— Valkyrie.[70] "In the most passionate and tempestuous show of sympathy"[71] that marks the beginning of her stretto, she stops him and announces her decision: "Sieglind' shall live—and Siegmund with her!"[72] She revokes the death sentence and promises protection in the upcoming battle with Hunding.

Thus the Duet marks the opera's, indeed the cycle's, turning point—the moment when Brünnhilde emancipates herself from her role as Wotan's obedient tool and acquires a will of her own. From this moment the possibility exists that she may eventually become Wotan's successor, the central protagonist in the transition from the traditional world shaped by the Wotan-Alberich competition to the brave new world of autonomous, loving humanity. It is the "sympathy" ("Mitgefühl") with human suffering that effects this transformation. The ability to feel what the suffering hero feels (already at the beginning of her cabaletta statement she tells him: "I can see the need that gnaws at your heart; I can feel the hero's holy sorrow") is what humanizes the divine daughter.[73] Only a short while ago, she could not quite comprehend how one might prefer to go to hell with one's beloved rather than enjoy the "bliss everlasting" of Valhalla without her. Now she understands, or rather feels, it: humans are autonomous, and there is something—love—that matters to them more than anything the gods might offer.

Alas, this is the turning point for Brünnhilde, not for Siegmund. Each of the first two acts of *Die Walküre* culminates in Siegmund's duets—the first one with Love, the second with Death. Both duets end on a note of rather frantic hope, the hope of a narrow escape from the fate that has been pursuing him since the first measure of the opera. This hope proves vain. Siegmund's Duet with Brünnhilde in scene 4 is framed by two shorter scenes of recitative dialogue supported by an almost continuous orchestral development, with some sections of pantomime action. The beginning of the frame, the beginning of scene 3 that accompanies the reappearance of Siegmund and Sieglinde on the stage, picks up where the Prelude to act 2 left off: both are based on the motive associated with the flight of the Wälsungs. It is as if everything that has happened in scenes 1 and 2 were put into brackets: while the gods haggle and brood, the ill-fated siblings run and run. In this respect nothing has changed since we first met Siegmund. In scenes 3 and 5, Sieglinde, racked by feelings of guilt (not at her adultery, to be sure, but at the dishonor of having submitted to the loveless marriage), intuitively senses how hopeless this running is; Siegmund trusts his prowess and his Sword. It is her intuition that proves right. Hunding catches up with the fugitives and in the ensuing duel Brünnhilde's protection proves inadequate when Wotan himself shatters Siegmund's Sword with his Spear, allowing Hunding to kill his disarmed rival. All that remains for Brünnhilde is to try to save Sieglinde and escape with her. All that remains for Wotan is to express sorrow over his son's death, contempt for his killer (he sends Hunding to "kneel before Fricka"),[74] and wrath for his disobedient daughter (whom he presently pursues).

Act 3: Waiting for the Hero

The first two acts of *Die Walküre* comprise the tragedy of Siegmund, overlapping with the beginning of the story of Brünnhilde's emancipation from Wotan in act 2. It is this latter story that is completed in act 3. Accordingly, if the music-dramatic forms of the first two acts were to a certain extent similar, the form of act 3 is different (see appendix 2: act 3). The act is divided into two parts, the first one (scenes 1 and 2) defined by the presence of all the Valkyries onstage (there are eight of those, in addition to Brünnhilde), and the more intimate second one (scene 3) with only Wotan and Brünnhilde present. The first part is additionally articulated into three sections, the first one involving the eight Valkyries only, the second marked by the additional presence of Brünnhilde and Sieglinde, and the third one by the arrival of Wotan. The closed musical numbers are now placed at the beginning of the first part (the ensemble usually referred to as the Ride of the Valkyries) and at the end of the second part (the aria commonly called Wotan's Farewell).

The first number, the Ride of the Valkyries, is largely orchestral, with voices superimposed. Thus it can take the double role of the act's prelude and opening scene. Its form is simplicity itself, alternating a predominantly orchestral and tonally stable refrain with tonally more fluid episodes in which the voices of the Valkyries take a more active, dialoguing role (table 8). It ends inconclusively with the second episode, implying, but not delivering, a final refrain. This does eventually materialize, but only at the very end of the whole first part of the act, with the Valkyries' exit, and not as a full-fledged repetition, but rather as a distant and much abbreviated echo. Its reappearance at the end of the first part ensures that the part is experienced as a single whole not only because of the visual-dramatic presence of the eight sisters, but also because of their aural presence.

In dramatic-expressive terms, the number, a tableau of a get-together of the Valkyries on their way from assorted battlefields back to Valhalla, is Brünnhilde's entrance from act 2 writ large, a cross between a witches' Sabbath and a Hells Angels gathering, a faintly ridiculous but immensely popular piece that, more than anything by Wagner, has contributed to his image as a composer of loud and pompous music. While the Ride continues the topic of incessant flight from the pursuing fate—now it is Brünnhilde who tries to escape Wotan's wrath—that had pervaded the opera throughout, it provides a well-calculated and much-needed

TABLE 8 *Die Walküre*, Act 3, The Ride of the Valkyries

Form	Key	Text incipit	Measures	CD.track.time
Refrain	b/B		1–78	IV.1.0:00–2:42
Episode		Zu Ortlindes Stute stell deinen Hengst	79–102	IV.1.2:42–3:29
Refrain	b/B		103–57	IV.1.3:29–5:26
Episode		In Wald mit den Rossen zu Rast und Weid'!	158–266	IV.1.5:26–8:25
[Refrain	b/B		937–79	IV.7.2:57–4:25]

respite after the tragedy of the first two acts and before the sublime and heartrending final scene still to come. (Like the Rhinedaughters in *Das Rheingold*, but unlike other characters we have encountered so far, the Valkyries are allowed to sing together: they are more a collective entity than fully individualized creatures, and it is unlikely that even the most devoted Wagnerians can recall all of their names.)

The most memorable passage of the ensuing dialogue between Brünnhilde and Sieglinde is its ending. Brünnhilde had revealed to Sieglinde that she (Sieglinde) is pregnant with Siegmund's child, and she (Brünnhilde) had decided to await the pursuing Wotan and thus shield the escape of the pregnant mother in the direction of the forest (where, we learn *en passant*, Fafner, transformed into a dragon, hides in a cave, guarding Alberich's hoard and the Ring). After all this, the Valkyrie announces, to the proleptic accompaniment of the Siegfried motive now heard for the first time, that "the world's noblest hero, o woman, you harbour within your sheltering womb!"[75] She gives Sieglinde her twin-husband's shattered Sword and names the unborn hero: "Let him who'll wield the newly forged sword receive his name from me—may 'Siegfried' joy in victory!"[76]

Sieglinde's ecstatic expression of gratitude (III.534–62) that concludes the dialogue begins with the famous melody (III.534–41) that will next be heard only at the very end of the cycle. This moment has been given numerous names and interpretations by the exegetes. According to his wife's *Diary* entry (July 23, 1872), the composer himself referred to it as "Sieglinde's theme of praise for Brünnhilde."[77] (Memorable though the melody is, one wonders, however, if Wagner's optimistic reckoning that we shall recall in a few days exactly where we have already heard it is not a miscalculation.) For a brief moment, we catch in close proximity motivic glimpses of the *Ring*'s heroic protagonists, the yet-to-be-born Siegfried and the yet-to-be-reborn-as-a-human Brünnhilde, and are even given a preview of the latter's final apotheosis.

Once Wotan catches up with his daughter, the focus of attention through the end of the opera is on him. Brünnhilde has already made her fateful choice and now needs only to submit to her father's punishment. Wotan, on the other hand, needs to learn how to transmute the consuming wrath he feels at his daughter's disobedience into a father's profound sorrow at the inevitable separation from the beloved being who is no longer the faithful agent of his will. It is this emotional trajectory that is the content of the remaining portion of the opera. The drama that had begun as the tragedy of the Wälsung twins, and that has centered on the fateful transformation of the Valkyrie into a human being, ends as the tragedy of the god who this once reveals himself to be vulnerable to suffering and hence sympathetic—the only one of the divine beings in the *Ring* with an interior life of human depth.

As long as the wrath dominates, and all the Valkyries remain onstage, the dialogue between Wotan and Brünnhilde remains stylistically close to the recitative. Once the Valkyries exit and the conversation between father and daughter becomes more intimate, the orchestral motivic web that accompanies the recitative gets gradually more dense and is interspersed with long arioso passages, thus creating a stylistic transition to the culminating, final, and longest arioso of them all: Wotan's Farewell, with the full revelation of the god's interiority reserved ultimately for the orchestra.

But first, in the presence of her sisters, Brünnhilde is cast out from the gods' circle. She will be put to sleep on the rock where they now find themselves, to be overpowered and domesticated by the first man who would find and awaken her, a fate that she, along with her proudly virginal sisters, perceives as deeply shameful. Once the Valkyries had been sent packing, Brünnhilde can explain to her father the motives that drove her to disobey him: she has followed what she took to have been his true intention, before Fricka managed to falsify it. More important, she has been profoundly shaken by the sight and sound of Siegmund's love and distress. This experience inspired her own love in turn and thus has been decisive: "Inwardly true to the will which lodged this love in my heart and which bound me to the Wälsung—I flouted your command."[78] The explanation cannot change Wotan's verdict: "You blissfully followed the force of love: now follow him whom you're forced to love!"[79] The emphasis, in the statements of both the daughter and the father, on love as the power overriding all other claims is noteworthy, since love will indeed become the sole content of Brünnhilde's gospel to humanity. Brünnhilde understands the consequences of her actions and asks only not to be dishonored by being exposed to the will of a random first comer. Surround my rock with a terrifying fire, she asks her father, so that only a fearless and free hero can penetrate it and reach me. She intimates that it is Siegfried she has in mind for herself—an intimation Wotan would rather not hear.

Wotan's Farewell—the act's main and final closed number—brings his answer. The number is laid out in three broad sections. The first two—respectively fast and slow and hence reversing the customary pattern—are lyrically dominated by the voice and each ends with an expansive orchestral postlude. The third, moderate, one is dominated by the orchestra with superimposed sections of vocal recitation, thus providing a largely orchestral peroration or coda to the two-part aria (see appendix 2: act 3, scene 3, b.).

The vocal line of the first section develops freely, without any obvious form-creating internal repetitions; it continues and intensifies the ariosos that preceded Wotan's Farewell in the scene. Similarly, the motivic content of the orchestral accompaniment freely follows the flow of Wotan's ideas as he bids farewell to his "valiant, glorious child"[80] and promises to shield her sleep with "a bridal fire"[81] that would be crossed only by "one freer than I, the god!"[82] The orchestra makes it clear that it is Siegfried who will be the liberating hero. It is impossible to decide with complete certainty in a moment such as this whether the orchestra spells out here Wotan's unverbalized thought, thus showing that he has taken in Brünnhilde's earlier revelations concerning the future of the Wälsungs, or whether it serves as a narrator speaking above Wotan's shoulders directly to the audience, but the former seems more likely. The father and daughter entertain similar hopes for the future. This too is a sign of their deepening reconciliation.

By contrast, the orchestral postlude that follows the first section of Wotan's arioso is highly unified motivically. It develops the idea that was most prominently featured in the preceding dialogue when Brünnhilde had explained what it was that most deeply motivated her—her love of the Wälsung—thereby intimating that this love will be transferred from the now-dead father to the yet-unborn son. In this way, the postlude links Brünnhilde's past with her future by giving voice to the power that matters most to her, that defines her identity: the "valiant, glorious child" is on her way to become a woman and an apostle of love. And the postlude ensures that, even as Wotan reveals his emotional vulnerability more intimately than ever before or after, Brünnhilde's character and destiny remain the center of attention.

Only in the last measures of the postlude (III.1572–79) is the musical-dramatic motive of the love of the Wälsungs transmuted into another one, one that will completely dominate the second section of Wotan's Farewell, its orchestral postlude included. This motive, too, has been featured in the dialogue that preceded the Farewell (at III.1430–53), specifically at the point when Brünnhilde begged Wotan to "shield the sleeper with hideous terrors that only a fearlessly free-born hero shall find me here on the fell!"[83] The motive is thus immediately associated with the idea of shielded sleep. But its roots go much deeper: it was first heard at the very beginning of *Das Rheingold* (137–38), in the opening, carefree Song of the Rhinedaughters frolicking under the protection of their father's waters. Brünnhilde's sleep, protected by her own father, is thus seen as a regenerating and cleansing return to the womb of nature, so that she may be reborn as fully new and human when she awakens. (As the *Ring* progresses, its music-dramatic motives develop increasingly rich and far-reaching associations, leaving behind any initial impression that they might be no more than simple, univocal, unambiguous musical signs.)

Not only is the accompaniment of the second section of the Farewell much more uniform motivically than that of the first one, but its vocal line, too, is much more structured, patterned into a Bar (AAB) form (table 9). Clearly now, this is no more

TABLE 9 *Die Walküre*, Act 3, Wotan's Farewell, Second Section

Form	Text incipit	Measures	CD.track.time
Introductory vamp		1580–81	IV.13.2:40–2:52
A	Der Augen leuchtendes Paar	1582–89	IV.13.2:52–3:35
A	dieser Augen strahlendes Paar	1590–97	IV.13.3:41–4:24
B	zum letzten Mal letz' es mich heut	1598–609	IV.13.4:31–5:47
Coda	Denn so kehrt der Gott sich dir ab	1610–24	IV.13.5:53–7:21
Postlude		1625–44	IV.13.7:21–9:58

an arioso, but a full-fledged aria. The orchestral postlude recapitulates the central ideas of the section—the accompanying motive of shielded sleep throughout and over it first the A (III.1628–31) and then the B phrase (III.1632–38) of Wotan's vocal line. The section is the emotional core of Wotan's Farewell: he kisses his daughter's eyes for the last time, predicting that, in the future, "on a happier man [happier than he, the god] their stars shall shine."[84] In so doing he kisses her godhead away and puts her into the regenerating sleep from which she will awaken a human and a woman.

What remains is a coda-like afterthought, an orchestral peroration with some superimposed vocal declamation, as Wotan summons Loge, surrounds the rock with fire, portentously announcing that "he who fears my spear-point shall never pass through the fire!" and sorrowfully departs.[85] Here the fear of the fire is secondary to the fear of Wotan's Spear. The long-awaited liberating hero, the main protagonist of the *Ring*, must confront the Spear fearlessly if he is to rid the world of the old regime of the traditionally accumulating contracts that the Spear safeguards. Throughout, the orchestra reviews and weaves together appropriate motives, most prominently the music of Loge (from III.1650 on) culminating in the tinselly Magic Fire (III.1674–85) that seems to have broken in straight from *The Nutcracker*, and (from III.1690 until the end) the music of Brünnhilde's shielded sleep that had played such a central role in the second section of the Farewell.[86] It now returns to dominate the ending of the third section as well, thus ensuring that we hear it as the completion of Wotan's aria rather than as a separate unit. This time it appears with a few motives superimposed, most prominently, the portentous double announcement of Siegfried as Wotan pronounces his just-quoted final words (at III.1693 and 1702) and (at III.1709) the B phrase of the second section of his aria ("zum letzten Mal...") as "he gazes sorrowfully back at Brünnhilde" before departing.[87]

Die Walküre begins as the tragedy of the Wälsungs, but it ends with the tragedy of Wotan. From the standpoint of the Aristotelian dramatic unities, this might be seen as a flaw and it would indeed be a flaw if the opera were to stand on its own. But of course this was never the intention. From the standpoint of the whole cycle, the tragedy of the Wälsungs is secondary: their job is literally to engender Siegfried and metaphorically to engender Brünnhilde by humanizing her; this accomplished, they are expendable. And the tragedy of Wotan is balanced by the hope that his rule might be replaced by something better—the rule of his daughter and grandson. Within this larger perspective, the real subject of *Die Walküre*, and one that gives the opera its dramatic unity after all and justifies its title, is Brünnhilde's painful but necessary separation from her father, her transformation from a callous teenage divinity into a compassionate and loving grown-up human being.

SIEGFRIED: HOW ONE BECOMES A HERO

It has often been noticed that each evening within the *Ring* represents a different genre, respectively: a myth, a tragedy, a fairy tale, and a grand opera. After the sublime tragedy of the divinity turned woman, the fairy tale of a boy turned hero is something of a letdown. If *Siegfried* is less gripping and profound than *Die Walküre*, this is not because Wagner's inspiration abandoned him; it is because Siegfried is less interesting a character than Brünnhilde, at this stage of his development at least. She discovers compassion and love, and through them discovers humanity. He discovers nothing really until he discovers her. What defines Siegfried is not reason, but healthy natural instinct, fearlessness, and rude strength. Himself built on the model compounded of Rousseau's natural man and his Emile, he is the prototype of Walther and Parsifal—Wagner's other exemplars of the overman, the improved future model of the human being, healthy of body and instinct, and a bit dumb so as not to smother the instinctual and creative under the pillow of the reasonable, of knowledge of tried and true past practices and traditions. When circumstances or instinct bring him face to face with his enemies, he is capable of confronting them in death-defying acts of bravery. This is admirable, but not terribly interesting. After a certain age, we just cannot warm up to fairy tales quite as much as to tragedies. Even the greatest artistic skill does not suffice to make us excited about a dumb but healthy superhero.

If a comparison between *Die Walküre* and *Siegfried* does not favor the latter, the root cause might be the respective functions assigned Brünnhilde and Siegfried in the allegory of the *Ring*. The new humanity that would replace the old order of Wotan and Alberich is to be free, free precisely of this old order and its constraints. Fearlessness in the face of death is a prerequisite of freedom; it is fear that makes us consent to an enslavement. But freedom needs to be given a specific content: the new humanity is not only to be free *from* the traditions inherited from the past, but also free *to* . . . , well, to what? Love is the answer, because love is something that can neither be bought (and thus come under the sway of Alberich) nor legislated (and thus come under the rule of Wotan) without being corrupted out of existence, while it can give content to freedom. Like fearlessness, love is the essential index of human freedom—the former its prerequisite, the latter its content. In the *Ring* it is Siegfried who stands for fearlessness, Brünnhilde who speaks for love; he is all about being free, but it is she who can give this freedom actual content. No wonder he seems lighter weight by comparison.

Act 1: Getting the Sword

The two operas invite also more immediate comparisons. Siegfried is to succeed where his father failed, and the first act of *Siegfried* is all about the hero acquiring a proper weapon, the very same Sword, just as the first act of *Die Walküre* was (the acquisition of a proper woman is this time postponed until act 3). The parallelism of the two acts is further underscored by their similar settings. The opening act of *Siegfried*, too, takes place inside a solitary forest dwelling of a profoundly unsympathetic character—this time it is Mime who conducts an Emile-like pedagogical experiment on the young Siegfried, raising the boy in total isolation for his own nefarious purpose. And, finally, the formal organization of the corresponding first acts is similar. Also in *Siegfried*, the opening act is, in spite of its nominal division into three scenes, an operatic *scena* writ large, with the recitative dialogues of the first two scenes preparing the large closed number of scene 3 with which the act culminates and concludes (see appendix 3: act 1).

To be sure, in keeping perhaps with the fairy-tale character of the story, the first scene is peppered with short folksy songs, but these are too short and lightweight to provide the recitative dialogue of the scene with a formal shape; they merely embellish it. Siegfried's and Mime's paired little single-stanza songs close to the beginning of their dialogue, in particular, are just brief precipitations from the surrounding recitative, held together by uniform accompaniments and keys, and designed to show off their respective temperaments as they interact with one another—the fiery impatience of the ward and the petulant whining of his guardian. Siegfried's second arietta is slightly more elaborate, consisting this time of two freely parallel stanzas ("Es sangen die Vöglein so selig im Lenz," I.773–97 plus "So ruhten im Busch auch Rehe gepaart," I.797–829). But the last arietta is again a single stanza of particularly folk-like, or even nursery rhyme–like, character.

Die Walküre was dominated by the image of flight—the flight of Siegmund, then of both ill-starred twins, finally of Brünnhilde with Sieglinde—a continuous flight that came to an end only with the Valkyrie's decision to stop running away and await Wotan. The first act of *Siegfried*, by contrast, is permeated by the image of going nowhere, of incessant, obsessive turning in circles, of being unable to break free—at least until the young hero manages to cut the Gordian knot of his enslavement with the newly forged Sword and run away. Mime, as we encounter him when the curtain goes up and even before, since the Prelude provides a portrait of his state of mind, is not in flight. On the contrary, he is going nowhere, his thoughts obsessively turning round and round, always pondering the same problem to which he is incapable of finding a solution. The Prelude and its continuation until Siegfried's entrance are dominated by the repetitive motive of the Nibelung hammering we remember from the visit to the Nibelheim in *Das Rheingold*, where it was the sound of the incessant automatic self-reproduction of the capital that enslaved its producers. Other motives and thoughts, most notably those of the Ring, the Sword, and of Fafner as a dragon, emerge from time to time as they cross Mime's mind; the repetitive hammering remains constant, the sound of his obsession. Mime's mind is running in circles. When toward the end of scene 1 Siegfried exits, leaving his guardian once again alone, we find him exactly where he had been at Siegfried's entrance—returning back to his repetitive, fruitless thoughts of the hammering, with those of the Ring, the dragon, and others thrown in. And during their dialogue, too, Mime manages to sound like a broken record. His pathetically whining arietta must have been heard by Siegfried many times, since the youth mockingly quotes from it (I.834–42) and Mime himself laces the dialogue with repeated excerpts from it (in I.1018–79).

We quickly learn what it is that has tied Mime's mind in knots: in spite of his reputation for being an expert smith, he is unable to forge an adequate sword for Siegfried, as the prodigiously strong youth breaks even his best products. The only weapon that would do, Mime knows, would be the restored Nothung. Alas, the dwarf is unable to put the shattered fragments back together. Nothing much happens in scene 1: its main purpose is to bring the audience up to date and to provide initial characterization of Siegfried. In *Die Walküre*, act 3, we left Sieglinde running off in the direction of Fafner's forest. Now we learn that in the forest she was found by Mime, who gave her shelter in his solitary cave, where she died in childbirth. (Mime, we realize, must have moved here in order to keep an eye on Fafner, whose Ring he covets no less than do his brother and Wotan.) Ever since, he has been raising the orphan alone, isolating the child from the world, pretending to be its father and hoping that the ignorant youth will kill their forest neighbor, Fafner the dragon, and thus win the Ring for the dwarf.

But now Siegfried is child no more and, a lad of healthy natural instincts, he cannot stand the hypocritical, lying, ugly dwarf, cannot believe him to be his father. Using force to pry the truth out of Mime, he learns his real parents' identities and fates, and that Mime hides the fragments of his father's Sword. It is from these fragments, he decides at once, that Mime should forge his Sword anew; with this weapon Siegfried would leave his repulsive tutor at once for the freedom of the forest. It is noteworthy, incidentally, that Siegfried makes his first appearance in the *Ring* emitting inarticulate cries ("Hoiho! Hoiho!," I.254–58), just as Brünnhilde did, or her sisters, or for that matter the Rhinedaughters. What all these characters have in common is their healthy, pre-reflective and pre-cultural proximity to primordial nature and hence also a proclivity to express themselves in a pre-linguistic fashion. Language itself, Wagner thought (dependent in this, whether directly or not, on an idea of Rousseau), had its origins in the sort of pre-conceptual emotive vocalizations in which music and language had not yet been separated.[88]

TABLE 10 *Siegfried*, Act 1, Scene 2

Form	Text incipit	Measures	CD.track.time
The Wanderer refrain	Heil dir, weiser Schmied!	1289–414	I.10.0:00–11.1:46
Mime's questions	Du rührtest dich viel auf der Erde Rücken	1414–601	I.11.1:46–10:23
The Wanderer refrain	Was zu wissen dir frommt	1601–57	I.12.0:00–2:29
Wotan's questions	Nun, ehrlicher Zwerg! Sag mir zum ersten!	1657–855	I.12.2:29–13.0:35
The Wanderer refrain	Dreimal solltest du fragen	1855–59	I.13.0:35–0:48
Wotan's answer	nach eitlen Fernen forschtest du	1860–903	I.13.0:48–2:51

And thus, at the end of scene 1, Mime is left not knowing how Nothung might be restored, or how his ward would be controlled once he has the Sword in his hands. The answer to the first of these two questions he gets in scene 2—Mime's encounter with Wotan, who roams the world under the guise of the Wanderer and now pays the dwarf an unexpected and unwanted visit. (Evidently, Wotan, too, keeps a wary eye on both Fafner and the competitors for the dragon's hoped-for inheritance.) Dramatically, the scene is a functional equivalent of the lengthy narrative monologue we have come to expect from Wagner at this point in an act. It provides the audience with background information as well as insight into the attitude of the narrator toward this information. Wagner varies the formula now by presenting it under the guise of a wager in which first Wotan and then Mime ask their respective interlocutor three questions each—the answers providing the information that would have normally been offered by the narrator. This varying of the formula is apt: not only is this use of a standard fairy-tale topos in keeping with the nature of the opera, but more importantly, it reinforces the hopelessly repetitive imagery of the act.

The circular shape is suggested also by the music-dramatic form of the scene. While the whole is basically a recitative dialogue, a rondo-like structure is intimated by the recurrence of the music associated with Wotan as Wanderer as a refrain: at length at the beginning when the first part of the wager, allowing Mime to ask three questions, is set up; more briefly in the middle when the second part of the wager, allowing Wotan his three questions, is set up; and most briefly after the second series of questions but before Wotan's final statement (table 10). (In addition, the repetitive question-and-answer structure suggests two smaller-scale rondos within the larger rondo—though only Mime's questions are all set to similar music.)

But the dramatic machinery creaks somewhat: up until Wotan's final statement, we learn nothing new really. An unsympathetic critic would say that Wagner is stretching his material in a redundant fashion just to fill time; a sympathetic one could argue as I have that the very redundancy is in keeping with the repetitive, obsessive hopelessness of Mime's situation. The first series of questions allows Wagner to remind us of the basic topography of his mythic world as well as of its nonhuman inhabitants: the Nibelungs led by Alberich in the underworld; the giants, with Fafner now transformed into a dragon, surviving on the earth's surface; and the gods led by Wotan up on heights. The Wanderer underscores the parallel positions of Alberich and Wotan by calling the former "Black Alberich"[89] and the latter "Light Alberich."[90] The second series moves on to the humans and their world-historical role: Wotan's favored but mistreated race of the Wälsungs, of whom Siegfried survives, and Nothung, the sword Siegfried must wield if he is to kill Fafner. The third question, however, Mime cannot answer: Who will forge Nothung anew? This question Wotan answers himself in the final section of the scene, providing the only really new information. Thus, it makes sense that Wagner sets this section after the final refrain, beyond the intimated rondo structure. It is as if Wotan cut short the final refrain and with it the circular shape of the scene in order to break out into new territory. He tells Mime: "Only he who never knew fear will forge the sword anew."[91] Fearlessness is indeed Siegfried's most essential defining virtue. But not Mime's: almost as an afterthought, Wotan adds that the dwarf's life is now in the hands of the one "who knows not the meaning of fear," leaving Mime in a paroxysm of terror.[92]

But the rondo shape of scene 2 is merely suggested. It is only in scene 3 that the act gets its fully developed closed lyrical number and hence its point of music-dramatic gravity, its formal point of arrival (table 11). In keeping with Siegfried's character, his two strophic songs are formally simpler than any large closed number we have heard in the *Ring* so far. However, the first of these proves more intricately put together than appears on the surface. More important, we discover that the two songs do not stand on their own, but are components of a single larger whole: the final cabaletta brings together elements from both songs, smelting them into a single aria consisting of not one but two moderate tempo cantabiles (the Smelting Song is marked "Bold, but not too fast"[93] and the Forging Song "Heavy and bold, not too fast")[94] followed by a fast and ever-accelerating cabaletta (marked "Lively"[95] at the beginning, then "Ever more lively,"[96] "Very fast and still more accelerating,"[97] and finally "As fast as possible").[98] The tonal plan, with the cabaletta coming back to the key of the first cantabile, additionally supports this reading of the whole sequence of events.

Each of Siegfried's songs gets interrupted by Mime. In the Forging Song Mime's interlude falls squarely in the middle, separating the two stanzas. In the Smelting Song Mime's interlude comes after the two main stanzas, but since the song is intricately framed, it is still an interlude, not a postlude. In addition to the regular refrain that separates and frames the two regular stanzas, the song also has a second refrain (labeled "super-refrain" in table 11) with which it begins and ends. Together with a phrase that pretends to begin a stanza but does not fulfill this promise (labeled "false stanza" in table 11), the super-refrain provides the song with a larger, outer frame. Yet another interruption from Mime initiates the caba-

TABLE 11 *Siegfried*, Act 1, Siegfried's Aria

Form	Key	Text incipit	Measures	CD.track.time
Cantabile 1: Smelting Song	d/(D)			
Super-refrain		Nothung! Nothung! Neidliches Schwert!	2430–39	II.4.0:00–0:24
False stanza		Zu Spreu nun schuf ich die scharfe Pracht	2440–47	II.4.0:24–0:41
Refrain		Hoho! Hoho! Hohei!	2447–56	II.4.0:41–1:05
Stanza		Wild im Walde wuchs ein Baum	2457–75	II.4.1:05–1:45
Refrain		Hoho! Hoho! Hohei!	2475–84	II.4.1:45–2:09
Stanza		Des Baumes Kohle, wie brennt sie kühn	2485–503	II.4.2:09–2:52
Refrain		Hoho! Hoho! Hohei!	2503–12	II.4.2:52–3:13
Mime's interlude with embedded refrain fragment		Er schmiedet das Schwert	2512–65	II.4.3:13–4:47
Super-refrain fragment		Hoho! Hoho! Hoho! Hohei!	2533–37	II.4.3:51–4:02
Stanza fragment disintegrating into a free arioso		Nothung! Nothung! Neidliches Schwert!	2565–71	II.4.4:47–5:01
False stanza		Im eig'nen Schweiße schwimmst du nun	2571–613	II.4.5:01–6:11
Super-refrain abbreviated		Nun schwitze noch einmal	2613–20	II.4.6:11–6:28
Recitative dialogue		Nothung, neidliches Schwert!	2621–27	II.4.6:28–6:43
		Was schafft der Tölpel dort mit dem Topf?	2627–92	II.4.6:43–8:27
Cantabile 2: Forging Song	F			
Refrain		Hoho! Hoho! Hohei!	2692–704	II.5.0:00–0:28
Stanza		Einst färbte Blut dein falbes Blau	2705–27	II.5.0:28–1:16
Mime's interlude		Er schafft sich ein scharfes Schwert	2728–40	II.5.1:16–1:41
Refrain		Hoho! Hoho! Hahei!	2741–53	II.5.1:41–2:08
Stanza		Der frohen Funken wie freu' ich mich!	2754–81	II.5.2:08–3:03
Cabaletta	d/D			
Mime's interlude		Den der Bruder schuf, den schimmernden Reif	2782–836	II.5.3:03–3:49
Super-refrain		Nothung! Nothung! neidliches Schwert!	2836–51	II.5.3:49–4:02
A variant of the Forging Song stanza with Mime in the background		Warst du entzwei, ich zwang dich zu ganz	2851–99	II.5.4:02–4:39
Super-refrain developed into a full final statement with Mime in the background		Nothung! Nothung! Neidliches Schwert!	2899–953	II.5.4:39–5:25
Orchestral postlude			2953–83	II.5.5:25–5:43

letta and even when Siegfried produces that section's main components, a variant of the stanza from the Forging Song framed by the super-refrain from the Smelting Song, Mime remains active in the background and the aural space is saturated with the sound of the frantic Nibelung hammering (now appropriated by Siegfried, just as he has appropriated the role of a master smith from Mime), a sound familiar to us from *Das Rheingold* and from the first scene of the act. In fact, Mime's backstage presence is so pervasive throughout that we might almost be tempted to consider the whole number a duet rather than an aria.

Indeed, throughout the number both Siegfried and Mime are engaged in important activities. To understand these, we need to go back to the dialogue that precedes the aria. The Wanderer has left the terrified Mime in a worse state than he had found him: the dwarf knows now that "only he who never knew fear will forge the sword anew" and that he himself will be killed by such a fearless person. Once Siegfried reappears in the cave, the dwarf's first thought is to teach his ward fear. He even manages to make the idea attractive to the youth, who had obviously never experienced this curious emotion. Hence he accepts with enthusiasm Mime's plan to lead him to Fafner's lair: the dragon will teach him fear. Moreover, since Mime had been unable to reconstruct the Sword, Siegfried decides to do this himself. Armed with the Wanderer's prophesy, Mime understands that the lad will succeed. He realizes, too, that there is no point in having Fafner teach Siegfried fear, as the young hero needs to remain fearless if he is to kill the dragon. Hence the dramatic content of the aria. In the foreground, Siegfried successfully restores Nothung. In the background, Mime brews a sleeping potion and refines his initial plan: once Siegfried kills the dragon, his guardian will put him to sleep, use Nothung to kill him in turn, and thus become the master of the Ring.

The triumphant ending of the act—Mime certain of the future success of his plan and prematurely jubilant, Siegfried splitting the anvil with one blow of his newly forged Sword—feels like an ironic repetition of the untroubled triumph at the end of the first act of *Die Walküre*, it too a duet during which the Sword is won, enabling its owner to cut enslaving ties and run away to freedom. Splitting the anvil, Siegfried cuts the Gordian knot of his guardian's obsessive and hopeless running in circles. He is ready to move out and run all the way to the summit of Brünnhilde's rock, ready to begin maturing toward independence and autonomy, perhaps even ready to lead the world beyond the traditional stagnation of the hopeless Wotan-Alberich stalemate and into a more hopeful future under the aegis of fearless, loving, and free humans.

Act 2: Using It

The second act of *Siegfried* is a music-dramatic anomaly. As the only act constructed by Wagner after *Das Rheingold* that is not focused on a formally closed vocal number, it is something of a structural experiment, an experiment the composer evidently did not consider successful enough to warrant repeating. The reason for this experiment lies in the plot continuity between acts 2 and 3. Once Siegfried leaves Mime's cave, he does not really stop until he reaches the summit of Brünnhilde's rock, or, rather, he stops only as long as is needed to overcome successive obstacles on his way: the dragon, Mime himself, and finally Wotan. Accordingly, Wagner treats acts 2 and 3 as if they were one continuous super-act formally focused on a large closed number at the end of the opera.

Act 2 consists of two sections, a large introductory scene 1 that reminds us of the mythological background by staging the central confrontation between Wotan and Alberich (central in more senses than one, this being the central act of the *Ring*, if you keep in mind that *Das Rheingold* was just an introduction) and, as the main body of the act, a series of shorter scenes spread among what Wagner labeled scenes 2 and 3, involving the actions and meditations of the drama's eponymous hero (see appendix 3: act 2). These shorter scenes form two similar cycles of four sections each (sections a.–d. in Wagner's scenes 2 and 3). Each cycle begins with a dialogue (a.) and culminates in one of Siegfried's essential deeds in this act, the killings of Fafner and of Mime (c.). These action scenes are surrounded by meditative scenes in which Siegfried communes with nature (b. and d.).

While the act dispenses with formally closed vocal sections, it does not dispense with all musical coherence. The burden of providing coherence, however, shifts from the voice to the orchestra and does so from the very beginning, when the orchestral part of scene 1 continues seamlessly from the music of the Prelude. What holds this large developmental f minor section together musically is the pedal point involving a diminished fifth (or tritone—the two intervals are treated as enharmonically equivalent throughout) between the fifth scale step, *c*, and a chromatically bent second (or first) scale step, *g-flat* (or *f-sharp*). The tritone pedal point completely stabilizes the Prelude itself (II.1–103). In the subsequent scene (II.104–529) the tritone begins to wander to other pitch levels and there are three significant sections from which it is absent (II.168–252, 286–375, and 451–99), but after each of these interruptions the tritone comes back (II.253–85, 376–450, and 500–529), settling on the original pitch level either immediately (in the first and third returns) or eventually (in the second return, by II.411). In short, the Prelude and scene 1 of the second act of *Siegfried* offer a classic lesson in how one may tonally stabilize and thus unify long stretches of music by means of a pedal point consisting not of a single tone as traditional pedal points do, but of an interval or even a chord, a lesson that would not be lost on subsequent generations of composers up to the First World War.

But what is particularly striking and exemplary about this scene is not just that it is unified by means of a pedal point, but that this pedal point is a tritone. What should have been a perfect fifth outlining the dominant is chromatically inflected and, as a result, a quintessentially unstable interval is used to stabilize the music. The paradoxical nature of the device is rooted in the dramatic content of the scene—the encounter of the cycle's main mythical antagonists, Alberich and Wotan, deadlocked in a hopeless struggle that offers no prospect of a satisfactory resolution. The tritone offers a perfect emblem for the paradoxically unstable stasis of the modern world. For radicals such as Wagner—and it is immaterial whether they are of the left or of the right—this very instability is intolerable. They dream of replacing it with a world from which all conflicts will have been rooted out, a world in which the tritone will be resolved to the D-flat major tonic once and for all—as it will be at the end of the *Ring*. By contrast, the centrists—and it is again immaterial whether they are of a liberal or conservative bent—dread all utopian visions of a perfectly harmonious world. They celebrate the institutions of modernity for their ability to tolerate and temporarily resolve conflicts and thus to keep our world permanently open-ended and unfinished.

Proximately, the tritone is associated with Fafner the dragon, himself the emblem of the unstable stasis of the Wotan-Alberich world. (Fafner hibernates on the Nibelung treasure, but does nothing to make his capital serve his ends, since he has none beyond sheer possession; clearly, this unproductive form of capital accumulation, keeping money under the mattress rather than investing it, cannot last forever.) The tritone is first heard (II.2-4) in the timpani that tap pianissimo the rhythmic pattern associated with the giants since *Das Rheingold*. But soon, still in the Prelude, the range of associations expands. The tritone shows itself (II.54-59) to be a component of the motive of Alberich's Curse (also remembered since the opening evening of the cycle), and it also settles (by II.73) on a motive that will accompany Alberich's opening words and thus get associated with his dark brooding. But it is in its timpanic, Fafner-related, shape that it will be heard most prominently throughout the scene.

Alberich is "brooding darkly" (stage direction at his first appearance) about Fafner and the future of the Ring.[99] Incessantly he guards the entrance to Fafner's cave, hoping for, and dreading, the arrival of the dragon's slayer. When, instead, it is Wotan who arrives in his guise as the Wanderer, Alberich recognizes his rival instantly. Their encounter is, predictably, a scene of mutual loathing. Alberich understands Wotan's predicament perfectly well and does not hesitate to rub it in: since Wotan paid the giants for their labor with the Ring, he cannot take it away from Fafner without ruining the whole structure of traditional contracts on which his power depends. But Wotan tells Alberich that his immediate antagonist now is his brother, Mime: it is he who leads Siegfried to the cave, so that Siegfried might kill Fafner and thus make the Ring, about which the young hero knows nothing, available to the dwarf. Wotan himself "came to watch and not to act."[100] Siegfried, whom he admits he loves, is a free agent: "Heroes alone can help me," he says, without explaining what sort of help he actually expects in this case.[101] (Perhaps he hopes that once Siegfried recovers the Ring he will freely offer it to his grandfather as a gift?) Wotan even wakes Fafner up to warn him of the approaching danger, telling Alberich that perhaps the dragon will give back the Nibelung his "toy" in order to escape death.[102] But Fafner remains unimpressed: "What I lie on I own:— leave me to sleep," he memorably tells both intruders, his magnificent final yawn outlining the c-G-flat tritone.[103] The attempt having failed, the Wanderer withdraws, telling Alberich to compete with Mime alone.

Considered purely in terms of plot development, the scene is even more redundant than the corresponding scene of the Wanderer's encounter with Mime in the preceding act. It tells us nothing essential that we do not know already. And yet it is not experienced as a dramatic miscalculation—quite the contrary. It is the one scene of the *Ring* in which the central conflict that, from the perspective of the cycle, wrecks the world today is presented with an emblematic force both dramatically and musically. Whether "today" is *anno* 1848, 1876, or 2008, the conflict is between the imperatives of economy and those of the state, between unfettered financial capitalism and law-governed legitimate politics. It makes artistic sense that the image of Alberich and Wotan circling Fafner's cave in mutual hostility, at once united and divided by the unresolved tritone, stands indelibly at the center of the cycle. It is this conflict and this tritone, Wagner thinks, that require resolution, or else a revolutionary sweeping aside.

After the introductory scene, the Fafner-related tritone is prominently heard in the timpani twice more in the main body of the act, first in the section in which Siegfried kills Fafner (II.961–1169), and second in the section in which he kills Mime (II.1412–701). In the former, the timpani tritone accompanies Fafner's words from the beginning (from II.1020 on) and is ubiquitous throughout at various pitch levels. In the latter, the tritone reasserts itself only in the last portion of the section (II.1672–701). There, Mime having been killed and his body thrown into the dragon's cave, Siegfried blocks the entrance to the cave with Fafner's carcass, leaving his two slain antagonists to guard what remains of the Nibelung hoard. Thus the introductory scene throws its long musical shadow over the main body of the act, linking the Wotan-Alberich contest with Siegfried's two murderous actions.

All the same, it is not the tritone that provides scenes 2 and 3 with their main unifying musical backbone. Rather, this is constituted by the recurrent orchestral music traditionally called the Forest Murmurs that accompanies Siegfried's contemplative monologues before and after each of the two murder scenes. The Forest Murmurs is another instance of Wagner's characteristically elemental music, like the Prelude to *Das Rheingold*, elemental in both senses of the word: because it represents nature reduced to its most basic building blocks (there, at the cycle's beginning, the river's flowing waters; now, the air gently caressing the leaves of the forest's trees), but also because in both cases it is a music made of almost nothing, here of strings quietly oscillating between adjacent tones of the diatonic E major scale, the kind of music that constantly intimates the birth of melody, but never quite delivers on this promise, never quite coalesces into a fully articulated melodic phrase. At most it provides a shimmering background to Siegfried's recitative monologues and to instrumental and vocal melodies emerging from this tapestry of sound—most prominently to the singing of the Woodbird, both before and after Siegfried can understand her words (before: II.833–56, 866–71, 894–900, 925–34, 1179–94; after: II.1198–206, 1386–95, 1797–809, 1826–37, 1855–61).

In only one of these Forest Murmurs passages, at II.1395–412, is Siegfried with someone else, and the moment is particularly interesting and unusual from the standpoint of musical dramaturgy. Siegfried and Mime observe one another at a certain distance, without engaging in conversation, and we hear the thoughts of both at the same time. While the dwarf is actually talking to himself, the orchestra stays with the Forest Murmurs that Siegfried had been listening to just before the appearance of Mime (II.1386–95, now in combination with a meditative theme associated since the first act of *Die Walküre* with the sufferings of the Wälsungs, with which the Murmurs had already been combined at II.771–86) and thus continues to express his, rather than Mime's, inner life.

For all its attenuated character, the Forest Murmurs recur with sufficient regularity and at sufficient length to provide scenes 2 and 3 with a musical point of gravity, the main unifying thread of the act. By the same token, they allow Wagner to shift the focus of attention somewhat from Siegfried's two murderous actions (ostensibly the act's main events) to the scenes of introspection that surround them and that, for the first time, throw a sympathetic light on the hero, show him capable of something more than just shouting and throwing his weight around, capable of self-reflection and hence of development into a more interesting person than he has been up until now. In those moments when he is alone, as he notices the sounds of nature around him, the rustling of leaves and the singing of birds, he also begins to explore his own deeper nature, to listen to himself, to think about his parents, about where he comes from. And it is from the nature without and within that he begins to learn who he is and what it is that he should accomplish. At the same time he also learns to understand the motives of those around him better. Until now he just instinctively loathed Mime, but now he also hears behind Mime's hypocritical words the dwarf's real thoughts and intentions. He may not have learned fear, as he had hoped when he embarked on this expedition into the forest, but he has learned something about himself and others after all.

But his education is not yet complete. The voice of nature that is his teacher is the voice of the Woodbird emerging from the Forest Murmurs, the voice whose meaning Siegfried learns to understand once he has tasted Fafner's blood. It is the Woodbird who instructs him to take the Tarnhelm and the Ring from the dragon's cave, warns him of Mime's intended treachery, and sends him onward toward Brünnhilde's rock, so that the experience of love might complete his education. It is thus by listening to nature that Siegfried gradually discovers his own true self.

Act 3: The Awakening

The boy who left his foster cave at the end of act 1 in order to learn fear has not concluded his quest by the end of act 2. As a result, act 3 is continuous with act 2 and, as I have mentioned, only the two together get a synthesizing closed number once Siegfried's goal is reached at the end of the opera. The last act consists of three scenes, of which the first two, respectively Wotan's encounter with Erda and Siegfried's with Wotan, are open-composition dialogues. The third one, Siegfried's encounter with Brünnhilde, is a love duet expanded to huge proportions by long sections of recitative dialogue (see appendix 3: act 3). Before the summit of Brünnhilde's rock is reached in scene 3, Siegfried must overcome one more obstacle on his way, Wotan himself in scene 2; on the other hand, scene 1 is an interlude, akin to scene 2 in act 1 and also the first scene in act 2, one of the three significant and self-revealing encounters Wotan has in this opera.

The act begins well—remarkably so, given that Wagner is returning here to the project he had interrupted more than a decade earlier. Musically, scene 1 is one of the opera's high points. While nominally Wotan's encounter with Erda is a recitative dialogue, the lengthy statements from both protagonists are ariosos of considerable nobility, rather than simple recitatives. The whole is held together by a unifying key as well as by the orchestra that develops the material of the Prelude. The passages of vocal recitation supported, recitative style, by sparse orchestral chords that were still occasionally to be heard in act 2 are for the most part gone now. The continuity of the instrumental texture, as well as its motivic density, is such that the music of the orchestra alone, without the voices, provides a musically coherent and self-sufficient discourse, though, of course, the voices and their words provide the motivation for the content of this discourse. All the same it is a freely developing, unstructured discourse that contrasts Wotan's restlessness with Erda's sleepiness, but does not attempt any formal architecture beyond that alternation.

The scene is no less important dramatically than it is impressive musically: this is where Wotan reveals himself most thoroughly since the monologue of the second act of *Die Walküre*, and what he reveals, or rather enacts, since he changes his mind in our presence, is the next stage in his evolution. The god awakens the presumably all-knowing Erda and insists on their conversation so "that I may now gain knowledge."[104] What he wants to know is "how to hold back a rolling wheel," the wheel of history.[105] Once in the past (in *Das Rheingold*) she instilled in him the fear of the impending end of the gods' rule. He now wants to know, "How can god overcome his care?"[106] In other words, he begins this conversation still filled with hope that the twilight of the gods might be averted, that the "rolling wheel" might be held back. But Wotan's question to Erda remains without an answer and, after a brief outburst of violent recriminations (she telling him that he is not really a god, he predicting that her wisdom is about to end, too), he resolves to will what he cannot avoid anyway: "Fear of the end of the gods no longer consumes me now that my wish so wills it!" he solemnly announces.[107] Thus, without Erda's help, he has found a way to "overcome his care." It is a moment of conversion of sorts, and a conversion for which one can find no clear motivation—an act of pure, willful self-overcoming. Erda does nothing really to contribute to this outcome. At most, Wotan uses her presence to talk himself into it.

To be sure, once in the past (in his monologue of the second act of *Die Walküre*) he made a similar decision, but this was taken in despair; now he is taking it freely "in gladness and joy."[108] On that earlier occasion he bequeathed the world to Alberich's son, since he realized that his own was not up to the task. Now he is passing his heritage on to his own grandson and, as he does so, the orchestra emphatically sounds the ecstatic motive that usually goes by the name of World Heritage (III.374–77). The motive is repeated (III.408–16) as Wotan predicts that the fearless hero will awaken Brünnhilde, which can only mean that she too is included in the inheritance. More, it is Brünnhilde who "will work the deed that redeems the world."[109] And the motive is heard one more time (III.425–29) as Wotan concludes: "Whatever they do—to one who is eternally young the god now yields in gladness."[110] He is no longer a Schopenhauerian, but rather a Nietzschean, filled with *amor fati*.

Thus the scene not only marks a stage in Wotan's development, showing him embracing the inevitable revolution of the rolling wheel of history in the spirit of acceptance and joy; it also looks forward to the (as yet unspecified) world-redeeming deed that will end the drama. But the very next scene demonstrates the limits of the god's conversion with admirable realism. Once the future ruler of the world shows up at the door, the old king is less ready to embrace the change than he had thought he was.

For Wotan's encounter with Siegfried, Wagner returns to a slightly simpler, less arioso, sort of recitative, though the supporting orchestral discourse remains continuous and, while not unified tonally as a whole, it stays in the key of E-flat at least some of the time (specifically for the part of the conversation extending from III.499 to 602). Initially Wotan greets the arrival of Siegfried with pleasure. But the mood quickly turns sour, since the god expects to be treated with courtesy if not reverence and Siegfried is his usual brash and irreverent self. He has suffered enough under the tutelage of an older authority figure and, having gotten rid of one, is not about to submit to another elderly tutor. Before long he sees the Wanderer as an obstacle on his way to Brünnhilde's rock, while Wotan cannot help but be increasingly unnerved by his grandson's affronts. The prospect of being unceremoniously crushed under the rolling wheel of history turns out to be much less appealing up close than it had been only a moment ago when contemplated in the abstract and at a safe distance. And so Wotan provokes a fight in which Siegfried shatters the god's Spear with one blow of the hero's Sword.

If the *Ring* is essentially the story of how the old regime of traditional rights and obligations safeguarded by the gods was replaced by the new anarchy dominated by the free, fearless, and loving heroes, this should be the turning point, the peripeteia, of the whole cycle. This, however, is not what Wagner's musical dramaturgy tells us: the dramatic turning point occurs in the musically least emphatic scene of the act. Scenes 1 and 2 of act 3 are merely preparatory. The main music-dramatic emphasis falls on scene 3—the goal of not just this act, but of acts 2 and 3 together. It is Siegfried's union with Brünnhilde that Wagner chooses to foreground in this opera; his vanquishing of Wotan, like the killing of the dragon, is merely a stage on the way to this final goal. On the face of it, this is a puzzling dramatic decision, and it requires an explanation. By playing down Siegfried's shattering of the Spear, Wagner suggests that this is not in fact the denouement of the drama, that another deed, still more important and still in the future, will be truly decisive. This other deed, we are led to assume at this point, must be "the deed that redeems the world," which Wotan foretold toward the end of his conversation with Erda would eventually be accomplished by Brünnhilde. In the largest perspective of the redemptive history of the world, Brünnhilde is as indispensable as Siegfried, perhaps even more important than he is. And hence the hero's union with the ex-Valkyrie has to be seen as the main goal. Alone, Siegfried is not sufficient as the agent of world redemption.

The two preparatory scenes of the act are separated from the main one by an orchestral Interlude of the kind we have not heard since *Das Rheingold*, a cinematic depiction of the scenery change as Siegfried ascends Brünnhilde's rock through a wall of fire that surrounds it all the way to the Alpine thin air and blue sky of the summit, a depiction in which the hero remains invisible, and, thanks to the combined efforts of the orchestra and the stage designer, we see the changing world through his eyes. It is precisely the formal function of the Interlude to set off the following scene as the goal and main event of the act.

I am tempted to hear the whole of scene 3 as a duet expanded to gigantic proportions by the introductory recitative monologue and a recitative dialogue intervening between the tempo d'attacco and the cantabile (see appendix 3: act 3, scene 3). To be sure, one might initially see the duet proper to begin only with Brünnhilde's cantabile and interpret the tempo d'attacco section as an independent lyrical number. But two kinds of considerations, motivic and tonal, suggest that Wagner had a single larger whole in mind. First, the centrally important motivic and textural event of the tempo d'attacco reappears prominently in the duet's cabaletta. At the culminating moment in the tempo d'attacco (III.1131–44) Siegfried and Brünnhilde sing for the first time a real duet, that is, they sing simultaneously using similar words and melody, a motive that might be called the Praise of Existence ("All hail to the mother who gave me/you birth; hail to the earth that gave me/you nurture") that is here heard for the first time.[111] A close variant of this music reappears in the cabaletta (III.1731–52), the first moment since the tempo d'attacco where the two sing a real duet, that is, simultaneously and sharing the

EXAMPLE 11. *Siegfried*

a. III.1131–44

EXAMPLE 11. *(continued)*

b. III.1731–52

(continued)

EXAMPLE 11. *(continued)*

motivic, though this time not the verbal, content (example 11). And second, the tonal relationship of the main portion of the duet, a cantabile in E and a cabaletta in C, is anticipated at the beginning of the scene where the recitative held together by the stable tonality of E, both major and minor, is followed by the tempo d'attacco in C that itself begins with a phrase emphatically and repeatedly juxtaposing the e minor and C major chords (at III.1067–68, 1079–80, 1088–89, 1096–97).

But even though the scene as a whole can be heard as a single duet, the proportions of this duet are strikingly skewed in favor of open discourse. The truly lyrical portions (the tempo d'attacco, cantabile, and cabaletta) are relatively short, taking little more than one-fourth of the total number of measures. As a result, the duet has a strikingly discursive, cerebral character, and, in spite of the undeniable beauty of some of its sections (the tempo d'attacco and the cantabile in particular), seems to me the biggest music-dramatic failure of this opera. A comparison with the love duet of Siegmund and Sieglinde that ended the first act of *Die Walküre* is telling. Siegfried's parents felt mutual erotic attraction long before they could verbalize it and the music left us in no doubt as to the authenticity and intensity of what they felt. Siegfried and Brünnhilde verbalize long before they feel anything and ultimately one is left unsure that they ever do feel anything much. They talk themselves into their relationship, and their enthusiasm for it seems forced. Theirs is a most cerebral kind of love: love as ideology, not as passion.

This, however, is not to deny the imaginative power of some of the scene, beginning with the extraordinary unaccompanied monody of the first violins (III.831–57) that precedes Siegfried's opening recitative monologue and manages to capture at once the rarified, cool Alpine atmosphere of the mountaintop just ascended by the hero and his astonishment at the scenery around him: "Blissful wasteland on wondrous heights!"[112] Siegfried's recitative is firmly anchored in E, both major and minor, but otherwise follows freely his thoughts as he discovers and awakens Brünnhilde, thoughts to which we have access thanks to the usual motivic activity of the orchestra and the unusual fact that Siegfried happens to talk aloud to himself rather than simply think silently (unusual, because a normal Wagnerian monologue is explicitly spoken aloud and addressed to a listener onstage). At first, he takes the sleeping Brünnhilde for a man and the discovery, once he removes her breastplate, that "No man is this!"[113] fills him with "burning enchantment"[114] and "fiery terror."[115] A brief moment ago he passed fearlessly through raging fire without; now he encounters the fire of enchantment within. The first inkling of erotic desire—"searing desire consumes my senses"—inspires anxiety as, presumably for the first time in his existence, he encounters a member of the opposite sex (his mother having died in childbirth).[116] Indeed, confronted with this new and terrifying fiery power, he twice calls upon his mother for protection (III.944–46 and 985–86); a little later (III.1161–88) he will momentarily confuse Brünnhilde with his mother. This, again, is Wagner the dramatist at his proto-Freudian best.

TABLE 12 *Siegfried*, Act 3, Love Duet, Tempo d'attacco

Form	Text incipit	Measures	CD.track.time
Opening solo	Heil dir, Sonne! Heil dir, Licht!	1067–103	IV.8.0:00–3:49
Developmental dialogue	Lang war mein Schlaf	1102–31	IV.8.3:49–5:25
Culminating duet	O Heil der Mutter, die mich gebar!	1132–44	IV.8.5:25–6:08
Closing solo	O Siegfried! Siegfried! seliger Held	1144–61	IV.9.0:00–0:54

Siegfried has left Mime's cave with the express purpose of learning fear. The thought now occurs to him that it is fear that he at last experiences: "A woman lies asleep:—she has taught him the meaning of fear!"[117] This, too, is subtle (on Wagner's part, if not on Siegfried's). To the outside public world, the hero remains as fearless as he has always been. But within the inner private world that begins to emerge here—the world of Siegfried, Brünnhilde, and their love—he discovers for the first time his vulnerability. He is potentially in her power and about to lose his individual autonomy, hence his momentary confusion between fear and love. And the power emanating from her proves irresistible. For a moment, the fairy tale about the boy who left home in order to learn fear is transformed into the one about the sleeping beauty as Siegfried awakens Brünnhilde with a kiss. Wagner's comment on this kiss, noted in Cosima von Bülow's *Diary* (August 15, 1869), is significant and perceptive: "The kiss of love is the first intimation of death, the cessation of individuality, that is why a person is so terrified by it."[118]

The moment of awakening itself gets a closed-form emphasis, staged as a four-section C major duet (table 12). The opening section of the duet is another example of Wagner's ability to create effects of elemental imaginative power out of the most limited of materials, similar in this respect to the airy violin monody at the beginning of the scene or, for that matter, to the watery Prelude at the beginning of the whole cycle. Like the opening of Brünnhilde's encounter with Siegmund in the second act of *Die Walküre*, this section, too, presents its entire material first in purely orchestral form (III.1067–87; example 12) and then again with the Valkyrie's voice superimposed (III.1088–102), her words explicating the dramatic content of the music. The music itself consists of little more than stark juxtapositions of triads, first e minor and C major (III.1067–72), then e minor and d minor (III.1073–78), and finally e minor and C major again (III.1079–87), juxtapositions so stark than we remain unsure as to whether the tonal center is e or C until almost the end, the moment when C gets its dominant (III.1083) and thus wins. Its victory, however, is almost at once undercut, as the phrase bends back toward e minor at the end (III.1087) so that the whole can be repeated. Wagner accomplishes the bending by means of a brief violin monody (III.1083–87) reminiscent of the one that opened the whole scene. Brünnhilde is every bit as astonished at the sight of the world now opening in front of her eyes as Siegfried has been.

EXAMPLE 12. *Siegfried*, III.1067–87

Brünnhilde greets "sun," "light," and "light-bringing day" and the emphatic, accented association of these words with the C major chords leaves no doubt as to the intended referent of this tonality.[119] Would then the e minor stand for the sleep from which she is just emerging, her very next words reminding us that "long was my sleep"?[120] Probably, the more so since E was also the key of the ending of *Die Walküre*, where this sleep was induced. In any case, we shall remember that the juxtaposition of e and C that dominates this opening section is also the tonal organizational principle of the Duet as a whole. Brünnhilde's emerging from long sleep into the light of day is clearly the subject of this final scene of the opera, although the last-moment deflection of C back to e suggests that this emerging will be a protracted process, not something accomplished all at once here.

The developmental dialogue that follows is less stable tonally, but it too ends with a musical and verbal variant of the pattern established in the opening solo. No sooner does Brünnhilde learn the identity of the hero who has awoken her (III.1102–16) than she breaks into the repeated and accented praises (III.1117–31) of the "gods," "world," and the "splendent earth."[121] Gods may seem out of place in the company of sun, light, day, world, and earth, but it is appropriate that the Valkyrie devotes one grateful thought to her father for having kept his promise and allowing a genuine hero to be her rescuer. Otherwise, however, her praise is reserved not for any transcendent realm, but simply for this realm of immanence, the earth, she is about to inherit.

The culminating phrase reestablishes C major with an emphatic cadence (at III.1144). As already noted, this is the first time in the *Ring* that we hear a genuine duet and the first time that we hear the Praise of Existence motive. Moreover, since a genuine duet will be heard in *Siegfried* only one more time, again in combination with this very motive, in the cabaletta of the Love Duet, this phrase can be heard as the first installment of the emphatic culmination of the whole Duet. Wagner is clearly insisting that we pay attention to this moment, and it is not difficult to understand why: he wants us to notice that the two heroic lovers hail existence, immanence, this actual world, and not some transcendent realm beyond: "Hail to the earth that gave me/you nurture."[122] The higher human beings who will inherit the earth will not want to look toward Wotan and Alberich for meaning; they will make their existence meaningful on their own. We might just as well rename this music the Praise of Immanence. This is Wagner anticipating Nietzsche.

The orchestral appendix that closes this culmination and frames Brünnhilde's closing solo (III.1144–50, 1157–61) seems like overkill, a music more fitting for the coming together of two allied armies than the encounter of future lovers. But perhaps the military tone is not altogether inappropriate, since what ensues in the lengthy dialogue that separates the tempo d'attacco from the cantabile is something that occasionally is reminiscent of combat. Brünnhilde's awakening has only just begun; it will not be accomplished without a considerable effort on Siegfried's part until almost the end of the opera.

TABLE 13 *Siegfried*, Act 3, Love Duet, Brünnhilde's Cantabile

Form	Key	Text incipit	Measures	CD.track.time
Main phrase	E/e	Ewig war ich, ewig bin ich	1478–96	IV.11.0:00–1:08
Subsidiary phrase	→G	O Siegfried! Herrlicher! Hort der Welt!	1497–516	IV.11.1:08–2:10
Main phrase developed	→E	Sah'st du dein Bild im klaren Bach?	1517–39	IV.11.2:10–3:12
Main phrase recapitulated	E	ewig licht lach'st du selig	1540–60	IV.11.3:12–4:08

Brünnhilde begins the conversation with an avowal of her love for Siegfried, love that began even before the hero's birth (indeed, recall that she sacrificed herself in order to protect his pregnant mother from Wotan's wrath), and proceeds almost immediately to articulate the Platonic doctrine that, to the extent that they love one another, they are one: "Your own self am I, if your but love me."[123] She is, however, far from ready for the carnal union Siegfried is urging upon her in no uncertain terms: "O woman, quench the fire now!"[124] The sight of her horse and weapons reminds her of who she once was—a virginal deity of war—in contrast to who she now is—"a weaponless, sorrowing woman"[125] whose "daughterly body's defenses"[126] "a keen-edged sword has cut . . . in two."[127] (She means the armor that Siegfried removed using his Sword.) She still experiences her new state as shameful: "Alas for the shame, for my ignominious plight!"[128] For once, Siegfried interprets her reluctance with uncharacteristic perceptiveness: "To me you are still the dream-struck maid: Brünnhilde's sleep I have not yet disturbed."[129] The process of awakening is far from completed.

Brünnhilde's cantabile is the most architectonic of all the closed-form sections of the Love Duet, a bow form consisting of four phrases of similar length (table 13). Throughout, the main melodic phrase is accompanied by a low-string counterpoint of the repeated motive associated with the idea of shielded sleep that we remember from the slow central section of Wotan's Farewell in the last scene of *Die Walküre*. But it is becoming clear now that the sleep from which the Valkyrie needs to awaken is not just the one that her father had induced; rather, it is the dream of the eternally divine existence from which she needs now to emerge into the waking and passing world of humans. "I was eternal, I am eternal"[130] "and so do not touch me,"[131] she tells Siegfried, while the orchestral counterpoint tells us that hers was the eternity of sleep.

It takes the considerable length and considerable amount of forced rhetoric of the following tempo di mezzo for Siegfried finally to break her defenses and persuade her to give up the eternity of transcendence for the transience of immanence. When at long last "she embraces him passionately," it is to the sound of the music that used to accompany the Valkyries to their battles (III.1682–85 and again at the very end of the tempo di mezzo, III.1706–9).[132] Even the hero recoils "in joyful terror,"[133] though immediately thereafter he reports, "my courage returns and the fear ... that I never learned ... I have quite forgotten it now!"[134] The choice of martial music to accompany Brünnhilde's embrace seems as absurd as it is unnecessary, given that Brünnhilde is no longer a Valkyrie. But perhaps Wagner wants to anticipate the horseback leap that will end Brünnhilde's life when she jumps onto Siegfried's funeral pyre at the end of the cycle. Her leap of love here is also a leap of death, and indeed, in a moment the two lovers will talk of love and death simultaneously. The confusion between fear and love has now been cleared. The boy who left his cave in search of someone who would teach him what fear was has found love instead. But the martial music is fear-inspiring and does little to convince us that it is erotic love and not intellectual argument that drives the protagonists. Again, this seems to me this duet's failing.

And so the cabaletta too is more interesting ideologically than persuasive emotionally. Much of it, we already know, is taken by a varied repetition of the culminating moment from the tempo d'attacco (III.1731–52, quoted in example 11 above) now accompanied by a forceful figure for horns that makes its appearance already at III.1719, migrates to the voices at III.1753, and permeates the whole cabaletta with a tone more suitable for a boisterous scene at a military encampment or a hunting party than for one of erotic ecstasy.

The words are more interesting than the music. "Laughing let us perish,"[135] says Brünnhilde near the beginning of the cabaletta, and this conjunction of laughter and death remains the main idea of the opera's closing section, the lovers' last words apostrophizing repeatedly "light-bringing love and laughing death!"[136] Meanwhile Brünnhilde bids farewell to the ancien régime of the gods and welcomes the rising star of Siegfried, while the hero himself hails again the day, sun, light, world. They look forward to the world of the future, the world of the free, fearless, loving human beings who no longer seek Wotan's or Alberich's tutelage. To be sure, in this new world of immanence Brünnhilde will be as mortal, as transient, as any human. But the heroic race of overmen faces this transience with laughter, not terror: they take delight in existence, in every aspect of existence, and turn away from the dream of transcendent essences. These are intriguing thoughts, presaging Nietzsche again. But while the ideas are interesting, the music is merely loud and ponderous. Instead of a genuinely persuasive erotic union of two passionate human beings, something he was by now, after *Die Walküre* and *Tristan*, perfectly capable of providing, Wagner chose to end *Siegfried* with the coupling of the man and woman of the future, a noisy but lifeless ideological construct.

GÖTTERDÄMMERUNG: THE APOCALYPSE
Prologue: The Past and the Future

Die Walküre and *Siegfried* are as different as their respective heroine and hero, but for all their differences there are also some similarities in the construction of the two operas. In both, the first act centers on the hero obtaining the Sword, the second on his using it, and the third is literally a culmination ending in the same place, the top of the Valkyrie's rock. *Götterdämmerung* is different, a huge *Abgesang* after the two preceding *Stollen*.

George Bernard Shaw, who loathed *Götterdämmerung*, seeing in it a regression from music drama to grand opera, thought that the *Ring* should have ended with *Siegfried*.[137] One can see his point: the grand-operatic character of the cycle's final evening is indeed unmistakable (though it is debatable whether one must consider this to constitute an artistic crime). More importantly, by the end of *Siegfried*, Wotan's Spear has been shattered and the union of the man and woman of the future that was expected to replace the old political order represented by the Spear has been accomplished. But Wagner thought otherwise and one can see *his* point, too: something essential still remains to be accomplished. The symbol of Wotan's political power has been destroyed, but the symbol of Alberich's economic order, the Ring, still remains in circulation, retaining all of its destructive potential. So long as the Ring has not been un-forged, returned to nature as an innocent, unformed lump of gold at the bottom of the Rhine, the revolution remains threatened and the story incomplete. The very existence of money threatens the revolution with the possibility that commercial practices (exchange, trade, contracts) might be reborn and with them some elementary notions of fairness and justice as well as the need for a political order to enforce them. Thus the Ring needs to be destroyed if the destruction of the Spear is not to be in vain. And there is perhaps one more thing that a satisfactory completion of the story requires. The "light-bringing love and laughing death" so tantalizingly apostrophized at the end of *Siegfried* should now be exemplified. The overmen should show mere humans what this formula truly entails, how humanity emancipated from the tutelage of superhuman powers should face existence. Contrary to what Shaw supposed, there is still room for one more evening. In fact, the actual tragedy of Siegfried and Brünnhilde has not yet begun. The three preceding evenings were just a preparation for it.

But before the tragedy begins in earnest, Wagner throws in one more introduction. The first act of *Götterdämmerung* is preceded by a lengthy Prologue, literally a Prelude ("Vorspiel") which, uniquely in the music dramas, is not simply an orchestral introduction to the act, but rather a mini-act of its own, consisting of two scenes followed by an orchestral transition (see appendix 4: Prologue). In fact, the Prologue as a whole is a huge transition between the world of *Siegfried* and the one of *Götterdämmerung*, picking up the story at the same place and time where we left it: on the Valkyrie's rock during Brünnhilde's and Siegfried's first night together.

Unique, too, so early in the evening is the closed-composition style of both scenes. The profoundly imagined Norns scene, one of the *Ring*'s more inspired moments, is a study in circularity, its shape partly preformed already by the structure of the text (table 14).

TABLE 14 *Götterdämmerung*, Prologue, The Norns Scene

Form	Key	Text incipit	Measures	CD.track.time
Orchestral prologue	e-flat		1–17	I.1.0:00–1:35
Prelude	e-flat	Welch Licht leuchtet dort?	18–49	I.1.1:35–4:10
First cycle				
First Norn	e-flat	An der Weltesche wob ich einst	50–111	I.1.4:10–7:46
Second Norn	→c	Treu berat'ner Verträge Runen	111–53	I.2
Third Norn		Es ragt die Burg, von Riesen gebaut	153–95	I.3.0:00–2:22
Second cycle				
First Norn		Dämmert der Tag? Oder leuchtet die Lohe?	195–207	I.3.2:22–3:08
Second Norn		Durch des Speeres Zauber zähmte ihn Wotan	207–37	I.3.3:08–4:13
Third Norn		Des zerschlag'nen Speeres stechende Splitter	237–59	I.3.4:13–5:26
Third cycle				
First Norn		Die Nacht weicht; nichts mehr gewahr ich	259–71	I.3.5:26–6:09
Second Norn		Des Steines Schärfe schnitt in das Seil	271–81	I.3.6:09–6:45
Third Norn		Zu locker das Seil, mir langt es nicht	281–85	I.3.6:45–6:54
Postlude		Es riß! Es riß! Es riß!	285–304	I.3.6:54–8:05

In terms of its dramatic genre, the scene is related to other Wagnerian narrative monologues (such as, most prominently, Wotan's monologue in the second act of *Die Walküre*) in which the speakers essentially tell the story of past events. But instead of a single speaker, here there are three, and the narration is distributed among them. The structure of the text suggests the circular music-dramatic form in that, first, the three Norns take up the thread of the narration one by one in three progressively shorter cycles, and second, the whole is punctuated by two verbal refrains that clarify the overall shape. First, a flexible refrain immediately precedes the beginning of each cycle. Just before the first cycle, one of the Norns asks, "If we're to spin and sing, on what will you stretch the rope?"[138] and another answers, "For good or ill, I wind the rope and sing."[139] Before the second cycle, a Norn sings, "If you know yet more, then coil the rope anew; from the north I cast it back to you: spin, my sister, and sing!"[140] And before the third, shortest, cycle, one says most succinctly, "If you want to know when that will be, sisters, wind the rope!"[141]

Another refrain punctuates the cycles internally. Thus, in the first cycle, a pair of Norns each ends her portion of the narration with "Sing, my sister,—I cast it to you—do you know what will become of it?"[142] In the second cycle, a Norn concludes with "do you know what became of him?"[143] and another with "do you know what will come of him?"[144] In the third cycle, Norns finish again with "do you know what became of him?"[145] and "do you know what will come of that?"[146]

A network of musical refrains helps to project this circular shape further. In order to mark the beginning of the first cycle (at 50) and separate it clearly from the introductory dialogue that precedes it (18–49), Wagner additionally deploys regular lyrical vocal phrasing. The First Norn begins her discourse with a balanced period of seven plus seven measures (50–56 + 57–63). Shortly thereafter, however, Wagner returns to the less regular arioso vocal style that is the norm in narrative monologues. Similarly he initially maintains tonal stability, keeping the music through the end of the First Norn's discourse in e-flat minor, but afterward the modulatory character typical of monologues prevails. It is left to the orchestral refrains to make the decisive contribution to the projection of the form, and these function similarly to the verbal ones. The most general articulation of the whole into cycles is accomplished by the strategic deployment of the Fate motive we first encountered at the beginning of the Brünnhilde-Siegmund scene in the second act of *Die Walküre*. This marks the beginning of the whole by opening the prelude (18–19), separates the first and second cycles by appearing twice toward the end of the first one (181–82, 184–85), and separates the second and third cycles by appearing twice toward the end of the second one (251–52, 253–54). It then marks the ending of the whole by closing the postlude, appearing three times (299–304).

But the cycles are further articulated internally by musical refrains partially coordinated with the verbal ones. In the first cycle, two of the Norns end their discourses with the same sequence of three motives: at the outset, a motive in even eighth notes that originally appeared at the beginning of the prelude (at 19) and that might be labeled Spinning (101–5 and 143–47); next, a sequence of chords in even dotted half notes that might be labeled the Norns' Song, since it is coordinated with the words "sing, my sister,—I cast it to you" (105–7 and 147–49); and finally, the Questioning Fate or Question motive that in the Brünnhilde-Siegmund scene closely followed the Fate motive, now associated with the words "do you know what will become of it?" (108–111 and 150–53). The Spinning (185–89 and 192–94) and the Norns' Song motives reappear also at the end of the discourse of the Third Norn, the latter again coordinated with the appropriate words. The internal refrain articulating the second, shorter, cycle is simpler: the two Norns end their discourses with the Question motive coordinated with the verbal refrain of "do you know what became/come of him?" (204–7 and 235–37). And in the still more compact third cycle, the last words of the First Norn, "do you know what became of him?" as well as those of the Second Norn, "do you know what will come of that?" are set to the Fate motive attenuated to the point of almost nonexistence (270–71 and 280–81). The circular shape is fraying to the breaking point; in fact, it breaks almost immediately, as the thread of the Third Norn's discourse is interrupted (at 285).

The three cycles are preceded by a prelude (18–49) dominated by the Spinning motive that is associated with the Norns' activity as they hand to one another a golden rope which is at once the thread of destiny or fate and the narrative thread, the plot or *mythos*, of the tale in which this destiny is told. Thus the motives that permeate the scene are all interconnected: the Spinning of fate and simultaneously of the narration; the Norns' Song in which the narration takes place; the Questioning Fate in which the outcome of the story is dimly and anxiously anticipated; and finally and most prominently Fate, the content of the story, itself. The interconnection of the motives shows how a profound insight (into the essentially narrative character of fate) can be projected by means that, if not purely musical, are nevertheless music-dramatic in nature.

The orchestral prologue (1–17) that precedes it all paints the scenery. It is essentially a repetition of the opening of the scene of Brünnhilde's awakening from the third act of *Siegfried* (what I have labeled the tempo d'attacco of the closing love duet of that opera), transposed a chromatic half step down and thus darkened. On that earlier occasion, the e and C, as well as e and d, triads were starkly juxtaposed (e-C; e-d; e-C), with C winning over e only in the end. Now the third juxtaposition is interrupted, so that C-flat never gets the chance to be established and in the end it is e-flat that seems stronger: e-flat-C-flat (1–8); e-flat-d-flat (9–16); e-flat (17). The awakening from sleep that the e-C sequence of triads represented then is now less conclusive and successful. The sleep not yet fully dispelled: indeed, Brünnhilde and Siegfried are presumably still asleep. Combined with the music we have come to associate with nature and Rhine, it all paints the tentative beginnings of the awakening of nature, night just before daybreak. For a full awakening and coming of the day, we have to wait until the orchestral interlude that follows the Norns scene.

The music-dramatic form of the Norns scene, then, projects circularity that gets progressively weaker and finally breaks altogether, its three cycles shorter and shorter, the final one significantly interrupted first (280) by the Sword motive and then (283–84) by the appearance of the motive originally associated with Siegfried as the child of nature and the forest (in the first act of the preceding evening). The eternal mythic order of which the Norns sing gradually decays, just as the rope that is the thread of their narration frays, and the implied appearance of the sword-wielding hero brings it to the breaking point. It is the world-historical role of Siegfried (and Brünnhilde), after all, to replace the unchanging cyclical order of the natural and divine powers with the future-oriented progressive order of heroic humanity.

This is the only scene of the *Ring* in which the Norns, the three daughters of Erda, appear, but we have heard of them earlier. In the first scene of the last act of *Siegfried*, Erda told Wotan that the Norns explicitly articulate her implicit universal knowledge: "My sleep is dreaming, my dreaming brooding, my brooding the exercise of knowledge. But when I sleep, then Norns keep watch: they weave the rope and bravely spin whatever I know."[147] Now they weave the rope of destiny and we hear them narrate the events past, present, and future—the mythic plot of the world's history that the rope stands for.

Some of their story we already know, or even have witnessed, but of some crucial events we now learn for the first time. We learn in particular that the original act of rape that disturbed the primordial natural world order was not Alberich's but Wotan's. Long before Alberich robbed the Rhine of its gold in order to forge of it his Ring, Wotan broke off a branch of the sacred world-ash in order to make of it the shaft of his Spear. This act has had devastating long-term effects on the natural world. Over many years, the world-ash gradually died and the spring of natural wisdom that it shaded dried out. One could not overestimate the importance of this information. It confirms what we may have merely suspected until now, namely that Wotan's political order is no less a problem in search of a solution than Alberich's economic order, that both need to be replaced if the original ecological harmony is ever to be restored. If anything, the original sin is Wotan's, his act of violence being the earlier of the two.

Once the Spear had been shattered by Siegfried, we learn further, Wotan ordered the world-ash to be hewn into pieces and the logs to be collected in Valhalla, thus preparing the timber for the conflagration that will consume the hall and mark "the downfall [or end] of the immortal gods."[148] The Norns foresee this future only dimly, as the destruction of the world-ash and the drying out of the spring has affected the clarity of their vision. But they talk of the approaching twilight of the gods clearly enough; they just do not know when this will come. As their rope snaps, their eternal wisdom comes to an end.

While the Norns do not sing of the reasons for the approaching end of the gods' rule, the story they tell strongly suggests what these reasons might be. Wotan's trespass seems to call for a restitution; the political order his Spear symbolizes cannot be satisfactory, since it rests on an act that had disturbed the harmony of nature. Even without the further instability introduced by Alberich's capitalist economy, the traditional rule of the gods is unsustainable. If the *Ring* is to provide a vision of final redemption, the logic of the Norns' narrative suggests an ending in which both Alberich and Wotan will be replaced by something better, something that will restore the natural order and leave it undisturbed in the future. Independently of the Norns, we know that Siegfried and Brünnhilde will play a role in bringing this future order about. What we do not know is what exactly this role, or this future order, might be. But in any case, the Norns scene, with which Wagner originally intended to open the whole drama, decisively inflects the sense of the *Ring* in a new direction. No longer just a story of the unstable and hence unsatisfactory traditional political regime of Wotan in competition with the economic regime of Alberich, it now appears to be also, and more fundamentally, a story of the natural world wounded and, one hopes, made whole again. That the Rhine should get back his gold has been known since *Das Rheingold*. But until the Norns scene it was less than perfectly clear why the rule of the gods has to come to an end. It is only now that we learn the reason: Wotan has sinned against nature no less than Alberich, and hence the twilight of the gods is not only inevitable but also justified and desirable.

If the first scene of the Prologue was a narrative with a sophisticated rondo design, the second is a more usual duet—usual by Wagner's standards, of course (see appendix 4: Prologue, b.). This is introduced by a brief orchestral prelude (305–54) that paints the awakening of nature (with the moments of the "Dawn," "Sunrise," and "Broad daylight" precisely indicated in the score at 304, 347, and 349, respectively)[149] and ends in E-flat, the key of the Duet (and, since the Norns scene began in e-flat, the predominant tonality of the whole Prologue). The awakening of nature is at the same time the awakening of Brünnhilde and Siegfried. The prelude introduces two new motives, his heroic and ponderous (first adumbrated at 312 and fully stated in 327–29), hers loving and lyrical (from 330 on), that will be associated with them throughout the Duet, the one of Siegfried emphatically marking the beginning of each of the Duet's three main sections (at 354, 417, and 593) as well as the beginning of the orchestral postlude. More than anything else, these two motives, ubiquitous throughout, as well as the unifying key of E-flat, keep the whole scene together.

The two lovers are just as wordy in the morning as they had been in the duet of the preceding evening, and hence also now much of the scene is taken by a modulating open-composition arioso dialogue (marked as tempo di mezzo in appendix 4, Prologue, b.). Only the framing cantabile and cabaletta, both in E-flat, have a closed-composition character. As often with Wagner, the cantabile stresses this character especially at the beginning: Brünnhilde starts her discourse with two balanced eight-measure phrases (362–69 + 370–77), but this regularity gradually disintegrates and the cantabile's unity is sustained essentially by the stable motivic content and key. It is the cabaletta that deploys the greatest number of closed-composition features, giving the whole duet, and even the whole of the opera's Prelude, its cadential stability. Brünnhilde provides the initial melodic gesture of stepwise ascent from c″ to a-flat″ followed by a jump back to c″ (596–99) as she addresses her "hallowed kinsmen,"[150] the "holy gods"[151] on high. Once she finishes her sentence (at 614), Siegfried picks up the gesture twice, each time allowing Brünnhilde to complete the phrase (615–21 and 622–26), but the second time around they both participate in these interlocking completions (625–28) in a true duet fashion, raising the ascending gesture through b-flat″ (625 and 627) all the way to the triumphant high c‴ (632–34), which cannot fail to reach the gods.

The intervening night has not made the two heroic lovers any less rhetorical and grandiloquent than they had been the evening before: she addresses him as "beloved hero"[152] and he her as "wondrous woman."[153] Having lost her virginity and with it all her supernatural strength and having otherwise spent the night teaching him "what gods have taught me"[154] (whatever this might be; Siegfried's subsequent story does not inspire confidence in his abilities as a student), she sends him into the world "to new adventures [deeds],"[155] adventures evidently being what a hero requires. As a token of his faithful love, he gives her Alberich's Ring and she reciprocates with the gift of her horse, Grane. She asks the gods to "feast your eyes on this blessed pair!" without mentioning, and perhaps without knowing, that the blessed pair would bring about the gods' twilight, and they part, hailing love, light, life, and one another.[156] An orchestral interlude known as Siegfried's Rhine Journey (670–892) depicts the hero's merry progress into the real human world, allowing for a change of scenery behind a lowered curtain. At long last, the actual drama can begin.

Act 1: The Entrapment 1

Brünnhilde has sent Siegfried in search of new adventures among the humans, and the one adventure he has, the adventure that is the content of *Götterdämmerung* and hence of the *Ring*, ends in disaster and death—Siegfried's death (the drama's original title). The hero, so successful in dealing with superhuman powers, victorious over Fafner, Mime, Wotan, and Brünnhilde herself, proves helpless when dealing with mere humans. Strictly speaking there is only one human who is relevant here—Hagen, Alberich's son by a mortal woman (we have heard of him from Wotan in the second act of *Die Walküre*). For a grand opera, *Götterdämmerung* is remarkably economical with characters, having only three principal ones. The tragedy of Siegfried's death involves essentially only the protagonist himself, Brünnhilde, and Hagen. Hagen's half siblings (they all have a mother in common), Gunther, the tribal chieftain of the Gibichungs who have their territory on the Rhine, and his sister Gutrune, are mere puppets in their half brother's hands.

The first act of the drama is divided into two parts that take place in two different settings, the royal hall of the Gibichungs on the Rhine and the summit of Brünnhilde's rock, with an orchestral interlude between the two (see appendix 4: act 1). Strictly speaking the interlude consists merely of a ten-measure modulation, the quietly expressive intensity of which looks forward to *Parsifal* (I.967–76), but since the preceding scene has a lengthy orchestral postlude (I.924–66) and the following scene has a similarly lengthy orchestral prelude (I.977–1017), there is ample time for a change of scenery behind a closed curtain downstage. The act contains only one fully developed closed musical section, the magnificent Hagen's Watch, one of the *Ring*'s most impressive set pieces, and this sits, unprecedentedly, not at the end but in the center of the act, surrounded on both sides by two scenes of recitative dialogue each. The two duets for Siegfried and Gunther embedded in the dialogue of scene 2 (the former must have been planned by Wagner already when he was writing the poem, since he gave Gunther and Siegfried two identically constructed stanzas) are too short to be of more than local significance, although the second of these involves some simultaneous singing from the two protagonists and is substantial enough to provide the scene with its culminating point, and the only section departing from

TABLE 15 *Götterdämmerung*, Act 1, Hagen's Watch

Form	Text incipit	Measures	CD.track.time
A	Hier sitz' ich zur Wacht, wahre den Hof	870–85	II.4.0:00–1:15
A'	Ihm führt das Steuer ein starker Held	886–910	II.4.1:15–3:12
B	Ihr freien Söhne, frohe Gesellen	911–23	II.4.3:12–4:11
Orchestral postlude		924–66	II.4.4:11–7:24

the recitative-dialogue norm in scene 3 is Waltraute's narrative monologue. Formally it is Hagen's Watch that provides the structure with its central stabilizing capstone.

It makes good sense to center the act on Hagen, as he is the one protagonist we still do not know, and he is the evil *spiritus movens* of the plot. The Watch, a rare case of a monologue without a listener (most monologues in the *Ring* and other music dramas are delivered for the benefit of someone listening onstage), allows us to overhear his thoughts just at the moment when he had set the action in motion, and thus to understand his intentions. Its six three-verse stanzas are grouped into three double stanzas and shaped into a single Bar form in e-flat minor, followed by a sizable orchestral postlude, also in e-flat (table 15 and example 13).

Within each Stollen, each stanza is preceded by a few measures of orchestral music presenting a similar configuration of motives: this ensures that the parallel construction of the two Stollen is clearly projected (compare I.870–72 with 886–88 before the first stanza of each Stollen, and 878–81 with 894–97 before the second stanza of each). The first of these configurations (I.870–72 and 886–88) twice intertwines a heavily accented diminished fifth, c-flat–F, which recalls the tritone pedal point that held together the Wotan-Alberich scene at the beginning of the second act of *Siegfried* (now shifted a half step lower). Here it is clearly associated with Hagen, in combination with an intimation of Siegfried's horn—a gesture that graphically reminds us just how hopelessly entangled with Hagen Siegfried now is, and to what extent he has become a pliant tool in Hagen's fingers. The second configuration (I.878–81 and 894–97) in turn twice involves the descending half step, the traditional figure of lament, that has become the generalized signature of Woe in the *Ring*. Moreover, while Hagen's thoughts turn around the two men who had just departed to do his bidding, Gunther and in particular Siegfried, who, Hagen notes with satisfaction, will bring him the Ring, he himself does not forget whose son he is: "Though you [Siegfried and Gunther] think him [Hagen] lowly," are his final words, "you'll serve him yet, the Nibelung's son."[157]

The orchestral postlude continues and develops this train of thought further. It consists of three phrases: first, the multiple Woe motive (I.924–35); next, the twice-presented configuration of ideas intertwining Hagen with Siegfried as well as the Ring and (something new) the Spear, that is, the sign of the contractual law (I.936–

EXAMPLE 13. *Götterdämmerung*, Hagen's Watch, I.870–966

(continued)

EXAMPLE 13. (continued)

EXAMPLE 13. *(continued)*

(continued)

EXAMPLE 13. *(continued)*

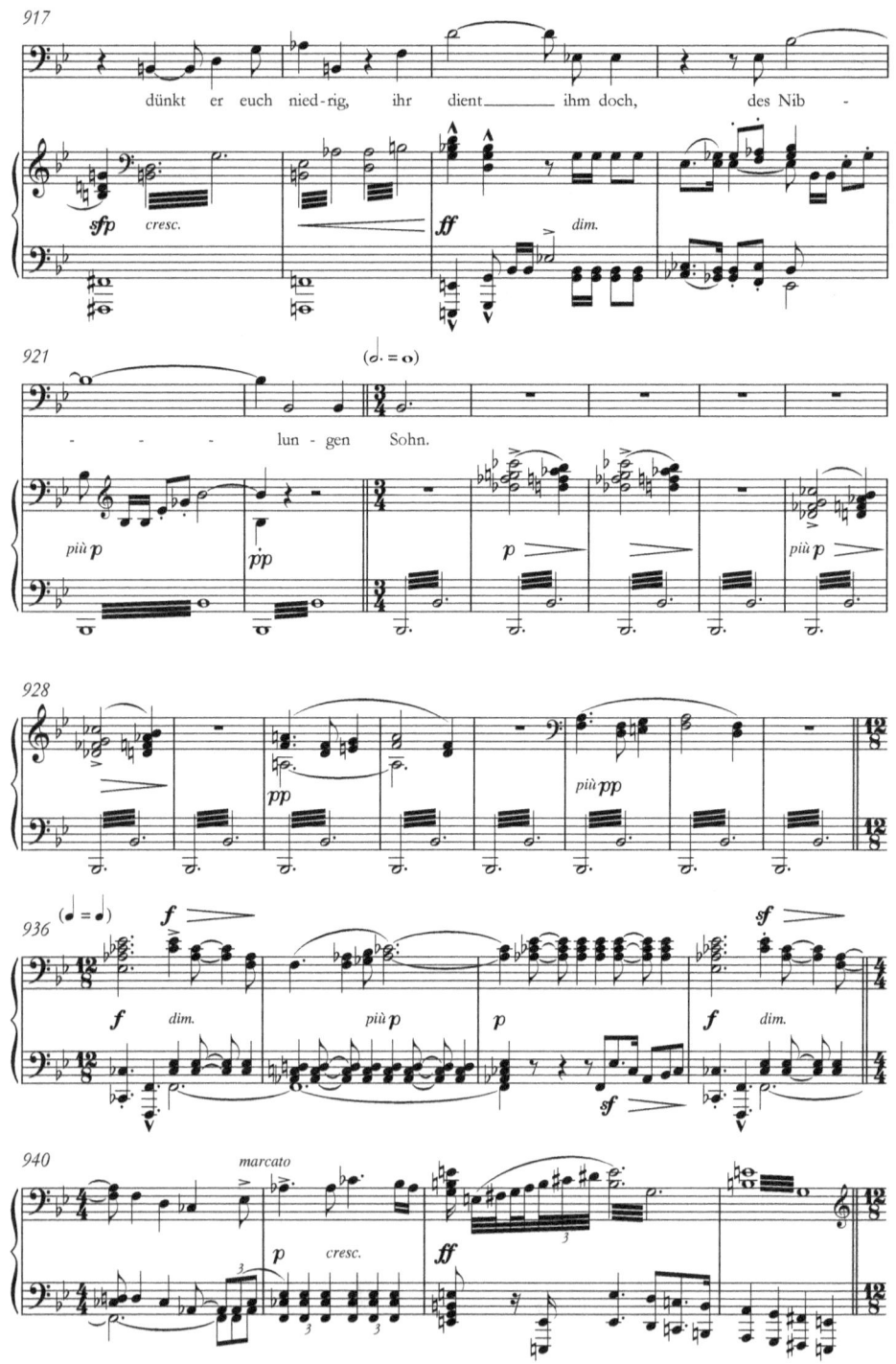

EXAMPLE 13. *(continued)*

51); and finally, an echo of the Abgesang melody ending with a triple repetition of the intertwined Ring and Woe motives (I.952–66). (Throughout, the multiple repetitions of motivic complexes underscore the brooding nature of Hagen's meditation.) The unexpected appearance of the Spear/Law idea is particularly interesting, reminding us just how much thinking can be generated in the *Ring* at this late stage simply by the associations of motives, without any verbal help. Siegfried, the free hero who has shattered the Spear and who comes to replace the traditional contracts with something better, has naively allowed himself to get entangled by Hagen in a new, binding contract that restricts his freedom in a most disastrous way. It is not surprising that the Spear motive (variously combined with the Alberich's Curse and the Alberich-Hagen's tritone) has played the central role also in the Oath Duet that has sealed Siegfried's blood brotherhood with Gunther, an oath that would so fatally bind him (at I.640–42, 658–60, 675–76, 687–90, 715–17, and 729–31).

The recitative dialogues that precede this central capstone of the act are designed to show how Hagen ensnared Siegfried, while those that follow it show the dreadful consequences of this entrapment.

The snare is simple. The Gibichung siblings are vain, weak, not too smart, and devoid of any moral scruples; their cunning half brother has no trouble manipulating such characters any way he wants. He dangles in front of them the prospect of marriages to the world's most desirable partners, Brünnhilde (for Gunther) and Siegfried (for Gutrune), and a way of bringing these improbable unions about: once Siegfried arrives (which he most obligingly does), Gutrune would offer him a magic potion that would make him instantly forget Brünnhilde and fall in love with Gutrune instead. And this is indeed what happens. Having completely forgotten his beloved and inflamed by his new passion, Siegfried offers to do something Gunther is incapable of doing, namely, crossing the fire surrounding Brünnhilde's rock yet again and, disguised as Gunther (with the help of the Tarnhelm), bringing her down as the Gibichung's bride in return for Gutrune's hand. Prompted by Gunther, they seal this arrangement with an oath of blood brotherhood that commits them to be faithful to it on pain of death, and they depart toward Brünnhilde's rock.

The potion of oblivion and love that makes all of this possible may seem a cheap and mechanical narrative device, and so it is, of course. But one should not condemn Wagner's dramatic technique too quickly. What matters here is *that* Siegfried forgets Brünnhilde and falls in love with a new woman, not *how* he does it: the potion is more the symbol of oblivion and love than its mechanical cause. True, had Siegfried simply quickly moved from one woman to another, we would have a good reason to find him morally culpable; the potion makes him look innocent. But we should not be taken in by this seeming innocence. In a *Diary* entry (March 12, 1872), Cosima noted these words of her husband: "'Siegfried lives entirely in the present, he is the hero, the finest gift of the will.'"[158] But living in the present means forgetting the past, and forgetting past commitments is indeed what Siegfried's character is all about. He has come to make the earth free of past commitments, to destroy the traditional legally binding contracts guarded by Wotan's Spear. His very first step into the real human world shows just how impossibly utopian this calling is. No sooner is one commitment forgotten than another replaces it, because making contracts is what humans do, and it is essential if a human community is to achieve any stability and relative permanence. Thus, the potion does not really cause anything; it merely reveals the tragic flaw in the hero's essential makeup, the character flaw with disastrous consequences for him and those around him.

In fact, the roots of the self-contradictory nature of Siegfried's character go even deeper. Once you give up on all gods and all transcendence, you necessarily give up on all permanence, too, and embrace change in a radical fashion. This is because only a transcendent order can give a permanent sense to the transient here and now. But Siegfried, like Søren Kierkegaard's Don Giovanni, turns his back on all that transcends the present moment, on all stable meaning, and hence even without the potion he is bound to forget the past. Nothing that happens to him can be linked with, or rooted in, the past; the overman of the future, if he ever abandons the present, it is only in order to rush headlong into the future, "to new adventures." What the *Ring* shows are the consequences of this kind of existence once it comes into contact with humanity as we know it. Indirectly it also suggests the chilling possibility that if the new world with which our heroes would want to replace the old order is ever to be successful, not only the gods, but also humanity as we know it, would need to be replaced.

It is the central paradox of *Götterdämmerung*, and hence of the *Ring*, that it demonstrates the hopelessly utopian nature of the anarchist ideal that it promotes. While some would conclude at this point that the whole project is incoherent, others (and probably Wagner himself) would claim instead that the incoherence characterizes not the project, but the human condition, or at least the present human condition, that the world as we know it is not a place where human flourishing and felicity will ever be realized. Be that as it may, if it is true that Siegfried gets corrupted by Hagen and his potion, it is also the case that the hero is a most appropriate victim for Hagen's machinations, as the potion brings out and expresses his true character.

The last scene of the act shows the first of the consequences of Siegfried's character flaw. But before Brünnhilde is forced by Siegfried into submission to Gunther, there is an interlude—the scene of the ex-Valkyrie's encounter with one of her sisters, Waltraute. The latter has braved Wotan's interdiction and come to visit in order to beg Brünnhilde to give back the Ring to the Rhinedaughters, since she has heard the god say, "If she gave back the ring to the deep Rhine's daughters, from the weight of the curse both god and world would be freed."[159] But Brünnhilde scarcely understands her sister's tale and request. For her, the Ring is "Siegfried's pledge of love,"[160] that is, something "more than the glory of the immortals,"[161] and she would not think of casting it away.

It is striking that, at this late stage, after the Spear had been shattered and the world ash tree felled and cut up for logs, Wotan still hopes that the end of the gods might be averted, that the restitution of the Rhine gold is all that is needed. The ending of the drama will show that his assessment of the predicament is incorrect: the giving back of the Ring will not avert the destruction of Valhalla. There are clearly limits to Wotan's knowledge and self-knowledge. He understands the transgression that was Alberich's rape of the gold, but not the one constituted by his own rape of the world ash tree. But in any case, for Brünnhilde love has become the supreme value, trumping all other claims, even those of the existing world order. "I shall never relinquish love,"[162] she proclaims to the same tune that was used by one of the Rhinedaughters when she announced that "only the man who forswears love's sway . . . can master the magic spell that rounds a ring from the gold"[163] and by Siegmund when he reversed the significance of the motive and dedicated himself to the "highest need of holiest love."[164] Brünnhilde's use of the tune paradoxically synthesizes these two earlier moments: like Alberich, she clings to the Ring, but it is Siegmund's inheritance she claims. The rule of law is to be replaced by the rule of love.

After this love-exalting interlude, the brisk final scene of the act is all the more cruel. It is hard to imagine love being betrayed and trampled upon more brutally than in this scene of a lover who violates his beloved on behalf of another man. Siegfried appears wearing the Tarnhelm, which makes him look and sound like Gunther, and as "Gunther" demands that Brünnhilde follow him as his wife. She is to wed him in the same cave chamber in which she had spent the first night of love with Siegfried. Her attempt to defend herself with the Ring is ineffective. It is not entirely clear why this is the case, but it is probably because the Ring has no power over those who do not know of its nature or do not covet it. At the beginning of act 2 Alberich explains that "even my curse grows feeble in face of the fearless hero: for he does not know what the ring is worth, he makes no use of its coveted power."[165] "Gunther" wrests the Ring from her and forces her into the cave. At the point of following her, Siegfried draws his Sword and, in his natural voice, announces that Nothung will chastely separate him from her during the night. Next morning he would bring the untouched bride down the rock to his waiting blood brother.

From the moment of Siegfried's appearance (I.1609) to the last measures of the act, the motive of the Tarnhelm that makes all this deception possible is much in evidence. Indeed, this is the one scene of the *Ring* in which the Tarnhelm, the characteristic weapon of Alberich and by extension also of Hagen, the weapon of those who do not fight openly but only by stealth, comes into its own. Only when Siegfried reverts to his natural voice is his own weapon, the Sword, mentioned. Nothing could symbolize better the full measure of Siegfried's degradation and corruption at Hagen's hands than this use of the Tarnhelm. At this point, Hagen dominates the story just as much as he dominates the act: he is the brooding center of both.

Act 2: The Entrapment 2

The music-dramatic paradox at the heart of *Götterdämmerung* has its source in the history of the opera's creation. The poem was the earliest of the cycle's libretti to be completed (essentially 1848–52), and the music came at the end of the composition process some two decades later (essentially 1869–74). As a result, there is a formal disjunction between the music and the text. While the former represents Wagner's experience of shaping not only the earlier installments of the cycle but also *Tristan* and *Die Meistersinger*, the latter predates the dramatist's most mature practice of centering a whole act on a single decisive event and limiting the number of scenes in an act to the necessary minimum. The advanced musical style of *Götterdämmerung* is put in the service of a grand-operatic dramatic structure in which each of the numerous scenes of an act may get a clear formal focus, but the overall shape of the whole act emerges only with difficulty.

All the same, some sense of overall form does emerge, even in act 2 with its profusion of individually shaped scenes (see appendix 4: act 2). The two orchestral interludes divide the act into three parts, the three central scenes dominated by a large number of protagonists accompanied by a crowd of the Gibichungs, and one framing scene of a more private character (that is, with a smaller number of protagonists and without the crowds) each at the beginning and end. The three central scenes get a common formal focus in the Duet of Siegfried's and Brünnhilde's oaths (II.1128–213) with which the sequence culminates. (The two choral Songs of the Vassals are of a more local significance.) Similarly, the final scene is formally focused on the concluding Trio (II.1619–704). But—and this is the decisive difference from Wagner's normal mature formal practice—neither of these two numbers can be said to dominate more than their respective scene or group of scenes, to dominate the act as a whole.

If there is a single number that does dominate the whole act, it is the Hagen's Dream with which the act opens and which takes the whole of the Prelude and scene 1, and hence is much longer and substantial than either the Oaths Duet or the Trio. But since this is placed at the beginning rather than the end of the act, it cannot function as a goal or point of arrival for the whole. Rather, it casts a shadow over the following act, not unlike the closely related Hagen's Watch that cast a shadow over act 1 from its center. Alberich's son pulls the strings of the intrigue in act 2 no less than he did in act 1. The immobile spider drew Siegfried into his net in act 1, and now he draws also Brünnhilde. This indeed is the point of these first two acts, to show how the free and loving overhumans fare when confronting the actually existing all-too-human humanity.

158   CHAPTER 2

TABLE 16 *Götterdämmerung*, Act 2, Hagen's Dream

Form	Text incipit	Measures	CD.track.time
Hagen's refrain (prelude)		1–38	III.1
Alberich's episode with verbal refrain	Schläfst du, Hagen, mein Sohn?	39–48 43–44	III.2.0:00–0:22
Hagen's refrain	Ich höre dich, schlimmer Albe	48–54	III.2.0:22–0:54
Alberich's episode	Gemahnt sei der Macht	54–60	III.2.0:54–1:12
Hagen's refrain	Gab mir die Mutter Mut	60–75	III.2.1:12–2:23
Alberich's episode with verbal refrain	Hagen, mein Sohn! Hasse die Frohen!	75–99 98–99	III.2.2:23–3:27
Hagen's refrain	Der Ewigen Macht, wer erbte sie?	99–105	III.2.3:27–3:57
Alberich's episode with verbal refrain	Ich – und du! Wir erben die Welt	106–29 128–29	III.2.3:57–4:57
Hagen's refrain	Zu seinem Verderben dient er mir schon	129–33	III.2.4:57–5:14
Alberich's episode with verbal refrain	Den gold'nen Ring, den Reif gilt's zu erringen!	133–63 161–63	III.2.5:14–6:32
Hagen's refrain with verbal refrain	Den Ring soll ich haben	163–202 167–68	III.2.6:32–9:06

The first scene is magnificently realized and visionary. Characterized by Wagner as "the ghostly, dreamlike dialogue between Alberich and Hagen" when he recalled the first performance with particular satisfaction, it dwarfs—in artistic terms as well as length—the rest of the act with its more conventional grand-operatic situations, sentiments, and procedures.[166] (This is not to criticize the rest of the act: the conventionality is required by the represented world, the human world of the Gibichungs.) The alternating ariosos of the conversation between Hagen and Alberich are given an overall shape primarily by the orchestra (table 16). Alberich does much more talking than his son and the motivic content of his interventions is varied, following, recitative style, their verbal content. By contrast, Hagen's ripostes, all relatively short except for the framing ones at the beginning and end, are all given similar music which thus provides the whole scene with a rondo-like refrain. The opening refrain is not a riposte, of course; in fact, it is a purely orchestral Prelude that depicts the silent Hagen's sleepy brooding. The contrasting tempi help to differentiate the refrain from the episodes: slow ("Sehr mässig bewegt") for the refrain and lively ("Lebhaft") for the episodes. A secondary refrain, this one verbal, punctuates Alberich's interventions, stressing the repetitive, obsessive nature of Hagen's Dream. (All three principal Nibelungs, Alberich, Mime, and Hagen, tend to tie themselves into obsessive knots.) Alberich, namely, begins his first intervention by asking, "Are you sleeping, Hagen, my son?" and then repeats the question at the end of each of his subsequent interventions except for the very short second one.[167] At the end of the last episode this verbal refrain takes a somewhat modified, but still recognizable, form: "Do you swear to it, Hagen, my son?"[168] and Alberich repeats these words, again somewhat modified, once more already within the final refrain of Hagen: "Do you swear to it, Hagen, my hero?"[169]

The close dramaturgical and musical proximity of Hagen's Dream to Hagen's Watch is unmistakable. Both scenes provide us with access to the solitary, brooding character's innermost and silent thoughts. In the Watch Hagen is awake and the singer articulates his thoughts aloud for our benefit. In the Dream the situation is left ambiguous, though most likely Hagen is asleep and Alberich is an apparition in his dream, disappearing toward the end the way night apparitions do, with the first light of dawn. In the opening stage direction he is described as "sitting asleep"[170] and a little later he "still seems to be asleep, even though there is a glassy stare in his permanently open eyes."[171] The stage direction at the beginning of Hagen's final refrain is particularly revealing: "From this point onward an increasingly dark shadow starts to envelop Alberich again. At the same time, the first streaks of light begin to appear in the sky."[172] However, the main argument for considering Alberich a mere apparition in Hagen's dream is musical: his final words occur not within an independent episode, but within Hagen's last refrain. Thus he gradually fades away ("During the following Alberich's form gradually disappears from sight, while his voice grows more and more inaudible") not as an actual independent character, but rather as a figure of Hagen's imagination.[173] All the same, one cannot completely exclude the possibility that Alberich is actually there and talks with Hagen, who remains half asleep. In either case, here too the singers articulate the content of the characters' thoughts, whether silent or actually spoken.

Again, whether Alberich is speaking on his own behalf or is Hagen's projection we shall never know for sure. But while the difference is real enough, it ultimately does not matter all that much, as we never see Alberich again in the *Ring* and for the remaining part of the drama it is Hagen who stands for the principle represented in the cycle as a whole by his father. Certainly one might read into the dialogue intimations that Hagen thinks of emancipating himself from his father and acting on his own behalf and thus makes Alberich anxious, but such intimations are left without any further consequences in the drama. Thus, for instance, asked by Hagen who would inherit the gods' power, Alberich answers, "I—and you,"[174] but any speculation as to whether this answer hides the anxiety that his son might replace him (if it is the actual Alberich we hear) or Hagen's hope that he might take over from his father (if what we witness is his dream) is idle. From the vantage point of the Wagnerian allegory, Alberich and Hagen are one. They stand for identical values. Their relationship is only partly similar to that of Wotan and Siegfried. Like Hagen, Siegfried is supposed to inherit his ancestor's mantle, but unlike Hagen, he also replaces his ancestor's values.

To make sure that we do not miss the relationship between the two numbers, Wagner quotes the Abgesang phrase from the ending of the orchestral postlude to the

Watch at the end of the Dream's Prelude (compare II.30–38 with I.952–66). Such a recall of a whole lyrical phrase, as opposed to a recall of a motive, is an uncommon occurrence in the *Ring* (Siegmund's evocation of the Rhinedaughter's phrase as he is about to get the Sword in *Die Walküre*, act 1, is another example), and its function here is clearly to draw attention to the proximity of the Dream to the Watch, to project the former as a continuation of the latter: at the beginning of act 2 we find Hagen where we had last left him in act 1. In essence the two scenes that dominate the first two acts of the opera are silent, brooding monologues of the character who completely controls the action, monologues that reveal this character's motivation as well as his dependence on his father. It cannot be an accident that just as at the end of the Watch Hagen identified himself as "the Nibelung's son,"[175] so also throughout the Dream Alberich repeatedly stresses the relationship in his verbal refrain of "Hagen, my son." Hagen does not forget for a moment who he essentially is—the son of the Nibelung.

Alberich, or rather his apparition, no longer lives in fear of Wotan, whom he sees as already defeated by Siegfried and doomed to fall together with the other gods. (Wotan's adversaries see his situation more clearly than he himself does.) The real antagonist now is not Wotan, but Siegfried, whose essential character Alberich captures shrewdly and economically, evoking the final words of *Siegfried*: "laughing, in loving desire, he burns his life away."[176] Indeed, laughter, love, and lack of concern for the past or the future, including lack of the fear of death, is what Siegfried is all about. What makes Alberich anxious is not that Siegfried might make use of the Ring, but rather that Brünnhilde, "a wise woman,"[177] might persuade him to give the Ring back to the Rhinedaughters: "The gold would be lost to me then, no cunning could ever reclaim it."[178] This must be prevented and the Ring regained, which is why Siegfried needs to be destroyed.

It is rather striking, in sum, that for all the important revelations of the Norns scene, in *Götterdämmerung* itself Wotan not only makes no appearance, but is essentially irrelevant. The conflict has now passed to the next generation (or two), to Hagen, who clings to Alberich's values and continues to crave the Ring and the power it bestows, and to Siegfried with Brünnhilde, who overthrew Wotan's values, care nothing for the Ring and its power, and stand for laughter, love, and fearlessness instead of legally constrained politics or money-driven economics. One can at this point imagine two ways in which this conflict might be permanently resolved: either Hagen will regain the Ring and the earth will be turned around by capital, or Siegfried-Brünnhilde will give the Ring back to the Rhinedaughters and thus wipe the slate clean and make room for a new and improved humankind animated by the example of their carefree love. Whether anyone will get hurt in the process is essentially irrelevant to the further course of world history, however vital it might be to the person in question. In the event, Wagner contrives to produce the desirable outcome *and* to have all three protagonists killed. Ever a maximalist, he can thus have it all, both a tragedy (*Siegfrieds Tod*) and a *lieto fine* (the passing of the ancien régime, or *Götterdämmerung*).

There can be no doubt as to which outcome we are supposed to crave, or about who is offered to us as the role model. Both the Watch and the Dream project evil, but it is evil of undeniable grandeur and depth. By contrast, the dramatic world of the remaining scenes of act 2 is shallow and tawdry, with music to match. It is particularly disappointing to see Brünnhilde, supposedly "a wise woman," fall into Hagen's trap just as easily as Siegfried—whom one would never accuse of wisdom—had.

The first two scenes of the second part of the act (scenes 2 and 3) are merely preparatory, designed to assemble onstage the required crowd with a maximum of tedious grand-operatic pomp. The essential events all take place in scene 4. Siegfried, ever impatient to wed Gutrune, arrives ahead of his party (scene 2) and is subjected by his bride to a bantering interrogation with tense undertones that foreshadows the rope Hagen would use to hang them all. Gutrune wonders: If Siegfried wooed Brünnhilde disguised as Gunther and spent a night with her before delivering her to the new bridegroom next morning, did he also consummate the relationship on Gunther's behalf? Gutrune tiptoes around this question and Siegfried provides naively ambiguous answers, needlessly so, since we have no reason to doubt that he kept his word and used Nothung to separate himself from Brünnhilde on that fateful night. The question whether he did or not is, in any case, without much interest (to us at least, as opposed to Gunther and his tribe). Even if he did not touch her, he *had* violated Brünnhilde in a most terrible way (by her and our lights, if not by those of Gunther and his tribe). The ambiguity of his answers now is a subtle way of making this point explicit to us. We should not care, but the Gibichungs will, and Siegfried's naïveté plays into Hagen's hands.

Scene 3, in turn, is devoted to Hagen's assembling the Gibichung vassals ostensibly so that they might give a properly festive reception to their approaching chief and his bride and help celebrate their wedding. But of course the primary purpose is that they might witness Brünnhilde's reaction to her inevitable discovery of Siegfried as Gutrune's betrothed. (Remarkably, neither Gunther nor his sister seem to anticipate that this discovery might create some difficulties. Hagen's half siblings are uncommonly dense.) Hagen initially pretends that he is calling the vassals to battle—in a sense, he actually is—and only gradually clarifies his purpose. It is noteworthy that his early recitatives are held together by the orchestral F-sharp-c tritone (at II.393–430, 503–12, and 549–56), the same pedal point that held so memorably together the opening Alberich-Wotan scene of the second act of *Siegfried*. Hagen inherits not only his father's strife-engendering values, but also the musical signifier that goes with them.

With the arrival of Gunther and Brünnhilde in scene 4, the inevitable, anticipated by Hagen but not by his half siblings, happens. Brünnhilde is appalled to see

Siegfried at Gutrune's side, and even more appalled to discover the Ring, which she thought had been wrested from her by Gunther, on Siegfried's finger. Smarter than anyone in the company bar Hagen, she quickly concludes that "he it was who wrested the ring away from me: Siegfried, the treacherous thief!"[179] Outraged by Siegfried's betrayal, she publicly announces that she is wed to him: "He forced delight from me, and love."[180] (Her quick rage and thirst for revenge is where she disappoints: not that they are unjustified, but why doesn't she probe deeper and try to find out how it happened that her lover abandoned her?) Siegfried, equally outraged, denies the accusation. Both are telling the truth; the trouble is that they refer to different events—she to their first night together (which he does not remember), he to what happened last night (which she deliberately ignores). (I am willing to give Brünnhilde the benefit of the doubt and assume that she talks of the first night only and ignores the last one in good faith; otherwise, the "wise woman" would disappoint even more.) And they both proceed to swear an oath on the point of Hagen's spear. May this be the weapon that kills me, says Siegfried, "if that woman's charge is true."[181] I bless this weapon that it kills him, follows Brünnhilde, "for . . . this man has now forsworn himself."[182] Ever lighthearted, Siegfried predicts that Brünnhilde's resentment will quickly pass and invites the vassals and their women to follow him to the wedding feast. They all withdraw into the hall, leaving the stage to Brünnhilde, Gunther, and Hagen alone.

The Oaths Duet with which the scene, and the whole second part of the act, culminates takes the form of two parallel statements, A + A' (II.1128–76 + 1176–213), from Siegfried and Brünnhilde respectively, of, phrase for phrase, very similar content—the form anticipated already in the libretto by the identical prosody and parallel content of the two oaths. Throughout the final portion of the scene, Hagen's F-sharp-c tritones are conspicuously present, associated specifically with the point of his spear, first as he makes it available for the oaths (II.1119–22); again during the oaths, as Siegfried and Brünnhilde mention the weapon (II.1146 and 1183); and finally at the very end of the orchestral transition to scene 5, as well as in the initial measures of the new scene itself (II.1328–36). It is not just that our attention needs to be focused on the fatal weapon that will kill Siegfried; more importantly, we cannot forget who is the master puppeteer and stage director here.

But we should not take the oaths themselves too seriously. Although they contradict one another, neither of the protagonists lies, and Siegfried's death in particular cannot be understood as a punishment for perjury (there is none). It is Hagen, not higher powers, that will kill Siegfried. Given a chance, Hagen would kill him anyway, perjury or no perjury. To be sure, when the time comes Hagen does justify the murder by invoking the perjury: "A false oath I avenged!"[183] But that is precisely what this oath is: an excuse for Hagen. As Brünnhilde dismissively puts it, "Oaths true or false—an idle concern!"[184] The Duet's function is simply to provide this part of the act with a suitably impressive formal culmination; it has no profound dramatic motivation. Should Wagner have decided to remove it, nothing much would change. The Duet is a formal effect without a dramatic cause.

The grand-operatic conventions are even more conspicuous in scene 5 with its final c minor Trio in which the three conspirators (Brünnhilde, Gunther, and Hagen) agree that Siegfried must die (II.1617–73) followed by a C major orchestral coda (II.1674–704). Throughout the Trio itself, Brünnhilde and Gunther, now Hagen's puppets, share the text; Hagen's words are his own, just as his mind is. The Trio is laid out in two broad phrases (1617–44, 1644–73). By the middle of the first one, from II.1632 on, Brünnhilde and Gunther sing not only the same text, but essentially simultaneously; Hagen keeps himself apart. By the beginning of the second phrase, from II.1644 on, all three sing largely together. An operatic alliance has been sealed with a traditional operatic number.

Hagen's tritone, featured so prominently already in scenes 3 and 4, is conspicuous also here, but now it is incorporated within a larger complex of motives (sometimes referred to as the Vengeance Alliance). The complex appears at the very beginning of the Trio first at the F-B level (II.1617–20) and immediately thereafter at the usual pitch level of c-f-sharp (II.1621–23). It is then featured prominently in the coda (affirming that the coda belongs together with the Trio) at II.1689–92 and again in the final measures of the act at II.1701–4. But the complex appears intermittently throughout scene 5, long before the Trio, thus making sure that this final number grows organically out of the scene. Within the scene, it is strategically placed to draw attention to important pronouncements, all referring to Siegfried's death as plotted by the allies: at II.1383–87 with Brünnhilde's "Who'll offer me now the sword with which to sever those bonds?";[185] at II.1462–65 with Hagen's "And there my spear shall strike him!";[186] at II.1517–24 with Hagen's fateful "only Siegfried's death can help you!"[187] this time first at a lower pitch level, E-flat-A, and then at the usual one of G-flat-c; and at II.1581–84 with Hagen's "His death will serve us all."[188]

The Vengeance Alliance complex binds the whole last scene of the act, just as Hagen binds Brünnhilde and Gunther to his purposes—which is the dramatic point of the scene. Hagen first offers his services as the avenger to Brünnhilde and coaxes out of her the invaluable information that the only part of Siegfried's body unprotected by her magic spells is his back (she knew the hero would never show it to the enemy). And then he turns his attention to the shame-stricken Gunther in order to convince him that his disgrace can be atoned for only by Siegfried's death, never mind the blood brotherhood they had sworn (after all, it was Siegfried who broke the bond first), or the grief Gutrune is bound to feel (she will be told that her husband was killed by a boar during a hunt they would undertake tomorrow). As they seal the alliance in the Trio, they offer their prayers, respectively, to Wotan (Brünnhilde and Gunther) and Alberich (Hagen), the old world's presiding antagonist divinities. Thus the ending of act 2 marks the cycle's deepest regression into the worlds of prerevolutionary politics and prerevolutionary opera.

Act 3: Death and Transfiguration

The ease with which the heroic couple has been degraded in acts 1 and 2 may disturb us, but it also makes sense: there is no room for the new humanity of love in the world populated by humanity as we know it, lusting after riches, power, and status. While the first two acts have been completely dominated by Hagen, in act 3 Siegfried and Brünnhilde snap back from the state of ensnared puppets to that of free independent agents and reoccupy the center of attention, he in the first part of the act and she in the second (see appendix 4: act 3). Even though they both die—to this extent Hagen succeeds—they, or rather one of them, manage also to wipe the slate of the world clean and make room for a humanity better than the one they knew, and we know—to this extent Hagen ultimately fails. Their valedictory scenes (scene 2 for Siegfried, scene 3 for Brünnhilde) both have a similar construction, with an introductory recitative dialogue followed by the essential content of the scene—a lengthy monologue of the protagonist that ends with his or her death and the narrator's orchestral peroration exalting the just-deceased hero or heroine. By contrast, scene 1 functions as a prologue, reintroducing one last time nonhuman characters and providing the act's only closed musical number. Indeed, it is striking that Wagner begins the act with a relatively light, and lighthearted, song and places greatest formal emphasis on the two developmental orchestral discourses that provide the act, the opera, and the cycle with a double ending. In other words, he reserves the last word for himself, or his narrator.

The first scene, Siegfried's encounter with the Rhinedaughters, takes the form of a lengthy recitative dialogue between them, framed on both sides by the Rhinedaughters' Song preceded by an orchestral Prelude. The brief Prelude serves to paint the scenery, introducing first the distant onstage horns of Siegfried and others in the hunting party against Hagen's cow-horn accompanied by his woeful F-sharp–c tritone (III.1–19); it then moves to the foreground (the curtain will open on a bank of the Rhine) with the music of nature, the Rhine, and Rhinegold we know from the Prelude and the opening scene of *Das Rheingold* (III.20–39). The hunters remind us of their distant presence briefly toward the end of the section (III.35–38). The Prelude finally zeros in on the characters about to appear, the Rhinedaughters themselves (III.39–50). Their ensuing Song is a similarly simple and lovely strophic affair (table 17) that manages to infuse the mood of careless frolicking with a sense of nostalgic longing for lost but recoverable innocence. The daughters sing about "how brightly you [the Rhinegold] used to shine" in the past and "how happily then you would shine" if returned in the future.[189] In their refrain they vocalize meaningless syllables that have been a trademark of these children of nature from the beginning. The formal simplicity is deliberate, of course, designed to make sure that this single closed number of the act does not challenge the weight of the much more important openly developmental monologues and perorations to come.

TABLE 17 *Götterdämmerung*, Act 3, The Rhinedaughters' Song

Form	Text incipit	Measures	CD.track.time
Orchestral refrain		51–73	IV.2.0:19–1:13
Stanza 1	Frau Sonne sendet lichte Strahlen	73–96	IV.2.1:13–2:12
Refrain	Weialala, weialala leila leila	95–114	IV.2.2:08–2:58
Interruption		115–22	IV.2.2:58–3:14
Stanza 2	Frau Sonne, sende uns den Helden	122–45	IV.2.3:14–4:10
Interruption		144–49	IV.2.4:06–4:18
[Recitative dialogue	Ich höre sein Horn. Der Helde naht	150–444	IV.2.4:18–5.5:13]
Refrain with Siegfried's voice superimposed	Weialala weialala leila leila	445–64	IV.5.5:13–5:59
Interruption with Siegfried's voice superimposed and with the refrain heard from a distance	dem kommt dann ihr Keifen dran!	465–72	IV.5.5:59–6:17
Orchestral postlude		473–93	IV.5.6:17–7:02

The return of the music, characters, and dramatic situations from the very beginning of the cycle is striking—a musical and dramatic signal that at this point the denouement and conclusion are near, that the seeds planted three evenings ago are about to bear fruit. And the specific choice of the music and characters that reappear is not accidental: they all represent Nature. Offended and despoiled by Wotan and Alberich, Nature awaits the atonement which, now that Wotan's Spear has been shattered, can only be accomplished by giving the Rhinedaughters back the Ring fashioned from their father's gold, the gold that Alberich had robbed at the beginning. The atonement requires memory: you cannot atone for a transgression you do not remember. The last act of *Götterdämmerung* is to a large extent about the recovery of memory, about how Siegfried comes back to his senses and restores his essential identity by recalling his life story. But for Siegfried the recovery comes too late and in any case he is unable to see his own story in the appropriate world-historical context. A note in Cosima's *Diary* (July 4, 1873) is revealing: Siegfried, she writes, is "not a tragic figure, since he does not become conscious of his position. . . . Wotan and Brünnhilde are tragic figures."[190] It is left to Brünnhilde to reflect on Siegfried's story *and* to see where it fits within the story of the world and thus bring about the desirable denouement. The gesture of recalling the music of the Rheingold Prelude near to the beginning of act 3 is singularly apt in this drama of the recovered memory of one's own, and the world's, origins.

But Siegfried will begin to recover his memory only in scene 2. In scene 1 he is still his old carefree self, living only in the present moment, and hence his encounter with the Rhinedaughters is bound to remain fruitless. The daughters await the hero's arrival with high hopes and, once he arrives, explicitly ask him for the Ring.

But then, just as he is inclined to comply with their request, they make the mistake of threatening him with dire consequences (Alberich's Curse) if he keeps the Ring for himself. Siegfried will not be threatened. Why should he care for the Curse, even if this had been woven "into the rope of primeval law,"[191] he whose Sword had splintered the Spear of laws and contracts? But he is wrong; he should care. True, it might seem that the Curse need not concern him, since, unlike all those who had died because of it, he does not covet the Ring for the power it brings. But on the other hand, as long as he owns the Ring his life is in danger, simply because others want it. His lack of interest made him immune to the Ring's power (in the final scene of act 1), but it does not make him immune to its Curse.

In making his lack of interest in the Ring's properties explicit, Siegfried articulates what it is that does interest him instead: "Though the ring were to win me the world's inheritance, for the sake of love's favours I gladly forgo it."[192] Siegfried lives for love and does not care for power or even life itself, if lived without love and in fear. He would give the Rhinedaughters the Ring in exchange for their favors (he is ready to move on from Gutrune as quickly as he was ready to move on from Brünnhilde), but not when they threaten his life. And he summarizes his contempt for life lived without love and in fear in a grand gesture of throwing a clod of earth behind him: "Thus do I fling them [life and limb] far away from me!"[193] The shrewd Alberich characterized him correctly: "Laughing, in loving desire, he burns his life away." The Rhinedaughters abandon "the fool,"[194] predicting that Brünnhilde will inherit the Ring this very day and that she will give them a fairer hearing.

The similarity of the scene to that which opened the cycle is obvious, and so is the purpose of this similarity: it makes the contrast between the values of Alberich/Hagen and those of Siegfried all the more striking. Both then and now the teasing Rhinedaughters encounter a sexually interested male who fails to win them over and in the process articulates his essential values in a grand summarizing gesture—Alberich's repudiation of love in favor of power, Siegfried's repudiation of power and of a loveless, fearful life in favor of love.

At first glance it might seem that the scene does not tell us anything about Siegfried we did not know already. It might seem, instead, that it summarizes for us the hero's essential character at its most sympathetic and most exasperating: sympathetic, because how can one not like someone who prefers love to power and who values life only insofar as it is lived fearlessly and filled with what he esteems; exasperating, because how is one not to get impatient with a fool who cannot see beyond what is right in front of his nose, has no notion of the past or future, of the causes and consequences of his actions? But actually we do learn something new, namely, we realize that Siegfried possesses more insight into his own nature than we had suspected. He not only *is* the way Alberich had described him, he also *knows* that he is this way. This deepens our interest in, and sympathy for, him.

Our sympathy deepens further as we observe him trying to enlarge his self-insight by looking back at the key events of his life in the second scene of the act. The centerpiece of the scene is Siegfried's monologue of self-discovery and self-revelation that begins at III.653, peppered in the usual monologue fashion with recitative interruptions from his listeners. It is briefly interrupted by the orchestral pantomime with recitatives that accompanies the scene of murder (III.835–66), and is then completed by the final vision of the dying hero (III.867–912). As they all settle down for a mid-hunt rest, Siegfried tells his hunting companions the story of his life, all of which we know and much of which we had witnessed. With remarkable clarity, he concentrates on just the key moments in his life before the Gibichung misadventure, the story dramatized in *Siegfried*. Inevitably the story leads from Mime's cave where he forged Nothung, through Fafner's cave where he found the Tarnhelm and Ring, to Brünnhilde's rock. The only important episode he omits is the splintering of Wotan's Spear; his self-insight has its limits and does not suffice to make him realize that this might have been one of his most important deeds.

But before Siegfried embarks on this last act of his story, Hagen hands him a drink designed to awaken the hero's memory, a sort of antidote to Gutrune's potion. His memory refreshed, Siegfried, oblivious to his surroundings and increasingly rapt by the ecstatic vision of the once again remembered glorious moment, proceeds to tell his companions how he found and awakened Brünnhilde with a kiss and how she embraced him in turn. Gunther, appalled, interrupts the narrative and Hagen promptly "thrusts his spear into Siegfried's back,"[195] to the accompaniment of his ubiquitous woeful F-sharp-c tritone combined with the Curse motive (III.840–42). What follows is a brief completion of the monologue of the mortally wounded hero, a continuation of the radiant vision of Brünnhilde's awakening that had begun right before the murder. It opens now with the same music that accompanied the actual awakening in *Siegfried*, act 3—the e-C, e-d, e-C triads (III.867–84)—and that was evoked, transposed, at the beginning of *Götterdämmerung*. Siegfried's final moments resemble those of Isolde: "Sweet extinction,—blissful terror—: Brünnhild' gives me her greeting!"[196]

We may have had many doubts about the foolish hero when he was alive, but there is no denying that he develops and deepens on this last day of his life. He dies having achieved as much self-insight as he is capable of, that is, having fulfilled his potential. His life lived only in the present has been both shallow and catastrophic. In his last moments he transcends this limitation and recovers memories of the past. What he remembers, finally, is the most important thing that has happened to him: his encounter with Brünnhilde on the summit of her rock, literally, the high point of his life. Characteristically he pays no attention to the coming death and clings to the recovered vision of love; he remains faithful to his exaltation of love and his contempt for mere life. In another feat of remarkable poetic insight, he interprets his meeting with Brünnhilde as an awakening, both hers and his. Indeed they both have been in need of awakening from forgetfulness and error. That the awakening is also death brings the scene into the proximity of *Tristan*. Siegfried dies groping toward a metaphysical vision of love that transcends life as lived here and now. This vision is his legacy.

His death unleashes the longest outpouring of the author-narrator's orchestral commentary heard in the *Ring* until now, and the most important one until the final peroration of the cycle: the so-called Siegfried's Funeral March that accompanies the vassals' carrying of Siegfried's body back home through the night (and the change of the scenery by an open curtain). According to Cosima's *Diary* entry of September 29, 1871, the composer himself thought of the March as a tragic chorus: "'I have composed a Greek chorus,' R. exclaims to me in the morning, 'but a chorus which will be sung, so to speak, by the orchestra; after Siegfried's death, while the scene is being changed, the Siegmund theme will be played, as if the chorus were saying: "This was his father"; then the sword motif; and finally his own theme.'"[197] A few months later (February 13, 1872), Cosima noted: "Some days ago, R. told me that perhaps the finest thing in this act would be the orchestral prelude following Siegfried's death."[198] One of the great set pieces of the cycle, the somber March allows the "choral"-orchestral narrator to grieve for, and honor, the fallen hero and to review in thought the whole story of the tribe of which he was the last representative.

It is noteworthy how the perspective broadens here. Siegfried himself could not see beyond his own life story; the narrator locates this story within a larger context of the history of the Wälsungs. In the final scene of the opera, Brünnhilde will open up the perspective still further, to that of universal history. As the funeral procession moves on, the narrator thinks of the protagonists and events of the tribal history one after another: the Wälsungs (III.931–34); Siegmund telling Sieglinde why he cannot call himself Friedmund (III.938–42); the love of Sieglinde and Siegmund (III.942–48); the suffering of the Wälsungs (III.949–53); the Sword (III.954–56); Siegfried in his usual motivic shape (III.960–69); Siegfried in his most heroic form in which we know him since his first appearance in *Götterdämmerung* (III.969–76); Brünnhilde from the same scene in which she urged him on to new adventures (III.877–83); Hagen's tritones with cries of woe (III.983–84); the Curse (III.985–87); and finally Siegfried as a hero, now in a mournfully minor mode (III.987–88). Not yet the whole story of the *Ring* (this would include the nonhuman mythological strand and go back to the beginning of *Das Rheingold*), it is nevertheless the cycle's whole human history, from the first appearance of human beings at the beginning of *Die Walküre* to Siegfried's death and thus more than a Funeral March for Siegfried. It is, rather, a threnody for all of the Wälsungs, an outpouring of grief for their suffering and admiration for their bravery.

But if the Funeral March is the final word on the destiny of the Wälsungs, it is not the final word on the destiny of the world. This requires one more broadening of perspective to the universal outlook of Brünnhilde. How does she reach this outlook? She has not shown herself to be particularly wise thus far. What happens to make her wise? Specifically, why does she change her mind and decide to be posthumously reconciled with Siegfried, to forgive and forget his treachery, and her own, too? And why does she change her mind and decide to give the Ring back to the Rhinedaughters, something she had refused Waltraute in the first act? In short, when and why does this double conversion take place?

Remarkably, Brünnhilde's conversion occurs offstage and we learn about it only obliquely and gradually. Wagner is more interested in letting us know *that* it occurred than in explaining exactly when and why. Gutrune, anxiously awaiting the return of the hunters, mentions hearing Brünnhilde's laughter and seeing her go down to the shore of the Rhine that night, after the murder of Siegfried took place. But what motivated the laughter, or the excursion, we never learn.[199] Later on Brünnhilde will thank the Rhinedaughters for their "sound advice."[200] By the time she reappears onstage, at any rate, she has already undergone the conversion. This is all Wagner tells us. We may assume with a good deal of probability that the Rhinedaughters advised Brünnhilde to give them the Ring. All else remains uncertain. Did Brünnhilde's laughter mark the moment of the conversion, or only the moment of her decision to consult with the Rhinedaughters? Did she penetrate the nature of the tragedy and reach the conclusion that Siegfried has been essentially innocent on her own, or only with the help of the Rhinedaughters? We shall never know for sure. But it is clear that, whatever help she did receive, the initial impulse to act rather than passively suffer has been Brünnhilde's own. As for her newly achieved understanding of Siegfried's tragic fate, this she will present in her final monologue.

Meanwhile, the matter of Brünnhilde's nocturnal excursion is dropped to make room for the return of the hunters with the hero's body. The hunters are accompanied by "men and women carrying torches and firebrands," so that the last scene of *Götterdämmerung* is witnessed by a silent crowd of the Gibichungs onstage.[201] A fight between Hagen and Gunther over who should now get the Ring promptly ensues and the latter falls dead: the first victims of the Curse have been brothers, and so are its last. Even so, Hagen is unable to get the Ring, since just as he reaches for it, Siegfried's hand "raises itself threateningly"[202] in one of the cycle's most unfortunate operatic touches, cheap and unnecessary, since Brünnhilde's authoritative and stately entrance at this point should have been enough to stop the son of the Nibelung in his tracks.

Nothing suggests that Brünnhilde even registers Gutrune's hasty confession that it was a potion that made Siegfried forget his love. Similarly, Brünnhilde is completely uninterested in the question of her own responsibility in Siegfried's death that Gutrune raises. She has much else on her mind, and she spells this out in her concluding monologue. The great monologue, while not quite a closed

TABLE 18 *Götterdämmerung*, Act 3, Brünnhilde's Monologue

Form	Content	Text incipit	Measures	CD.track.time
Part 1	Siegfried			
Section 1	Brünnhilde addresses the Gibichungs	Starke Scheite schichtet mir dort	1232–66	IV.16.0:00–2:45
Section 2	Brünnhilde addresses herself	Wie Sonne lauter strahlt mir sein Licht	1267–302	IV.16.2:45–4:48
Section 3	Brünnhilde addresses Wotan	Wißt ihr, wie das ward?	1303–64	IV.16.4:48–8:55
Part 2	The Ring			
Section 4	Brünnhilde addresses the Rhinedaughters	Mein Erbe nun nehm' ich zu eigen	1365–416	IV.17
Section 5	Brünnhilde addresses Wotan's ravens	Fliegt heim, ihr Raben!	1417–55	IV.18.0:00–1:30
Section 6	Brünnhilde addresses Grane and, at the end, Siegfried	Grane, mein Roß! Sei mir gegrüßt!	1456–501	IV.18.1:30–3:40

number, is considerably more structured than the corresponding monologue of Siegfried (table 18). Unlike other monologues of the *Ring*, this one is not punctuated by interruptions from the listeners, as the Gibichungs dare not interrupt Brünnhilde and her other addressees are either not present or not able to speak. Instead it is punctuated by brief orchestral interludes that separate its six individual sections. In addition, the return of the initial music at III.1365 divides the whole into two parts.

In each section Brünnhilde addresses a different listener, and with each she raises a different issue. Accordingly, each section is characterized by an individual mood and kept together by its own set of dominating orchestral motives. The first one, addressing the Gibichungs, is permeated by the stately dotted rhythm of the orchestra, expressive of the "mood of solemn exaltation" with which she speaks.[203] The second is dominated by a more lyrical music as "her features get increasingly transfigured" in solitary contemplation of Siegfried's face.[204] As she turns to Wotan in the third section, the motive of Questioning Fate permeates the orchestral discourse through III.1343. The fourth section, in which she addresses the Rhinedaughters, is filled (from III.1380 through 1408) with the orchestral music associated with them. As her thoughts turn to the impending conflagration in the fifth section, the orchestra burns with the music associated with fire. The sixth section, finally, addressed to her horse, Grane, presents the music of the Valkyries' Ride in continuing association with fire (III.1456–67, 1474–80, and 1499–501) in alternation with the theme we have last heard from Sieglinde in the third act of *Die Walküre*, and which from now on takes increasing importance (the whole cycle will end with it), "Sieglinde's theme of praise for Brünnhilde," as Wagner himself called it, or Brünnhilde's Apotheosis, as I shall call it for short (III.1468–71 and 1481–98).

The topics Brünnhilde discusses are precisely the ones we wanted to know about: Concerning the past in part 1, how does she finally understand Siegfried's character and fate? And concerning the future in part 2, what will she do with the Ring? The first section is merely preparatory: she bids the vassals to erect a funeral pyre for Siegfried and herself on the shore of the Rhine. The second section is devoted to the paradox of Siegfried: he was "the purest of men"[205] and yet "no one betrayed as he did!"[206] The question this paradox raises is stated at the beginning of the third section: "Do you know why that was so?"[207] Brünnhilde does not even mention Gutrune's potion; clearly this is a surface phenomenon, and she wants to get to the bottom of things. Similarly she does not consider the possibility, suggested by me above, that Siegfried's actions resulted from a character flaw. For her, he is blameless.

The guilt lies with Wotan: "Oh you, eternal guardians of oaths! . . . Behold your eternal guilt!"[208] Brünnhilde's newly acquired wisdom tells her to shift the perspective from acting and suffering human individuals to the larger superhuman mythical forces that govern the course of the world; an individual's destiny begins to make sense only within this larger context. Siegfried's tragic death was the result of Alberich's Curse, which he brought on himself when he acquired the Ring, as Wotan secretly desired: "By the bravest of deeds [the killing of the dragon], which you [Wotan] dearly desired, you doomed him who wrought it to suffer the [Alberich] curse to which you in turn succumbed."[209] Hence the ultimate responsibility for the tragedy lies least with Siegfried and Brünnhilde, somewhat more with Hagen and Alberich, but mostly with Wotan himself. So much for Siegfried's death. The explanation of the other, lesser, fact about the hero, his betrayal of Brünnhilde, is simpler but similar: "It was I whom the purest man had to betray, that a woman might grow wise."[210] Also here, what matters is not the individual's responsibility and guilt, but the larger, world-historical purpose his actions serve.

Having discussed the *cause* of Siegfried's tragedy, Brünnhilde now moves to the final and most important topic of the third section, the *purpose* Siegfried's death served. "Do I now [with my newfound wisdom] know what you [Wotan] need?" she asks.[211] Yes, she does: "All things, all things, all things I know, all is clear to me now!"[212] The tragedy was needed to put Wotan's mind at ease: "Rest now, rest now, you god!"[213] This is the answer to the motive of Questioning Fate that has permeated the third section through much of its course. But a step seems to have been missed in this explanation and answer. It is clear that Siegfried had to get the Ring (otherwise it would have fallen back into Alberich's hands) and, as a result, die because of the Curse; it is not clear that these events are enough to hasten the end of the gods' rule, or to put Wotan's mind at ease. The gods' rule is at an end in any case: the Spear has already been splintered. If we are to understand Brünnhilde's reasoning, we must assume that Wotan cares about the inheritance he leaves to his successors, that he cares about the fate of the world after the demise of the gods. Should the Ring end up in Hagen's hands, Wotan cannot rest. He can get true "rest" ("Ruhe") only once he knows that the Ring is beyond his antagonist's reach, safely in the possession of the Rhinedaughters. The orchestra suggests this as it accompanies Brünnhilde's words about the god's rest with the Rhinegold music (at III.1358–60). What happens with the Ring now: this remains the missing link in Brünnhilde's explanation.

The ultimate destiny of the Ring, and thus the world-historical significance of Brünnhilde's newly acquired wisdom, is the subject unveiled in the second part of her monologue. In the fourth section, Brünnhilde bids the vassals to place Siegfried's body on the pyre, claims the Ring as her rightful inheritance, and bequeaths it to the Rhinedaughters: "Let the fire that consumes me cleanse the ring of its curse: in the floodwaters let it dissolve."[214] Cleansed by fire, dissolved by water, the Ring is to return to the natural elements as pure gold. All that remains is to send Wotan's ravens back to their master with good news, to summon the god of fire to Valhalla, and to ignite the pyre (the fifth section). As she does so, Brünnhilde equates the pyre with Valhalla: "Thus do I hurl the torch into Valhalla's proud-standing stronghold."[215] Now that she has properly disposed of the Ring, Wotan's mind has been put to rest and Valhalla can go down. The last section of the monologue is devoted to her desire for a union with Siegfried, her final words as she leaps on horseback onto the burning pyre addressed directly to him: "Siegfried! Siegfried! See! In bliss your wife bids you welcome!"[216] Brünnhilde's monologue ends similarly to Siegfried's, with a Tristanesque final vision of a love union that transcends the limiting conditions of earthly existence.

We have seen how, toward the end of the cycle, the horizon opens up from Siegfried's narrow self-understanding of his own biography only, to the narrator's putting this biography into the context of the story of the Wälsungs, to Brünnhilde's all-embracing view that places everything in the context of the history of the world. Not even the narrator's peroration that follows now will surpass Brünnhilde's universal standpoint. How could it? Siegfried has accomplished a lot, what with his getting the Ring, smashing the Spear, and uniting with Brünnhilde, but his self-insight remained relatively limited. Brünnhilde is the self-consciousness of this heroic couple, which allows her to complete the one deed Siegfried has left undone: the returning of the Ring to its rightful owners. Thus she surpasses him both in deed and in wisdom. But in the end they are one and they both end up in the same place—with a vision of transcendent love, which is what ultimately they have to offer as a replacement for the this-worldly values of Alberich and Wotan. In *Art and Revolution*, one of the Zurich reform essays in which Wagner clarified to himself and the world his basic thinking at the time he was working on the *Ring*, we read: "Only the *Strong* know *Love*; only Love can fathom *Beauty*; only Beauty can fashion *Art*. The love of weaklings for each other can only manifest as the goad of lust; the love of the weak for the strong is abasement and fear; the love of the strong for the weak is pity and forbearance; but the love of the strong for the strong is *Love*, for it is the free surrender to one who cannot compel us."[217] And further: "The Tragedy [of the future] will be the feast of all mankind; in it, . . . free, strong, and beauteous man will celebrate the dolour and delight of all his love, and consecrate in lofty worth the great Love-offering of his Death."[218] Siegfried's and Brünnhilde's legacy is the example of the beauty- and art-begetting love of the strong.

Brünnhilde's monologue presents the richest self-interpretation we can find in the drama. Understandably, Wagner devoted a great deal of attention to it and revised the text more often than that of any other portion of the *Ring*. While in all the versions Brünnhilde returns the Ring to the Rhinedaughters and joins Siegfried on the funeral pyre, in the earliest preliminary stage of Wagner's work on his story, the prose narrative entitled *Die Nibelungensage (Mÿthus)* begun in late September 1848 and finished on October 4 of the same year, she also announces the end of the Nibelungs' and Alberich's slavery. Wotan continues to rule the world and Brünnhilde brings Siegfried to Valhalla, just as she used to bring fallen heroes there in the past.[219] Similarly, in the first version of the poem (November 12–28, 1848), Brünnhilde expressly tells the Nibelungs that her deed makes them, and even Alberich himself, free, which is consistent with, but not articulated in, the final version.[220] More important, however, also here there is no twilight of the gods: Wotan is left to rule the world alone and to "rejoice in the freest of heroes."[221] Clearly at this stage the ancien régime was not yet to be swept completely aside to make room for the self-governing free heroes, but rather reformed as a popular monarchy. The people, made free by the revolution that would abolish the power of both the traditional aristocratic and the modern financial elites, would legitimize the continuing rule of the king. And presumably the free hero-artist would create his works expressing the deepest values of the people under the direct protection of the ruler and without interference from court officials or profit-seeking entrepreneurs.

Wagner's thinking at this stage is spelled out in the speech he delivered on June 14, 1848, at the Fatherland Association, a republican-minded political club in Dresden (it was published anonymously in *Dresdner Anzeiger* a day later), in which he discussed the attitude that those attempting to establish a republic in Saxony should take toward the existing monarchy. The goal, Wagner thought, should be "*the extinction of the last glimmer of aristocratism*," that is, the abolition of court aristocracy and the establishment of an egalitarian classless society ("that henceforth we may all be children of *one* father, brethren of *one* family!").[222] The monarchy, however, should be preserved, leaving only the people and the prince, "the whole blithe happy Folk, where every member of that people through its joyous deputies may smile upon its Prince, may tell him he is First of a free Folk!"[223]

Thus, "we durst ask *the King to be the first and sterlingest Republican of all*" and to represent the whole people, not merely the court aristocracy, to be "the genuine free Father of his Folk."[224] This people would then address "*the question of the root of all the misery in our present social state, . . .* whether Man, that crown of the Creation, whether his lofty spiritual, his artistically stirring bodily powers and forces, were meant by God to serve in menial bondage to the stubbornest, the most lifeless product in all Nature, to sallow *metal?*"[225] Money, Wagner hopes, will be abolished, giving way to an economy based on exchange of goods: "That will be the *full emancipation of the human race.*"[226] Four days later (June 18, 1848) the composer felt compelled to explain his speech to his boss, the intendant of the Dresden Court Theater, Baron August von Lüttichau, stressing that his aim was to defend the monarchy against those who would want to abolish it, but not hiding his agreement with those who would want to abolish the court.[227]

At this stage, then, Wagner's hopes did not go beyond the position reached already in *Lohengrin* of 1846–48 (and recovered in a revised form two decades later, in *Die Meistersinger*). But in the year of the revolution, this initial spirit of reform did not last. In what might be considered the second version of the poem (December 1848) the end of the old regime is already envisaged as Brünnhilde tells the gods: "Depart without power whom guilt now shuns."[228] With the revolutionary radicalization, the monarchy is now no longer to be reformed, but replaced. In an article published anonymously on April 8, 1849, in *Volksblätter*, a radical journal edited by his Socialist political mentor and friend August Röckel, Wagner gave full vent to the revolutionary enthusiasm that corresponds to this stage, making his revolution proclaim: "Whatever stands, must fall. . . . I will destroy the dominion of one over many . . . ; I will break the power of the mighty, of law, of property. . . . Annulled be the fancy that gives One power over millions. . . . *I will destroy all rulership of one over other.*" And further, in what reads like the epitome of the *Ring*'s ending: "From the ruins of this ancient world let rise a *new*, instinct with happiness undreamt!"[229] About Röckel, the composer will write in his autobiography: "On the basis of the socialist theories of Proudhon and others . . . , he constructed a whole new moral order of things to which . . . he little by little converted me, to the point where I began to rebuild upon it my hopes for the realization of my artistic ideals."[230]

The ending we know, the burning down of Valhalla included, appeared in the third version (by December 15, 1852), with, however, a substantial interpolation between the present fifth and sixth section of the monologue, an interpolation often referred to as the Feuerbach ending.[231] In it, Brünnhilde addresses the humanity surviving in "a world without rulers,"[232] spelling out the bequest of her wisdom: "Not wealth, not gold, nor godly pomp; . . . not troubled treaties' treacherous bonds, not smooth-tongued custom's stern decree: blessed in joy and sorrow love alone can be."[233] Note that the interpolation does not really add anything new.

Rather, it heavy-handedly spells out Brünnhilde's lesson for the benefit of the densest among the Gibichungs and Bayreuthians: the love of the free is to replace Alberich's enslaving quest for riches and Wotan's entangling quest for traditional legitimate power based on custom and agreed-upon contracts. In order to avoid didacticism, Wagner could have safely removed it from the final version without changing the message in any way.

Before settling on the final version, however, he toyed with yet another idea, replacing the Feuerbach ending, or rather interpolation, of the third version with the so-called Schopenhauer ending in the fourth version (sketched in prose in mid-May 1856, but versified only in 1871 or 1872).[234] Here Brünnhilde lays stress not on the vision of transcendent love, but on something the experience of love has taught her. She tells her listeners: "To the holiest chosen land, free from desire and delusion, ... the enlightened woman now goes." And further: "Grieving love's profoundest suffering opened my eyes for me: I saw the world end."[235] Love is here no longer the goal, but only a means to an end; the real goal is enlightenment as to the delusional nature of the world and liberation from all desire and delusion. If kept, this ending would have radically inflected the meaning of the cycle, bringing it in line with *Tristan und Isolde*. No longer a story about how the world might be improved by a replacement of the old regime with something better, the rule of love, it would have become the story about how the world should end.

Wagner mentioned the contemplated revision in a letter to Franz Müller of June 22, 1856: "Namely, I shall, however, write quite new poetry for Brünnhilde's ending, since it has become clear to me that the poem has progressed far beyond its original schematic tendency still contained in this ending, which thus represents a narrowing and curtailment of the achieved result. Naturally, in essence it remains the same; only the interpretation of Brünnhilde who has become all-knowing will be different, broader and more decisive."[236] A more detailed explanation of the contemplated revision can be found in the letter to Röckel (August 23, 1856) in which Wagner describes how the reading of Schopenhauer opened his eyes to the contradiction between his (Wagner's) superficial optimistic (that is, left-Hegelian revolutionary) beliefs and the deeply pessimistic (proto-Schopenhauerian) tendency of his art. The passage is of great interest and deserves to be quoted at some length:

> My most striking experience in this respect came, finally, through my Nibelung poem; it had taken shape at a time when, relying upon my conceptions, I had constructed a Hellenistically optimistic world for myself which I held to be entirely realizable if only people wished it to exist. . . . I recall now having singled out the character of my Siegfried with this particular aim in mind, intending to put forward here the idea of a life free from pain; more than that, I believed I could express this idea even more clearly by presenting the whole of the Nibelung myth, and by showing how a whole world of injustice arises from the first injustice, a world which is destroyed in order to teach us to recognize injustice, root it out and establish a just

world in its place. Well, I scarcely noticed how, in working out this plan, nay, basically even in its very design, I was unconsciously following a quite different, and much more profound, intuition, and that, instead of a single phase in the world's evolution, what I had glimpsed was the essence of the world itself in all its conceivable phases, and that I had thereby recognized its nothingness, with the result, of course—since I remained faithful to my intuitions rather than to my conceptions, what emerged was something totally different from what I had originally intended. But I also recall once having sought forcibly to assert my meaning—the only time I ever did so—in the tendentious closing words which Brünnhilde addresses to those around her, a speech in which she turns their attention away from the reprehensibility of ownership to the love which alone brings happiness [that is, the Feuerbach ending]; and yet I had (unfortunately!) never really sorted out in my own mind what I meant by this "love" which, in the course of the myth, we saw appearing as something utterly and completely devastating.... It required a complete revolution in my rational outlook, such as was finally brought about by Schopenhauer, to reveal to me the cause of my difficulty and provide me with a truly fitting key-stone for my poem, which consists in an honest recognition of the true and profound nature of things.[237]

One can readily see how the creator of the Flying Dutchman, Tannhäuser, and Lohengrin, disillusioned with the midcentury revolutionary failure and inflamed by the reading of Schopenhauer, might be tempted retrospectively to see in Buddhist resignation the deepest tendency of his art. One can even see how he might see the ultimate self-understanding reached by Brünnhilde in this light. But as an overall interpretation of the *Ring*, this will not do. The traces left by Wagner's original revolutionary-optimistic intentions are too numerous to be simply obliterated, no matter what Brünnhilde says.

When he set the last portion of the score in 1872, Wagner stepped back from this radical revision and settled in the final, fifth, version on an ending substantially identical with that of the third one, but without the Feuerbachian interpolation; that is, he came back to the understanding of the story he had reached and put into verse already by the end of 1852. (Cosima Wagner thought that the final orchestral peroration was "in fact a paraphrase of the words not set to music, 'Not the glitter of gold, etc.—in joy and sorrow let love alone prevail,'" that is, of the Feuerbach interpolation, and noted this thought in her *Diary* on April 23, 1875.)[238] This is important to note because, dazed by the apocalyptic conflagration that ends the *Ring*, some listeners and viewers might leave the theater under the impression that they had just witnessed a staged ending of the world, a view occasionally shared by Wagner himself, as, for instance, in his letter to Liszt (February 11, 1853): "Mark well my new poem—it contains the world's beginning and its end!"[239] This would be a mistake. What they have witnessed is not the end of the world (much of the world—nature, humans—remains intact), but only the end of Alberich's stand-in, Hagen, of Wotan with his gods, and of the heroic couple that brought about the downfall of the Wotan-Alberich order. The world has not been annihilated, but only burned and washed clean of the old regime so that a new order might replace it. In short, we have witnessed an apocalyptic revolution, but not the apocalypse itself. It is true that in 1856, at the height of his new philosophical infatuation, Wagner was toying with the idea of inflecting the *Ring* in the end-of-the-world direction, but he abandoned it, allowing Wotan to play the role of the Schopenhauerian pessimist but restoring the epic as a whole to its original left-Hegelian or Feuerbachian intellectual-political universe.

If Brünnhilde's monologue is considerably richer in both dramatic and musical content than Siegfried's, the same cannot be said of the following orchestral peroration (this too, like Siegfried's Funeral March, was understood by Wagner to be like a Greek tragic chorus, "'as it were a hymn to heroes,'" as Cosima noted on July 23, 1872).[240] In Siegfried's Funeral March, the orchestral narrator moved beyond the horizon of the preceding monologue. But precisely because Brünnhilde's outlook attained universality, the narrator cannot enlarge it even further. The orchestral peroration is mostly devoted, instead, to illustrating in a rather straightforward manner the pantomime of the drama's final events. This involves three stages: the violent flaring up of the blazing pyre (III.1502–10); its sudden subsiding as the Rhine overflows its banks and the Rhinedaughters swim over to regain the Ring, dragging Hagen to his watery death (III.1511–26); and the gradual subsiding of the flood, with the Rhinedaughters rejoicing over the Ring, and with a growing red glow over the horizon finally revealing a distant vision of the burning Valhalla (III.1527–93). The Ring and Valhalla, the main symbols of Alberich's and Wotan's will to power, the symbols whose proximity has been explicitly revealed by the narrator at the beginning of the cycle (in the transition between the first two scenes of *Das Rheingold*), are destroyed simultaneously and their destruction is the *Ring*'s final event.

In the last of these three stages, intermittently, the voice of the narrator can be heard, increasingly loud and emphatic, over and above the illustrative motives that have to do first with the Rhinedaughters in combination with Valhalla, and then with Valhalla alone. The narrator invokes twice the Apotheosis of Brünnhilde near the beginning of this stage (III.1539–42 and 1549–52) and then Siegfried near its ending (III.1590–92). After much sequential instability, the D-flat major tonic is reached only at III.1594 for the final, subdominant-colored, cadential phrase. These last measures of the opera are the narrator's alone and his subject is again Brünnhilde's Apotheosis (III.1594–98) in combination with the Rhinegold motive, so redolent of Wotan's finally achieved "rest" ("Ruhe"), in the background. Or perhaps this is actually the apotheosis of the heroic couple, if we consider the following remark of the composer, registered by Cosima (July 23, 1872): "'I am glad that I kept back Sieglinde's theme of praise for Brünnhilde, to become as it were a hymn to heroes.'"[241]

In short, when the peroration is not simplistically illustrative (as it is for the most part), it serves to express the authorial admiration for the heroic role-model couple of the humanity of the future, and in particular for Brünnhilde, with a passing thought devoted also to their ancestor god whose rule they came to end and replace. That the cycle that had begun so memorably in nature's own E-flat major ends a step lower, in D-flat, is noteworthy.²⁴² Recall that the main key of *Das Rheingold* was D-flat, the key of the Valhalla music at the beginning of scene 2 and ending of scene 4; this was preceded in scene 1 by the introductory E-flat key of the Rhine. The cycle ends in D-flat rather than E-flat precisely because it ends with the annihilation of Valhalla, not of the entire natural world. Moreover, it only seems that, with the destruction of the Ring and Valhalla atoning for the original rape of nature, we are back where we started. Actually, we are not. The sufferings of the Wälsungs, of Siegfried and Brünnhilde, the whole slaughterhouse of history, were not in vain. Humanity's restored unity with healed nature is something else than the original innocence. The trials and errors of history have been the laboratory that has produced useful lessons for the postrevolutionary future.

THE MYTH OF REVOLUTION

But what actually are these lessons, and how useful are they?

In February 1848, that is, shortly before Wagner conceived a plan for his Siegfried drama, as a new wave of revolutions broke out in Paris and began to sweep through much of continental Europe, Wagner's Dresden included, Karl Marx and Friedrich Engels published in London a short tract entitled *Manifesto of the Communist Party*. The political-economic-social condition of the age in the advanced countries of Europe and North America as diagnosed by the authors of this catechism is characterized by the already largely victorious, though perhaps still to be completed, struggle of the modern bourgeoisie against the premodern feudal aristocracies. The premodern, feudal society was fairly static, or, at any rate, changing very slowly and gradually, and it was held together by countless bonds of traditional allegiances, rights, and duties, the mutual allegiances of parents and children, guild masters and apprentices, vassals and lords, some codified in positive law, some merely rooted in custom, but all accompanied by deeply felt and unquestioned sentiments. The victorious advance of the bourgeoisie during and since the French Revolution has been destroying these traditional bonds and disenchanting the world, creating a dynamic, perpetually changing society: "Constant revolutionizing of production, uninterrupted disturbance of all social conditions, everlasting uncertainty and agitation distinguish the bourgeois epoch from all earlier ones," the authors claimed in their famous and, in this respect compelling, diagnosis. "All fixed, fast-frozen relations, with their train of ancient and venerable prejudices and opinions, are swept away, all new-formed ones become antiquated before they can ossify. All that is solid melts into air, all that is holy is profaned, and man is at last compelled to face with sober senses, his real conditions of life, and his relations with his kind."²⁴³

The solvent by means of which the bourgeoisie has been destroying all traditional bonds and emotional attachments and replacing them with cold "naked self-interest" is private property in its most abstract monetary form, capital: "The essential condition for the existence, and for the sway of the bourgeois class, is the formation and augmentation of capital."[244] Capital is at once the means (the weapon that gives the bourgeoisie their victories) and the aim (since the bourgeois wants nothing but to form and augment his capital). As a result, as it progresses, the bourgeoisie transmutes everything into capital:

> The bourgeoisie, wherever it has got the upper hand, has put an end to all feudal, patriarchal, idyllic relations. It has pitilessly torn asunder the motley feudal ties that bound man to his "natural superiors," and has left remaining no other nexus between man and man than naked self-interest, than callous "cash payment." It has drowned the most heavenly ecstasies of religious fervor, of chivalrous enthusiasm, of philistine sentimentalism, in the icy water of egotistical calculation. It has resolved personal worth into exchange value, and in place of the numberless indefeasible chartered freedoms, has set up that single, unconscionable freedom—Free Trade. In one word, for exploitation, veiled by religious and political illusions, it has substituted naked, shameless, direct, brutal exploitation.[245]

In short, the bourgeoisie has replaced all that has been traditionally valued and loved by one thing alone: monetary ("exchange") value. This goes even for the most hallowed and natural of all human bonds, that linking family members: "The bourgeoisie has torn away from the family its sentimental veil, and has reduced the family relation to a mere money relation."[246]

The modern order represents an advance over the premodern one, as it has unleashed humanity's productive potential and created a more dynamic society, but nevertheless it is intolerable, since it creates social conditions in which a small minority (bourgeoisie) ruthlessly exploits the vast majority (proletariat) and in which all bonds of human solidarity are destroyed and replaced by pitiless competition for money among thus isolated individuals. Hence it needs to be destroyed and replaced by something better. To be sure, the authors are rather vague as to what this something better might be, what will be the specific nature of the bonds and values holding the society of the future together. They know for sure that there will be no exploitation of one class by another, because all classes will disappear; the society will be egalitarian. Beyond that, the best they can come up with is something remarkably vague, a general vision of a universal human brotherhood of free individuals (though neither "free" nor "individuals" in the bourgeois sense of these words): "In place of the old bourgeois society, with its classes and class antagonisms, we shall have an association, in which the free development of each is the condition for the free development of all."[247]

But if what needs to be constructed remains murky, what needs to be destroyed, and by what means, is perfectly clear. The desired change requires yet another violent revolution, this time proletarian, not bourgeois, one that will abolish private property: "The theory of the Communists may be summed up in the single sentence: Abolition of private property."[248] This entails also the abolition of trade, of buying and selling, including the buying and selling of labor. "The proletariat will use its political supremacy, to wrest, by degrees, all capital from the bourgeoisie, to centralize all instruments of production in the hands of the State, i.e., of the proletariat organized as the ruling class; and to increase the total of productive forces as rapidly as possible."[249] What this last clause involves is explained more clearly at a later point in the program, when the authors propose "equal liability of all to labor. Establishment of industrial armies, especially for agriculture."[250] If these proposals to put all capital at the disposal of the state, and to mobilize compulsory labor armies (in other words, though not the words the authors would have chosen, to replace wage labor with slave labor), entail violence, coercion, and despotism, so be it: "Of course, in the beginning, this cannot be effected except by means of despotic inroads on the rights of property, and on the conditions of bourgeois production."[251] This does not trouble the authors, since the goods and values to be abolished all have a bourgeois character: "The abolition of bourgeois individuality, bourgeois independence, and bourgeois freedom is undoubtedly aimed at."[252] Eventually, they promise, the state itself will disappear, since the state is nothing but a tool of class exploitation: "When, in the course of development, class distinctions have disappeared, and all production has been concentrated in the hands of a vast association of the whole nation, the public power will lose its political character. Political power, properly so called, is merely the organized power of one class for oppressing another."[253]

Wagner was not a Marxist, of course, and while he certainly read the essay "On the Jewish Question" and probably also some of Marx's other writings, and while he certainly was aware of who Marx was, it remains uncertain whether he ever read the *Manifesto*.[254] In his speech to the Fatherland Association, delivered four months after the *Manifesto* had been published, the composer talks of Communism as a "preposterous and senseless doctrine," which may, but does not have to, suggest that he did read Marx's tract and certainly suggests that he did not like the idea that property might be owned in common by all.[255] In the slightly later *Art and Revolution*, the term "communism" (which Wagner explicitly states to have borrowed from Ludwig Feuerbach) is given a positive sense akin to "brotherhood" and is contrasted with "egoism," that is, individualism.[256] In any case, the source of his glorification of human love was Feuerbach, his left-Hegelian of choice and an author we know he did read, while his hatred of capital and generalized anarchism owed a lot to the ideas of Pierre-Joseph Proudhon (about whom he learned from his friend Röckel and whom he also read) and Mikhail Bakunin (with whom he was in direct contact at the time immediately preceding and during the Dresden rebellion).

But for all the undeniable differences between their positions, the similarities between Wagner and Marx are even more striking—striking and unsurprising, given their common left-Hegelian, and ultimately Rousseauist, heritage. No less than Marx in the *Manifesto*, also Wagner in the *Ring* was driven by the contrast between what is and what should be, between the actual present condition of humanity—a condition characterized by man's alienation from his fellows and from nature—and the desired future condition in which the alienation would disappear, leaving men and women free to relate to one another like siblings or lovers (or both) rather than like deadly competitors for economic advantage and political power. No less than Marx, also Wagner reckoned that to reach this goal one would first have to identify and then destroy the root causes of alienation. Where Feuerbach located these causes in the human propensity to worship gods, to displace our own human values onto another, transcendent realm, and where Marx thought that he found the causes of alienation in the institutions of the market economy (the division of labor, trade, money, and above all privately owned capital), Wagner's *Ring* represents a synthesis of these two views, with both Wotan's gods and Alberich's capital standing in the way of the unalienated humanity of the future. Wagner's anticapitalist beliefs at the time of the *Ring*'s conception are documented in an interesting entry (December 2, 1848) in the diary of Eduard Devrient. After a reading of the *Siegfrieds Tod* poem, the conversation took a political turn, "at which point he [Wagner] again mounted his hobby horse, the annihilation of capital."[257]

Finally, no less than Marx, also Wagner thought that the only way to achieve the desired goal was a violent revolution that would push Wotan aside, shattering his Spear and burning Valhalla, and equally would permanently deprive Alberich of his Ring. My claim is not that the *Ring* put the *Communist Manifesto* onstage. Bakunin was surely a much more immediate influence on the composer than Marx, and it was with Bakunin that Wagner shared the gospel of the necessity of revolutionary destruction. "The annihilation of all civilization was the objective on which he [Bakunin] had set his heart," the composer remembered in his autobiography.[258] My claim, rather, is one of close family resemblance. Both the *Ring* and the *Manifesto* are characteristic, and arguably the most prominent and influential, documents of the state of mind widely shared by radical intellectuals at mid-nineteenth century, expressing their converging diagnoses and hopes at the time of what Lewis Namier so memorably dubbed "the revolution of the intellectuals," the century's high-water mark of revolutionary fever.[259]

To see both the similarities and the differences still more clearly, one needs to consider three aspects of the positions elaborated in the *Manifesto* and in the *Ring*: what the authors claim needs to be destroyed; by what means; and what should be put in its place.

The diagnosis of the modern condition of the developed world, the world that needs to be destroyed, offered in the *Ring* is remarkably close to that of the

Manifesto. Both Wagner and Marx see their world as defined by the struggle for dominance between the older and declining feudal aristocracy—the defenders of slowly accumulating rights and obligations, some customary, some legally codified, all firmly rooted in human sentiment—and the newer and ascending bourgeoisie intent on replacing all custom and law by the naked power of privately owned capital. To be sure, their diagnoses are not identical. For Marx, the bourgeoisie has already been largely victorious; more realistically, Wagner saw the struggle between Wotan with his Valhalla and Spear and Alberich with his Ring and Tarnhelm as still ongoing and unresolved (realistically, since in most of Europe aristocracies retained significant power and influence though the First World War). Marx had a tendency to underestimate the importance of the political. Wagner's picture of the painfully uncomfortable intertwining of politics and money is richer, more realistic, and more illuminating of the world of his and of our time than Marx's picture of money largely dominating and replacing politics.

Moreover, the fundamental motivation behind their respective diagnoses of modernity differs in at least one important respect: Marx wants to emancipate the downtrodden and exploited majority, the proletariat, while Wagner, an artist to the core of his being, is interested mostly in the fate of art, and more especially his own art, the art of opera, under modern conditions. In the earliest—and today perhaps least read—of his Zurich reform essays that accompanied the gestation of the *Ring*, the one that allows us the best insight into his overall political-cultural outlook at the time, *Art and Revolution* (written in 1849 and published in 1850), Wagner made clear that modern conditions, involving as they did the rule of commerce, were even more inimical to art than the far-from-perfect premodern forms of church and aristocratic patronage. Under these conditions, he wrote, "Art, instead of enfranchising herself from eminently respectable masters, such as were the Holy Church and witty princes, preferred to sell her soul and body to a far worse mistress—*Commerce*."[260] As the result, "This is Art, as it now fills the entire civilized world! Its true essence is Industry; its ethical aim, the gaining of gold; its aesthetic purpose, the entertainment of those whose time hangs heavily on their hands."[261] Wagner's anticapitalism is driven not so much by the desire to liberate the Nibelungs as by the wish to emancipate opera from Alberich's profit motive, which debases ethically and aesthetically demanding art into low entertainment.

Similarly, both Wagner and Marx see the present world not as crying for reform and improvement, but as requiring wholesale destruction, a violent revolution. In *Art and Revolution* one reads: "Only the great *Revolution of Mankind* ... can win for us this Art-work [of the future]."[262] And further: "From the dishonouring slave-yoke of universal journeymanhood, with its sickly Money-soul, we wish to soar to the free manhood of Art ... ; from the weary, overburdened day-labourers of Commerce, we desire to grow to fair strong men, to whom the world belongs as an eternal, inexhaustible source of the highest delights of Art. To this end we need the mightiest force of Revolution."²⁶³ (The composer's enthusiasm for revolution, by the way, did not begin in 1848. Already *Das Liebesverbot* of 1834–36 is marked by it, as it is by the glorification of the love of the free, or rather free love, which a popular uprising that resolves the opera's plot makes possible.) Siegfried's Sword, the flooding waters of the Rhine, and above all the cleansing final conflagration are all needed to destroy both the declining rule of custom and law and the ascending rule of capital.

Indeed, the extent to which Wagner's imagination was fired by the spectacle of a cleansing conflagration in the years in which he was working on the *Ring* poem is striking. Each evening of the cycle takes a fiery ending, with Brünnhilde being enclosed in a ring of flames at the end of *Die Walküre*, her heroic lover penetrating this ring at the end of *Siegfried*, and both, as well as the gods, going up in flames at the end of *Götterdämmerung*. Retrospectively, even the final vision of *Das Rheingold*, "the rainbow bridge of blinding radiance" leading to Valhalla, "which now glints in the glow of the evening sun," seems a prefiguration of the conflagration that will consume the gods' castle in the end.²⁶⁴ During the Dresden rebellion, on hearing that the opera house burned down (May 6, 1849), the composer jotted down this note in his *Annals*: "Opera House now burnt down. Strange feeling of comfort."²⁶⁵

Wagner's letters of the period, too, overflow with pyromania. In a letter to Theodor Uhlig (September 20, 1850), he envisages three performances of *Siegfrieds Tod* within one week to be given in a purpose-built theater in Zurich, after which the theater would be torn down and the score burned.²⁶⁶ And in a letter to Clara Brockhaus (March 12, 1854) we read: "After the performance [of the *Ring*] I shall throw myself with the score on Brünnhilde's funeral pyre so that everything burns down."²⁶⁷ Perhaps the most telling example occurs in a letter to Theodor Uhlig (October 22, 1850): "I no longer believe in any other revolution save that which begins with the burning down of Paris." He continues: "Look, just as we need a water-cure to heal our bodies, so we need a fire-cure in order to remedy (i.e., destroy) the cause of our illness—a cause that is all around us."²⁶⁸ In this, his most radical period, the composer, a firm believer in the healing efficacy of spas and their waters, burns with the desire for a "fire-cure," a cleansing conflagration that would engulf and consume the utterly unredeemable existing order. And still long after the subsiding of the revolutionary fervor, during the Franco-Prussian war, Wagner's hope that Paris might be burned down lives on. On August 18, 1870, his wife notes: "R. says he hopes Paris ('this kept woman of the world') will be burned down; . . . the burning of Paris would be a symbol of the world's liberation at last from the pressure of all that is bad."²⁶⁹ One does not need to be a particularly perspicacious psychologist to see that Wagner's obsessive hatred for Giacomo Meyerbeer, overdetermined though it undoubtedly was, must have been motivated also by his realization that, for all the gulf that separates mere talent from genius, he had a lot in common with the composer of *Le prophète* (1849), not least a penchant for fiery denouements.

Moreover, in Wagner's mind the political and the artistic revolution embodied in the *Ring* blend into one. His self-characterization in "A Communication to My Friends" (July–August 1851) is unambiguous and emphatic: "I am neither a republican, nor a democrat, nor a socialist, nor a communist, but—an artistic person and as such, everywhere were my sight, my wish and my will reaches, a revolutionary through and through, a destroyer of the old in the creation of the new!"[270] Similarly radical sentiments are expressed with vehemence in a letter to Theodor Uhlig (November 12, 1851): "I ... can no longer suffer—the torments of *halfmeasures*.—With this new conception of mine I am moving *completely* out of touch with our present-day theatre and its audiences: I am breaking decisively and for ever with the formal present." And he continues, again conflating the artistic and the political:

> A *performance* [of the cycle] is something I can conceive of only *after the Revolution*; only the Revolution can offer me the artists and listeners I need. The coming Revolution must necessarily put an end to this whole *theatrical business* of ours.... Out of the ruins I shall then summon together what I need.... I shall then run up a theatre on the Rhine and send out invitations to a great dramatic festival: after a year's preparations I shall then perform my entire work within the space of *four days: with it* I shall then make clear to the men of the Revolution the *meaning* of that Revolution, in its noblest sense.[271]

Where Wagner and Marx differ is in their identification of the potential revolutionaries. Wagner's revolutionaries are not Marx's proletarians: the composer did not envisage an active world-historical role for the Nibelungs enslaved by Alberich. Instead, his revolutionaries, Siegfried and Brünnhilde, are naturally free individuals of no particular class, in fact, of socially uncertain origin and status, unanchored individuals driven by passion and instinct and not by the values of an inherited or assumed social position—in short, modern artist types, unfettered by any social role, without a church or court salaried employment, like so many Wagnerian heroes (think Tannhäuser, Lohengrin, Walther, or Parsifal, in addition to Siegfried), or like Wagner himself, coming from nowhere and bringing good tidings—part artists, part Rousseau's men of nature, part Nietzsche's overmen, but wholly men of the future.

Even so, the vision of the future offered by Wagner is not entirely unrelated to that offered by Marx, and remarkably similar in its vagueness. What is clear is that for both it would be a future without Alberich or Wotan, without privately owned capital and without legally enforceable rights and obligations—that is, without a market-regulated economy and law-regulated politics, with their inherent exploitation and competition. Marx proposed to put all capital and labor in the hands of the state, vaguely promising that eventually the state, and with it the need for politics, would disappear. Wagner, not obliged to write a party program, did not bother to indicate what the intermediary stage between the dismal present and the radiant future might look like. Both hoped that eventually instead of competing for economic advantage and political power, humans would relate to one another through spontaneously arising bonds of sympathy and love. The vision of the future presented in the *Manifesto* is condensed into the single already-quoted sentence: "In place of the old bourgeois society, with its classes and class antagonisms, we shall have an association, in which the free development of each is the condition for the free development of all." The vision of the future presented in the *Ring* is intimated in Siegfried's and Brünnhilde's perorations with their paeans to love. Where Marx dreams of a brotherhood of the free, Wagner follows Feuerbach and dreams of a sexual union of the free.

Common to both is a characteristic Romantic Prometheism or Faustianism. Neither Marx nor Wagner wants to restore or preserve the traditional values and allegiances of the premodern past, with its unjust hierarchies, inequalities, and privileges. Both believe that traditional injustices can and need to be swept aside, that humankind's ability to remake itself according to its own (or, rather, their own) design is unlimited. And neither is deterred by the thought of the violence needed to realize their Faustian projects. Along with other radicals of 1848, both have thoroughly forgotten or ignored the prophetic diagnoses and warnings issued by Edmund Burke in his 1790 *Reflections on the Revolution in France*.

Common to both, too, is a Romantic revulsion toward the recently emerged industrial society seen as dissolving all traditional values and allegiances and replacing them with naked, ruthless competition for money and power among isolated individuals, as well as a revulsion toward the theoretical underpinning of this society in the philosophy of liberalism that assumed the natural egoism of individuals requiring a theory of social contract that would harmonize conflicting interests through legal mechanisms that safeguard collective and individual security by putting limits on individual freedom. The thought stemming from Bernard Mandeville and Adam Smith that competing individual egoisms can actually produce socially beneficial outcomes does not persuade them. The Romantics, such as Wagner and Marx, do not see the society as necessarily consisting of naturally isolated and egoistic individuals; such a society is for them a contingent product of recent historical development. Instead they assume the primacy and desirability of a community held together by bonds of naturally arising sympathy and solidarity among its equal members, bonds that spontaneously cause each individual to identify with the community as a whole. Unlike the society of the present, the community of the future will not need the mediation of a social contract or law to maintain its unifying bonds. It will be held together by spontaneous sympathy, without any such mediation. For all their differences, both Marx and Wagner postulate for us some sort of vaguely imagined post-political and post-legal future, and neither is deterred by the thought of the despotism such a future entails. In practice, the abolishing of legal limits on individual freedom cannot but lead to the domination of the strong over the weak.

To Wagner in his most radical anarchist period the thought does not seem to have occurred. It did occur to Marx, only to be dismissed: the despotism of the state, he promised, would be only a temporary stage on the road to the perfectly unified, conflict-free society which, being conflict-free, would have no need of politics or law. A (bourgeois) liberal, attached to his (bourgeois) freedom within legal limits and skeptical as to the prospects of ever creating a perfectly unified society held together by the glue of spontaneous solidarity and love, is likely to remain unconvinced that giving up his individual and legally limited freedom for a most uncertain promise is a sensible bargain. And hence, just as he is unlikely to be swayed by the ringing rhetoric of the *Manifesto*, the ending of *Götterdämmerung*, for all the persuasive power of the orchestral narrator's peroration, is likely to leave him with considerable misgivings.

I have suggested that the similarities between Wagner's and Marx's positions can be explained by their common heritage in the strain of modern thinking initiated by Rousseau. But their common roots go even deeper, all the way back to the teachings of Jesus. Wagner's *Ring* in particular, with its picture of the essential historical progress consisting in the replacement of Wotan's rule of law by Siegfried's and Brünnhilde's rule of love resonates with Jesus's (and Saint Paul's, and Saint Augustine's, and Luther's) doctrine that spontaneous solidarity among humans and between humans and God, solidarity rooted in love, renders the prescriptions of the Mosaic Law superfluous, that the bonds of love should replace the bonds of contracts. This fundamental intuition is also the deepest root of all the utopias of universal human brotherhood, the Marxist one included. Needless to say, neither Marx nor Wagner at this stage can be considered Christians. In particular, the love Wagner preaches in the *Ring* is the erotic love of Feuerbach, not the love of one's neighbor proclaimed by Jesus (for the composer's conversion from eros to agape we need to wait until *Parsifal*). More importantly, the Promethean belief common to the mid-nineteenth-century radicals that the kingdom of universal brotherhood can be fully realized on earth is profoundly at odds with the wiser and safer Christian understanding that the Earthly City driven by envy and competition for earthly goods is unlikely ever to be fully replaced here on earth by the City of God animated by charity, no matter how hard we try to follow Jesus's teachings. Thus, it would be a mistake to consider the *Ring* simply as an attempt to dress Christianity in Germanic garb. But equally it would be a mistake not to notice its Christian roots—a mistake that would render Wagner's evolution from the *Ring* to *Parsifal* puzzling and incomprehensible. It might be worth recalling here that in early 1849 Wagner was planning an opera on *Jesus von Nazareth* in which Jesus was cast in the role of a revolutionary who wants to replace the society based on private property with a society based on love. In a note to a sketched scenario, Wagner wrote: "The law is lovelessness and even when it would command love, I would not practice love in observing it, since love acts only from itself, not according to a commandment. The atonement of the world is therefore to be brought about only through the abolition of the law."²⁷²

The problem with this way of thinking—indeed, the central problem with the worldview promoted in Wagner's *Ring*—is that the rule of law means justice, and justice is no less a virtue than love. We need both and, in this world at any rate, one cannot replace the other. This is because their spheres of validity do not completely coincide. Justice is the virtue we need primarily in the public sphere, love in the private one. Wagner's dream of replacing justice with love goes hand in hand with his dream of a post-political future, a dream prophetic of the utopian political experiments of the early twentieth century.

Der Ring des Nibelungen may have been conceived and received as an answer to the call for a German national opera, the mythic material of the *Nibelungenlied*, published by Friedrich Heinrich von der Hagen in a modernized version in 1807, that is, a year after the traumatic dissolution of the Holy Roman Empire, having been widely taken in nineteenth-century Germany as the national epic, a Germanic equivalent of the Homeric poems. (It was dubbed *Nationalepos* by the brothers Grimm as early as 1810.)²⁷³ Precisely such a call to use the *Niebelungensage* as the stuff for a grand heroic opera was issued by Friedrich Theodor Vischer in 1844, and the author repeatedly stressed the national character of the material: "This material is *national*, this is the first thing for which it is to be praised."²⁷⁴ And when Wagner offered the yet-to-be-completed score to the publishers Breitkopf and Härtel, he wrote (June 20, 1856): "I hope to deliver with my 'Nibelungs' a popular-national work in the most noble sense."²⁷⁵ It is for this reason probably, and surely also because of his rapidly growing prestige as the nation's preeminent artist, that Wagner managed the seemingly impossible feat of assembling for its premiere at Bayreuth in the summer of 1876 the political, economic, and social elites of the newly minted German Reich, the Kaiser himself included.

It has to be seen as an act of unprecedented impudence and audacity, however, that what the composer offered these elites for their contemplation was not in fact the expected national epic, but the spectacle of their own impending demise. What Wagner made of his mythic materials is not a national opera (this he offered elsewhere, in *Die Meistersinger*), nor the foundational story for an emerging unified Germany, but something much more universal, a foundational story for the yet-to-be-created new postrevolutionary world. Wagner did think of himself as a German Aeschylus, but his tetralogy turned out to be something of an anti-*Oresteia*: while the last installment of the Aeschylean trilogy, *The Eumenides*, leads the tormented hero to a trial by the Athenian jury and thus celebrates the power of the city's law to replace the archaic cycle of violence and revenge with a civilized order, Wagner's tetralogy, on the contrary, celebrated the revolutionary destruction of a civilized legal order and its replacement by more primordial and instinctual bonds. In *Art and Revolution* the composer wrote: "The Art-work of the Future must embrace the spirit of a free mankind, delivered from every shackle of hampering nationality; its racial imprint must be no more than an embellishment."[276] A remark made in *My Life* is also worth recalling in this context: "I was delighted even in those days to find in the German mind the capacity to transcend national barriers and appreciate purely human qualities, . . . a faculty that seemed akin to the Greek spirit."[277] Another remark by Cosima in her *Diary* (September 6, 1875), reveals something of Wagner's thinking: "R. reflects: . . . How can one speak of a national work of art? What does a stonemason . . . get from the *Ring des Nibelungen*? . . . Only individuals, the chosen few, can enjoy art."[278]

Indeed, instead of a national myth, the composer has fashioned in the *Ring* what must be considered the artistically most significant embodiment of one of the two most pernicious ideological legacies of the nineteenth century, the myth of revolution (the other one being the myth of nation), of the necessary and violent destruction of the old world of economic markets and political legalities to make room for something unprecedented, new, and immeasurably better, a perfectly unified society free of exploitation and competition. According to Cosima's *Diary*, still on May 2, 1874, Wagner emphasized the intimate connection of his project with the uprisings of "'48, the spring of the people. . . . I believe I myself should never have conceived the *Ring* but for that movement.'"[279] As the revolutions of 1848–49 failed, the attractiveness of the myth seemed gradually to have faded, too. By 1876 the political and economic potentates of Germany could contemplate it without terror (and perhaps without much comprehension).

The catastrophes of the twentieth century, however, have shown that this fading has been only temporary, that in the conditions of acute crisis created by the First World War, the promises of the myth of the revolution, whether in its red or brown version, may regain their attractiveness. Even today, with the period that ended in 1989 long behind us, it is far from certain that the myth has lost all of its allure, that the virus is dead rather than dormant. "It might seem mysterious," writes Alain Badiou, "that the two philosophers who are instigating the resurrection of the word 'communism' today [he has himself and Slavoj Žižek in mind] should also be those who are passionately following the public fate of Richard Wagner and are fighting upstream against the opprobrium cast on him." But of course there is actually nothing mysterious in the fact that, in spite of its composer's dark reputation as Hitler's favorite artist, the *Ring* continues to excite the enthusiasm of Leninist-Stalinist thinkers such as Žižek and Badiou, thinkers ready to wax lyrical in the early twenty-first century about "the rediscovered vitality of the idea of revolution."[280] After all, we are as troubled now as Wagner's contemporaries were then by money's uncanny power to corrupt all the values that we hold dear, and as unsure that we know how to hold this power in check, more troubled than they were by our continuing despoilment of nature, and as ready to think that solidarity among equals might be preferable to competitive struggle and exploitation. The hope is that we have become more skeptical than they were about the prospects of our ever mastering the technique of producing perfect social cohesion without resorting to despotism.

But if the *Ring* stands as the nineteenth century's grandest artistic monument to the myth of revolution, its standing, both ideological and music-dramatic, within Wagner's own oeuvre is less certain. Undoubtedly the composer's most ambitious and monumental project, it must be seen as the centerpiece of his life's work. And this was for a time how he regarded it. In a letter to Breitkopf and Härtel (July 10, 1856), the composer himself characterized it as the "full and sumptuous main work of my life."[281] He called it again the "main work of my life" in a letter to Ludwig Schnorr von Carolsfeld (October 8, 1864).[282] The project was made even more ambitious and monumental by the conjunction with the Bayreuth Festival, itself a stupendous and unprecedented entrepreneurial achievement created expressly to provide this work with an appropriate vehicle: the embryonic idea of a festival to present *Siegfrieds Tod* appears already in Wagner's letters to Ernst Benedikt Kietz of September 14, 1850, and to Theodor Uhlig of September 20 of the same year.[283]

But, ideologically, the *Ring* represents a position that Wagner had largely left behind by the time he managed to complete the cycle. Yes, he did identify himself as a socialist even in his late regeneration essays, but the social, political, and philosophical positions projected in his last three dramas do not fit comfortably with the world of *Der Ring des Nibelungen*. The metaphysics of the cycle has been transcended by that of *Tristan*, its politics by *Die Meistersinger*, and its ethics by *Parsifal*. In purely artistic terms, too, for all its great and undeniable dramatic and musical beauties, the cycle is uneven, considerably more so than the other three late music dramas (among the evenings of the *Ring*, only *Die Walküre* sustains their high level of achievement from beginning to end). Surpassed, in short, as a work of art and thought by Wagner's three late masterpieces, the *Ring* remains nevertheless at the center of his legacy.

PART TWO

3

Tristan und Isolde
The Erotic Utopia

Always only the yearning to die and the yet-maintaining-oneself; this is love.
FRANZ KAFKA, *DIARY*, OCTOBER 22, 1913

What else then is the magic of the highest love if not that we forget the whole world and what else oppresses us in it in a single longing of love? My Tristan says this quite clearly: but he teaches also that love itself remains as the last, highest torment and that the only redemption through death is not so easy to achieve.
RICHARD WAGNER, LETTER TO BLANDINE OLLIVIER, MARCH 3, 1858[1]

If *Der Ring des Nibelungen* embodies Wagner's most radical vision of the public realm, his understanding of its past, present, and future, *Tristan und Isolde* is the *Ring*'s equally radical and uncompromising counterpart in the private sphere. The anarchist's utopia projected in the *Ring* left the outlines of the postrevolutionary world remarkably vague, promising only that such a world might be populated by humans who, rather than competing for advantage, would relate to one another through spontaneously arising bonds of sympathy and love. The revolution would make room for sexual unions of the free and fearless, would create conditions under which such unions would not necessarily have to end in disaster. In *Tristan* the sexual union of the free and fearless gets a closer look, and as a result the optimism of the *Ring* is put into question. A disaster is discovered woven into the very fabric of the erotic, regardless of the social and political circumstances under which the union takes place. The metaphysical radicalism of *Tristan* leaves the prospects of human happiness and flourishing projected by the revolutionary utopia of the *Ring* in shreds. A letter to his political mentor and friend, August Röckel, of August 25–26, 1856, shows that already at that early date Wagner was fully aware that the *Ring* rested on shaky foundations: "I shaped it [the Nibelungen poem] at a time when I had built for myself with my concepts only a Hellenically optimistic world the realization of which I considered entirely possible as soon as people only wanted it, whereby I attempted rather artificially to avoid worrying about the problem why actually they did not want it."[2]

THE LYRICAL AXIS

The normal kind of discourse in Wagner's music dramas consists of an arioso recitative dialogue accompanied by a motivically significant orchestral development. This kind of discourse makes use of the "open" system of composition with its irregular phrasing, key instability, developing motivic variation, and contrapuntal texture in which both vocal and orchestral lines can take leading roles and in which the main melodic line frequently shifts its position. Three modes depart from this neutral norm—the zero degree of the music-dramatic discourse. First there is what might be called the lyrical mode, in which the composer abandons the musical prose of the declamatory recitative to approximate the musical poetry of fully developed numbers in traditional opera: songs such as aria, duet, and larger ensembles that stick out from the traditional opera's own neutral discursive norm, the recitative dialogue. He does so by introducing some or all of the traditional song elements, elements of the "closed" system of composition— the regular hierarchical phrasing, key stability, patterns of melodic units based on contrast and repetition, and homophonic texture in which the voice lords over the orchestra. Second, there is what might be called the narrative mode in which the composer retains the normal discourse of arioso recitative over motivically significant orchestral development, but applies it to a prolonged monologue rather than a dialogue—a form of departure from the norm with less obvious ancestry in traditional opera (though with a link to the accompanied solo recitative or arioso). And third, an orchestral mode is constituted by sections of music provided entirely by the orchestra, with the voices either silent or reduced to melodically perfunctory declamation. All three modes are present in *Tristan und Isolde*, forming three intertwining strands that together give the music drama its overall shape.

Putting aside a few simple closed items, such as the derisive song of Kurwenal early in act 1 or Isolde's song in praise of Frau Minne early in act 2—these are too short to have more than local formal significance—one finds that the center of the lyrical axis falls at what is the center of the opera. The Love Duet (II.1117–631), which is the second of the three sections of the second of the opera's three acts, is, with its 515 measures of music that can take as much as twenty-five minutes in performance, by far the largest and most complex lyrical form of the work. Wagner was particularly proud of this music. His wife noted his words in her *Diary* (April 4, 1879): "'The key to *my* music is the A-flat major from *Tristan*: Beethoven, Bach, and Mozart, well and good, but *that* is my music.'"[3] Its organization is, in a characteristically Wagnerian way, unique and yet recognizably related to the *solita forma* with its backbone of a slow cantabile followed by a fast cabaletta. But the backbone is much obscured and overgrown, there being not one but two cantabiles with a double cabaletta to match and with each cantabile followed by a postlude and a section of recitative dialogue (see appendix 5: act 2, part 2, section 3).

In both cantabiles the most obvious mark of difference from discursive normality is the almost complete shift of the melodic substance from the orchestra to the vocal parts. To be sure, in the first cantabile the orchestral motive of the Day which opened the second act (II.1-3) and dominated the long recitative dialogue that preceded the Duet (II.682-1116) continues to make appearances (II.1138-55, 1184-92) as the lovers implore the Night to drive away the Day with its illusions. But for the most part, already in the first cantabile and even more completely in the second one, it is striking to what extent the orchestra's role has been reduced to that of a discreet accompaniment that at most doubles the voices and leaves them in command of the attention.

Yet how imaginative such doubling can be! The accented appoggiaturas with which both Tristan and Isolde end the initial lines of their Duet are at first doubled by the orchestra (II.1126-33), but then acquire a life of their own and continue to be echoed by the orchestra without any provocation from the voices (II.1134-37), thus achieving, however fleetingly, an independent motivic identity. This identity is confirmed with augmented emphasis when the orchestra uses the motive, again independently of the voices, to punctuate the half cadence in the middle of the cantabile (II.1158-61). And this is why, when the appoggiaturas reappear repeatedly in the orchestra as an accompaniment to the beginning of Brangäne's Warning that follows the cantabile (II.1210-25), we hear the Warning as a postlude rather than a completely independent new section of the whole. (Brangäne, Isolde's maid, keeps watch during the lovers' assignation in the castle garden.) Born of the lovers' voices and passed on to the orchestra, the appoggiaturas provide the regular breath of the nocturnal atmosphere that, without challenging the primacy of Brangäne's line, allows it to soar over their supportive counterpoint, and they ensure that the lovers' presence in the night's embrace is not forgotten. They become the musical symbol of Night, the counterpart of the Day motive. The Day motive has long been identified by the compilers of leitmotivic guidebooks, but if you ever wondered where the Night motive is in the act devoted to the exploration of the Day-Night opposition, here it is.[4] The Night motive is prominently emphasized in the last of the *Wesendonck Lieder*—one of the two designated by Wagner as a "study" for the opera, in this case for the Love Duet—and there its content is unambiguously specified as "dreams" ("Träume").

But the shift of the melodic center of gravity from the orchestra to the voices is just one mark that lifts the cantabiles above the discursive norm. Its effect is reinforced by other marks of the lyrical mode—the clarity of metric definition and the stability and unity of key, of course, but also and more importantly the relative regularity of phrasing correlated with the regularity of a motivic pattern based on some repetition. Because of these each cantabile is perceived as a clearly articulated but also unified melodic period.

Thus two strong half cadences (II.1158–61 and 1200–1201) articulate the first cantabile into two phrases (II.1123–61 and 1162–201) of almost identical length (respectively, thirty-nine and forty measures) framed by a brief six-measure instrumental introduction (II.1117–22) and a similarly brief nine-measure coda (II.1202–10) that modulates to the key of the postlude. The melodic similarity of the way the two phrases begin—both ascend from the fifth scale step—as well as the similar order of the significant motivic events in both phrases (compare the appoggiaturas in II.1126–37 with those in II.1167 and 1173, and compare the Day motives in II.1138–55 with those in II.1184–92) together suggest their A-A′ relationship. Brangäne's postlude (II.1210–57), with its closely corresponding length of forty-eight measures, rounds off the cantabile with a B-section, casting this whole first lyrical portion of the Duet in a Bar form (AA′B).

The regularity of phrasing and of motivic patterning is even more pronounced in the second cantabile and its postlude. The cantabile is again articulated by two half cadences into two phrases (II.1377–400 and 1401–24), this time identical in length and melodic content, except that what in the first phrase was sung by Tristan alone is in the second distributed between the two voices. Moreover, the twenty-four measures of each phrase are grouped with a most un-Wagnerian quadratic regularity into three eight-measure incises each consisting of two four-measure units. Brangäne's twelve-measure postlude (II.1424–35) echoes the ending of her previous Warning (II.1246–57), now a half step higher (her G major coming this time on the heels of the Duet's A-flat major without any modulation), and provides the A-A of the cantabile with a B that completes another Bar form. In giving his two Bars a common B section (much abbreviated on its second appearance to match the smaller proportions of the second cantabile), Wagner ensures that the two cantabiles are perceived as related, as parts of a single larger lyrical whole, rather than as two independent songs.

Similarly he ensures that this large lyrical whole is not limited to the cantabiles and their postludes by motivically relating both cabalettas to the cantabiles. The melody of the first cabaletta develops the climactic ending of the first cantabile (compare the beginning of the cabaletta with II.1198–201), and that of the second cabaletta clearly develops that of the second cantabile. But the relationship of the two cabalettas to one another is the reverse of what the relationship of the two cantabiles had been: where the first cantabile was considerably more complex and approximately twice as long as the second one, now it is the first cabaletta that is roughly half the size of the second one. Moreover, the tonal plan of the two cabalettas ensures that the first—which modulates to the V of B—is heard as a mere introduction to the second—which stays in B.

Both cabalettas share one characteristic marker of the lyrical mode: the melodic substance is carried for the most part by the voices, and the orchestra is given an accompanying or at most a doubling role. But in the second, main, cabaletta the doubling is so consistent that the whole might be played by the orchestra alone without any loss of the melodic substance. More: here and there one suspects that it is the orchestra that carries the main line and the voices that provide counterpoints. This seems to be the case already in II.1544–45 and 1548–49, but it is certainly the case from II.1598 on when, all the way through to the end of the Duet, the orchestra takes over the melodic burden of the discourse and the voices either provide counterpoints or double the instruments. It is as if the rising erotic tension overwhelmed the protagonists and rendered them relatively inarticulate, drowning their individual subjectivities in the common stream that carries them both on toward the conclusion.

Only two sections of the Duet do not depart from the Wagnerian discursive norm of recitative dialogue and do not share in the lyrical mode—the modulating interludes that follow each Bar and get back from the key of its B section to the main key of the double cantabile. To be sure, the first interlude (II.1258–376) gets something of a rounded ABA' form (the middle section extending from II.1295 to 1335), but this shape does not depend on anything provided by the voices. Rather, it relies on the orchestral phrase that opens the interlude (II.1258–65), and especially on its head motive, which pervades much of the outer sections and thus unifies the whole first interlude. The same motive unifies also the earlier portion of the second interlude (II.1436–80) until II.1460—the point at which the interlude begins gradually to accelerate and heat up emotionally so that the music may function analogously to a tempo di mezzo, moving seamlessly on to the frenzied double cabaletta.

But here too Wagner makes sure that the interludes are heard as parts of the larger whole. It is not only that he relates them to one another, basing them both on the same unifying orchestral motive. More important is the derivation of the motive from an earlier lyrical portion of the Duet. The motive insinuates itself into the orchestral contrapuntal fabric well before the first interlude begins—from II.1234 on through the end of Brangäne's Warning it is scarcely ever absent from the background, so that the interlude is well prepared in advance, just as the Warning itself had been, and by a similar method. And also in this case the orchestral motive originates in the voices doubled by instruments: its source is in Isolde's "heart on your heart, mouth on mouth."[5] Thus, when in the postlude the motive emancipates itself from the voices, its presence in the orchestra suggests, again, that all through Brangäne's Warning the lovers, though silent and perhaps scarcely visible, are still there, hidden in the enveloping night, "Herz an Herz dir, Mund an Mund." And it is appropriate that this very motive keeps the following dialogues together since the lovers' "Herz an Herz" becomes the subject of their conversation as they agree (in the first interlude) that their union could not be destroyed by death, but, on the contrary, that death in common would make this union perfect and permanent, and hence decide (in the second interlude) to die together.

Death was not yet present in the first cantabile, at least not explicitly. The opposition that governs the two lovers' self-understanding in the Duet and beyond is that of existing in a world split into two metaphysically distinct levels—in their language, Day and Night. Day is the realm of consciousness, that is, of separation between subject and object, between the I and the world with its multiple phenomena, and this unbridgeable separation necessarily breeds unappeasable desire. Night is the realm of oblivion where the separation between subject and object, between the I and the world, is cancelled, where the multiplicity of phenomena turns out to be illusory, where all is one, where the desire born of separation is appeased. Since what love aims at is, precisely, the appeasement of desire and the cancellation of any separation between subject and object, clearly what the lovers wish for, in their Duet and beyond, must be to leave the world of Day behind and merge together into the Night. In the first cantabile each implores the "night of love"[6] to "descend"[7] upon them and "bring forgetfulness that I live,"[8] "release me from the world."[9] What each wants is the state in which "I myself am the world."[10] It is from this "wish of never to waken again" that Brangäne desperately but unsuccessfully tries to tear them away in her Warning.[11]

But, of course, the wish to escape Day and merge into Night implies death. It is the logic of love that, since it aims at obliterating the distance between subject and object, if pursued with sufficiently radical single-mindedness and exclusivity, it has to issue in oblivion and death. As Cosima noted in her *Diary* (November 20, 1878): "From this he goes on to *Tristan* and says in the second act he wanted to do just that, to describe happiness, the feeling that there are no more barriers and all else is forgotten, and the desire to perpetuate this condition through death."[12] (Throughout death also doubles as a metaphor of erotic fulfillment: Wagner knew his troubadours and *Minnesänger* well.) The subject of death becomes explicit in the colloquy of the first interlude, where Tristan immediately gets to the point: "Let me die!"[13] and, a little further, "Let Day give way to death!"—a formula in which death replaces Night as its synonym.[14] But Isolde worries that perhaps death will rather replace Day and interfere with their love: "What if Day and death unite to strike at our love?"[15]

Tristan has no such worries: "Our love? . . . What strokes of death could ever make it yield?"[16] Love is eternal and hence "how could love . . . , the eternally living, end with me?"[17] And, in the final twist of his argument, he concludes: "But, if his love would never die, how could then Tristan die of his love?"[18] Yet Isolde has further worries. What is at stake here, she reminds her lover, is bigger than just him and his love; it affects them both together, Tristan *and* Isolde. Should Tristan die, will "the union of love"[19] symbolized by "this sweet little word: and" not be destroyed?[20] No, he answers: "All that would die is what prevents us from doing what matters to Tristan—always to love Isolde."[21] In other words, all that would die are the annoyances of Day. At this point in the argument Isolde realizes that Tristan's death implies her death, too: "How else but together with Isolde's own life would death be given to Tristan?"[22]

The upshot of this colloquy is that their common death would not be in alliance with Day, it would not interfere with their love and bring it to an end. On the contrary, it would in alliance with Night remove all obstacles to their complete and permanent union. It would be hard to maintain at this point that the logic of the argument is entirely faultless; only at the end of this chapter will I be able to explain how this logic can be made to work. But for the lovers at this point it is already strong enough to allow them to talk themselves (or, to be precise, to allow Tristan to talk Isolde) into what an unsentimental observer can only call a suicide pact. Only now, in the second cantabile, can Tristan spell out the conclusion toward which their argument was driving them. And only now can Isolde obediently repeat after him, "We would die so as to live only for love—unseparated, for ever endlessly united, without waking, without fearing, namelessly enveloped in love, given completely to one another!"[23] The form of the cantabile, with its seemingly redundant, almost exact repetition of the same words and music (exceedingly rare in late Wagner), brings to mind a solemn oath taking, with one party reciting the text of the oath first and then both parties repeating it. What began in the first cantabile as a love duet is transformed by the second one into a death, or love-death, duet. Where death is a synonym of Night, a "night of love" ("Nacht der Liebe" or "Liebesnacht") is bound to be transmuted into a "love death," or literally, a "death from love" ("Liebestod"). Shortly the preparatory cabaletta, an invocation addressed first to "Liebesnacht" and then to "Liebestod," will make this equation explicit.

It is precisely to make possible this transformation of the *Liebesnacht* into a *Liebestod*, to show how and why the lovers' decision to die together is taken, that the Love Duet needs not one but two cantabiles and the intervening argumentative interlude. What follows the second Bar form—the new interlude and the double cabaletta—can only serve to show how the decision is put into practice. The lovers have reached the point when nothing more remains to be said and everything remains to be done. Words and arguments matter here less and less, and accordingly Wagner's syntax grows more and more disjointed. Words give way to the steadily mounting erotic frenzy whipped up by the orchestra which in the main cabaletta first consistently doubles the voices and then takes over the rushing melodic stream and nearly drowns the voices in it.

Nearly, but not quite. The expected *Liebestod* does not come, they do not die, at least not yet. The single most conspicuous feature of the Love Duet is of course its lack of conclusion. The much-prolonged dominant in II.1619–30 should get its

TABLE 19 *Tristan und Isolde*, Act 2, Postlude to the Love Duet

Form	Text incipit	Measures	CD.track.time
Prelude	Wohin nun Tristan scheidet	1914–27	III.7.1:53–2:48
Tristan's question:			
A	Dem Land, das Tristan meint	1928–43	III.7.2:48–3:50
A'	Was, da sie mich gebar	1944–61	III.7.3:50–5:02
Interlude	Als für ein fremdes Land	1962–73	III.7.5:02–5:45
Isolde's answer:			
A"	Nun führst du in dein Eigen	1974–92	III.7.5:45–7:05
Postlude		1992–97	III.7.7:05–7:39

tonic resolution in 1631, but does not—or rather, not yet, not here. Instead, in II.1631 "the desolate Day" intervenes "one last time,"[24] as Tristan puts it, in the form of the inopportunely returning aggrieved husband and his entourage. It is this interruption that explains why, in what must be the largest recapitulatory gesture in opera since *Don Giovanni* (or, at least, since *Lohengrin*), a portion of the Love Duet is repeated and completed at the end in, as Wagner called it, Isolde's "Transfiguration" ("Verklärung") that closes act 3 (III.1621–99).[25]

Long before this occurs, however, the Love Duet gets a kind of delayed postlude toward the end of act 2 (II.1914–97; table 19). A brief song duet takes the form of Tristan's question and Isolde's answer, both in the Love Duet's original key of A-flat and beginning with the motive that dominated the Duet's interludes (compare II.1914–17 with II.1258–61). Together these features create the impression of a postlude to the Love Duet rather than an independent lyrical unit in its own right. Framed by a brief prelude, interlude, and postlude, the song duet itself is almost entirely dominated by the voices and consists of three similar phrases (AA'A"), two for Tristan and one for Isolde. Tristan's question to Isolde is whether she will follow him into the realm of Night, "from whence my mother sent me,"[26] the realm that was "her [his mother's] fortress of love."[27] Isolde answers in the affirmative: "How could I flee the land that spans the whole world?"[28] Thus the postlude-like song duet is a promise that what has just been interrupted shall be completed.

And it is completed in the Transfiguration (appendix 5: act 3, part 2.3). In III.1621–31 Isolde appropriates Tristan's music—but not the words—from II.1377–98, in the same key of A-flat; that is, she recapitulates practically the entire substance of the second cantabile, missing only its final half cadence (II.1399–400), since the remaining part of the cantabile (II.1401–24) simply repeated Tristan's music, dividing it now between him and Isolde. The missed half cadence after III.1631 allows Wagner to shift effortlessly from A-flat to B, so that in III.1632–80 Isolde can repeat in turn the music she and Tristan sang in II.1530–630, again in the same key of B, that is, recapitulate the complete second cabaletta. In III.1621–

80, in short, Isolde repeats the music of the second cantabile and second cabaletta of the Love Duet. Thus, the Duet is recapitulated in a most economical fashion: the second cabaletta needs to be repeated because this was the section that got interrupted in the first place and hence has to be completed now; and the second cantabile is there because it is from this cantabile that the cabaletta derived its material. The two belong together. And, lest we forget, they belong together also textually and dramatically, containing the Duet's most essential points. The cantabile was where the lovers solemnly committed themselves to their common *Liebestod* ("We would die so as to live only for love"), and the cabaletta was where they attempted to fulfill their pact.

All these repetitions required that, when he composed the Transfiguration, Wagner had to have the score of the Duet in his hands. But because he had not appeared before the public with a new work for nearly a decade—*Lohengrin* having premiered in 1850—and because he was eager to secure a performance of the opera as quickly as possible, in *Tristan und Isolde* Wagner did not follow with his normal practice of not sending the score to the publisher until it was completed. Instead he supplied Breitkopf and Härtel with finished installments while continuing to work on the score.[29] No wonder then that by the time he was ready to compose the final portion of his opera, he was bombarding his publishers with requests for the proofs of the second act. Thus he writes from Lucerne on June 5, 1859: "I long for the proofs of the second act very much; it is very important for me to use this opportunity to go in detail over this preceding act one more time."[30] On July 18 he repeats: "I urgently ask . . . that you let me see at least a copy of the as yet not corrected printing of the last third of the same [act II], since I need to look into this in order to be able to finish my work."[31] And again, on July 26: "I urgently ask that you do not let me also wait now for the promised proofs of the last third of the second act: I need these to finish my score."[32] The analysis of the score makes it perfectly clear why he was so insistent and impatient.

The remaining measures of the Transfiguration (III.1681–99) are new (there is nothing left to recapitulate). They provide the prolonged dominant in III.1674–80 (corresponding to the one in II.1619–30) with the tonic resolution that had been so rudely denied to the Love Duet. But the character of this resolution is as different from what might have been expected in II.1631 as the character of the preceding tension. What in act 2 was a steadily mounting and increasingly noisy erotic frenzy *à deux* is now a solo mystical rapture (Tristan is already dead and Isolde is about to follow him), equally intense in its way, but also "mild and quiet."[33] Appropriately, instead of the blatant male tonic release we almost got in act 2, act 3 brings a tonic subtly weakened and attenuated by the subdominant—a gradual female subsiding of tension until the final release and disappearance.

Wagner's control over this resolution is truly admirable. Instead of an unambiguous tonic, he provides first, in III.1681–84, an oscillation of the tonic and subdominant chords (over the tonic pedal), placing the subdominant on the stronger and the tonic on the weaker measure and thus making sure that we hear the subdominant as an accented appoggiatura that weakens the tonic. In III.1685 the subdominant takes over entirely, becoming minor in III.1688. In III.1690–94 the tonic and the subdominant go back to their oscillation, but this time it is the tonic that takes the stronger metric position and hence, if not yet fully in charge, it is more prominent than it had been in III.1681–84. But for a completely satisfying and unclouded tonic we have to wait until the final cadence of the opera (III.1695–99). Here Wagner brings in one last time the so-called *Tristan* chord (III.1695)—the same one first heard at the very beginning, in I.2—resolving it this time to the minor subdominant of B (III.1696) rather than to the V^7 of a (as in I.3). In a sense he transforms the dominant into the subdominant and hence pushes the tonic a whole tone up, finally moving to the B tonic (III.1697–99). In other words, he gives us the tonic three times, in III.1681–84, 1690–94, and 1697–99, purifying and making it stronger with each progressive appearance until, at the end, it sounds completely unclouded and brings final appeasement.

Throughout the Transfiguration the main melodic line is carried by the orchestra; Isolde sometimes doubles it and at other times provides free counterpoint. Such spots of vocal counterpoint against the main instrumental melodic line appear almost immediately (for instance III.1625–26), making it clear where the principal melody lies and who is doubling whom. As in the later portion of the main cabaletta of the Love Duet, here too the voice is meant to be carried along by the orchestral stream, to swim, and this time eventually to drown, in it. Over Tristan's dead body Isolde fulfills their mutual promise of the Duet (to "die so as to live only for love—unseparated, for ever endlessly united"), her final words literally invoking the image of drowning, of loss of consciousness as subject merges with object: "In the heaving swell, in the resounding echo, in the blowing all of the world-breath, to drown, to be absorbed, unconscious, highest joy!"[34] "All the mystics of all religions," writes Arthur Schopenhauer, "ultimately arrive at a kind of *ecstasy*. In this each and every kind of *knowledge* together with its fundamental form, *object and subject*, entirely ceases."[35] Elsewhere the philosopher notes: "In some sense or other (made clear only by philosophy) we are one with the world."[36] Both musically and dramatically, what was meant to happen but did not at the end of the Love Duet happens now, at the end of the opera.

Together, the Love Duet with its postlude and Isolde's Transfiguration constitute the lyrical axis of the opera—its lyrical center of gravity (table 20). And together they articulate musically the central event of the dramatic action—the *Liebestod* that is the lovers' aim, interrupted and eventually successfully completed. In other words, Wagner the musician makes sure that what is bound to be experienced as the formal center of gravity will articulate what Wagner the dramatist wants us to experience as the central event of the music drama.

TABLE 20 *Tristan und Isolde*, The Lyrical Axis

Form	Key	Content	Text incipit	Measures	CD.track.time
Love Duet	A-flat/B	Liebestod interrupted	O sink hernieder, Nacht der Liebe	II.1117–1631	II.12–III.3
Duet Postlude	A-flat	Promise of completion	Wohin nun Tristan scheidet	II.1914–97	III.7.1:53–7:39
Transfiguration	A-flat/B	Completion	Mild und leise wie er lächelt	III.1621–99	IV.11

The sections of closed-form music are in bold.

THE NARRATIVE AXIS

The components of the lyrical axis, however, are not the only moments in the opera when Wagner departs from his discursive norm of recitative dialogue. Running parallel with the lyrical axis there is a second, narrative, axis consisting of those moments when the normal discourse of an arioso recitative over a motivically significant orchestral development is applied to long monologues rather than to dialogues (table 21). By "monologue" I mean a scene in which a single personage speaks at considerable length, usually though not always with one or more witnesses. Three such moments are particularly conspicuous in *Tristan und Isolde*, one in each act. They provide points of music-dramatic gravity alternative to the lyrical ones and, together, constitute the opera's narrative axis.

If the lyrical axis is where the characters enact the main events of the drama and thus objectively present the story, the narrative axis is where they reflect on these events, where they present their subjective understandings of the story. In a striking reversal of traditional operatic practice, according to which the action is set in recitative and a passionate reaction to a new situation is set in a lyrical number, Wagner reserves his most lyrical utterances to present the action, and uses recitative for moments of reflection. But there is a clear logic to this reversal. First, the action here is what happens in the depths of the characters' minds rather than in their external world; also traditional operatic practice reserved lyrical numbers for the revelation of characters' interiorities. Second, the recitative in question is deployed in long monologues rather than dialogues and hence is suitable for moments of sustained individual reflection. But in addition to allowing us to learn what the characters think about their story, all three monologues are also occasions when the protagonists can simply tell the story, and especially some of the antecedent events, as they see it—hence the prominently narrative flavor of the monologues. The narratives are not redundant precisely because they fill in gaps in the background, but even more importantly because it is in a retelling of the story that the teller reveals his or her attitude to it.

TABLE 21 *Tristan und Isolde*, The Narrative Axis

Form	Text incipit	Measures	CD.track.time
Isolde's Monologue	Wie lachend sie mir Lieder singen	I.602–862	I.6.0:00–8.2:25
Marke's Monologue	Tatest du's wirklich?	II.1689–890	III.5–6
Tristan's Monologue		III.1–1324	III.9–IV.7

The open-form but non-dialogical sections are in bold italics.

It has been observed that, because of the role played by the orchestral narrator, Wagnerian dramaturgy approximates that of the novel. In fact, those moments when the orchestra takes on the function of an independent narrator are quite infrequent in Wagner's music drama. The affinity with the novel may have less to do with the use of the narrator and more with the frequent deployment of the double perspective whereby we both witness events and, thanks to the monologues, hear what the characters think about these events.

In the final analysis, while the narratives have their addressees and are spoken aloud, they—and especially Tristan's—come close to being interior monologues. No less than the lyrical, the narrative axis also serves to reveal the depths of the protagonists' minds. The devaluation of the public, external world of Day in favor of the private, interior world of Night characterizes not only Tristan's and Isolde's view of the world, but also Wagner's music-dramatic method. Wagner deserves to be taken seriously not only as an innovative composer of genius, but also—in this opera at least—as a dramatist of first importance. In his own time, only Ibsen might be considered a peer. The relentless emphasis his method places on interiority is one of the reasons why *Tristan und Isolde* has to be seen as an early and key monument of high modernism—literary as well as musical, a milestone on the road to *Erwartung*, to be sure, but also to *Ulysses*.

Marke's Monologue (which takes some fourteen minutes in performance) is the least elaborate of the three—appropriately so, since Marke is the least important member of this triangle and his point of view is the one that interests us least. All the same, it is this Monologue more than anything else that justifies Wagner's repeated claim that his opera has not two but three main roles.[37] Formally the Monologue centers on an arioso (II.1750–831) held together by a single orchestral motive that is exposed right at the beginning (II.1750–52) and permeates much of the orchestral texture, often penetrating the vocal part as well (for instance at its beginning in II.1758–60). The central arioso is framed by more conventional solo recitatives (II.1689–749 and 1831–90). The first of these, too, is dominated by an orchestral motive exposed at the outset (II.1693–97). The motive returns at the beginning and toward the end of the second recitative (II.1831–37 and 1876–83), but now it starts with an allusion to the arioso motive (II.1831–33 and 1876–79), which then seamlessly transforms itself into the recitative motive (II.1833–37 and 1879–83).

Like Marke himself, the Monologue is beautiful and noble, but also, in context, somewhat dull. By the time the king makes his case, we are already so taken in by the lovers' point of view that we have little patience for Marke's common decency and sense of honor. We want to brush it aside as Tristan does when he interrupts the Monologue, as if trying to conjure away an annoying vision: "Day's apparitions! Morning's dreams! deceitful and desolate! Vanish! Go away!"[38] For him, and for us, Marke is the main representative of "the desolate Day" that intervenes "one last time." Cosima correctly noted (June 17, 1874): "King Marke, that symbol of moral order and consequently herald of death."[39] (The opera that does justice to Marke's point of view is *Die Meistersinger.*) Dramatically the main point of the Monologue is to allow Day's main representative to make the strongest possible case for it, and thus to allow Tristan to reject this case publicly (immediately following the Monologue, as we shall see) and to make Isolde, equally publicly, promise to reject it, too (as we have already seen).

Otherwise about the only thing that is intriguing about Marke is just how little he is interested in his wife and concerned about her betrayal of him, and how exclusively his attention is focused on his rival. To be sure, Isolde is dutifully apostrophized as "this wonderful woman,"[40] and Marke rhetorically asks, "Who [could] proudly call her his own without considering himself blessed?"[41] But he immediately makes sure that we (and the rest of the world) learn that he himself could not really call her his own, since he never dared to approach and possess her: "She, whom my will never dared to approach, she, whom my wish reverently renounced."[42] This indiscreet revelation takes us aback until we reflect that it might have been dictated by a chivalrous wish to free Isolde from the adultery charge, given that the marriage had not been consummated. Now, whether out of reverence or because of indifference, he does not address a single word to his wife and concerns himself solely with the heartbreaking and incomprehensible betrayal by his "most loyal of all the loyal,"[43] "most friendly of friends,"[44] his nephew and chosen heir.

But Marke's narrative of background events allows us to learn something of considerable interest that we (and presumably Isolde, too) had not known until now: his marriage with Isolde was Tristan's idea. When Marke's first wife died childless, the king, wishing that Tristan inherit his realm, decided not to remarry and reluctantly changed his mind only when Tristan threatened to leave his court and country forever unless he were "sent to win a bride for the king."[45] It appears then that, like a troubadour, Tristan had intended to channel his dangerous passion into the safe waters of the conventions of courtly *fin'amor*, making sure that the object of his love be at once near (in Cornwall rather than Ireland) and inaccessible (the wife of his feudal lord). In other words, he wanted to spread a safety net—or, in the language of Schopenhauer and young Friedrich Nietzsche, a veil—of civilization between himself and raw, elemental, cruel, and indifferent nature. He underestimated both the power of his passion and Isolde's determination. The whole external action of act 1 consists of Isolde's ultimately successful efforts to break the decorous distance between them and force Tristan to face her.

Isolde's own narration of the antecedent events and her own perspective on what is going on is, obviously, more interesting and more important. Accordingly her Monologue is formally considerably more differentiated and shapely than his. Of roughly comparable length to Marke's, the narrative itself requires less than ten minutes in performance, but together with its coda, the song of Brangäne, it runs more than fifteen minutes. Wagner signals its relatively greater interest and weight by moving Isolde's arioso partly in the direction of an aria, that is, by introducing some of the traditional song features. Moreover he follows the Monologue itself (I.602–862), after a brief postlude transition recitative of Brangäne (I.862–82), with Brangäne's simple and soothing arietta (I.883–1036), thus providing the Monologue with a coda-transition before returning to his discursive norm of recitative dialogue (I.1036). It is precisely because the normal recitative dialogue comes back for good only in I.1036 that Brangäne's Song is experienced as belonging with Isolde's Monologue, that is, with the departure from the discursive norm it initiated in I.602. The Monologue and the Song belong together for dramatic reasons as well: Isolde tells Brangäne her story and the maid responds, attempting to calm her agitated mistress.

The Monologue itself (see appendix 5: act 1, part 1.2, Isolde's Monologue) is articulated into three sections, each opened by a brief prelude introducing the narrative, and closed either (in the first two sections) by a brief interlude as Brangäne interrupts the narration or (in the last section) by a coda. The songlike features are particularly pronounced at the beginning, where Wagner takes pains to signal a break with the recitative norm. Even the text of the first prelude (I.602–8) is enlisted to help in the task. Having just heard a derisive song of Tristan's servant, Kurwenal, echoed by the sailors (I.510–37), Isolde introduces her narrative with "As they mockingly sing songs for me, so could I well respond!" thus suggesting that what follows is like a song, too, if not literally a song.[46] Indeed, the narrative proper begins with phrasing so regular that it could easily be heard as an antecedent (I.611–14) followed by a consequent (I.615–18). But immediately after, its job done, the regular phrasing is abandoned and Wagner settles for his normal arioso, the texture in which the voice predominates over the orchestra without the latter ever being conventionally perfunctory for long, but in which the vocal line is not shaped by the traditional song means, such as, in particular, the hierarchical organization of phrases into antecedents and consequents, or repetitive formal patterns (ABA, AAB, and others). Initially the music is held together by a single accompanimental motive that had been introduced already in the prelude (I.602–4) and that continues to dominate the orchestral texture through the end of the first section. In the following two sections, even this one unifying motivic element is abandoned, as is the unity of key. The first section of the Monologue was in e; the remaining two sections are tonally unstable.

What shapes the Monologue as a whole is Isolde's steadily mounting agitation. The generally moderate ("mässig") tempo into which she settles in the first section of her narration gives way to something fiery ("sehr feurig") in the second section, to culminate in a very fast ("sehr schnell") and furious fortissimo coda as she curses both Tristan and herself: "Curse upon you, villain! Curse upon your head! Vengeance! Death! Death for us both!"[47]

The prose of the arioso recitative is abandoned for the poetry of song only with Brangäne's arietta at the end. Clearly it is at the beginning and end that Wagner is most concerned to mark the distance from the discursive norm and thus frame the whole. Indeed, Brangäne's arietta *is* a strophic song (see appendix 5: act 1, part 1.2, Brangäne's Song). Its first two stanzas are separated by a fleeting orchestral gesture that choreographs Isolde's turning away at hearing her maid's well-meant but misguided consolations, and its second and third stanzas by a brief dialogue interpolation.

The simplicity and regularity of Brangäne's poetry, coming after the stormy complexity of Isolde's prose, is obviously indicative of their contrasting personalities, and of the maid's wish to pour calming oil over her mistress's troubled waters. This being Wagner, the simplicity is relative, of course. The successive stanzas are variations rather than literal repetitions of the first one (and the key of the first stanza, E-flat, is fully reestablished only at the end of the third), and while there is a single main melodic line, it is carried sometimes by the voice, at other times by the orchestra, and at yet other times by both at once. Each stanza consists of three phrases that together form the AA′B pattern, with the last part of B returning to the motivic ideas of A (table 22).

But the artful simplicity of Brangäne's consolations could not be effective, could not turn Isolde away from her decision to seek "death for us both," since the maid has not really understood (or did not wish to understand) the story her mistress had told her: In a duel Tristan, the nephew and heir of Cornwall's king, killed Morold, the betrothed of the Irish crown princess Isolde, but not before receiving a grievous wound. Aware of Isolde's healing powers, he drifted incognito to Ireland to seek her help. While nursing him, she discovered his identity and, furious, attempted to avenge Morold's death with Tristan's own sword. It was then that something unexpected but decisive happened: "He looked up from his bed, not at the sword, not at the hand, he gazed into my eyes. I felt pity for his wretchedness; I dropped the sword! I healed the wound smote by Morold so that he might recover and return home, not to burden me with his gaze any more!"[48]

What Isolde describes with remarkable precision here, at the end of the first section of her narrative, is the single most important event in the drama's

TABLE 22 *Tristan und Isolde*, Act 1, Brangäne's Song Stanzas

Form	Measures	CD.track.time
Stanza 1		
A	883–91	I.9.0:17–0:32
A'	891–99	I.9.0:32–0:48
B	899–917	I.9.0:48–1:26
	(891 return to A)	
Stanza 2		
Orchestral anticipation of A	920–21	I.9.1:33–1:36
A	922–30	I.9.1:36–1:52
A'	930–42	I.9.1:52–1:56
B	942–58	I.9.1:56–2:51
	(946 return to A)	
Stanza 3		
Orchestral anticipation of A	984–91	I.9.3:46–3:56
A	991–96	I.9.3:56–4:04
A'	996–1008	I.9.4:04–4:22
B	1008–36	I.9.4:22–5:08
	(1028 return to A)	

prehistory—the moment of falling in love marked by the meeting of the glances, the moment when each subject became vulnerable, dependent on the other. At this point she does not yet know what this event meant to him, just that it rendered her defenseless.

Given this fateful glance, it is understandable that the memory of Tristan's subsequent action, which Isolde narrates in the second and third sections of the Monologue, would arouse her fury and motivate the vehement curse in the coda. He returned to Ireland, now under his own name, to ask for her hand in marriage not to himself, but to his uncle. From this perceived rejection Isolde draws the only conclusion that her radical, maximalist, all-or-nothing character makes possible: "Death for us both!" What to Isolde must seem an outrage and betrayal, Brangäne chooses to interpret more conventionally as an act of gratitude: Tristan offered Isolde a royal crown and relinquished his own inheritance in her favor. Having heard King Marke's revelations, we suspect yet another motive: Tristan's wish to preserve his invulnerability *in*, if not *from*, the elemental passion of love by means of civilizing courtly conventions.

All this we can as yet only surmise. We still need to hear directly from Tristan how he himself understands his story and his own motives, and for this we need to wait until the first part of the last act. Even if we single out only the monologue sections proper (III.277–440, 516–840, 866–999, 1209–324), Tristan's Delirium (as it is sometimes called) takes just more than half an hour in performance; the scene as a whole (III.1–1324) lasts about twice that long. It is by far the longest musical-dramatic unit of the opera, so much so that it not only dwarfs the other two Monologues, but also challenges the claim of the Love Duet to represent the main center of gravity of the work. It has been often experienced as the opera's alternative center, especially by more advanced musicians impressed by the symphonic-developmental character as well as the expressive intensity of some of its sections.

But not only by musicians: Nietzsche, in *The Birth of Tragedy* (1872), directed a question to "genuine musicians" ["those who . . . are related to things almost exclusively through unconscious musical relations"], asking "whether they can imagine a human being who would be able to perceive the third act of *Tristan and Isolde*, without any aid of word and image, purely as a tremendous symphonic movement, without expiring."[49] Nietzsche's words bring to mind the famous passage in one of Wagner's letters to Mathilde Wesendonck, written in mid-April 1859 while the composer was working on the music of the third act: "Child! This Tristan is turning into something *terrible*! This final act!!!———————- I fear the opera will be banned—unless the whole thing is parodied in a bad performance -: only mediocre performances can save me! Perfectly *good* ones will be bound to drive people mad,—I cannot imagine it otherwise."[50] It may be that Wagner was still talking about Tristan's Monologue in this fashion when he and Nietzsche were in close contact, the time when Nietzsche worked on *The Birth of Tragedy*, and that Nietzsche's book reverberates with this sort of talk. Whether or not Nietzsche's words here contain echoes of something he had heard from Wagner himself, they surely betray the avant-garde musician's bias in favor of purely instrumental, symphonic, developmental discourse and, tellingly, single out the third act (its first part, as Nietzsche's following discussion makes clear) for particular attention in this respect. Wagner himself claimed in *My Life* that it was while working on the earlier part of act 3 that he first fully realized what a bold score he was writing: "It was in just those first scenes of this act that I realized with complete clarity that I had written the most audacious and original work of my life in this very opera, which it was believed, quite unwarrantably, would turn out to be easy to produce."[51]

In short, if the Love Duet (or rather the Love Duet completed by Isolde's Transfiguration) is the opera's most sustained moment of lyrically expressed internal action, Tristan's Monologue is its most extended moment of narratively embodied, passionate self-reflection. And there is a good reason why Wagner gave Tristan's, rather than Isolde's, reflections so much weight: Isolde's Monologue comes at a point in the story when much is still not known. She does not even know whether her passion is reciprocated. By the time Tristan begins his reflections, all the elements of the story are already in place; he even knows how it will, or at any rate should, end.

The Monologue (see appendix 5: act 3, part 1) is shaped into two similarly organized series, each consisting of three main sections separated by more conventional recitative-dialogue interludes. Each main section is a monologue except for the first section of the first series, which is almost entirely orchestral (the first section of the second series expands on this, combining a monologue with an orchestral development). The main sections in both series correspond. The first ones are related in the manner of an exposition and a development of one theme; the middle monologues in both series are quiet and contemplative in character; and the final monologues are fiery and frantic.

The functions of the four interludes are obvious. For the most part they come back to the normal recitative-dialogue discourse, providing points of articulation that help to shape the long scene; two of them (the second and fourth) help to change Tristan's mood between individual sections of his Monologue; they give Kurwenal, Tristan's servant and listener, something to say and do and thus justify his presence onstage through much of the scene (he leaves only at the beginning of the last monologue—the only one where Tristan is alone onstage); and last but not least they give the tenor periods of respite within what must count among the most gruesomely exhausting hours for any operatic singer. Except for the last one, all interludes are dominated by Kurwenal, and the third one is in effect Kurwenal's brief recitative monologue.

The three main sections of each series are, naturally, more interesting. The first one (III.1–163) is almost entirely instrumental, with the orchestra continuing to provide the main melodic substance even when the voices (the Shepherd's, Kurwenal's, Tristan's) begin to get superimposed over it (from III.97 on). Two kinds of music are heard here. First there is the music coming from the pit (its main motivic content exposed in III.1–15), unheard by the characters onstage. It performs the usual operatic functions of providing external and internal ambience as well as the more specifically Wagnerian leitmotivic function of giving a musical embodiment to some of the ideas later expressed in the dialogue. Thus, III.1–6 get associated later in the dialogue (III.101–9) with the deep sleep (or, rather, coma) into which Tristan—who had allowed himself to be wounded by Marke's courtier, Melot, and was brought over the sea by Kurwenal to his ancestral Breton castle—has fallen; the chain of infinitely ascending dyads in III.7–10 will represent (III.114–19) the empty waste of the sea ("Desolate and empty the sea!")[52] between Brittany and Cornwall, desolate, because the eagerly awaited ship that would bring the only person capable of healing Tristan's wound, Isolde, is nowhere to be seen; and the tenderly expressive III.11–15 will be linked (III.109–13) with the thought of the awaited healer. But gripping and vivid as these gestures may be, they are just a foil to the second kind of music—more striking still, and in the long run more important. More striking because this music is played onstage, presumably piped by the Shepherd (whose melody is exposed in full in III.52–93 and partly echoed in III.145–60), and hence heard by the characters—even by Tristan, whom it awakens and who recognizes "the old tune."[53] This music is thus itself a dramatic event. Its full significance will be unfolded only in the corresponding first section of the second series, where it provides the main subject of the orchestral development.

But before it can be unfolded, Tristan has to begin his self-searching meditation and push it deep enough, to the level where the significance of the old tune lies buried. Tristan's monologues, even more than those of Marke and Isolde, explore and retell the past so that the present might be rendered less obscure. The first one (III.277–440) starts with the immediate past, with a laborious recollection of the realm he had inhabited in his coma, a realm that cannot really be captured in words and positively described. All that Tristan is able to do is to say what it is not: there is no sun there, nor land, nor people—nothing. But he knows it to be the realm in which he was born and where he will go when he dies ("where I had ever been, where I for ever go"),[54] the "wide realm of the universal night"[55]—the Night the lovers had invoked at the beginning of their Love Duet, and the orchestra makes sure that the association is not missed (III.310–14). It is above all the realm of "divinely eternal, primordial oblivion"—the cessation of memory and consciousness.[56] In short, it is no-being, nothingness. What brought him back from this realm of Night into the light of Day, Tristan says further, was the recollection of his love for Isolde. He wants "in her alone to expire, to disappear."[57] The aim of the union celebrated in the Duet, after all, was not a solitary death, but a *Liebestod à deux*, with and in each other. But there is a price to pay for this return: he is now again delivered to the suffering of desire in the separating light of Day. Appropriately, the first monologue culminates in the evocation of the "accursed day, with your apparent glow," supported by a powerful double statement of the Day motive in the orchestra.[58]

What is clear thus far is that the escape from the separating illusions of Day into the unifying truth of Night remains Tristan's goal, but a goal he cannot accomplish in Isolde's absence, since they need to escape together. Without her, the Night will have nothing to unify him with. Understandably, then, in the dialogue of the interlude (III.441–516), when Kurwenal informs him that he had already sent for Isolde and that she is about to arrive, Tristan's mood changes from the despondency and exhaustion of his first monologue to the exaltation of the second one (III.516–625). This monologue culminates and ends (III.611–25) with Tristan's feverish vision, or mirage, of Isolde's approaching ship, accompanied, in a bold imaginative metaphor, by the orchestra's motivic and tonal evocation of the accented appoggiaturas that surrounded the beginning of Brangäne's Warning (II.1210–27) with the atmosphere of the gently breathing night in whose womb the united lovers hid. It is that night's breath that fills the sails of the ship Tristan sees now with his mind's eye— the real infinity of the separating empty sea is transfigured by the imagined infinity of the unifying Night.

In reality, however, "das Meer" remains "öd' und leer." The Shepherd's "alte Weise" is heard again and Kurwenal confirms its outward significance: "There is as yet no ship to be seen!"⁵⁹ The return of the "old tune" with which the scene had begun initiates its second series and Tristan's third monologue (III.626–840). Both musically and verbally this is the center of gravity of the whole scene, and, for Nietzsche's "genuine musicians," of the whole work ("the actual *opus metaphysicum* of all art," as Nietzsche called this opera).⁶⁰ (At more than eleven minutes in performance, it is also the longest of the five monologues.) Its musical rank and reputation is due to the developmental richness of the orchestral discourse. With only the slightest of exaggerations one might claim that the orchestral part played alone, without the voice, would make a credible continuous symphonic development.

Most of this development is based on the "alte Weise." Other motives come and go, but the "old tune" is the subject of, initially at least, almost uninterrupted obsessive scrutiny. At first, the Shepherd's piping (English horn onstage) is heard directly, though from early on (from III.656) its motives begin to insinuate themselves into the orchestra, precisely—Wagner is precise about such things—when the tune becomes less what Tristan actually hears and more what he remembers from early childhood: "It [the tune] anxiously broke through the evening wind, when once it announced to the child the death of his father."⁶¹ (One is reminded of how subtly, early in act 2, Wagner conveys the difference between what everyone onstage can actually hear—the calls of distant hunting horns—and what Isolde chooses to hear instead—the rustling of leaves and murmurs of a stream—simply by moving the music from the onstage horns to the strings; see II.112–85.)⁶² After III.718 the orchestra takes it over entirely. Until III.727 the music remains in the tune's key of f minor (the accented and obsessively repeated plangent flat second its most prominent feature, accounting for what Tristan refers to as its "plaintive tone,"⁶³ its peculiar mélange of anxiety and yearning)⁶⁴ and, except for a fleeting appearance of the "yearning" ("Sehnen") motive (III.708–9) when the subject crosses Tristan's mind, it completely dominates the orchestral discourse. Only when Tristan starts (from III.727 on) to recall the events that led to his present predicament, beginning with his first fateful encounter with Isolde when wounded by Morold, does the participation of other motives of recollection become richer and the discourse get modulatory, returning to the f minor tonic only at the end of the monologue (in III.840). But even then, throughout this second, motivically and tonally more complex half of the monologue, the "old tune" is the one subject to which the orchestral discourse keeps coming back.

Kurwenal, we have heard, explained the outward significance of the tune: "There is as yet no ship to be seen!" Its more profound inner significance is the subject of Tristan's exploration in the monologue, which is why it is the main subject of the orchestral development, too. It is the principal function of the orchestra to reveal, and comment on, what is on the protagonist's mind. That the tune is "old" is essential. It awakens Tristan's earliest memories, it is his madeleine, and the exploration of the past, including its most deeply buried layers, is how one comes to understand oneself and one's predicament. Tristan's Monologue is a model psychoanalytic session, couch included, though Wagner's is psychoanalysis minus the pseudo-science. The Monologue's aim is to dramatize the process of self-reflection that makes Tristan aware of his wounded, incomplete condition, with its root in childhood trauma—the condition that makes him seek healing completeness in Isolde's arms. Not only did the tune once announce "to the child the death of his father," it was also heard when he became aware that his mother died in (his) childbirth. Then and now the tune gives rise to the question: "To what chosen fate was I then born?"[65] Then and now Tristan hears in it the answer: "The old tune tells me this again: to yearn—and to die!"[66]

Yet this answer does not go far enough; it is too generic. It describes the universal human condition of senseless and unappeasable desiring until death, not the particular predicament of this particular orphaned-at-birth individual. And so Tristan rejects it as soon as he pronounces it: "No! Oh, no! This is not its [the tune's] meaning!"[67] In his individual fate, he sees now, yearning and dying cannot be so neatly separated—first one, then the other. His fate is rather "to yearn in dying, not to die of yearning!"[68] In his case, death would not bring the appeasement of desire. Only the arrival of Isolde, only death in her presence and with her, would bring it: "The never dying, yearningly calls now to the distant physician for the peace of death."[69]

Thus at the end of the first half of the monologue (by III.727) Tristan has understood that his yearning, with its roots in the early loss of his parents, is a condition that death alone cannot heal. It can be healed only by Isolde, in Isolde's presence. He seems at this point no further along than he was at the end of the first monologue, but in fact he did make some progress: thanks to the old tune, he has brought his orphaned childhood into the picture. He needs, however, to probe deeper, and this is what he does in the second, developmental half of the monologue. He begins by recapitulating the crucial events in his and Isolde's story. Characteristically, only the internal events matter to him, just as only the internal events really mattered to Wagner. Morold, King Marke, and Melot are not even mentioned.

In Tristan's mind the story is reduced to two episodes only. First there was his fateful encounter with Isolde in Ireland. Mortally wounded, the tune's "yearning complaint" in his ears, he sailed to Ireland to seek her help.[70] There she indeed did close Morold's wound, but opened another—her own: "The wound, which she healingly closed, she reopened again with the sword."[71] Tristan's words confirm something we had suspected, but did not know for sure—that this encounter was as important, as "wounding," for him as we know it was for Isolde. It was then that they both fell in love, though they did not yet acknowledge it to one another. Noteworthy too is that in Tristan's mind his wounds are closely related, even one—namely, the real wound inflicted by Morold and the metaphorical wound inflicted by Isolde. To these we might add both the real wound inflicted most recently by

Melot's sword and the metaphorical one inflicted in earliest childhood by the death of his parents.

These are all signs of the wounded condition that from the start has marked his existence. Tristan is essentially someone existentially wounded, someone who yearns to be healed, to be made whole again. Tellingly, the old tune accompanies the chain of four wounds that runs through his life. At this point the tune is set free of its exclusive association with Tristan's early childhood losses and acquires a more general significance of a sign of his wounded condition. The ever-reopening real wounds inflicted by his enemies, and the even more painful metaphorical ones inflicted by the absent loved ones, his lost parents, and above all the distant Isolde, are all connected, and the plaintive tune expresses his yearning for the healing physician. It is here that the outer and inner meanings of the "alte Weise" get linked: the desolate empty waste of the sea that separates Tristan from Isolde is the outward sign of his inner desolation so long as he remains separated from the awaited healer. Without Isolde, Tristan is adrift on the sea of existence that is "öd' und leer."

The second episode that matters to Tristan is his next encounter with Isolde, the one on board the ship bringing them both to Cornwall. There, he recalls, she gave him the "poisoned potion," which he drank in the hope that it would heal him completely.[72] Instead the potion delivered him to a different fate: "that I should never die, but inherit eternal torment!"[73] The torment is that of yearning: "No healing, no sweet death can now ever set me free from the affliction of yearning."[74] This is of course the episode we witnessed in act 1, the one where love was mutually acknowledged. Wagner, and Tristan, separate the falling in love and the avowal into two distinct episodes because the mutual avowal raises the stakes—the defenselessness and vulnerability that love brings—to a new level. Until the avowal, Tristan had a realistic chance to be able to control the frightening power of love by the civilizing conventions of *fin'amor*. Until that moment, too, he could misunderstand his love as no more than one more wound, one more sign of his participation in the universal human condition of senseless longing to be terminated by death. With the avowal all the defenses are down and love takes over as the only power that matters. The exclusive desire now unleashed, the desire to bridge the gap between the subject and object can be set aside, or physically terminated, by death, but it can find its fulfillment and appeasement only in a part-physical, part-mystical *Liebestod* that would merge subject and object into one. In this sense it is stronger than simple death, which cannot be a solution to the problem it raises. A subject overpowered by the passion of love transfigures a finite object of his passion and the passion itself into something infinite. This is why he cannot expect death alone to bring a suitable and sufficient conclusion to his desire; this is why Tristan needs a love-death with Isolde. After the avowal, too, Tristan can no longer see himself as simply participating in the general human condition of senseless longing. His desire, rather, has acquired a specific individual object and goal, and more, he has become a specific individual subject with a specific individual life story.

Death, however, would have been sufficient before the avowal—sufficient to terminate the condition of senseless longing. This is why the lovers willingly drink the potion they both believe to be poisoned. In his recollection, Tristan confirms what we had reason to suspect already in act 1—that, just like Isolde, he was convinced that the potion Brangäne had prepared for them was one of death. The "oath of atonement"[75] he pronounced on drinking it ended with these words: "Eternal mourning is the only consolation: Good potion of forgetfulness, I drink you unflinchingly!"[76] It was the expectation of imminent death that made the mutual avowal possible. In the face of death—Tristan clearly, and Isolde probably, understood death to bring eternal forgetfulness, that is, the annihilation of the self—the vulnerability and defenselessness of the self stripped bare by love seemed irrelevant. The paradox of the potion is that the real potion the lovers drink, the love potion, has no efficacy whatsoever, is not the cause of anything. Tristan and Isolde had fallen in love long before, in Ireland. On the other hand, the potion they imagine they drink, the death potion, causes them to take the irreversible step of avowal, and thus to forfeit the "only consolation"—the eternal forgetfulness of death—that had been available to them until then.

Thus Brangäne need not feel guilty, as her deception is not the cause of the lovers' misery-cum-bliss. Tristan's next and final step in his monologue is to acknowledge precisely this point: "The fearful potion . . . I myself . . . , I brew it!"[77] He goes through the ingredients that went into the preparation: "I found the potion's poisons in father's distress and mother's woe, in everlasting tears of love, in laughing and crying, delights and wounds."[78] He admits that he enjoyed drinking it, curses the drink and himself: "The fearful drink I brew, . . . [and] enjoyed slurping with bliss—be accursed! Be accursed he that brew you!"[79] And then he faints.

Until this final step, Tristan was basically just repeating himself. Already by the end of the first half of the monologue he knew that he needed more than death, that he needed a *Liebestod* with Isolde. Now he also acknowledges that his predicament is no one's "fault" but his own: the falling in love may have been a matter of fate (or blind Cupid's arrow shot disguised as Isolde's sword), but the avowal and the subsequent transformation of love into the exclusive and overwhelming force trumping all else, everything finite, with its infinite claims, the way he chose to experience and live his love—for these only he himself is responsible. This is not just because the avowal was made as a result of his own free choice. It might be argued, after all, that he did not fully realize what its consequences would be. It is rather because the avowal and its consequences express who, at the deepest level, he is: a particular individual with these parents and that biography. The acknowledgment of his own responsibility for his own fate, which strictly speaking is the only real result of the self-analysis undertaken in the third monologue, may not seem like much (and in fact it isn't much), but it makes a difference—the difference between his (and our) ability to see Tristan as a hero rather than as a victim, a subject rather than an object. The whole point of the self-analysis is to allow Tristan to get reconciled with himself and thus get ready to die and turn himself into a story, a work of art—to be able to say, like Nietzsche, to his fate: "Thus I willed it."[80]

We should not take too seriously the curse with which the monologue ends. This is an expression of Tristan's physical and nervous exhaustion at that moment, not his final verdict on his existence. Were it the final verdict, there would be no point in his impatient awaiting of Isolde's arrival. And yet this is precisely what happens next. Everything that needed to be realized and said has been realized and said; Tristan's self-understanding is now as complete as it is ever going to get. All that remains for him to do at this point is wait. Accordingly, his first words as he regains consciousness are: "The ship? Don't you see it yet?"[81]

The fourth monologue (III.866–999) is framed by a preparatory recitative dialogue on one end (III.866–913) and a brief recitative on the other (III.963–99). At its center (III.914–63) stands a "very quiet and not dragging"[82] E major cantabile kept together by the same orchestral motive that gave unity to the recitative-dialogue interludes of the Love Duet (compare the beginning of the first interlude in II.1258–65). (There is little point in worrying about the exact extent of the fourth monologue: the sections that frame the center are transitional and might also be assigned to the preceding and following interludes; what matters is the cantabile at the center.) While in reality no ship can yet be seen, the monologue paints Tristan's anticipatory vision of Isolde coming to him across the sea: "Smiling, she brings me consolation and sweet rest, she gives me last comfort."[83] It will be recalled that in the conversation of the Love Duet interlude to which the orchestra now refers, the lovers discussed for the first time their desire for erotic extinction in common. Tristan's quiet vision of the approaching final bliss is linked to that earlier conversation and gives a concrete sense to the "consolation," "rest," and "comfort" he expects now.

The immediately following brief transitional recitative monologue (III.963–99) impatiently anticipates the last interlude (III.999–1208), as Tristan insists that what he so clearly sees, Kurwenal must see too: "You must see it!"[84] And indeed as the last interlude begins (III.999), the Shepherd's pipe is heard playing a different, merry tune—the signal that Isolde's ship has been spotted. Already earlier (from III.988 on) splinters from the Shepherd's new tune had been heard in the orchestra: Tristan "hears" it internally, just as he had internally "seen" the ship before they could actually be heard and seen. The interlude completes, then, the business of Isolde's arrival, as Kurwenal exits to help her ascend to the castle and Tristan's mood changes from the visionary quiet of the cantabile to the ecstatic frenzy of the "very lively"[85] last monologue (III.1209–95) followed by a postlude (III.1295–324). Tristan's diction now is a matter of exclamations rather than complete sentences, just as his music, famously, cannot settle on any one stable meter, moving irregularly back and forth between measures of two, three, four, and five beats. Since everything that needed to be said had already been said in the central (third) monologue, what matters at this point is not words but action—Tristan's last and long-anticipated deed of erotic suicide, as he tears off his wound's dressing to be able to bleed to death in Isolde's arms.

THE ORCHESTRAL STRAND

The two separate axes we have identified as the organizational principle of the opera—the lyrical and the narrative—are not the whole story. Intertwined with both, a third strand runs through Wagner's drama (table 23): a series of repetitions, with one exception (that of the Falling in Love episode), always at the original pitch, of all or some of the opening twenty-one measures of the orchestral Introduction to the first act.[86] Such long-range recalls of relatively long musical units are quite exceptional in opera and hence stand out from the surrounding normal discourse. Involving as they do not a single motive but rather extended musical discourses, they represent something qualitatively different from the mere recurrence of motives of reminiscence that is so central to Wagner's mature practice. The recapitulations shape the whole work, while the significance of motivic recurrences is local.

Strictly speaking, there is only one such repetition in each act, accompanying, respectively, the Avowal, Tristan's Answer, and Tristan's Death. The two additional episodes I have assimilated to this series, the Falling in Love in act 1 and Isolde's Death in act 3, are only tenuously related to these main repetitions—tenuously, but also significantly.

Only one of these repetitions does not intersect with either the lyrical or the narrative axes of the work (table 24). At the beginning of the final section of the first act (I.1754–97), the first twenty-one measures of the orchestral Introduction to the act are repeated almost literally, though with interpolations motivated by the dramatic action they accompany.

Apart from Isolde's opening toast ("I drink to you!")[87] and both lovers' disjointed exclamations at the end ("Tristan! Isolde! Faithless sweetheart!"),[88] the repeat is purely orchestral and accompanies a wordless pantomime described in detailed stage directions, the most important of which states: "In highest excitement, but motionless, both . . . look fixedly into each other's eyes in the expression of which the defiance of death soon yields to the glow of love."[89] This is the essential dramatic content of the pantomime and it is this content that is implicitly anticipated in the opening measures of the Introduction. The music captures the wordless and motionless moment when glances are exchanged as tokens of mutual recognition and avowal of love—the main event of act 1 (indeed, its only event, remembering that the action that truly matters in this drama is purely internal)

TABLE 23 *Tristan und Isolde*, The Orchestral Strand

Form	Key	Text incipit	Measures	CD.track.time
Introduction	a		I.1–21	I.1.0:00–2:12
Falling in Love		er sah mir in die Augen	I.666–78 [= I.16–21]	I.7.0:30–1:37
Avowal of Love	a	Ich trink' sie dir!	I.1754–97 [= I.1–21]	II.3.1:15–4.2:04
Tristan's Answer	a	O König, das kann ich dir nicht sagen	II.1891–913 [= I.1–17]	III.7.0:00–1:47
Tristan's Death	a		III.1301–24 [= I.1–20]	IV.7.2:18–3:50
Isolde's Death and Transfiguration	B		III.1695–99 [complete and resolve I.2–3]	IV.11.6:15–7:07

The open-form but non-dialogical sections are in bold italics.

and its emotional high point. Precisely because the essential action of the opera is internal, its musical embodiment can on occasion (as here in act 1) be left to the orchestra alone. Long before Wagner, the orchestra had become opera's principal tool for disclosing the characters' interiority. Its function here is to communicate the lovers' fundamental experience—that of mutual desire (I.1–17 have been commonly identified by the compilers of leitmotivic dictionaries as expressive of the lovers' desire or yearning), avowed and sealed by the encounter of glances (I.18–21 commonly identified by the exegetes as expressive of the glance).[90]

It is this experience that is communicated also in the remaining repetitions of the opening measures of the Introduction, all of which intersect with either the lyrical or the narrative axes. Three are attached, one each, to the three Monologues. Thus the second of the main repetitions, that in act 2, occurs at the point of transition between Marke's Monologue and the Promise Duet (II.1891–913). To King Marke's reproachful demand to disclose the "inexplicably deep mysterious cause"[91] of his disgraceful act, Tristan can only answer, "O King, ... what you would know, that you can never learn,"[92] after which he turns to Isolde. The transition (II.1891–913) is set as an orchestral recapitulation of the music of desire from the opening of the introduction (I.1–17) in the original key of a, with Tristan's answer superimposed. Thus it is the orchestra that discloses what the king can never experience, the deep and mysterious cause of the desire that again turns the lovers toward one another and separates them from the intervening world of Day.

The main repetition in act 3 is also attached to a monologue—it closes the scene of Tristan's delirium and composes his death. Accompanying the lovers' final embrace, the postlude to Tristan's Monologue returns to the music with which the opera began, that is to say, also the music that accompanied the pantomime of their first embrace in act 1 (III.1301–24 of Tristan's Death recapitulate I.1–20 of the Introduction and I.1754–96 of the Avowal). This last section of Tristan's Monologue is no longer self-reflective (all the self-reflection that was needed has already

TABLE 24 *Tristan und Isolde*, Act 1, Avowal of Love

Form	Measures	CD.track.time
REFRAIN	1754–56 [= I.1–2]	II.3.1:15–1:21
Interpolation	1756–57	II.3.1:21–1:24
REFRAIN	1758–60 [= I.2–3]	II.3.1:24–1:37
Interpolation	1761–70	II.3.1:37–2:26
REFRAIN	1771–74 [= I.4–7]	II.3.2:26–2:47
Interpolation	1775–83	II.4.0:00–0:30
REFRAIN	1784–97 [= I.8–21]	II.4.0:30–2:04

been accomplished). Rather, it presents another crucial episode in the internal action of the drama.

The remaining two repetitions are much more partial but no less significant. The first of these, also attached to a monologue, occurs near the end of the first section of Isolde's narration as she recalls the crucial moment of their falling in love (I.658–88). Shortest and least literal, the return at the Falling in Love breaks with the patterns of the other returns. It does not pick up the music of the Introduction from its beginning, and it moves what it does pick up to a new key. This is fitting, since it is the only one of these episodes that is narrated rather than enacted; it returns as if refracted through Isolde's memory. This clearly is not yet the moment of mutual recognition and avowal of love. Rather, it is a rehearsal for what is to come—the Avowal scene later in the act. Not only dramatically, but also musically, this is the most expressively intense and important moment in the act between the Introduction and the Avowal, and it mediates between these two. The music of the Introduction that will return in the Avowal scene now accompanies Isolde's narration of Tristan's gaze and its effect on her (I.666–78, with an echo when the gaze is mentioned once more at the end, in I.685–86). Specifically, I.666–78 are derived from I.16–21—that is, the music of the glance (I.18–21; the glance music begins in the second half of I.17) introduced by the last measure and a half of the preceding desire music.

The final return, the ending of Isolde's Transfiguration, is the shortest of all, but, placed at the very end of the opera, it is no less important or conspicuous than the others—quite the contrary. It is the one that brings the only full tonic resolution to the chord first heard at the beginning of the Introduction (III.1695–99 complete and resolve I.2–3) and brings it, moreover, at a whole tone higher than what we were led to expect throughout the opera. Thus it simultaneously appeases and transfigures the desire that drove the lovers throughout the internal action of the drama, leaving us in no doubt that a Transfiguration has indeed occurred, that the lovers have passed to a new ontological level, different from the one on which they had operated until now. In other words: the placement of the chord at the same pitch level as on its previous appearances underscores its identity with its predecessors as the symbol of the lovers' yearning; the resolution of the chord to the tonic for the first and only time serves to assure us that the yearning has finally been appeased; and its resolution in a new key tells us that what has occurred is no mere consummation of the erotic act, but its transfiguration—whatever this means, and we should not pretend at this stage that we know what it means.

Thus the desire that is the essential expressive content of the orchestral strand weaves its way through the opera and reaches its conclusion only in these final measures, with the final cadence acting like a clasp that brings the beginning and ending of the drama together. Wagner himself was of course fully aware that they do belong together. Cosima Wagner reports (February 5, 1873) that her husband "said that this Prelude [Introduction to *Tristan*], together with the postlude [presumably the Transfiguration], express the whole will in its longing and resolution (the modulation to E major); no escape from the longings of individuality except in death!"[93] (The reference to E rather than B major is probably a slip on Cosima's part—an understandable one, given the prominence of the subdominant E/e, instead of the Introduction's dominant E^7, in the last measures of the Transfiguration, from III.1681 on.) Ten years earlier, on February 26, 1863, to be exact, in St. Petersburg, the composer inaugurated the tradition of orchestral performances of the Introduction and Transfiguration as a single continuous whole (that is, I.1–111 immediately followed by III.1621–99), his preferred form for the presentation of the Introduction in concerts.[94] The idea is first mentioned in a letter of October 5, 1862. There and in other early documents of the practice, the first component of the whole is referred to as "Liebestod," and the second as "Verklärung."[95] It was probably for this performance that Wagner prepared a short program note, which he subsequently used also for other early performances. About the Prelude he wrote: "From the most timid complaint of the unappeasable longing, from the most delicate shaking to the terrifying eruption of the avowal of hopeless love, the feeling traverses all the phases of the struggle without a victory against the inner fervor until, powerlessly falling back onto itself, it seems as if going out in death." And the following was his comment on the closing piece: "But what fate separated for life, revives now transfigured in death: the gate of unification is opened. Over Tristan's body, the dying Isolde is granted the most blessed fulfillment of ardent yearning: eternal unification in measureless spaces, without limits, without bounds, inseparable!"[96] It is evident that the composer considered the Introduction with Transfiguration to offer an orchestral epitome of the opera—and rightly so.

THE MUSIC-DRAMATIC FORM

I summarize our results thus far in table 25, where the components of the lyrical axis are marked in bold, those of the narrative one in bold italics, and those of the

TABLE 25 *Tristan und Isolde*, The Music–Dramatic Form

Form	Key	Measures	CD.track.time
Introduction with	a	I.1–111	I.1
REFRAIN		I.1–21	I.1.0:00–2:12
Isolde's Monologue with		I.602–862	I.6.0:00–8.2:25
REFRAIN (Falling in Love)		I.666–78	I.7.0:30–1:37
REFRAIN (Avowal of Love)	a	I.1754–97	II.3.1:15–4.2:04
Love Duet	A-flat/B	II.1117–631	II.12–III.3
Marke's Monologue with		II.1689–890	III.5–6
REFRAIN (Tristan's Answer)	a	II.1891–913	III.7.0:00–1:47
Duet Postlude	A-flat	II.1914–97	III.7.1:53–7:39
Tristan's Monologue with		III.1–1324	III.9–IV.7
REFRAIN (Tristan's Death)	a	III.1301–24	IV.7.2:18–3:50
Transfiguration with	A-flat /B	III.1621–99	IV.11
REFRAIN (Isolde's Death)	B	III.1695–99	IV.11.6:15–7:07

The sections of closed-form music are in bold; the open-form but non-dialogical sections are in bold italics; the refrain is in bold capital letters.

orchestral strand in bold all-capital letters (appendix 5 shows how these components fit into the overall music-dramatic plan of the opera).

The form of Wagner's music drama involves two independent parallel axes: the lyrical, consisting of the Love Duet with its delayed postlude and Isolde's Transfiguration; and the narrative, consisting of Isolde's, Marke's, and Tristan's Monologues. Intertwined with both axes there runs through the opera a third, orchestral, strand, periodically recapitulating all or some of the initial twenty-one measures of the Introduction and accompanying the episodes of Falling in Love, Avowal of Love, Tristan's Answer to Marke, Tristan's Death, and Isolde's Death. The musical form serves dramaturgical purposes. It emphasizes certain portions of the story at the expense of others, and it shows how various portions are related to one another. Thus it clarifies both the shape and the meaning of the drama.

The lyrical axis articulates musically the central dramatic event of the story, the lovers' interrupted but eventually completed *Liebestod*. The single-minded, radical pursuit of the logic of love to its final consequences, in full knowledge that the aim of obliterating the distance between subject and object has to result in oblivion and death, is what the internal action of this drama is all about: "no escape from the longings of individuality except in death!"

The lyrical axis tells us that at the center of the story stands the love's consummation in a transfiguring death. It is in the Love Duet where the most fundamental tenets of the lovers' self-understanding get articulated, where they decide on a course of action that follows from these tenets, and where they put their decision into practice. Their outlook, we recall, is based on the opposition between the phenomenal realm of Day—a realm of consciousness, of separation between subject and object that necessarily breeds unappeasable desire—and the noumenal realm of Night—that of oblivion, where the separation between subject and object is cancelled and hence the desire born of separation appeased. Aiming at the cancellation of all separation between subject and object and the appeasement of all desire, the radically single-minded lovers necessarily want to leave the world of Day behind and merge together into the Night, to commit an erotic double suicide of a *Liebestod*, which is to say (in the language of Day) to die in common, or (in the language of Night) to reach a complete and permanent union: "We would die so as to live only for love—unseparated, for ever endlessly united . . . !" And they reach their goal when, at the end, "Isolde gently sinks, as if transfigured, . . . upon Tristan's body" (as the stage direction has it),[97] transfigured perhaps, but also unmistakably dead, as is made clear in the plural in the stage direction, "Marke blesses the bodies,"[98] Isolde's final words ecstatically pointing toward the desired drowning of conscious individuality in the undifferentiated metaphysical totality: "in the blowing all of the world-breath, to drown, to be absorbed, unconscious, highest joy!"

The narrative axis, in turn, allows the protagonists to articulate their subjective understandings of the story. In particular it allows Tristan to come to see himself not as a passive, dumb victim of blind fate, but as someone who actively chose his fate—a man existentially wounded by the loss of his parents in early childhood and yearning for a healing wholeness in Isolde's arms. Tristan's remarkably perspicacious self-analysis is conducted at such length and with verbal and motivic-developmental resources of such richness that his Monologue becomes the alternative center of gravity of the whole music drama—its pole of reflection on par with the pole of action in the Love Duet–Transfiguration.

Moreover, Tristan stresses that solitary death will not do. The goal is an at once physical and metaphysical *Liebestod à deux*, with and in each other. This is because the lovers are subject not only to the universal human condition of senseless and unappeasable desiring (which can be terminated by solitary death), but also to the very individual condition of being in love with this particular person and no other—a condition that transfigures a finite object of desire and the desire itself into something infinite and hence aims at transcending the human finitude. Accordingly their condition is no mere life, but rather love, and hence it cannot issue in mere death, but has to seek *Liebestod*.

The orchestral strand, finally, plays a more complex role in the articulation of the drama. On most of its appearances it obviously accompanies all the remaining important dramatic events: the recollected moment of falling in love, the actually enacted moment of the mutual avowal of love, as well as the individual deaths of the lovers. Tristan's Answer to Marke is its only appearance not obviously connected with an important event. On reflection, however, one realizes that Tristan's decisive and final turning away from the world of Day at this point, and—what is crucially important here—a turning away not in secret but in the presence of the Day's most central representative, is clearly an indispensable event, too. If it were not so long and cumbersome, one might be tempted to label this event not simply Tristan's Answer, but Tristan's Public Repudiation of Day.

The repetitions of the orchestral strand remind us of the experiential content of the lovers' mutual yearning that links all of these episodes—both the experience of desire in general (which is the content of I.1–17) and the experience of desire focused on this particular partner fixed with the glance (which is the content of I.18–21). The dramatic aim of the strand, then, is to articulate all of the important events of the story save the central one and to make palpable the experience that links them all. Running through the piece from beginning to end and connected on most of its appearances with elements of the other two axes, the strand powerfully unifies the whole and in particular brings together the beginning and ending—the beginning and ending of the desire that is the subject of the drama, the desire that can conclude only in a transfigured form—but also the beginning and ending of the music drama itself.

By comparison with the Love Duet and Transfiguration, the remaining five events of the story, the Falling in Love, Avowal, Public Repudiation of Day, and the protagonists' respective Deaths, are subordinated and almost mute. They do not add anything essential to our understanding of the protagonists' outlook and goals. Accordingly, all five are almost entirely silent: Tristan's Answer is verbally a non-answer, with the actual answer made by the orchestra; only glances, but no words, are exchanged at the Falling in Love as narrated by Isolde; the Avowal is again a matter of exchanged glances plus, this time, an embrace, with hardly a word spoken; Tristan's Death involves an embrace and the protagonist's collapse, but not much in the way of a dialogue; and, similarly, Isolde's Death involves her collapsing on Tristan's body after all the words have been pronounced. In all these cases it is the orchestra that does most of the talking, accompanying Isolde's narration and the lovers' pantomimes with the music from the opening of the Introduction, the language of glances and desire.

But the orchestra's final peroration, though brief, is singularly eloquent and indispensable, as without it we could not be sure how this story ended. The first and last appearances of the Tristan chord provide the whole with an instrumental frame that begins with the symbol of endless desire (the dissonant chord resolves by means of chromatic polyphony to another, only slightly less dissonant dominant chord and no further—this is its essential point) and ends with the symbol of desire finally appeased and transfigured (as the chord gets at last a fully consonant subdominant-colored tonic resolution a whole tone higher than expected). Both of these features of the ending need to be kept firmly in mind. The music assures us that the story ends with the lovers and their desire at once appeased (rather than merely terminated by death) and transfigured to a different ontological plane (rather than provided with a merely terrestrial erotic consummation).

Who speaks through the orchestra? Whose voice does the orchestra represent? This is a question related to, but not identical with, the one asked on a number of occasions by Carl Dahlhaus, namely: Who expresses himself through the leitmotifs?[99] Leitmotifs, Dahlhaus argued, sometimes embody the memories, conscious or not, of the singing character. At other times, however, they represent the narrative voice, for Dahlhaus identical with the voice of the author (and I agree that it would be needless pedantry to distinguish the author from the narrator in the music drama), who speaks directly to the audience about the characters and their dramatic situations. This might seem right at first, except that one soon realizes that the situations when a leitmotif has to be attributed to the narrator-author are quite rare in the *Ring* and even rarer in the remaining music dramas. For the most part, the orchestra, although remarkably eloquent and motivically rich, functions in late Wagner similarly to how it long functioned in earlier opera: rather than opening up a new, separate subjectivity, it provides the audience with direct access to the speaking character's interiority. The leitmotifs tell us what is on the character's mind, whether or not the character is fully conscious of what it is, just as an agitated accompaniment to a traditional operatic aria tells us that the personage is, well, agitated. It is of course true that, where in the traditional opera the orchestra usually tells us only of the character's mental state, his or her mood or emotion, Wagnerian leitmotifs extend this narrow range of reference considerably to include also the thought of such entities as specific persons, objects, and even fairly abstract notions that cross the character's mind. But for the most part the Wagnerian orchestra does not speak in the name of a separate subjectivity. Rather, it simply amplifies our insight into the subjectivity of the presently acting and speaking character—just as the traditional operatic orchestra does.

On rare but crucially significant occasions, however, a true narrative-authorial voice does seem to emerge in the orchestra. This may happen when the orchestra stops speaking in isolated motives and begins to provide a longer, continuous discourse, a discourse that makes musical sense independently of the vocal lines even when these are present. It is at such moments that we become aware of the emergence of a voice that seems to emanate from a subjectivity independent of the characters onstage. The length and in particular the continuity of the independent orchestral discourse, I am suggesting, makes the crucial difference. This is probably at least in part because continuity is the essential attribute of human consciousness. It is characteristic of us that we are aware not only of what is happening in the present moment, but also of how this present is connected with the remembered past and anticipated future. Melody, which can be comprehended only when its continuity is grasped in terms of the constantly shifting interplay of the experienced present with the remembered past and anticipated future, has frequently served philosophers—from Saint Augustine through Schopenhauer to Edmund Husserl and Martin Heidegger—as the key example of how consciousness works.[100] Once an independent orchestral melody acquires a certain length and degree of continuity, it becomes less and less plausible that what we hear is the voice of the character's subconscious or nonverbalized consciousness, and more and more tempting to attribute the orchestra's discourse to a new subjectivity, that of the narrator-author, speaking independently of the characters.

In *Tristan* it is this voice of the narrator-author that seems to articulate what I have identified as the opera's orchestral strand—from the Introduction, through the several episodes when some or all of the initial twenty-one measures of the Introduction are repeated (perhaps the Falling in Love, certainly the Avowal, Tristan's Answer, and Tristan's Death), all the way to the final measures of the opera (Isolde's Death). But is it really the voice of the narrator-author we hear in those episodes? We may have jumped to this conclusion too hastily.

Consider the situation obtaining in the second cabaletta of the Love Duet and in the Transfiguration. In the Duet's main cabaletta, the orchestra consistently doubles the voices and gradually emerges as the carrier of the main melodic line to which the voices provide counterpoints. In the Transfiguration, the orchestra carries the main melodic line throughout, with Isolde's voice sometimes doubling it and at other times providing a subordinated counterpoint. The suggestion in both the cabaletta and the Transfiguration is of the voices carried along by the orchestral stream, swimming in it and eventually drowning—of linguistically articulate rational subjects gradually submerged and overpowered by something nonverbal and irrational.

There is no good reason, however, to attribute this something to another human subject, to a narrator. Rather, the orchestra seems to speak for something quite different than a rational, articulate individual, something that overwhelms all individuality, rationality, and language. In the cabaletta this something is clearly the mounting power of erotic desire. In the Transfiguration it seems to be something related, but more general—the metaphysical ground of all being, the Will itself, the All, or the Nothing. It will be remembered that, for Schopenhauer, erotic desire is the most obvious of the phenomenal objectifications of the noumenal will: "The sexual impulse is the kernel of the will-to-live, and consequently the concentration of all willing," he says. And he repeats: "The sexual impulse is therefore the most complete manifestation of the will-to-live."[101] In the cabaletta the will appears in its erotic disguise; in the Transfiguration it speaks directly. It does not seem necessary to think that we are told about these rising sub- or supra-verbal powers by a narrator or author who speaks above the heads of the characters. Rather it seems more natural to fall on traditional operatic habits and think that in these cases the orchestra provides us, as usual though at unusual length, with insight into what goes on in the characters' minds but what they leave unspoken, perhaps because it cannot be captured in words, or because they are not fully conscious of what it is.

We may think similarly of the episodes of the orchestral strand. Also there it is not necessary to posit a new, authorial or narrative, speaking voice; also there one may hear the orchestra as expressing the endless longing for transcendence felt by the characters onstage. The only exception is the Introduction itself, since at this point there are as yet no characters onstage. But this exception is irrelevant to our discussion. After all, Dahlhaus's idea that the music drama introduces the voice of the narrator concerns the role of the orchestra after the curtain has been raised, not before. Initially the idea seemed attractive, not the least because a narrator would fit a dramatic genre that leans so heavily toward the epic. On reflection, however, it turns out to be unnecessary and unconvincing. Wagner's orchestra is given music of greater motivic and melodic substance than is usual in opera, but its dramatic role, with rare exceptions, is not unusual.

THE MYTH OF WILL

One advantage of the kind of music-dramatic analysis we have just completed is that it allows us to identify the interpretative problems at the center of the work. A story of love's consummation in a transfiguring death raises two obvious questions: Is death as inevitable a result of love, as this opera suggests? And what exactly is the sense of the "transfiguration" at the end, meaning, how does it differ from death *tout court*? The first of these questions is answered within the opera. The second is not and hence is more challenging. The final orchestral cadence assures us that the "transfiguration" hinted at in the accompanying stage direction does indeed take place, but it does not explain what the precise content of that transfiguration might be. By leaving us without a clear answer, Wagner forces us to come up with something on our own.

The two questions are related and troubling, and they go to the heart of the unease with which the work leaves us. No matter how highly we value Wagner's artistic (musical and dramatic) achievement in *Tristan und Isolde* (and it would not be easy to overestimate that), it is hard not to entertain some doubts about the ultimate significance of the work. After a performance of any of Wagner's music dramas, one leaves the theater exhausted and full of highest admiration, but also with a more or less distinct undertone of resistance. A serious consideration of a music drama should account for both the admiration and the resistance, and indeed, from Nietzsche on, the most interesting Wagner critics have attempted to account for both.

In *Tristan*'s case, the source of the resistance is easy to identify, although it is surprising how rarely it is explicitly acknowledged, perhaps precisely because it is so obvious: the protagonists of this story are in love with death. Death is not something they accept as a necessary evil, a high price worth paying for their ecstasy.

Rather it is a good worth longing for in its own right, the desired outcome and fulfillment of their passion. Mindful of the Fascist cult of death and of its roots in Romanticism, mindful of how the wish to escape the terrestrial reality that is the essence of Romanticism fed the Fascist wish to invent a new aestheticized politics-beyond-everyday-politics, we cannot be wholly indifferent to the veritable orgy of necrophilia unleashed in *Tristan* even if we remember, as we should, that the opera is concerned exclusively with the private sphere.[102] The orgasmic "screaming-with-joy haste"[103] with which Tristan tears the dressing from his wound and greets the free flow of his blood ("Ahoy, my blood! Flow now cheerfully!")[104] just before he dies leaves even the unsqueamish disturbed and ill at ease.

To be sure, it is not simply death the two lovers seek: they wish to die together, in each other's arms. The easiest way to assuage our doubts about the opera's infatuation with death would be to see death in *Tristan* as nothing more than a time-honored metaphor of erotic fulfillment and to see the opera as a whole as a dramatization of a particularly drawn-out and satisfying sexual encounter. But the temptation should be resisted. It is not that death in *Tristan* does not function as a stand-in for erotic fulfillment—it does, of course. But to reduce the issue to no more than that would be to trivialize it beyond recognition. It is not difficult to see where the trivialization lies in this case: it consists in the depriving of sex of its metaphysical dimension, a dimension that evidently mattered a great deal to Wagner.

To recapitulate: the intertwining of love and death is the central issue this opera raises. To understand *Tristan* is to understand this intertwining. And while death does stand for erotic fulfillment, it cannot be wholly reduced to it. We need to go deeper.

Wagner himself spelled out his intention for what he hoped to achieve in *Tristan und Isolde* with unusual clarity. It was "to erect a ... monument to this most beautiful of all dreams"—that is, the "true happiness of love" that he has never known in real life—"a monument in which this love will be properly sated from beginning to end," as he wrote to Franz Liszt on December 16 [?], 1854—that is, after he first conceived the work in the fall of 1854, but long before he began the prose draft (August 1857) or composition (October of the same year).[105] "Dream" is the key word here. Erotic love, whose monument the opera was to become, was not love as it exists among us humans, which even at its best is transient, intermittent, and shot through with disappointments and compromises exacted from it by our finitude and by the social world, the world of Day, that we cannot completely escape. It was not love as it is, but as it should be, purified of all accidental imperfections, love as an ideal in the world of Night, a "dream." The aim of the opera was to capture what was essential about love. (An examination of love in the light of Day, love suitable for the finite and social beings that we are, was to be undertaken in *Die Meistersinger.*)

As Tristan and Wagner both thought (there is no need to distinguish the two in this case), death clearly belongs to the essence of love. It is its proper goal, its consummation, and this for reasons spelled out in the opera. Erotic love begins with two distinct, separate persons, each reciprocally the subject and object of a desire to become one with the other, to cancel the separation. Hence it is bound to end—if pursued radically enough to its logical conclusion, and if successful—with precisely this: the annulment of the distinction between subject and object, a merger and disappearance of the two separate persons. Thus death is the appropriate name for the ultimate destination of erotic desire. More positively, one might also talk of a complete and permanent union of two individuals, without forgetting, however, that the death of the individuals is what such a union implies.

This seems to be the strongest case one can make in defense of the intertwining of love and death in the opera. But death remains death, even when it is dressed up in fancy philosophical vocabulary. From the standpoint of Day, Frau Minne (the tutelary goddess of love) is to be feared and avoided, or at least civilized, but surely not worshipped unconditionally—unless one can give some concrete positive sense to the final "transfiguration," unless, that is, one can show that the lovers not only die but are also "transfigured," and can explain what the value of such a transfiguration might be.

In other words, to be transfigured is to be raised to a different, higher, ontological plane, to transcend existence as it is here and now, and erotic desire is precisely a desire of transcendence. The separation of subject and object, the subject's lack of immediate access to the object, is what defines human finitude. To overcome the separation of subject and object is to go beyond the limitations of the human condition, to leave behind the finitude of Day for the infinity of Night. No less than Plato in the *Symposium*, Wagner understood that eros drives us to transcend our limits, to reach beyond the confines of self and nature, to raise ourselves from our transient and conditioned state toward the permanent and unconditioned realm beyond—in short, that erotic love is the closest approximation we have of the mystical experience of immediacy. It is on purpose that I invoke the *Symposium* here. On April 9, 1870, Cosima noted in her *Diary*: "R. places this work [the *Symposium*] above everything else: ' . . . what would the world know of redeeming beauty without Plato?'" She further quoted Wagner as saying: "'I, too, thought today of *Tristan* and the *Symposium*. In *Tristan* it is also Eros who holds sway, and what in the one is philosophy is music in the other.'"[106]

Ultimately it is this Platonic view of eros as driving us to transcendence that lies behind the intertwining of love and death and that needs to be confronted in any interpretation of *Tristan und Isolde*. The desire for transcendence, if satisfied, has to end in self-annihilation. What is its point, then? Does it have a point? Or is it rather—as Nietzsche and his numerous successors, John Dewey and Martin Heidegger, Richard Rorty and Jacques Derrida, urged in their various idioms—

merely a self-destructive temptation to be avoided at all costs, a siren song that accompanied European philosophical and religious tradition for a few millennia, bringing us nothing but grief, a song we should finally stop listening to and leave behind?

A quick clarification: even if we answered this last question in the affirmative, this would not count against Wagner's opera. Wagner can be, and has been, accused of many sins, but moralism is not one of them, at least not in this opera. His aim in *Tristan und Isolde* was surely not to teach us how we should live, but, as he suggested, to erect a monument to a particularly glorious and terrifying divinity, and this aim he did accomplish, brilliantly. Success in cases like this one is measured by the truthfulness and depth of the portrayal, and Wagner's picture of love is both true and probing. Eros, on his account, inspires and deserves worship as a giver of ecstatic bliss; equally he inspires and deserves fear as a bringer of most terrible suffering and destruction. When Isolde apostrophizes Frau Minne in a brief aria at the end of the first scene of act 2 (II.370–471), what she finds important about this "administrator of the world's becoming"[107] is that "life and death, which she weaves out of bliss and sorrow, are subordinated to her."[108]

But in any case it is not clear that our question will be answered in the affirmative. The simplest, and only preliminary, answer might take a clue from Isolde's words: Frau Minne dispenses both bliss and sorrow, brings ecstasy that takes us beyond our narrow everyday limits as well as suffering and annihilation. Each one of us will have to calculate the benefits and risks individually, but Isolde's and Tristan's heroic choice to worship at Frau Minne's altar (assuming that one has a choice in such matters) might be taken to be the less craven, more admirable, one.

An answer of this sort, however, while an acceptable first step and correct as far as it goes, is insufficient; it does not go to the heart of the matter. For both Plato and Wagner, more was at stake in the erotic drive to transcendence than the decision whether to take life-threatening risks for the sake of life-transforming ecstatic experiences. The question raised, at least implicitly, by them both is, rather, whether or not the pursuit of transcendence is the pursuit of a chimera that brings us nothing worthwhile, a bargain whereby we stop paying attention to the only existence we have in order to chase an empty dream.

In a certain sense of the term, transcendence is something we could not avoid even if we wanted to. We may, and should, be wary of Platonic, or Christian, or Kantian dualisms, of the splitting of reality into two distinct levels, the realms of appearance and truth, of human earthly temporal mutability and divine heavenly eternal permanence, of the phenomenal and noumenal—the former invariably mediated and contingent, the latter available immediately if at all and unconditional, the rock-bottom foundation of all there is. Much intellectual effort of the modern era (Baruch Spinoza, Georg Wilhelm Friedrich Hegel, Nietzsche and the pragmatic tradition he inaugurated) has gone into the overcoming of such dualisms, into providing a monist vision of reality. But even the most hard-nosed monists, convinced that the realm of appearance is all there is (and hence that calling it "appearance" does not make much sense), cannot avoid going beyond the world immediately at hand. Unlike most other earthly creatures, humans do not live in the present moment alone. In addition to experiencing the world in the present, they also recollect it in the past and anticipate it in the future. Even a most rigorous monist could not limit him- or herself to the present only; our world is necessarily split between the actually experienced present and the imagined past and future. It is in this modest sense that transcendence, going beyond the actually experienced present, is something inevitable. Since, to use a Hegelian idiom, we humans must supplement dumb nature with the self-conscious spirit, we cannot but confront the actual with the imagined.

But normally, when we talk of transcendence, we have in mind something stronger than that, something that requires a full-blown dualist worldview. The transcendent realm in this stronger sense is the realm not only beyond here and now, but one representing a completely distinct ontological level. In this sense it is not so much the realm of personal imagination, remembrance, and expectation as it is one of abiding truth beyond changeable appearances, the unconditional foundation of everything.

Both kinds of transcendence have a similar point: their job is to provide a standard against which the actual can be evaluated. This is obviously the case with the strong transcendence. The value of items in the realm of appearances, or in the earthly city, is measured by their proximity to or distance from their models in the realm of ideas, or in the heavenly city. But it is also the case with the weaker form of transcendence. Our ability to imagine the future is particularly relevant here. It implies that we have available to us not only the world as it is and was, but also the world as it might or should be. We do not just confront the actual with the imagined; we confront what is with what should be. Moreover we evaluate and judge what is in the light of what should be. This is how real things, persons, and events acquire sense and value for us. "Transcendence" in the most general sense is the name for our best and most comprehensive vision of what should be and how it relates to what is. If the pursuit of transcendence is to have any value for us, if it is to be more than a pursuit of a chimera, it is here that we should look for this value.

What then is the content of the transcendence our lovers pursue and attain at the Transfiguration?

It would be hard not to notice that the protagonists speak the dualist language. We have seen that their fundamental outlook is articulated in terms of the opposition between Day and Night, between the surface realm of illusion and the deep realm of truth. The world of Day is the normal world they share with all of their contemporaries, the social world of separate individuals relating to one another through a system of traditional feudal rights and obligations (the "custom" [*Sitte*] that is the initial subject of Isolde's and Tristan's conversation when they finally face one another in act 1). The world of Night is one whose very existence is not suspected by most of their fellows, even by such socially exalted personages as King Marke, not to mention Kurwenal or the Shepherd. When Marke inquires after the deepest causes of his nephew's actions, Tristan tells him: " O King, . . . what you would know, that you can never learn."[109] And Kurwenal tells the Shepherd when the latter asks what is wrong with their lord: "Do not ask, since you can never know [or, learn],"[110] but it is doubtful that Kurwenal himself knows much more. The world of Night is the world beyond, preceding and succeeding all individuality, and hence one in which traditional rights and obligations are irrelevant. Most importantly, Day is where consciousness reigns and hence where subject and object, the I and the multiple phenomena of the world, are separate; thus it is also where unappeasable desire can arise. Night is where oblivion reigns, and hence where the separation between subject and object is cancelled, where the very multiplicity of phenomena turns out to be illusory. Thus it is also where the desire born of separation can be appeased.

The Schopenhauerian origin of this outlook is obvious, well documented, much discussed, and undeniable. ("It was no doubt in part the earnest frame of mind produced by Schopenhauer, now demanding some rapturous expression of its fundamental traits, which gave me the idea for a *Tristan und Isolde*," Wagner recalled in *My Life*.[111] Significantly, as soon as the poem of *Tristan und Isolde* became available in print, Wagner asked the publisher to send a copy to Schopenhauer, among others.[112] The philosopher did not react.)[113] Equally obvious is the composer's one signal departure from the philosopher: making eros into the royal road to transcendence and oblivion must have struck Schopenhauer as bizarre, as the philosopher preferred to think that sexual desire should be renounced, not intensified and sublimated. Wagner's letter of December 1, 1858, to Mathilde Wesendonck makes clear that he was fully aware of his departure at this point from the philosopher: "During recent weeks I have been slowly rereading friend Schopenhauer's principal work, and this time it has inspired me, quite extraordinarily, to expand and—in certain details—even to correct his system. . . . It is a question . . . of pointing out the path to salvation . . . which involves the total pacification of the will through love . . . engendered on the basis of sexual love, i.e., the attraction between man and woman. . . . In love there lies the possibility of raising oneself above the individual impulse of the will to a point where total mastery over the latter is achieved."[114] But precisely because the outlook of the protagonists (and of Wagner, at this point) is in essence Schopenhauerian, its ostensibly dualist structure may not matter all that much. (It is not even clear that Schopenhauer himself should be considered a dualist: he rather talks as if the realm of representation and that of will are two different perspectives on the same worldly reality. The world is representation when it appears to us; in itself it is will.) The realm of Night as the protagonists conceive it, like the realm of Schopenhauer's will, is certainly neither the domain ruled by God, nor even one ruled by reason. For Isolde of the Transfiguration it is "the blowing all of the world-breath" in which she asks "to drown, to be absorbed, unconscious"—the realm where all consciousness ceases. For Tristan in his first monologue it is the domain of "divinely eternal, primordial oblivion"—again the realm where all consciousness ceases, the kingdom of no-being, of nothingness, from whence one emerges at birth and with which one will merge again when one dies.

However, whether all or nothing, it is clear that Night cannot provide us with a standard for evaluating the actual, that it offers no models against which the multiple items in the realm of Day could be measured. The world of Tristan and Isolde is closer to that of Schopenhauer and Charles Darwin than to that of Jean-Jacques Rousseau, Immanuel Kant, and Hegel, let alone to the world of Saint Paul, Saint Augustine, or Martin Luther. Neither God nor an autonomous, self-legislating Reason underwrites the meaningfulness of the opera's universe—in fact, it is hard to see this universe as intrinsically meaningful at all. The vision of fulfillment the lovers aim at has obviously nothing in common with the moderns' desire to live within bounds drawn by their own autonomously self-legislating Reason, but neither has it anything in common with the Christian desire to be reconciled and united with the loving Creator. Human existence, as they see it, comes from nowhere and goes nowhere. Since neither God nor Reason will be found there, not even the most intimate acquaintance with Night will tell us anything about what "should be."

But if this is the case, can Tristan's desire to go back to the realm of Night and Isolde's wish to follow him there be at all justified? Enthusiasm for death can be justified only when death is the door through which one escapes a deficient reality to enter a better world, or when it offers the only available respite from a wholly insufferable existence. These conditions do not seem to obtain here. Tristan and Isolde are not (nor are we) led to believe that in their final Night they will be vouchsafed a beatific vision of one sort or another. All they and we can expect is eternal unconsciousness and oblivion, and one can imagine a fate much worse than Isolde's at King Marke's court, even if, "unloved," she must "see the most glorious man always nearby."[115]

Briefly put: eros drives our lovers to transcendence, makes them leave the finitude of Daily existence and enter the infinite Night, but the Night offers them nothing. Unless one is able to take Schopenhauer's thoroughgoing pessimism seriously, unless one truly believes that nothing is better than something, one's doubts about the ultimate significance of Wagner's work seem to be confirmed at this point. The opera appears to be no more than yet another Romantic glorification of the nihilistic death wish—entrancing and sublime, to be sure, but all the more pernicious for its sublimity.

And yet both the protagonists and we experience the ending of *Tristan und Isolde* as a success, not a failure. Now *they* may be mistaken about this—they may take a failure for a success—but we cannot be. Wagner's resolution of the *Tristan* chord at the end is calculated, we have seen, to make sure that we understand the ending not as a mere cessation but as a triumph, that we believe in the final transfiguration. Is this sense of final triumph simply a lie, a mendacious consolation proffered by skillfully deployed cadential resources of tonal harmony?

One might argue at this point that this, after all, is a story of a couple that in the end triumphs rather than fails. In the second cantabile of the Love Duet the lovers solemnly undertake to "die so as to live only for love—... for ever endlessly united" and, while unable to fulfill this oath then and there, they do fulfill it in the end. In this one crucial respect Wagner and his protagonists part company with Schopenhauer. The lovers' trajectory does not aim at resignation—they want their love perfectly and completely fulfilled, not abandoned. And what is more, they succeed: their project ends in triumph, not failure. Here Wagner's heroes might be seen to anticipate early Nietzsche, accepting Schopenhauer's premises (the world is at bottom nothing but pointless striving that produces incessant oscillation between the torments of desire and the boredom of satiety), but rejecting his conclusions (that the wise will opt for resignation as the only sensible attitude to existence).

To this argument a skeptic will respond: yes, they do manage to die at the end, but surely not to "die so as to live ... for ever endlessly united." The realm they enter at the end, the realm of Night, is where all individuality and all consciousness ceases. This is not the kind of place in which the idea of living forever endlessly united, in the posthumous manner of, say, Paolo and Francesca, makes any sense. The dissolution of all particularity in the Night's solvent makes nonsense of any notion of unity of particulars. If Tristan and Isolde think they triumph at the end, they are deluded.

There is only one way that we can take our unmistakable final sense of triumphant success rather than tragic failure seriously, in spite of the natural skepticism aroused by the fact that what we see as the curtain goes down contradicts what the orchestra is telling us. What we see are two dead bodies on top of one another instead of the apotheosis that opera since Claudio Monteverdi's *L'Orfeo* (1607) has accustomed us to expect, that Isolde imagines, and that the orchestra confirms. From now on, after the opera's ending, we can tell ourselves, Tristan and Isolde will "live only for love—... for ever endlessly united" in our memory, in cultural memory, transfigured (not for nothing did Wagner call the final tableau a Transfiguration and directed that we see Isolde "as if transfigured") into protagonists of an endlessly repeated myth of a love that trumped all competing considerations. The complaint that they will not literally live so, permanently and perfectly united, will be seen to lose much of its force once we reflect that finite beings like ourselves cannot really know or imagine what it would mean for such a union to be literally permanent and perfect. We can see such things only through a glass, darkly, if at all. Nevertheless the complaint is well taken: for the lovers themselves, their project ends in failure. But not for us. Tristan's and Isolde's permanent and perfect union as uniquely single-minded lovers in a myth that our culture endlessly recycles, not least in Wagner's own telling, is the only form of such a union we can truly imagine and understand.

And this is also the only way one can make sense of the protagonists' eagerness for death. Their dying together is the prerequisite for their transformation into figures of myth. As long as they live, their story is not completed and hence not ready to be told. More importantly, perhaps, as long as they live they are subject to the usual earthly contingencies and accidents that stand in the way of any permanent and perfect union and may at any moment spoil their story: aging, disease, the unexpected withdrawal of the passionate tide in which they drown now—the list is endless. As long as they live, their story cannot be "a monument in which this love will be properly sated from beginning to end."

Without the aesthetic transfiguration of their lives into a story, their existence would have to be considered a tragic mistake and failure. With that aesthetic transfiguration it still remains a failure for them, but not for us. The transfiguration leaves them empty-handed: the content of the transcendence they attain turns out to be nothing (or, what amounts to the same thing, all). But it does not leave us empty-handed. We are left with "a monument to this most beautiful of all dreams," a vision of love at its most radical and uncompromising and hence necessarily tragic. The lovers' transfiguration into a myth does take place, and although it is of no use to them, it is of use to us. They may be under the impression that they sacrifice themselves on the altar of love, but in fact, they sacrifice themselves on the altar of art.

POSTSCRIPT

1.

In a classic essay of 1956, Joseph Kerman argued that *Tristan und Isolde* is not a tragedy but a religious drama.[116] In recent years this claim has been reiterated by Michael Tanner and given a book-length treatment by Roger Scruton.[117] The argument is obviously relevant to the interpretation presented above and so, in closing, I would like to return to Kerman's original argument and to Scruton's development of it and offer a critique of both of them.

It has been often observed that the "action" of *Tristan und Isolde* ("Handlung" is how Wagner, paradoxically, specified the genre of the work)[118] is internal rather than external. What matters in this drama is not so much what the characters do to one another as what they experience—feel, desire, believe—while doing things. Cosima reports her husband's comment on the opera (September 15, 1873): "'In my other works the motives serve the action; in this, one might say that the action arises out of the motives."[119] Now, the internal experience of the protagonists, Kerman claims, is religious in character: it is the experience of conversion. The conversion is from a normal, everyday, commonplace outlook on life, an outlook one shares with one's community, to the view that passionate erotic love is "the compelling higher reality of our spiritual universe," and hence that its value trumps the value of anything else we might otherwise esteem.[120] It is a commitment to (in Francis Fergusson's words, which Kerman invokes with approval) "passion as the one reality."[121] The *Handlung* of this opera, one might say, involves the conversion from the world of action to one of passion. As a result of this conversion, the action that to an agnostic might seem to issue in a tragic catastrophe issues instead in what the protagonists experience as a triumph, "a state of illumination which transcends yearning and pain."[122]

To be precise, according to Kerman the conversion we actually witness onstage is Tristan's and it takes place in the so-called Tristan's Delirium scene—the long monologue, or series of monologues, that constitutes the first part of the last act. We do not witness Isolde's conversion, but can infer that it did take place from the so-called *Liebestod*, her peroration that concludes the opera. These are, for Kerman, the main events of the opera, whose "fundamental rhythm" is punctuated by "Tristan's conversion and the concluding 'Liebestod' of Isolde."[123] Both events take place in "the last act . . . [which] is concerned specifically with the conversion of Tristan . . . , and with a reflection of this conversion in Isolde's 'Liebestod.'"[124] At the climactic moment of the conversion, "suddenly there is a flood of revelation—that fearful drink: he himself was the one responsible . . . and the curse, the purgation, of his own guilt."[125] As a result of this revelation, "Tristan finds in death no longer oblivion, but triumph."[126] "Isolde's concluding 'Liebestod,'" in turn, "achieves the intense, ecstatic concentration on and identification with the ultimate reality of Passion, sharing Tristan's experience from a more inspired standpoint."[127]

Even if one is not completely persuaded by it, one can see the point of Kerman's fundamental claim that Wagner's *Handlung* is not a tragedy but a religious drama. If a drama necessarily involves a conflict, the tragic conflict is one between values, or systems of values, that cannot possibly be reconciled and harmonized with one another. Consequently a tragedy ends in failure, typically in death: at least one of the heroes, committed to one set of values, is defeated and destroyed. Moreover, not only the audience, but the protagonist him- or herself understands their ending as a defeat. A comedy, by contrast, succeeds in harmonizing the conflicting values and reconciling the protagonists. It ends in triumph, typically in marriage. *Tristan und Isolde* does not comfortably fit either of these schemata, although it borrows some features of both.

We have seen that two value systems do collide in the opera and that they carry the names, respectively, of Day and Night—roughly, the values of the feudal court and those of the erotic love, or, if you will, the values of the lovers' society and those of their antisocial passion. As in a tragedy, the protagonists do die at the end, their values unreconciled with and—here and now at least—defeated by those of the world. On his wife's testimony (May 10, 1882), Wagner himself considered his opera a tragedy for this very reason, because in it erotic love is defeated: "*Tristan* is the greatest of tragedies, R. says, for here Nature is thwarted in its finest work."[128] An almost identical note from May 29, 1882, makes it clear that Nature's finest work is love.[129] Yet it would be hard to claim that they simply fail. They do fail from Marke's, or Day's, perspective. But otherwise their end is rather a triumph, perceived as such both by the protagonists (whose perspective is that of Night, or love) and by the audience (whose perspective is one of art). From both standpoints one understands that the lovers succeeded in what they had set out to accomplish: a complete, perfect, permanent union, not here and now but in the metaphysical realm of "the blowing all of the world-breath," or the imaginary realm of myth. Thus their story is a tragedy, but only for Marke. All the same, in spite of their success and happily-ever-after union, no one is likely to classify the opera as a comedy. The protagonists do die at the end, after all, and they remain unreconciled with the world. A comedic reconciliation and marriage should be played out in the same world in which the preceding conflict took place. The union to which Tristan and Isolde aspire, and which they eventually accomplish, is not of this world. This is one of the reasons why the term "religious drama" sounds plausible. The other reason is the one offered by Kerman: the drama centers on the experience of conversion.

Less persuasive is Kerman's claim that the conversion is Tristan's, taking place during his third-act Monologue, and that in her final Transfiguration Isolde merely identifies with this conversion, "sharing Tristan's experience from a more inspired standpoint." The conversion that is relevant here is the one from the values of Day to those of Night, and this takes place long before Tristan's Monologue and involves both protagonists equally: it takes place toward the end of act 1, in what I have called the Avowal scene, where both lovers take the irreversible step that will separate them from now on from their society. Surely by the time they embark on the Love Duet of act 2 with its invitation to the Night to descend upon them, the lovers had been long converted. (In Kerman's reading acts 1 and 2 are rather pointless; accordingly, he has to plead that the last act "is the greatest in every way.... The preliminaries are long, sometimes undramatic and tedious.")[130] Tristan's Monologue does not involve him in any change of values; rather, we have seen that it involves him in a self-analysis at the end of which he is able to take responsibility for his own predicament. What Kerman describes is not a conversion, but this sort of self-revelation.

Why this misstep? One can only guess. My impression is that it is the result of Kerman's wish to put together two independent convictions, both persuasive: first, his own intuition that *Tristan und Isolde* is a religious drama centering on the experience of conversion; and second, the traditional claim that can be traced back to Wagner himself to the effect that this is a new kind of opera, "opera as symphonic poem," and that the main locus of its claim to symphonic status is Tristan's Delirium. It is not surprising if the wish to place the moment of conversion at the climax of the orchestral development in the Delirium proved irresistible.

2.

Kerman's idea of the opera as a religious drama is crucially intertwined with his analysis of the music. In developing this idea further, Scruton has many sensible and sensitive things to say about the music, but his overall interpretation of the opera is largely independent of those things and would not be much different had he discussed the libretto alone. In summarizing this interpretation now, I shall translate it into an idiom that differs somewhat from that used by Scruton, without, I hope, doing too much violence to its spirit.

Scruton locates Wagner in close proximity to the anti-liberal moderns, within the intellectual family most prominently represented by Rousseau and his progeny through Karl Marx. Members of this family reject the classical Lockean liberalism that would allow individuals to pursue any desires they might wish to pursue, without limits, or rather subject only to minimal regulation designed to make sure that all individuals may be equally able to follow their individual visions of happiness. What is wrong with liberalism, such thinkers claim, is that it leaves individuals enslaved by endlessly multiplying and artificially stimulated desires (makes them into "consumers," as the contemptuous label of choice among thinkers of this sort today would have it), without any eternal, or at least relatively permanent, supra-individual standards, without any "sense of the ideal, without which human life is worthless."[131] At the same time, thinkers of this family are not simply reactionaries wishing to restore the premodern standards of the revealed religion, although, like Wagner, they may make use of traditional religious images and concepts, such as that of "redemption." (Thus, not being an orthodox Christian, Wagner "set out to discover a redemption that needs no God to accomplish it."[132] Our task, in turn, is "to understand what redemption could mean when detached from every promise of a life after death.")[133] Human dignity, for modern critics of liberalism, rests not on a submission to God's will but rather on our ability to set standards for ourselves, to be neither enslaved by myriad empirical desires nor by a God, but self-directed and autonomous. In embracing freedom and autonomy as the basis of human dignity, such thinkers are as modern as their liberal opponents. They represent an alternative, anti-liberal strand within modernity. Their task as they see it is to discover standards by which we might live in a worthwhile fashion, rules that impose limits on desire (and in this sense require "renunciation"—a key Wagnerian term), but, being self-legislated, also underwrite our claim to autonomy and hence to dignity (and in this sense bring us "redemption"—an even more central Wagnerian term).

To explain in what sense the love of Tristan and Isolde brings them redemption, Scruton needs to make explicit the theory of erotic love that underlies Wagner's creation. "Among German intellectuals of Wagner's generation, Kantianism had replaced Christianity as the background system of belief," he writes,[134] and it is clear that a version of Kantianism retains its validity for Scruton too and provides the background for his own thinking about erotic love and about Wagner's opera. Even those who have left all religious belief behind are compelled to see themselves simultaneously and paradoxically as both *natural objects*, organisms bound by the same laws as the rest of nature, and as entities different from the rest of nature because capable of making choices free of all external determination and of rationally justifying these choices with reference to self-established rules, that is, as *autonomous subjects*, persons. Accordingly, while we share with other animals a variety of instinctual needs, including the desire of sexual gratification, we also transform these drives into something distinctly human. Human erotic love in particular is distinct from the animal sexual drive that can be satisfied by a genital transaction with any partner of a suitable species, gender, and age. Rather, erotic love engages equally both the animal and the rational sides of the desiring subject and it is, similarly, directed at both the body and the soul of the desired object. That it concerns the bodies of the lover and the beloved is fairly obvious. If it does not, it is not erotic love (*eros*) but something else—charity (*agape*) perhaps, or friendship (*philia*). Less obvious, but no less true, is that it can be felt only by, and toward, a rational animal. It is, in essence, the desire of one particular freely choosing embodied self to possess totally and exclusively another particular freely choosing embodied self.

The possibility—nay, certainty—of disaster and tragedy shadows the erotic. The beloved may not reciprocate the lover's desire, and even when the desire is reciprocal, both selves are embodied and hence subject to inevitable decay and eventual demise. The exclusivity of the desire invites the torments of jealousy, and in any case the desire to possess another totally is impossible ever to satisfy fully. The desire itself, moreover, is not a choice. It is "a destiny"[135] or "an affliction,"[136] something we may hide from others, even from the beloved, but not from ourselves. It would seem a misfortune, a disease to be avoided as best we can, if it were not also frequently our most profound and exalting experience. (Thus Marcel Proust correctly calls love *le mal sacré*; it is a disease, but a sacred one.)[137] "The suffering of love," writes Scruton, "is also a vindication: a sign that the lovers have risen above the natural order and possessed themselves of the individuality and the freedom which justify the trouble of existence, and of which bereavement is the price."[138] In desiring a complete and exclusive possession of one another as free and irreplaceable embodied persons, the lovers expose themselves to inevitable sufferings, but they also defy and rise above their merely natural lot and prove that they are not entirely of this world. Certainly they remain as vulnerable and mortal as any animal, but they also transcend this vulnerability and mortality by proving to themselves, as Tristan and Isolde do, that "for him, as for her, the love that united them was supremely important—more important than death."[139] Thus they "remake as a choice what begins as a bodily compulsion."[140] Scruton concludes: "This is, for me, the ultimate proof of my freedom, that I can make an offering of myself to another."[141]

And so the experience of erotic love brings us with a particular clarity face to face with the sacred, the sacred that we encounter whenever we realize that our freedom, reason, and self-consciousness make of us beings not wholly of this world: "The sacred derives from and elaborates a day-to-day revelation: the sudden glimpse of the free and transcendental being in the most ordinary things of this world."[142] The "redemption" consists in reestablishing the sense of the sacred: "When writing of the 'redemption' achieved by his lovers, Wagner is using this term in its true religious sense, to mean a regaining of the sacred."[143] "By scorning death for the sake of a goal that only free beings can embrace or conceive, the act of sacrifice sanctifies the one who performs it."[144] The redemption consists in "a recognition that freedom really does exist in this world and that we too possess it."[145]

Much of what Scruton says about Wagner's opera is both profound and plausible. Much of it, however, also stimulates disagreement. To begin with, Scruton is obviously right to think that for Tristan and Isolde love matters infinitely more than death, but I do not see much evidence in Wagner's opera for the claim that his lovers wish to die in order to affirm their transcendental freedom, and I see plenty of evidence that they wish to die because the dissolution of the self is what an existence driven exclusively by erotic love must ultimately aim at: the desire of two selves to possess one another completely, to abolish all separation between them, the abolition of selfhood itself. It is this logic of erotic love in its pure state that Wagner captures in *Tristan und Isolde*.

If one decides that in willingly embracing death Wagner's lovers demonstrate that they transcend their merely natural embodied finitude, one is likely to find the opera's vision consoling. Given the realities of human existence, its precariousness and the inevitable decay and demise we all face, we need all the consolation we can get and it is churlish on my part to deny such consolation to those who feel they get it here. But Wagner's self-confessed aim in writing the opera was nothing more than "to erect a monument to this most beautiful of all dreams." I doubt that he wanted also to derive consolation or hope from the contemplation of his monument, and indeed the vision of the human condition captured in the opera is hardly consoling or hopeful. Wagner's is not a picture of human beings who express their autonomy by making rational choices and thus are capable of raising themselves over the merely natural lot of other animals. Rather it is a vision of human beings in the grip of an instinctual power that descends on them like a bird of prey and drives them to extinction.

Moreover, even if Scruton were right to claim that in embracing death Wagner's lovers affirm their transcendental freedom, I could not follow him in deriving any consolation from this thought (and neither, I am afraid, could Kant). It is true, of course, that I never give more emphatic proof of my freedom than when I choose to die rather than sacrifice something I value even more highly than life. But what we choose to value more highly than life should be truly valuable, and we should be able to defend its value on rational grounds. Otherwise, the actions of any suicidal terrorist would serve equally well as those of Tristan, and would afford us similar encouragement. And it simply will not do to reach for the music when all other arguments fail: "Its [the music's] success is sufficient dramatic proof that love can be fulfilled in death, when death is chosen, and that this fulfillment is a genuine redemption."[146] Would you find this persuasive if the subject of the opera was not the erotic passion of two human beings for one another but the enthusiastic devotion of young Hitlerians for their Führer, provided the music were sufficiently ardent and compelling?

What is more, if my conviction that I am free is as inescapable as Scruton thinks it is, we hardly need proofs of this sort. What we need, as critics of classical liberalism tell us, are not death-defying proofs of our transcendental freedom, but publicly available and binding standards by which to live worthwhile lives, alone and with others, self-legislated limits on desire, the only "redemption" post-Christians can hope for. By the late 1850s Wagner had lost much of his earlier enthusiasm for this-worldly redemptive schemes of this sort. He did not send Tristan into the world to renew it (as he arguably did in the case of young Siegfried), and, indeed, Tristan left his immediate world in ruins and the larger world just as he found it. We should not blame Tristan and Isolde for not offering us any glimpse of redemption, whether in this or in another world. It is not redemption they sought, after all, but oblivion, dissolution into the *Welt-Atems wehendem All*. To claim that Tristan and Isolde are "redeemed"[147] in the end is to succumb to wishful thinking, to the very human need to be consoled.

Scruton is right when he affirms that Wagner's generation took as its point of departure the paradoxical double perspective on human beings as at the same time natural objects and autonomous subjects. But he is not sufficiently mindful of the decisive change of emphasis that affected the relation between these two components in the wake of the failed revolutions of 1848–49. The pre-1848 spirit was predominantly optimistic and hopeful, confident that, no matter how repressive the current political and social arrangements, we humans can, and perhaps eventually will, remake them to extend the realm of autonomy and rationality. By the mid-1850s much of this optimistic confidence was gone, to be replaced by a century's worth of multiplying social and political theories that emphasized not our rationality and autonomy but our utter dependence on natural and social forces we cannot hope ever to control. What began to matter more now than any transcendental freedom was animal instinct, race, *Blut und Boden*. Will to power rather than reason was to determine humanity's future, to the extent that it had any future worth bothering with. Schopenhauer replaced Hegel as the privileged reader of Kant.

Wagner participated in, and powerfully shaped, this changing climate of opinion; he was one of the prophets of the new iron age. It is hardly plausible to see in *Tristan und Isolde* a monument raised to human rationality and autonomy. On the contrary, the vision of the human condition here is one in which reason and autonomy count for very little. Even the ruthless radicalism with which the lovers embrace and pursue their passion to the exclusion of all else speaks to the new, harsher spirit. If the effect of Wagner's opera is consolatory, it is not because of what it says about the human lot, but because it says something important about it at all. It is a consolation, or vindication, of sorts for us to know that for all our misery, we are the only sort of beings who can create self-images and self-understandings, and thus distance ourselves to a certain extent from the immediacy of our misery. But this is a kind of consolation that any great work of art brings. Thus, again, the religion celebrated in *Tristan und Isolde* is surely not the religion of human rationality and autonomy. Rather, the protagonists celebrate the religion of love, and we who witness their self-immolation celebrate the religion of art.

4

Die Meistersinger von Nürnberg

Politics after Tristan

> More than anywhere else in the world, in Germany one was of the opinion that an artist carries a narrower social responsibility than other people, more, that he leads his own life so to say outside of the political, social, and economic orders, a life on the ground and under the skies of, precisely, the atemporal world of the arts, eternity, the cosmos, a realm of dreams, that is not subordinated even to any religious authority, only to a divinity intimated by the artist himself.
>
> CARL ZUCKMAYER, GEHEIMREPORT[1]

The optimistic Feuerbachian erotic utopia of *Der Ring des Nibelungen* has been undermined by the pessimistic Schopenhauerian metaphysics and erotics of *Tristan und Isolde*. *Die Meistersinger von Nürnberg* might be understood as an attempt to salvage the social-political optimism of the *Ring* without repudiating the implications of *Tristan*'s metaphysics. Indeed, the drama does seem to offer a way forward, beyond the impasse reached in *Tristan*. It might seem, too, that in this comedy Wagner abandons the radicalism of his earlier tragic dramas and tries on the mantle of the wise and moderate sage. The prospects of human happiness and flourishing are once again on the agenda and seem no longer to require a revolution as their prerequisite. In the end, however, the vision of the future offered in *Die Meistersinger*, while a genuine enrichment of that of the *Ring*, turns out to be no less radical and revolutionary.

ACT 1: THE KNIGHT'S FAILURE

The first act of *Die Meistersinger* is anchored by five major closed-form sections: the opening Chorale, David's Monologue with its cabaletta, Pogner's Aria, Walther's Admission Aria, and his closing Trial Song (table 26). Additional minor, closed forms—the Terzetto at the end of scene 1, the Ensembles of the Apprentices introducing David's Monologue and framing his cabaletta in scene 2, and

TABLE 26 *Die Meistersinger*, Act 1, Closed Forms

Form	Key	Text incipit	Measures	CD.track.time
Scene 1				
Chorale	C	Da zu dir der Heiland kam	222–85	I.2.0:00–3:14
[Terzetto]	C	Für euch Gut und Blut	545–65	I.4.3:07–4:07]
Scene 2				
[**Ensemble of the Apprentices**	D	Was der sich dünkt!	576–88	I.5.0:21–0:48]
David's Monologue	D	Aller End' ist doch David	619–862	I.5.2:02–8.1:15
[**Ensemble of the Apprentices**	G	Ja, lacht nur zu!	880–901	I.9.0:00–0:31]
David's Cabaletta	G		902–62	I.9.0:31–2:39
[**Ensemble of the Apprentices**	G	Das Blumenkränzlein aus Seiden fein	963–75	I.9.2:39–3:05]
Scene 3				
Pogner's Aria	F	Das schöne Fest, Johannistag	1167–265	I.12.0:00–4:27
Walther's Admission Aria	D	Am stillen Herd in Winterszeit	1478–590	I.15
[Kothner's Arietta]	C	'Ein' jedes Meistergesanges Bar'	1646–85	I.16.2:58–5:11]
Walther's Trial Song with **Ensemble Finale**	F	'Fanget an!' So rief der Lenz in den Wald	1699–2082	II.1.0:11–3.6:33

The sections of closed-form music are in bold; the open-form but non-dialogical sections are in bold italics.

Kothner's Arietta separating Walther's Trial Song from his Aria in scene 3—serve to shape individual scenes rather than the act as a whole.

Of the five closed-form sections, by far the largest and structurally most intricate is the last one, the Trial Song. Moreover, since the last section of the Song (I.2029–82) echoes both verbally and musically Walther's earlier Admission Aria, the whole second half of scene 3 (I.1427–2119), the half where Walther for the first time in the drama is the center of attention, constitutes an even larger formally articulated and closed unit (see appendix 6: act 1, scene 3, part 2). As a result, everything that precedes this final unit feels like mere preparation: the act's formal center of gravity is placed at its end, in the scene of Walther's Trial.

As usual with Wagner, the musical form fits a dramatic purpose. Everything before Walther's Trial merely provides background information that we and the protagonists need to understand its significance. What happens in act 1 happens in the Trial scene and can be summarized in one sentence: on the eve of Saint John's Day in mid-sixteenth-century Nuremberg, Walther von Stolzing, a young knight from Franconia newly arrived in the city, fails the trial and as a result is not admitted to the mostly middle-class guild of the mastersingers. (The trial is lost *de jure* but not *de facto*, since Walther wins over the only judge who really matters, but this we shall realize much later.) The prehistory of this event is laid out in the preceding scenes. There we learn (scene 1) that on the preceding day, Eva (the only daughter of a rich Nuremberg goldsmith and a mastersinger himself, Veit Pogner) and Walther fell in love at first sight, and that tomorrow Eva is to become the bride of the winner of a singing contest in which only mastersingers can participate, which means that Walther needs to try to join the guild in a hurry by taking part in the admission trial that is about to take place.

Joining the guild, however, is not a simple matter. David, an apprentice to the greatest of the mastersingers, the shoemaker Hans Sachs, explains in a lengthy monologue (scene 2) that an aspiring member must demonstrate that he has mastered all the rules governing the making of poems, the composition and singing of melodies, and the fitting of poems with melodies. To be admitted Walther would have to sing his own poem correctly fitted to his own melody in front of the masters and without breaking their rules. Singing by the rules is obligatory: the marker (who officially marks the candidates' efforts) allows only seven mistakes. Thus David explains the rules Walther must follow if he is to be admitted to the guild.

Pogner, in turn, in his Aria and the following dialogue explains the rules of the singing contest that will take place in front of the whole population of Nuremberg on the very next day, when the town celebrates the feast of Saint John (the first part of scene 3). Eva's hand and Pogner's wealth are the prize; the masters will again be the judges, but Eva will be free to refuse their choice, in which case she will have to remain single forever. The winner "must be a mastersinger: she should marry only him whom you would crown," as Pogner tells the mastersingers.[2] The first scene is there so that we understand why Walther has to become a mastersinger; the second, so that we know the hurdles he faces; and the first half of the third, so that we grasp the full extent of the catastrophe that his failing the trial would be for him and his beloved.

Of the three closed forms that precede the Trial scene, perhaps the most interesting is the shortest, first one (I.222–85). Taking place at the end of a service in Saint Catherine's church, the section that opens the act confronts the stage congregation chorus singing a chorale harmonized in Johann Sebastian Bach's style with the modern passionate love duet of solo instruments of the pit orchestra. The instruments intervene at first between the chorale's verses and eventually also during the singing, with the full orchestra providing a postlude to the chorale. It is a confrontation of a number of opposites at once: the stage versus the pit music, the vocal versus the instrumental, an old versus a modern style, the sacred versus the profane, the communal versus the individual. This is the series of oppositions that the drama will attempt to reconcile: it is the wisdom of tragedy that not all conflicts of values people live by can be harmonized; it is the wisdom of comedy that we should try to harmonize them anyway. *Die Meistersinger* is a comedy. The stage congregation sings a hymn addressed to Saint John the Baptist. This is a Christian community, one that would live by the "commandment of salvation,"[3] Jesus's commandments to love the Lord and to love one's neighbor. The pit orchestra expresses a different love, the erotic current running between Walther and Eva that animates their silent exchange of gestures and glances. Thus the music-dramatic form itself embodies one of the central issues this opera will raise, the question of whether it is possible to integrate a private erotic love within this sort of public world. In *Tristan und Isolde* this question receives an unambiguously negative answer; a possibility of reconciliation is not even considered. *Die Meistersinger* reopens the question, tries to see how the worlds of Night and Day, the realms of private passions and public obligations, might be brought together. The orchestra's peroration after the chorale (I.267–85) anticipates motives from Walther's Prize Song that will bring the drama its resolution (they reappear again in the Terzetto that provides scene 1 with closure) and thus suggests that the issues raised by this opening will resound through to the end.

Almost all of the second scene is taken by David's Monologue, with simple ensembles of the apprentices providing a frame for the whole scene and dividing the Monologue into two large parts, the slower "cantabile" (I.619–862) in D and the faster "cabaletta" (I.902–62) in G (see appendix 6: act 1, scene 2). Otherwise, the Monologue eschews any architectonic organization beyond brief interruptions by Walther and the apprentices that punctuate its considerable length at logically appropriate junctures.

As usual, the dramatic function of the Monologue is not to articulate any events (nothing happens, really), but to impart background information. This is introduced systematically, subject by subject, with pedantry worthy of a diligent apprentice. In part 1 of the cantabile David confronts Walther with the numerous rules of prosody a student of poetry must master and establishes a close parallel between "shoemaking and poetizing"—to his mind both equally crafts.[4] Walther's impatience ("God help me! Do I want to be a cobbler?")[5] is the first hint that he might want to aspire to a different, higher, conception of poetry. Part 2 is where the "art of singing,"[6] that is, of composing and singing melodies, is introduced, this too consisting of innumerable traditional figures and turns of phrase, "the masters' tones and tunes,"[7] and rules. In the coda, finally, in which Walther and the apprentices participate more equally with David, we learn that to be a "poet"[8] one needs to be able to join the words with the tones correctly. David concludes, "The poet who through his own effort joins a new melody made of tones to words and rhymes of his own invention will be recognized as 'mastersinger.'"[9] All that remains for the cabaletta is to introduce the dreaded figure of the marker,[10] who allows a candidate for a mastersinger only seven mistakes.

The third and last closed form before the Trial scene, Pogner's Aria at the center of the first half of scene 3, is more structured than David's Monologue but still exceedingly simple: ABA′ with a drastically abbreviated recapitulation (see appendix 6: act 1, scene 3, part 1.b, Pogner's Aria). Pogner, a mature and successful master, has a broader view of art than David, a mere apprentice anxiously wondering if he will ever pass the trial—though still far from broad enough to be likely to satisfy the aspirations of Walther, let alone Sachs. While David is obsessed by everything he needs to learn, Pogner shares with other members of the guild different worries. In Germany, burghers—their class—are generally looked down upon as stingy materialists interested only in money. No one remembers that we alone cultivate art, he tells his fellows. This is why he, Pogner, has decided to challenge this negative opinion by offering the impressive prize to the winner in tomorrow's contest (he does not realize that some might see in his gesture a confirmation rather than refutation of his class's materialism). Just as the relatively unstructured monologue has been replaced by a somewhat more shapely aria, the narrow concern with art's rules has been replaced here with the somewhat broader concern with art's social function, its ability to project a flattering class image.

But the chorale, monologue, and aria are just warm-up exercises. The one large and elaborately structured closed form of the act is the trial scene consisting of three parts: the culminating Trial Song—the act's longest and most elaborate form—which is preceded by the related and simpler Admission Aria, and separating the two Kothner's unassuming Arietta (for its overall plan, see appendix 6: act 1, scene 3, part 2). All three units have something in common: the two songs of Walther exhibit the same form, the rules of which are explained by Kothner, one of the mastersingers.

Kothner's recitation from the guild's rulebook, *Leges Tabulaturae*, full of mock-Baroque French-overture pomposity, each phrase ending with a mechanical flourish echoed by the orchestra, could not be more different from Walther's passionate effusions. Nevertheless it is precisely the rules underlying these effusions that the mastersinger pedantically spells out. The pedantry Wagner gently mocks here is obviously not only the masters', but also his own. Ostensibly Kothner enumerates the rules for the benefit of Walther, who is to follow them. But he, or rather Wagner, enumerates them in the first place for our benefit, so that we might understand how Walther's Admission Aria and Trial Song are constructed. Kothner articulates the one matter David left insufficiently explained, namely, how to put together a master song or "Bar." This must consist of several identically built stanzas, each formed of two "Stollen" sung to the same melody and an "Abgesang" sung to a different melody (in other words, poetically each stanza has the ABC form, while melodically it has the AAB form), every one of these units made of several rhyming verses.

Whether consciously or instinctively, Walther had already constructed precisely such a stanza in his preceding Admission Aria (see appendix 6: act 1, 3, part 2.1). Its three units are answers to Kothner's interrogation. The master with whom he did his apprenticeship, Walther claims in his first Stollen, was Walther von der Vogelweide, or rather "an old book"[11] of his (the good master himself died more than two hundred years ago), a book in which he could read of past and future springs in the middle of winter. The school where he studied singing, he goes on to explain in the second Stollen, was that of the wood birds when the summer returned. And he devotes the Abgesang to affirm that he is prepared to present now his own new master song that will show off what he has learned from the "book and grove."[12] While the masters and their apprentices are obsessed with rules, Walther learns by experiencing compelling examples of art and nature, the great poetry of the past and the enchanting world around him. He is a poet and a musician of a new kind, relying less on consciously learned craft and more on instinct and inspiration.

After Walther's second Stollen, Vogelgesang, one of the masters, remarks with approval: "He has stitched together two proper Stollen."[13] Here Wagner allows himself a joke to gladden a deconstructionist's heart. There is such a thing as stage (or "diegetic") poetry, just as there can be stage (or "diegetic") music, but Walther's Admission Aria is neither of those. It is an "aria" only for us, not for the characters onstage. For them, Walther simply answers Kothner's questions, speaking in prose. But for a Pirandellian moment Wagner allows the unwitting Vogelgesang to step out of his fictional world and stumble into ours, to notice what has been destined for our ears only.

Really to hear an aria, the characters onstage have to wait for Walther's Trial Song (the act ends as it has begun—with stage music). This too displays the form described by Kothner, but at much greater length and with additional internal articulation, so that, we now realize, Kothner's lesson was perhaps not superfluous. Whether or not it helps Walther, it surely helps us to understand what Walther is doing (see appendix 6: act 1, 3, part 2.2.c). Walther, namely, constructs his Stollen of two contrasting sections (marked A1 and A2 in the appendix). He does not break the rules, but creatively extends them. It is perhaps this extension, in addition to the similarly extended style and content of the poetry and melody, that confuses the already ill-disposed marker (the town clerk Sixtus Beckmesser, who happens also to be Walther's rival for Eva's hand), so much that by the end of the first part of the second Stollen he interrupts Walther's song. To be sure, Walther does pick up where he was interrupted and finishes the song later on, but not undisturbed: he has to sing the second part of the second Stollen as well as the Abgesang over the steadily increasing noise made by the quarrelling masters eventually joined by their apprentices. Hence his completion of the song is simultaneously an ensemble finale.

Walther has no patience for the rules; he relies instead on the inspiration of the moment. Unexpectedly and intriguingly, this is provided by Beckmesser. (By contrast, inspiration is not something Beckmesser can rely upon. His creative method later on in the drama will be to steal from Walther. The contrast is telling: Beckmesser "borrows" Walther's ideas only to spoil them, while Walther borrows Beckmesser's and transforms envy into love, ugliness into beauty.) Walther begins his song by repeating Beckmesser's signal, "Begin!"[14] and finding in it an impulse to paint in the first half of the first Stollen a picture of Spring awakening in the woods with the clamor of birds' voices. Also the second half of the Stollen is inspired by Beckmesser— this time by the scratching of the chalk with which he marks what he takes to be Walther's mistakes. Walther now paints a contrasting picture: the envious Winter, concealed in a thorny hedge (as Beckmesser is in his marker's booth), broods over the question of how he might confound the joyous singing. Undeterred by the scratching, Walther goes on then to develop an image of the first part of the first Stollen in the corresponding part of the second one and compares the awakening of Spring to the awakening of love in his breast, the love that inspires his song. The second part of the second Stollen is similarly a development of the corresponding part in the first Stollen: to confound this song, a screeching owl (Beckmesser) arouses from the thorny hedge a hoarse chorus of ravens (the remaining masters). In vain: Walther's Abgesang, rising above the noise made by the quarreling masters, unfolds the image of a wonderful bird soaring on golden wings and inviting him to fly away from "the urban tomb"[15] "to the native hill,"[16] "to the green meadow of birds [Vogelweid']"[17] of Master Walther [von der Vogelweide], where he would sing in praise of his beloved, undeterred by the crow-masters.

The thought of the "green hill" ("grüne Hügel") on which Wagner will build his festival theater in Bayreuth, away from the disagreeable, meddling politicians of urban centers such as Munich, is irresistible at this point. Walther is obviously a self-portrait of the artist as a young man, just as—we are about to learn—Sachs is a self-portrait of the mature master. But more important than any autobiographical allusions is the fundamental opposition the Trial Song embodies, the opposition between two conceptions of art. For Beckmesser and the masters, art rests on the bedrock of inherited artificial rules. An artist, in their premodern conception, is someone capable of ingenious manipulation of traditional formulas and materials. Walther's conception, by contrast, is modern. For him self-expression is paramount. What matters is the life-giving natural inspiration provided by the artist's own passion. If the opening scene of the act raised the question of how the private mutual erotic attraction of two individuals can be integrated with the larger public economy of rights and obligations in a Christian society, the act's closing scene raises the question of whether any reconciliation is possible between the two contrasting understandings of art. As the drama unfolds, it will also become increasingly clear that these two central questions are closely related, as both involve the opposing claims of tradition and innovation, the social and the individual. Together they are the central issue this opera dramatizes.

The Song embodies then the question of whether the two visions of art might be reconciled, and the dialogue that interrupts the Song spells out the relevant issues in a more discursive fashion. Beckmesser enumerates all the faults he has found in the Song: there were problems with meter and form, the meaning was unclear, the tune combined various traditional turns that did not go together. He concludes with accusations well familiar to Wagner himself: "There is no break, no coloratura, also not a trace of melody!"[18] All the masters agree, except for Sachs. He found the song "new, but not confused";[19] it followed its own rules, not the traditional ones. Here Beckmesser objects: Sachs opens the way "to bunglers"[20] who would do whatever pleases them. For Beckmesser, *tertium non datur*: there is either strict adherence to traditional rules or complete anarchy and the disappearance of all criteria of aesthetic judgment. He thinks in the aesthetic domain as Ivan Karamazov did in the ethical one when he claimed that "if there is no God, everything is permitted." Sachs, however, sees a third way: the criteria can be adhered to, abandoned, or renovated. (He also points out that it is inappropriate for a rival to serve as the marker.) This third way is the first inkling we get of the sort of reconciliation the comedy will eventually reach. At this point, however, any reconciliation is still a distant prospect. For now, Walther picks up his Song, encouraged to do so by Sachs, against the noisy objections of the remaining masters who in the end vote the candidate down.

ACT 2: THE CLERK'S FAILURE

The basic construction of the second act is strikingly similar to that of the first one (table 27). (One does not have to be Alfred Lorenz to recognize that the idea of the Bar form was much on Wagner's mind when he was shaping *Die Meistersinger*, as the contrasting last act will play the role of an Abgesang to the two Stollen acts preceding it.)[21] Also the second act concentrates most of its dramatic and formal energies in its final portion. Beckmesser's Serenade and the following Ensemble Finale belong together (the Finale is based on a cantus firmus derived from the Serenade) and constitute by far the largest and most elaborate closed form of the

TABLE 27 *Die Meistersinger*, Act 2, Closed Forms and the Refrain

Form	Key	Text incipit	Measures	CD.track.time
[Song of the Apprentices	G	Johannistag! Johannistag!	1–99	II.4.0:00–3:24]
[Pogner's Arietta	B-flat	Will einer Selt'nes wagen	141–98	II.5.0:37–3:56]
Sachs's [Elder] Monologue	[G]/F	Was duftet doch der Flieder	274–371	II.7
REFRAIN	B	Geliebter, spare den Zorn	773–810	II.10.3:59–12.0:05
Sachs's [Cobbler] Song	B-flat	Jerum! Jerum! Hallahallohe!	878–1023	II.14.0:00–15.0:26
REFRAIN	B	Welch toller Spuck!	1202–17	II.15.7:01–7:46
Beckmesser's Serenade with	G	Den Tag seh' ich erscheinen'	1217–357	II.16.0:00–17.1:16
Ensemble Finale and	G	Zum Teufel mit dir	1357–439	II.17.1:16–3:09
Coda = REFRAIN	E	He! Lene! Wo bist du?	1439–85	II.17.3:09–5:45

The sections of closed-form music are in bold; the open-form but non-dialogical sections are in bold italics; the refrain is in bold capital letters.

act, its formal point of gravity. At the same time this is also where the act's most important dramatic events take place. Both musically and dramatically, Beckmesser's Serenade and Ensemble Finale have obviously been made with the corresponding "numbers" of act 1 (Walther's Trial Song and Ensemble Finale) in mind, maximizing at once the similarity and the contrast between the two rivals for Eva's hand. All that precedes the Serenade is of lighter weight formally, and merely preparatory dramatically.

Beckmesser's Serenade is his Trial Song and, similar to Walther's, it fails in its aim and only manages to sow general discord. And just as Walther had managed to convince the only judge who matters, so Beckmesser fails with this very judge. The central event of the act can again be summarized in one sentence: early that night, between ten and eleven o'clock, Beckmesser attempts and fails to win Eva's heart with a serenade below her window (but he succeeds in putting most inhabitants of Nuremberg at each other's throats). The parallelisms and contrasts between the two contestants are striking and obvious. Both sing Trial Songs, are judged by Sachs, and cause communal strife, but unlike Beckmesser, Walther is able to persuade Sachs of his merits. The pain he gave the remaining masters will eventually prove to have been productive, pregnant with a future renewal of their tradition, while the strife generated by Beckmesser is, like his art, mechanical and sterile.

In addition, however, act 2 has a second central event, one without a parallel in act 1. This too takes place during the final section of the act, specifically during the Coda to the Serenade and Finale, and likewise can be easily summarized: at the same time, Eva's and Walther's desperate attempt to elope is thwarted by Sachs. This second event is also articulated by a music of structural importance for the organization of the act as a whole. The music of the Coda appears twice before in the act and thus forms a kind of a refrain that punctuates the act's second half. The two central dramatic events and the musics that articulate them are closely intertwined. The events take place simultaneously and involve each of the rivals misbehaving in his own fashion and being judged by Sachs, and they are linked musically in that the refrain serves at the same time as the coda to the last scene.

Of the closed forms that precede the Serenade, the most substantial ones are Sachs's Monologue and Song—indicative of his growing importance in the drama. He now emerges as this opera's main protagonist, the arbiter of all its conflicts, towering over both Walther and Beckmesser. The Song of the Apprentices that opens the act is merely a *couleur locale*–painting frame to some initial dialogue. And Pogner's Arietta is so attenuated that it is hardly there at all. It begins lyrically enough (II.141–52) and ends rather grandly (II.171–98), but its tone quickly begins to approximate recitative (II.153–58) and its very slender body consists mostly of recitative dialogue (II.159–70). The Arietta precipitates for a moment from the surrounding dialogue and merges back with it almost as soon as it is registered.

Sachs's substantial Monologue towers over it (see appendix 6: act 2, 1.c). Its main body (II.315–71, in F) is held together essentially by the orchestra developing a three-measure-long orchestral motive (II.315–17) derived from Walther's Trial Song (compare with I.1719–20)—appropriately so, since this song provides the subject of the shoemaker's meditation (and this is not the only motive from Walther's songs that goes through Sachs's mind). It follows an introduction in G based on the same motive, a modulating recitative transition, and a brief moment of orchestrally accompanied pantomime in F that anticipates the Cobbler Song yet to come and thus creates a link between Sachs's two important statements in the act.

Sachs needs to finish some work, but he has a hard time concentrating on it (the cobbling pantomime before the main body of the Monologue is short and somewhat desperate). He cannot get the memories of Walther's singing out of his mind. It was clear already in act 1 that his artistic horizon exceeds that of his fellow masters. But the encounter with Walther's art stretches this horizon further, forcing Sachs to reflect on the nature of what he has experienced earlier that day. He is now doing the job that the narrow-minded marker should have done, the job of the true critic who should remain faithful to his authentic experience: not smother it under familiar rules, but rather try to comprehend its novelty, originality, and uniqueness. It is an object lesson in how the modern art of self-expression should be experienced and reflected upon.

Sachs begins where a genuine critic should begin, with the admission that something mysteriously significant, incomprehensible but demanding comprehension, had happened: "I feel it and cannot understand it; I cannot retain it, yet also cannot forget it."[22] One would want to capture and give a measure of this experience, "but how would I measure what seemed to me immeasurable."[23] The known rules do not fit this novel case, and yet one senses that it is not lawless: "No rule would fit it, and yet there was no mistake there."[24] And then Sachs comes closer to capturing the essence of what happened: "It sounded so old, and yet was so new."[25] This is a formula we need to keep in mind, as it goes to the heart of the vision of art promoted and exemplified in *Die Meistersinger*, an art that is open to, and demands, innovation but remains rooted in tradition. Finally Sachs reflects also on the source from which such new creation springs: "The command of Spring, the sweet need, she placed it in his breast: now he sung as he had to; and as he had to, so he could."[26] The modern art of self-expression has its ultimate origin in the depth of the individual personality of the artist, in his nature, in life as he experiences it. It is this that the artist expresses and that the critic needs to experience and comprehend.

What this beautiful and profound meditation reveals is a character in the process of spreading his wings. This is when Sachs becomes interesting. Not only does he know more, see further, than his fellows, but he is still capable of growth under the pressure of new experiences. And the inchoate conclusion he reaches now is the first tentative outline of the aesthetic theory that will ultimately dominate the opera: a vision of art demanding innovation but rooted in tradition, capable of innovation *because* rooted in tradition, the sense that vital art is the result of an encounter between a living social practice in which a tradition is sedimented and a living experiencing individual, an individual whose experience demands expression and whose expression demands experiencing.

Sachs's second big statement in the act, his Cobbler Song, is a simpler affair, full of the humorous vigor of the shoemaker busy at work and doing well-intended mischief on the side. Formally a strophic song in B-flat, there are three stanzas with dialogue interruptions between them (and some dialogue in the background even while the song is going on) and a short dialogue postlude at the end (see appendix 6: act 2, 2.c).

Whereas the Monologue was all contemplation, the Song is all action. It is a piece of stage music, music heard as such by other characters, and very much a performative act. Since these other characters are Beckmesser in the foreground preparing to sing his Serenade below Eva's window, on the one hand, and Walther and Eva hiding in the background and preparing to elope, on the other, the very fact of performing the Song thwarts the plans of both parties. Beckmesser cannot sing while Sachs is making so much noise, and the lovers cannot escape while the two bickering masters block the way. Less obviously and significantly, the Song intertwines the act's two central events: the failed Serenade and the failed elopement. From now on the two will run simultaneously.

Sachs sings a good-natured complaint to Eva (Adam's Eve, that is), blaming her for causing the expulsion from Paradise and hence for making it necessary for humans to wear shoes and for shoemakers like himself to work. But a serious intent obviously hides behind the humorous facade: Eva (Walther's Eva, that is) is about to commit a grave transgression and her fall too would result in an expulsion from a nurturing community where the daughter of a patrician family is treated like a princess. Whether Eva gets the complete message or not, she is troubled by the song and takes Sachs's complaint seriously, as she should: "The song pains me, I do not know how! . . . Oh, best of men! That I should distress you so!"[27]

All of this, however, is preliminary to the main business of the act, which begins with Beckmesser's Serenade in G (see appendix 6: act 2, 3.b). This consists of full three stanzas in (what else?) Bar form, with dialogue interruptions and in the third stanza increasingly many voices (Sachs, David, and the men of the neighborhood) in the background. The Serenade then leads to the Ensemble Finale, also in G (though eventually sequentially rising and inconclusive in the end), as the background voices take over and more and more groups of people step in, following the male neighbors already present, also apprentices, journeymen, female neighbors, and finally the masters (of the individuals, only Magdalena holds her own throughout). The voices are superimposed on a motoric orchestral fugato and the intricate whole is held together by a variant of Beckmesser's Serenade melody. Sung by the masters as the cantus firmus, it ensures that we hear the Finale as a completion of the Serenade rather than as a separate unit.

The whole is an infernal parody of the Trial Song. Since Sachs would not be quiet and let Beckmesser sing his Serenade in peace, the two come to an agreement: the shoemaker will act as the clerk's marker, continuing to work on his shoes, but making noise with his hammer only when the singer breaks the rules. And, to make sure that we do not miss the similarity to the Trial scene, Sachs orders Beckmesser to begin, just as Beckmesser had ordered Walther: "Fanget an!" (II.1215). Unsurprisingly, the clerk's song, with its absurdly mechanical vocal ornamental runs of even sixteenth notes echoing equally mechanical lute accompaniment, not to mention its inane and tactless text (the father's riches seem to be as much on this suitor's mind as the daughter's charms), shows no trace of artistic sense or talent. But for someone who prides himself on his mastery of the rules ("I know well all the rules, observe proper measure and number"),[28] Beckmesser turns out to be also astonishingly incompetent when it comes to such an elementary matter as matching accented syllables of the verse with strong beats of the melody, and Sachs quickly delivers a caustic lesson: "I would think that the tune and verse should fit?"[29]

This singer is beyond learning. By the end of the second stanza Sachs has had plenty of opportunities to use his hammer, the shoes are ready, and Beckmesser has to finish his song against growing background noise, just as Walther had. Sachs now loudly proclaims his opinion: "A good song needs measure."[30] He repeats the word "Takt" so insistently that one gets the impression that the singer's tactlessness offended the marker's sense of propriety as much as did his inability to match the meters of the verse and melody. At the Serenade's end, David looks out of the window, mistakenly takes Beckmesser to be wooing his own beloved, Magdalene (Eva's nurse), and, enraged, throws himself at the singer.

The pandemonium of the Ensemble Finale ensues, driven by the Serenade-based cantus firmus. More and more neighbors, raised from early sleep by the noise, come out, and before long the sight of David and Beckmesser fighting proves contagious and results in a chaotic war of all against all. Beckmesser's infernally mechanical music, lacking "Takt" (both "tact" and "measure"), has un-tuned the civilized polis and returned it to the Hobbesian state of nature. It is a Gioachino Rossini opera buffa finale to the nth power and more frightening than comic, with the peaceful and reasonable citizens of Nuremberg turned into marionettes gripped by folly—the giddy Rossinian *follia* transformed into the altogether more threatening Wagnerian *Wahn*.

The dissonant (F-sharp^9) climax of the Ensemble Finale in its final measure (II.1439) is at the same time the beginning of the Refrain music we have already identified as the second structural backbone of the act. Here, at the beginning of the act's Coda, the two musics meet. Throughout the second half of the act, the three appearances of the Refrain articulate the theme of the lovers' elopement. The Refrain consists of three components, the main one of which is what I will call the Night Music, joined by two subordinate stage-music elements—the cow-horn and the Call of the Night-Watchman (table 28).

All three components are heard for the first time when they interrupt the recitative dialogue between Walther and Eva (II.647–877) in the scene that precedes Sachs's Cobbler Song. This is the lovers' first meeting since the trial and an occasion for Walther to vent his rage at the masters and all "the glue and paste of their rhyming rules"[31] as well as to exhort Eva: "Away, to freedom! I belong there, where I am the master at home. If I should marry you today, I beseech you now, come away and follow me!"[32] Walther's is a call in which the young artist's desire for freedom from traditional prescriptions of the craft and the young man's desire for freedom from traditional constrains on sexual mores (the two central and closely related issues debated in *Die Meistersinger*) are indistinguishable. In other words, for all its artistic idealism, it is a call for Eva to elope.

Walther now indulges his rage to the point of a hallucinatory vision in which he sees himself surrounded and trapped by jeering masters ("Everywhere masters, like evil spirits, I see them ganging up to mock me").[33] But at the climactic diminished-seventh point of this phantasmagoria, the spell is suddenly broken by the stage sound of the Night-Watchman's cow-horn (II.773–75), whose long-drawn fortissimo f-sharp becomes the dominant-pivot that temporarily stabilizes the B major key of the following Night Music (II.775–97). A quiet orchestral discourse with superimposed recitative dialogue, a discourse of great poetic beauty, the Night Music seems imbued with the summer-night fragrance of the linden tree under which Eva bids Walther to hide until the Night-Watchman passes. Eventually (from II.787) it intimates Walther's Prize Song of the third act, the song that will win him his beloved. Indeed, in the hushed, superimposed dialogue, Eva

TABLE 28 *Die Meistersinger*, Act 2, The Night Music Refrain

Form	Pitch or key	Text incipit	Measures	CD.track time
Refrain 1				
The Night-Watchman's Cow-Horn	F-sharp/G-flat		773–75	II.10.3:59–4:08
Night Music	B	Geliebter, spare den Zorn	775–97	II.11.0:00–1:11
The Night-Watchman's Call	F	Hört, ihr Leut', und laßt euch sagen	798–808	II.11.1:11–1:44
The Night-Watchman's Cow-Horn	F-sharp /G-flat		809–10	II.12.0:00–0:05
Refrain 2				
The Night-Watchman's Cow-Horn	F-sharp		1202–3	II.15.7:01–7:04
Night Music	B	Welch toller Spuck!	1203–17	II.15.7:04–7:46
Refrain 3				
The Night-Watchman's Cow-Horn	F-sharp /G-flat		1439–42	II.17.3:09–3:19
The Night-Watchman's Call	F	Hört, ihr Leut', und lasst euch sagen	1456–66	II.17.3:54–4:28
The Night-Watchman's Cow-Horn	F-sharp /G-flat		1467–69	II.17.4:28–4:38
Night Music	E		1469–85	II.17.4:38–5:45

promises Walther to escape the court of the masters, which under the circumstances can only mean one thing—her agreement to elope.

It is at this point that the Night-Watchman himself appears to recite his Call (II.798–808) in the jarringly incongruous, tritone-removed key of F, made even more incongruous when he caps his Call with the same long-drawn f-sharp /g-flat (II.809–10) with which the whole interruption in the recitative dialogue had begun (in II.773–75). The Night-Watchman reminds the citizens to take care of their fires and lights so "that no one comes to harm."[34] He is completely oblivious to the imminent danger of the planned elopement and the wrong key of his Call captures to perfection the sleepwalking fashion in which he moves through the city. And yet, for all his absentmindedness, he sounds his horn and Call at the exactly right moment—the moment when Walther asks Eva to escape with him and she consents. While his words are recited in the wrong key, his horn gets the key right, stabilizing the B major of the Night Music. A personification of the civic spirit of Nuremberg, the Night-Watchman indirectly assures us that no one will come to harm after all, that for all its susceptibility to temporary accesses of folly, the unconscious spirit of this community is essentially sound. As the recitative dialogue resumes (in II.810), we realize that Sachs has overheard the preceding conversation and is determined to prevent the elopement.

The f-sharp of the Night-Watchman's cow-horn (II.1202–3) introduces the B major of the Night Music again (II.1203–17) right after Beckmesser strikes his bargain with Sachs to serve as his marker and before he begins to sing his Serenade. This second appearance of the Refrain is much abbreviated: the Night-Watchman's horn is heard only from afar. He himself does not materialize and does not recite his Call, and the Night Music is shorn of its anticipations of the Prize Song. The hushed dialogue superimposed over it momentarily brings Walther and Eva from their background hiding under the linden tree, reminding us that they are still unable to escape. Significantly, both experience the encounter between Beckmesser and Sachs as a crazy hallucination, an echo of Walther's earlier vision of jeering masters. Walther: "What a mad spell! To me it seems a dream."[35] Eva: "It wraps my temples like a folly."[36]

But as we already know, this hallucination actually does become reality in the Ensemble Finale, where Walther and Eva find themselves in the midst of folly-driven masters, and other citizens of Nuremberg, tearing each other apart. Just as the earlier phantasmagoria had been interrupted at its climactic moment by the first Refrain, so too the actual mayhem of the Finale is interrupted at its climactic moment by the third Refrain, which doubles as the coda of the whole Serenade-Finale scene. The long-drawn fortissimo f-sharp of the Night-Watchman's cow-horn is heard again (II.1439–42), and it is enough to bring the city to its senses. While Sachs gets hold of Walther and pushes Eva toward her father's house, the riot quickly calms down and the fighting citizens disperse, leaving the stage empty. The Night-Watchman, as oblivious as ever, now appears to deliver his Call, again in the wrong key of F

(II.1456–66) and again corrects himself by his horn's g-flat/f-sharp (II.1467–69). Significantly, this time the Call itself does not mention any fire or light. Instead the Watchman warns his city of hallucination and folly: "Defend yourselves from ghosts and spells, so that your souls are not troubled by an evil spirit!"[37]

The unconscious collective spirit of Nuremberg is again wiser than its conscious individual citizens, the sleepwalking Night-Watchman included. It prevents the elopement and calms the riot at exactly the right moment, much as the Night-Watchman's horn knows better than its master what the right key should be, providing the fulcrum that allows for the tonic to be reached. As the Night-Watchman walks away, the stage remains empty, illuminated by the full moon of the midsummer night and the fragrant Night Music (II.1469–85). But this time, in the final measures of the act, the g-flat of the Night-Watchman's horn (II.1467–69) is reinterpreted from the dominant to the secondary dominant resolved to the dominant (II.1474) and the tonic (II.1481) as the Night Music shifts a fifth lower from B to E major in a gesture of complete appeasement.

The two intertwined musical strands that together give act 2 its shape, the Serenade-Finale and the Refrain, are opposed to one another in both form and content. Beckmesser and his antics remain in the foreground, Walther and Eva are hidden in the background. The clerk offends by the sterile, excessive rigidity of his traditionalism, the knight by his overexuberant readiness to tear up all customary arrangements. But for all their opposition, they are both threatening to disrupt and harm the normal healthy life of this community, what Georg Wilhelm Friedrich Hegel would call its *Sittlichkeit* (uprightness, custom-based ethical life). In act 2, the Night-Watchman had embodied Nuremberg's *Sittlichkeit* but, like the city itself, was quite unconscious of it. In act 3 Nuremberg's *Sittlichkeit* will acquire self-consciousness in the person of Sachs—triumphantly, perhaps all too triumphantly, so.

ACT 3, PART 1: A LESSON IN POETICS

The first act takes approximately one hour and twenty-five minutes in performance; the second, one hour; the third, two hours. In the gigantic Bar form of *Die Meistersinger*, the concluding Abgesang dwarfs the two initial Stollen in size—as is usually the case, at least in the examples of the form Wagner provides in the opera. As usual, too, the Abgesang is constructed differently than the two parallel Stollen, but makes reference to them toward its end. If acts 1 and 2 culminate in stage songs of Walther and Beckmesser, respectively, act 3 seems to culminate in stage songs of both contestants, first the clerk's and then the knight's. Otherwise, however, the colossally long act is constructed quite differently than its predecessors (table 29).

The main novelty is the division of the act into two parts, the first taking place indoors, in Sachs's workshop, the second outdoors, in an open meadow on Nuremberg's river, the Pegnitz. The very shape of the act is indicative of how, in this opera,

TABLE 29 *Die Meistersinger*, Act 3, Closed Forms

Form	Key	Text incipit	Measures	CD.track.time
Part 1				
1.				
Prelude	g/G		1–64	III.1.0:00–6:28
[David's Little Verse]	D	'Am Jordan Sankt Johannes stand'	201–28	III.3.0:00–0:58
Sachs's [Folly] Monologue	→C	Wahn! Wahn! Überall Wahn!	301–437	III.3.3:05–4:6:30
2.				
[Sachs's Arietta]	B-flat	Mein Freund, in holder Jugendzeit	545–611	III.6.0:00–3:02]
Walther's Dream Song begins	C	'Morgenlich leuchtend in rosigem Schein'	651–801	III.7.0:00–7:47
3.				
[Beckmesser's Arietta]	d	Die ich mir auserkoren	1007–48	III. 8.4:54–6:16]
4.				
Walther's Dream Song ends	C	'Weilten die Sterne im lieblichen Tanz?'	1431–94	III.10.3:44–11.0:28
[Sachs's Arietta]		Hat man mit dem Schuhwerk nicht seine Not!	1495–544	III.11.0:28–2:01]
[Eva's Arietta]		O Sachs! Mein Freund!	1545–97	III.11.2:01–4:32]
[Sachs's Baptism Speech	(D)/(a)/C	Ein Kind ward hier geboren	1624–90	III.12.0:00–IV.1.1:04]
Quintet	G-flat	Selig, wie die Sonne	1691–730	IV.1.1:04–5:33
Part 2				
5.				
Marches and Choruses of the Guilds	F/C	Sankt Krispin, lobet ihn!	1779–876	IV.2.0:00–3:42
Dance of the Apprentices	B-flat	Herr Je! Herr Je!	1876–2058	IV.2.3:42–3.2:39
March of the Mastersingers	C		2059–146	IV.3.2:39–4.0:22
Reformation Hymn with	G	'Wach auf! es nahet gen den Tag'	2154–70	IV.4.0:42–2:39
Acclamation of Sachs	C	Heil! Heil! Heil!	2171–87	IV.4.2:39–3:23
6.				
Sachs's Harangue I	G	Euch macht ihr's leicht	2188–280	IV.5.0:00–4:11
Beckmesser's Prize Song	e/G	'Morgen ich leuchte in rosigem Schein'	2379–454	IV.6.1:51–5:49
Walther's Prize Song	C	'Morgenlich leuchtend im rosigem Schein'	2610–732	IV.8.0:00–6:02
Sachs's Harangue II with	C	Verachtet mir die Meister nicht	2771–897	IV.9.0:00–5:48
Acclamation of Sachs	C	Heil Sachs!	2897–910	IV.9.5:48–6:30

The sections of closed-form music are in bold; the open-form but non-dialogical sections are in bold italics.

the narrower private world, the world of Eva, Walther, and Beckmesser, needs to open up and be integrated into, and confirmed by, the broader public world, the world of the masters of Nuremberg, the city "in Germany's center,"[38] and perhaps even the still-wider German world up- and downstream beyond the city, the world glimpsed by Sachs. Indeed we have seen that from the beginning, from the Chorale scene that had opened act 1, the question of how private desires fit into public obligations, how the freedom of individuals can be reconciled with the traditions of the community, loomed as the central issue driving the narrative.

The main pillars that structure the first part of the act are the orchestral Prelude (not labeled in the score) and Sachs's Monologue at the beginning (the two belong together, as we shall presently see), the interrupted and later completed Dream Song of Walther in the middle, and the Quintet at the end. Several smaller closed forms additionally punctuate this part of the act, and as usual these have a more local formal significance, shaping a scene in which they occur rather than the first part of the act as a whole.

The first pillar extends through the whole first scene (III.1–437). While Sachs's Folly Monologue itself occupies only its final part, in a sense the whole scene from the beginning of the act is devoted to the shoemaker's meditation (as in the Elder Monologue, here too he broods over what he had witnessed in the preceding act). Since the Folly Monologue (III.301–437) comes back to the musical ideas first heard in the Prelude (III.1–64), at least retrospectively it becomes obvious that the Prelude had represented in a purely instrumental form some of the thoughts verbalized in the Monologue. To make sure that we do not miss the connection, throughout the earlier portion of the intervening recitative dialogue that separates the two sections (III.65–300) Wagner periodically invokes the Prelude's opening motive (at III.81–86, 98–102, 148–53) as Sachs clings to his private thoughts even as he converses with David.

The motive will play a crucial role not only in the opening scene but in the whole act, functioning as a motto invoked at a number of crucial moments. The composer himself noted its derivation in an interesting comment on the third-act Prelude made in a letter to Judith Gautier (November 1868):

> The first motive of string instruments has been heard, to be sure, simultaneously with the third couplet of the cobbler's song in the second act [see the woodwinds and horns beginning in II.984]. There it expressed the complaint of a resigned man who shows the world a brave and energetic face. Eva has understood this hidden complaint and, touched to the depth of her soul, has wanted to escape so as not to hear any more this seemingly so joyful song. This motive is now played alone and it develops its intimacy to die in the sadness of resignation.[39]

The Monologue proper, a freely developing vocal arioso, proceeds in four stages, each defined by its own dominating orchestral motives and its own key (see appendix 6: act 3, part 1, 1.c). Its first part is based on the just-discussed motive, or, strictly speaking, on the two motives the Monologue shares with the Prelude, both associated with the idea of "folly" ("Wahn") and Sachs's despondency in the face of folly, one a monophonic motto in the cellos and double basses (III.301-7; compare III.1-4 from the Prelude), the other an imitative low-tessitura string counterpoint (III.313-24; compare III.5-15). Folly, Sachs thinks, makes the world go round. It drives the history of the city and of the world, it accounts for their senseless frenzy and violence: "Nothing may happen without it."[40] This is a crucial insight. In Sachs's reflection, *Wahn* acquires the metaphysical status of the Schopenhauerian *Wille*.

The thought is crucial, since eventually a necessary conclusion will be drawn from it, namely that not only frenzied violence, but also the magic of peaceful harmony, requires *Wahn* if it is to happen at all. At the end of the Monologue Sachs will be even more explicit: "A noble work"[41] can "never succeed without some folly."[42] The same underlying active force can be put to destructive and to creative uses. On June 17, 1874, Cosima noted in her *Diary*: "*Maneia Manteia Wahn*: R. explains to Richter that he is in fact mad to undertake something like the festival theater . . . and yet from madness of this sort all greatness springs—like, for example, the ideal of a united Germany as well; analogy with animal instinct—also 'mad.'"[43]

Part 2 of the Monologue starts again with the monophonic motto (III.336-38), but then is dominated by a stately dotted-rhythm motive associated with the idea of Nuremberg (III.339-54) as Sachs considers "with joyful exaltation"[44] the peaceful customs of his beloved city. In the development that follows (III.355-83), the motive gradually transforms itself into the theme of the fugato that kept together the war-of-all-against-all ensemble finale of the second act (the transformation is partly accomplished already by III.364, but compare especially III.375ff with II.1361ff). Sachs's thoughts turn from the normally peaceful Nuremberg to the general mayhem of the previous night and the motivic transformation neatly captures that civic meltdown. Why did it happen?

Part 3 brings the answer. It begins with the Night Music of the Refrain from act 2 (III.384-88) in the key with which it was associated there, B major, and then picks up the fugato theme again (III.389-403), now completely transformed in character—from one of frantic strife to one of gentle midsummer-night magic replete with flickering glowworms and elder fragrance. The mayhem was the work of "an impish sprite"[45] of the midsummer night, Sachs says. The orchestra identifies the imp more precisely. The Night Music has been closely associated with the theme of the young lovers' elopement, and the fugato theme with the distemper brought about by Beckmesser's serenading. We may admire Walther and despise Beckmesser, but in act 2 the actions of both were threats to public order.

In the fourth part, finally, the thought of the past midsummer night gives way to that of the just-beginning Saint John's Day. The motive that dominates the whole discourse is the one associated with the day since Pogner's Aria of act 1 (compare

III.407ff with I.1167ff) combined with the closely related dotted-rhythm Nuremberg idea from the second part of the Monologue. Sachs is determined to use the unavoidable driving mechanism of folly to bring about a desirable outcome, one that would reconcile private desire with public good: "Now let us see how Hans Sachs does it that he can subtly drive folly to do a noble work."[46] On April 19, 1873, Cosima noted the following words of her husband in her *Diary*: "'A great statesman is one who recognizes the prevailing influence of unreason and guides it as best he can.'"[47]

In more ways than one, this magnificent Monologue is the opera's pivotal turning point, the moment of Sachs's reflection into the deepest nature of things, the Schopenhauerian will at the bottom of all that happens, but also the moment of his decision to bend this will away from works of violence to works of peace. (It is characteristic of the modernity of Wagner's dramatic art that the *peripeteia* occurs here within a meditative monologue, that it is a matter of internal reflection rather than external action.) Nota bene: Sachs (and—in this opera at least, but not only in this one—Wagner) accepts Arthur Schopenhauer's metaphysics of the will, but not his ethics of renunciation. On the contrary, he wants to bend will to his own purposes, to be its active manipulator, not its passive victim.

The Prelude, we know, shares with the Monologue the two opening motives, both associated with the notion of *Wahn*. The monophonic motto at the beginning (III.301-7) and the following passage of imitative part-writing (III.313-24) are the content of the Prelude's framing sections (III.1-15 [= 1-4 + 5-15] and 51-64 [= 51-54 + 55-64]). If the Prelude maps Sachs's earlier, silent train of thought, it is clear that the idea of *Wahn* is the one to which this thought constantly comes back (also during the following dialogue with David, as we have seen, and of course at the beginning of the Monologue itself). The insight into the deepest ground of being and becoming has to precede any decision as to sensible and effective future action. In the center of the Prelude (III.16-50), reminiscences of the last night's events (III.26-43) are again firmly framed (III.16-25 and 43-50), this time by a solemn brass chorale we shall eventually get to know (in the last scene of act 3) as the Reformation Hymn. The communal hymn, a vision of the coming dawn, literally and metaphorically, suggests that for all the seriousness and sorrow of his nighttime thoughts, Sachs is not wholly despondent, not quite ready for full-blown Schopenhauerian resignation. The decision to act and change the world rather than to accept it as it is will come, and when it comes, it will keep the common good of the polis firmly in view.

The dramatic point of David's Little Verse ("Sprüchlein"), a simple single stanza embedded in the recitative dialogue that intervenes between the Prelude and Sachs's Monologue, is to make David (and us) realize that his master has the same first name as Saint John the Baptist, about whom the apprentice sings and whose day this is. This is when we begin to grasp also the full significance of the day and of the constant reminders of its patron saint that have permeated the opera from its beginning.

Hans Sachs, who will shortly baptize Walther's song and later in the day exhort the whole city to honor German art and its masters, is like his saintly namesake a prophet of a new faith, this one a religion of the art of the future being just born and of the national culture within the framework of which such an art might flourish. Sachs's stature has been steadily growing throughout the opera. Now, at the beginning of act 3, he emerges as something of an alter ego of, and spokesman for, the opera's author. Like Sachs, the late Wagner was regularly referred to as "the master" ("der Meister") in the circle of his intimates, for instance in Cosima's letters to young Friedrich Nietzsche. The scene promotes a vastly idealized self-portrait of the mature artist—Wagner as he would like to have been (Walther, by contrast, is an equally idealized self-portrait of the artist as a young man).

The pillar at the center of the first part of act 3 is constituted by Walther's Dream Song, of which he first presents two stanzas to Sachs alone (scene 2) and then, after a sizable interruption, the last stanza also to Eva (scene 4). Thus Eva gets to hear at least some of what Walther can do as an artist before the contest itself, just as she has already heard what her other suitor can do. The interruption provided by scene 3 serves essentially to emphasize the contrast between the two suitors (what Walther creates, Beckmesser steals) and to inject some comic relief between the more serious scenes (the scene approaches in tone the lower comedy of Richard Strauss's *Der Rosenkavalier* [1910], just as the Quintet will get us close to the latter opera's more serious tone of the Trio). Spanning in this fashion three scenes, the Dream Song is a significant component in the formal organization of this part of the act. Moreover, since Walther's Prize Song, the culminating event of the second part of the act, is a variant of the Dream Song, the formal significance of the latter extends beyond the act's first part. Between them, the Dream Song and the Prize Song are a structural backbone of act 3 as a whole.

Like all the major efforts of the two suitors, the Song itself again exemplifies the Bar form (see appendix 6: act 3, part 1, 2.b). One would think that by now even the densest among us understand how the form works, but Wagner, never particularly reluctant to repeat what one already knows, behaves here like the most pedantic of his masters and recapitulates the lesson once more through the mouth of Sachs, who makes brief comments after each verse of the first stanza telling Walther what is expected of him next.

More interesting and subtle are his reactions when each stanza is completed. Walther's song and singing move Sachs deeply, and Wagner's redundant stage directions after the first two stanzas leave us in no doubt as to his intentions: Sachs is "moved"[48] and "very moved."[49] We of course are moved, too, and Wagner's emphatically non-redundant orchestra embodies both these emotions—Sachs's and ours—all at once. Here is one of those moments in this intensely self-referential drama when the characters onstage and the audience offstage become one, something that is bound to happen when a performance is staged in a theater-within-a-theater fashion. The specific content and quality of the emotion are interesting, too. With each of the three reactions, the orchestra invokes the act's motto, the *Wahn* motive. Folly, we already know, is the source of everything that happens, destruction as well as creation, hence also the deepest source of Walther's creativity, and it is to folly that Sachs's thoughts return yet again.

Good opera composers, throughout the genre's history, have known how to represent and express simple, distinct passions, passions that can each be named with one word: sadness, joy, anger. Great opera composers—Wolfgang Amadeus Mozart and Giuseppe Verdi are Wagner's most obvious peers in this respect—have also known how to capture the complexity of emotion, an amalgamation of many often-conflicting shades of feeling. On December 5, 1881, Cosima noted in her *Diary*: "'Oh music!' he exclaims. 'Here one will be able to see for the first time what potentialities it contains for conveying sorrow in bliss!'"[50] The composer's words here refer to the score of *Parsifal*, but they are applicable to his music dramas in general and capture one of his most signal and enduring achievements. Thus Sachs is delighted by what Walther brings forward and also awed by it, awed by folly's creative potential. Perhaps (who knows?) there is even a shade of jealousy here, of an older artist confronted with the work of a greater and younger one. The orchestra's music of folly at the end of each stanza captures this ambivalence and ambiguity to perfection, blending the feelings of delight and admiration with the tragic sense of the inseparability of creation and destruction, the sense that the old will be pushed aside to make room for the new. (The *Wahn* motive, by the way, was implicated in emotionally complex situations from its first appearance. Recall Wagner's description in his letter to Judith Gautier quoted above of how its secret sadness infiltrated the third stanza of the Cobbler Song and how Eva was able to hear its message hidden behind the boisterous facade of Sachs's singing.) Even the generally resistant Theodor Adorno admired moments like this one:

> This intermediate stratum of expression, which is indeed the epitome of the musical modernity of the nineteenth century, did not exist before Wagner. That suffering can be sweet, and that the poles of pleasure and pain are not rigidly opposed to one another, but are mediated, is something that both composers and audience learned uniquely from him, and it is this experience alone that made it possible for dissonance to extend its range over the whole language of music. And few aspects of Wagner's music have been as seductive as the enjoyment of pain.[51]

After the last stanza, the orchestra's particularly passionate music of folly is left without immediate vocal exegesis and the stage direction describes a whole pantomime of responses from the overwhelmed onstage audience. Eva has listened "as if enchanted"[52] and "now bursts passionately into tears,"[53] sinking on Sachs's breast. He, in turn, needs to force himself to turn away, leaving her on Walther's shoulder. The emotions unleashed by the song are indeed complex. Eva is confused in her feelings between the older and the younger man, and the older man relinquishes her with notable reluctance. In this moment of generational succession, not only the older artist, but also the older (potential) lover, needs to make room for the newer one.

The moment is sufficiently complex emotionally to require some verbal exegesis, and this is provided by the two ariettas, Sachs's (III.1495–544) and Eva's (III.1545–97), that immediately follow Walther's Song. Sachs covers up his confusion and ambivalence with a gruff variant of the Cobbler Song (this was attached also to Beckmesser's Serenade—the clerk's counterpart to the knight's Song—but to rather different effect): a cobbler's work is never done!; were I not also a poet, I would have long dropped it. Artistic self-assertion comes more easily at this point than the erotic kind. Eva's passionate arioso is more explicit and goes to the heart of the matter: you have awakened me, she tells Sachs, and "if I had a choice, I'd choose only you."[54] "But now," she continues, "it has chosen me [and the orchestra identifies the 'it' as folly in a particularly chromatic-ecstatic shape] to a previously unknown anguish and if I marry today, it was without any choice."[55] Both verbally and musically we are in the vicinity of *Tristan und Isolde* here, in the realm of Frau Minne, who strikes her victims unexpectedly and condemns them to a life of endless torment. But *Die Meistersinger* is a comedy and Wagner deftly brings the temperature down via a famously self-referential move: Sachs's response to Eva (III.1597–610) brings an orchestral quotation of the Yearning motive and an evocation of King Mark's music from *Tristan* as the shoemaker tells her that he knows "a sad play"[56] about Tristan and Isolde and is wise enough not to want "the happiness of Lord Mark."[57] This is more than clever: the self-referential quotation from the "sad play" brings a distance between the play we remember and the one we watch, assures us that not only is Sachs no King Mark, but *Die Meistersinger* is no *Tristan und Isolde*. Indeed it offers an alternative to *Tristan*, a way of cutting the "sad play's" hopeless knot even in the universe governed by *Wahn*.

Explaining a work of art by its creator's biography is one of the worst critical habits. Not to notice the relevance of the work to the biography, on the other hand, would be unnecessarily fastidious and doctrinaire. Let us notice, then, that unlike his hero, in the later part of his own life Wagner did gamble repeatedly on the happiness of Lord Mark with much younger women, and won the gamble with Cosima von Bülow. As Schopenhauer was reported to have answered, when someone complained that in his own life the sage did not follow the ascetic ways he recommended in his writings, "It is a strange demand upon a moralist that he should teach no other virtue than that which he himself possesses."[58] Indeed, "it is just as little needful that a saint should be a philosopher as that a philosopher should be a saint."[59]

Sachs's reaction to the second stanza of the Dream Song is notable for one other reason. The first two stanzas, he tells Walther (using strikingly Freudian language), provided a successful "image of a dream";[60] if you want to create the third stanza, this should provide "an interpretation of the dream."[61] A whole poetics of artistic creation is implied here, a poetics made explicit in the dialogue that preceded the Song (III.438–650). The conversation begins with Walther telling Sachs that he has had "a wonderful dream,"[62] one that he scarcely dares to think about for fear that it might evaporate. "This," Sachs tells him, "is precisely the work of the poet that he memorizes and interprets his dreams."[63] And he immediately follows with this poetic credo: "Believe me, our truest folly is disclosed to us in dream: all art of poetry and poetizing is nothing but the interpretation of true dreams."[64] There we have it: the function of art is the disclosure of truth, and the deepest truth about the world is the Schopenhauerian will or the Wagnerian folly that is the foundation of all being and that drives all becoming. Such truth is disclosed in dreams, and it is the job of the poet to capture and interpret it.

Another centrally important issue that comes up in the conversation is Sachs's conviction that Walther's individual dreams should be integrated with the social practices of the mastersingers and his hope that this can still be accomplished—a hope, he significantly tells Walther, without which "instead of preventing your flight, I would have run away with you myself!"[65] When artistic innovation and artistic tradition come into an irreconcilable conflict, Sachs is on the side of innovation. But the conflict need not be irreconcilable, he thinks. There is a good reason, he tells Walther, why your song frightened the masters: "With so much passion of poetry and love one seduces daughters to adventure; but for the blissful matrimony one finds other words and tunes."[66] From the start, this opera raised two parallel questions: how to integrate individual erotic desires with the social practices and traditions of the community, and how to reconcile artistic innovation with artistic tradition. Sachs brings the two questions together and suggests that they are closely related, perhaps even that there is a single question here. Indeed, it is a single question, since the same folly drives both erotic desire and artistic creation.

But this is a dialogue on poetry rather than eros, and Walther now frames the question as follows: what the difference is between "a beautiful song" and "a master song."[67] Sachs's arietta (III.545–611) provides the answer. Many, when young and driven by powerful erotic desires, succeed in making "a beautiful song." As one ages, marries, and encounters the usual vicissitudes of life, if then one still is able to make a beautiful song, one deserves to be called a master. My aim, Walther interjects, is a marriage that lasts. Then Sachs continues the arietta: "Learn in good time the rules of the masters, so that they guide you faithfully and help you preserve what in youth, with hallowed drive, spring and love placed unconsciously in your heart, so that it is not lost and you can nurture it."[68] What begins to emerge here is a part of the reason why the reconciliation of innovation and tradition is so important. From the standpoint of the individual artist, traditional craft learned early on helps to sustain creativity even after youthful, biologically driven inspiration begins to dry out. Whether it is marriage or poetic work, the durability of what individuals make depends on the sustenance provided by the context of social practices and traditions.

The answer is partial, since one would want to know also why the reconciliation matters from the larger standpoint of the community. This, indeed, is the subject Sachs picks up next. The rules have been made up by aging, careworn masters to help them remember and re-create "an image"[69] of "youthful love."[70] So far, this is nothing new: the rules serve to sustain the creative drive. But now, the arietta finished, Sachs elaborates briefly: an aging master refreshes this image as well as he can and "therefore, I would like, as one in need, that if I teach you the rules, you should explain them to me anew."[71] Individual innovative creativity helps to keep the communal traditional rules alive, ensures that they do not ossify.

The whole dialogue is clearly of great importance to the opera, elucidating as it does the views of Sachs and Wagner on one of the central issues of this drama: the relationship between individual innovation and communal tradition, whether in the matter of art or of sexual relationships. This is no longer a "dream image." It is a "dream interpretation" and Wagner evidently thinks that while "images" may well be captured in closed forms, an interpretation requires an open recitative-dialogue (or monologue) form of discourse. Only briefly does the dialogue get condensed into an arietta, and one that, being twice interrupted by Walther, does not stand out from the surrounding dialogue too sharply.

The "dream image" comes with the first two stanzas of Walther's Song. What was his dream, then? He dreamed of entering a delightful garden one morning, finding there a tree overhung with desirable golden fruit, and, better yet, an even more desirable woman, who embraced him like a bride and pointed to the fruit from the tree of life. In the evening he only desired "to suck bliss from her eyes";[72] in the night he saw two stars appear in the sky, stars that multiplied and replaced the fruit of the laurel tree. What Dr. Freud would say to all that we can only guess, perhaps that the dream expresses a repressed desire for the woman and poetic laurels alike. But Walther does not need Dr. Freud, since he offers his own interpretation in the third stanza. There the stars form "a wreath of stars"[73] around the beloved's head, which she places on his head in the new day. Not much of a surprise here: Walther dreams of winning the poet's crown and thereby winning the girl, too. For all the intriguing but ultimately inconsequential biblical typology of the song, the poetic theory in this case surpasses in interest the actual poetic practice. But let us not forget that this is *poesia per musica*, and it is the *musica* that counts here for more than the embarrassingly conventional and overwrought *poesia*.

The Dream Song having been completed and sung, all that remains is to give it a name. The third structural pillar of the first part of the act comes at its end and consists of the Quintet introduced by Sachs's Baptism Speech. Throughout this book, I have been repeatedly claiming that closed musical forms provide Wagner's late music dramas with points of gravity that focus the long-term organization of each act and even of the whole opera. I have carefully *not* been claiming that these points of formal emphasis are necessarily also the aesthetic high points of the works. Wagner's extraordinary ability to make his recitative dialogue interesting and gripping both musically and dramatically has to count among his signal achievements. In the case of the Quintet, however, the formal emphasis and the aesthetic interest coincide: the Quintet belongs among the most memorable and beautiful moments in *Die Meistersinger*, its quiet rapture providing the first part of the act with an intensely moving culmination. It is, literally, a moment: the five participants (in addition to the Song's father, Walther, also the godparents, Eva and Sachs, as well as the baptism's witnesses, Magdalena and David) do not act or interact. They look inward, removing themselves from the real time of the action to the timeless realm of contemplation. Wagner underscores this removal by the choice of the key for the Quintet, G-flat, which is as far away as possible from the C major of Walther's Song, of Sachs's Baptism Speech, and also of the second part of the act. We are perhaps intended to relate it to the equally otherworldly f-sharp/g-flat of the Night-Watchman's horn.[74]

The formal organization of the Quintet could not be simpler: ABA (III.1691–702, 1703–15, 1716–26) plus an orchestral postlude (III.1726–30), with the central section based on the Dream Song and with the postlude combining the motives of the A and B sections. In the preceding Baptism Speech, Sachs has given Walther's song a rather unwieldy name, "The tune interpreting the blissful morning dream,"[75] and invited Eva as the godmother to pronounce a verse over the newborn: hence the first section of the Quintet is sung by Eva alone. But it is hard to decide whether the remaining four listen to her verse or not. Each seems to be lost in thoughts regarding the significance of the song and of the moment, thoughts that make them glance from the private present to the public future. For Eva and Walther, the Song is a promise of his winning the contest. For Sachs it is a token of his renunciation of Eva and of bidding farewell to his youth, as well as a promise of a more durable youth that only poetry can provide. In the background, finally, Magdalena and David think that their own union is at hand, too.

ACT 3, PART 2: THE SHOEMAKER'S TRIUMPH

Thus the first part of the act ends as it has begun, with an intense emphasis on interiority. The second part, by contrast, leaves this private interior world behind, or, more precisely, attempts to blend it with the public world of the city. This part itself is divided into two sections, the lengthy—and to this listener-spectator, a bit tedious and conventional—introduction, which allows all the inhabitants of Nuremberg to arrive at the meadow for the Feast of Saint John, and then the singing contest itself. Each section ends similarly, with the assembled people acclaiming Sachs with loud—and to this admittedly anachronistic listener-spectator, distinctly unpleasant-sounding—"Heils" (table 29 again). With *Parsifal*, *Die Meistersinger* is Wagner's most self-referential music drama, and it is only appropriate that this story of poet-musicians should culminate with a singing competition within the context of a public festival, just as its creator's life story culminated with the Festival of Bayreuth.

The introductory succession of Marches and Choruses of the Guilds (III.1779–876), Dance of the Apprentices (III.1876–2058), and March of the Mastersingers (III.2059–146) are all a buildup to the real point of the opening section—the Reformation Hymn (III.2154–70) sung by all the assembled people. All stand, the men with bared heads (stage direction at III.2153) except for Sachs, the author of the hymn, who thus symbolically places himself above the community, and, significantly, Beckmesser (desperately trying to learn by heart the text of Walther's song he had stolen earlier that day), who thus symbolically excludes himself from the community even before the contest begins. Sachs's poem, by itself, seems innocuous enough: a picture of the approaching day announced by the singing of a nightingale.

The solemn communal Lutheran-chorale style of the musical setting, however, imbues the hymn with significance that goes far beyond the textual surface. In the singing of this individual nightingale-artist, the poetic "I" hears a promise of an awakening of the whole people to a new day, the community's rebirth in which the religious reformation in Sachs's sixteenth-century Nuremberg and the national regeneration in Wagner's nineteenth-century Germany blend into one. The poet's call, "Awake!"[76] is clearly addressed to the whole community; indeed, the new art is to awaken the nation of Nuremberg to new life. Appropriately the poem was written not only by the fictional Sachs of the opera, but also by the historical Hans Sachs on which the fictional one is modeled. In his autobiography, Wagner refers to it as "Sachs's poem on the Reformation" and describes how its melody occurred to him at the Palais-Royal in Paris in January 1861—probably the earliest musical idea of the opera.[77] We heard this sort of music at the very beginning of the opera, in the opening chorale, a hymn addressed to Saint John the Baptist. Now the prophet announcing the coming of a new day is Hans Sachs (Wagner had equated him with Saint John already at the beginning of the third act). But the equation is far from perfect. That earlier faith aspired to universality, and addressed a community in which "there is no difference between the Jew and the Greek" (Romans 10.12), while the new faith is distinctly more parochial, even tribal.

Sachs's apotheosis does not stop here. The shoemaker's appearance has excited the assembled people already before the singing of the hymn (III.2146–54): "Seeing him all push forward, taking off hats and caps."[78] The hymn finished, "the people take up again a jubilant attitude,"[79] acclaiming Sachs with resounding and repeated cries of "Heil!" (III.2171–87). Sachs meanwhile remains the "motionless"[80] center of this excited cyclone and "looks over the mass of people."[81] A motionless far-seeing leader and the thronging adoring masses below yelling "Heil!"—the image seems a rehearsal for many a twentieth-century dictator, but for none more than Adolf Hitler and his people at the 1934 outdoor Nuremberg Nazi Party Congress staged by Leni Riefenstahl. *Triumph des Willens*, her 1935 film of the event, made memorable use of *Die Meistersinger* music and thus emphatically claimed the ancestry of the *Johannistag* for her *Parteitag*; the congress itself was opened with a festive performance of the opera in the Nuremberg Opera House.[82]

In the last scene of the opera, a new protagonist enters the stage, "the people" ("das Volk"), and its presence transforms both Sachs and the opera. Not that we have not been warned: Sachs's populism surfaced briefly already in the first act, in the dialogue among the masters that followed Pogner's Aria with its announcement of the contest (I.1265–426). Pogner has reserved for his daughter the right to refuse as a husband whomever the masters would choose as the winner, which to the masters seemed an unwelcome limitation on their judgment. Not to Sachs, however: he suggested something even more radical, arguing that "the sense of women, quite untutored, seems to me to equal in worth the sense of the people. If you now want to show the people how highly you honor art, and if you let the child have her choice, but do not want her to refuse the verdict, allow also the people to be the judge, they will certainly agree with the child!"[83] Sachs shows himself here a radical democrat, ready to enfranchise women and commoners, that is, those who do not meet the education and property requirements of the patrician males. Not surprisingly, the masters loathe the idea, seeing in it a further infringement on their prerogative as experts in the matter of art and its rules.

Sachs, however, does not give up. He is all for the rules, "but I would find it wise once a year to test the rules themselves whether they had not lost their force and life through lazy habitual use. And whether you are still on the right track of nature, this will tell you only he who knows nothing of the tablature."[84] Sachs respects tradition, but only a tradition that lives, not a dead one. The test of a living tradition is that its products may interest and move not just specialists, but also the untutored: women and especially the people. Therefore, he continues, once a year, at the Feast of Saint John, we should turn to the people for judgment so "that the people and art may equally flourish and grow."[85] Suddenly and only for a moment, we catch a glimpse of the full scope of Sachs's concerns: what matters to him is not just that art should live, but equally that the people flourish. Nota bene: the masters reject the proposal.

But only in the final scene of the opera does Sachs's populism become the central theme. The jovial and wise elderly adviser and protector to Walther and Eva is transformed in front of our eyes into the prophet of the nation, a nation awoken to new life by its new and vital art, as well as the far-seeing leader of his adoring people. What transforms him is the presence of "the People" ("das Volk"). Who, actually, is *das Volk*? Everybody and no one in particular: it is of the essence of "the

People" that it is a collectivity. As such, the People can only sing in one voice, so to speak, as a chorus—not an ideal condition to articulate an individual point of view or a dissenting opinion, of the kind, for instance, that individual masters put forward when they debate Pogner's and Sachs's proposals in act 1. The People sing best in homophonic harmony hymns written by someone else. They need someone to articulate their collective thoughts—a Leader. Sachs, who now emerges into full view, is as much a creation of the People as they are being formed by him. It is a symbiotic, reciprocal relationship.

This relationship drives the rest of the opera. To be sure, the singing contest that now takes place is articulated primarily by the Prize Songs of Beckmesser and Walther (III.2379–454 and 2610–732, respectively). But these are preceded and followed by Sachs's harangues to the People (III.2188–280 and 2771–897), and this frame acquires at least as much weight in the second part of the final scene as do the contestants' offerings. Here again the "dream image" can be captured in closed forms, but the "interpretation of dreams" requires a more open, monologic form of discourse. In his speeches Sachs interprets the dream the People and we have been dreaming, the dream called *Die Meistersinger*; he reveals his final thoughts and tells the People and us what to think.

The contest itself seems, inevitably perhaps, rather anticlimactic. If you like to watch public executions, you will love the scene of Beckmesser's humiliation. Even before he starts to sing he is greeted by the People with a brief derisive fugal-scherzando chorus (III. 2321–65): the suitor is too old. Beckmesser had stolen Walther's poem as written down by Sachs (presumably only the words, not the melody), and he now delivers it to a tune of his own. But he finds the poem incomprehensible (which, given its quality, is perhaps not surprising). Failing to learn it by heart, he garbles it mercilessly. His song is absurd and after a single stanza he is laughed offstage.

By rather predictable contrast, Walther acquits himself with honors. He too produces only one stanza, sensibly expanding its tune and modifying the text so that we are not treated to a literal repetition of something we have already heard. His Prize Song is a spontaneously improvised, improved version of the Dream Song interspersed with comment-interruptions from the ensemble of the masters and chorus of the People (see appendix 6: act 3, part 2, 6.b4). Wagner's thinking about the relationship between the Dream Song and the Prize Song is probably faithfully captured in Cosima's letter (January 31, 1867) to King Ludwig II of Bavaria in which she reports:

> The Friend [that is how Cosima refers to the composer in her letters to the King] found namely that it is completely impossible to allow the same poem to be said twice in the same act; it had to be therefore the same and yet different.... The difficult task which unusually preoccupied the Friend in recent times was crowned in my view with a wonderful success; the second poem is like an interpretation of the

dream and its sharpened image, it is a master song about the dream. . . . The Friend has also both changed and yet not changed its music wonderfully, one does not know, is it the same, is it different.[86]

The object of desire in Walther's "dream of love"[87] is identified in the first Stollen as Eva under a tree—presumably of life, rather than knowledge—in Paradise. When before his trial Walther had announced that the subject of his song would be love, one of the masters remarked disapprovingly that "we deem this secular."[88] But Walther, like Wagner, elides the difference between the secular and the sacred. Indeed, in the second Stollen the love object is transformed into the Muse of Parnassus standing under the laurel tree (the poet's reward), as sexual desire flows into poetic inspiration. My singing, Walther triumphantly concludes in the Abgesang, wins me both Parnassus and Paradise. The secular and the sacred, the artistic and the erotic, are one, and Walther will have it all. To both the masters and the People, the words, previously garbled by Beckmesser, suddenly make sense, especially when enveloped by Walther's music, and they unanimously declare him the winner while Eva crowns him with a wreath of laurel and myrtle.

But how did Walther get to compete in the first place, given that he had failed the trial and was not a mastersinger at all? This is clarified in the recitative dialogue that separates the two competing songs (III.2454–609), although the ground had been prepared by Sachs already before the contest, in his first harangue to the people (III.2188–280). There, Sachs, as the designated speaker, introduced the contest, explaining that out of his love of art, Pogner had offered his daughter and wealth as the prize. What the speaker does not mention, however, is the condition the masters had accepted, namely, that only a mastersinger can compete. Instead, he turns to the people with this ambiguous request: "Let the recruitment be free to a poet."[89] This is an act of usurpation: addressing the People above the heads of his fellow masters, Sachs attempts to change the rules of the contest by opening it to all comers.

The full implications of this act become clear to the masters only after the Beckmesser fiasco. The clerk, furious at his failure, publicly announces that it is Sachs who is the author of the song just presented. (Indeed, he had stolen it from the shoemaker's desk and has no idea that the song had been dictated by Walther.) Sachs in turn announces first that he is not the author, second, that it is a great song that was ruined in performance, and third, that properly sung, its author would be called a master by impartial judges. And, as the accused, he calls upon Walther to be his defense witness. Now at last the masters begin to see what it is that Sachs is doing and, understandably, they express some annoyance, but then immediately and spinelessly give in: "Hey, Sachs, you are so clever! But for today let it be."[90] He makes light of their objections: "The good of the rules can be recognized from the fact that every now and then they can take an exception."[91]

(Nietzsche will in turn make light of this maxim: "A marriage proves itself a good marriage by being able to endure an occasional 'exception' ["Ausnahme"]."[92]) The people side with Sachs ("A good witness"),[93] and he promptly pronounces the decision: "The masters and the people are willing to find out what my witness is worth."[94]

This is how Sachs makes good on the promise of the Folly Monologue to "subtly drive folly to do a noble work." He manipulates the folly of Beckmesser, of the masters, and of the People. No blood gets spilled and all (except the hapless Beckmesser) are having such a good time that we may not notice that what has just happened is a rehearsal for a coup d'état. The rules of the game established by the legitimate if spineless patrician assembly have been put aside by the alliance of a cunning demagogue invoking an "exception" with the unquestioningly adoring and disenfranchised crowd. "Sovereign is he who decides on the exception" ("Souverän ist, wer über den Ausnahmezustand entscheidet"), Carl Schmitt, Hitler's preeminent jurist, famously opined in 1922.[95] A modern dictator is one capable of calling a state of emergency in which the constitutional order and rule of law are suspended; the capability involves skills in crowd manipulation, in the subtle driving of its folly. Sachs is the prophet not only of a new art and a renewed national community, but also of the politics of the future, the mass politics in which the legitimate liberal bourgeois order will be undermined and overthrown by the usurping leaders of the people. In his time, by the way, Wagner was not alone in noticing the peculiar modernity of the Leader-People symbiosis. In early August 1859, the brothers Goncourt made the following observation in their *Journal*: "Strange thing! Modern despotism, yesterday as today, has a new and anti-natural foundation: the public opinion. This is what it seems always to address."[96] The Goncourts were thinking here of Napoleon and indirectly also of his nephew, Louis-Napoleon, but their reflection loses nothing of its actuality even today.

We have seen how in the first part of the act each stanza of Walther's Dream Song was greeted by Sachs with awed enthusiasm, articulated in the orchestra by the *Wahn* motive (see the three Reactions in appendix 6: act 3, part 1, 2.b), which has acted as a motto and periodically punctuated the whole act, reminding us of what was most deeply on this Schopenhauerian shoemaker's mind. The Prize Song itself gets a Postlude (appendix 6: act 3, part 2, 6.b4) in which the motive is allowed to reverberate in the minds of those to whom it was addressed: the People, the masters, and Eva. Once the Postlude is over the *Wahn* motive is heard one last time (III.2732–35) as Sachs addresses the crowd, asking what they think of his witness (a rhetorical question if ever there was one). At this point he clearly thinks more of the folly of those he had cleverly manipulated than of the creative folly of Walther.

The immediate motivation for Sachs's final thoughts in his second harangue to the People is Walther's momentary refusal to accept the status of a mastersinger that the guild now wants to bestow upon him: "Not a master! No! I want bliss without masters!"⁹⁷ Like those other youthful geniuses in Wagner's late dramas, Siegfried and Parsifal, Walther must be a bit dense if he still does not get the point that this will not do. Earlier in the act Sachs spent considerable time trying to explain to his protégé that, whether in art or in sexual relationships, nothing enduring can be achieved by individuals, no matter how talented, if they remain unmoored in a traditional social practice. Now the tutor delivers the lesson one last time, generalizing it for the benefit of the whole People, and the People repeat the lesson's final portion to signal they have internalized it well.

Much of the harangue (III.2771–897) as well as the People's final acclamation of Sachs (III.2897–910) is held together musically by the orchestra, which delivers a free recapitulation of the recapitulation music from the opera's Prelude, thus providing the whole drama with a formally satisfying frame (III.2771–825 and 2849–910). The only interruption takes the form of a stylistically jarringly conservative accompanied recitative (III.2826–48) that might have come straight from *Lohengrin*. Sachs begins by addressing Walther: "Do not disdain the masters and honor their art!"⁹⁸ It is your art alone, not your birth or weapons, that won you your happiness today, and this art has been preserved by our guild, "German and true."⁹⁹ In this way Sachs reaffirms his conviction that individual creative achievement would not be possible without the ongoing social practice that is the indispensable framework for this individual effort.

And then, with the central recitative, Sachs turns to the People: "Watch out! We are threatened."¹⁰⁰ The threat is that of the loss of national identity. Should the German people and state decay under the influence of "foreign [literally: French or Romance] pretense and trumpery,"¹⁰¹ "no one would know any more what is German and genuine, if it did not live on in the honor of German masters."¹⁰² The argument has subtly but unmistakably changed: artistic tradition needs to be cherished not only because it is what makes individual achievement possible, but also because it is a specifically national tradition and as such a guarantee, more sure than the state, of the survival of national identity. It is this nationalist sentiment, coupled with the enmity toward the French "other," that more than anything else in this opera has often given offense. With the music of the opera's Prelude coming back, Sachs concludes and all present (Beckmesser is absent by now) repeat after him: "Honor your German masters! . . . Even if the Holy Roman Empire [of the German Nation] goes up in smoke, we would still have the holy German art!"¹⁰³ At the time of the opera's premiere in 1868, the Holy Roman Empire, dissolved in 1806, was a distant memory and the new German Empire, about to be established in 1871, still only a nationalist hope; the shop was minded by the master of German art. All that remains is for Walther to accept the master's chain, for Eva to move the poet's wreath from Walther's to Sachs's head, for Pogner to kneel in front of the shoemaker, and for the masters to point to Sachs "as to their head":¹⁰⁴ the apotheosis of the Leader is complete.

The final words of the opera clearly show that the nationalist sentiment would be emphasized even without the interpolation; only the anti-French aside would be missing. Wagner seems to have entertained considerable doubts about Sachs's second harangue. To be sure, a close variant of Sachs's final couplet was added in pencil already on the margin of the prose draft of 1845: "Zerging' das heil'ge röm'sche Reich in Dunst, / Uns bliebe doch die heil'ge deutsche Kunst."[105] But neither there, nor in the two prose drafts of 1861, nor in the first version of the poem dated January 25, 1862, is there any trace yet of the warning that eventually will be issued in the central recitative of the speech (III.2826–44).[106] The warning itself condenses the thoughts Wagner articulated in a lengthy essay that best captures his thinking on these issues at the time, "German Art and German Policy" of 1867, in which the composer painted a picture of contemporary Europe as a scene of "the contest between French civilization and the German spirit," the former superficial and materialistic, imposed on the people from above, the latter deep, spiritual, and rooted in the people. German identity, Wagner argued, is safeguarded by German art, not by the thoroughly alien French civilization of local princes and their courts.[107] Nietzsche captured this aspect of the opera in a pithy formula found among his preparatory notes for *Richard Wagner in Bayreuth* (1876): "Meistersinger—the opposite of civilization, the German versus the French."[108] In an important letter of January 31, 1867, Cosima reported to King Ludwig II:

> The sublime Friend [the King] will be amazed to find on the sheet [enclosed with the letter] the new stanza of Hans Sachs ["Habt acht! Uns dräuen üble Streich"]; it was written in the night of 28 January between 2 and 3 AM, after I have spent almost the whole day discussing with the Friend [Wagner] the ending of the work; he thought, namely, that the drama was actually closed with Walther's poem and that the great speech of Sachs did not belong there, was more an address of the poet to the audience, and that he would rather do well to leave it out; at which I made such a miserable face, and told him also that "Will ohne Meister selig sein" belonged still so completely to the characterization of Walther, that he became reflective, even if he also naturally kept his opinion. It gave him no peace in the night, he wrote the stanza, crossed out what I had given him, and also sketched the music to it with a pencil.[109]

Wagner's doubts are understandable and believable. It was not his normal practice to tell his audiences directly what they should think, and his artistic instinct must have made him uneasy in the face of so much didacticism. His normal practice was well captured in the words Cosima transmitted in her *Diary* on March 4, 1869: "It is that which distinguishes the true poet, R. says, the ability to depict everything as it is, without explanation or solution. The latter is provided by the philosopher."[110] A similar sentiment was expressed on November 26, 1878: "Conveying messages always fails in art, however good the intention."[111] If in the end Wagner decided to keep, and even expand, Sachs's final speech, he might have been motivated by more than Cosima's views, or even his own ideological zeal. There were purely musical, formal reasons, too. Some kind of text and action was simply indispensable after Walther's Prize Song, if the formal design of the last scene was to be completed. Here is why:

The decisive contribution to our sense that the frame of Sachs's harangues outweighs in significance the kernel of the contestants' songs is made by the orchestra. The second part of the last act is dominated by an orchestral recapitulation (with or without superimposed voices) of the opera's Prelude. This proceeds in three stages, the first directly preceding Sachs's first harangue, the second accompanying the contest, and the third accompanying and following the ending of the second harangue and thus constituting the ending of the opera itself. In this way the stages provide the backbone and the outer frame for the last scene of the opera and, together with the Prelude itself, the outer frame for the opera as a whole—the opera's largest-scale and hence most weighty formal feature. Wagner lets us know that the Prelude will play an important role in the last scene already in the bass line of the orchestral transformation that begins the second part of the act (III.1764–78). A similar bass line resumes when the arrival of the mastersingers is announced (III.2059–75) and the recapitulation begins in earnest with the March of the Mastersingers (III.2076–135). A brief postlude follows as the apprentices call all the assembled to silence (III.2135–46). Wagner himself thought of the Prelude as a preview of the events in the last scene of the opera. The interpretation of the Prelude that he offered concert audiences long before the opera was completed (its earliest use is documented for the concerts in Karlsruhe on November 14 and 19, 1863) begins: "The Mastersingers march up with festive pomp in front of the people of Nuremberg."[112]

While a full-scale analysis of the Prelude would be superfluous here, a brief outline is necessary if we are to understand precisely what is being recapitulated and why (table 30). The Prelude is laid out in a tripartite ABA' form, the outer sections in C major, the central one modulatory. Wagner described the form to Cosima (November 26, 1879) as "a march with a trio, the theme of the trio appearing first of all in a whispered, fragmentary way before emerging in its full breadth."[113] Section A (I.1–89) presents four ideas in a row, two of which are particularly stressed (somewhat in the manner of the main and secondary themes in a sonata allegro, though here they are both in the tonic key): the theme representing the masters (I.1–27) and the one representing the guilds (I.37–58). This one is often referred to also as the King David theme; indeed, the composer's program for his Prelude does mention a "banner with the picture of King David playing a harp" at this point.[114] Wagner derived it from an example in Johann Christoph Wagenseil's book of 1697, the book that provided him with much of his information concerning the historical Meistersinger.[115] In his 1870 essay "About Conducting," Wagner gives it a more neutral name of "fanfare," which is precisely what it is.[116] (Of the

TABLE 30 *Die Meistersinger*, Prelude

Form	Key	Measures	CD.track.time
A.	C		
Masters		1–27	I.1.0:00–1:04
Transition		27–36	I.1.1:04–1:37
Guilds		37–58	I.1.1:37–2:30
Masters variant		59–89	I.1.2:30–3:41
B.	→		
Transition		89–96	I.1.3:41–4:06
Walther		97–121	I.1.4:06–5:14
Beckmesser against Walther		122–50	I.1.5:14–6:27
Retransition—Masters		151–57	I.1.6:27–6:44
A'.	C		
Masters with Walther and Beckmesser		158–73	I.1.6:44–7:20
Masters with Walther variant and emerging Guilds		174–87	I.1.7:20–7:53
Guilds		188–211	I.1.7:53–8:58
Masters		211–22	I.1.8:58–9:27

remaining two ideas, the one in I.27–36 functions as a transition and the one in I.59–89 is a variant of the Masters theme.)

The developmental section B (I.89–157) stages a preview of the contest, pitting Walther and Beckmesser against one another, Walther represented by his Prize Song (introduced at length in I.97–121) and Beckmesser by a scherzando transformation of the Masters theme (introduced at I.122 and struggling with Walther's song in I.122–50). Section A' (I.158–222), finally, begins with a synthesis: in I.158–73, the Masters theme in the bass is combined with Walther's theme in the soprano, thus indicating that Walther's integration into the mastersinger guild is the long-term goal of the drama. "The love song sounds together with the Masters' tunes: pedantry and poetry are reconciled," writes Wagner in his Prelude program.[117] In addition, the sixteenth-note figuration of the violins suggests the scherzando theme of Beckmesser, and the suggestion is made unmistakable in I.170–73, thus indicating that even Beckmesser will not be excluded from the final reconciliation—pity that Wagner left this indication discreetly hidden in the Prelude and did not make it explicit in the drama itself. The rest of the Prelude is devoted to the recapitulation of the main ideas from section A, in particular the Guilds theme (I.188–211) and the Masters theme (I.211–22).

With this background in mind, we can now see clearly what happens in the March of the Mastersingers (table 31, where the sections directly involved in the recapitulation are in bold print). At this stage of the recapitulation, Wagner ignores the two contestants and concentrates on the two main themes of the Prelude, presenting first the masters as they have been shown at the beginning of section A

TABLE 31 *Die Meistersinger*, Act 3, The Recapitulation of the Prelude

Form	Measures	CD:track:time	Recapitulated measures	CD:track:time
Stage 1				
Arrival of the Mastersingers	2059–75	IV.3.2:38–3:19		
March of the Mastersingers	2076–102	IV.3.3:19–4:19	I.1–27	I.1.0:00–1:04
	2102–28	IV.3.4:19–5:23	I.188–211	I.1.7:53–8:58
	2128–35	IV.3.5:23–5:42	I.211–22	I.1.8:58–9:27
Guilds	2135–46	IV.3.5:42–4:0:22		
Acclamation of Sachs with	2171–81	IV.4.2:39–3:06	I.74–88	I.1.3:04–3:40
Guilds	2182–87	IV.4.3:06–3:23		
Stage 2				
Beckmesser greeted with derision by the People with	2321–65	IV.6.0:24–1:27	I.122–50	I.1.5:14–6:27
Guilds	2366–78	IV.6.1:27–1:51		
[**Walther's Prize Song**	2610–732	IV.8.0:00–6:02	I.97–121	I.1.4:06–5:14]
Stage 3				
Sachs's Harangue II	2771–77	IV.9.0:00–0:22	I.151–57	I.1.6:27–6:44
	2778–93	IV.9.0:22–1:01	I.158–73	I.1.6:44–7:20
	2794–801	IV.9.1:01–1:20	I.174–87	I.1.7:20–7:53
	2802–25	IV.9.1:20–2:21	I.41–89	I.1.1:47–3:41
[interruption	2826–48	IV.9.2:21–3:41]		
Sachs's Harangue II cont. with	2849–65	IV.9.3:41–4:23	I.158–73	I.1.6:44–7:20
	2865–82	IV.9.4:23–5:11	I.188–205	I.1.7:53–8:40
	2883–97	IV.9.5:11–5:48	I.59–89	I.1.2:30–3:41
Acclamation of Sachs	2897–910	IV.9.5:48–6:30	I.211–22	I.1.8:58–9:27

(III.2076–102 = I.1–27) and then the Guilds and Masters themes from the end of section A' (III.2102–28 = I.188–211; III.2128–35 = I.211–22). The March, in other words, brings together the beginning and the end of the Prelude. It is then followed by the Guilds as the apprentices call for silence and, after the interpolation of the Reformation Hymn, by the general Acclamation of Sachs, which recapitulates this time the ending of the A section of the Prelude (III.2171–81 = I.74–88), followed by the Guilds again. The first stage of the recapitulation corresponds then to the section A of the Prelude, beginning and ending as this opening section did.

The second stage, in turn, corresponds to the B section of the Prelude, its two main ideas presented in reverse order. First, Beckmesser's scherzando version of the Masters theme from the Prelude (I.122–50) is used for the derisive fugato with which the People greet his appearance as a contestant (III.2321–65). The other thematic element of the B section, Walther's Prize Song (I.97–121), is the only significant idea from the Prelude that is, strictly speaking, not a part of the orchestral recapitulation. Instead of appearing in its orchestral guise, it simply appears as itself (III.2610–732), as an orchestral recapitulation would be redundant and tedious.

The third stage of the recapitulation, corresponding to the A' section of the Prelude, begins with Sachs's final harangue (III.2771) and, except for a brief interruption at the central recitative within the speech (III.2826–48), extends through the end of the opera. In the portion that precedes the interruption, the orchestra that accompanies Sachs begins with the retransition from the end of section B of the Prelude (III.2771–77 = I.151–57) and continues with the first two ideas of section A' (III.2778–93 = I.158–73 and III.2794–801 = I.174–87). There is one notable difference, however: where the beginning of section A' (I.158–73) synthesized the Masters, Walther, and Beckmesser themes, now (III.2778–93) Beckmesser is not included in the synthesis—at this point it is all about Walther getting integrated with the masters. At III.2802 the source of the recapitulated material changes and the orchestra now goes back to the second half of the A section of the Prelude, beginning with Guilds and continuing through the end of the section (III.2802–25 = I.41–89). In short, the Prelude material recapitulated before the interruption consists essentially of the first two ideas from section A' followed by the last two ideas from section A.

After the interruption, the recapitulation of the material from section A' begins anew with the section's first idea (III.2849–65 = I.158–73). Walther's integration with the masters is again emphasized, but this time there may also be the faintest whiff of Beckmesser's presence in the sixteenth-note runs of the violins in III.2852–56. It is hard to decide whether the allusion is there or not, since the runs never crystallize into a thematically distinct idea (as they had in the Prelude at I.170–73). If Wagner really wanted to include Beckmesser in the final synthesis, he should have been more explicit. At any rate, since his humiliation through the end of the drama, Beckmesser is not physically present onstage. (But we should not agonize all that much over Beckmesser's fate. First, his public humiliation is richly deserved; second, and more importantly, unlike Walther, Beckmesser does not need to be integrated with the masters because he is one of them already and no one thinks of expelling him from the guild. He stands for the most hidebound and ossified aspects of the tradition, the aspects that Walther's fresh talent should help to minimize and overcome, as it should if the tradition is to live.) When the People's chorus repeats Sachs's words, the orchestra moves on to the as-yet-not-recapitulated Guilds from section A' of the Prelude (III.2865–82 = I.188–205) and then yet again to the final idea from the A section (III.2883–97 = I.59–89). The recapitulation of the triumphant final idea of the Prelude is kept for the concluding Acclamation of Sachs (III.2897–910 = I.211–22). To summarize, then, there are in effect two recapitulations of the A' section, one each before and after the interruption, both beginning with the crucial Masters-Walther synthesis with which A' starts. While the first recapitulation ends with the final two ideas from A, the second corrects this by incorporating the final two ideas from A'.

As I have suggested, there were purely musical, formal reasons why Wagner decided to retain Sachs's second speech, in spite of the unease he felt on account of its overtly didactic nature. Now it should be clear what these reasons were. Some kind of text and action were simply indispensable after Walther's Prize Song if the formal design of the last scene, consisting of a recapitulation of the Prelude, was to be completed. And the interpolation, while strictly speaking not necessary, allowed Wagner to recapitulate A' twice, thus making the ending of the opera still more emphatic.

THE MYTH OF NATION

Thus the orchestral recapitulation of the Prelude underlies the whole last scene of the opera, providing it with a sturdy frame—the only formal feature that transcends the dimensions of a single act and embraces the entire drama (table 32 summarizes the overall formal organization of the opera). Until we become aware of this feature, it might seem that each of the three acts of *Die Meistersinger* is designed to lead toward and culminate in the final stage song: Walther's Trial Song with the Ensemble Finale in act 1; Beckmesser's Serenade with the Ensemble Finale in act 2; and in the two-part act 3, for all its Abgesang contrast to the two Stollen of the preceding acts, the Prize Songs of both Beckmesser and Walther in the second part of the act. The latter runs through the whole act as its backbone, since it is anticipated in Walther's Dream Song in the first part of the act.

This domination of each act by the culminating songs of the contestants, however, is not the full story. Already at the end of act 2, Beckmesser's Serenade is shadowed by the Night Music refrain in which some elements of the unconscious

TABLE 32 *Die Meistersinger*, Formal Organization

Form	Key	Text incipit	Measures	CD.track.time
Prelude	C		I.1–222	I.1
Walther's Trial Song with Ensemble Finale	F	'Fanget an!' So rief der Lenz in den Wald	I.1699–2082	II.1.0:11–3.6:33
REFRAIN	B	Geliebter, spare den Zorn	II.773–810	II.10.3:59–12.0:05
REFRAIN	B	Welch toller Spuck!	II.1202–17	II.15.7:01–7:46
Beckmesser's Serenade with Ensemble Finale and	G	Den Tag seh' ich erscheinen'	II.1217–357	II.16.0:00–17.1:16
	G	Zum Teufel mit dir	II.1357–439	II.17.1:16–3:09
Coda = REFRAIN	E	He! Lene! Wo bist du?	II.1439–85	II.17.3:09–5:45
Walther's Dream Song	C	'Morgenlich leuchtend in rosigem Schein'	III.651–801	III.7.0:00–7:47
			III.1431–94	III.10.3:44–11.0:28
The Prelude recapitulated:				
March of the Mastersingers	C		III.2059–146	IV.3.2:39–4.0:22
Acclamation of Sachs	C	Heil! Heil! Heil!	III.2171–87	IV.4.2:39–3:23
Sachs's Harangue I	G	Euch macht ihr's leicht	III.2188–280	IV.5.0:00–4:11
Beckmesser greeted with derision by the People	E-flat	Zum Teufel! Wie wackelig!	III.2321–65	IV.6.0:24–1:27
Beckmesser's Prize Song	e/G	'Morgen ich leuchte in rosigem Schein'	III.2379–454	IV.6.1:51–5:49
Walther's Prize Song	C	'Morgenlich leuchtend im rosigem Schein'	III.2610–732	IV.8.0:00–6:02
Sachs's Harangue II with	C	Verachtet mir die Meister nicht	III.2771–897	IV.9.0:00–5:48
Acclamation of Sachs	C	Heil! Sachs!	III.2897–910	IV.9.5:48–6:30

The sections of closed-form music are in bold; the open-form but non-dialogical sections are in bold italics; the refrain is in bold capital letters.

civic spirit of Nuremberg get to be articulated in purely musical terms, nonverbally. In the second part of act 3, the songs of the two contestants are framed and dwarfed by Sachs's harangues to the People. Ultimately it is on Sachs, not on Walther, that the act culminates, and it is Sachs who speaks for Nuremberg's people, articulating their communal spirit now in a fully conscious, verbal manner. And the People respond with the Acclamations of Sachs that in turn frame the two harangues and thus additionally underscore the shoemaker's dominance, or rather the dominance of the Leader and the People in a symbiotic embrace. The Prelude-and-its-recapitulation frame additionally deemphasizes the formal importance of the contestants' songs. The songs are significant for the organization of each act, to be sure, but the frame embraces all three acts. And since the last portion of the frame articulates the final harangue and acclamation, Sachs and the People emerge as the predominant protagonists of the drama.

Moreover, the dramatic functions of the songs, on the one hand, and the frame, on the other, are different. The songs articulate the most important events of the plot (this *is* a story of the contest between Walther and Beckmesser), while the frame, and in particular its final portion, articulates Sachs's (and Wagner's) ultimate interpretation of the story (as Sachs tells the people, and Wagner tells us, what to think about the events they, and we, have witnessed). By providing an outside point of view on them, the frame comes to dominate the songs. The story of individual rivalry is submerged in, and overpowered by, the image of the awakening collective spirit of Nuremberg, Germany, nation. The linear time of the contest is ultimately devalued or made relative by what matters even more, what matters absolutely: the enduring and permanent social-national tradition in the context of which the contest takes place.

We have seen that the issue of how the individual and the social should be properly related to each other dominated *Die Meistersinger* from the start. Throughout the opera this issue took the shape of two closely intertwined questions: Can and should private erotic passions and desires be harmonized with the public world of socially established traditional customs and obligations, and if so, how should the former be properly integrated into the latter? And: Can and should individual artistic talents and innovations be harmonized with the social aesthetic practices and traditions of the community, and if so, how? It is really one question in two variants: How can, and why should, individuals make something new within the social context of traditional practices, enriching rather than destroying this context? And the two variants come together as well, because whether in the erotic or the artistic arena, only individuals driven by the Schopenhauerian will, or folly, make something new.

The first question received a negative answer in *Tristan und Isolde*, but it is reconsidered and offered a more hopeful answer in *Die Meistersinger* (and the quotation from *Tristan* in the third act helps make this relationship between the two operas explicit). It now turns out that passionate love and enduring marriage are not mutually exclusive, and, more, that the vitality of the latter depends on the former just as the staying power of love depends on the social institution of marriage. And the second question, too, receives a similarly conciliatory, middle-of-the-road answer: artistic innovation does not need to revolutionize and overthrow artistic tradition, but may also renew and revitalize it. The social artistic tradition ossifies and dries out if not fertilized by individual innovation, just as individual creativity needs the context of the social tradition if it is to be more than a flash in the pan and, in fact, if its innovations are to be of any value at all. Nothing worthwhile in art has ever been created in a complete vacuum, independent of any preexisting tradition.

But in the last scene the opera shifts gears and goes into overdrive. It turns out that the issues that have dominated the drama up until now need to be seen from a still-larger perspective. Up to the last scene we would have been justified to hear in *Die Meistersinger* a wise plea for a moderate, conciliatory, balanced relationship between an individual's claim to be allowed to make something new and society's need to maintain stable traditions. This is how Nietzsche saw it in his 1876 *Richard Wagner in Bayreuth* pamphlet: "And will the *Meistersinger* not speak of the German nature to all future ages—more, will it not constitute one of the ripest fruits of that nature, which always seeks reformation not revolution, and though broadly content with itself has not forgotten that noblest expression of discontent, the innovative deed?"[118] In the last scene, however, this balance is disturbed as the needs of the social overpower any claims an individual can make. What is really important, we now discover, is not that Walther can have his way without ruining the proprieties of Nuremberg; what matters is that Nuremberg flourishes. The distinction might seem subtle, but it makes all the difference in the world. It matters whether the community is there to enable individuals to flourish, or whether individuals are there for the sake of the flourishing community. It matters because in the latter case, but not in the former, individuals may be easily pushed aside when they are in the way of the community.

We may have thought that the whole point of an artistic tradition was to provide context enabling individual accomplishment. But Sachs explains that this is not the whole point: a *national* artistic tradition defines the nation's identity and, more than statehood itself, guarantees its survival. A nation, *this* nation, is its art ("the holy German art"), not its state ("the Holy Roman Empire [of the German Nation]"): "even if the Holy Roman Empire were to dissolve into thin air, we would still have the holy German art!"—this is the opera's emphatic conclusion.[119] A passage in Wagner's 1865 essay "What Is German?" reads like a gloss on the opera's concluding words: "The outcome of the Thirty Years' War destroyed the German nation; yet, that a German Folk could rise again, is due to nothing but that outcome. The nation was annihilated, but the German spirit had passed through."[120] The emphasis at the end of the opera is on the German nation's identity and survival; the flourishing of Walther with Eva is a secondary matter. The social categories of the artistic tradition and the national community trump the claims of any individual artist or lover.

Voltaire famously quipped that the Holy Roman Empire was neither holy, nor Roman, nor an empire. This is not the case with Wagner's alternative: every word in the formula "holy German art" deserves to be taken seriously. The only question we may see as remaining open at the end of the opera is: What is more important, the art or the nation? Is the art there for the sake of the nation's survival, or the reverse: Is the nation there so that its art might flourish? Carl Dahlhaus tried to explain away the unpleasantly nationalist emphasis of the opera's ending by claiming that "Nietzsche's tenet that art is the only thing that justifies life . . . summarizes the theme of *Die Meistersinger*."[121] But if the function of art is to define, express, and preserve a nation's identity, then it is far from certain that it is life that serves art here; the opposite may well be the case. In the end, our question does not allow a clear answer: art and nation seem to be equiprimordial in *Die Meistersinger*, each existing in order to make the other possible. In this opera, "German" and "art" are equally important notions and both are "holy" in the sense that both transcend and trump any claims any individual might make, it being of the essence of the divine that it transcends the merely human.

The best argument that one might make for the primacy of art over nation in Wagner's thinking would have to go beyond the confines of this particular opera and point out that in no other of the late music dramas is the nation-building role of art at all important. Certainly Wagner wrote his poems in German and drew his material from Germanic mytho-poetic sources, but neither the *Ring* nor *Tristan* nor *Parsifal* is about establishing and preserving the German national community. Contrary to what one might think, it is not the *Ring* but *Die Meistersinger* that is Wagner's *Oresteia*, or, rather, *Oresteia* crossed with *A Midsummer Night's Dream*, the furies and folly unleashed during the community-threatening *Johannisnacht* riot appeased and productively directed toward the state-founding energies of the *Johannistag* festival.[122] Nationalism is an issue, *the* issue, in *Die Meistersinger* alone. More than the other three works, this one, written and composed between 1861 and 1867 and premiered in 1868, is contemporary with Bismarck's most intensive efforts to reestablish the German Reich. "In sum, particularly in the present time I estimate to have touched the very nerve of the German life," Wagner wrote on November 20, 1861, to his publisher, Franz Schott, with regard to the prose draft of the new project.[123] And on March 16, 1873, Cosima noted her husband's words in her *Diary*: "'This is the form in which I visualized Germans in their true character, their best light, with a popular poet like Hans Sachs, an enthusiastic youth who, though not a mastersinger, feels poetically, and a respectable pedant. This is their level in life; everything else, elegance, for instance, is affectation; but their feelings are of the highest.'"[124]

Clearly Wagner did think of the opera in national terms. (And, just as clearly, his remarks should give pause to all those who confidently assume that Beckmesser was intended as a Jewish caricature.) As I have argued in an earlier discussion of *Die Meistersinger*, nationalism is much more sympathetic when it is the ideology of a community struggling for unity, independence, recognition, and statehood, and much less so when it is the ideology of an aggressive and successful state.[125] In Wilhelminian Germany, *Die Meistersinger* was regularly understood to embody the national spirit in its struggle against foreign powers, and so it was understood after the defeat of 1918 and again in Hitler's Germany. When on July 22, 1924, the Bayreuth Festival reopened after a ten-year interruption with this very opera, the audience followed the performance with a performance of its own, singing "Deutschland über alles."[126] Curiously, Hitler himself disapproved of such manifestations and let it be known during the 1934 Festival that "The Führer wishes to see an end to the singing of 'Deutschland über alles' or the Horst Wessel Lied and similar demonstrations at the close of the performances."[127] The last two festivals of the Nazi period, those of 1943 and 1944, presented only one opera, *Die Meistersinger*, in a production that involved the participation of both Wilhelm Furtwängler (who conducted) and the composer's grandson, Wieland Wagner (who designed the sets and costumes), and that featured members of the SS-Division Viking in the role of the People.[128]

To Wagner's credit, it has to be said that his nationalist ardor cooled down considerably within a decade after the empire has been established in 1871. At the time of the first Bayreuth Festival in 1876, with so many potentates of the new empire in attendance, it was possible to mock the composer as a "state *musicus*" ("Staatsmusikant," in Karl Marx's contemptuous formulation).[129] In a similar spirit, Nietzsche proclaimed: "What did I never forgive Wagner? That he *condescended* to the Germans—that he became *reichsdeutsch*."[130] But Nietzsche's accusation, accurate for the early and mid-1870s, was out of date by 1888, or even a decade earlier. Once it became clear that Bismarck and the emperor of the Germans would do much less for the Bayreuth cause than the generous King of Bavaria, the disillusioned composer quickly stopped being *reichsdeutsch*. Recalling the difficulties of financing the first Bayreuth Festival two years after the fact in 1878, he concluded: "I soon had enough of Reich and Kanzel."[131] (I assume that by "Kanzel" he means "Kanzler," the chancellor, Bismarck.) On July 15, 1878, he wrote to King Ludwig II: "And this new Germany nauseates me!"[132]

More broadly, in the 1865 essay "What Is German?"—that is, at the time when he was composing *Die Meistersinger*—Wagner clearly expressed his preference for a cultural rather than political Germany, for a *Kulturnation* over a *Staatsnation*: "German poetry, German music, German philosophy," he wrote, "are nowadays esteemed and honored by every nation in the world; but in his yearning after 'German glory' the German, as a rule, can dream of nothing but a sort of resurrection of the Romish Kaiser-Reich, and the thought inspires the most good-tempered German with an unmistakable lust of mastery, a longing for the upper hand over other nations. He forgets how detrimental to the welfare of the German peoples that notion of the Romish State had been already."[133] And he added a warning: "Woe to us and the world, if the nation itself were this time saved, but the German spirit vanished from the world!"[134] In short, Dahlhaus may have been wrong about nationalism's subordinate status to art in *Die Meistersinger*, but he was surely right about art's preeminence in Wagner's long-term thinking. The composer's paramount cause was art, especially his own art, and not the nation. And even in *Die Meistersinger* the nation celebrated by Wagner (though not necessarily all of his listeners) was likely to be cultural rather than political.

Before Dahlhaus, it was Thomas Mann who thought that the final lines of the opera expressed "a downright anarchic indifference to political structures, as long as German intellectual and spiritual values ... are preserved intact,"[135] and in the wake of Dahlhaus, both Dieter Borchmeyer and Udo Bermbach interpreted the opera as an apolitical aesthetic utopia.[136] "Wagner's Nuremberg," Borchmeyer points out, "is wholly depoliticized.... The town of Nuremberg lacks any municipal authority.... It is impossible to escape the conclusion that Nuremberg has been transformed into a kind of 'aesthetic state.'"[137] Moreover, "In Wagner's imaginary Nuremberg [the masters] replace the town councilors of history.... Art and artists alone set the tone in this totally aestheticized community."[138] Bermbach argues similarly: "The 'myth of Nuremberg': for Wagner this meant to put all one's hopes for the future in art, to place art as the decisive medium of the radical social self-renovation and thus also to show that the politics practiced until now has become superfluous."[139] Like Borchmeyer, Bermbach concludes that "politics is absent in *Die Meistersinger.*"[140] And he argues that the intention of Sachs's final monologue is to give art primacy over politics.[141]

All of this may be literally correct, but if it is designed to justify Sachs's final monologue, it misses the point. Far from solving the *Meistersinger* problem, the opera's apolitical aesthetic utopian character *is* its problem. It might have been slightly preferable had Wagner ended the opera unambiguously with a glorification of art rather than nation, but only slightly. There is nothing all that admirable in the artist's megalomania and self-aggrandizement. Should we want, with Wagner, artists to be kings or political leaders? Modern liberal democracies, in any case, should be properly esteemed when they make high culture available to those citizens who want access to it. They should not additionally provide creators of such culture with positions of social and political leadership for which they are not necessarily qualified. Not much imagination is needed to see how the final apotheosis of Sachs as a poet-dictator might inspire an admiring but untalented imitator, a failed artist like Beckmesser, to attempt a political career (as Stefan Herheim suggested in his intelligent and imaginative Salzburg staging of 2013). In his public pronouncements if not his actual practice, Hitler himself completely agreed with Wagner that art and culture should have priority over politics and economy.[142] And already in 1938, Thomas Mann recognized in Hitler a fellow artist, "brother Hitler."[143]

More importantly still, the hypothetical *Die Meistersinger* that had ended with a glorification of art and artist would be problematic for yet another reason. The devaluation of, and contempt for, grubby everyday politics, partisan struggles for power and influence over policy, haggling and voting masters, in favor of art and spirit, of culture, has been one of the central tenets of the German intellectual tradition. In this respect nothing separates Wagner from Nietzsche, for example. At the time when he still identified himself as a "non-political man" (1918), Thomas Mann captured this aspect of Wagner's thinking with revealing clarity and, unfortunately, equally revealing approval: "But why did he hate democracy? Because he *hated politics per se*, and because he recognized that *politics and democratism are one and the same thing*. . . . A nation's taste for democracy is in inverse proportion to its distaste for politics. If Wagner was in any sense an expression of his nation, if in anything he was German, German-humanistic, German-bourgeois in the highest and purest sense, it was in his hatred of politics."[144] By 1940 Mann's approval of this attitude was withdrawn when he bluntly asserted in a text devoted to the subject of Wagner and Hitler: "National Socialism, in all its ineffable empirical vileness, is the tragic consequence of the mythical political innocence of the German spirit."[145] There is nothing surprising in that intellectuals and artists, the creators and main consumers of high culture, think that they deserve positions of leadership in their societies (recall the role Plato envisaged for philosophers in the *Republic*). But the apolitical or even antipolitical tenor of their intellectual tradition was one of the reasons why most German intellectuals were so ineffective and defenseless in the face of Hitler's rise to power.

It is more than likely that Wagner's nationalism of the 1860s was inspired by Johann Gottlieb Fichte's *Addresses to the German Nation*, delivered in Berlin in 1807–8 and published in 1808. I mentioned some of the points of convergence in the prologue to this book. Particularly striking perhaps is Fichte's emphasis on the middle-class, rather than aristocratic, nature of the Germans:

> The Germans who stayed behind in the motherland had retained all the virtues that were once native to their soil: loyalty, integrity, honour, simplicity; but as for cultivation to a higher life of the spirit, they had received no more than the Christianity of that time. . . . This did not amount to much, and they lagged a long way behind their emigrated kin in this respect. Though honest and upright, they were yet half-barbarians. Among them, however, there rose up cities built by members of the people. In these cities every branch of the life of culture rapidly put forth the most beautiful blossoms. . . . The German burghers were now cultured and the others barbarians. . . . This epoch is also the only one in German history in which this nation stands in all its splendor and glory. . . . As its prosperity is destroyed by princely greed and

thirst for power, and its freedom trampled underfoot, so the whole sinks gradually ever lower and approaches to its present state. . . . The decisive influence of this class, which was in effect the ruling class, on the development of the German imperial constitution, on Church reform, and on everything that was ever characteristic of the German nation and exported abroad is manifest everywhere one looks, and it can be shown that everything that is still venerable among the Germans arose in its midst. And with what spirit did this German class bring forth and enjoy its heyday? With the spirit of piety, respectability, modesty, community.[146]

Fichte continues with a passage that reads like a direct call to Wagner encouraging him to create *Die Meistersinger*:

Of the individual and particular means of raising the German spirit once more, a very effective one would be the publication of an inspiring history of the Germans during this period, which would become a national book, a book for the people, . . . until the day when we in turn accomplished something worthy of being recorded. Only instead of enumerating deeds and events like a chronicle, such a history ought to grip us in the most marvelous fashion and, without our co-operation or clear consciousness, transport us right into the midst of the life of those times, so that we seem to walk, to stand, to deliberate, to act with our forebears. . . . That time was the youthful dream of a nation moving in limited circles, a dream of future deeds, struggles and victories: and it was the prophecy foretelling what it would one day be when in full possession of its power. The blandishments of society and the allure of vanity have carried away the rising nation into circles that are not its own and, because it desired to shine there also, it finds itself covered with shame and fighting for its very survival. . . . Let us first turn this nation back from the wrong path it has taken; show it in the mirror its childhood dreams, its true inclination, its true vocation, until in the midst of these meditations its power unfolds to embrace mightily its destiny. May this appeal help to bring forth a suitably equipped German man who very soon will solve this preliminary task![147]

Recall Wagner's remark quoted above: "This is the form in which I visualized Germans in their true character, their best light."

In its understanding of politics, art, and their mutual relationship, *Die Meistersinger von Nürnberg* returns in many essential points to the positions originally articulated in *Lohengrin* (1845–48). Reading one Wagnerian drama in the light of another, incidentally, is a procedure that would probably meet with the poet's approval. In a pamphlet dated December 7, 1871, and published in 1872, in which he reported on the circumstances attending the realization of his *Ring* project, Wagner talks of "the grand concordance of all sterling Myths" as well as "the wondrous variations standing out amid this harmony," and he provides an example: "Both Tristan and Siegfried, in bondage to an illusion which makes this deed of theirs unfree, woo for another their own eternally-predestined bride, and in the false relation hence-arising find their doom."[148] As Wagner made clear in *A Communication* to *My Friends* (written in 1851 and published a year later), Lohengrin was conceived as a figure of the modern artist, a genius whose inspired work redeems his society—provided, however, that it is taken on faith, by feeling, without irksome questions dictated by reason.[149] The political arrangement idealized in *Lohengrin* is in essence the one Wagner will advocate in his speech to the Fatherland Association during the heady days of June 1848 (the speech discussed above in connection with the evolving conception of how the *Ring* might end), a popular monarchy in which the relationship between the king and his people is immediate, rather than mediated by the court aristocracy and the town money lenders. In such a society, an artist would be allowed to articulate the people's deepest convictions under the direct protection of the king and he, the artist, in turn would protect the king and the people by the guidance provided by his redeeming art.

Lohengrin, the God-sent champion of Elsa of Brabant (who has been falsely accused of having murdered her brother, Duke Gottfried), can not only successfully defend the innocent maid, but also, as Elsa's husband and the realm's ruler, the Protector of Brabant, bring peace to the duchy troubled by political uncertainty, but only under the condition that his wife would not ask his name or origin: "You should never ask me, nor trouble yourself to know, wherefrom I have come, nor what is my name and origin."[150] For a time Elsa seems to have internalized Lohengrin's requirement to be taken on faith. As she tells the conniving Ortrud: "Poor thing, you cannot conceive how my heart loves without a doubt? You have never had the happiness that is given us only through faith?"[151] A little later she announces, "His being is so pure and noble, the sublime man is so full of virtue, that he who can doubt his sending will never recover from disaster!"[152] Alas, this is precisely what happens to her. She asks the fatal question, Lohengrin reveals his name and origin (he is one of the Knights of the Grail, a brotherhood of divinely inspired and supported do-gooders ruled by his father, Parsifal), and, to universal regret, departs back for the Grail castle of Monsalvat, but not before giving the Brabantians a consolation prize in the shape of a new ruler, the miraculously restored Duke Gottfried himself: "Behold the Duke of Brabant, let he be named your Leader."[153] (It is possible that Hitler got the idea of calling himself the "Führer" from *Lohengrin*.)[154]

It is thus that the symbiotic—or, if you will, organic—triangle of the king, the people, and the artist provides the essential structure of *Lohengrin*, with the artist expressing the people's values and thus offering them guidance and even legitimizing the rule of the king, provided his sending is emotionally accepted rather than intellectually examined, just as it does in the case of *Die Meistersinger*, and will again in that of *Parsifal*. Even the nationalism, later so pronounced in *Die Meistersinger*, is already in place in *Lohengrin* where the king is heard proclaiming, and all the men repeating after him, "For the German soil the German sword! So will the power of the Empire be validated!"[155] and again where Lohengrin is heard delivering himself of a prophesy, "The hordes from the East shall never, even in the most remote days, draw victoriously toward Germany."[156] Already at this stage the roles of the king and the artist begin to blend: Lohengrin's is primarily that of the artist, but he is also a ruler, the Protector of Brabant, himself under the protection of a still more important ruler, the head of the empire of which Brabant is but a province, King Henry the Fowler. The step from this art-political vision of *Lohengrin* to the one in which the figure of the artist blends with that of the king even more, as it does in *Die Meistersinger*, is a short one. In *Parsifal* the evolution will reach its logical conclusion, the king and the God-sent redeeming artist becoming one.

In this context one can make sense of the call Wagner issued in 1863 (in the "Preface to the public issue of the poem of the Bühnenfestspiel 'Der Ring des Nibelungen'") to "a German Prince" to come to his rescue and provide him with the material means that would make regular festival performances of the *Ring* possible: "Thus would he [the Prince] found an institution that needs must give him an incalculable influence upon German art-taste, on the development of German artistic genius, on the cultivation of a genuine, not arrogated national spirit."[157] In retrospect it becomes clear that the revolutionary radicalism of *Der Ring des Nibelungen* has been something of an aberration or detour in Wagner's oeuvre; or, perhaps better, one might see in *Lohengrin* and *Die Meistersinger* the outlines of the political order for which the revolution of the *Ring* would make room. *Die Meistersinger* would thus provide us with an insight into the post-political politics (or "metapolitics," to use the concept introduced by Constantin Frantz, a political theorist Wagner much admired) implied but left wholly unspecified by the *Ring*.[158] From *Lohengrin* through *Die Meistersinger* (and on to *Parsifal*), Wagner's political ideal has been a kind of artocracy (an ideal he may have hoped to have come close to in real life when King Ludwig II offered him his protection), a popular monarchy untroubled by political and economic struggles for advantage and providing a luxurious shelter to the artist, who like the church of old returns the favor and provides the secular realm with his spiritual guidance, or even blends with the monarch. Given Germany's and Europe's subsequent history, it is a vision at once prophetic and chilling, an invitation to an artistically minded usurper to come and save the nation in trouble, a blueprint for Hitler's popular dictatorship. No matter how biased one is in favor of art, there is nothing consoling in the kind of aesthetic post-political politics envisaged here. Incidentally, we should not be misled by Walter Benjamin's famous but facile formula that assigned such aestheticizing of politics to Fascism alone. "The logical result of Fascism," claims Benjamin, "is the introduction of aesthetics into political life. . . . Communism responds by politicizing art."[159] Actually, the aestheticizing of politics is characteristic of totalitarian practice regardless of whether its coloring is brown or red.

The claim that Wagner's metapolitics anticipates that of Hitler should not be taken to mean, as some of the more enthusiastic proponents of the Wagner-as-proto-

Nazi view of the artist sometimes argue, that all of Hitler is already there in Wagner and that there are no differences between them.[160] Wagner's clear preference for Germany as a cultural rather than political nation as well as his equally clear and explicit opposition to violence, militarism, and imperialism (something we shall encounter in the following chapter), the militarism and imperialism of the contemporary Prussian Reich emphatically included, make his wholesale appropriation by the Nazis a grotesque act of usurpation equal to that of their appropriation of Nietzsche. All that I claim here is that the composer's aesthetic metapolitical utopia has proto-totalitarian features and hence should trouble rather than console us.

In short, both the music-dramatic formal analysis and an examination of what the protagonists say and do point in the same direction: the carefully calibrated balance between the claims of individuals and those of the society that prevails through much of *Die Meistersinger* is disturbed in the last scene of the opera, where the individuals are sidelined and the emphasis is all on the social side, on the side of artistic and national traditions. The opera that, we had thought, was about how Walther's needs as an artist and lover were integrated with the common practices of Nuremberg's masters turns out at the end to be about the need to preserve the national identity of the German people under the tutelage and leadership of Hans Sachs. And we should not mistake the final apotheosis of Sachs for a celebration of human individuality. Sachs and the People, we have seen, are one. Far from being a free individual, he is the Leader articulating the People's deepest collective aspirations.

On both levels, then—that of form and that of content—the last scene of the opera springs a surprise. But consider how much more surprising (and wiser) it would have been if it did not surprise us in this way. The moderate liberal-conservative wisdom of *Die Meistersinger* without its last scene is quite un-Wagnerian. Artistically, socially, and politically, Wagner's temperament was fundamentally radical—revolution, not reform, its byword. The composer was not one of those who dream of improving the existing world; he was one of those who dream of destroying it in order to make room for something completely different. This was obviously the case in his most revolutionary phase between 1848 and 1854, when both his poems and his letters abounded in images of a desired world conflagration. But Wagner remained radical also after he exchanged the company of Mikhail Bakunin for the patronage of King Ludwig II and the optimism of Ludwig Feuerbach and other left-Hegelians for the pessimism of Schopenhauer. The temperament, the imagination behind *Tristan* and *Parsifal*, no less than those behind the *Ring*, are of the world-rejecting and -overturning, not world-improving, sort. Thus the radical political vision of the last scene of *Die Meistersinger* comes as a surprise in the context of what preceded it in the opera, but not in the context of Wagner's late oeuvre as a whole. On the contrary: the last scene brings this opera into line with other late music dramas.

There are two other respects in which *Die Meistersinger* turns out to be much less of an anomaly among Wagner's late works than it might seem at first, when it appears to us as a comedy among works of tragic character and as a drama based on historical rather than mythological materials. Joseph Kerman, we have already seen, argued that *Tristan und Isolde* should be considered a religious drama rather than a tragedy, and similar claims could also be made about the *Ring* as well as, obviously, *Parsifal*. To be sure, the comic tone of *Die Meistersinger* does differentiate it from the tragic one of the remaining music dramas but nevertheless, all of the late operas end similarly, on a note of triumphant exaltation in the face of a vision of a transcendent reality. Thus we should be fooled neither by the comic nor by the non-mythological nature of *Die Meistersinger*, as both are put in doubt by its final scene. A myth is a story of an encounter between the human and the divine. At the opera's end Sachs unveils an exalting vision of a transcendent reality, the absolute national reality that relativizes all the individual struggles that went on before. No less than the remaining music dramas, also this one stages a myth, the nationalist myth of Nuremberg.

Those of us troubled by the damage nationalist ideology did to Nuremberg, Germany, Europe, and the world within some eighty years following the opera's premiere will find the triumphant exaltation of the finale regrettable, even revolting. The problem of *Die Meistersinger* is not, as has been commonly supposed, the final speech of Sachs, but the last scene as a whole. (In any case, as I have argued above, what Sachs says is relatively harmless when compared to what he does in this last scene, subverting the legitimate order and staging a coup.) To my mind, the final scene considerably weakens both ideologically and artistically what might have been Wagner's wisest work ("my finest work," as the composer estimated it while drafting the third act,[161] or "really his masterpiece," as Cosima reports him to judge it on March 14, 1882, that is, close to the end of his life),[162] drowning the sublime subtlety of the Quintet and much that had preceded it under the bombast of a folk festival-turned-political rally led by a new Rienzi, the people's tribune, a triumphalist monument to the artist's will to power and megalomania. In fact, I can think of no other example of a masterpiece so profoundly wounded by its ending.

But this ending also makes the work so much more interesting and prophetic, if less coherent. The opera resembles its main protagonist: behind the jovial, *altdeutsch* facade lurks something much less *gemütlich*. The artistic, social, and political vision of *Die Meistersinger*, I have claimed here, returns to, and updates, the position embodied already in *Lohengrin* and the earliest version of the *Ring*: the ideal of a popular monarchy or dictatorship, with the people legitimizing the rule of the leader or king directly, without any interference from the mediating political and economic elites, a system under which the artist would be able to express the people's deepest values under the leader's or king's protection, without having to bow to the wishes of the elites. And if the leader happens to be an artist himself, so much the better. No less than Walther's art, also Walther's politics of art and Sachs's art of politics may seem so old, and yet are so new. Walther had no chance of succeeding under the old patrician regime of the masters. He succeeds only thanks to the patronage of Sachs, who, in alliance with the people he manipulates, subverts the legitimacy of the masters' rule. The modern artist, feeling lost, helpless, and neglected within a society that has no clear role for him, longs for the protection of a prince, old or new, be his name that of King Ludwig II or, with the gradual waning of aristocratic patronage in the twentieth century, of some future dictator.

Die Meistersinger marks the moment of Germany's transformation, soon to be regretted by Wagner himself, from a national community defined by its culture into one defined by its state power. It offers a glimpse of the alliance between the Leader and the People that will be one form politics will take in the coming age of mass democracies, and of the eagerness with which artists will seek the protection of dictators under these new conditions. It is perhaps this opera's most fascinating feature that it offers these glimpses of a radical future, as if unaware that such a future is incompatible with the moderate liberal-conservative bourgeois order that it has otherwise depicted with so much genuine insight and sympathy.

5

Parsifal
Ethics after Tristan

If *Die Meistersinger von Nürnberg* offered an improved, richer, more differentiated alternative to the social and political issues raised in *Der Ring des Nibelungen*, *Parsifal* seems to offer an improved, more hopeful alternative to the ethical issues raised in *Tristan und Isolde*. That the hope requires an act of faith is only to be expected. Less expected, however, is that this hope is built on a transformed understanding of the notion of love. No less than *Die Meistersinger*, so too does *Parsifal* repudiate the free love extolled in the *Ring* and the radical eros celebrated in *Tristan* in favor of another deity. In the public realm, the sacred takes the shape of the nation, we learned in Nuremberg; at Monsalvat we learn that, in the private sphere, the sacred takes the shape of the love of neighbor—eros is replaced by agape.

THE COMMUNION SEQUENCES OF ACTS 1 AND 3

The simplicity and clarity of formal organization in *Parsifal* is quite unprecedented in Wagner's oeuvre. Even the most inattentive member of the audience must notice the ABA' plan of the whole, with the contrasting central act that takes place in Klingsor's magic castle and garden surrounded by acts of parallel construction, each beginning in the forest and ending in the castle in the domain of the guardians of the Grail (the cup used by Christ during the Last Supper, which received the blood shed at the cross). Not much more attention is required to observe how in each of the framing acts the loosely structured, open, outdoor beginnings, dominated by prosaic recitative dialogues and narrative monologues, give way to more tightly organized, closed, indoor endings that contain the longest stretches of lyrical utterance in the opera. But the parallels between the two acts go much further.

The closing portion of act 1, from the music that accompanies the forest-into-castle transformation of the scenery to the end of the act, is the opera's longest sequence of nondialogic, mostly lyrical, closed forms, laid out in five broad sections that in turn can be grouped into three parts (see appendix 7: act 1, B).

The Transformation is almost entirely orchestral, with some superimposed dialogue at the beginning and end. It is modulatory, as is appropriate for music designed to accompany the transition of the elderly Grail knight, Gurnemanz, and the mysterious young intruder, Parsifal, from the God-made to the human-made forest of the dome-covered, pillared hall in the castle. Arriving in C only at the end, it is saturated by the characteristic dotted march rhythm, especially at the beginning and end. Its "slow and solemn"[1] march finds its natural continuation in the three choruses that follow in the same tempo and, for the duration of the first two at least, the same meter and rhythm. This is natural, since the Knights of the Grail enter the hall in Gurnemanz's and Parsifal's footsteps, with the same purpose of participating in the Feast. The Processional of the Knights in C is answered by the Youths from the mid-height of the dome as the wounded king, Amfortas, and the shrine of the Grail are brought onstage. They enter in an inconclusive transitory e-flat, and the Boys from the top of the dome intone one of the central motives of the Communion—usually identified as the motive of Faith—in the concluding A-flat. Thus the two sections—Transformation and Processional—while distinct, clearly belong together and serve to assemble all the participants in the expected Feast and get us from C through an unstable and inconclusive e-flat to A-flat—the key of the Communion.

Once the Communion concludes, the same tonal and thematic trajectory rewinds in reverse, though much faster, in the brief orchestral and modulatory Recessional (a succinct recitative emerges toward the end, I.1635–53). This begins with the same motive of Faith and in the same key in which the Processional ended. Eventually it becomes dominated by a return to the slow and solemn march that takes Amfortas, the shrine, and the Knights out of the hall and leads from the A-flat of the Communion through a brief moment of stability in E-flat back to the final C. This frame of the Transformation and Processional on one end and Recessional on the other—its two components mirroring one another in their mostly orchestral delivery, motivic and tonal content, and dramatic function—ensures that the entire proceedings from the beginning of the Transformation to the end of the act are taken in as a single whole rather than a succession of independent units.

At the center of this freely symmetrical arch, the Communion itself stands as its tonal and dramatic capstone. A few introductory measures (I.1422–39) accompany the uncovering of the Grail cup, then come "voices from above,"[2] presumably the Youths from the mid-height of the dome judging by the voice ranges. These intone in unison a "very slow"[3] A-flat major phrase, the Love motive, which is then repeated by the trumpet while the hall is gradually submerged in complete darkness (I.1440–58). Wagner's term for "Communion," "Liebesmahl," literally "feast of love," brings out the connection, lost in translation, between the name of the ritual and that of the motive that is the ritual's central musical theme. This sequence of musical events is then repeated a third higher, in c minor, with the phrase intoned by the Boys "from above,"[4] presumably from the top of the dome, except that this time the orchestra does not allow the trumpet to conclude the phrase. Instead it develops further to finish in C major (I.1459–78) while "a dazzling ray of light falls from above upon the crystal cup, which now glows, ever-deeper, a shining wine-purple color, shedding a soft light on all around."[5] All the while, Amfortas raises the Grail and consecrates the bread and wine. A postlude based on the musical idea I shall call the Hope motive modulates back to A-flat (I.1479–92) as daylight returns and the Grail is set again in its shrine. The first half of the Communion is over.

In the second half, as the consecrated bread and wine are distributed to the Knights, three separate choral groups—the Boys, the Youths, and the Knights—are divided first into two half choirs and then reunited. In four consecutive phrases (I. 1493–509, 1510–26, 1528–44, 1544–61) they transmute the Love motive into something that sounds more and more like a triumphantly goose-stepping military march in E-flat—the Knights of the Grail at their most unattractively Teutonic ("Definition of the Teuton: obedience and long legs").[6] The orchestra, however, deflects the final cadence so that the Communion can end with all three choirs intoning the Hope motive in A-flat (I.1563–74) as the Knights solemnly embrace.

Thus, in spite of this articulation into two halves—the first devoted to the consecration of the sacramental bread and wine, the second to the partaking of the sacrament by the Knights—the Communion is a tonally and motivically unified whole, with each half based on the Love motive and rounded off by the Hope motive and a return to the main key of A-flat.

This capstone of the formal arch that closes the act is anticipated in the opening portion of the Prelude. It begins with the two phrases of the Love motive that had begun the Communion, the ones in A-flat and c respectively, each intoned in unison by strings doubled by woodwinds and repeated by an accompanied trumpet. As a result, I.1440–78 are nearly identical to I.1–38, except that in the Prelude the second trumpet phrase is allowed to repeat the second string phrase literally, while in the Communion scene it undergoes a slight development at the end. As in the scene, so also in the Prelude: the Love music is followed by the Hope theme in A-flat, but this time the literal repetition of the Prelude phrase occurs not at the end of the first half of the scene (where a modulation back to A-flat was needed), but at the end of the second half, where the Prelude's Hope motive (I.39–41) is repeated three times (I.1563–74). This repetition is subtly anticipated in the Prelude, where the motive is extended by the echo of the so-called Dresden Amen (I.42–43). The only additional new material in the Prelude, introduced immediately thereafter, is the Faith motive (I.44–55), which completed the preparation for the Communion scene at the end of the Processional and initiated its immediate aftermath at the beginning of the Recessional.

On the one hand, not only the key but also all of the motivic material of the Communion scene is derived from the Prelude, much of it literally; on the other, the Faith motive aside, the complete thematic exposition of the Prelude (I.1–43) is reproduced almost measure for measure in much of the first half and the ending of the second half of the Communion scene (I.1440–78 and 1563–74). As a result, the Prelude is retrospectively experienced as an anticipation of the Communion and assimilated to the structure of which the Communion scene is the center—the two lyrical, or at least nondialogic, pillars at the beginning and end of act 1.[7]

The thematic exposition of the Prelude is peculiar in that its ideas are simply presented one after another, without any transitions. An entry in Cosima Wagner's *Diary* (September 23, 1879) throws an interesting light on this unusual mode of presentation, suggesting that in the composer's mind it went hand in hand with the liturgical use to which this material was to be put: "During the evening R. played to us the Prelude to *Parsifal*, which he called a preamble [*Vorrede*], like the preamble to a sermon, since the themes are merely laid out side by side."[8] Wagner's own names for the themes can be found in a program he prepared for King Ludwig II when the Prelude was to be given a private performance on November 12, 1880.[9] The composer describes the Prelude as consisting of two parts (I.1–79 and 80–113), the first of which is devoted almost entirely to the presentation of the themes. Surprisingly he divides this first part into two, rather than three, sections. The first (I.1–38) he calls "Love" ("Liebe," the name I have retained here), and the second (I.39–79) "Faith" ("Glaube"). But he then clarifies that within this second section, there are really two ideas: first, the "Promise of Redemption through Faith" ("Verheißung der Erlösung durch den Glauben," I.39–43) which I am calling Hope, and second, the "Faith" proper ("Glaube," I.44–55), the name I retain.

But to come back to the Communion sequence, my description of the ending of act 1 as a freely symmetrical arch formed by the Transformation and Processional, the central capstone of the Communion, and the concluding Recessional is incomplete. Before the Communion can begin, the structure of the arch is disrupted by Amfortas, who in a lengthy monologue attempts to prevent the ritual over which he should be presiding from taking place. Preceded by a brief recitative dialogue and followed by a brief chorus and recitative, the monologue avoids all features of the "closed" compositional system. Regular phrasing, stable tonality, and patterns of motivic contrast and repetition, features that dominate the remaining portions of the arch (where the only "open" moment is the succinct recitative added toward the very end, I.1635–53), are absent. Clearly calculated for maximum contrast with its surroundings, the monologue is like an alien, tortured body inserted into the stately and steadily progressing celebration—a disruption or interruption (it would be entirely possible to go directly from the ending of the Processional to the beginning of the Communion, from I.1244 to 1422), in short, not only in dramatic but equally in musical terms.

Why this interruption? We need to consider the significance of the disrupted ritual. The Feast of Love ("Liebesmahl"), as the Knights call it at the very beginning of the Processional (I.1169–79), is obviously a Christian sacrament, a version of the Eucharist, a thanksgiving commemoration of the Last Supper. It involves the consecration of bread and wine as Christ's body and blood (long and inconclusive wars were to be fought over the precise meaning of this "as") and their reception by the assembled faithful in communion. Wagner's fictitious Knights of the Grail are a military order like the historic Knights Templar, Knights of Malta, or the Teutonic Knights. Devoted to performing good works and guarding the relics of the Crucifixion (the Grail as well as the Spear that wounded Christ on the cross) from the infidel other, in this case the rejected magician Klingsor. Significantly, while the domain of the Knights lies in the mountains of northern Gothic Spain, that of Klingsor lies to the south, toward the part of Spain held by the Arabs. The meaning that the Feast holds for the Knights is straightforwardly Christian: it gives them new strength to do their good works. They themselves spell this meaning out during the Processional: "He who rejoices in a good deed will be renewed by the feast."[10]

This is the meaning that the Communion should hold also for their leader and king, Amfortas. But Amfortas's situation and hence his attitude toward the sacrament is much less straightforward. Amfortas tried to defeat Klingsor, but proved unequal to the task—weak and sinful. The Knights vow chastity ("it is given only to the pure [to become] one of the brothers"),[11] but Amfortas succumbed to sexual temptation, falling into a trap set by Klingsor. After the magician stole the Spear and wounded the king with it, Amfortas, helped by Gurnemanz, barely escaped with his life. But he now has an open wound in the same place where Christ had his, and inflicted with the same weapon. He is permanently incapacitated and suffering. Being, as he puts it in his monologue, the "only sinner among all [the Knights],"[12] there is no question of him being able to perform any good deeds, or of the sacrament to renew his strength. He can only yearn for the Lord's mercy in the spirit of repentance: "I must reach Him by the healing repentance of my inmost soul."[13]

Meanwhile, the blood of the sacrament only renews his torment, and it does so in a way that deserves our close attention: "I feel the fount of the most holy blood pour into my heart: the ebb of my own sinful blood . . . must then flow again, gushing with wild terror into the world of sinful passion. It breaks open the door anew [and] now streams through it, here, through the wound, like His, . . . and from which now . . . flows my hot sinful blood, ever renewed from the fount of yearning that, ah!, no repentance of mine ever appeases!"[14] This baroque conceit of the divine blood transfusion and its effects might strike us as bizarre, but it is actually not all that distant from the normal Christian view of the Eucharist, where the receiving of Christ's blood restores the communicant in some sense, if the sacrament is taken in good faith. It does not restore Amfortas, however, in his sinful state. On the contrary, the infusion of Christ's blood only renews his lustful yearning, reopens the wound, and makes his own blood flow through it. This is why he does not want to perform his office of the main celebrant, and when he finally and reluctantly does perform it, he does not participate in the sacrament (as the stage direction that accompanies the Recessional makes clear); his wound bleeds anew (the stage direction again).

Thus the musical form—a closed arch disrupted by an open monologue—makes a dramatic point. This is a story of a sinner at odds with the community of saints that he leads (and, lest we forget, for the premodern Christians the contrast between saints and sinners was as meaningful as that between autonomous mature individuals and dependent immature ones has been for enlightened moderns), a story that is likely to end either with the destruction of the community, or with the reintegration ("redemption") of the leader.

They all know that the redemption can come only from the Lord's mercy, and also that it will be brought by the Lord's chosen representative. They know this because Amfortas told them that his fervent prayer has been answered by a message emanating from the Grail: "Await him, whom I have chosen—the pure fool, made knowing by compassion."[15] And we know it, too, since the promise is periodically repeated throughout the first act as a refrain: we hear it, incomplete, from Amfortas himself when we first meet him (I.320-26); we hear it complete from Gurnemanz at the end of the monologue in which the prehistory of the drama is laid out (I.729-41); we hear it again when the Boys and Youths sing it at the close of Amfortas's monologue (I.1405-12); and, finally, we hear its promise from the voice coming down from the dome at the end of the act (I.1655-58).[16] I shall call it the Redeemer Refrain when the music appears together with the words; the music alone will be called the Redeemer motive.

The knowledge of this promise allows us to understand that, in addition to the Knights and Amfortas, there is a third party at the Communion, another participant with his own particular expectations. Gurnemanz comes to the Communion in the same attitude as the remaining Knights and participates in it with the rest of them. But in addition he is there to test Parsifal, to see whether or not this is the promised redeemer. Parsifal had stumbled upon the Grail domain earlier that day in pursuit of a wild swan. He has no idea where he came from or who his father was; he does not even know his own name. Naive, unself-conscious, ignorant—there can be little doubt that he is a fool. But is he *the* fool—is he pure, and is he the promised redeemer? Gurnemanz has reasons to hope so: "I think that I have recognized you correctly: no earthly way leads to it [the Grail], and none could tread it whom the Grail itself would not want to guide."[17] He needs to make sure, and so he brings Parsifal to the Communion to find out, telling him: "If you are pure, the Grail will presently sustain you";[18] and little later, as they both enter the hall: "Now pay attention and let me see: if you are a fool and pure, what knowledge may be imparted to you."[19]

Parsifal seems to have failed the test. To be sure, as the stage directions inform us, on hearing Amfortas's cry for mercy, "Parsifal . . . had made a violent motion toward his heart, which he clutched convulsively for a length of time"[20]—a clear sign of compassion mentioned in the Redeemer Refrain. What is unclear is if this compassion led to any knowledge. In spite of Gurnemanz's express invitation, Parsifal did not take part in the Eucharistic meal, and afterward was unable to explain what it was that he saw. Gurnemanz understandably concludes that the innocent he has brought in is only a fool, and pushes him out.

The Communion in act 1 is thus not only disrupted, but more a failure than a success. The community of the Knights may be satisfied with it, but even they must be aware that their king did not receive the sacrament, and Gurnemanz is aware in addition that Parsifal, too, kept apart. For a fully successful Communion, one that would satisfy the Knights *and* redeem their king, we need to wait until the end of the opera, until the last portion of act 3.

This begins again with the forest-into-castle transformation of the scenery and repeats most of the trajectory traversed in act 1 (see appendix 7: act 3, B). The whole is much shorter and simpler this time, but the succession of events— the progression from the orchestral Transformation to the choral Processional to the solo recitative Monologue to the Communion itself—is sufficiently similar that no one is likely to miss the parallelism between the endings of acts 1 and 3. Yet there are important differences. The two most significant ones are, first, that this time there is no Recessional to follow the Communion, and second, that the Communion is preceded by not one but two Monologues.

The lack of a Recessional transforms the formal shape of the whole. From the capstone of the asymmetrical arch it was in the first act, the Communion becomes now the goal of the teleological linear progression. The reverse rewinding of the events of the Processional in the Recessional we have observed in act 1 is not needed in act 3 because, as we shall see, this time the Communion is a success: the desired outcome has been reached. In other words, the ending of act 3 is no mere recapitulation of the ending of act 1. Rather, it gets things right, repairs what went wrong on the first try.

The Communion itself is for the most part made of the same materials it had been made of in act 1, but it is now quite differently structured. In act 1, it will be recalled, it was articulated into two halves—the consecration of bread and wine, and the communion—each half based on the Love motive and each completed by the Hope motive and a return to the main key of A-flat. What we get now is, rather, an orchestral and choral peroration in A-flat, based on the motives familiar since the Prelude, that is, the Love and Hope motives again, plus the motive of Faith that in act 1 framed the Communion on both ends.

The peroration develops in three stages. First the orchestra weaves together in A-flat the three motives familiar from the Prelude: the Hope motive (III.1090–92) is followed by a variant of the Love motive, which, in a moment, will be revealed to carry the significance of the Redemption (III.1092–94), and this in turn is followed by the Faith motive (III.1094–97), after which the whole sequence is repeated (III.1098–100, 1100–1102, 1102–5). This first stage accompanies the unveiling of the Grail as it gradually begins to glow, while the bottom part of the hall grows dark and illumination increases in its top part.

Stage two (example 14) is a famous harmonic progression moving from the tonic to the subdominant of A-flat and involving all the choirs (the Boys from the top of the dome, the Youths from the middle, and the Knights on the ground divided into two half choirs). They begin by intoning the motive of the Redeemer that in act 1 functioned as the refrain ("the pure fool, made knowing by compassion"); now that the redeemer has come they simply gush, "The miracle of supreme salvation!"[21] Only the first half of the refrain music is used here. Had the refrain been completed, it would have ended on the local tonic of D-flat, the harmonic goal of this second stage. But since it is not completed, it stops on the chord of D in the first inversion (III.1109). Subsequently the three choirs proceed with the variant of the Love motive already introduced by the orchestra, which is now revealed to stand for the mysterious idea of "Redemption for the Redeemer!"—the last words of the drama.[22]

This is the Feast of Love, and the transmutation of the Love motive into the Redemption motive carries a clear, and clearly Christian, message, namely that redemption flows from love—not erotic love, of course, but the love of neighbor, the compassion or pity through which the pure fool gained knowledge. The D-flat that has been implied but not explicitly given already in III.1109 (which expired on D) is reached only at the end (III.1119), by the way of enharmonically spelled ascending fifths (A, E, C-flat, and G-flat) articulated every second measure. In other words, a move from the tonic to the subdominant is drawn out by a chain of subdominants—an anti-dominant gesture designed to drain the harmony of all its goal-directed drive, just as the community of Knights give up the drives of the will for the appeasement of compassion.[23]

The last words of the drama—except that the last word belongs to the orchestra. The third and last stage of the peroration articulates a large-scale plagal cadence back in A-flat, beginning with the Faith motive on the subdominant (III.1119–22), while a white dove descends from the dome to hover over Parsifal's head (the stage directions throughout are precise, and precisely placed). This third stage continues with the Hope motive moving from the subdominant back to the tonic (III.1123–27) while all the protagonists present—Amfortas, Gurnemanz, and Kundry (about whom more soon)—pay homage to Parsifal, who waves the Grail, blessing the worshipping Knights. Kundry sinks lifeless to the ground at the precise moment

EXAMPLE 14. *Parsifal*, III.1108–19

(continued)

EXAMPLE 14. *(continued)*

EXAMPLE 14. *(continued)*

when the subdominant chord of D-flat gets embellished by the a minor triad—another famous harmonic touch that casts an ostensibly diatonic and consonant chord in a chromatic and dissonant role, the old Klingsor's final act of harmonic sorcery, melding together dissonance and consonance, death and redemption.[24] It all ends in the tonic with the Faith motive (III.1127–34) followed by the beginning of the Hope motive completed by the once Love and now Redemption motive (III.1135–41) while the curtain slowly closes.

Not only musically but also dramatically, some events here are similar to those of the original Communion, but quite a few are unprecedented. Strictly speaking, the Eucharistic sacrament is now only suggested, but not enacted: the Grail is again unveiled to similar lighting effects and waved to bless the Knights, but there is no consecration of bread and wine, and no communion takes place. The emphasis shifts from the idea of the communion, the periodic renewal of the community's strength and commitment, to the idea of the redemption, the much more infrequent event that the communion commemorates. This community was in serious trouble, even mortal danger, ever since Amfortas's fall, and it needs more than a simple Mass. It can be truly restored only if its leader is redeemed—and replaced. The white dove that descends to hover over Parsifal's head—an obvious evocation of what according to the Gospels (Matthew 4.16–17, Mark 1.10–11, Luke 3.21–22, John 1.32–34) happened immediately after the baptism of Jesus—makes it perfectly clear who the new redeemer is. And the final action of the drama is the recognition of Parsifal's new authority (which Gurnemanz and Kundry had already recognized earlier that day) by Amfortas and the Knights, and hence the transfer of the community's leadership to the new king.

The second, even more important, difference between the sequences of musical units in acts 1 and 3 is that the orderly progression from the Transformation and Processional to the Communion is interrupted not only by the disrupting Monologue of Amfortas, as in act 1, but also by the unprecedented Monologue of Parsifal, who mends the disruption by bringing the long-awaited answer to Amfortas's and his Knights' prayers.

Many years have passed between the two Communions (we do not know how many, but recognize that in the meantime Gurnemanz has grown very old). The disintegration of the community of Knights is almost complete. Amfortas, maddened by his suffering and craving death, has long refused to perform the office of the Grail that renews his and his Knights' strength, thus hoping to hasten the end. But this refusal enfeebles the whole community, not only him. The Knights are too exhausted and dispirited to perform any good works. Today's Communion is to be performed "for the last time,"[25] as the Knights woefully and repeatedly intone during their Processional and as their king had promised.

But during his Monologue, Amfortas reneges on this promise, refuses to perform the rite, and instead of uncovering the Grail he uncovers his wound and challenges his Knights to plunge their swords in it: "Kill the sinner with his torment, then the Grail will illuminate you on its own!"[26] A this point Parsifal steps forward and touches Amfortas's wound with the Spear he had recovered from the enemy: "Only one weapon will do: only the Spear that opened the wound closes it."[27] ("But where danger is, grows / The saving power also," says Friedrich Hölderlin, in verses that Martin Heidegger put to good use.)[28] The recovered Spear in Parsifal's hand is the sign of hope of renewal for the community of Knights, of salvation for their fallen king ("Be healed, absolved, and atoned!"),[29] and of transfer of power from Amfortas to his redeemer ("For I now perform your office").[30] And indeed, it is Parsifal, not Amfortas, who officiates at the Communion.

In short, the denouement of this drama takes place in the two Monologues that separate the Communion from the introductory Transformation and Processional, in the confrontation of Amfortas and Parsifal. As in the Hölderlin verses, and more to the point, as in the Christian drama of redemption where the salvation comes from the sacrifice, the nadir in the plot's trajectory is transformed into its apex. Lest we forget, the final act of Wagner's opera takes place on Good Friday. The Communion in act 1 failed because the longed-for redeemer that the king's fallen state required did not appear; or, rather, he appeared but was not ready and remained silent, limiting himself to the dumb language of gestures that suggested unself-conscious compassion, pity without knowledge. Now, in act 3, Parsifal is ready. No longer a mere fool, he understands the meaning of the compassion he feels; he has been "made knowing by compassion." Hence he now speaks, telling Amfortas: "Blessed be your suffering that gave the hesitant fool the highest force of compassion and the power of purest knowledge!"[31] Parsifal's Monologue—not just what he says, but the very fact that he speaks, structurally the main difference between the sequences of musical units in acts 1 and 3—makes all the difference also dramatically.

Together, the two parallel Communion sequences in acts 1 and 3 (I.1073–666 and III.800–1141), each extending from the beginning of the Transformation music to the end of the act, and each involving primarily closed musical forms and subordinating these smaller units into a large-scale shape (arch-like in act 1 and teleological in act 3), constitute the two pillars of structural stability that define the architecture of the opera. The sequences provide the work's longest stretches of music that is not recitative-based. Individually, each gives its respective act its point and center of gravity (the music that precedes them in the act is dominated by the recitative) and together, precisely because of their parallelism, and as much because of the similarities as because of the differences, they provide the whole with its ABA' architecture.

Again, the dramatic import is inseparable from the musical shape. The musical form is calculated to make sure that the second Communion is experienced as the main event and goal of the drama and that its significance depends at least in part on a comparison with the first Communion, which turns out to have been a failed rehearsal for the ultimately successful performance. What emerges most strikingly from this comparison is the idea that, in order to survive, a Christian community in serious trouble may need more than the communion, the periodic commemoration of the redemptive act that forms the core of the community's beliefs and the foundation for its activities. It may need, rather, to witness a repetition of the redemptive act itself. Hence the shift of emphasis between acts 1 and 3 from the idea of communion to that of redemption.

The shift may seem a departure from the traditional Christian doctrine. There has been, after all, only one act of redemption—God's sacrifice of his Son on the Cross. But the idea is not as heterodox as it might seem at first. The periodic commemoration of the sacrifice, sufficient to keep a community of believers in good order in normal times, may become routinized, mechanical, and insufficient for a time of crisis, when a stronger, more vivid identification with the original Redeemer is required. *Imitatio Christi* has been a devotional ideal widely shared over the centuries by most impeccably orthodox believers, Catholic and Protestant alike. A faith that is fully alive asks for the closest possible identification with Jesus, with his teachings and actions.

It is in this light that the potentially mystifying final formula of the "Redemption for the Redeemer" should be considered. This is a Christian community and the original Redeemer was, needless to say, Christ himself. But both Amfortas and Parsifal take on a number of features that make them Christlike: Amfortas was wounded by the same weapon and in the same spot at his side as Jesus; Parsifal is marked as God's chosen representative in the same way as Jesus was when the dove descends to hover over his head; and his decisive, successful act takes place on Good Friday. The similarities are so many and so obvious that, it seems to me, Wagner was protesting too much when, on October 20, 1878, he told his wife: "W.[olzogen] goes too far in calling Parsifal a reflection of the Redeemer: 'I didn't give the Redeemer a thought when I wrote it.'"[32] But it is true that neither Amfortas nor Parsifal is a usurper; neither pretends to be a second Christ. They are, rather, Christ's imitators and, like Jesus, actual or potential leaders of their community. Their *imitatio Christi* is necessary, if Jesus's example is to be kept alive. It is in this sense that they are the Redeemer's "redeemers." The redemption here involves embodying Christ's example in such a way as to make it fully alive for the community and thereby provide the community with leadership. The "Redemption for the Redeemer" means no more and no less than that. Amfortas, the fallen and failed "Redeemer"-leader, requires and gets his "Redemption"—the replacement by a new leader, the one who did not fall and fail—so that the community can continue to thrive, defend the faith, and do good works. Moreover, Parsifal's act of redemption travels further up the mimetic chain of Christ-Amfortas-Parsifal: not only is the fallen Amfortas redeemed, but also the Grail itself, the mystical symbol of Christ profaned by Amfortas's fall.

The mimetic chain does not end here. The *imitatio Christi* is performed by the leaders for the benefit of the faithful and is expected to be picked up and continued by them. It is the Knights who are addressed in the two Communions, the Knights whose faith and strength are to be renewed and sustained. But not only the Knights. Recall that the first Communion repeats literally the opening portion of the Prelude, thus assimilating the Prelude to the architectural structure on which the opera rests. As a result, the opera itself becomes the Communion enacted in it, and the opera's audience assumes the position of the Knights that the sacrament addresses and, presumably, renews and sustains. *Parsifal*'s Prelude thus functions similarly to the Overture to *The Magic Flute*, which was also designed to draw the audience into direct participation in the ritual enacted onstage. Not incidentally, the parallels with Wolfgang Amadeus Mozart's opera are numerous: it, too, featured an endangered male brotherhood, as well as a young and initially naive saving hero who achieved enlightenment and withstood the blandishments of a dark seductress and her messengers.[33]

Another indication that the distance and even distinction between the audience and the Knights is to be attenuated and elided comes at the junction between the Prelude and the act itself. Strictly speaking, the Prelude ends in I.113, at which point the curtain opens, but the motives of the Prelude continue to resound through I.146, coming partly from the orchestra and partly from stage brass and accompanying the morning prayers of Gurnemanz and his two youthful Esquires. The stage action begins in earnest only in I.147. The stage brass provides the music the characters onstage hear, and the orchestra echoes this music, allowing us to hear how the music reverberates within the characters. Right at the start, we, the audience, are given a lesson in how to listen—how to take in, internalize, what we hear. And the consecration music heard and internalized by the audience during the Prelude turns out to be the music heard and taken in by Gurnemanz and his companions. We are them.

Even more than with his other works, Wagner took pains not to allow this drama to enter the normal operatic market. "What good would it do now to release this most Christian of works of art into a world which recoils in its cowardice in the face of the Jews!" he wrote to King Ludwig II on August 25, 1879.[34] Further on in the same letter, he wrote: "I have to insist that it would be a sacrilege equal to the profanation of the Eleusinian mysteries if this work was to be exposed to our urban theater audience, with its late comers and early leavers, its rattle, being bored, etc."[35] A year later (September 28, 1880) he insisted again: "How, indeed, might it be possible or permissible for a drama in which the most sublime mysteries of the Christian faith are openly presented on stage to be performed in theaters such as ours, side by side with an operatic repertory and before an audience such as ours?"[36] *Parsifal* was to be reserved for performances at the Bayreuth Festival only (the copyright guaranteed the festival exclusive rights to the opera for thirty years), and was referred to as the *Bühnenweihfestpiel* (a "feast play for the consecration of the stage"). The opera, in short, was conceived as a new kind of dedication Mass for a new kind of temple.

The temple was to be in some sense Christian rather than simply Wagnerian. The exact sense is captured with remarkable clarity in the opening sentence of the 1880 essay "Religion and Art": "One might say that where Religion becomes artificial, it is reserved for art to save the spirit of religion by recognizing the figurative value of the mythic symbols which the former would have us believe in their literal sense, and revealing their deep and hidden truth through an ideal presentation."[37] Christians circa 1880, Wagner thinks, are in a similarly precarious state as his Grail Knights, and similarly in need of a redeemer who would give their faith renewed life and strength. On July 15, 1879, he tells Cosima: "For me Christianity has not yet arrived, and I am like the early Christians, awaiting Christ's return."[38] His *Parsifal* was to "redeem" Christianity by providing the moderns, no longer capable of taking the message of the Gospels literally, with a figurative interpretation disclosing its deep truth. Wagner sought to bring his contemporaries what Parsifal brought Amfortas and his Knights: a revitalized Christian faith. In *Parsifal* the idea of the religion of art does not imply that in the modern age art should take over from religion its function of providing society with the fundamental beliefs that keep it together. Rather, it meant that theater would take over from the church—that art would make the truth of religion alive once again.

THE MONOLOGUES OF ACTS 1 AND 3

The dialogue between Gurnemanz and Parsifal that is superimposed over the beginning of the Transformation music in act 1 ends with this celebrated exchange:

Parsifal: "I hardly stride, yet imagine I am already far."
Gurnemanz: "You see, my son, here time becomes space."[39]

"Here" is the sacred realm, the domain of the Grail, where the flow of time that defines human existence in the profane everyday world gets suspended in favor of numinous timelessness: "time becomes space." The linear time of profane human history, including the history that had been narrated during the earlier portion of the act, is now left behind as the two pilgrims, together with the Knights, are about to enter the sacred cyclical time of the regularly enacted commemorative ritual. But in addition, Gurnemanz's words also imply a musical-formal transformation: up to this moment, the discourse of the act was dominated by recitative, but from now on, it is going to be dominated by more regularly structured musical forms. Also in this sense, "here," that is, at this point, "time becomes space" as the open logical discourse gives way to closed architectonic forms.

Much of the first part of act 1, the part preceding the Transformation music, is composed as the normal recitative dialogue. But not all: at the center of this first part there is a long narrative Monologue of Gurnemanz (see appendix 7: act 1, A.2). Gurnemanz, together with Amfortas, Parsifal, and Kundry, and more than Klingsor, is undoubtedly a first-rank role, but unlike those others he is hardly a character at all. Rather he is a narrative device, someone who, both here and in the corresponding opening part of act 3, makes sure that we hear about all the essential events that had not been enacted on the stage. In act 1 he makes sure that we learn what we need to know about Amfortas's past and the roles that Kundry and Klingsor played in that past, as well as about Amfortas's future and the role to be played in it by the promised redeemer.

It is not easy to decide where the Monologue really begins, since Gurnemanz's confidences are only gradually coaxed out of him by the two youthful Esquires who are his companions. The scene starts as a conversation between Gurnemanz and these acolytes, and even when he gets going with his story in earnest it continues to be punctuated by interruptions from his listeners. Thus Gurnemanz slips into the narrative gradually and almost imperceptibly (Wagner's "art of transition" again), perhaps by I.458 ("Ja, wann oft lange sie uns ferne blieb"), or by I.499 ("Das ist ein And'res, jedem ist's verwehrt") at the latest. From that point on, the Monologue becomes more continuous, with only two brief dialogue interruptions separating part 1 from part 2 (I.546–63) and part 2 from the coda (I.704–9). Since the second part (I.564–704) is its longest uninterrupted section, it emerges as the Monologue's main body.

In part 1 we begin to get acquainted with the opera's most extraordinary and intriguing character, Kundry—though only begin, since Gurnemanz does not know much himself and only offers tentative guesses. "Wild"[40] is the first epithet we hear applied to her. The stage direction describing her on her first entrance (if this is the right word—she "hastily hurls in, almost staggering")[41] confirms this, talking of her "wild garb."[42] And now the conversation that precedes the Monologue begins with one of the Esquires attacking her: "Hey, you there! Why do you lie there like a wild beast?"[43] Like a wild beast, too, she is given throughout to producing inarticulate screams and uses language, the essential medium of the human spirit, haltingly and unwillingly. In this realm of spirit Kundry is supposed to be on the wild side. Among all those saintly, disembodied, celibate males, she stands for the body, for female animality, perhaps—who knows?—even for sex. She delivers an answer that convinces us that she is the one to watch, the interesting one: "Aren't beasts holy here?"[44] This complicates the spirit-nature opposition, as the realm of the spirit may also be where nature gets sanctified and transfigured.

Kundry, Gurnemanz reminds the Esquires, serves the brotherhood as a worldwide rapid delivery system, selflessly and without any recompense. Beyond this, he is unsure himself: perhaps she is "cursed"[45] and atones by her services to the Knights for some "guilt from earlier life" (note the ambiguity as to whether what is meant is Kundry's former life, or her former incarnation).[46] Maybe even, as one of the Esquires suggests, her guilt has something to do with Amfortas's downfall. Gurnemanz does not reject this possibility, but he leaves it to us to connect the dots he now draws. Amfortas, armed with the Spear, waged a war against evil Klingsor. Close to the sorcerer's castle he was seduced by "a frightfully beautiful woman,"[47] and while he lay in her arms, Klingsor stole the phallic Spear and wounded the king with it—an act of symbolic castration that parallels the real one we soon come to.

But who is Klingsor, actually? This we learn in part 2 of the Monologue, though also in this case Gurnemanz does not know everything: "It remained unknown to me what sin he committed over there,"[48] but "over there" being the "voluptuous land of heathens,"[49] the transgression was likely of sexual nature—the standard European fantasy of debauchery with the oriental other. Klingsor wished to atone for it by joining the brotherhood, but the membership was open only to "the pure," and pure was one thing he was not. And here Gurnemanz's report gets drastic: "Powerless to stifle the sin in himself, he turned his blasphemous hands against himself; then he turned them toward the Grail, whose guardian repulsed him with contempt."[50] But Klingsor's self-castration was not all wasted. True, it did not gain him the membership he craved, but it endowed him with magical powers. He has transformed the desert into a "garden of delights,"[51] grows there "devilishly beautiful women,"[52] and uses them to bait the Knights "to evil lust":[53] "Many of us has he already ruined."[54] Now that the Spear is in his hands, he expects to win the Grail, too. Gurnemanz ends his narrative with a coda recounting the message of the promised redeemer we already know, the message about "the pure fool, made knowing by compassion."

Clearly, the narrative does more than merely inform us about the prehistory of the events we are about to witness. It also sketches a characterization of the evil realm faced by the Grail Knights. It is, we learn, the realm of "wild" nature, populated by "wild beasts," the realm of the untamed body and of femininity that, through sexual attraction, threatens exclusive self-possession of the males with emasculation (that lost Spear that leaves behind a permanently bleeding wound!). Evil consists precisely in this: the abandonment of good works in the Grail's service, works on behalf of one's neighbors, and the succumbing to sexual temptations, to the satisfaction of one's own desires. In the world of *Parsifal* sex is unambiguously evil, so much so that one is left to wonder how exactly Amfortas's saintly father, Titurel, managed to beget him (was it a case of parthenogenesis?). Already Friedrich Nietzsche wondered: "One fact, finally, which leaves us dumbfounded: Parsifal is the father of Lohengrin. How did he do it?"[55]

But if sex is unmistakably evil, the position of nature is ambiguous. For one thing, while nature is sinful, it can also be sinned against. Sexual desire should be stifled by the power of will, and self-castration, the act of violence against nature, is "blasphemous" and deserving of "contempt." Klingsor's self-inflicted wound is a monstrous and mocking echo of Amfortas's, just as the latter imitates the wound received by Christ on the cross. And there is a fourth bleeding wound in the opera that echoes these three: the wound in the breast of a wild swan wantonly hit by Parsifal's arrow in act 1. This too is the result of an act of violence against nature. The relationship between the swan's and Amfortas's wounds goes deeper: it is when confronted with the result of the violence he has perpetrated on the swan that Parsifal experiences for the first time in his life the pang of compassion that he will soon experience again when witnessing the agony of the king. All of this accords with the background of Christian assumptions behind the opera: the Creation, as the work of the benevolent Creator, cannot be simply evil, and can be sinned against. More generally *Parsifal* seems to assume two kinds of nature: the "wild" untamed and sinful nature of Klingsor's garden of sexual delights, and the redeemed nature sanctified by the spirit, the nature in the Grail's domain where even animals can be holy. The task the Knights face, or should face, is not so much how to keep nature at bay, but rather how to redeem wild nature by bringing it under the spirit's dominion.

As in act 1, also in act 3 much of the first part up to the Transformation music involves recitative dialogue. And as in act 1, here too the exceptions take the discursive form of monologues. But in act 3 Parsifal is no longer dumb; instead it is now Kundry who is struck dumb. Although present onstage throughout the act, she manages to emit two words at the beginning ("To serve, . . . to serve")[56] and otherwise communicates by gestures and glances only—seen but not heard, like a good child or servant. We have already seen that, in the last part of the act, Amfortas's Monologue was followed by one by Parsifal. Similarly, in the first part of the act, the first of the two Monologues of Gurnemanz—there are two rather than only one this time—is provoked by the immediately preceding Monologue of Parsifal, and the second is framed by Parsifal's prologue and epilogue (see appendix 7: act 3, 1.a and 3.a). Where in act 1 we had a single long multipartite Monologue of Gurnemanz, now we have two shorter monologue complexes involving both characters.

The first monologue complex is a straightforward, functional narrative: we have not seen Parsifal and Gurnemanz for many years and they use their arioso recitatives to tell us, as well as each other, what has happened to them in the meantime. Parsifal, long unable to find his way back to the Grail's domain, has finally arrived there "by the path of error and suffering"[57] with the aim of restoring the recovered Spear to the community and thus bringing Amfortas salvation. What his story emphasizes is not the aim, however, but the tortuous way lost "in pathless straying."[58] Meanwhile, the community's disintegration, Gurnemanz tells him, has progressed much further. Communion is no longer celebrated and the exhausted Knights, deprived of its sustenance, no longer engage in good works: "The dispirited and leaderless knighthood wander about, pale and miserable."[59]

Thus the two stories parallel one another, Parsifal's "pathless straying" echoed by the Knights' aimless wandering. The image the two narratives have in common, that of tortuous moving without knowing the way forward, is where act 3 began. The harmonically extraordinarily complex and tortuous (unnamed) Prelude contains some of the most advanced music Wagner ever wrote, constantly modulating and changing direction all the time—a perfect image of "wandering about." And the wandering it depicts is not only Parsifal's (as is often claimed), but also the knighthood's. It is true that much of the motivic substance of Parsifal's Monologue is derived from the central, main body of the Prelude—compare in particular the Monologue's beginning, III.285–89, where the "path of error and suffering" is first mentioned, and ending, III.308–32, where the subject of "pathless straying" returns, to the Prelude's III.10–38. To this extent the traditional view of the Prelude as depicting Parsifal's roundabout way back to the Grail's domain is correct. Moreover, the view is supported by the testimony of the composer in a letter to King Ludwig II (October 15, 1878): "But I must first introduce it [act 3] with an orchestral prelude to accompany Parsifal's effortful wanderings up to the point where he rediscovers the realm of the Grail."[60] But the music that frames the Prelude, III.1–9 and 39–44, and in particular the opening nine measures of the act, play a central role in Gurnemanz's Monologue: they come back almost literally and in the original key of b-flat minor close to the beginning of the Monologue (III.354–66; example 15a and b), that is, as soon as Gurnemanz comes to the subject of the state of the knighthood, and the music is evoked again, and again in the original key, at the end of the Monologue (III.400–19), when the Knights' dispirited wandering about is described. The link between the opening measures of the Prelude and the dismal state of the knighthood will be made explicit yet again, and again in b-flat, at the very beginning of the Processional that will bring them "for the last time"[61] to the Grail's hall (III.857–61; example 15c).

Thus, on the one hand, the Prelude is assimilated into the first monologue complex as its anticipation, and, on the other, it clarifies what the two monologues that make up this complex have in common: the image of pathless straying. That Wagner himself was fully aware of the connection his Prelude was supposed to establish between Parsifal's straying and the knighthood's disintegration is made clear by an entry his wife made in her *Diary* (October 24, 1878): "R. talks about the sad strains he will now have to compose [the Prelude to act 3]; they must not contain a single ray of light, he says, for that could lead one far astray. Parsifal's sad wanderings, which must lead up to the situation on Monsalvat."[62]

Because of its functionality, the first monologue complex recalls Gurnemanz's Monologue in act 1: this too served to narrate the events that could not be enacted onstage. But it is the second monologue complex in act 3 that offers an answer to Gurnemanz's Monologue in act 1, and it is this second complex that, in its musical and verbal substance, constitutes the point of gravity of the whole first part of the last act.

EXAMPLE 15. *Parsifal*

a. III.1–9

b. III.354–66

(continued)

EXAMPLE 15. *(continued)*

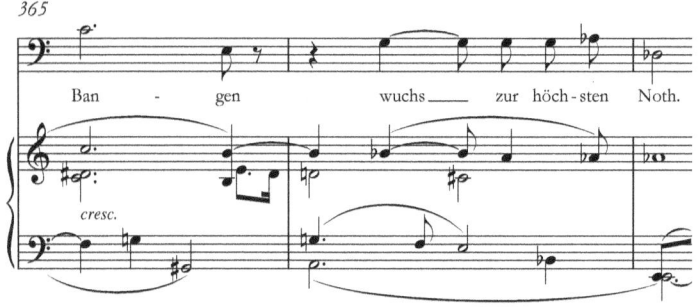

c. III.857–61

Its musical weight derives from its being the single lengthy stretch of lyrical utterance in this part. Moreover, in this utterance the melodic substance is carried almost entirely by the orchestra, with the voices superimposing their counterpoints above it. Not much rewriting is needed to present the whole as an orchestral piece, and, of course, it has often been so presented, as the *Good Friday Spell*.[63] Its main portion (see appendix 7: act 3, A.3.a), in D major, is given to Gurnemanz (III.675–770); this is framed by Parsifal's prologue in B major (III.626–74) and epilogue in D major (III.770–99), "the spot that he [Wagner] himself called 'elegy,'" as the composer's authorized biographer reports.[64]

What is striking about the Good Friday music, in its context, is how deliberately, serenely stable and regular it is (example 16)—a complete reversal of the character of the music that opened act 3 and pervaded the first monologue complex. After three introductory measures (III.626–28), Parsifal's prologue begins with two almost identical phrases of eight measures each (III.629–36, 637–44), the first one ending on the dominant and the second on the tonic chord, but otherwise harmonized with utmost simplicity: four measures of the tonic followed by four measures of the dominant for the antecedent; four measures of the tonic, three measures of the dominant, and final tonic measure for the consequent. This is followed by a new eight-measure phrase (III.645–52), this one also sounding like an antecedent and ending on the dominant, though harmonically more animated than the first. The consequent, however, is less regular this time: consisting of only six measures (III.653–58) and ending on the dominant, it sounds inconclusive, and so does its even shorter repeat (III.659–63) that brings the main body of Parsifal's prologue to an end. But by this point the harmonic stability and the regularity of phrasing have been so firmly established that the inconclusive ending does nothing to erase them.

All this expressive serenity serves a dramatic purpose, of course. In order to understand this purpose fully, however, we need to look back at what has happened between the two monologue complexes—a series of highly symbolic actions, presented to a considerable extent in wordless, orchestrally accompanied pantomime, the sort of pantomime that has been prominent in act 3 from the start. All involve the pouring of liquids. As Parsifal reacts to Gurnemanz's story with despair and is about to faint, Kundry fetches some water with which to revive him. Parsifal's fainting and Kundry's gesture, incidentally, are other prominent parallels between acts 1 and 3, as they echo similar events in the first act. In act 3, however, the water Kundry brings triggers a whole cascade of flowing liquids. First, Gurnemanz orders that Parsifal be washed of the dust of his pilgrimage in the water of the nearby "holy spring,"[65] where indeed Kundry bathes the pilgrim's feet, while Gurnemanz sprinkles his head. Next, Kundry produces a vial of ointment and, in a gesture that clinches our suspicion that her figure is partly modeled on the traditional image of that other repentant sinner, Mary Magdalene (thereby providing Parsifal with yet another Christlike feature), anoints the pilgrim's feet and dries them with her own hair. At Parsifal's own request, the vial now passes from Kundry to Gurnemanz, who uses its contents to anoint the pilgrim's head and thus to proclaim him the new king. And finally, the new king performs his first office, using the water of the spring to baptize Kundry, who "sinks her head deep to the ground; she appears to weep fervently."[66]

This is where the Good Friday music begins. According to the stage direction, "Parsifal turns around and looks in mild rapture at the forest and meadow which

EXAMPLE 16. *Parsifal*, Good Friday Spell prologue, III.626–63

EXAMPLE 16. *(continued)*

(continued)

EXAMPLE 16. *(continued)*

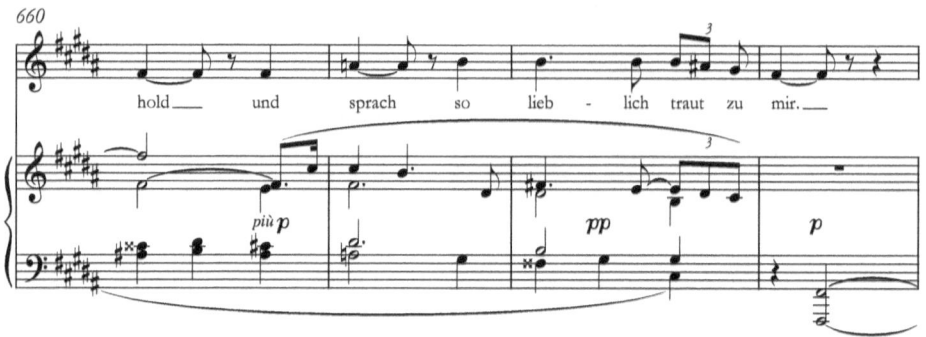

now glow in the morning light."⁶⁷ The ointment, the water of the spring, Kundry's tears, and the morning dew blend together, bringing Parsifal, Kundry, and the meadow a new life. Kundry has been associated with "wild" nature already in Gurnemanz's Monologue of act 1. And at the beginning of act 3, nature's renewal with the coming of spring after harsh winter and Kundry's revival after a deep coma are explicitly correlated: "Up! Kundry! Up! Winter has fled and Spring is here!"⁶⁸ Gurnemanz addresses her as he tries to wake her up from her hibernation. But now, thanks to the baptism, "nature" is no longer "wild"—it has been brought under the dominion of the spirit. On this spring morning, nature is renewing itself and Parsifal looks at it with new eyes: "How beautiful does the meadow seem to me today!"⁶⁹ And he contrasts the present serenity of the transfigured meadow with the remembered wild erotic temptations of Klingsor's enchanted garden. The black magic of untamed desire has been defeated by the white magic of spiritual transformation. Gurnemanz explains: "This is . . . the Good Friday spell, my Lord."⁷⁰

Gurnemanz's words usher in a transition between the prologue and the main portion of the Good Friday Spell (III.663–74), a brief modulatory intrusion of passionate suffering as Parsifal recalls that Good Friday is the day of the crucifixion and thus should be one when all creation mourns and weeps. His tutor's answer (III.675–770) is both musically and verbally the core of the scene—a lecture in theology, or rather a sermon, that lies at the center of the opera (example 17).

Musically, Gurnemanz's sermon is constructed on scaffolding made of the two diatonic phrases of Parsifal's prologue, whose periodic reappearances, all in the tonic key of D major, are separated by two new heavily chromatic and modulatory interpolations (in table 33 the material based on Parsifal's first phrase, III.629–36, is marked A, that based on his second phrase, III.645–52, is marked B, and the interpolations are marked x and y). It begins with an introduction made of Parsifal's first phrase, short-

EXAMPLE 17. *Parsifal*, Gurnemanz's Good Friday sermon, III.675–770

(continued)

EXAMPLE 17. *(continued)*

EXAMPLE 17. *(continued)*

(continued)

EXAMPLE 17. *(continued)*

EXAMPLE 17. *(continued)*

TABLE 33 Gurnemanz's Good Friday Sermon

Form	Measure	CD.track.time
Introduction		
A	675–84	IV.8.0:00–0:30
Part 1		
x	685–98	IV.8.0:30–1:10
A	699–704	IV.8.1:10–1:30
Part 2		
y	705–15	IV.8.1:30–2:01
B	716–37	IV.8.2:01–3:05
A	738–52	IV.8.3:05–3:52
Peroration		
B	752–70	IV.8.3:52–4:50

ened and inconclusive, presented in two overlapping statements (III.675–84). There follows as the first part of the sermon the first interpolation (III.685–98), and this culminates in a single repetition of Parsifal's first phrase (III.699–704), again incomplete and inconclusive. The second interpolation (III.705–15) begins the second part of the sermon and again issues seamlessly in a presentation of, this time, Parsifal's second phrase (III.716–37), much developed and consequently much longer than in its original form, as well as, equally seamlessly, the first phrase (III.738–52) repeated three times and given this time a triumphant conclusion. The whole is rounded off with a peroration based on the second phrase (III.752–70).

Once the sermon is finished, Parsifal completes the Good Friday music with an elegiac epilogue-peroration of his own (example 18) consisting first of a brief chromatic interpolation (III.770–80), and then of the first phrase of his prologue, presented this time in a complete and conclusive form (III. 781–88). It is rounded off with an echo of Gurnemanz's peroration (III.788–99) that dissolves into a transition to the Transformation music, which follows immediately.

The periodic refrain-like returns of the diatonic phrases in the tonic key calm down and neutralize the tortured quality of the chromatic interpolations, just as divine love redeems and consoles suffering mortals—the sermon's theme. In this respect the Good Friday music is the epitome of Wagner's score as a whole, where, similarly, outbursts of lush, colorful, and tortured chromatic polyphony are becalmed by austere, monochromatic, and serene diatonicism. The music thus mirrors the way most of the protagonists (Amfortas, Klingsor, and above all Kundry) are internally split between two equally strong but contradictory desires—for abandonment in decadent sensuality and for redeeming, ascetic "purity."[71]

Parsifal has been mistaken, Gurnemanz teaches, in thinking that this day is an occasion for all the creation to mourn and weep only. This, after all, is the day

EXAMPLE 18. *Parsifal*, Good Friday Spell epilogue elegy, III.770–99

(continued)

EXAMPLE 18. *(continued)*

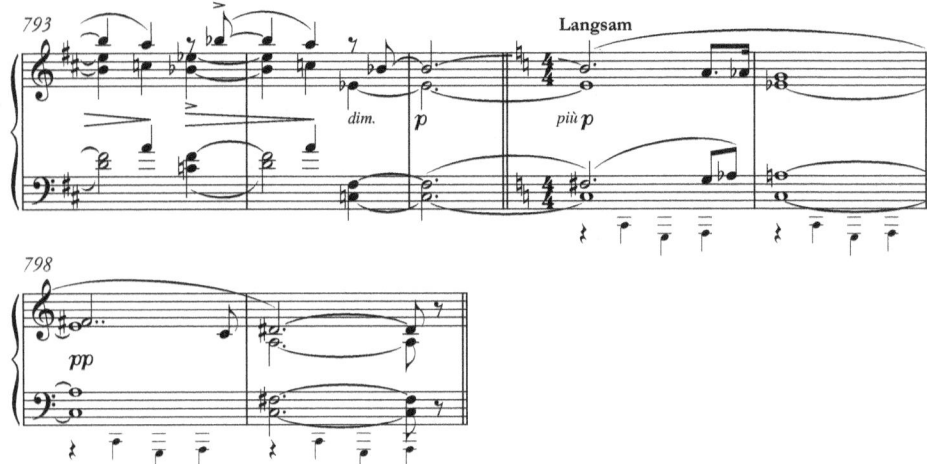

when God's loving self-sacrifice redeemed humanity, "who feels liberated from the burden of sin and dread."[72] Thus today's tears have a regenerative power, and the day itself calls for rejoicing.

So far, so traditionally Christian. But Gurnemanz goes further, and it is here that the Christian message acquires an unmistakably Wagnerian accent. The sacrifice of the cross has a significance that extends beyond humanity to all of nature. Through human mediation the divine act of redemption spreads to the rest of creation. To be sure, creation "cannot itself glimpse Him [the Savior] Himself on the Cross,"[73] but "therefore it looks up to the redeemed man."[74] And "the sinner's tears of repentance . . . besprinkle field and meadow with holy dew and thus make it flourish"[75] so that "all the creation rejoices."[76] More: the repentant sinner becomes nature's guardian rather than exploiter. Here is the key passage of the sermon: "Now grass and flower in the meadows notice that today the foot of man does not step on them, but rather that—as God with heavenly patience pitied him and suffered for him—so also man today in pious grace spares them with soft steps."[77] Just as God has shown humans His compassion, so now humanity is compassionate toward "all that blooms and soon dies here."[78] Thus also nature is "made free of sin"[79] and regains its "day of innocence."[80]

In short, the divine compassionate love pours its redeeming grace over the sinful humans, whose tears of repentance, in turn, shed in love and compassion over dumb and mortal nature, include it in the salvation plan, and make it flourish and rejoice. In Wagner's recension, thanks to humanity's channeling of divine love further down, the good tidings embrace all of nature. Wagner's Christianity takes on a distinctly ecological coloring. Thus the question suggested by Gurnemanz's Monologue in act 1—how to redeem wild nature by bringing it under the spirit's dominion—finds its answer in his Good Friday sermon.

Parsifal's epilogue elegy is designed to make sure we understand that nothing escapes this embrace—neither the blooming meadow in front of his eyes, nor the remembered flowers of evil, the seductive Flowermaidens in Klingsor's enchanted garden, nor finally the most evil flower of them all, the "rose of hell"[81] herself, Kundry, now repentant and newly baptized. He wonders if Klingsor's flowers he once saw wither "today long for redemption."[82] He assures Kundry that her tears of repentance are a "dew of blessing":[83] "You weep, . . . behold, the meadow smiles!"[84] And he seals this assurance with a chaste kiss on her forehead—a kiss of charity that reciprocates the (yet to be discussed) erotic kiss she had given him in Klingsor's garden.

Since in the Good Friday Spell the melodic substance belongs almost entirely to the orchestra with the voices assuming a subordinated role, the scene raises again the question we have confronted when discussing the similarly textured Transfiguration of Isolde and the final portion of the Love Duet: Does the orchestra here become the mouthpiece of a new subjectivity, distinct from the characters onstage, and in particular does it speak for the narrator or author? Let us step back for a moment to see why such passages raise this question with a particular urgency.

If there is one thing that everyone knows about later Wagner it is that in his music dramas he assigned a demanding role to the orchestra, giving its part a melodic and motivic content of unprecedented density. As a result, the orchestra abandoned its subordinate, accompanimental role and became, some of the time at least, an equal partner of the voices. But who is it, actually, that speaks through the orchestra in Wagner's music dramas? Whose voice does the orchestra represent? To ask this question is to give the subject of representation in Wagner a somewhat unusual slant. Normally no sooner is the subject mentioned than someone will talk of leitmotifs, and no sooner are leitmotifs mentioned than someone will ask, What do they represent? My question here is not so much about what is represented by leitmotifs as who does the representing, who expresses himself through the leitmotifs.

Recall Carl Dahlhaus's argument discussed in the *Tristan* chapter that leitmotifs sometimes embody the memories, conscious or not, of the singing character and at other times they embody the narrative voice, speaking about the characters and their dramatic situations directly to the audience, above the characters' heads.[85] Recall, too, what we found out: outside of the *Ring* the situations when a leitmotif has to be attributed to the narrator are exceedingly rare and even in the *Ring* they are not common. To attribute the information provided by leitmotifs to a separate speaker is unnecessary—a needless multiplication of entities against which Ockham would be justified in wielding his razor. For the most part, in later Wagner it is not that the narrator raises himself up from the pit to provide us with the information; it is, rather, that a window opens up in the character through which we may peek inside and access the intentional mind behind the gestural and verbal behavior. Wagner's orchestra, like the operatic orchestra in general, acts usually as an extension of the singer's body, amplifying and supplementing his or her comportment, gestures, and tone of voice so that we might know better what is on the character's mind.

Does a true narrative voice ever emerge in the orchestra? As I have suggested in the *Tristan* chapter, this may be particularly likely to happen when the orchestra stops speaking in isolated motives and begins to provide a longer continuous discourse, a discourse that makes musical sense independently of the vocal lines even when these are present. It is at such moments that we may become aware of the emergence of a voice that seems to emanate from a subjectivity independent of the characters onstage. This is why the temptation to hear in the orchestral melody of the Good Friday Spell the voice of the narrator or author is perhaps stronger than at any other moment in the music dramas (purely orchestral passages, such as Siegfried's Funeral March, aside). But is the temptation irresistible? In the *Tristan* passages mentioned above—the final portion of the Love Duet and Isolde's Transfiguration—the impression was of the characters whose conscious, rational selves were being overpowered by a force stronger than they, but not necessarily distinct from them—rather, a force emanating from the deeper, sub-rational layer of the self. There was, therefore, no need to postulate a separate subjectivity speaking through the orchestra. Something similar happens at the outset in the Good Friday Spell and hence also in this case one is initially inclined to reach for Ockham's razor. Parsifal is seized by a philosophical-religious vision of "wild" suffering nature transfigured by spirit, consoled by divine compassion, of eros brought under the dominion of agape, a vision he cannot coherently and rationally articulate in words but that is nevertheless his own, and is articulated for him by the orchestra speaking the language that can access deeper layers of the self than his words could at this stage. Just as in *Tristan*, then, so too in *Parsifal* there seems no need at first to postulate that the orchestra speaks for a separate subjectivity, that it assumes the authorial voice. Subsequently the more experienced Gurnemanz brings this orchestral vision into fully rational linguistic awareness in his sermon. Throughout, the orchestra articulates a way of experiencing the world that Parsifal and Gurnemanz share, even if only the latter is able to express this way in words, to make it fully conscious and rational. Thus there seems to be no need to postulate that the orchestra speaks for a separate subjectivity, that it assumes a narrator's voice.

But things will begin to look different when we consider the Good Friday Spell in the larger context, the context of the whole opera. Before we can do this, however, we need to complete the discussion of the opera's music-dramatic organization.

ACT 2: THE KISS OF SELF-KNOWLEDGE

That earlier kiss, Kundry's kiss, coming in the center of act 2, is the opera's turning point, its peripeteia, and Parsifal's moment of conversion. This is what transforms him from a mere fool of act 1 who fails at the task he does not even comprehend to one who has been "made knowing by compassion" and hence able to succeed.

The kiss is the fulcrum of the long confrontation between Parsifal and Kundry that is the main scene of the act ("Parsifal! Weile!," II.739–70, and "Dies Alles hab' ich nun geträumt?," II.781–1539). This is preceded by two much shorter and less weighty scenes: the (unnamed) Prelude (II.1–60) and initial dialogue between Klingsor and Kundry ("Die Zeit ist da," II.60–426); and the scene of Parsifal among the Flowermaidens ("Hier! Hier war das Tosen!," II.427–739, and "Dich zu lassen! Dich zu meiden!," II.771–81). The ending of the Flowermaidens scene and the beginning of the Parsifal-Kundry confrontation overlap not only because Wagner does not like sharp articulations, but also because the erotically seductive flowers of Klingsor's magic garden and Kundry—his seductress-in-chief and "rose of hell"—have so much in common. The Flowermaidens can only soften Parsifal up for Kundry; her appointed task is to complete what they could only initiate and to deliver the *coup de lance*. Both the Flowermaidens scene and the Parsifal-Kundry confrontation take place in Klingsor's magic garden, and the former, much the shorter and more lighthearted of the two, serves to introduce the latter. The Klingsor-Kundry conversation, which takes place in a tower of Klingsor's castle, contains, unlike the other two scenes, no departures from the recitative-dialogue norm and hence has an even more preparatory character. In other words, the three scenes of the act are successively increasingly substantial.

The dialogue between Klingsor and Kundry confirms our guesses with regard to her. Yes, she is his unwilling but obedient tool, a sexual bait whom the magician had used to entrap Amfortas and whom he would now use similarly to entrap the approaching Parsifal. But we also learn new things. Above all, we learn that sex is the central ingredient in the worldview projected by the opera.

Consider the nature of the "curse" hanging over Kundry and of Klingsor's power over her. Kundry's problem is that all men fall for her erotic charms: "All fall with me victim to my curse."[86] How might she be released from her curse? Simple: "He who would spurn you, would set you free."[87] In *Parsifal* sexual desire is unambiguously evil, and the ability to resist its temptations unambiguously good. Klingsor has control over Kundry, "because with me alone your power can do nothing."[88] But his resistance is not of the kind that might set her free: he spurns her not because of superior self-control, but because of violent self-castration. By that act he "had stifled in himself the pain of unbridled yearning, the most awful, hellish desire, to the silence of death."[89] "Hellish desire": again, one could not be more explicit in one's condemnation of sex.

Parsifal, we also find out, is "protected" from the danger that awaits him in Klingsor's domain "by the shield of foolishness."[90] Since, as we already suspect and soon will learn for sure, the danger in question is that of erotic seduction, the meaning of Parsifal's "foolishness" emerges as having to do with his sexual innocence. And since "purity" throughout the opera serves as the code word for chastity (the Grail's Knights, for instance, are supposed to be "pure"), what may have been confusing at first now becomes clear: the promised redeemer is to be a "pure fool" because he is expected to be chaste and sexually innocent—a "fool" at least until compassion makes him "knowing." (We shall see that Wagner also took the word "fool" more generally to designate someone ignorant but endowed with genius.)

The Flowermaidens' attempt to enlighten Parsifal fails, perhaps because they are too eager, and there are too many of them: they crowd each other out. Like the adolescent that he is, like a Cherubino, Parsifal is at this early stage erotically unfocused—he will concentrate on a single object of desire only later, when Kundry drives the Flowermaidens away. In any case, the scene is just an hors d'oeuvre—a flowery exercise in erotically charged orientalism, a belated answer to the Jockey Club's call for an appropriately titillating second-act *divertissement*. While the scene contains the act's only closed musical number (another is possibly the Narrative Aria of Kundry), and has as a whole a loosely closed form, it is no more a match for the musical and dramatic weight of the subsequent Parsifal-Kundry confrontation than the Flowermaidens are for Kundry herself.

The closed musical number at the center of the scene, the choral dance of the Flowermaidens, is surrounded by more open conversational framing sections and followed, after the interruption created by Kundry's appearance, by a brief coda of the departing Flowermaidens (see appendix 7: act 2, 2.). Thus the framing sections and the coda give shape to the whole scene. The choral dance, however, is the only section characterized, at least initially, by a stable key and regular phrasing—initially, because as it proceeds, it too acquires a more and more developmental and open character.

Given that Klingsor and Gurnemanz had led us to expect something demonic—the magician talked of a throng of "beautiful witches"[91] and the knight of "devilishly lovely women"[92]—the Flowermaidens turn out to be not only harmless and ineffective, but also surprisingly innocent children of nature, the Rhinemaidens in a harem. Parsifal addresses them as "beautiful children"[93] and a stage direction says that they dance "as if in a graceful children's play."[94] Wagner would have had no difficulty introducing a sinister undertone into their song, and his failure to do so is unlikely to have been a miscalculation. Rather, it suggests that in addition to the view of sexuality as unambiguously evil, the view projected in the opera thus far, there is room in *Parsifal*'s world also for a view of sexuality as a fairly innocent and shallow, amoral (or, better, premoral) feature of the natural world, the world of flowers blooming in spring and quickly withering thereafter.

More immediately, the childish innocence of the Flowermaidens is a foil for what is to come next: the much more dangerous and decidedly neither childish nor innocent Kundry. Characteristically she dismisses them as "childish wantons"[95] and "early withering flowers."[96] But for all the difference in character, she is not completely unrelated to them. She too is erotically alluring, flowery, and exotic: as the stage direction describes her, she appears now as "a youthful woman of highest beauty . . . on a couch of flowers, in . . . a fantastic robe of an approximately Arabic style."[97] (Privately, Wagner would emphasize the erotic aspect, as his wife noted in her *Diary* on January 4, 1881: "A sketch of Kundry, brought along by Jouk.[ovsky], pleases us a lot. 'Actually,' says R., 'she ought to be lying there naked, like a Titian Venus.'—Now this has to be replaced by finery.'")[98] In his initial confusion, Parsifal wonders if she, too, is a flower: "Do you also bloom on this bed of flowers?"[99]

Kundry's unexpected call to Parsifal is, literally, an arresting moment, one of the most arresting in all of opera, and her appearance is enough to send the eager throng of chorus girls packing. Her confrontation with Parsifal is the real content of act 2; what has happened up to this point has been mere foreplay. The confrontation itself takes the form of substantial monologues embedded within a long recitative dialogue, the whole framed by the brief moment of Kundry's appearance on one end and the equally brief moment of Klingsor's downfall on the other (see appendix 7: act 2, 3.).

Kundry begins immediately with the essential point, with Parsifal's name now pronounced for the first time in the opera. Its sound seems to surprise him no less than it surprises us. When in act 1 Gurnemanz asked him for his name, he was not sure what it was: "I had many, but know none of them any more."[100] And now he asks: "Did you call me, the nameless one?"[101] The name, in *Parsifal* as in the first act of *Die Walküre*, is *the* locus of identity, and Parsifal is about to embark on a voyage of self-discovery, with Kundry his guide and catalyst. And for Parsifal as for Tristan, the voyage of self-discovery is the voyage to the most deeply buried and most distant past, to infancy and childhood, to the male infant's relationship with its parents and above all with its mother, the relationship understood to be the sexual wellspring of identity (next to the Tristan's Monologue, the Parsifal-Kundry confrontation shows Wagner in his most proto-Freudian mode). In fact, Parsifal needs to recall and consider his past even more than Tristan did. One cannot gain an identity, one cannot become someone, if one lives only in the present and sleepwalks through life, as Parsifal has done until now.

Like Kundry, Parsifal too immediately moves on to what is essential: "Parsifal? . . . Thus called me once my mother in her dream."[102] The name, she now explicates, dotting another "i," means "pure fool": "I named you, foolish pure one: 'Falparsi'—you, pure fool: 'Parsifal.'"[103] In his correspondence with Judith Gautier, Wagner indulged in a bit of fanciful etymologizing: "This is an Arabian name. . . . 'Parsi fal' means: 'parsi' . . . 'pure'; 'fal' means 'mad' in a higher sense, in other words a man without erudition, but one of genius," he suggested in an undated letter of late fall 1877.[104] But shortly thereafter, in another undated letter of December 1877, he admitted: "The 'Arabian dialect,' in which 'Fal'—mad, raw—was supposedly found, was of my invention: I wanted to inflict this word on any dialect, because it suits me! ... What do I care of the real meanings of Arabic words."[105] But if the etymology is playful, the matter is serious: the name is the identity. In one sentence Kundry imparts all the information he needs to have concerning his father: Gamuret died in battle while Parsifal was still in his mother's womb. It is the mother who matters and it is to her that Kundry now devotes a lengthy narration—perhaps the second and last closed musical number of the act.

"Closed" in late Wagner is a relative notion, of course. As usual, the architectonic features are stressed at the beginning in order to clearly establish the new formal unit. Thus Kundry's aria begins regularly enough with two identically constructed six-line stanzas set as a clear antecedent-consequent period in G major, the antecedent (II.825–39) ending with a half cadence and the consequent (II.840–58) with a full cadence. After that, however, the architectonic features recede and the main key is never again reconfirmed with a full cadence; in fact, the aria ends in D rather than G major. Undecided, the narrative hovers between a closed and open character.

The story Kundry tells Parsifal in her aria is simple: His mother, Herzeleide (her name, too, encapsulating an identity and destiny), grieved for her fallen husband but found joy in her newborn son. To spare him the fate of his father, she raised him ignorant of weapons and war (a "fool" also in this respect). He roamed the world, and when one day he finally left for good, she died brokenhearted.

Her narrative triggers the first stirrings of self-awareness in the young sleepwalker. Tellingly, the awakening self-consciousness is linked to feelings of guilt. Being self-conscious equals having a conscience, or a sense of responsibility for one's actions, and memory is the prerequisite of both—memory of others and of oneself. Desperately Parsifal asks himself: "O fool! Stupid, blundering fool! Where did you stray, forgetting her, forgetting even yourself?"[106] Once triggered, the process of remembering, of becoming self-aware, will not be stopped: "Ah! What else have I forgotten?"[107] But more than Kundry's storytelling is needed for him to be able to answer *this* question.

Meanwhile, Kundry would use his distress for her own purposes and offers him a consolation: herself. Her strategy of seduction is to occupy the place abandoned by the departed mother and thus to transform infantile eroticism into mature sexuality: "She who once gave you body and life, ... she offers you today, as the last greeting of a mother's blessing, the first kiss of love."[108] With these words, she "fixes now her lips in a long kiss on his mouth."[109]

This is the kiss that fully awakens the sleeping beauty, the second and final trigger of the emerging self-awareness which is at the same time awareness of the world (the self and world are inextricably linked, or, as Heidegger put it, "*Dasein ... has*

Being-in-the-world as its essential state").[110] It unleashes Parsifal's great Monologue of self-understanding—his equivalent of Tristan's Monologue. Thanks to the kiss he knows now what else he has forgotten: "Amfortas! . . . The wound!"[111] What has been predicted has now happened, and the "pure fool" has been made "knowing by compassion": "I saw the wound bleed, now it bleeds in me!"[112] And then Parsifal realizes what the true nature of the "wound" is, what it is that he experiences: "No! No! It is not the wound. . . . The yearning, the dreadful yearning which seizes and compels all my senses! O! Agony of love! How everything trembles, quakes, and palpitates in sinful longing!"[113] The torment he experiences is that of erotic desire. The nature of the "wound"—not only his, but also Amfortas's—is now clear to him. He not only experiences it in an act of compassion, he also understands what it is that he experiences—he has become knowing. This is how Wagner explained the significance of the kiss to King Ludwig II (letter of September 7, 1865):

> The kiss which causes Anfortas to fall into sin awakens in Parzival a full awareness of that sin, not as his own sin but as that of the grievously afflicted Anfortas whose lamentations he had previously heard only dully, but the cause of which now dawns upon him in all its brightness, through his sharing the feeling of sin: with the speed of lightning he said to himself, as it were: "ah! that is the poison that causes him to sicken whose grief I did not understand till now!"—Thus he knows more than all the others, more, especially, than the assembled Knights of the Grail who continued to think that Anfortas was complaining merely of the spear-wound! Parzival now sees deeper.[114]

Because he knows more than the knights, can see deeper, Parsifal now understands, too, what it was that he witnessed in the Grail's castle, "the lament of the Savior":[115] "Redeem, save me from the hands stained by guilt!"[116] He understands, in short, that he has been called to become the redeemer's redeemer. Finally he understands too the role played by Kundry the "corrupter"[117] and pushes her away.

There is only one thing he does not seem to understand: he owes all this enlightenment, and hence also the ability to fulfill his calling, to Kundry's kiss. Naturally compassionate he was already earlier—we saw traces of this in act 1. But compassion alone was not enough to produce knowledge. Without the corrupter, he would be nowhere. It is thanks to her kiss only that he experiences for the first time in earnest the anguish of erotic desire, that he realizes what it is specifically that torments Amfortas, and that he comes to recognize his calling.

Clearly the meaning of sexuality in this opera, initially characterized as simply an evil to be avoided and then somewhat enriched by the Flowermaidens' shallow but natural and premoral innocence, is more complicated than it had appeared until now. Erotic desire is not something that can be simply ignored or bypassed. Rather it has to be experienced, and only then rejected. Sexuality is evil, but also essential—a mark of the human condition. Kundry should be pushed away, but not before her kiss is experienced. Both of these actions are indispensable if

Parsifal is to be the redeemer—and, by the way, the redeemer of not only Amfortas and his community, but also of Kundry (as Klingsor made clear).

By the conclusion of his Monologue, Parsifal has been fully enlightened and transformed. He knows who he is and how he has become who he is, and he is ready for his mission. It is now Kundry's turn. Her great Monologue of self-revelation follows his immediately. Gurnemanz had guessed correctly: Kundry, we learn, is under an ancient curse. She had been a witness to Christ's way of the cross, perhaps among those women to whom, according to Luke's report, Jesus said, "Daughters of Jerusalem, weep not for me, but weep for yourselves, and for your children" (23.28). This, even more than one of her earlier reincarnations as Herodias, makes her into a possible candidate for the only explicitly Jewish character in Wagner's music dramas, the only personage whose claim to Jewishness requires no speculative, and necessarily inconclusive, arguments, and the only one who is not an implicit caricature—as all the other possible candidates—Alberich, Mime in *Siegfried*, Beckmesser—would have to be.[118] This said, I should admit that there is something more than faintly absurd in the idea of considering the ethnicity or religion of a person who goes through a number of reincarnations. Under the circumstances, it seems most sensible to settle on Kundry's identity as a female Wandering, or Flying, Jew, a late version of Wagner's early hero, the Flying Dutchman.

But Kundry did not weep in Jerusalem. On the contrary, she laughed, and "then . . . his gaze hit me!"[119] Kundry's sin, laughter at another's suffering, that is, *Schadenfreude*—for Arthur Schopenhauer "the worst trait in human nature"—is the exact opposite of compassion, *Mitleid*, the ethical ideal to the pursuit of which Parsifal had been called.[120] This was *her* moment of awakening conscience. "Now I look for him from world to world, to meet him again."[121] She has been waiting for him, the savior, "since eternities."[122] That she is looking for another Christ should not surprise us, since we already know that *imitatio Christi* is built into the worldview of *Parsifal*, and for that matter into the Christian worldview in general. All she yearns for is "to be united with you for one hour only, . . . in you be cleansed of sin and redeemed!"[123] It is her own redemption that she seeks in his arms: "If you are a redeemer, what prevents you, evil one, from uniting also with me for salvation's sake?"[124] But no sooner does she meet someone who looks like a savior than "the accursed laughter takes hold of me again: a sinner sinks into my arms!"[125]

Strictly speaking, what Kundry reveals about herself here is, for the most part, nothing essentially new. We had already understood what she stands for: female sexuality at its most seductive and most dangerous to males seeking to devote their lives to good works on behalf of their neighbors, rather than to the satisfaction of their own egoistic desires. We had also understood her inner conflict—her wanting, but being unable, to escape her own nature, her "curse."

There are four important new points we learn from her narrative. First, her abnormal longevity, or rather her going through a long series of reincarnations, accentuates her symbolic character: she is *das Ewig-Weibliche*. Second, we learn how it happened that she is under the curse, what sin she committed: she laughed at Jesus's suffering. Note that the crime and the punishment are intimately related. Her sin consists in a lack of compassion, an inability to feel with the suffering other; her curse is to be condemned to infecting the male world with egoism. Third, we learn why she experiences her state as a curse, that is, why she repents: she is haunted by the memory of the suffering Christ's gaze, the gaze that awoke her conscience, that made her aware of the suffering other. Fourth, and perhaps most crucially, for the first time we clearly see just how self-defeating Kundry's quest for redemption is: her nature compels her to try to seduce her potential saviors and hence to unmake them as saviors. Klingsor had clearly told her, "He who would spurn you, would set you free." Either she has not registered this, or, more likely, she has but can do nothing about it. It appears that her own actions are of no avail; she is at the mercy of the redeemer. Here, too, the theology of *Parsifal* seems to agree with orthodox, Augustinian Christianity.

Once Kundry's Monologue is completed, there is little more to learn, no real revelations remain to be made. The rest of the act is disposed of in the third and last recitative-dialogue struggle between Parsifal and Kundry as well as the final battle between Klingsor and Parsifal, which takes the form of an orchestral coda with a superimposed dialogue. Predictably, Parsifal is able to withstand Kundry's seductive assaults, fierce though they are, and equally predictably, he is able to defeat Klingsor, regain the Spear, and, making with it the sign of the cross, turn the magic castle into rubble and the magic garden into a desert—a veritable triumph of the Cross. The only spike Kundry is able to throw into the inexorably turning wheels of salvation is that she will not show Parsifal how to get back to the Grail's domain and that, for good measure, she curses him to stray and not be able to find his way: "Stray! Stray!"[126]

The final dialogue between Parsifal and Kundry, however, does enrich our understanding of the opera's theology in one important respect. It is not entirely true that Kundry can do nothing to hasten her deliverance. She should renounce her sinful sexual longings and thus make herself receptive to the workings of divine grace, Parsifal tells her: "I am sent also for your salvation, if you turn away from your longings. The solace that ends your sorrows is not offered by the source from which they flow. Salvation shall never be bestowed upon you until that source closes in you."[127] She is, it turns out, not all that different from the Knights: also she is capable of the willed suppression of sexual desire, and nothing less is expected of her than of the males. There is a role for free will in *Parsifal*: it is to stifle the will.

THE MUSIC-DRAMATIC FORM

Table 34 summarizes the opera's main structural events as well as their principal dramatic functions. There are three principal kinds of events here, each performing

TABLE 34 *Parsifal*, Main Structural Events

Form	Key	Measures	CD.track.time
Act 1			
Prelude	A-flat	I.1–113	I.1
Gurnemanz's Monologue		I.373–741	I.5.0:46–7.11:19
Communion Sequence I:			
Transformation	→C	I.1073–167	II.1.0:00–3.1:23
Processional	C→e-flat / (E-flat)→A-flat	I.1168–244	II.3.1:23–7:01
Amfortas's Monologue		I.1245–421	II.4.0:00–6.0:22
Communion	Ab	I.1422–574	II.6.0:22–7.4:46
Recessional	→E-flat →C	I.1575–666	II.8
Act 2			
Choral Dance	A-flat	II.567–702	III.1.0:00–4:23
Parsifal-Kundry Confrontation:			
Prelude (Kundry appears)		II.739–70	III.2.0:00–2:10
Recitative dialogue (Parsifal's name)		II.781–823	III.3
Kundry's Narrative Aria	G	II.824–915	III.4
Recitative dialogue (Kundry's kiss)		II.916–83	III.5.0:00–4:41
Parsifal's Monologue		II.983–1126	III.5.4:41–6.7:45
Kundry's Monologue		II.1126–275	III.7.0:00–6:26
Recitative dialogue (Kundry's curse)		II.1275–486	III.7.6:26–8.1:39
Postlude (The Spear regained)		II.1486–539	III.8.1:39–4:06
Act 3			
[Prelude]		III.1–44	III.9
The first monologue complex:			
Parsifal's Monologue		III.285–332	IV.2.0:52–3.1:58
Gurnemanz's Monologue 1		III.332–419	IV.3.1:58–4.5:10
The second monologue complex:			
Good Friday Spell	(B)/D	III.626–799	IV.7.0:44–9.0:18
Communion Sequence II:			
Transformation	→e	III.800–56	IV.9.0:18–4:30
Processional	b-flat →e	III.857–920	IV.9.4:30–10.4:07
Amfortas's Monologue	d→	III.921–1029	IV.10.4:07–11.7:06
Parsifal's Monologue		III.1029–88	IV.11.7:06–12.3:44
Communion	A-flat	III.1088–141	IV.12.3:44–13.4:09

The sections of closed-form music are in bold print; the open-form but non-dialogical sections are in bold italics.

a distinct dramatic role. First, the opera's main structural pillars of closed-form stability: the two Communion sequences that close acts 1 and 3, the first sequence shaped as an asymmetrical arch with the Communion itself serving as its capstone, the second shaped as a teleological linear progression with the Communion as its goal. Retrospectively, the Prelude is assimilated as a component of the first sequence, once we realize that its first forty-three measures anticipate the first Feast. The two

Communions themselves emerge in this reading as the most important sections of the whole. According to Cosima Wagner's *Diary* entry of August 11, 1877, it was while composing the first Communion sequence in the summer of 1877 that Wagner came to see that "this scene of Holy Communion will be the main scene, the core of the whole work."[128] Second, these two pillars of closed-form stability are separated by the opera's largest open-form sequence—the Parsifal-Kundry confrontation of the second act, with the pivotal kiss, the drama's turning point, at its center. And third, standing outside of this symmetrical ABA' structure, there is the unique combination of a closed-form orchestral discourse with superimposed monologues—the Good Friday Spell directly preceding the second Communion sequence.

The dramatic function of the first of these structural elements is to enact the ritual that is the main content and point of the opera—the ritual that, in a sense, *is* the opera. It has to be performed twice, since it is not initially successful: it accomplishes everything it is meant to accomplish only on the next try. The ritual action has two aspects, as it is, or is expected to be, at once a communion and a redemption. The first of these two roles it successfully accomplishes even on the first run-through, but not the second, since the designated redeemer is not yet ready. The second Feast, the emphasis now shifting from the communion to the redemption, is a full success.

The dramatic function of the second structural element is to show how the merely potential redeemer was transformed into the actual one, how the conversion of the saving hero was accomplished. If the ritual enacted by the first structural component is the essential content of the opera, the conversion enacted by the second component is the prerequisite for the ritual's success.

The dramatic function of the third structural element differs in kind: it presents no action, but rather offers a commentary on one. Even without the Good Friday Spell, the drama would be complete. Like any sermon, the Good Friday Spell interprets the ritual action it accompanies, and thus the Good Friday music plays a peculiar role in the music-dramatic organization of this opera, being at once central and eccentric. In one sense, it does not belong to the drama at all; in another, it is its core.

Wagner, a practical man of theater from the beginning, was increasingly aware in his later years that his task did not end with the creation and publication of the dramatic poem and score. Increasingly he sought to shape and control the initial productions and performances of his dramas and thus to establish performance traditions for each one. The Festival Theater at Bayreuth was only the most visible and permanent institutional embodiment of this awareness and interest. But in *Parsifal* Wagner went one step further. In addition to assuming control over the way his dramas would be performed, as well as the conditions under which they would be seen and heard, with *Parsifal* the composer also attempted to control the way in which the drama would be understood. This, in a nutshell, is the function of the Good Friday Spell. Although the sermon is delivered by Gurnemanz, not by Wagner himself, the temptation to identify the two in this case is strong simply because, as we shall see, the views expressed by Gurnemanz are consistent with the views Wagner was putting forward in his later years.

And thus the question left in suspension at the end of the second section of this chapter, the question of whether in the case of the Good Friday Spell one may postulate that the orchestra speaks for a separate subjectivity, for the author, does indeed look different when we consider the scene in the larger context of the whole opera. While hardly incontrovertible, these then are my two interrelated arguments in favor of considering the orchestral voice of the Good Friday music as speaking for the author: first, the section stands outside of the drama, it does not serve to present the story, but rather to interpret it; and second, there are good, and yet to be presented, reasons to think that the interpretation is Wagner's own. The shifting of the melodic substance from the voices to the orchestra is at most merely a hint that the author's voice may be taking over. In his sermon Gurnemanz speaks for the composer and, consequently, can be taken to articulate by means of concepts what the composer's voice embodied in the orchestra is telling us directly.

When he recalled in his autobiography, many years after the fact, how he wrote the first (now lost) prose sketch of his poem on the Good Friday of 1857, Wagner stressed that the thoughts of Good Friday were the inspiration: "From the idea of Good Friday I quickly sketched out an entire drama."[129] There are reasons to think that Wagner's memory was inexact and that the sketch could not have been written on that particular day, April 10, 1857.[130] But this does not seem terribly important. What is important is that in his memory the work was conceived "from the idea of Good Friday." The Good Friday Spell is indeed the spiritual and musical core of the work. In his autobiographical writings, Wagner was less interested in factual accuracy than in the symbolic significance of the recollected events. Cosima's *Diary* for April 22, 1879, confirms: "R. today recalled the impression which inspired his 'Good Friday Music'; he laughs, saying he had thought to himself, 'In fact it is all as far-fetched as my love affairs, for it was not a Good Friday at all—just a pleasant mood in Nature which made me think, "This is how a Good Friday ought to be."'"[131]

But even this most successfully dictatorial of artists could control the performances and interpretations only to a certain extent. Even at Bayreuth, performances of *Parsifal* did not freeze forever into exact museum replicas of those produced by the master himself. And the interpretation history can be immobilized even less than the performance history. We hear Gurnemanz's interpretation of the ritual, we hear Wagner's interpretation of the drama, and then we interpret both the drama and the authorial interpretation in turn. We could not do otherwise even if we wanted to, as we have no immediate, uninterpreted access to anything, Wagner's work included.

EROS AND AGAPE

The world as it is in itself, *Parsifal* tells us, the world of "wild" nature, is the domain of senseless and endless longing and torment. To live is to desire, and to desire is to suffer and inflict suffering. This is not only because any attempt to satisfy a desire involves some sort of effort and struggle. It is also because of the endless character of desire: individual longings may find temporary fulfillments, but as long as life goes on, the movement of desire itself never stops and can never find ultimate appeasement.

Sexual desire lies at the heart of this vision of the world. But the exact role played by sex in this worldview should be neither underestimated nor overestimated. Above all, the role of sex in the outlook projected in the opera should not be simply attributed to the long tradition of Christian condemnation of eros. Rather, the erotic in *Parsifal* is the powerful emblem of the most fundamental structural feature of the natural condition, the condition in which humans participate, but which is not exclusive to them.

Up to this point Wagner's vision remains consistent with that of Schopenhauer, and, for that matter, of Charles Darwin. (Wagner, we have seen, stressed the affinity between Darwinian naturalism and Schopenhauerian metaphysics.) Moreover, it does not go beyond the vision of things embodied already in *Tristan*. But *Parsifal* contains also an attempt to look beyond *Tristan*, to glimpse a horizon beyond that opera's "desolate and empty" sea.

The two operatic projects were closely intertwined. In his autobiography, Wagner recalled that in the fall of 1854, that is, at the time when he was beginning to sketch his *Tristan* poem, he planned to have Parsifal, on his long erratic way back to Amfortas's Grail domain, visit wounded Tristan in Brittany. The reason for the visit was the close similarity Wagner discerned between the figures of Tristan and Amfortas: "I identified Tristan, wasting away but unable to die of his wound, with the Amfortas of the Grail romance."[132] The similarity is indeed unmistakable and goes beyond the wounds with which the two heroes are afflicted to what these wounds stand for: unappeasable erotic longing. The composer continued to entertain the idea of the visit until at least late August 1857.[133] It was probably also by April of 1857, and certainly by October 1, 1858, that is, at the time when he was working on *Tristan*, that Wagner began to think of a Parsifal opera.[134] Wagner's early thoughts on it are mostly documented in his letters to Mathilde Wesendonck dating from the time of his work on *Tristan* and immediately afterward, 1858–60.[135] Even after the idea of a Parsifal visit to Kareol was dropped, the affinity of the two operatic projects, and specifically the affinity between Tristan and Amfortas, continued to haunt the composer. On May 30, 1859, as he worked on the music of the first part of act 3, he wrote from Lucerne to Mathilde Wesendonck in Zurich: "This last act is now a real intermittent fever:—the deepest and most unprecedented suffering and yearning, and, immediately afterwards, the most unprecedented triumph and jubilation. . . .

It is this thought that has most recently turned me against Parzival again. You see, it has again dawned upon me of late that this would again be a fundamentally evil task. Looked at closely, it is *Anfortas* who is the center of attention and principal subject.... It suddenly became dreadfully clear to me: it is my third-act Tristan inconceivably intensified."[136] Further down in the same letter we read: "And you expect me to carry through something like this? And set it to music, into the bargain?—No thank you very much! I leave it to anyone who has a mind for such things; *I* shall do all I can to keep my distance from it!"[137] Composing the music of Tristan's Delirium was an emotionally draining experience. That the composer might have been reluctant to revisit these sorts of emotional states yet again on account of Amfortas is not difficult to understand.

But if Amfortas is an intensified Tristan, Parsifal has no counterpart in the earlier opera. "Over coffee, when our conversation turns to Eros and Anteros, scorned love, R. says that Anteros is Parsifal," Cosima noted (September 20, 1881).[138] Wagner mistook the meaning of Anteros, who was the god of love requited, but no matter—it is easy to follow his line of thought: Parsifal is the anti-Eros, the answer to what afflicts Tristan and Isolde as well as Amfortas and Kundry, the answer to what afflicts all nature in its wild state. His role is to heal the erotically afflicted, to redeem raw nature.

In a January 31, 1865 letter to King Ludwig II, Wagner explained the program of a concert to take place next evening:

> We want to begin with the tone picture of the most untroubled repose of the most sublime blessedness of love that we imagine as the original source of all pure, transfigured love, the love of the world redeemer: 1. this will be proclaimed by the *orchestral Prelude* to *Lohengrin*—the mystery of the holy Grail. 2. We should then be made to feel the opposed unsatisfied longing of love by the Prelude to *Tristan*: the *Liebestod*, however, should be followed by the Transfiguration (the final section) leading us through the highest ecstasy finally back to this state of highest purity of love which allows us again to glimpse the holy Grail.[139]

At this point *Parsifal* is an as yet unrealized project, and it is the Prelude to *Lohengrin* that has to represent the significance of the Grail symbol. But the letter illustrates Wagner's understanding of how the love monumentalized in *Tristan* is related to the love celebrated in the Grail temple. The former is a yearning that brings torment and can never be fully appeased; the latter is the transfiguration of the former, the bliss of appeasement itself, the ultimate fulfillment of all desire that comes from the "original source of all pure, transfigured love, the love of the world redeemer." Wagner's Anteros, the answer to eros, is agape, the Christian love of neighbor, charity, pity, compassion.

In the last years of his life the composer's conversation returned frequently to the opposition between the senseless cruelty of nature on the one hand, and the only power that can transcend nature and provide it with meaning, the compassion introduced by Jesus. Thus for instance on July 30, 1881, Cosima writes in her *Diary*: "In the evening prolonged discussion about the relationship of animals to human beings; about Nature's cruelty, which does, however, allow for the possibility of good. It is our task to conform to this possibility, and from all else arises the sorrow which afflicts us and the significance of religion."[140] Similarly, on December 8, 1881, she notes: "When I tell him about an episode in Pisan history (the Battle of Meloria and its consequences), he says what happened there is just as in Nature, the same naive cruelty, and so it was everywhere up to the moment which he calls *Jesus*; for a sensitive person, he says, the impulses of Nature are horrible!"[141] This is the one possible answer to the Schopenhauerian-Darwinian world of *Tristan*, the meaningless world of raw, natural, unending desiring and suffering, the world driven by the self-serving eros. As an alternative *Parsifal* proposes a vision of nature transfigured and redeemed by charity—a world guided by the other-serving anti-eros, a world in which natural desires and torments find their ultimate appeasement and meaning in a vision of supernatural bliss. Such symbols as the Grail allow one to perceive visions of this sort in the only way that finite beings can perceive the infinite, mediated by signs, as if in a dark mirror. Wagner follows Schopenhauer to the letter: "Selfishness is *eros*, sympathy or compassion is *agape*," the philosopher wrote.[142] Having been "made knowing by compassion," that is, feeling pity for another suffering being and understanding this feeling, is one act capable of stopping the meaningless wheel of torments and imbuing dumb nature with sense.

It might appear then that we are getting a Christian answer to a Schopenhauerian question. But in fact there can be little doubt that the Christianity of *Parsifal* takes on a distinctly Schopenhauerian coloration, too. This is particularly noticeable in Gurnemanz's Good Friday sermon—the one section of the drama where Wagner speaks most directly his own mind. More explicitly than Jesus, Schopenhauer was ready to extend the love of neighbor to animals, since he saw no essential break between the human and the animal worlds; animals suffer, and hence deserve pity, no less than humans, he thought.[143] The noble person is touched by the suffering of another and wants to alleviate it: "He recognizes immediately, and without reasons or arguments, that the in-itself of his own phenomenon is also that of others, namely that will-to-live which constitutes the inner nature of everything . . . ; in fact, he recognizes that this extends even to the animals and to the whole of nature; he will therefore not cause suffering even to an animal."[144]

Wagner was clearly impressed, as his preoccupation with such issues as vegetarianism (which he was for, at least some of the time) and vivisection (which he was against) in his late years shows. "*For our conclusion should be couched as follows:—That* **Human dignity** *begins to assert itself only at the point where Man is distinguishable from the Beast by pity for it*," we read in his 1879 open letter against vivisection.[145] In the same letter the composer made clear that he was aware that his views in this regard departed from Christian orthodoxy, regrettably rooted as it was (he thought) in Judaism: "Unfortunately it will sorely strain the strict ecclesiastic dogma, which still reposes on the First Book of Moses, if the pity of God is to be claimed for beasts created merely for the use of man."[146] The so-called regeneration essays of 1880–81 are full of similar sentiments. Moreover, if Wagner's autobiography is to be believed, the composer did not need to read Schopenhauer to discover compassion with suffering animals: "The sufferings of others, and particularly those of animals, have always affected me almost too deeply, even to the point of filling me with a strange kind of disgust at life itself," he writes in *My Life*.[147] Cosima suggests (January 27, 1882) just how central a role the notion of compassion played in the composer's understanding of religion and how closely the issue of vivisection was intertwined with this notion in his mind: "In the evening, after telling us that the antivivisection petition has again been rejected (Reichstag), he says that he recognizes no religion except compassion."[148]

This religion of compassion, then, is what Gurnemanz preaches in the Good Friday Spell. He extends compassion not only to undeniably human beings such as Amfortas, but also to creatures whose fully human status may be somewhat in doubt, creatures that bridge the gap between the human and the animal (wild, erotically supercharged, possibly Jewish females such as Kundry), or even the human and the vegetal (such as the Flowermaidens), and finally to all living beings, even the flowers of the meadow. In the eco-theological vision of *Parsifal*, divine compassion is channeled through its elected male vessels (such as Parsifal himself) to the rest of living nature, and humanity becomes not the exploiter, but the loving guardian, of creation.

In fact, long before his late years, already at the time of Wagner's initial involvement with the *Parsifal* project, which was contemporary with the composition of *Tristan*, the compassion for dumb nature seems to have been even more important to him than the compassion for fellow humans. Self-consciousness gives humans the ability to rise above their sufferings and embrace resignation, he thought; suffering animals lack this ability and hence deserve compassion even more. A fascinating entry of October 1, 1858, in a diary he kept for Mathilde Wesendonck deserves to be quoted at length:

> But I am also clear in my own mind why I can even feel greater fellow-suffering for lower natures than for higher ones. A higher nature is what it is precisely because it has been raised by its own suffering to the heights of resignation, or else has within it—and cultivates—the capacity for such a development. Such a nature is extremely close to mine, is indeed similar to it, and with it I attain to fellow-joy. That is why, basically, I feel less fellow-suffering for people than for animals. For I can see that the latter are totally denied the capacity to rise above suffering, and to achieve a state of resignation and deep, divine calm. And so, in the event of their suffering, as happens

when they are tormented, all I see—with a sense of my own tormented despair—is their absolute, redemption-less suffering without any higher purpose, their only release being death, which confirms my belief that it would have been better for them never to have entered upon life. And so, if this suffering can have a purpose, it is simply to awaken a sense of fellow-suffering in man, who thereby absorbs the animal's defective existence, and becomes the redeemer of the world by recognizing the error of all existence. (This meaning will one day become clearer to you from the Good Friday morning scene in the third act of Parzival.)[149]

Animal suffering plays a similar role in Wagner's thinking to that played by the suffering of infants and small children in the thinking of Saint Augustine and Fyodor Dostoevsky: it is the stumbling block in any effort to make sense of existence. ("Oddly enough," writes Leszek Kołakowski, "the question which appears to be most embarrassing and most difficult to accommodate within a Christian theodicy arises from the fact of the suffering of animals.")[150] The suffering animal, able to die and thus terminate its torment, but not to rise above it, shows existence to be meaningless. The only glimpse of sense appears with human compassion for the suffering animal. It is this act of compassion that allows self-conscious humans to recognize the senselessness of existence and thus to redeem it by world-transcending resignation.

Thus the core ideas of Wagner's last opera were evidently in place even before the completion of *Tristan*. It is clear, again, that these ideas go beyond the horizon of *Tristan*. A slightly later letter to Mathilde Wesendonck, sent from Venice on March 2, 1859, may perhaps suggest that much—that Wagner sees *Parsifal* as an answer, enrichment, and completion of the Schopenhauerian drama he was then composing: "Then I occupied myself a lot with philosophy and succeeded in that to reach great results, which supplement and emend my friend Schopenhauer.... Parzival occupied me a great deal."[151] Even before he settled on the Parsifal project, the composer was thinking of *Tristan* as the first part of a diptych of sorts, a statement of the problem to which another opera would provide the answer, planning to complement, or answer, *Tristan*'s portrayal of the erotic torment with a redemptive solution, embodied at this point in a drama on a Buddhist subject: "In addition to the Nibelung dramas, I have in my head a Tristan and Isolde (love as fearful torment) and my latest subject 'the Victors' (supreme redemption, Buddhist legend)," he wrote to August Röckel from Zurich on August 23, 1856.[152]

Soon thereafter the position of the answer to *Tristan* was taken over by *Parsifal*, and the two dramas remained coupled in Wagner's mind to the end. As Cosima noted (October 6, 1882): "He observes that *Tannhäuser*, *Tristan*, and *Parsifal* belong together."[153] They do belong together, obviously, because all three center on a hero suffering erotic torments. But the contrast of Eros (the sinful love of Venus) and Anteros (the redeeming love of Elisabeth) that in the 1840s could have been handled in a single drama was by the next decade developed and distributed among two separate installments. *Tannhäuser*, in fact, was the matrix for not two but three late music dramas. Its motif of the singing contest was to be picked up and developed in *Die Meistersinger*, and Wagner himself reported that he had conceived of the latter drama as a comic satyr-play pendant to the earlier one, with the middle-class masters of Nuremberg replacing the knightly *Minnesänger* of Wartburg.[154]

It is undoubtedly true that the Christianity of *Parsifal* departs in its ecological emphasis from strict orthodoxy. But it is also the case that Wagner, for all his devotion to Schopenhauer, was well aware of the Christian sources of the ideas he was exploring in this last opera, just as he was aware of where the difference between *Tristan* and *Parsifal* lies. From the start the two works were closely associated in his mind, and he frequently liked to confront them. Spurred by his wife, he did so again on December 18, 1881, in Palermo, at a time when *Parsifal* was constantly in his thoughts as he was completing the orchestration of the third act. On that day his wife noted in her *Diary*: "When we are alone, I say to him, 'Tristan and Parsifal, one dies because of his will to live, the other lives because of his dying will.' R: 'You must always have a *mot*,' then, after a pause, 'Parsifal sees Tristan' (in Amfortas), and, after another pause, 'Something has come between them—the blood of Christ.'"[155] If *Parsifal* is to be seen as an answer to, or an amplification of, *Tristan*, it is precisely the ideal of compassion, and moreover compassion for all suffering nature, that it adds to the earlier work's ideal of renunciation. Where exactly this ideal comes from, whether from Jesus, or Schopenhauer—or, most likely, Jesus rendered philosophically respectable by Schopenhauer—matters less.[156]

Thus the religion celebrated in *Parsifal* is not, like the one celebrated in *Tristan und Isolde*, the religion of art. Rather it is the religion of universal compassion; the operatic art is used here to promote a genuine ethical ideal. It is a particular merit of Lucy Beckett's book on the opera to recognize that the work involves more than a purely self-referential play of art, that what is at stake there is not just beauty, but also truth:

> It is easier, perhaps, to decide with Chamberlain, Dahlhaus, Tanner and many others that Wagner uses the trappings of Christianity only to exploit the symbolic charge they retain from the past; that it is not only possible but correct, since "Art was the only idea in which Wagner believed" (Dahlhaus), to sit through a performance of the work without feeling to any degree threatened or persuaded by the idea it embodies. But although to reject this purely aesthetic approach is to plunge into the far deeper water of actual belief, actual truth, this is the demand that *Parsifal* does make—in fact and not only in Wagner's intention.[157]

This is persuasive. Where Beckett errs, however, is in her positing a simple opposition. For her, the opera can be either a purely aesthetic phenomenon or a religious event. She forgets the principal lesson of Heidegger's and Georg Wilhelm Friedrich Hegel's lectures on art: no less than religion or philosophy, art serves to disclose truth. *Parsifal* is an aesthetic phenomenon, of course, but it also makes a claim to truth. The opera uses art to do more than simply worship art itself; it uses it to tell its audience how to change their lives.[158]

THE MYTH OF REDEMPTION

The conclusions reached thus far seem to suggest that Wagner embraced a hopelessly self-contradictory position. We have established, first, that *Parsifal* promotes an ethical ideal and, second, that the specific content of this ideal is what Wagner saw as the Schopenhauerian kernel of truth in Christianity—compassionate insight into the inescapable and unjustifiable suffering of all will-driven nature, and the resulting renunciation of all willing as the only sensible answer to the senselessness of the world. Cosima's *Diary* (June 10, 1875) is worth recalling in this context: "Schopenhauerian philosophy and *Parcival* as the crowning achievement! That is what we resolve."[159] And four years later (February 19, 1879): "He says, 'Yes, it was Schopenhauer who revealed Christianity to me.'"[160] But the promotion of resignation is hardly compatible with the renouncing of all willing; resignation can only be practiced, not preached. A hermitlike withdrawal from all engagement with the world is what is required here, not the writing of operas and the establishing of festivals for their presentation.

Regardless of whether we decide that Wagner is contradicting himself or not, he clearly goes beyond Schopenhauer. Like Wagner himself, his Parsifal too elects in the end not to withdraw from the world. On the contrary, he assumes the role of a leader to a revitalized, regenerated community. There is no place for any hope of social regeneration in Schopenhauer, but there is one in late Wagner. Yes, the language of regeneration is not absent from *The World as Will and Representation*, but the only kind of regeneration Schopenhauer is interested in pertains to the individual, not to society. Thus, he writes: "We . . . need a complete transformation of our nature and disposition, i.e., the new spiritual birth, regeneration, as the result of which salvation appears."[161]

The composer articulated this hope not only in the opera, but also in a series of the so-called regeneration essays he put forward in his house organ, the *Bayreuther Blätter*, as he was working on the score: "Religion and Art" (1880), supplemented by "'What Boots This Knowledge?'" (1880), "'Know Thyself'" (1881), and "Hero-dom and Christendom" (1881).[162] The essays paint the scenario of past and present societal degeneration as well as the possible future regeneration.

In "Religion and Art," Wagner continues to see both the natural world and the historical human world in essentially Schopenhauerian-Darwinian terms: the world is a slaughterhouse where the strong devour the weak, the arena of senseless violence driven by the ever-striving but ultimately aimless and meaningless will.

346   CHAPTER 5

As Schopenhauer put it, "This world is the battle-ground of tormented and agonized beings who continue to exist only by each devouring the other."[163] But unlike Schopenhauer, for whom these features of the world were rooted in its metaphysical structure and hence inescapable and unchanging, Wagner now thinks that the world might once have been otherwise, and consequently might become otherwise yet again: its present state is one of degeneration of the human race that is the result of humans, prompted by scarcity and hunger, turning from peaceful vegetarians into violent carnivores; a future regeneration, while not guaranteed, is possible, provided we become pacific vegetarians once again. The hope lies in an alliance of vegetarians with those who defend animals from cruel treatment, with advocates of temperance and sobriety among the dis-privileged, and with socialists. (If old Wagner were not a music dramatist of genius, he would have made a first-rate street-corner crank.)

Such an alliance would build on the teachings of "the two sublimest of religions, Brahminism with its offshoot Buddhism, and Christianity,"[164] that brought sense into the meaningless world by advocating vegetarianism and nonviolence, a turning away from the self-directed will to the other-directed compassion with all living and suffering creatures (animals included), that is, resignation. "The deepest basis of every true religion we find in recognition of the frailty of this world, and the consequent charge to free ourselves therefrom," Wagner wrote.[165] Christ, "the quintessence of all pitying Love, stretched out upon the cross of pain and suffering," beckoned "to the highest pity, to worship of suffering, to imitation of this breaking of all self-seeking Will."[166] Vegetarianism, according to Wagner, was "the most intelligible core of Christianity."[167] You may have missed this in reading the Gospels, but Wagner was convinced that "his own flesh and blood he [Christ] gave as last and highest expiation for all the sin of outpoured blood and slaughtered flesh, and offered his disciples wine and bread for each day's meal:—'Taste such alone, in memory of me.' This the unique sacrament of the Christian faith; with its observance all the teaching of the Redeemer is fulfilled."[168]

But the vegetarian alliance could not simply rely on the present-day Christian churches, since these degenerated, too, forgetting for instance Christ's teaching of vegetarianism and dogmatically insisting on the literal truth of its mythic symbols. The cause of this degeneration was Christianity's unfortunate drawing upon Judaism: once Christianity became a state religion, it had to offer support to political structures based on the will to power and violence, and it did so by invoking the Jewish God of domination and power. "But what was bound to prove her [the Church's] ruin . . . was the tyrant-prompted thought of tracing back this Godliness upon the cross to the Jewish 'Creator of heaven and earth,' a wrathful God of Punishment who seemed to promise greater power than the self-offering, all-loving Saviour of the Poor," writes Wagner.[169] And further: "For us it is sufficient to derive the ruin of the Christian religion from its drawing upon Judaism. . . . However, it is precisely hence that the Church obtained her source of might and mastery; for wherever Christian hosts fared forth to robbery and bloodshed, . . . it was not the All-Sufferer whose name was invoked, but . . . all the . . . captains of Jehova who fought for the people of Israel."[170] By this drawing upon Judaism, the Church got its power, but the Christian religion was ruined: "Without this intrusion of the ancient Jewish spirit, . . . how were it possible to the Church till this day to claim for her own a 'civilised world' whose peoples all stand armed to the teeth for mutual extermination . . . ?"[171]

Wagner, alas, might have found support for some of this ignorant nonsense in his beloved Schopenhauer. "New Testament Christianity," Schopenhauer thought, "is Indian in spirit, and therefore, more than probably, Indian in origin, although only indirectly, through Egypt. Such a doctrine . . . is . . . little suited to the Jewish stem on which that Indian wisdom had to be grafted in the Holy Land."[172] For an anti-Semite, the news that the original Christianity had little or nothing to do with Judaism must have been good tidings indeed. The philosopher opined further: "It is to be regarded generally as a great misfortune that the people whose former culture was to serve mainly as the basis of our own were not, say, the Indians or the Greeks, or even the Romans, but just these Jews."[173] The truth that had been grafted on the alien Jewish stem, the denial of the will to live, was common to Christians and to Hindus and Buddhists, Schopenhauer thought.[174] But the grafting diluted it:

> But we find what we have called denial of the will-to-live still further developed [further than in Christianity, that is] . . . in the ancient works in the Sanskrit language. . . . That this important ethical view of life could attain here to a more far-reaching development . . . is perhaps to be ascribed mainly to the fact that it was not restricted by an element quite foreign to it, as the Jewish doctrine of faith is in Christianity. . . . Christianity is composed of two very heterogeneous elements. Of these I should like to call the purely ethical element preferably, indeed exclusively, the Christian, and to distinguish it from the Jewish dogmatism with which it is found. If . . . that excellent and salutary religion should completely decline, then I would look for the reason for this simply in the fact that it does not consist of one simple element, but of two originally heterogeneous elements. . . . Yet after this dissolution, the purely ethical part would still be bound always to remain intact, because it is indestructible.[175]

Already in a letter of June 7, 1855, Wagner explained to Franz Liszt that "we may allow that Christianity is such a contradictory phenomenon because we know it only through its contamination by narrow-minded Judaism . . . , whereas modern research has succeeded in proving that pure, uncontaminated Christianity is no more and no less than a branch of that venerable Buddhist religion which, following Alexander's Indian campaign, found its way . . . to the shores of the Mediterranean."[176] In any case, as Wagner concludes his argument in "Religion and Art," today art alone might accomplish what the degenerate church is no longer capable of doing: autonomous art, free of the petrified church dogmas, can give the essential teachings of religion (Schopenhauer's "purely ethical element") a new life and provide guidance to the vegetarian alliance. It might be mentioned in passing that this last step in Wagner's argument is indebted, without acknowledgment, to E. T. A. Hoffmann's classic 1814 essay "Old and New Church Music."[177] Hoffmann's spirit, in general, presides over much that Wagner has to say on the relationship of music and religion in the regeneration essays. We have already heard the crucial statement concerning the relationship of religion and art: "Where Religion becomes artificial, it is reserved for Art to save the spirit of religion by recognizing the figurative value of the mythic symbols which the former would have us believe in their literal sense, and revealing their deep and hidden truth through an ideal presentation."[178] The path to a "better state of future man" is one from which "all violence is quite shut out."[179] If there is any hope of a regeneration of the human race, it is only art (presumably and specifically the art of the Bayreuth master) that will allow humankind to find this path.

The first two supplements to "Religion and Art" do not add anything essentially new to this argument, although the anti-Semitic component becomes notably more astringent in the second of these, "'Know Thyself,'" with its ominous final chord: "Only when the fiend [the Jew] ... no more can find a where or when to lurk among us [Germans], will there also be no longer—any Jews."[180] But however ominous this sounds, I agree with Dahlhaus that this and similar pronouncements by Wagner, including the notorious ending of "Jewishness in Music," where one hears of "self-annihilation" ("Selbstvernichtung"), should not be anachronistically interpreted as calls for the physical annihilation of the Jews. Rather, they are calls to the Jews to "annihilate" themselves by ceasing to be Jews, that is, world-oriented "optimists" in the Schopenhauerian sense of term.[181] A similar conclusion, at least with regard to how the "redemption" of the Jews is to be understood in "Jewishness in Music," has been reached by Saul Friedländer: "Therefore, one cannot interpret Wagner's first anti-Jewish pamphlet as a call to a violent extinction of the Jews; rather, one must read it as a call to an abolition of Jewishness as a culture, to a removal of the 'Jewish spirit.'"[182]

There is something new, however, in the third supplement, "Hero-dom and Christendom." According to Cosima's *Diary*, in Venice, on October 22, 1880, Wagner renewed his acquaintance with the aristocratic French author Arthur de Gobineau, whom he had previously briefly met in late 1876.[183] According to Cosima again, the composer was reading Gobineau's *Essai* by March 18, 1881, and he finished reading it on May 28.[184] The *Diary* mentions Wagner working on "'Know Thyself'" on February 2, 1881, and correcting the proofs on March 1.[185] "Hero-dom and Christendom" was written from August 23 to September 4, 1881.[186] It seems then that Wagner's reading of the *Essai* occurred after the time he wrote "'Know Thyself'" but before his work on "Hero-dom and Christendom." This reading accounts for the latter essay's innovations.

Wagner did not need Gobineau to become an anti-Semite, of course. His "Jewishness in Music," published under a pseudonym in 1850, and again, in a revised and expanded version and this time under the author's own name, in 1869, marks a stage in the evolution from the deadly, premodern, Christian anti-Judaism to the even more deadly, modern, secular, racist form of anti-Jewish sentiment and is one of the classics of modern German and European anti-Semitism—from at least the mid-nineteenth century until our own day a characteristic component of the outlook of left- and right-wing radicals who identify Jews with financial capitalism. Before Wagner there is in particular the slightly earlier 1844 tract by Karl Marx, "On the Jewish Question," with which the composer was certainly familiar and on which he partly drew,[187] though in Wagner's case anticapitalist animus was typically amalgamated with resentment and envy of his more successful Jewish competitors, Felix Mendelssohn and, in particular, Giacomo Meyerbeer.[188] As Thomas S. Grey demonstrated, by the second edition of 1869 Wagner added a good deal of persecution mania into the mix, shifting the main target of his attack from Jewish composers to the supposedly hostile and supposedly Jewish-dominated press led by Eduard Hanslick.[189]

Wagner's historical responsibility for having lent the prestige of a great artist to helping make a vulgar and deadly prejudice acceptable—even respectable—among the educated classes, for making anti-Semitism seem compatible with culture, is incontestable.[190] Even if Adolf Hitler had felt no particular affinity with Wagner, and even if Winifred Wagner, the English widow of Wagner's son, Siegfried, had not committed the Bayreuth Festival to the Nazi cause, the question of Wagner's role in the prehistory of the annihilation of European Jews would pose itself. But compared to the earlier regeneration essays, the racism of "Hero-dom and Christendom" is something new, and this novelty shows the fingerprints of Gobineau. The causes of the historical degeneration of humanity, we now learn, go beyond turning away from the vegetarian diet:

> Quite apart from such an explanation, one of the cleverest men of our day has also proved this fall to have been caused by a corruption of blood, though ... he has derived it solely from the crossing of races, whereby the noblest lost more than the less noble of them gained. The uncommonly circumstantial picture of this process supplied us by Count Gobineau in his *Essai sur l'inégalité des races humaines* appeals to us with most terrible force of conviction.[191]

Miscegenation has thus joined the eating of animal flesh as a cause, perhaps even *the* cause, of the degenerating "corruption of blood." "Indeed this one relation [the mixing of races] might suffice to explain our fall," Wagner writes.[192]

The corruption of Christianity is now attributed to the fact that it took root among the racially mixed "Latino-Semites" of the Roman empire ("that ... blend of races white and black which ... supplied the basic character of the nations of the later Roman empire"),[193] giving rise to "the Semite-Latin Church": "The falsehood of our whole Civilisation bears witness to corrupted blood of its supporters."[194] The crucial chapter in the history of degeneration occurred when the heroic Germanic tribes, the last purebred Aryans, became the masters of the racially mixed "Latino-Semites" of the falling Roman empire, embraced their "Semite-Latin" Christian faith, and thus got contaminated and ruined: "The accident of their ["the last pure-bred Germanic branches" "of the Aryan race"] becoming masters of the great Latino-Semite realm ["the falling roman world"] was fatal to them."[195] The results can still be felt today: "It certainly may be right to charge this purblind dullness of our public spirit to a vitiation of our blood—not only by departure from the natural food of man, but above all by the tainting of the hero-blood of noblest [Aryan] races with that of former cannibals now trained to be the business-agents of Society [the materialist Jews]."[196]

In "Religion and Art" and its earlier supplements, degeneration resulted from the abandonment of vegetarianism and regeneration was predicated upon a return to a vegetarian diet. Since in "Hero-dom and Christendom" degeneration is the result of the mixing of races, it would seem that now Wagner should make the next logical step and advocate a return to racial purity, however accomplished, as a prerequisite for regeneration. Surprisingly, however, this is not the step he makes. Instead he asserts "the oneness of the human *species*" consisting in our common "capacity for conscious suffering," though, to be sure, in "higher natures" this capacity is more developed than in lower ones. This capacity is what differentiates humans from other animals.[197] "This faculty [of conscious suffering] we can only regard as the last step reached by Nature in the ascending series of her fashionings; thenceforth she brings no new, no higher species to light, for in it she herself attains her unique freedom, the annulling of the internecine warfare of the Will."[198] Thus, in spite of its division into unequal races, the human species is one, and its ultimate destiny is resignation, the self-overcoming of the will. Wagner was willing to follow Gobineau only that far; ultimately he was a wholehearted anti-Semite, but a halfhearted racist.

The self-annihilation of the will was also the whole point of Christ's sacrifice. Christ might have come as the answer to the plight of humankind confronted with racial degeneration: "The blood in the Redeemer's veins might thus have flowed, as divine sublimate of the species itself, from the redemptive Will's supreme endeavour to save mankind at death-throes in its noblest races."[199] But his sacrifice was not for the benefit of Aryans alone. Rather, it was for the benefit of the whole species: "The blood of suffering Mankind, as sublimated in that wondrous birth, could never flow in the interest of howsoever favoured a single race; no, it shed itself on all the human family."[200] The sacrament of communion symbolically purifies the blood of all the communicants, even the racially low or impure: "Thus, notwithstanding that we have seen the blood of noblest races vitiated by admixture, the partaking of the blood of Jesus, as symbolized in the only genuine sacrament of the Christian religion, might raise the very lowest races to the purity of gods. This would have been the antidote to the decline of races through commingling."[201] The antidote to the degenerating miscegenation, then, is not racial purification but rather the sacrament of communion that symbolically raises even the racially most suspect communicant to full membership in the universal human family and makes him capable of self-transcending renunciation.

Even without the racist supplement, the essential historical vision of the regeneration essays, the discourse of the past and present degeneration to be followed by potential future regeneration, cannot be easily synthesized with Schopenhauer's metaphysics. The philosopher's outlook was fundamentally ahistorical. For Schopenhauer, humankind's predicament was always the same and remained inescapable even if a rare select individual managed to transcend it by attaining the self-cancellation of the will. When he supplemented the essays with Gobineau's racism, Wagner did not make his task of synthesizing the regeneration discourse with Schopenhauer any easier. The regeneration essays remain an uncomfortable and not entirely coherent compromise. But—the crucial point—it is a compromise in which the last word belongs to Schopenhauer, rather than to the Aryan supremacist. This is because of how the content of the regeneration is understood. For Wagner, the regeneration of humankind consists not in the supremacy of vegetarian Aryans over racially inferior and mixed carnivores, but rather in universally attainable resignation, the silencing of the selfish will so that the voice of knowing compassion for all suffering creatures may be heard. To be sure it is not difficult to guess that humankind would be led toward regeneration by the example of the Aryan-vegetarian elite. It may even be that only the elite would achieve regeneration. These matters are not really spelled out. All the same, ultimately, the claims of the universal human condition as conceived by Schopenhauer trump those of racial particularism inspired by Gobineau.

The point is crucial, because what is at stake here is more than just the interpretation of the last stage in Wagner's development as a moral and social thinker. What is at stake is also the sense we can make of *Parsifal*, of the opera's significance for Wagner, perhaps even of the composer's whole oeuvre, given that *Parsifal* may be seen as something of a testament. As he confided to Cosima (March 28, 1881), "'Gobineau says the Germans were the last card Nature had to play—*Parsifal* is my last card.'"[202]

The central argument of the regeneration essays is closely and obviously related to the concerns of the opera. Both—the essays and the opera—share a grand historical narrative of a community's degeneration followed by its regeneration. Less straightforward is the relationship between understanding the causes or conditions offered by the essays, on the one hand, and the opera, on the other, to explain either the degeneration or the regeneration. In *Parsifal* the degeneration of the community is caused by the king's failure to remain "pure," that is, chaste. And the reverse: the regeneration of the community is possible only under the leadership of a "pure" king who has experienced sexual desire but was capable of mastering it, not by the unworthy expedient of self-castration, but by an act of self-cancelling will. Sexual desire, we know, was for Schopenhauer the central manifestation of the noumenal will in the phenomenal world. "The sexual impulse is the kernel of the will-to-live, and consequently the concentration of all willing," the philosopher wrote. And again: "The sexual impulse is therefore the most complete manifestation of the will-to-live."[203] In *Parsifal*, too, sex may be understood as the *pars pro toto* emblem of the will. Hence the central value of sexual abstinence in the drama that makes "resignation," the will's self-overcoming, the turning away from the self-serving desire toward the other-serving compassion, into the focus of its vision of regeneration.

The regeneration of society is understood in the essays just as it is understood in the opera: it will occur when society, or at any rate the elite, abandons the selfish will to power as well as the violence that is the instrument of the will and embraces instead altruistic compassion for the suffering. The essays differ from the opera in what they choose to emphasize as emblematic of the will: the stress falls now not on sexual activity, but on the eating of animal flesh supplemented and perhaps replaced in "Hero-dom and Christendom" by the mixing of the races.

It is not difficult to see how Wagner might have come to treat vegetarianism as an equivalent of celibacy—another example of abstinence from satisfying selfish, fleshly desires. The racism of the final supplement, however, is another matter, and a stumbling block to any attempt to see the essays and the opera as expressing a single ethical vision. Not surprisingly, it has given rise to the suspicion that the opera contains a hidden, anti-Semitic and racist, agenda.

An early formulation of the suspicion appeared in Robert Gutman's 1968 study of the composer.[204] "In *Parsifal*," Gutman claimed, "Wagner's canon preaching the identity of denial, death, redemption, and love was to amalgamate with racism to reach a strange apotheosis."[205] The opera presented the problem of racial degeneration in allegorical form: "The catchwords of Wagner's early and middle periods were 'redemption' and 'renunciation.' To these the dying composer added the arresting war cry—'racial decline.' It was the rather ambitious duty of *Parsifal* to provide a framework in which all three could be expounded and reconciled."[206] Moreover, Wagner's last work did not limit itself to the presentation of the problem; it also offered a solution: "Although embracing Gobineau's ideas about man's degeneration, Wagner could not accept a scenario lacking a redemptive finale. . . . Racial mixture was not ineradicable; adulterated blood could again be made pure. At hand was a savior long hinted at . . .—the Aryan Jesus, whom the vaticanations of '*Heldentum*' first revealed."[207] Wagner's "purpose in '*Heldentum*' and its artistic counterpart, *Parsifal*," Gutman concluded, was "to confront Germany with the seriousness of its racial crisis—to outline the perfection, decline, and hopes for regeneration of the debased Aryan."[208]

To bolster this reading of the opera, Gutman specifically claimed that "the Grail community in *Parsifal* was alarmed to observe natural selection working against its distinctive Aryanism."[209] The objective of the community was to preserve its racial purity: "Racial heredity and strict breeding, not natural selection, formed the new mechanism of salvation."[210] Like the story of the community, also the story of its leader could be read in racial terms: "On its darkest level . . . *Parsifal* is an allegory of the Aryan's fall and redemption. . . . Amfortas, stands at the very center of the drama."[211] Furthermore, "Amfortas contrasts the divine blood of Christ in the Grail with his own sinful blood, corrupted by sexual contact with Kundry, a racial inferior, this criminal miscegenation epitomizing the Aryan dilemma. Both blood streams contend within his own wracked system. . . . The evil blood spilling from the wound is fed by a craving to repeat the transgression."[212] In short, "Amfortas . . . hungers for both non-Aryan sex and Aryan salvation."[213] And finally, not only the community and its leader, but the redeemer, too, was driven by racial considerations, according to Gutman: "Parsifal's sudden insight in the magic garden was the realization that by yielding to Kundry he would dilute his purebred strain."[214] According to Gutman, redemption in *Parsifal* amounts to the restoration of racial purity: "Parsifal reclaimed the spear, that holy apparatus of Aryanism outrageously appropriated by Jewry, and returned this stolen symbol of power to the temple." In this way, "the Aryan world was again . . . in order."[215]

According to Gutman, then, *Parsifal* allegorizes the racist scenario of "Herodom and Christendom": the Aryan Monsalvat community suffers from racial degeneration, which is the result of Amfortas's sexual union with the Jewish Kundry, and the community's regeneration involves racial purification under the new leadership of the racially uncontaminated Parsifal. By contrast, I have suggested above that the community's degeneration is the result of its king's failure to remain chaste, and that regeneration can be achieved only under a chaste leader. With sexual desire standing for the will and with regeneration understood as the turning away from the selfish will toward altruistic pity, chastity becomes an emblem of the will's self-overcoming. "Voluntary and complete chastity is the first step in asceticism or the denial of the will-to-live," says Schopenhauer.[216] In Gutman's reading, sexual activity as such would be unobjectionable; what is fatally compromising is intercourse with a racial inferior.

It may seem that the essential difference between the two interpretations turns on the meaning of the concept of "purity" in Wagner's dramatic poem. When Wagner uses "rein" and other closely related words, does he mean sexual purity (that is, chastity), or purity of race? The question cannot be answered by means of analysis of each instance when such words occur in the poem. Whether we assume one answer or the other, we end up with a coherent reading of *Parsifal*. An interpretation of the opera as a racist allegory of Aryan degeneration and regeneration cannot be dismissed as internally incoherent.

But is it what Wagner intended? To answer this question we need to read the text of *Parsifal* in appropriate contexts, and the contexts likely to prove productive in this case include Wagner's other writings, his readings, and reports of his oral pronouncements. The interpretation claiming that the concept of purity in the poem is synonymous with chastity relies primarily on Wagner's well-documented decades of infatuation with Schopenhauer, lasting from 1854 through the end of the composer's life; the claim that what is really meant is racial purity invokes primarily the regeneration essays. (Additionally, Hartmut Zelinsky has used excerpts from Cosima Wagner's diaries, which were unavailable to Gutman, in support of a similar claim that "the anti-Semitic blood ideology is central to *Parsifal*."[217] Zelinsky's readings of the excerpts, however, are not persuasive.)[218] But the evidence of the essays weakens rather than strengthens Gutman's case. We have seen that Gobineau's racism makes an appearance only in the last supplement (written August 23 to September 4, 1881). Earlier essays (1880–81) are free of it, since at the time of their writing Wagner was not yet familiar with Gobineau's theory. *A fortiori*, he could not have had it in mind when writing the *Parsifal* poem (January 25 through April 19, 1877) a few years before the essays. It is, in short, implausible that Wagner intended his opera to be interpreted as a racist allegory.[219]

It is not implausible, alas, to assume that, once he became acquainted with Gobineau's *Essai*, he might have welcomed a racist reading of *Parsifal*, but even so, his reading would have been somewhat different from Gutman's. Gutman, it seems to me, has not read "Hero-dom and Christendom" carefully enough and has misrepresented some aspects of the essay, reading into it, in particular, a call to racial purification that I do not find there. For all its undeniable and revolting racism, the supplement offers a vision of social regeneration that does not involve the domination of the inferior races by the purebred Aryans, but rather a return to nonviolence and universal compassion.

To show that the opera is not racist, however, is not the same as to show that it is not anti-Semitic. In a recent survey of issues raised by Wagner's anti-Semitism, Thomas S. Grey observed that "the question of anti-Semitism in the works [as opposed to Wagner's later writings, about the anti-Semitic character of which "there has never been any question"] begins and ends, probably, with *Parsifal*."[220] "The case 'against' *Parsifal*," Grey explains, "differs from hypotheses about anti-Semitic elements in the other works in concerning precisely the fundamental themes and textures of the drama, not merely isolated caricatures or allusions to ethnic-cultural stereotypes"[221] that scholars propose to identify in the figures of Alberich, Mime, and Beckmesser, following the lead of Theodor Adorno's typically apodictic and inaccurate remark to the effect that "all the rejects of Wagner's works are caricatures of Jews."[222] "The gold-grabbing, invisible, anonymous, exploitative Alberich" got on

Adorno's list as a Jewish plutocrat, an identification that is neither completely implausible nor obligatory; the "shoulder-shrugging, loquacious Mime, overflowing with self-praise and spite" made the list because of his fidgety manner, a case considerably less plausible than that of his brother, but like that of Alberich impossible to disprove with certainty; and "the impotent intellectual critic Hanslick-Beckmesser" is on the list because in the 1861 prose draft of the libretto Wagner named the personage Hanslich, a case discussed at greatest length in the literature of the subject and the most plausible of the three.[223] Alberich's son, Hagen, by the way, although a "reject" too, does not appear on the list of the usual suspects probably because he is the one late Wagnerian villain who does not fidget, talks little, has nerves of steel, and bides his time. (To be sure, a sentence in a 1945 essay suggests that Adorno considered also Hagen to be a "Jewish" figure: "The whole plot of Wagner's *Ring* suggests some kind of a gigantic Nazi frame-up, with Siegfried as an innocent, lovable Teutonic hero who, just by chance, conquers the world and ultimately falls victim to the Jewish conspiracy of the ark dwarfs and those who trust their counsel.")[224] And what of Klingsor, a reject if there ever was one?

And then there is Kundry. The very universalism of the vision of redemption on offer in *Parsifal* means that there will be no room in the regenerated society for any alternatives and particularisms. Wagner was surely not a prophet of a tolerant multiculturalism. But whether we identify an anti-Semitic intent in *Parsifal* or not depends entirely on whether we consider that Kundry was intended to be taken as a Jewish character or not. (Thus, once the claim that the opera projects a racist blood myth has been answered, as I believe it has been above, the case of *Parsifal* turns out not to be fundamentally different from that of the *Ring* or *Die Meistersinger*.) Kundry, with her multiple reincarnations, is undoubtedly a personification of the ever-resurgent will, but, as we have seen, it is not completely implausible to think of her also as specifically Jewish, at least in one of her incarnations. Once we assume this part of her identity, we cannot fail to notice that the redemptive compassion in *Parsifal* does include in its embrace even a Jew, but only at the price of baptism. In a spirit consonant with "Jewishness in Music," a Jew is acceptable only when she self-destructs as a Jew. (After Hitler, we forget sometimes that it is possible to be an anti-Semite without advocating genocide.) Granted, an anti-Semitic interpretation of the opera is optional rather than necessary, because the decision to see Kundry as a Jewish character is optional, just as it is in the cases of Alberich, Mime, and Beckmesser. But the option in this case is not completely implausible, though hardly compelling and, given Kundry's principal role as the personification of metaphysical will, not particularly interesting. Even so, it needs to be noticed that, given the universalist assumptions of the plot, a denouement in which a Jew was both redeemed *and* allowed to remain a Jew was not a possibility. The only possible alternative was a denouement in which Amfortas gets redeemed and Kundry is left behind. Wagner's solution was clearly the more humane one.

Still, there is little evidence that the opera's putative racist or anti-Semitic subtexts were properly decoded by those who should have been most skillful at hermeneutic exercises of this sort. Instances of racist or anti-Semitic interpretations of *Parsifal* stemming from Nazi Germany or from the Bayreuth circle are uncommon.[225] In general, the Nazis did not need such interpretations to make the high-quality Furtwängler-Tietjen-Preetorius productions in Bayreuth and Berlin work in their favor by providing the regime with a prestigious sheen of cultural legitimacy. As Jens Malte Fischer observed, "It is undoubtedly the case that performances of Wagner's works [in the Third Reich], no matter how little specifically propagandistic they were, served to stabilize the system.... Already around 1900 and then during the period of the Weimar republic, has the work of Wagner become for broad circles of the public so much the symbol of German national art, and Wagner himself the leading figure of an anti-Semitic artist of world rank, that a decisive propagandistic turn after 1933 was altogether unnecessary."[226] Similarly, Saul Friedländer pointed out: "But it appears that for the German public of, above all, the Twenties their [Wagner's music dramas'] political-ideological dimension was impossible to miss.... Parts of this public might have easily associated 'Wach auf' [chorus from *Die Meistersinger*] with 'Deutschland erwache!' [a favorite Nazi song]."[227] Given the widespread nationalist reception of Wagner's oeuvre already before 1933, additional anti-Semitic or racist emphases after the Nazi assumption of power were simply not needed.

For an affinity between the opera and the Nazi, or more generally Fascist, ideology we would have to look elsewhere than to specific more or less veiled racist or anti-Semitic messages. Students of Fascism have long singled out the discourse of regeneration as its essential feature. Fascist identity is built on the narrative of society's degeneration that can and should be reversed by extreme measures, in particular redemptive violence, to produce a regeneration of national and racial unity and purity.[228] It is this discourse of regeneration that links *Parsifal* to later Fascist ideologies. The family resemblance is far from perfect (neither *Parsifal* nor the regeneration essays can be accused of advocating violence), and its significance should not be exaggerated. The history of opera does not lack stories of endangered communities that successfully overcome their crises (think of *Idomeneo* or *The Magic Flute*). All that can be claimed here is that, if a Nazi wanted for whatever reasons to claim *Parsifal* as his own, such a claim might be built on the common foundation of the regeneration discourse and would require that he overlook the specific content the opera gave to the notion of regeneration.[229]

There was one listener who seems to have done precisely that and may have interpreted the opera in racist terms: Adolf Hitler.[230] (Strangely enough, it appears that not a single one among the Führer's numerous documented remarks on Wagner mentions the composer's anti-Semitism.)[231] Hitler's attitude to *Parsifal* was ambiguous. On the one hand, he declared already in 1936: "From Parsifal I build my religion."²³² And he thought sufficiently well of it to plan a performance in celebration of the expected final war victory. Hence it is possible that he did see in *Parsifal* a symbolic image of Germany's "awakening" and contemplated the idea of making the opera into the liturgical centerpiece of a future National Socialist religion for his *Reich*. It is also possible that in the elite order of the Knights of the Grail he saw a prefiguration of Heinrich Himmler's SS.²³³ On the other hand, he may have sensed that the reality to which he wanted Germans to awake did not fully correspond to what was explicitly advocated by Wagner. It is noteworthy that *Parsifal*, since 1882 with one exception an annual fixture of the Bayreuth Festivals, was not performed there after 1939.

In particular Hitler disliked the opera's Christian symbolism, rejected the notion that the opera projected a Christian-Schopenhauerian ethics of compassion, and, if Hermann Rauschning's admittedly controversial testimony is to be believed, preferred to understand the work in racist terms as a defense of the purity of blood: "We must interpret 'Parsifal' in a totally different way to the general conception, the interpretation, for instance, of the shallow [Hans von] Wolzogen [from 1878 to 1938 the editor of the *Bayreuther Blätter*]," Rauschning claims he heard him say (which, by the way, would show that Hitler was aware that his interpretation diverged from the official Bayreuth line). "Behind the absurd externals of the story, with its Christian embroidery and its Good Friday mystification, something altogether different is revealed as the true content of this most profound drama. It is not the Christian-Schopenhauerist religion of compassion that is acclaimed, but pure, noble blood, in the protection and glorification of whose purity the brotherhood of the initiated have come together."²³⁴ A devotee of the hermeneutics of suspicion, Hitler anticipated the readings promoted some three decades later by Gutman and his followers.²³⁵

Accordingly the Führer advised his youthful Bayreuth protégés, the composer's grandsons Wolfgang and Wieland, to tone down the religious symbols in future productions (it was Wolfgang who conveyed Hitler's ideas to the budding opera director, Wieland). Whether conscious that he was following "Uncle Wolf's" advice or not, this is precisely what Wieland Wagner did in the celebrated 1951 production with which he reopened the Bayreuth Festival after the war—arguably the most important and influential staging in the whole history of Wagner performance, a staging designed at once to set the way Wagner operas were presented free of literal adherence to the composer's stage directions and to purge Bayreuth of its politically tainted past. If the war itself did not turn out quite as Hitler had hoped, the opera's production, at least to some extent, did. Wagner's work was presented in a highly abstract fashion, emphasizing timeless myth and psychology and playing down most historical and cultural associations, its Christian symbols much attenuated. As Udo Bermbach demonstrated, the new Wagner interpretation promoted in the postwar years until the epoch-making centennial Chéreau-Peduzzi-Boulez *Ring* of

1976 on the pages of the *Bayreuther Programmheften* (which continued to be dominated by ex-Nazis such as Zdenko von Kraft, Otto Strobel, Hans Grunsky, and Curt von Westernhagen) promoted a line similar to Wieland's, a Wagner of timeless myth and Jungian-depth psychology.[236] It is an ironic twist characteristic of the whole convoluted reception history of Wagner's oeuvre that this artistically and politically important production, designed to wipe Wagner's work clean of the fingerprints left on it by the Nazis and thus make both this work and the Bayreuth Festival culturally palatable in the new liberal democratic Germany, may have been partly inspired by the memory of conversations with the fallen dictator.

Epilogue
Wagner contra Nietzsche

> *In admiring the Bayreuth master, I had none of the scruples of those who, like Nietzsche, are bidden by a sense of duty to shun in art as in life the beauty that tempts them and who, tearing themselves from* Tristan *as they renounce* Parsifal, *and, in their spiritual asceticism, progressing from one mortification to another, succeed, by following the most painful of* viae Crucis, *in exalting themselves to the pure cognition and perfect adoration of* Le Postillon de Longjumeau.
>
> MARCEL PROUST, *THE CAPTIVE*[1]

The trajectory of Richard Wagner's artistic and ideological development from the late 1840s to the early 1880s needs surely to be counted among the most extraordinary adventures in the arts of the period. Had Wagner's career and life ended with the Dresden uprising of May 1849, as well it might have, he would be remembered, performed, and studied today as the most important composer of German opera in the nineteenth century. But, improbably, he did survive the crisis of 1848–49 and went on to reinvent himself—even, against great odds, to fashion for himself a second and much grander career. He thus became one of the few composers who decisively influenced the course of the history of Western art music and one of the key figures in European culture of his time, a central example of this characteristically nineteenth-century type—the artist as a prophet. In this and some other respects he is close kin to two Russian contemporaries: Fyodor Dostoyevsky (also for the anti-Semitism, the sensitivity with regard to the sufferings of inarticulate innocents, and the revulsion against London as the embodiment of Western modernity) and Leo Tolstoy (also for a fascination with Arthur Schopenhauer, the attempts to revive Christianity independent of the churches, the insistence on nonviolence, even the vegetarianism, an affinity noticed already by Thomas Mann).[2]

The strength of character and purpose that this refashioning required needs to be taken into account by those who would have us believe that he was a great artist but otherwise an awful man, a most commonly repeated received opinion about him today and not an altogether incorrect, though rather too simplistic, one. What also needs to be taken into account is the extraordinarily intense love and devotion this man inspired in a great number of people throughout his life, from the time of the Parisian misery 1839–42 (Minna, Kietz, Lehrs), through the period of bourgeois stability in Dresden 1842–49 (Röckel, Semper, Uhlig, Julie Ritter), the exile in Zurich 1849–58 (Liszt, Sulzer, Jessie Laussot, the Wesendoncks, the Willes, Herwegh), the years of wandering 1858–64 (Cornelius, the von Bülows, Mathilde Maier), Munich 1864–65 (King Ludwig II), Tribschen 1866–72 (Nietzsche, Malwida von Meysenbug, Judith Gautier, Tausig, Richter, Schuré), all the way to Bayreuth 1872–83 (Feustel, Rubinstein, Joukowsky, Gobineau, Levi). Moreover, and this is perhaps most admirable about this complex person, the reinvention never stopped. From the beginning to the end he remained faithful to his prophetic mission, but was never fully satisfied with the content of the prophesy nor with the artistic means designed to project this content, and so he continued to develop and deepen both from one music drama to the next. The second most popular *idée reçue* about him is that he was a great composer and a miserable poet. This assessment, too, needs to be reconsidered. The verbal music of his poetry may indeed be of questionable value (unless you cannot have too many alliterations), but this matters little, since Wagner had real music at his disposal. As a dramatist, however, he deserves to be taken seriously.

The process of reinvention began with *Der Ring des Nibelungen*, the work that transformed the German romantic opera composer into the bard of the universal postrevolutionary future. We have seen that, in spite of its prolonged gestation and belated premiere, the cycle's ideological and artistic premises belong to Wagner's politically most radical anarchist period of the late 1840s and early 1850s when, inspired by Ludwig Feuerbach, Pierre-Joseph Proudhon, and Mikhail Bakunin, the composer expected a successful pan-European revolution that would sweep away the old regime of traditional aristocratic political elites and new plutocratic financial ones and usher in a world in which humans would stop competing for political power and economic advantage and instead relate to one another by spontaneously arising bonds of solidarity and love. The *Ring* was designed for a utopian festival, akin to dramatic celebrations of ancient Athens, that would reveal to the men and women of the new postrevolutionary world the meaning of the transforming apocalypse they had brought about. Accordingly, its revolutionary content and performance situation required an equally revolutionary musical and dramatic means that transcended traditional operatic practice to such an extent as to merit a new generic appellation of the music drama.

The project became outdated, however, long before it was completed. By late 1854 Wagner's expectations of an impending successful revolution faded away and the composer found an explanation for his disappointment in the pessimistic philosophy of Schopenhauer. Moreover, *Tristan und Isolde*, the first music drama for which he interrupted the composition of the *Ring* in the late 1850s, was dedicated to the celebration of a conception of love that profoundly undermined the very foundations of the Nibelung cycle. Erotic desire, a phenomenal manifestation of the noumenal will—ceaseless, pointless, and senseless—drives the protagonists of the new music drama inexorably to transcend the finite daily realm of customary social rights and obligations for an infinite metaphysical night of nothingness. Love, it turns out, is hardly a force that might underwrite any new society, let alone a society based on spontaneous solidarity. The metaphysical pessimism of *Tristan* exploded the social optimism of the *Ring* and forced Wagner to rethink his political and ethical vision.

The first fruit of this rethinking was the main project of the 1860s, *Die Meistersinger von Nürnberg*. I have proposed to read this new music drama as an attempt to see whether something like the social-political optimism of the *Ring* might still be possible after the pessimistic revelations of *Tristan*. Wagner did arrive at an affirmative answer to this question, but the results were fascinatingly ambiguous. Much of the drama seems to propose a retreat from the revolutionary radicalism of the *Ring* toward a richer, moderate vision of a progressive-conservative society that puts the incessant and potentially destructive will to creative uses, attempts to balance traditions with innovations, and moves forward by revitalizing rather than abandoning its past. In the end, however, this vision is undermined by something no less radical than the *Ring*, a prospect of a post-political national community, a revolutionary symbiosis of the leader-artist with the people over the heads of the silenced political and economic elites of the past.

The time immediately preceding and following the establishment of Bismarck's new German Empire in 1871 was spent on the completion of the *Ring* and the creation of the theater and festival at Bayreuth. But the empire evidently did not live up to the hopes embodied in *Die Meistersinger* (to say nothing of those in the *Ring*). By the late 1870s, in his final music drama, *Parsifal*, Wagner turned his back on larger national politics and on the increasingly militaristic, aggressive, and triumphalist empire in search of a direction for a smaller cultural community, such as the one that he hoped would emerge in Bayreuth, a community that would prepare a regeneration of humanity by cultivating the pacific Schopenhauerian-Buddhist-Christian virtues of renunciation and compassion. Resignation and agape are now offered as the only possible hopeful answers to the hopelessness of will and eros.

In short, I have proposed to see the trajectory of Wagner's development in the second part of his career as centering on the artistic and ideological crisis embodied in the composer's most radical masterpiece, *Tristan und Isolde*. The crisis prompted the search for political and moral outlooks that would salvage something of the optimism of *Der Ring des Nibelungen* without traducing the metaphysical pessimism of *Tristan*. The resulting new political vision received an ambiguous articulation in *Die Meistersinger von Nürnberg*. *Parsifal*, finally, embodied the moral outlook that, while consistent with the premises of *Tristan*, allowed for some measure of personal and social hope. Strikingly, in traversing this trajectory the eclectic artist managed to come into contact with every major component of the modern worldview that challenged the Reason of the Enlightenment (to use the shorthand of my prologue), flirting with a quasi-Marxist vision of History in the *Ring*, absorbing the Schopenhauerian philosophy of Will in *Tristan*, temporarily embracing the Fichtean faith in the Nation in *Die Meistersinger*, and leaving the stage with the testament of a partly Schopenhauerian and partly Wagnerian version of Christianity in *Parsifal*.

Today, 130 years later, we are not noticeably further than Wagner got in the end, in that we have not developed any new ideological positions. In the West, we still recycle the basic options provided by the God of the Judeo-Christian tradition, the Reason of the Enlightenment, and the Counter-Enlightenment forces beyond Reason; History, Nation, and Will. What has changed since 1883 is that the experiences of the past century have revealed to us the practical consequences of these fundamental ideological options. The twentieth century was not a time of ideological innovation, but rather an era of practical experimentation that revealed the full murderous potential of nineteenth-century ideas, in particular the ideas of History and Nation, ideas that could be put into practice only with the arrival of mass politics and with the political, social, and cultural breakdown provoked by the catastrophe of the First World War. This is in part why Wagner remains so astonishingly alive and contemporary: the first artist to consider, and to be torn between, all the basic worldviews still on offer today.

His ideological legacy, for all its flashes of genuine insight and even wisdom and for all its late emphasis on compassion, is a decidedly mixed bag. This writer, in any case, cannot summon any enthusiasm for Wagner's radical revolutionary fervor or for his dreams of a post-political aesthetic social order. His artistic legacy is music of unsurpassed subtlety and expressive power, capable of capturing the most complex states and chiaroscuro shadings of the human soul. Unforgettable, too, are some of his dramatic scenes. Far from being the master of only individual states of mind, he also knew how to picture the mind's evolution over time and how to dramatize vividly complex human interactions: In *Die Walküre*, the rapid and violent onset of love and the brief moment of happiness of Siegmund and Sieglinde (act 1), the encounter in which Fricka breaks Wotan's spirit (act 2, scene 1), the encounter in which Siegmund humanizes Brünnhilde, stretching her spirit's range (act 2, scene 4), and the heartbreak of Wotan's farewell to Brünnhilde (act 3, scene 3). In *Götterdämmerung*, the crepuscular rounds of the Norns scene (act 1, prelude), the solitary brooding of an evil mind in Hagen's Watch (end of act 1, scene 2), the closely related hallucinatory colloquy of Hagen with Alberich (act 2, scene 1), and finally Siegfried's dying words and the orchestral retrospective narration that follows his death (end of act 3, scene 2). In *Tristan*, though admittedly it is hard to single out individual moments from this miraculous score (as is also the case with *Die Meistersinger* and *Parsifal*), the Prelude and the mounting fury of Isolde's narration (act 1), the central Love Duet (act 2) and its echo toward the end of the act as well as its completion in Isolde's Transfiguration that ends the opera, and Tristan's symphonic auto-analysis (that is, the larger part of act 3). In *Die Meistersinger*, Sachs's monologue (act 2), the Prelude and Sachs's meditative monologue as well as the contemplative Quintet (the first part of act 3). And in *Parsifal*, the Prelude, the transformation music, and the agony of Amfortas's monologue (act 1), the pivotal Parsifal-Kundry confrontation (act 2), and the Prelude together with the Parsifal and Gurnemanz monologues that belong with it as well as the transfiguration of the Good Friday music (act 3). Not to be overlooked is also the unprecedented and unsurpassed control over large spans of time, the particular subject of this book. Like only the very greatest composers can, Wagner extended our conception of what music is capable of. It is also worth remembering that he created the (thus far) last significant epic of Europe—the *Ring* is the successor of *Paradise Lost* and *Faust* in this respect—providing an artistic embodiment for one of the continent's (so far) last significant myths, the myth of the revolution.

Friedrich Nietzsche was undoubtedly the most interesting among the contemporary witnesses and critics of this Wagnerian progress and arguably the single most indispensable figure in the whole history of the reception of the composer's work. In any case, no figure of comparable intellectual stature has ever lavished as much attention on this oeuvre. More: the whole history of European culture offers no other example of such a prolonged and intense encounter between a truly major composer and a philosopher. The Wagner-Nietzsche relationship is unique. An analysis of the issues involved in this relationship is unavoidable if one wants to grasp more fully the significance of the composer's or the philosopher's legacies. Their encounter surely defines the spiritual situation of their age and perhaps throws some light on our situation, too.

WAGNER AND NIETZSCHE: A HISTORY OF THE RELATIONSHIP

Nietzsche, Wagner's junior by thirty-one years, first encounters the composer's works, among them *Tristan*, in 1861–62 (Hans von Bülow's vocal score appeared in 1860) when he is still at the Pforta boarding school.[3] (In *Ecce Homo*, his autobiography-testament, he will recall: "From the moment when there was a piano score of *Tristan*—my compliments, Herr von Bülow—I was a Wagnerian. Wagner's older works I deemed beneath myself—still too vulgar, too 'German.'")[4] While still at school (Nietzsche will remain at Pforta until 1864) he associates the composer-dramatist with the ancient Greek tragedians who, he thinks, similarly combined the roles of poet and composer. In 1865, that is, early in his student years (he studies classical philology in Bonn 1864–65 and in Leipzig 1865–69), he encounters the work of Schopenhauer, the other central patron of his spiritual development. A letter of October 8, 1868, to a friend and fellow student, Erwin Rohde, shows that from the start Nietzsche associated the two: "In Wagner, as in Schopenhauer, I like the ethical air, the Faustian odor, Cross, Death, Grave, and so on."[5] When on November 8, 1868, Nietzsche met Wagner personally for the first time, they had "a longish conversation ... about Schopenhauer," as he reported to Rohde the next day.[6] Early in 1869, Nietzsche witnesses in Dresden and again in Karlsruhe performances of *Die Meistersinger*, now his "favorite opera," as he reports to his mother and sister on April 20, 1869.[7]

From 1869 to 1879 Nietzsche works as a professor of classical philology at the university in Basel. During the earlier part of this period, until late April 1872, when the Wagners move to Bayreuth, the composer lives in relative isolation not far away, in Tribschen near Luzerne (where he settled in 1866), since 1868 together with Cosima, daughter of Franz Liszt and estranged wife of Hans von Bülow (Wagner marries Cosima, his junior by twenty-four years, on August 25, 1870). In the three years between May 17, 1869, and April 25, 1872, Nietzsche visits and stays at the house in Tribschen twenty-three times (by his own count in a letter of May 1, 1872, to another friend, Carl von Gersdorff),[8] quickly becoming an intimate friend of the family—during his second visit, on June 6, 1869, Cosima gives birth to Wagner's only son, Siegfried—and a close intellectual interlocutor of his hosts.

The Tribschen idyll is undoubtedly the happiest period in the relationship between the philosopher and the composer as well as the happiest period of Nietzsche's life. Nietzsche admires the *Meister* boundlessly as artistic genius personified. (Still at the beginning of the period, he reports to von Gersdorff in a letter of August 4, 1869: "Moreover, I have found a man who, as no other, reveals to me the image of what Schopenhauer calls 'the genius.'")[9] But the Wagners, too, are aware of the potential stature of their young friend. On June 25, 1871, Cosima notes: "He is certainly the most outstanding of our friends."[10] They are also aware of the potential usefulness of a university professor to the Bayreuth cause, these being the years of Wagner's most intense efforts to build his theater and establish the festival. Already in 1870 Nietzsche proposes to take a leave of absence from the university for a few years and devote all his energies to the propagation of the cause. "In the matter of Bayreuth, I have considered that it should be best for me, if I ceased my professorial activity for a couple of years and also joined the pilgrimage into the Fichtel Mountains," he writes to Cosima (June 19, 1870).[11] Beyond the immediate propaganda needs, there are also longer-range plans of establishing a periodical at Bayreuth mentioned by Cosima (May 22, 1871): "Prof. N. tells us that he intends to found a periodical, under R.'s auspices, two years hence."[12] There are, however, also early signs that Nietzsche may be aware of the dangers that the intimacy with the Wagners may pose to his independence and development. A note of August 3, 1871, in Cosima's *Diary* is particularly telling (it is also a testimony of the diarist's perspicacity): "The latter [Nietzsche] is certainly the most gifted of our young friends, but a not quite natural reserve makes his behavior in many respects most displeasing. It is as if he were trying to resist the overwhelming effect of Wagner's personality."[13]

The publication of Nietzsche's first book, *The Birth of Tragedy*, at the beginning of 1872 marks the high point of the friendship. The Wagners greet the precocious masterpiece with euphoria, which is not surprising, given that the book gives the composer a world-historical role of someone who, after centuries, brings the tragic spirit of ancient Greece back to life and given that it shows the profound influence of Wagner's own *Oper und Drama* of 1851 and *Beethoven* of 1870 in some of its most fundamental ideas, such as that tragedy was born of music, and that there is a parallel between the Greek chorus and the modern orchestra.[14] On January 6, Cosima notes her husband's first reaction immediately upon finishing reading the book: "'This is the book I have been longing for,' says R."[15] To the author, the composer writes still in early January: "Never have I read anything more beautiful than your book! . . . I told Cosima that you are second only to her."[16] On January 10, Wagner continues: "I . . . cannot understand how it is that I may experience something like that."[17] Cosima confirms in a letter of January 18: "I think that there is only one omniscient Wagnerian; I do not say who this is."[18] After a meeting with the composer in Basel on January 24, Nietzsche writes to Rohde (January 28): "I have made an alliance with Wagner. You cannot imagine how close we are now and how our plans coincide."[19] Wagner confirms in a letter of February 5 to Nietzsche: "Still I was almost frightened to have been understood by you so clearly in Basel!"[20] The philosopher again thinks of taking a leave of absence from the university and devoting himself full-time to the Bayreuth propaganda.

Another high point in the relationship is reached when Nietzsche hears Wagner conduct Ludwig van Beethoven's Ninth Symphony on the occasion of the foundation-stone-laying ceremony for the Festival Theater in Bayreuth (a highly symbolic choice designed to suggest the role of Beethoven's work as a stepping stone on the way to the music drama). On June 25, Wagner writes Nietzsche: "Strictly speaking, you are the only real gain that life has brought me, and second only to my wife in that respect: fortunately, of course, I now have Fidi [the Wagners' son, Siegfried], too; but I need a link between him and me, and only you can forge that link, much as the son is linked to the grandchild."[21] In the summer, Nietzsche witnesses three performances of *Tristan* in Munich and writes to the conductor, von Bülow, on July 20, 1872: "You have opened an access for me to the most sublime art impression of my life."[22]

After this high point, the harmony of the relationship begins slowly to unravel. Classical scholars receive *The Birth of Tragedy* with almost universal hostility and by the next academic year Nietzsche cannot attract a single student of philology to Basel. It is also at about that time that he begins to experience seriously incapacitating health problems (migraines that last for days on end, near-blindness) that will plague him for years to come. With the Wagners' move to Bayreuth, frequent visits are no longer possible; Nietzsche's absence in the Christmas season annoys the composer. Nietzsche does not waver in his commitment to the Bayreuth cause, but seems to be increasingly aware that his continuing independent development requires that he put some distance between himself and his overwhelming friend. In a letter to von Gersdorff of March 2, 1873, he writes: "I cannot at all think how one might be more faithful and more deeply devoted to Wagner in all the main matters than I am. . . . But . . . I must preserve a freedom for myself in a certain abstention from *more frequent* personal contact, an abstention that is necessary for me and could be almost called 'sanitary,' if I am only to be able to maintain this faith in a higher sense."[23]

From 1874 on, his private notes begin to demonstrate a much more critical attitude toward the composer and his work than what his publications, or even letters to friends, show.[24] One is astonished, in fact, to find that most of the essential objections to both the artist and the man raised much later in *The Case of Wagner* (1888) can be found already in the sketches made in early 1874 in preparation for the *Richard Wagner in Bayreuth* pamphlet (1876). What these private notes jotted down long before the experience of the first Bayreuth Festival demonstrate is that by 1876 Nietzsche was prepared and ripe for his disappointment. For health reasons, he does not witness the Bayreuth *Ring* rehearsals in the summer of 1875. The premiere of the complete *Ring* during the first Bayreuth Festival in the summer of 1876 deepens the growing distance. To be sure, to help the cause Nietzsche pleases the composer with a laudatory pamphlet, *Richard Wagner in Bayreuth*, which he has been planning since 1872 and sketching in earnest since early 1874 (in the published version the author kept his private reservations to himself), and he does appear for the festival, but bad health allows him to witness only some of it. It is a telling symptom of his progressing emancipation that on September 27, 1876, he sends the composer the first letter in which he talks to him more or less like an equal and even dares to address him as "Hochverehrter Freund," instead of the usual "Verehrtester (or at best "Geliebter") Meister." He spends the autumn and winter recuperating in Sorrento in the company of new friends, among others a self-described "idealist" German writer, Malwida von Meysenbug, who is also a good friend of Wagner, and a German "materialist" empiricist philosopher of Jewish origin, Paul Rée.

It is in Sorrento in November–December 1876 that Nietzsche meets the Wagners for the last time. In his annual birthday letter to Cosima (December 19, 1876) he announces his growing distance from Schopenhauer and presents it as a return to "reason": "Will you be surprised, if I admit to you a gradually appearing difference with Schopenhauer's teaching of which I became almost suddenly aware? In almost all general propositions, I am not on his side; already when I wrote about Schopenhauer, I noticed that I got over all that is dogmatic in it; all that mattered for me was the man. In the meantime, my 'reason' was very active."[25] In her answer (January 1, 1877), Cosima recalls the "magic" of their common life in the isolation of Tribschen as a "paradise lost" to the business of the Bayreuth Festival.[26]

The break comes in 1878. On January 1, Wagner sends Nietzsche his just published *Parsifal* poem, with a warm dedication in which he facetiously styles himself as "Oberkirchenrath."[27] This is the last surviving communication from either of the Wagners to Nietzsche. On January 4, Nietzsche shares his mixed impressions with Reinhart von Seydlitz:

> Yesterday *Parsifal* reached me, sent by Wagner. First impression: more Liszt than Wagner, spirit of the Counter-Reformation; for me, all too accustomed as I am to Greek things, to what is human in a generally valid way, it is all too Christian, time-bound, limited; sheer fantastic psychology; no flesh, and much too much blood (especially too much blood at the Holy Communion); also, I do not like hysterical women.... But the situations and their sequence—is not this the highest poetry? Is it not an ultimate challenge to music?[28]

On April 25, the Wagners receive from Nietzsche his most recent book, *Human, All Too Human*, a collection of aphorisms dedicated to the memory of Voltaire that marks the author's decisive turn away from Schopenhauer's metaphysics toward a hard-nosed scientific experimentalism and that contains judgments such as the following: "It is the mark of a higher culture to value the little unpretentious truths which have been discovered by means of rigorous method more highly than the errors handed down by metaphysical and artistic ages and men, which blind us and make us happy."[29] Aphorism 220, in particular, hit close to home (even though Nietzsche removed Wagner's name from it):

> *The Beyond in art.*—It is not without profound sorrow that one admits to oneself that in their highest flights the artists of all ages have raised to heavenly transfiguration precisely those conceptions which we now recognize as false: they are the glorifiers of the religious and philosophical errors of mankind, and they could not have been so without believing in the absolute truth of these errors. If belief in such truth declines in general, if the rainbow-colours at the extreme limits of human knowledge and supposition grow pale, that species of art can never flourish again which, like the *Divina Commedia*, the pictures of Raphael, the frescoes of Michelangelo, the Gothic cathedrals, presupposes not only a cosmic but also a metaphysical significance in the objects of art. A moving tale will one day be told how there once existed such an art, such an artist's faith.[30]

For the Wagners this is enough to break all contact with the author. The dedication to the French leader of the Enlightenment was of course provocative, too, as were the remarks directed against anti-Semitism and nationalism and in favor of pan-European cosmopolitanism in Aphorism 475.

On May 31, 1878, Nietzsche writes to his friend, Heinrich Köselitz: "It [the book] has been practically banned by Bayreuth; what is more, the grand excommunication seems to have been pronounced against its author too. . . . Wagner has failed to use a great opportunity for showing greatness of character. I must not let that disconcert me in my opinion either of him or of myself."[31] Wagner attributes Nietzsche's intellectual turn to the baleful influence of Rée,[32] and so does his no less anti-Semitic wife, who writes to her friend, Marie von Schleinitz: "A process which I have long seen coming and against which I have fought with my limited strength has been completed in the author. A lot has contributed to the sad book! In the end also Israel was added in the shape of a Dr. Rée, very smooth, very cool, at the same time thoroughly taken over and subjugated by Nietzsche, but in reality outwitting him, in small the relationship of Judea and Germania. . . . I know that here the evil has won."[33]

In August Wagner publishes an article, "Public and Popularity," in his periodical, *Bayreuther Blätter*, where, without referring to Nietzsche's book or naming the author, he bitterly rejects the suggestion that art has become now "a mere rudiment from an earlier stage of human reason" and reminds his readers that the people ("das Volk") care not a bit for scholars, but instead "it [das Volk] knows its great men, and loves the Genius those others [scholars] hate; and finally, to them an abomination, it honours the Divine."[34] (Note the proximity of the concepts of "people" and "public" in Wagner's mind.) For his part, the philosopher declines the publisher's invitation to collaborate with the periodical ("I have never had anything to do with partisan journals of any kind," he writes to Ernst Schmeitzner on May 16, 1878)[35] and eventually even asks him to stop its delivery ("Why should I engage myself to take in monthly doses of the angry Wagnerian drooling!" he writes on September 10, 1878).[36]

On July 15, 1878, Nietzsche sends an important letter to Mathilde Maier in which he summarizes his current attitude to Wagner and Bayreuth:

> It cannot be helped—I must bring distress to all my friends by declaring at last how I myself have got *over* distress. That metaphysical befogging of all that is true and simple, the pitting of reason *against* reason, which sees every particular as a marvel and an absurdity; this matched by a baroque art of overexcitement and glorified extravagance—I mean the art of Wagner; both these things finally made me more and more ill, and practically alienated me from my good temperament and my own aptitude. I wish that you could now feel as I do, how it is to live, as I do now, in such pure *mountain air*, in such a gentle mood vis-à-vis people still inhabiting the haze of the valleys, more than ever dedicated as I am, to all that is good and robust, so much closer to the Greeks than ever before; how I now *live* my aspiration to wisdom, down to the smallest detail, whereas earlier I only revered and idolized the wise—briefly, if

you could only know how it feels to have known this change and crisis, then you could not avoid wishing to have such an experience yourself. I became fully aware of this at Bayreuth that summer [1876]. I fled, after the first performances which I attended, fled into the mountains, and there, in a small woodland village, I wrote the first draft, about one-third of my book."[37]

The relationship is broken and there is no further contact between the Wagners and Nietzsche within the composer's lifetime, but, judging by the relative frequency with which he is mentioned in Cosima's *Diary* between late 1878 and early 1883 (Wagner dies on February 13), the philosopher is frequently on the composer's mind. The apostasy continues to rankle to the end. Thus for instance on September 7, 1878, Cosima notes: "Talk in the morning about all sorts of things, about Nietzsche—how from this corm we raised a flower, but the corm itself remains an ugly thing."[38] On March 22, 1979, Cosima reports her husband's words that show what it was that particularly bothered him: "N. wrote his thoughts out of season, thus acknowledging that what he admires does not belong in our time but goes beyond it, and now he uses the fact that my enterprise is out of season to criticize it! Can one imagine anything worse than that?"[39] Still in the last month of his life, Nietzsche is much on his mind. Cosima again, on January 17, 1883: "Then he goes through our disloyal friendships—Nietzsche, von Gersdorff—and feels we should be downright ashamed of not having been able to keep a better grip on them."[40] On February 3, Wagner opines about Nietzsche: "The things in it [*The Gay Science*] of any value, he says, have all been borrowed from Schopenhauer, and he dislikes everything about the man."[41] Two days later, "Nietzsche's wretchedness also comes back into his mind."[42]

For his part, Nietzsche also never manages to forget his old friend, though his opinion of him is considerably more nuanced. In 1879 Nietzsche retires from his university post on account of bad health and begins his most creative decade, leading a nomadic existence of a freelance author, mostly outside Germany, in Switzerland (where he particularly loves Sils-Maria) and Italy (Venice, Genoa, Nice, Turin, and numerous other towns). His published books and private notes, as well as his letters, show that Wagner continues to be a central reference point to the end, which comes in Turin with Nietzsche's mental collapse on January 3, 1889. If anything, the composer's importance grows as Nietzsche comes to define himself simultaneously as Antichrist and anti-Wagner. All at once he suffers at the loss of intimacy with the Wagners, is retrospectively grateful for the way the friendship of the man and artist whose greatness he intermittently acknowledges stimulated his development, exults at his hard-won spiritual independence, and, almost against himself, continues to be mesmerized by Wagner's art. Painfully aware of the composer's human, all too human side, he nevertheless confides to his private notes in April–June 1885: "I have loved him and no one else. He was a man after my heart, so non-moral, atheistic, antinomistic, who ran alone."⁴³ But also the reverse: "With the exception of R. Wagner, until now no one encountered me with a slightest iota of passion and sorrow, so as to 'understand' himself with me; thus I was already as a child alone, I am alone still today, in my 44th year," he tactlessly tells his loyal Basel friend and colleague Franz Overbeck on November 12, 1887.⁴⁴

As for the music, still in the last days of sanity, on December 27, 1888, he writes to his musician friend Carl Fuchs: "Do not shirk *Tristan*: it is the central work and of a fascination which has no parallel, not only in music but in all the arts."⁴⁵ At the same time he confesses publicly in *Ecce Homo*: "But to this day I am still looking for a work that equals the dangerous fascination and the gruesome and sweet infinity of *Tristan*—and look in all the arts in vain.... This work is emphatically Wagner's *non plus ultra*; with the *Meistersinger* and the *Ring* he recuperated from it."⁴⁶ The music of *Parsifal*, a work otherwise so deeply deplored, elicits from Nietzsche one of the most penetrating and beautiful pages ever devoted to Wagner's art when he finally hears an orchestral performance of the Prelude in early 1887 in Monte Carlo (he stayed away from the Bayreuth premiere in the summer of 1882 and knew the music only from the vocal score). In a letter to Köselitz of January 21, 1887, Nietzsche writes:

> Did Wagner ever compose anything better? The finest psychological intelligence and definition of what must be said here, expressed, *communicated*, the briefest and most direct form for it, every nuance of feeling pared down to an epigram; a clarity in the music as descriptive art, bringing to mind a shield with a design in relief on it; and, finally, a sublime and extraordinary feeling, experience, happening of the soul at the basis of the music, which does Wagner the highest credit, a synthesis of states which will seem incompatible to many people, even "loftier" people, with a severity that judges, an "altitude" in the terrifying sense of the word, with an intimate cognizance and perspicuity that cuts through the soul like a knife—and with a compassion for what is being *watched* and *judged*. Something of that sort occurs in *Dante*—nowhere else. Has any painter ever painted such a melancholy gaze of love as Wagner did with the last accents of his prelude?⁴⁷

This last sentence, by the way, shows that even at this late date Nietzsche retained an impressively intimate knowledge of the music of the opera as a whole, that his study of the vocal score was not in vain. How else would he know that "the last accents" of the Prelude (he must be referring specifically to I.98–100) look forward to the "melancholy gaze" of Christ Kundry will recall in act 2 (II.1184–89)?

It is about the time of Wagner's death that Nietzsche begins to identify the composer's Christian turn in *Parsifal* as the main cause of his opposition toward him. On February 21, 1883, he writes to Malwida von Meysenbug: "W[agner] has offended me in a mortal way—I will tell you this!—I have experienced his slow going and creeping back to Christianity and to the Church as a personal offense: my whole youth and its direction seemed to me besmirched, since I have worshiped a spirit who was capable of this step."[48] Increasingly Nietzsche sees himself as remaining true to the ideals the "late Wagner" (that is, the Wagner of *Parsifal*) had betrayed. As he puts it in a letter to Overbeck on October 27, 1886, the followers of Wagner remain faithful also to him, Nietzsche, because "they know that today as ever I still believe in the ideal in which Wagner believed."[49] Above all perhaps he sees himself as an heir to Wagner's mantle as a cultural prophet, though of course he understands the contents of their respective prophesies as diametrically opposed. Already on March 21, 1882, he writes to Malwida von Meysenbug: "Last, if I do not deceive myself completely about my future, the best part of Wagner's impact will survive in my impact."[50] On April 6, 1883, he writes to Köselitz wistfully how good it would be for him to have "the authority of the 'later Wagner.'"[51] Letters from (still very few) admirers provoke this premature outpouring to Overbeck, on April 7, 1884: "What I long ago prophesied is now beginning—my becoming in some ways Wagner's heir."[52] He hopes that his teaching will be the antidote to the poison of late Wagner, and in his last year of sanity he writes and publishes *The Case of Wagner* to this end. To prove that his anti-Wagnerian turn is already ten years old, he also prepares in his last month an anthology of his published statements on Wagner, *Nietzsche contra Wagner*, but to the last moment hesitates whether to publish it and, one day before the breakdown, withdraws it (it gets published anyway).

The international resonance he has hoped for all along comes almost immediately after the catastrophe of January 3, 1889. By the turn of the century, Nietzsche is at least equally famous as, and probably more influential than, his antagonist, and while his views do little to dampen the enthusiasm of the Wagnerians or to counteract the poison seeping from Bayreuth, from that point on until our own day they indelibly mark the reception of Wagner's work. Nietzsche, of course, knows nothing about this. One of the three drafts of the letters to Cosima he pens immediately after his breakdown on January 3 addresses her as "Princess Ariadne, my beloved," and announces his coming "as the victorious Dionysus who will make the earth into a festive day."[53] Even in his insanity there is a method: at least since 1883 he had hoped to replace the departed Theseus.

. . .

The purely personal dynamics of the Wagner-Nietzsche relationship are not particularly mysterious. Consider what the two protagonists expected of one another, what they actually got, and how they reacted to the gap between expectation and realization:

At the time of their first meeting in 1868 Wagner is fifty-five, already a controversial international celebrity, the triumphant Munich premiere of *Die Meistersinger* just behind him. Thanks to Cosima, his turbulent private life is about to acquire a happy domestic stability; thanks to King Ludwig, his precarious finances seem secure at long last. Above all he knows who he is and what he wants. An artist-prophet, totally dedicated to his calling, he needs to complete the composition of the *Ring* and establish the festival and a cultural center of some sort so that his artistic and ideological legacy might be preserved. There is no reason to doubt that his affection for, and eventually even admiration of, his young friend is genuine, that he considers him almost a family member, a substitute son mediating between himself and his actual son, Siegfried, who is so young that he might as well be a grandson. Wagner also clearly appreciates the quality and potential significance of the friends Nietzsche draws in with him, such as Rohde or von Gersdorff. On October [28] 1872, he writes to Rohde: "I find that, with and through Nietzsche, I have got into excellent company. You cannot know what it means for a man who has spent his entire life in bad company, or at least among stupid people, finally to be able to say: God be praised, here is a genus, perhaps even a whole generation, for the sake of which it has been worth my while to have spent half a century shut up in prison!— But this new direction to my life really only began with Nietzsche."[54] But it is equally clear that what Wagner expects of Nietzsche (as well as his friends) is not the friendship of equals. Rather, he sees in Nietzsche a particularly gifted and promising acolyte who brings with him the prestige of a respected member of the academic guild, utterly devoted to the Bayreuth cause; someone who would be an able propagandist, and eventually, as the editor of the *Bayreuther Blätter*, a young intellectual guardian of the legacy; and perhaps as a tutor to Siegfried also a sort of a guardian of his son after the composer's death. As early as November 5, 1869, an entry in Cosima's *Diary* shows that Wagner plans for Nietzsche the role of Siegfried's tutor; the composer himself would observe the dauphin's education from a distance, "as Wotan watches the education of Siegfried."[55]

He reacts with annoyance to Nietzsche's earliest attempts to create some breathing space for himself after the Wagners' move to Bayreuth in 1872, and with anger to the philosopher's 1878 declaration of independence in *Human, All Too Human*. The book did represent an intellectual development away from the composer, and it did suggest that the whole Wagnerian enterprise belonged to the past rather than the future (a hurtful suggestion for a *Zukunftsmusiker*), but it did so without naming names, and implicitly putting Wagner right there with Dante, Raphael, Michelangelo, and the creators of the Gothic cathedrals. It was a declaration of independence, not of war. Wagner certainly did not need to react to it with quite the bitterness he did. (In the same letter in which she deplored Dr. Rée's Judaic influence on the book, Cosima admitted that the initial reaction of the Bayreuth faithful had been admiring.)[56] A genuine older friend would have rejoiced at seeing the younger man find his own way and his own voice. Wagner, disappointed in his plans for Nietzsche, chose to break off the relationship. In other words, once it becomes clear that Nietzsche would be useless to the Bayreuth cause, he is cut off with ruthless egoism. Nietzsche's verdict is measured and persuasive: Wagner missed an opportunity to demonstrate magnanimity. The composer emerges from this sorry affair looking small, self-absorbed, and peevish.

Unlike Wagner, in 1868 Nietzsche is still finding out who he is. He is barely twenty-four, an idealistic and naive enthusiast, and no more than a promising student and young scholar. At Tribschen he finds a substitute family (Nietzsche lost his own father very early, in 1849). His admiration and love of both the artist and the man is unconditional. Next to Schopenhauer—whom he, of course, does not know personally—Wagner is his introduction to the living world of spirit much larger than that offered by his academic discipline and proof that the cultural vitality he finds in the poets and philosophers of ancient Greece, and of Germany of the time of Johann Wolfgang von Goethe, is still possible today. As he puts it in a letter to Rohde in the first flush of enthusiasm at his Tribschen experiences (September 3, 1869), "Dearest friend, it is indescribable what I learn and see, hear and understand over there. Schopenhauer and Goethe, Aeschylus and Pindar are still alive, believe me."[57] And still on February 7, 1875, that is, at a time when the relationship is no longer untroubled, he writes to Malwida von Meysenbug: "In sum, I am actually doing better than all my fellow men, since I am on this way lit up by two suns, Wagner and Schopenhauer, and covered by a fully Greek sky."[58] Most important perhaps, Wagner is for him more than just Wagner: he is the promise of a whole movement (code name Bayreuth) that will draw in the best of German youth and revitalize, or Hellenize, national culture. In a letter addressed to the "Verehrtester Meister" (January 2, 1872), he writes with hope of "the time of 'fulfillment,' the Bayreuth cultural period."[59]

An instinct of self-preservation draws him back from this precipice: he could either remain Wagner's tool, or become himself. Between the Wagners' removal from Tribschen in 1872 and the first festival in 1876, he begins to distance himself from their home, probably sensing that this is needed if he is to become an independent creative person in his own right. He continues to be convinced of the importance of Wagner's art, but begins to discover that the man is not without some character flaws. Thus for instance he writes to von Gersdorff on July 4, 1874: "We both know that Wagner's nature tends to make him *suspicious*."[60] But it is the slowly growing realization that the Bayreuth movement will not live up to his hopes that seems to be the single most important factor in his turning away from Wagner. He had hoped that Bayreuth would become, if not a new Athens, then at least a new Weimar, a cultural alternative to the prosaic and philistine new German Empire he has distrusted from day one, or actually even before the Reich was established.[61] Wagner's Bayreuth, an artistic and cultural utopia under the patronage of a generous prince, was unmistakably modeled on Goethe's Weimar, mediated by memories of the town's silver age under Liszt in the 1850s, when the alliance of the two composers—Liszt had produced both *Tannhäuser* and *Lohengrin* at the court theater—was consciously designed to evoke that of Goethe and Friedrich Schiller.[62]

The 1876 festival itself seems to have been a tremendous disappointment and the decisive turning point. The following note, dated from the summer of 1878, can be found in Nietzsche's *Nachlaß*: "It was my mistake that I came to Bayreuth with an ideal: thus I had to experience then the most bitter disappointment."[63] Instead of an alternative to the empire, the festival was, he felt, the embodiment of the empire's culture, its public dominated not by the young intellectuals, like his friends, but by the Reich's political and economic elites. "What did I never forgive Wagner? That he *condescended* to the Germans—that he became *reichsdeutsch*."[64] Thus he remembered it twelve years later in *Ecce Homo*, but there is no reason to suspect that this was just a retrospective reinterpretation of the experience. We have already heard Karl Marx similarly dismissing Wagner as *Staatsmusikant* during the festival itself.

In the immediate aftermath of this disappointment, Nietzsche removes himself for a time to Sorrento and, less than two years later, publicly declares his independence in *Human, All Too Human*. As a human being, he emerges from the crisis looking much better than Wagner. He is an apprentice who has managed to emancipate himself from his master without doing anything improper or offensive. After the master's death, and especially in Nietzsche's last sane, but increasingly frantic, year, his tone can get biting and harsh and one does occasionally blush for him when he succumbs to the very *ressentiment* against which he had so often warned his readers, never more so as when, in a footnote to the "Postscript" of *The Case of Wagner*, he asks, "Was Wagner a German at all?" and answers, among others, "His father was an actor by the name of Geyer. A Geyer [vulture] is practically an Adler [eagle; a common Jewish name],"[65] thus managing to compound two mistakes (Wagner's stepfather, Geyer, was neither Jewish nor the composer's biological father) into the one insinuation that he, the declared enemy of anti-Semites, should not have made. Even in this case, however, one would do well to remember that in Nietzsche's mouth such an insinuation was meant rather as a compliment, designed at once to remove Wagner from the nationalist camp and perhaps to explain his anti-Semitism as a case of Jewish self-hatred. Already in spring–summer 1878, we find in his *Nachlaß* a private note that contains a speculation to this effect: "Would Wagner be a Semite? Now we understand his dislike for the Jews."[66] Curiously, Thomas Mann, too, was given to speculations as to Wagner's Jewish origin, speculations as unfounded as they were widespread already in the composer's lifetime. Writing in an article of 1940, Mann ruminated: "Perhaps—though this is not certain—Jewish blood did its share. Certain qualities of this art—its sensuousness and intellectualism—speak in favor of the assumption."[67]

The relationship was surely unequal. If Wagner had never met Nietzsche, he would be still the Wagner we know; if Nietzsche had never met Wagner, or had never managed to emancipate himself from the composer, he would not have become Nietzsche. Nevertheless, for all the disappointment and suffering that it caused on both sides, it was a relationship that benefited them both. Each, however, benefited in different, symmetrically opposite, ways. Wagner learned nothing from Nietzsche personally, but the posthumous reception of his work has been tremendously enriched by the philosopher's reaction to it. Without Nietzsche, this reception would have been completely dominated by the anti-Semitic nationalist ideology in which Wagner's oeuvre was enveloped at the most official and authoritative source, the Bayreuth of the composer's widow and of Houston Stewart Chamberlain.[68] Thanks to Nietzsche, there has always been a powerful alternative—critical to be sure, but one that has made Wagner's work look so much more interesting and vital. There is a genuine paradox here: Bayreuth, seemingly the composer's greatest entrepreneurial triumph, has turned out to be a long-term curse, drowning his legacy in the racist-nationalist mud from the time of Cosima and Chamberlain, through that of Siegfried's widow Winifred and Hitler, all the way to the post-1945 evasions of Siegfried's sons, Wieland and Wolfgang. Nietzsche, seemingly Wagner's greatest personal disappointment, has turned out to be a long-term blessing, bringing out the intellectual, cultural, and artistic significance of the legacy. Bayreuth turned Wagner's work into the property of anti-Semitic German nationalists; Nietzsche continues to offer a way of reflecting on this sorry turn of events and seeing beyond it.[69]

Nietzsche, by contrast, derived an incalculable personal benefit from his relationship with Wagner. His whole work, from *The Birth of Tragedy* to *Ecce Homo*, is one continuous dialogue with the composer. For the reception of this work, on the other hand, the relationship is of limited interest. Nietzsche scholars will continue to ask which motifs in his thought were borrowed from Wagner and which were developed in opposition to the composer, but these are questions of relatively limited interest. The philosopher's thought can be, and has been, fruitfully interpreted without reference to them.

As I have suggested, what turned Nietzsche decisively away from Wagner was likely not the composer's overweening personality or overwhelming art, but disappointment with the Bayreuth project: an alternative to the Reich had to be looked for elsewhere. In the immediate aftermath of the 1876 fiasco Nietzsche finds his own aphoristic literary voice and begins to search for his own way, still under the Greek skies but no longer lighted by the twin suns of Schopenhauer and Wagner. In this initial stage, a critique of Wagner's art is still very much in the background. It steps into the foreground only gradually and only after Nietzsche has found out who he is and where he stands on the issues that matter most to him; only then is he ready to consider the question of what it was about Wagner's art that made the failure of Bayreuth possible and perhaps even inevitable. And only then is he ready to use Wagner as a foil to himself in order to give his own views higher relief. Unquestionably his published writings and private notes have been peppered with critical remarks about Wagner the artist all along, eventually making it possible for him to prepare the late anthology *Nietzsche contra Wagner*. But it is only in *The Case of Wagner* of 1888 that the composer's artistic legacy comes under sustained scrutiny. What this suggests is that we need to consider who the mature Nietzsche was, or rather who he has become, before we consider the substance of his critique of Wagner.

BECOMING NIETZSCHE

Schopenhauer's outlook consisted essentially of two parts, one descriptive, the other prescriptive—a diagnosis and a remedy, if you will. First, his metaphysics asserted that the world is at bottom nothing but a universal will to live, a purposeless striving, and consequently that human existence swings pointlessly and endlessly between the pain of unsatisfied desire and the boredom of desire fulfilled, that "essentially *all life is suffering*." Then, his ethics taught how we might escape from this cruel trap of life: temporarily, by the expedient of aesthetic contemplation, or permanently, by the saintly road that leads from the virtue of active compassion for all suffering creatures (the love of neighbor) to the renunciation of the will to live. "Nothing else can be stated as the aim of our existence except the knowledge that it would be better for us not to exist. This . . . is the most important of all truths, and must therefore be stated, however much it stands in contrast with the present-day mode of European thought."[70]

The outlook was profoundly pessimistic, rejecting all optimism as wicked mockery of human suffering. Indeed, for Schopenhauer there was no more fundamental difference between worldviews than that between the optimistic and pessimistic ones. "I cannot," he wrote, "as is generally done, put the *fundamental difference* of all religions in the question whether they are monotheistic, polytheistic, pantheistic, or atheistic, but only in the question whether they are optimistic or pessimistic, in other words, whether they present the existence of this world as justified by itself, and consequently praise and commend it, or consider it as something which can be conceived only as the consequence of our guilt, and thus really ought not to be."[71] And he opposed the profound pessimistic wisdom of Brahmanism, Buddhism, and Christianity (all three reflecting "the ancient, true, and sublime faith of mankind")[72] to the shallow optimism of the paganism of Greece and Rome as well as Judaism "and its variety, Islam."[73]

This is where Nietzsche comes in: his main effort was to reverse this pessimism. Nietzsche encountered Schopenhauer's work in 1865,[74] at the tender age of twenty-one, and this work became the main, perhaps even with Immanuel Kant the only, philosophical point of reference for the budding classical philologist. His first book, *The Birth of Tragedy* (written in 1870–71 and published in 1872), rests on fully accepted and unquestioned assumptions of Schopenhauer's metaphysics, but it shows early traces of independence from the sage's ethical conclusions. Looking back at this brilliant debut from the mature perspective of 1886, when he supplied a new edition with a fresh preface significantly titled "Attempt at a Self-Criticism," Nietzsche writes: "How I regret now that in those days I still . . . tried laboriously to express by means of Schopenhauerian and Kantian formulas strange and new valuations which were basically at odds with Kant's and Schopenhauer's spirit and taste!" For Schopenhauer, the tragic spirit leads to resignation; "How far removed I was from all this resignationism!"[75]

Indeed, the formulas of Schopenhauer's metaphysics are there, but not the spirit of resignation and pessimism. To be sure, already at the time of writing the book Nietzsche entertained doubts about his master's metaphysical claims. In an unpublished fragment dating from 1871, "On Music and Words," we read: "It is only through representations that we know this kernel [the "inmost essence" of the world]. . . . Even the whole realm of drives . . . is known to us . . . —as I must interpose against Schopenhauer—only as representation and not according to its essence. . . . even Schopenhauer's 'will' is nothing but the most general manifestation of something that is otherwise totally indecipherable for us. . . . We . . . can never get beyond representations."[76] This is more Kant than Schopenhauer. Nevertheless, even in the fragment Nietzsche goes on to construct a theory of music and its relation to language that is remarkably close to that of Schopenhauer and that will enter also *The Birth of Tragedy*. All representations, Nietzsche thinks, are accompanied by sensations of pleasure and displeasure (which are also a species of representation), and these are "expressions of *one* primeval ground that we cannot see through" and "our only clue to all . . . willing."[77] They "find symbolic expression in the *tone* [of voice] *of the speaker*,"[78] which is a universal aspect of language and "an ever more adequate symbolical expression in the development of music";[79] all other representations are captured by the more arbitrary "*gesture symbolism* of the speaker,"[80] which is different in each particular language. Thus "*the will is the subject of music but not its origin*," while specific feeling is "already permeated and saturated by conscious and unconscious representations and hence no longer directly the subject of music," but only of language.[81] And Nietzsche relates the distinction between music, on the one hand, and language and image, on the other, to the distinction his book will make celebrated: "The single sound . . . is already Dionysian, and the single image, together with concept and words, is already Apollonian."[82]

But in *The Birth of Tragedy* all traces of doubts about Schopenhauer's metaphysics are suppressed. "Metaphysics" itself is clearly an honorific term for Nietzsche at this stage, as pronouncements such as this one make clear: "Art represents the highest task and the truly metaphysical activity of this life."[83] The central opposition famously proposed in the book, the one between "the Apollonian art of sculpture, and the nonimagistic, Dionysian art of music," the art of dreams and the art of intoxication, the two opposed tendencies that together generated "an equally Dionysian and Apollonian form of art—Attic tragedy,"[84] rests on the distinction between "mere appearance"[85] or "illusion,"[86] the realm governed by the *principium individuationis* and presided over by Apollo, and the realm where the *principium individuationis* collapses and "the veil of maya"[87] is annihilated to reveal the "terror" and "ecstasy"[88] of the undifferentiated ground of being presided over by Dionysus. "Despite all its beauty and moderation, his [the Apollonian Greek's] entire existence rested on a hidden substratum of suffering and of knowledge, revealed to him by the Dionysian."[89] It is clear that Nietzsche relies on Schopenhauer's distinction between the world as will (the terrifying Dionysian substratum captured in the music of tragedy) and the world as representation (the beautiful Apollonian appearance of the tragic poetic images that veil this substratum and thus allow the Greeks to endure it) to interpret ancient Greek culture in general and Attic tragedy in particular. It is also clear that he has absorbed Wagner's appropriation of Schopenhauer's theory in his *Beethoven* of 1870, an essay Nietzsche greatly admired and quoted in his book, when he proposed that the Dionysian gives birth to the Apollonian, the step that Schopenhauer himself would not make, but that was necessary to the composer who found absolute music insufficient and demanded that it be completed in the music drama. It is this distinction between will and representation that underwrites one of the book's most celebrated dicta: "It is only as an *aesthetic phenomenon* that existence and the world are eternally justified."[90]

And yet the saying also marks the distance between Schopenhauer and Nietzsche even at this early stage. Schopenhauer would be unlikely to talk of existence as eternally justified. In a revealing passage of his book, Nietzsche writes of "the metaphysical comfort—with which . . . every true tragedy leaves us—that life is at the bottom of things . . . indestructibly powerful and pleasurable."[91] The "profound Hellene" looks "boldly right into the terrible destructiveness of so-called world history as well as the cruelty of nature" and hence is "in danger of longing for a Buddhistic negation of the will."[92] He is saved for life by art. "She [art] alone knows how to turn these nauseous thoughts about the horror or absurdity of existence into notions with which one can live: these are the *sublime* as the artistic taming of the horrible, and the *comic* as the artistic discharge of the nausea of absurdity."[93] Thus, having accepted Schopenhauer's metaphysical diagnosis, Nietzsche rejects his ethical remedy and chooses "life" instead of the negation of the will to live.

Will is now celebrated as the instinctual basis of all creativity (Wagner has recently celebrated it as such under the name of *Wahn*) and opposed to rationality, knowledge, critical consciousness—the new values introduced by Socrates that proved fatal to Greek culture (and, as the values of Beckmesser, would endanger German culture as well). "While in all productive men it is instinct that is the creative-affirmative force, and consciousness acts critically and dissuasively, in Socrates it is instinct that becomes the critic, and consciousness that becomes the creator—truly a monstrosity *per defectum*!"⁹⁴ Socratic reason, Nietzsche argues, undermined the primacy of will and thus undermined also the sources of Greek creativity, making its central flower, tragedy, wither: "Optimistic dialectic drives *music* out of tragedy with the scourge of its syllogisms; that is, it destroys the essence of tragedy, which can be interpreted only as a manifestation and projection into images of Dionysian states, as the visible symbolizing of music, as the dream-world of a Dionysian intoxication."⁹⁵ (The thought has been anticipated in, and perhaps borrowed from, the earliest of Wagner's Zurich reform essays, *Art and Revolution*, written in 1849 and published in 1850: "At the bitter end, every impulse of Art stood still before Philosophy.... To *Philosophy* and not to Art, belong the two thousand years which, since the decadence of Grecian Tragedy, have passed till our own day.")⁹⁶ For Nietzsche, "Socrates is the prototype of the theoretical optimist . . . with his faith that the nature of things can be fathomed,"⁹⁷ and the modern world is dominated by the Socratic or Alexandrian scientific culture, characterized by "optimism, with its delusion of limitless power."⁹⁸ But this faith has proven illusory as science encounters "limits where its optimism . . . suffers shipwreck."⁹⁹

There can be little doubt that what Nietzsche has in mind here is the boundary of the Kantian noumenal, the realm inaccessible to intellect but hinted at by will, since a little later he explains: "While this optimism . . . had believed that all the riddles of the universe could be known and fathomed, . . . Kant showed that these really served only to elevate the mere phenomenon . . . to the position of the sole and highest reality."¹⁰⁰ The recent shipwreck of reason offers hope that culture might once again be revitalized by the instinctual energies of will, once again become artistic and tragic. "When they see . . . how logic coils up at these boundaries and finally bites its own tail—suddenly the new form of insight breaks through, *tragic insight* which, merely to be endured, needs art as a protection and remedy.... Here we knock ... at the gates of present and future."¹⁰¹

Nietzsche's take on Schopenhauer at this early stage, the acceptance of the metaphysical diagnosis and the rejection of the ethical remedy, resembles that of Wagner and was likely influenced by him. After all, Wagner too embraced the diagnosis, but resisted the remedy. It might be worth recalling in this context the composer's remark recorded by Cosima on February 17, 1870: "In the evening a letter from Prof. Nietzsche, which pleases us, for his mood had given us cause for concern. Regarding this, R. says he fears that Schopenhauer's philosophy might in the long run be a bad influence on young people of this sort, because they apply his pessimism, which is a form of thinking, contemplation, to life itself, and derive from it an active form of hopelessness."¹⁰² Wagner need not have worried. His young acolyte rejected the pessimism most decisively, more decisively than the composer himself. In the last thirty years of his life Wagner often preached renunciation, but neither his life nor his works show that he ever practiced it, not when, with iron will worthy of Bismarck himself, he realized his Bayreuth project, and not when he decided to end every single one of his post-1848 operas on the note of a musically articulated triumph rather than resignation. Even his two most Schopenhauerian music dramas contain elements that run contrary to the philosopher's teaching. In *Tristan* Schopenhauer would have approved of the protagonists' choice of nothingness, but not of the fact that it was eros-driven. In *Parsifal* he would have approved of the hero embracing love of neighbor rather than love of self, but not of any hopes of communal regeneration.

In the years that followed *The Birth of Tragedy*, Nietzsche explicitly emancipates himself from Schopenhauer's metaphysics, just as, in a parallel and closely related development, he will emancipate himself from Wagner. But he remains faithful to the fundamental valuations first articulated in the book: that will matters more than reason, being the source of all creativity (here he agreed with Schopenhauer), and that will and life (the terms are nearly synonymous for Nietzsche) are to be cherished and celebrated, not denigrated (here he reversed Schopenhauer's verdict).

The emancipation involved the abandonment of the very distinction between appearance and reality, or becoming and being. Nietzsche came to agree with modern science: there is only appearance, only becoming. Thanks to Charles Darwin, he discovered (as Wagner did at about the same time) that it was possible to maintain a strictly naturalistic standpoint and yet arrive at a vision of humanity's place in the uncaring universe that was similar to, and just as bleak as, that of Schopenhauer. In the first of his *Untimely Meditations* (1873), one reads: "According to Darwin, he [man] is precisely a creature of nature and nothing else, and has evolved to the height of being man ... by always forgetting that other creatures similar to him possessed equivalent rights, ... by feeling himself the stronger and gradually eliminating the other, weaker examples of his species."[103] Nietzsche may not be reading Darwin correctly, but what he grasps is quite clear: a vision of nature as the arena of "the *bellum omnium contra omnes* and the privileges of the strong."[104] A year later, in the second *Untimely Meditation*, Nietzsche speaks of "the doctrines of sovereign becoming, of the fluidity of all concepts, types and species, of the lack of any cardinal distinction between man and animal—doctrines which I consider true but deadly," thus testifying not only to his allegiance to Darwinian naturalism at this point, but also to his abandoning of the distinction between being and becoming.[105] By 1878, in the first volume of *Human, All Too Human*, the notion of the noumenal is openly derided: "The thing in itself is worthy of Homeric laughter: ... it ... is actually empty ... of significance."[106] By 1883, in *Thus Spoke Zarathustra*, the book from which Nietzsche's full maturity might be dated, he pronounced: "Evil I call it, and misanthropic—all this teaching of the One and the Plenum and the Unmoved and the Sated and the Permanent. ... It is of time and becoming that the best parables should speak: let them be a praise and a justification of all impermanence."[107]

Immanence, not transcendence, is the gospel Nietzsche preaches from now on. This will be his conviction to the end: "Being is an empty fiction. The 'apparent' world is the only one: the 'true' world is merely added by a lie," he writes in one of his last books, *The Twilight of the Idols* (written in 1888, published in 1889).[108] A little further down, he adds: "*With the true world we have also abolished the apparent one.*"[109] And finally, in his last authorized book, the masterful self-portrait of *Ecce Homo* (written in 1888, published in 1908), he confirms: "The affirmation of passing away *and destroying*, which is the decisive feature of the Dionysian philosophy; saying Yes to opposition and war; *becoming*, along with a radical repudiation of the very concept of *being*—all this is clearly more closely related to me than anything else thought to date."[110]

Thus there is no foundation, no noumenal ground of being, no real world behind the apparent one, nothing firm to which our statements might correspond. Our interpretations are all we have. At the same time that he was abandoning metaphysics and with it any thought of the ultimate unshakable foundations of being, Nietzsche also let go of its epistemological counterpart, the traditional notion of truth as correspondence to reality. Instead he worked his way toward a pragmatic notion of truth as never more than provisionally confirmed by effective social practice. Already in 1873, in an essay he left unpublished, "On Truth and Lie in an Extra-Moral Sense," we read: "What, then, is truth? A mobile army of metaphors, metonyms, and anthropomorphisms—in short, a sum of human relations, which have been enhanced, transposed, and embellished poetically and rhetorically, and which after long use seem firm, canonical, and obligatory to a people: truths are illusions about which one has forgotten that this is what they are."[111]

In one of the central texts of his maturity, *Beyond Good and Evil* (written in 1885–86, published in 1886), Nietzsche confirms this sort of radical pragmatism: "It is perhaps just dawning on five or six minds that physics, too, is only an interpretation and exegesis of the world (to suit us, if I may say so!) and *not* a world-explanation."[112] In 1887, in the fifth book of *The Gay Science*, he presses further: "We simply have no organ for *knowing*, for 'truth': we 'know' (or believe or imagine) exactly as much as is *useful* to the human herd, to the species: and even what is here called 'usefulness' is finally also just a belief, a fiction, and perhaps just that supremely fatal stupidity of which we some day will perish."[113] A true statement is not one that adequately captures an independent reality, but one that helps us get what we want. Objectivity does not involve reaching a standpoint independent of all perspectives (there is no such Godlike, perspective-less view available to mere humans), but rather the ability to play multiple perspectives against one another. Nietzsche will affirm in another central text of his mature years, *On the Genealogy of Morals* (1887): "There is *only* a perspective seeing, *only* a perspective 'knowing'; and the *more* affects we allow to speak about one thing, the *more* eyes, different eyes, we can use to observe one thing, the more complete will our 'concept' of this thing, our 'objectivity,' be."[114] In passages like these Nietzsche offered a persuasive theory of truth as pursued by modern science, a theory that matched the scientific conception of reality, and anticipated the most radical tenets of the late twentieth-century postmodernists. What he could not offer was a persuasive argument explaining why we should accept the scientific conceptions of reality and truth as *the* truth; even he could not step over this difficulty that the pragmatic conception of truth cannot be self-ratifying.

He was much less persuasive, however, when he presented his own interpretation of the world of becoming and appearance, one designed to replace that of Schopenhauer and rival that of Darwin. For Schopenhauer, will was will to live: "As what the will wills is always life, . . . it is . . . a mere pleonasm if, instead of simply saying 'the will,' we say 'the will-to-live.' . . . The will is the thing-in-itself, . . . but life, . . . the phenomenon, is only the mirror of the will."[115] Naturalized and applied to the organic world only, this might easily be translated into Darwin's notion of the universal struggle for existence. For Darwin, too, all life is will to live. In *Zarathustra* Nietzsche proposed his alternative: "not will to life but . . . will to power."[116] Living organisms do not merely want to preserve themselves and go on living; they want to *increase* and *exercise* their power. Against Darwin, Nietzsche asserted in *Beyond Good and Evil*: "Physiologists should think before putting down the instinct of self-preservation as the cardinal instinct of an organic being. A living thing seeks above all to *discharge* its strength—life itself is *will to power*; self-preservation is only one of the indirect and most frequent *results*."[117] Elsewhere in the same book he proposed: "Suppose . . . we succeeded in explaining our entire instinctive life as the development and ramification of *one* basic form of the will—namely, of the will to power, as *my* proposition has it; suppose all organic functions could be traced back to this will to power . . . then one would have gained the right to determine *all* efficient force univocally as—*will to power*. The world viewed from inside, . . . it would be 'will to power' and nothing else."[118] The problem is that these "suppositions" are no more than that: Darwin's claims have been empirically confirmed, Nietzsche's have not. Having committed himself to scientific conceptions of reality and truth, Nietzsche owed us a scientific—that is, empirically tested—interpretation of the world; instead he offered a dubious postulate about how the world should be viewed. The organic world is life and life is will to power, which is to say not to self-preservation merely, but to increasing and exercising power. Before he finished writing his book, Nietzsche managed to convince himself that "life simply *is* will to power," no longer merely that it might be so viewed.[119] And he remained attached to this conception to the end. "The struggle for survival is only an *exception*, a temporary restriction of the will to life; the great and small struggle revolves everywhere around preponderance, around growth and expansion, around power and in accordance with the will to power, which is simply the will to life," he wrote in the fifth book of *The Gay Science*.[120]

And in *On the Genealogy of Morals*, he expanded on the content of his central notion: "Every animal . . . instinctively strives for an optimum of favorable conditions under which it can expend all its strength and achieve its maximal feeling of power."[121]

In short, Nietzsche emancipated himself from the Schopenhauerian metaphysics of the noumenal will and distanced himself from Darwin's empirically tested claim about the essence of life only to replace them with his own metaphysics of will to power, a non-empirical postulate about how life should be viewed. Martin Heidegger's point is persuasive: with the theory of will to power, Nietzsche betrays his anti-metaphysical perspectivalism and claims to know what reality fundamentally is.[122] But just how little this emancipation and this replacement really mattered to Nietzsche's overall outlook! As before, the world was still devoid of all sense or purpose and it still did not contain any authority that might provide it with sense by offering humans direction, aims, values. The problem with Schopenhauer's worldview is that even if we accept the metaphysical diagnosis, whether prompted by Darwin or not, the ethical remedy does not follow with quite the self-evident force the philosopher believed it had. There is actually no necessary connection between Schopenhauer's metaphysics and his ethics—any ethics, in fact. Nothing specific follows from the belief that all is at bottom will to live. We may choose to reject this will with revulsion, or enthusiastically embrace it; either choice is equally arbitrary. By the same token, nothing follows for ethics when this metaphysics is abandoned and replaced with the belief that all is at bottom will to power. Unlike God or autonomous communicative reason, will (whether to live, or to power) can offer us no ethical guidance; we might just as well believe in nothing. The philosophy of will is in fact a belief in Nothing which one then may fill with Something at will; in this sense it is nihilistic. Schopenhauer's ethics of compassion is admirable, to be sure, but if we find it admirable it is for reasons independent of his metaphysics. We find it admirable if we assume the Judeo-Christian ethos. Nothing in the doctrine of the primacy of will prevents us from preferring cruelty to compassion rather than the reverse.

Nietzsche saw this point clearly. When in the fifth book of *The Gay Science* (1887) he assessed yet again the significance of Schopenhauer, he signaled his fundamental agreement with his predecessor's diagnosis, his "question," but equally fundamental disagreement with the proposed remedy, the "answer": "As a philosopher, Schopenhauer was the *first* admitted and uncompromising atheist among us Germans: this was the background of his enmity towards Hegel. The ungodliness of existence counted for him as something given, palpable, indisputable. . . . This is the locus of his whole integrity." And Nietzsche continues: "*Schopenhauer's* question immediately comes at us in a terrifying way: *Does existence have any meaning at all?* . . . What Schopenhauer himself said in answer to this question was—forgive me—something hasty, . . . a way of remaining and staying stuck in precisely those Christian and ascetic moral perspectives in which one had *renounced faith* along with the faith in God. But he *posed* the question."[123]

From the beginning to the end, from *The Birth of Tragedy* to *Ecce Homo*, Nietzsche's answer was to be different: in favor of life rather than against it. This fundamental choice was arbitrary and he knew it: "Judgments, judgments of value, concerning life, for it or against it, can, in the end, never be true: they have value only as symptoms."[124] From early on, too, he understood "life" to be the realm of action rather than contemplation or knowledge and hence to be driven by will or instinct rather than reason. To be in favor of life meant to embrace will and treat reason as instrumental, as nothing but will's tool. ("Reason is merely an instrument [of instinct]," Nietzsche says in *Beyond Good and Evil*.)[125] This is how things stand already in *The Birth of Tragedy*, where arid Socratic-Alexandrian scientific rationalism is seen as deadly to the vital instinctual energies of the tragic culture of earlier Greeks. And so it will continue. In the second *Untimely Meditation* we read: "Life thus dominated [by science] is not of much value because it is far less *living* and guarantees far less life for the future than did a former life dominated not by knowledge but by instinct and powerful illusions."[126] Twelve years later, in *Beyond Good and Evil*, it is no different: "Skepticism and paralysis of the will: for this diagnosis of the European sickness I vouch."[127]

Thus, in explicit opposition to Schopenhauer, who (arbitrarily) chose to turn away from will and embrace Nothing, Nietzsche (equally arbitrarily) chose to endorse will and embrace Something, namely, life driven by the irrational will. It might seem that this committed him to approve of everything and anything, but in fact Nietzsche does have a standpoint from which to evaluate all that is. From the beginning to the end, his main criterion of value remains constant: of every examined phenomenon he asks if it supports the ascending or the declining life, growth or decadence, and approves or disapproves accordingly. This is how the study of history is evaluated in the second *Untimely Meditation*: "We need it [history] ... for the sake of life and action, not so as to turn comfortably away from life and action.... We want to serve history only to the extent that history serves life."[128] In *Beyond Good and Evil* he generalizes this criterion: "The falseness of a judgment is for us not necessarily an objection to a judgment.... The question is to what extent it is life-promoting, life-preserving, species-preserving perhaps even species-cultivating."[129] But "life" here is an abbreviation for ascending or growing life. "Life itself is ... the instinct for growth, for durability, for an accumulation of forces, for *power*: where the will to power is lacking there is decline," late Nietzsche will affirm.[130] Life ascends when one's power, one's ability to act, increases; otherwise it declines. Only now does it become clear why Nietzsche needs the doctrine of will to power: it allows him to distinguish those phenomena he approves of from those he deplores. Without it, he would be reduced to having to say yes to absolutely everything that exists. The only problem is that the doctrine itself is non-empirical and arbitrary: on reflection it turns out to be just a flourish that pretends to justify the phenomena Nietzsche wants to endorse anyway, when in fact it merely gives these phenomena a general name and leaves them without any justification. The approval of the ascending life is just as arbitrary as the approval of life itself.

It might seem that to support and approve of the ascending life is simply to support and approve of the stronger, that the doctrine of will to power is an iteration of the teaching of Thrasymachus that might is right. This, however, is not quite so. Will to power is not (or, not primarily) will to domination; it is rather will to creativity. To be sure, Nietzsche does get carried away every now and then and exults in domination: "Life itself is *essentially* appropriation, injury, overpowering of what is alien and weaker; suppression, hardness, imposition of one's own forms, incorporation and at least, at its mildest, exploitation," we read in *Beyond Good and Evil*.[131] But the main tenor of his teaching is different: creation of something new, not domination of the weaker, is what he demands. "Creation—that is the great redemption from suffering.... But that the creator may be, suffering is needed and much change," says Zarathustra.[132] "To will liberates, for to will is to create," he adds.[133] In *Beyond Good and Evil* Nietzsche demands of a philosopher "that he *create values*."[134] And here we finally get close to the heart of the matter. The choice in favor of life and will to power is the choice in favor of creation. Be creative, make your own values and aims, shape your own self: this is the essence of Zarathustra's teaching. It is on the exceptional potential for creation that human dignity will rest in an age that can no longer believe in the essential difference between humans and other animals.

Together with some of his more perceptive contemporaries—Fyodor Dostoevsky's Ivan Karamazov, for instance—Nietzsche correctly concluded that if God does not exist, everything is permitted. For Dostoevsky this meant that there must be God (and that he must speak Russian), since moral experience, and in particular the experience of guilt at having violated a taboo (for instance the experience that resulted from Raskolnikov's experiment), shows that not all is permitted. Nietzsche, for all his admiration for Dostoevsky—a "kindred" spirit whose *Notes from the Underground* he accidentally discovered early in 1887[135]—went in the opposite direction, resolutely—nay, enthusiastically—accepting Zarathustra's announcement that *"God is dead!"*[136] Karl Jaspers considers the period between 800 and 200 BCE as the "axial age" that introduced in Greece, Judea, Persia, India, and China similar visions of ideal transcendent eternal realms from the universal perspective of which the particular transient actuality could be evaluated.[137] Nietzsche might be seen as someone determined to undermine all such visions by rejecting first Socratic rationalism (in *The Birth of Tragedy*) and then (from *Thus Spoke Zarathustra* on, with increasing vehemence) the Judeo-Christian ethical revelation. In one of his last publications he even styled himself as *The Antichrist*.

Neither Socrates nor Jesus, neither Reason nor God—Nietzsche rejected all transcendence.

It is surprising, by the way, that Zarathustra's slogan achieved such notoriety. After all, by 1883 the news that God was dead was old news. Nietzsche should have pronounced rather that, in addition to God, Reason had died, too. Indeed, this is how Zarathustra's slogan should be understood in the context of Nietzsche's full maturity. In *Twilight of the Idols* (1888) we see him troubled by "the basic presuppositions of the metaphysics of language, in plain talk, the presuppositions of reason" and fearing that "we are not rid of God because we still have faith in grammar."[138] Faith in God stood for him also for faith in Reason and "God is dead" meant also "Reason is dead." The former slogan was old news, the latter was not, but in any case the two went together.[139]

Unlike for Dostoevsky, for Nietzsche Zarathustra's call meant that from now on, in a universe devoid of intrinsic meaning, one will have to create one's own values, find one's own way. If, imitating the tribute Nietzsche paid to Schopenhauer in his third *Untimely Meditation*, one were to write an essay on "Nietzsche as Educator," one would have to single this out as the thinker's main achievement: since the last years of the nineteenth century until our own day, he has encouraged generations of young people on both sides of the Atlantic not to despair in the face of the empty and indifferent universe, but to think of themselves as authors of their own life stories and creators of their own values. Nietzsche's importance and influence in this respect cannot be overestimated. He is as central and seminal a figure for the period that began in the late nineteenth century and still continues as Jean-Jacques Rousseau was for the period from the late eighteenth century through the first half of the nineteenth. Rousseau gave earlier moderns the courage to rely on the foundation of autonomous reason rather than revelation. Nietzsche gave us the courage to live without foundations.

Our aims are neither revealed by a transcendent authority, nor found woven into the structure of rationality, but rather freely formulated by ourselves. An unpublished note of 1873 shows that Nietzsche was aware of this from the beginning: "[Georg Wilhelm Friedrich Hegel's] Conclusion: Every story must have an aim, hence also the history of a people and the history of the world. That means: Because there is 'world history' there must also be some aim in the world process. . . . But . . . it [is] a swindle to talk about it [the world process]. That my life has no aim is evident even from the accidental nature of its origin; that *I can posit an aim for myself* is another matter. But a state has no aim; we alone give it this aim or that."[140] A decade later Zarathustra publicly confirmed: "Verily, men gave themselves all their good and evil. Verily, they did not take it, they did not find it."[141] And he stressed that his disciples need to create their own values, not take them from him—that what he teaches are not specific aims but the need freely to create one's own aims: "Now I bid you lose me and find yourselves; and only when you have all denied me will I return to you."¹⁴² You need to follow yourself, if you would follow me, Zarathustra teaches. "Do whatever you will, but first be such as are *able to will*."¹⁴³ Again: "'This is *my* way; where is yours?'—thus I answered those who asked me 'the way.' For *the* way—that does not exist."¹⁴⁴ It is crucially important to grasp this point, because in addition Nietzsche also formulates and proclaims specific personal aims and values and it is tempting to conclude that he teaches primarily those. This is not the case. What he teaches in the first place is that we become self-directed. Everything else (his campaign against Christianity included) is *his* "way," not *ours*, not mine or yours.

Thus Nietzsche not only makes the choice in favor of life, will to power, and creation, he also specifies what it is that I should create: my own self. He is emphatically not interested in the creation of anything else, certainly not new forms of community, of living together with others, of society and state. It would be a mistake to think that he simply reinvents the wheel, that he too advocates autonomy, like Rousseau and his successors. For Rousseau, Kant, and Hegel, autonomy or self-rule was the rule of reason and reason was shared by all humans. Nietzsche by contrast is a radical individualist, profoundly suspicious of any values that can be shared by many or all; he wants individual freedom, not collective autonomy. What matters, he pleads against Hegel in the second *Untimely Meditation*, is not humanity, but individual and exceptional humans:

> The time will come when one will prudently refrain from all constructions of the world-process or even of the history of man; a time when one will regard not the masses but individuals, who form a kind of bridge across the turbulent stream of becoming. These individuals do not carry forward any kind of process but live contemporaneously with one another.... It is the task of history to be the mediator between them and thus again and again to inspire and lend strength for the production of the great man. No, the goal of humanity cannot lie in its end but only in its highest exemplars.¹⁴⁵

Against Hegel, too, he was profoundly suspicious of the state: "It will probably be increasingly the sign of spiritual superiority from now on if a man takes the state and his duties towards it lightly," he remarked in the third *Untimely Meditation*.¹⁴⁶ As Zarathustra he was equally suspicious and contemptuous of the small-thinking individual conformist, the "last man" who would be like everyone else and cares only for his own little comforts, not for the creation of the new:

> Let me speak to them of what is most contemptible: but that is the *last man*.... One must still have chaos in oneself to be able to give birth to a dancing star.... Alas, the time is coming when man will no longer give birth to a star.... Behold, I show you the *last man*. "What is love? What is creation? What is longing? What is a star?" Thus asks the last man, and he blinks. The earth has become small, and on it hops the last man, who makes everything small.... "We have invented happiness," say the last

men, and they blink.... No shepherd and one herd! Everybody wants the same, everybody is the same.¹⁴⁷

This is the tenor of Zarathustra's sayings:

> To lure many away from the herd, for that I have come.... Behold the good and the just! Whom do they hate most? The man who breaks their tables of values ...; yet he is the creator.¹⁴⁸

> The creation of freedom for oneself and a sacred "No" even to duty—for that, my brothers, the lion is needed. To assume the right to new values—that is the most terrifying assumption.¹⁴⁹

> The noble men want to create something new, and a new virtue. The good want the old, and that the old be preserved.¹⁵⁰

> Only where the state ends, there begins the human being who is not superfluous.¹⁵¹

> They bite at me because I say to them: small people need small virtues—and because I find it hard to accept that small people are needed.¹⁵²

> They are becoming smaller and smaller; *but this is due to their doctrine of happiness and virtue.* For they are modest in virtue too—because they want contentment.¹⁵³

> At bottom, these simpletons want a single thing most of all: that nobody should hurt them.¹⁵⁴

> Who represents the greatest danger for all of man's future? Is it not the good and the just? Inasmuch as they say ... , "We already know what is good and just ... ; woe unto those who still seek here!"¹⁵⁵

These examples could be multiplied at will and they point in the same direction: do not worry about values and aims you might share with others. What one creates when one formulates one's own aims and values is a self, one's own self.

This is Nietzsche's main demand: "*One thing is needful.* To 'give style' to one's character—a great and rare art! It is practiced by those who survey all the strengths and weaknesses that their nature has to offer and then fit them into an artistic plan until each appears as art and reason and even weaknesses delight the eye. Here a great mass of second nature has been added; there a piece of first nature removed—both times through long practice and daily work at it."¹⁵⁶ You are simultaneously the material that needs to be formed and the form-giver: "In man *creature* and *creator* are united: in man there is material, fragment, excess, clay, dirt, nonsense, chaos; but in man there is also creator, form-giver."¹⁵⁷ In *Ecce Homo* he compared the job of self-formation to that of a sculptor: "Man is for him [Zarathustra] an un-form, a material, an ugly stone that needs a sculptor."¹⁵⁸ You give style to your character and become what you are (the subtitle of *Ecce Homo* was *How One Becomes What One Is*) not by suppressing the chaos of your conflicting passions and impulses, which would make you sterile, but by organizing it into a harmonious whole, by giving an Apollonian rational form to the Dionysian instinctual material. Curiously, Wagner anticipated Nietzsche's formula in a letter of September 16, 1849, from Zurich to his Dresden friend, Theodor Uhlig, as he was embarking on his own project of self-transformation: "Only that man is free who is what he *can* be and therefore what he *must* be. . . . I do not care what becomes of me, as long as I become what my nature dictates I should become."[159]

It might seem that anything new one might create will do, that any new aim, new value, new virtue will be equally valid, but this again is not quite the case. Nietzsche does have a standpoint from which to evaluate what has been created, but this standpoint is aesthetic rather than moral—it is a standpoint "beyond good and evil," as the title of one of his later books proclaims. Morality has to do with our living with others, something with which Nietzsche does not want to concern himself. His talk of artistic plans, of form givers, of sculptors, implies that the resulting self will be evaluated by the same aesthetic criteria by which one evaluates the form of a work of art: newness and originality, the coherence of the whole, the appropriateness of each part to this particular whole, complementarity and balance among the parts. My task as Nietzsche sees it is to create an unprecedented, aesthetically satisfying, rich and coherent life story. At the end I need to be able to look back with satisfaction at the whole I have created, just as an artist would look back at a completed artwork, not wanting to change anything, the way Nietzsche himself did in finishing his life story by writing it up in *Ecce Homo*. "My formula for greatness in a human being is *amor fati*: that one want nothing to be different, not forward, not backward, not in all eternity."[160] In a world that can no longer believe in either God or immutable Reason, the only plausible standards of value are aesthetic.

This seems to be the significance of the doctrine Nietzsche saw as central to *Thus Spoke Zarathustra*, the doctrine of the eternal recurrence. "The fundamental conception of this work," he writes in *Ecce Homo*, "the idea of the eternal recurrence, this highest formula of affirmation that is at all attainable, belongs to August 1881."[161] He wants to be able to look back at a completed life story and not wish to change anything, even if this story were to be repeated over and over again, forever. Indeed Nietzsche often talks as if the doctrine was designed to affirm everything that ever was, the whole course of history. In *Ecce Homo* one reads: "The psychological problem in the type of Zarathustra is how he that . . . has the hardest, most terrible insight into reality . . . nevertheless does not consider it an objection to existence, not even to its eternal recurrence."[162] And again: "Zarathustra once defines . . . his task—it is mine, too . . . : he says Yes to the point of justifying, of redeeming even all of the past."[163] This, however, would be inconsistent with his rejection of "all constructions of the world-process or even of the history of man" quoted above. The test offered by the thought experiment (Can I say yes to everything that happened even if it were to recur over and over again?) is better thought of as applying to the kinds of stories Nietzsche did care about, individual life stories, not the kind he preferred to ignore, the history of the species. The test was not designed to encourage me to close my eyes to everything questionable in the past, but rather to see that all that was questionable has been refined and chipped away as the raw materials with which I began have been shaped in the course of my life into an ultimately coherent and satisfying narrative.

More radically than even Schopenhauer's, Nietzsche's thought laid bare the implications of a philosophy that would go beyond reason and promote will as the ultimate authority and source of values. First, it demonstrated the essential nihilism of such a philosophy: unlike the Revelation or the communicative Reason, unlike History or Nation, Will does not generate any obligations. The phenomenal world (the only world there is) is devoid of purpose and meaning; these can be generated only by will, whose decisions are inescapably arbitrary and individualistic. My way does not have to be your way. The very decision to embrace and admire will, rather than deplore it or simply recognize its existence, is groundless. Second, Nietzsche demonstrated this philosophy's essential aestheticism: if one wanted nevertheless to evaluate will's decisions, one needed to turn away from ethics toward aesthetics. The relevant criteria were not good versus evil, but new, interesting, ambitious, coherent, and formally satisfying and thereby somehow favoring flourishing (increasing one's power and freedom to act) versus old, boring, mediocre, chaotic, and disorderly and thereby somehow promoting decadence (diminishing power and freedom). And here too Nietzsche leaves us without a persuasive explanation of why we should admire the former and deplore the latter—why, for instance, a classicist ideal of closed, coherent form is preferable to the romantic ideal of open, self-contradicting form, why the former promotes flourishing and the latter decadence.

As often happens, what is best in Nietzsche's thought can be distinguished from what is worst in it only with difficulty. His radically apolitical individualism would have to be counted among his great merits as an educator of generations that have had to confront threats to individual freedom from increasingly powerful bureaucratic or totalitarian states. It is, however, also the source of his greatest weaknesses. In his maturity he recognized, as Hegel did, that values are inescapably historical and criticized Schopenhauer, who "with his unintelligent wrath against Hegel . . . has succeeded in wrenching the whole last generation of Germans out of the context of German culture—a culture that was, considering everything, an elevation and divinatory subtlety of the *historical sense*."[164] He remained deaf, however, to the other aspect of the Hegelian inheritance and did not want to recognize that values are not only inescapably historical, but also at least in part social. He understood that when I shape my own self and become who I am, I do not create this self out of nothing. Rather, I form it out of the materials already there, my own contradictory impulses. But he was apt to conceive of these materials as purely individual biological givens and to forget that they are also social-historical givens, that the culture of my ancestors has contributed at least as much to the chaotic pool of my impulses as did their biological makeup; there would be precious little to harmonize if my only desires were biological. He was right to urge his disciples to care for the self, not to sacrifice it on the altar of unexamined communal aims and values. He was wrong not to recognize that care of the self can, and needs to, be balanced by care for others, or that one can care for the self only within the context of a liberal rule-governed society and polity. Accordingly, he was right when he wanted individuals to spread their wings and be as free and nonconformist as possible, but wrong when he thought that his allegiance to freedom committed him to a total rejection of the other two catchwords of the French Revolution, equality and solidarity.

Convinced that aesthetic standards are all we need, he neither could, nor wanted to, provide ethical standards of evaluation. He did not want to recognize that it was possible to give style to one's character, to become who one was, to organize one's chaotic impulses, to shape one's life story into a coherent narrative, and still be a scoundrel or worse. Indeed he is at his least attractive when he intimates that violence and cruelty might be aestheticized, too, "that one has duties only to one's peers; that against beings of a lower rank, against everything alien, one may behave as one pleases . . . and in any case 'beyond good and evil,'"[165] when the sickly professor waxes lyrical upon seeing "at the bottom of all these noble races [he has in mind "the Roman, Arabian, Germanic, Japanese nobility, the Homeric heroes, the Scandinavian Vikings"] the beast of prey, the splendid *blond beast*."[166] He would have done better if, instead of pleading for "a liberation from all moral values,"[167] he had limited himself to reminding us that we needlessly moralize and even criminalize vast areas of human behavior, especially those having to do with pleasure, and that it would be preferable to think of *those* areas as beyond good and evil.

He is at his most sympathetic when he argues against *ressentiment* that makes us necessarily dependent on those we powerlessly resent ("Nothing burns one up faster than the affects of *ressentiment*"),[168] conformism, lazy mediocrity, fearful craving of complete safety and avoidance of all risk, when he urges us not to give in to despair but to try to surpass ourselves and create something new and better, to turn a man into an "overman," to strive after perfection. (Zarathustra: "*I teach you the overman. Man is something that shall be overcome.*")[169] He is much less attractive when, prompted by the conviction that as a species we are just another animal and that only exceptional individuals attempt self-creation and self-overcoming, he talks of "superfluous" human beings,[170] affirms that he finds it "hard to accept that small people are needed,"[171] or rants against democracy, which for him is nearly synonymous with equality: "To us the democratic movement is not only a form of the decay of political organization, but a form of the decay, namely the diminution, of man, making him mediocre and lowering his value."[172]

One can understand and sympathize with his worries: "The diminution and leveling of European man constitutes *our* greatest danger."[173] The advent of mass societies and commercially driven cultural products designed to cater to the lowest common denominator have made such worries sound prophetic. But Nietzsche was far too hasty to conclude that such worries commit him to turn against Kant: "We hold it absolutely undesirable that a realm of justice and concord should be established on earth (because it would certainly be the realm of the most profound leveling down to mediocrity and *chinoiserie*)."[174] In moments such as this his prophetic talent deserts him; he forgets that the realm of justice is the only kind of realm in which someone like Nietzsche might be allowed to flourish. He seems to think that his defense of hierarchy, of rank, of merit, of distinction between a higher and lower accomplishment is incompatible with any kind of legal or political equality: "To *me* justice speaks thus: 'Men are not equal.' Nor shall they become equal! What would my love of the overman be if I spoke otherwise?"[175] It may well be, however, that not only is it possible to love both the overman and justice with legal and political equality at the same time, but that it is only within the framework of justice and legal-political equality that the project of self-perfection is practically realizable.

In short, Nietzsche was profound on the subject of care of the self and shallow on the subject of care for others; his thinking was not only "beyond good and evil," but also fundamentally antipolitical and hence counterproductive in a world in which politics cannot be avoided. In *Ecce Homo* he calls himself "the last *antipolitical* German."[176] Alas, he was not the last, and the proudly unpolitical German cultural elite he helped to educate proved largely useless when confronted with the state's takeover by supremely political thugs.

Moreover, put to political uses, the implications of his thought would turn out to be quite sinister. His fundamental choice in favor of "life" understood as will to power, of action guided by instinct rather than reason, and of unfettered creativity implies a statesman-artist freely shaping the collective history of his society the way an individual might shape his own character and biography, his decisions subject to aesthetic criteria "beyond good and evil." The appropriation of Nietzsche's legacy by the National Socialists was an act of usurpation even more grotesque than their appropriation of the legacy of Wagner, but it did not rely on a complete misunderstanding. In his published writings Nietzsche made it emphatically clear that he held German nationalism and anti-Semitism, destined to become the twin pillars of Nazi ideology, in contempt. For instance, in the fifth book of *The Gay Science* one reads: "We are not nearly 'German' enough . . . to advocate nationalism and racial hatred" and "we are not inclined to participate in the mendacious racial self-admiration and obscenity that parades in Germany today."[177] This and the concentration of this free spirit on individual self-overcoming and self-perfecting make him a most implausible ancestor of the mass movement that subjected all individual aspirations to the collective demands articulated by the party and its Leader. All the same, his enthusiasm for the creative potential of the pure, unfettered will is not completely unrelated to the Nazi worship of the *Führer*'s will and its inevitable triumph. What the two have in common is the essential nihilism and aestheticism of the philosophy of will.

NIETZSCHE CONTRA WAGNER, WAGNER CONTRA NIETZSCHE

In Nietzsche's objections "contra Wagner" it is good to distinguish two fundamental targets, closely intertwined to be sure, but nevertheless separable. First, there are the institutions Wagner created to promote and perpetuate his art, the whole phenomenon of "Bayreuth:" the festival, the periodical, as well as the Wagnerites—the patrons and associated propagandists and hangers-on. And second, there is the art itself.

For Bayreuth Nietzsche had nothing but contempt. The reality, as opposed to the ideal, of Bayreuth represented for him everything he hated most about the contemporary German Reich—the narrow-minded, philistine, self-satisfied nationalism and anti-Semitism. In the retrospective summary of *Ecce Homo* he recalled once more his "profound alienation from everything that surrounded me" during the first festival of 1876: "*What had happened?*—Wagner had been translated into German! The Wagnerian had become master over Wagner.—*German* art. The *German* master. *German* beer. We others, who know only too well to what subtle artists and what cosmopolitanism of taste Wagner's art speaks, exclusively, were beside ourselves when we found Wagner again, draped with German 'virtues.' I think I know the Wagnerians.... Not a single abortion is missing among them, not even the anti-Semite."[178] Nietzsche's most fundamental objection to the Germans was that in opposing Napoleon's unification of Europe, they invented nationalism. In the section of *Ecce Homo* that, significantly, was devoted to a retrospective glance at *The Case of Wagner*, he wrote: "The Germans with their 'Wars of Liberation' did Europe out of the meaning, the miracle of meaning in the existence of Napoleon; hence they have on their conscience all that followed, that is with us today—this most *anti-cultural* sickness and unreason there is, nationalism."[179] And his most fundamental objection to Wagner the man was that he allowed himself to be enslaved by the institution he had called into being, that he became a Wagnerian, a nationalist icon. "What did I never forgive Wagner? That he *condescended* to the Germans—that he became *reichsdeutsch*," we have already read in *Ecce Homo*.[180]

As I have argued in the discussion of *Die Meistersinger* above, Nietzsche was right about Wagner at the time of the first festival, but overlooked the fact that his hero's flirtation with the new empire was relatively short-lived. On January 19, 1874, in preparation for the festival, Wagner could write to Emil Heckel, "I have now had the idea of offering our victorious Emperor the first performances of this work [the *Ring*] of mine as a quinquennial celebration to mark the glorious peace concluded with France in 1871,"[181] and on October 1, 1874, to King Ludwig II of Bavaria, "Grant this festival of German art the true solemnity of a festival marking the birth of a nation."[182] But no sooner was the festival over than this honeymoon with the empire was over, too. Already on August 13, 1876, he reported to King Ludwig II: "In a few friendly words, the Emperor told me that he had come to the inauguration of my stage festival because he saw it as a matter of 'national' importance. Of course he meant well, but his word struck me as somewhat ironical: what has the 'nation' to do with my work and its realization?"[183] The composer's last years were marked rather by growing alienation from the Reich, and the second festival of 1882 might even be seen as consecrating Bayreuth as a cultural community preparing humanity's and not just Germany's future regeneration against the disappointing background of the contemporary state of the empire and its politics. Moreover, Nietzsche was certainly one-sided, overlooking the Bayreuth Festival's contribution to the establishment and preservation of a performance tradition the composer thought his works required, as well as the festive performance conditions that undoubtedly contributed to the unique prestige of Wagner's oeuvre, lifting it above the usual operatic practice.

And yet it is a testimony to Nietzsche's sensitivity and cultural acumen that he got "Bayreuth" fundamentally right, more so even than he could have known in 1888. The late Wagner stopped being *reichsdeutsch*, but he did not stop being an anti-Semite. The Bayreuth circle inherited from Wagner not only the music dramas but also the writings. Its members could rightly claim that they did not invent the anti-Semitism, but got it from the founder himself; all they did was combine it with nationalism. As Udo Bermbach has shown, the Bayreuth circle consistently inflected the reception of Wagner's oeuvre in a conservative, nationalist, and eventually radically right-wing direction.[184] With Chamberlain moving in as Cosima's court philosopher in 1909 and warmly welcoming Hitler as early as 1923, and with Winifred's and her sons' close ties to the dictator through the Nazi period, the racist nationalism that was a component of the Bayreuth ideology from early on got amplified in ways that fully justified Nietzsche's prophetic intuitions. The reality of Bayreuth would have probably exceeded his worst expectations.

It did not have to turn out this way, Nietzsche thought, since Wagner's art was in fact diametrically opposed to what "Bayreuth" made of it. Far from being German and nationalist, the philosopher claimed, Wagner's art was cosmopolitan, Parisian, perhaps even Jewish (we recall Nietzsche's speculations about his friend's putative Jewish biological father), decadent. "Jewish," "Parisian," "cosmopolitan"— in the vocabulary of the day these were near synonyms and they were all calculated to annoy the nationalists, and to suggest that Wagner's art was pan-European and not a local-tribal phenomenon. But it was "decadence" that lay at the center of the diagnosis given in *The Case of Wagner*, Nietzsche's most comprehensive late (1888) reckoning with the art that had obsessed him all his life. And in his vocabulary "decadence" was at once a term of praise and an objection.

It was a term of praise precisely because it lifted Wagner's art above the narrow confines of atavistic tribalism and characterized it as European and modern—if not the art of the future, then certainly the art of the present, not the past. Nietzsche's Wagner is not a party comrade of Adolf Stoecker, Karl Lueger, or Édouard Drumont, but a *confrère* of Eugène Delacroix and Charles Baudelaire. Wagner's "closest relatives," Nietzsche summarized in *Ecce Homo*, are "the late French romantics, that high-flying and yet rousing manner of artists like Delacroix, like Berlioz, with a characteristic *fond* of sickness, of incurability—all of them fanatics of *expression*, virtuosos through and through. Who was the first *intelligent* adherent of Wagner anywhere? Charles Baudelaire, who was also the first to understand Delacroix."[185]

Here, too, Nietzsche was largely right. Unquestionably *Die Meistersinger* is profoundly marked by nationalism and it is possible, though by no means obligatory, to find anti-Semitic caricatures there and in the *Ring*. All the same, to reduce the significance of Wagner's work to nationalism and anti-Semitism, as both his more blinkered admirers and detractors have been inclined to do, is to miss most of what really matters about this oeuvre—some of its most problematic aspects, such as the revolutionary enthusiasm of the *Ring* or the ecstatic nihilism of *Tristan*, emphatically included. And the positive side of Nietzsche's claim rings plausible, too, at least to the extent that Baudelaire's 1861 essay on *Tannhäuser* in Paris was indeed a key landmark in the international reception of Wagner's oeuvre and that the French artistic avant-garde of the late nineteenth and early twentieth centuries were among the composer's most ardent admirers. In any case, in the decades preceding the First World War Wagner was indisputably an artistic event of pan-European resonance.

But at a more fundamental level, decadence is an objection, *the* objection. The term names at once an attitude to existence and an artistic style in which this attitude is embodied, and it is the style that I would like to consider first.

"What is the sign of every *literary decadence*?" Nietzsche asks in *The Case of Wagner*. And he answers: "That life no longer dwells in the whole. The word becomes sovereign and leaps out of the sentence, the sentence reaches out and obscures the meaning of the page, the page gains life at the expense of the whole—the whole is no longer a whole."[186] It has long been known that Nietzsche's unacknowledged source here is an observation by the French writer Paul Bourget in his 1883 essay on Baudelaire: "A style of decadence is the one where the unity of the book disintegrates to leave place to the independence of the page, where the page disintegrates to leave place to the independence of the phrase, and the phrase disintegrates to leave place to the independence of the word."[187] Nietzsche must have read Bourget's book when it was fresh off the press, since already in winter 1883–84 his private notes include the following: "The *style* of *decline* in Wagner: an individual turn of phrase is sovereign, the subordination and subsumption becomes accidental. Bourget p. 25."[188] It is clear that from the start Bourget's thought struck Nietzsche as being relevant to Wagner's style.

How relevant? Nietzsche explained in the same section of *The Case of Wagner*: "Wagner begins from a hallucination—not of sounds but of gestures. Then he seeks the sign language of sounds for them. If one would admire him, one should watch him at work at this point: how he separates, how he gains small units, how he animates these, severs them, and makes them visible. But this exhausts his strength: the rest is no good. How wretched, how embarrassed, how amateurish is his manner of 'development.'" Again: "Wagner is admirable and gracious only in the invention of what is smallest, in spinning out the details. Here one is entirely justified in proclaiming him a master of the first rank, as our greatest *miniaturist* in music who crowds into the smallest space an infinity of sense and sweetness." In sum, "Wagner disguised as a principle his incapacity for giving organic form."[189] Thus for Nietzsche Wagner's music dramas were like his own collections of aphorisms ("I am, no less than Wagner, a child of this time; that is, a decadent: but I comprehended this, I resisted it," one reads in the preface to *The Case of Wagner*).[190] The composer was the great master of brief, pregnant, plastic, and expressive gestures, "short things of five to fifteen measures," but he was incapable of subordinating such gestures to an overarching totality, incapable of creating large organic forms.[191]

The first part of this diagnosis is correct, the second could not be more wrong but has been tremendously influential, as from Nietzsche's day to our own this has been perhaps the most commonly repeated criticism of Wagner the composer. That the criticism would be formulated, and that it would stick, seems in retrospect inevitable. On the one hand, Wagner claimed to have inherited the mantle of Beethoven, the preeminent master of music in the grandest style, of large "organic" forms in music. On the other, he did not cultivate instrumental genres such as the sonata, string quartet, and symphony (the quintessential Beethovenian genres) in which the mastery of such forms was commonly demonstrated and for which our analytical tools and vocabularies designed for the purpose of such demonstrations have been developed. These tools and vocabularies proved inadequate when confronted with the radical novelty and originality of the large-scale Wagnerian forms, especially since these forms were being reinvented with each work; they did not congeal into any single standard pattern. This, after all, more than anything else made Wagner into the essential figure inaugurating musical modernism.

In these circumstances the complaint that the Wagnerian music drama did not live up to the principles of the Beethovenian symphony was to be expected. Indeed, it runs as a not-so-secret pedal point through much of Theodor Adorno's essay on the composer, for instance. Much of my motivation for writing this book was to develop an alternative analytical approach that would make it possible to show how seriously misguided is Nietzsche's and his successors' claim of Wagner's "incapacity for giving organic form." Writing to Mathilde Wesendonck on May 30, 1859, that is, at the time of his early thoughts on *Parsifal*, Wagner remarked: "But I cannot choose to work on such a broad scale as Wolfram was able to do: I have to compress everything into *three* climactic situations of violent intensity."[192] Even his pre-compositional dramaturgy was directed toward a *single* situation giving unity to each act. Wagner's ability to invent turns of phrase that would capture the expressive essence of the dramatic moment, of the character's present situation, gesture, thought, and state of mind, was indeed prodigious and Nietzsche was right to praise it. But if the analyses presented in this book are at all persuasive, the composer was equally the great master of large form, capable of controlling, shaping, and giving direction to spans of time of unprecedented (and still today unsurpassed) length. In this respect, Nietzsche's diagnosis is interesting in that it reveals something about the way this music was heard by him and probably by many others after him, but not because it reveals something about Wagner's compositional deficiencies.

The diagnosis of decadence was closely related to another central aspect of Nietzsche's critique. From the very start of their acquaintance, Nietzsche was struck by Wagner's histrionic talents. He alluded to these already in a letter of November 9, 1868, in which he reported to Rohde his impressions of the first meeting with the composer at the Brockhauses: "Before and after dinner Wagner played all the important parts of the *Meistersinger*, imitating each voice and with great exuberance. He is, indeed, a fabulously lively and fiery man who speaks very rapidly, is very witty, and makes a very private party like this one extremely gay affair."[193] The idea that Wagner's talent was primarily that of an actor begins to appear regularly in Nietzsche's private notes surprisingly early. From early 1874 on, one finds it all over the preparatory sketches for *Richard Wagner in Bayreuth* and already there such remarks are hardly complimentary, although their thrust will be veiled in the published version of the essay. Thus, for instance, Nietzsche notes: "If Goethe is a transposed painter and Schiller a transposed orator, Wagner is a transposed actor."[194] A little later, he amplifies: "The other characteristic is a great acting talent which is transposed, which finds for itself another trail than the nearest one: for this, namely, he lacks figure, voice, and the necessary modesty. Not one of our great musicians was in his 28th year still such a bad musician as Wagner."[195] Also: "As an actor, he wanted to imitate men only at their most effective and real: in highest affect. Since his extreme nature saw in all other states weakness and untruth. The danger of painting of affects is extraordinary for the artist. The intoxicating, the sensuous ecstatic, the sudden, the being-moved at any price—awful tendencies!"[196] The examples could be multiplied and they all come from before the end of 1874.

Wagner as actor remained a leitmotif to the end. "Wagner was *not* a musician by instinct," we read in *The Case of Wagner*. "He showed this by abandoning . . . all style in music in order to turn it into what he required, theatrical rhetoric, a means of expression, of underscoring gestures, of the psychologically picturesque. . . . *He has increased music's capacity for language to the point of making it immeasurable.*"[197] The main part of the book ends with great vehemence: "But who could still doubt what I want—what are the *three demands* for which my wrath, my concern, my love of art has this time opened my mouth? *That the theater should not lord it over the arts. That the actor should not seduce those who are authentic. That music should not become an art of lying.*"[198]

On the face of it, this anti-theatrical, anti-acting outburst might seem puzzling—*is* puzzling. Are acting, theater, performing necessarily "an art of lying"? Is this so because the truth is lodged in the work, the drama, and it is traduced in performance? Such thoughts would be worthy of Aristotle, who in the sixth chapter of his *Poetics* argued that, of the six components that make a tragedy, the ones that truly matter are the plot, the moral characters of the agents, and the agents' intentions that revealed these characters; the agents' words and melodies matter less, and the performance of the drama least of all. But are such thoughts worthy of Nietzsche? A hierarchy of the sort that Aristotle is promoting is rooted in the underlying hierarchy of essence and appearance: the plot, the characters, and their intentions are of the essence, the actual words and melodies that allow these plots, characters, and intentions to appear are secondary, and what the actors do with these words and melodies is tertiary, an appearance to the second degree. But this is precisely the kind of distinction that late Nietzsche taught us to leave behind. Of all people, Nietzsche had least right to defend the truth of the work against the lie of the performance. In this respect, it is as if Wagner and Nietzsche have exchanged the roles they should have played. Wagner's *Opera and Drama* relies to a remarkable extent on categories developed by Aristotle in his *Poetics*; had Wagner asserted the primacy of the enduring and unchanging work in relation to the ephemeral and variable performance, we would find it only natural. But instead Wagner's theories and practices suggest the opposite. On July 20, 1850, the very time of his most intense theorizing, he wrote from Zurich to Franz Liszt in Weimar: "Only the *performer* is the real, true artist. All that we create as poets and composers expresses a *wish*, but not an *ability.*"[199] His subsequent activities show that this was not a case of false modesty, but indeed the expression of his genuine conviction. His tireless efforts to train singers and orchestras in the art of the proper rendition of his works, and the creation of the festival itself, all show that he was not the kind of artist for whom it was enough to produce works; the real, true work of art existed only in actual performance. Thus, after the premiere of *Tristan*, he writes to King Ludwig II of Bavaria (June 13, 1865): "Yet—one thing has been achieved! This wayward Tristan has been completed . . . for—it was not complete until it actually came alive for us, as a drama, and spoke directly to our hearts and senses."[200] (Occasionally, however, even this committed man of the theater had enough, as the celebrated remark quoted by Cosima on September 23, 1878, shows: "He comes to his *Parsifal* and says: 'Oh, how I hate the thought of all those costumes and grease paint! . . . Having created the invisible orchestra, I now feel like inventing the invisible theater!'")[201] That the singing, and not only the song, is of the essence is dramatically demonstrated in the contest of the third act of *Die Meistersinger*, the contest Beckmesser loses because he garbles the stolen poem and is inept in the invention and rendition of the melody. Surprisingly, in this respect Wagner was much more radically modern than Nietzsche.

But perhaps we are on the wrong track here. Perhaps what Nietzsche meant when he railed against the lie of the theater and acting was not theater, acting, or performance in general, but how Wagner in particular treated these. Wagner, we have heard Nietzsche claim, begins with a vision ("a hallucination") of an actor's "gesture" or "attitude," the more intense and extreme, the better, and only then does he invent a musical shape in which such a gesture finds its expression. The actor's vehement gesture and the expressive musical shape in which this gesture gets embodied are the aim in itself. They do not serve any larger goal, and are not there to reveal the character or further the plot. Like details in the style of Bourget's decadents, they are emancipated from any larger whole. This is why they have to be considered inauthentic and mendacious: they do not express an integrated authentic personality. Nietzsche is implicitly turning against Wagner the latter's famous accusation that Giacomo Meyerbeer was the creator of "effects without causes."[202] If I am right, the anti-acting bias that runs through the whole length of Nietzsche's Wagner critique has to be seen as an aspect of his objection to the decadent style of the composer. It stands and falls (falls, in this case) together with the claim of the composer's inability to create large forms. Behind the critique of Wagner the actor and the associated critique of Wagner the miniaturist incapable of large organic forms lies the philosopher's bias in favor of classic absolute music. This part of Nietzsche's objections to Wagner reads as if written by an adherent of Johannes Brahms disappointed that the music drama is not like the symphony and incapable of noticing that the principles of the music-dramatic form are different from, but no less compelling than, those of the symphonic form.

But if Nietzsche stumbled over the centrally important question of the large form, otherwise his characterization of Wagner's style is generally perceptive and correct. In the second volume of *Human, All Too Human* (1879–80), he devoted an aphorism to the question of "*How modern music is supposed to make the soul move.*"[203] "Earlier music," we read there, "constrained one . . . to *dance:* in pursuit of which the needful preservation of orderly measure compelled the soul of the listener to a continual *self-possession.* . . . Richard Wagner desired a different kind of *movement of the soul:* one related . . . to swimming and floating. Perhaps this is the most essential of his innovations. . . . What he fears is petrification, crystallization, the transition of music into the architectonic." Building on this essential insight, Nietzsche constructs in *The Case of Wagner* an opposition between the "aesthetics of *decadence*" or "romanticism" (the two terms are nearly synonymous) and "*classical* aesthetics," and, of course, places Wagner firmly in the romantic camp.[204] He has opposed classicism and romanticism already in the second volume of *Human, All Too Human* and left no doubt as to which of the two was life-affirming and which decadent: "Both those spirits of a classical and those of a romantic bent—these two species exist at all times—entertain a vision of the future: but the former do so out of a *strength* of their age, the latter out of its *weakness*."[205] The classical style is the style of firmly contoured architectonic shapes, which in music involves forms made of identical-similar or contrasting blocks (forms like ABA' or AA'B) and relying on dancelike simplicity of rhythm and meter, clear opposition of stable and unstable tonal areas, and regular "poetic" phrasing. The romantic style, the style that Wagner pushed to its limits, dissolves such firmly contoured shapes into a web of developing motivic relationships, and it does this by eschewing rhythmic and metric clarity, making tonality float continuously, and replacing regular phrasing with an irregular prose-like syntax. Wagner's is the art of soft, gradual transitions rather than hard articulations, of imprecise rather than sharply defined boundaries, of veiling that extends even to the continuously mixed and remixed colors of the orchestra, and Nietzsche's metaphors of dancing versus swimming capture the resulting sensations of motion accurately.

Imprecise boundaries, moreover, suggest infinity. Wagner's art, Nietzsche correctly points out, is not satisfied with what is finite; it aims at what in eighteenth-century terms would be called the sublime rather than the beautiful, and what in the terms of *The Birth of Tragedy* was renamed the Dionysian rather than the Apollonian. "The beautiful in nature," wrote Kant in his third *Critique*, "is a question of the form of the object, and this consists in limitation, whereas the sublime is to be found in an object even devoid of form, so far as it immediately involves, or else by its presence provokes, a representation of *limitlessness*, yet with a super-added thought of its totality."[206] "Why, then, have beauty? Why not rather that which is great, sublime, gigantic?" scoffs Nietzsche in *The Case of Wagner*.[207] Wagner's art, he thinks, is immeasurable and monumental rather than cut to human scale, and it aims to make us swim and drown in the infinite ocean or the void of space, not dance amid the sharply delineated shapes of the *terra firma*. In this respect, too, it is a romantic rather than a classic art. And here, too, it is difficult to quarrel with Nietzsche's characterization of the style.

But decadence is more than just an artistic style; it is an attitude to life embodied in the style. What then is decadence as a worldview, and what is wrong with it? Nietzsche has said it a number of times before and he says it once more in the epilogue to *The Case of Wagner*: "Aesthetics is tied indissolubly to these biological presuppositions: there is an aesthetics of *decadence*, and there is a *classical* aesthetics."[208] And he immediately links the two to the contrast between "a *master morality* and the morality of *Christian* value concepts"[209] that he has been exploring since at least the *Genealogy of Morals* ("this book, my touchstone for what belongs to me"):[210] "The Christian wants to be *rid* of himself.... Noble morality, master morality, conversely, is rooted in a triumphant Yes said to *oneself*.... All of *beautiful*, all of *great* art belongs here: the essence of both is gratitude."[211] Already in the preface Nietzsche had linked the aesthetic and moral areas: "Nothing has preoccupied me more profoundly that the problem of decadence.... 'Good and evil' is merely a variation of that problem."[212] The aesthetics of the decadent (or romantic) sublime, like Christian ethics, is hostile to life, increases exhaustion, spreads nausea with life. Nietzsche's prime example in *The Case of Wagner* of its opposite, the classic "Mediterranean" aesthetics of beauty, is Georges Bizet's *Carmen* (*pace* Marcel Proust, not quite the *Postillon de Longjumeau* though there is some evidence that, even if his enthusiasm for *Carmen* was genuine,[213] Nietzsche's proposal of Bizet as Wagner's counterpart was somewhat tongue-in-cheek).[214] *Carmen*, like the master morality, has the opposite effect: "Bizet makes me fertile. Whatever is good makes me fertile. I have no other gratitude, nor do I have any other proof for what is good."[215]

We have seen that this is indeed Nietzsche's main criterion in evaluating anything: he always asks, Does this support ascending life, does it make me more powerful, more creative, or the reverse? I shall return to his evaluation of the two contrasting moralities. For now, we need to decide whether his evaluation of the two contrasting aesthetics is persuasive. How compelling, really, is the association of the romantic style with decadence understood as exhaustion with life? That five and a half hours in the theater will exhaust an audience is undeniable, but Nietzsche had something else in mind altogether—not audience fatigue but, rather, an art that effected a more fundamental and long-lasting change in one's attitude to life in general, an art that discouraged instead of encouraging.

In *The Birth of Tragedy* Nietzsche clearly favored the limitless Dionysian sublime as revealing the ultimate truth and reality. In *The Case of Wagner* he favors the limited Apollonian beauty. Why this change of mind? Because now he no longer believes that there is a difference between truth and appearance; he has gotten rid of bad metaphysics and hence does not believe any more that the Dionysian gives him access to the "ultimate reality." And he prefers the Apollonian as somehow favoring life. But how, exactly? I can find no compelling arguments in Nietzsche's writings that would convince me that a discouragement is indeed the effect of the romantic style. In fact it is difficult to find any arguments, compelling or not; in this matter Nietzsche asserts instead of arguing. He also makes his assertions immune to all those who would want to tell him that the effect Wagner's music has on them is actually revitalizing. He tells such people that they are themselves typical decadents, exhausted with life and hence attracted to this art: "Wagner increases exhaustion: that is why he attracts the weak and exhausted."[216] He attracts them because he provides the stimulants they crave: "In his art all that the modern world requires most urgently is mixed in the most seductive manner: the three great *stimulantia* of the exhausted—the *brutal,* the *artificial,* and the *innocent* (idiotic)."[217]

If there is an implied argument here, it seems to be based on the idea that the style that aims at the beautiful, the style of clearly delineated finite forms, clings to this phenomenal world, the only world there is. By contrast, the style aiming at the sublime, the style of formless limitlessness, gestures toward the infinite beyond, toward a transcendent world that Nietzsche thinks we do not need and that poisons our delight in the real world we have, since we are compelled to evaluate the real from the perspective of the transcendent and inevitably find the former wanting. But does this have to be discouraging? Could not the effect be revitalizing, spurring us to further efforts designed to bring the real closer to the ideal? Kant is more persuasive in this matter: "For the beautiful is directly attended with a feeling of the furtherance of life, and is thus compatible with charms and a playful imagination. On the other hand, the feeling of the sublime is a pleasure that only arises indirectly, being brought about by the feeling of a momentary check to the vital forces followed at once by a discharge all the more powerful, and so it is an emotion that seems to be no sport, but dead earnest in the affairs of the imagination."[218] Both the beautiful and the sublime may revitalize, though the former does it more playfully and directly, the latter more indirectly and earnestly.

In his attempt to attribute moral, political, and worldview implications to features of the composer's artistic style, Nietzsche paved the way for many Wagner critics in the twentieth century, most notably Theodor Adorno in his influential *In Search of Wagner* (written 1937–38, published 1952). The temptation is easy to reconstruct and understand. One begins with being enchanted by the art. One then discovers oneself in the company of the most unsavory fellow enthusiasts, whether the Wagnerians of the 1870s and 1880s, or the Nazis of the 1930s. This naturally raises the question: What is it about this art that makes it suitable for appropriation by such people? It is natural, too, that in answering this question one does not want to limit oneself to the overt ideological content of the works, that one wants to examine their stylistic features as well. Inevitably one finds what one is looking for: the overblown monumental, the false sublime, the mendacious histrionic—these seem to be the links between Wagner's art and the state-sponsored taste of the second or third empires. But such findings are too pat to be persuasive. Nietzsche's equation of the romantic style with a turning away from life seems to me far too simplistic and schematic.

Moreover, even if Nietzsche were right in his claim that Wagner failed with large forms, it would not be immediately obvious why a style in which a detail becomes sovereign and "gains life at the expense of the whole" would necessarily have to be "decadent" and hence reprehensible. In any case, here again Nietzsche does not offer convincing arguments. Adorno provides an intriguing clue as to what Nietzsche's rationale might have been. In a celebrated 1938 essay "On the Fetish-Character in Music and the Regression of Listening," a piece that is nearly contemporary with his *In Search of Wagner*, Adorno argues that, under the conditions of capitalism, art, whether high or low, inevitably gets commodified and this results in a consumption that privileges details and downplays the structures within which the details are embedded.[219] The similarity of this claim with Nietzsche's critique of Wagner is striking. Adorno claims in effect that under the conditions of the capitalist market, art becomes inevitably decadent (to use Nietzsche's term), and he criticizes contemporary modes of music consumption in terms remarkably similar to Nietzsche's case against Wagner. But what exactly is wrong in privileging details at the expense of structures? Why is this sort of listening "regressive"? Couldn't we just as well celebrate the liberation of detail from the repressive straitjacket of totalizing form? (Adorno's essay was a direct riposte to Walter Benjamin's starry-eyed endorsement of a distracted mode in which the "masses" absorbed popular culture in his 1936 essay "The Work of Art in the Age of Mechanical Reproduction.")[220] Adorno suggests an answer right at the beginning of the essay: "Music represents at once the immediate manifestation of impulse and the locus of its taming."[221] In one brilliant move, Adorno revises *The Birth of Tragedy*: whereas Nietzsche opposed the Dionysian art of music, nonrepresentational, intoxicating, and revealing the terrifying truth about the world, to the Apollonian art of sculpture, representational, moderating, and throwing the consoling veil of appearances over this truth so that it might be endured, Adorno wants music to be both Dionysian and Apollonian, expressive of the explosive energies of human psyche and capable of taming these energies by means of its formal organization. He identifies the "impulse" with the expressive detail and the "taming" with the structure or large form. It is this revision that allows us to understand what is wrong with the "regression of listening": "Regressive listening represents a growing and merciless enemy not only to museum cultural goods but to the age-old sacral function of music as the locus for taming of impulses."[222] It might be that something like this intuition lies also behind Nietzsche's critique of Wagnerian decadence. All the same, Nietzsche's accusation that Wagner was incapable of creating large forms is no more convincing than Adorno's claim that our abilities to take in such forms withered under the impact of capitalist markets.

But if Nietzsche's attempt to base his objections to Wagner on stylistic criteria fails, perhaps this is because the true ground of his opposition lies elsewhere, not in the composer's style, but in the content of his message; perhaps it was *what*

Wagner had to say that was decadent, not *how* he said it. Bizet, Nietzsche tells us in *The Case of Wagner*, aims to give pleasure, whereas Wagner wants to edify and ultimately redeem us: "There is nothing about which Wagner has thought more deeply than redemption: his opera is the opera of redemption."[223] What seems to be decadent and life-denying is the very idea that we are in need of redemption, as those who embrace this world and life do not feel they have to get redeemed. Nietzsche scoffs again: "'Man is corrupt: who redeems him? . . .'—Let us not answer. . . . Let us resist our ambition which would found religions. But nobody may doubt that *we* redeem him, that *our* music alone saves.—(Wagner's essay, *Religion and Art.*)"[224] *Amor fati* ("that one want nothing to be different")[225] versus redemption (because one wants everything to be different): here Nietzsche is indeed on much firmer ground.

We have seen above that, from about the time of Wagner's death on, Nietzsche began to think of himself as the guardian of what the master stood for at the time of their friendship and what he (Nietzsche) believed the composer betrayed at Bayreuth and most particularly in his last work, the work with which he consecrated the festival stage in 1882. In *Ecce Homo*, *Parsifal* is presented as the bone of contention: "When the book [*Human, All-Too-Human*] was finally finished and in my hands . . . I also sent two copies . . . to Bayreuth. By a miraculously meaningful coincidence, I received at the very same time a beautiful copy of the text of *Parsifal*, with Wagner's inscription for me, 'for his dear friend, Friedrich Nietzsche, Richard Wagner, Church Councilor.'—This crossing of the two books—I felt . . . as if two swords had crossed.—At any rate, both of us felt that way; for both of us remained silent."[226] An early version of this confabulation can be found in a letter to Lou von Salomé written on July 16, 1882, close to the time of the *Parsifal* premiere.[227] Dieter Borchmeyer and Jörg Salaquarda soberly observed that Nietzsche's story could not be literally true: First, Wagner's poem and dedication arrived at the very beginning of 1878; Nietzsche's book was received in Bayreuth only on April 25. Second, and more important, Nietzsche had been familiar with the 1865 prose draft of the *Parsifal* libretto since 1869, when he read it during Christmas vacation at Tribschen[228] and nothing suggests that he found it objectionable at the time; quite the contrary.[229] As late as October 10, 1877, he wrote to Cosima: "May the glorious promise of Parcival console us in all matters where we need consolation."[230] But this misses the larger point: Nietzsche's story may be literally untrue, but its self-stylization conveys a deeper truth all the same. (In this respect, too, Nietzsche, who in the early Tribschen idyll years helped Wagner to see the limited private printing of his autobiography through the press, learned from the composer.) From at least 1882 on, the philosopher understood his opposition to Wagner as first and foremost an opposition to the content of *Parsifal*.

Indeed, he had no fundamental objections to the contents of the remaining music dramas. In *The Case of Wagner* Nietzsche tells the story of how the good, optimistic Wagner of the *Ring* as it had originally been conceived had been transformed into the bad, pessimistic one: "Half his life, Wagner believed in the Revolution.... He believed that in Siegfried he had found the typical revolutionary. 'Whence comes all misfortune in the world?' Wagner asked himself. From 'old contracts,' he answered, like all revolutionary ideologists.... 'How can one rid the world of misfortune?' ... Only by declaring war against 'contracts' (tradition, morality). *That is what Siegfried does.*"[231] The reef on which this optimistic outlook got stranded was Schopenhauer's philosophy: "What had he transposed into music? Optimism. Wagner was ashamed.... So he translated the *Ring* into Schopenhauer's terms.... The new world is as bad as the old: the *nothing*, the Indian Circe beckons.... *Wagner was redeemed.* ... Only the *philosopher of decadence* gave to the artist of decadence—*himself.*"[232] Nietzsche evidently believed that the so-called Schopenhauer ending of the *Ring* that Wagner sketched in 1856 was the tetralogy's true conclusion, and he either did not realize or decided to ignore that the actual ending Wagner composed went back to the original revolutionary conception of the work, the optimistic conception he found sympathetic, just as sympathetic as was its hero, the prototype of the overman (in his view). But, justified or not, his words get us at long last closer to the core of his objections to Wagner: what remains when the scintillating but dubious rhetoric dictated by personal hurt and *ressentiment* is stripped away is disappointment that the composer did not remain faithful in his later dramas to the revolutionary gods-abolishing message of the *Ring*, that he embraced Schopenhauer instead.

But this still cannot be the whole story. After all, Wagner embraced Schopenhauer also in *Tristan*, and yet that opera remained for Nietzsche untouchable to the end: "This work is emphatically Wagner's *non plus ultra*; with the *Meistersinger* and the *Ring* he recuperated from it. Becoming healthier—is a retrogression, given a nature like Wagner's."[233] And not only *Tristan*, but *Die Meistersinger*, too, has never become subject to anathema. In fact, in 1886 in *Beyond Good and Evil* Nietzsche devoted to the prelude of *Die Meistersinger* one of the most perceptive pages ever written on the subject of a Wagnerian score ("a truly genuine token of the German soul which is at the same time young and superannuated").[234] Only to *Parsifal* was his opposition implacable—in print, at any rate. Privately we have seen that in a letter to Köselitz (January 21, 1887) he wrote a page about the opera's prelude that was even more insightful and sympathetic than the one on the prelude to *Die Meistersinger*. Clearly the decadent metaphysical pessimism of Schopenhauer was not enough to disqualify a Wagnerian drama in Nietzsche's eyes. Something else was needed in addition, and this something else came to the fore only in *Parsifal*: the philosopher's pessimism had to be combined with the ethical ingredient Schopenhauer inherited from the Christian tradition—agape, love of neighbor, pity, compassion for the suffering creation, and not only for humans, but for all living nature. Thus, it is not only that from at least 1882 on, Nietzsche's principal objection to Wagner centered on the content of *Parsifal*, but also that it involved an interpretation of this content as essentially Christian. Recall what he told Malwida von Meysenbug upon learning of the composer's death: "W[agner] has offended me in a mortal way—I will tell you this!—I have experienced his slow going and creeping back to Christianity and to the Church as a personal offense." The offense was to abandon Siegfried for Parsifal. Nietzsche summarized in *Beyond Good and Evil*:

> Perhaps Wagner's strangest creation is . . . the figure of Siegfried, that *very free* man who may indeed be much too free, too hard, too cheerful, too healthy, to *anti-Catholic* for the taste of ancient and mellow cultured peoples. He may even have been a sin against romanticism, this anti-romantic Siegfried: well, Wagner more than atoned for this sin in his old and glum days when—anticipating a taste that has since then become political—he began, if not to walk, at least to preach, with his characteristic religious vehemence, *the way to Rome*. . . . What I have against the "final Wagner" and his *Parsifal* music: . . . What you hear is *Rome—Rome's faith without the text*.[235]

Parsifal, with its "insane hatred of knowledge, spirit, and sensuality," represented "a self-negation, a self-cancellation on the part of an artist who had hitherto aimed with all the power of his will at the reverse, at the *highest spiritualization and sensualization* of his art."[236]

Nietzsche began to distance himself from Christianity early, and his opposition got more and more strident with time. Once this son of a Lutheran pastor lost his faith, Greek paganism became an alluring alternative. Athens, not Jerusalem, gives direction to Nietzsche the writer and thinker from the beginning to the end, from *The Birth of Tragedy* to *Nietzsche contra Wagner* and other feverish books of his last year. But it is only in 1884 that he begins to articulate explicitly, at first only in letters, the idea that his historical role might be to overturn traditional values and that he begins to see himself as a new Christ, or rather Antichrist, as someone who will split the history of humankind into two parts. Letters to Overbeck from this period are particularly revealing. On March 10, 1884, he writes: "It is possible that for the first time a thought occurred to me that splits humanity in two. This Zarathustra is nothing but a preface. . . . Is it [the thought] true or better: will it be believed as true, then everything changes and turns, and all values until now are devalued."[237] On May 21, 1884, he comes close to a self-presentation as a new Christ: "If I do not go to such an extreme that whole millennia will make their loftiest vows in my name, then in my own eyes I shall have achieved nothing. Meanwhile, I do not have a single disciple."[238] (Toward the end, in 1888, he will make this role explicit in the titles of two books, *The Antichrist* and *Ecce Homo*.) On July 25, 1884, he spells out the "thought": "My teaching that the world of good and evil is only an apparent and perspectival world is such a novelty that I sometimes lose the ability to hear and see when I think about it."²³⁹ By 1888 this conception of his own world-historical significance often comes close, or even oversteps, the bounds of sanity: "My life reaches now its zenith: another couple of years and the earth will shudder from a tremendous thunderbolt.—I swear to you that I have the power to change the way time is reckoned.—There is nothing that today is standing that will not fall, I am more dynamite than man," he writes to Paul Deussen on November 26.²⁴⁰ And there can be no doubt that what the dynamite was supposed to explode was Christianity: "What is at stake is an attempt at Christianity that will impact just like dynamite everything that had in the slightest grown together with it. We shall change the way we reckon time," one reads in a draft of a letter to Helen Zimmern, probably of December 8.²⁴¹ The year 1888 was supposed to count as the new Year One.²⁴²

It is also only in the mid-1880s that the opposition to Christianity becomes explicitly a central and growing concern. Its early symptom is the peculiar and mannered biblical diction this great master of German prose chose in 1883 for *Thus Spoke Zarathustra*. The thought that "good and bad is for a long time the same thing as noble and base, master and slave," appears already in 1878 in *Human, All Too Human*,²⁴³ but gets a fuller articulation only in 1885–86 in *Beyond Good and Evil*. Aphorism 260 sounds the keynote: "I finally discovered two basic types [or moralities] and one basic difference. There are *master morality* and *slave morality*.... The moral discrimination of values has originated either among a ruling group whose consciousness of its difference from the ruled group was accompanied by delight—or among the ruled, the slaves and dependents of every degree.... In this first type of morality the opposition of 'good' and 'bad' means approximately the same as 'noble' and 'contemptible.'"²⁴⁴ The values originating among the ruled are different:

> Suppose the violated, oppressed, suffering, unfree, who are uncertain of themselves and weary, moralize: what will their moral valuations have in common? Probably, a pessimistic suspicion about the whole condition of man will find expression, perhaps a condemnation of man along with his condition. The slave's eye is not favorable to the virtues of the powerful.... Conversely, those qualities are brought out ... which serve to ease existence for those who suffer: here pity, the complaisant and obliging hand, the warm heart, patience, industry, humility, and friendliness are honored.... Slave morality is essentially a morality of utility. Here is the place for the origin of that famous opposition of "good" and "evil."²⁴⁵

Above all, "The slave wants the unconditional," wants to submit himself to the one revealed law, denies the plurality of perspectives; understandably, Nietzsche much prefers the "noble and frivolous tolerance" of the ancient pagans.²⁴⁶ "Christianity is Platonism for 'the people,'" and "it meant standing truth on her head and denying *perspective*, the basic condition of all life, when one spoke of spirit and the good as Plato did," that is, as unconditional.²⁴⁷

Today, "The *democratic* movement is the heir of the Christian movement,"[248] itself the work of the Jewish people ("they mark the beginning of the slave rebellion in morals").[249] Nietzsche's fondest hope is to see both movements not as the goal, but as a parenthesis in European history. To be sure, the Jewish-priestly mode of valuation was not simply an unfortunate mistake; rather, it was on this basis "that man first became *an interesting animal,* that only here did the human soul . . . acquire *depth* and become *evil*—and these are the two basic respects in which man has hitherto been superior to other beasts!"[250] Nevertheless it needs to be overcome because it is inimical to life. "The two *opposing* values 'good and bad,' 'good and evil' have been engaged in a fearful struggle on earth for thousands of years. . . . The symbol of this struggle . . . is 'Rome against Judea, Judea against Rome': there has hitherto been no greater event than *this* struggle."[251]

Master morality versus slave morality, the perspectival aesthetic code of the Homeric and Norse heroes versus the unconditional moral code of Hebrew prophets and Christian saints—this is the theme of Nietzsche's next book, *On the Genealogy of Morals* of 1887 ("this book, my touchstone for what belongs to me"). It dominates the thoughts of his two remaining years of precarious sanity and defines his conception of his own world-historical role, his self-image as the Antichrist-Dionysus. "Have I been understood?—*Dionysus versus the Crucified.*" Thus ends *Ecce Homo*, his testament.[252]

One might think that someone for whom the ability "to employ a *variety* of perspectives" was of paramount importance would appreciate the validity of both Athens *and* Jerusalem, or, to use Nietzsche's terms, of both Rome *and* Judea.[253] Indeed, at times Nietzsche does precisely that. Thus we read in the epilogue to *The Case of Wagner*: "These opposite forms in the optics of value [master morality and Christian morality] are *both* necessary: they are ways of seeing, immune to reasons and refutations."[254] But most of the time the Antichrist forgets his own better instincts. Christianity is objectionable for three reasons. First and foremost, its very unconditionality makes it inferior to the aristocratic perspectivalism. After all, Nietzsche's aim is not to replace one moral code with another, but to do away with moral valuations altogether and replace them with aesthetic valuations. The other two objections are more specific: Christianity's supposed hostility to life and this world as the realm of torment, its repudiation of joy in life, of sensuality, of sexuality; and its ethics of compassion with all suffering humans.

The first of these latter two objections, while far from completely wrong, of course, in particular with regard to sex, shows Nietzsche at his most Voltaireian and one-sided. He assumes that to postulate the existence of a transcendent realm from the perspective of which this world is to be judged necessarily implies denigration of the earth and forgets that his own unconditional praise of the actually existing world is closer to the Judeo-Christian tradition that recognized that what God created must be good than to Schopenhauerian pessimism and rejection of the creation. He is right, on the other hand, to suggest that Christianity encourages us to place our hopes in the hereafter, that it encourages resignation about the here and now. But in any case it is the second of the two objections that is paramount for him.

Nietzsche's two optics (that of the masters and that of the slaves) brings to mind Augustine's two cities, the heavenly one and the earthly one. Citizens of the former, recall, are governed by well-directed love, whereby love of self is subsumed in, and transcended by, love of neighbor (charity), and that in turn is subsumed in, and transcended by, love of God. With citizens of the earthly city, love gets arrested before it reaches its ultimate goal, arrested at the self (becoming selfish cupidity) or at the neighbor (becoming a kind of idolatry, setting up of a lesser good in the place of the supreme one). Nietzsche's two optics can be re-described in Augustinian terms: the master favors the love of the self, the slave the love of neighbor, and the love of God is of no particular interest. Thus Nietzsche's Christianity is reduced to the bare ethical minimum. Transcendent judgment and grace recede into the background, and all that really matters is immanent love for one's neighbor, charity, with a corresponding turning away from love of self, from cupidity and sensuality.

That he would reduce religion in this fashion was inevitable. Like so many of his contemporaries and successors, Nietzsche thought that modern science, and Darwin in particular, has revealed the universe to be without purpose and hence put the onus of responsibility for our, and our world's, welfare on ourselves. To this extent the death of God was probably irreversible. This development, however, did not obliterate religion, but merely transformed it: the God of judgment and grace may have died, but Christ and his exemplary behavior, and the altruism that defies the senseless struggle for existence that prevails in nature, continue to provide us with moral guidance even now.

In short, Nietzsche's Christianity is at bottom a morality of pity and it is to be opposed as such, opposed above all because it detracts from care of self. The failures are to be shunned because they undermine our self-confidence, our trust in life: "That the sick should *not* make the healthy sick ... should surely be our supreme concern on earth."[255] In sum, "Christianity is called the religion of *pity*.... We are deprived of strength when we feel pity."[256] Moreover, though this is a lesser consideration, pity is bad not only for us, but also for those toward whom we feel it: we thus indulge their weakness and throw in a good deal of condescension toward them.[257] Here Nietzsche may well be right, provided one does not forget that there are situations in which a neighbor genuinely needs help, cannot get him- or herself out of the hole by his own efforts alone. Merely to feel pity is indeed useless and self-indulgent; active help, however, is another matter. And in fact, at times Nietzsche does seem to advocate active charity without passive pity: "One should, to be sure, *manifest* pity, but take care not to possess it.... The thirst for pity is thus a thirst for self-enjoyment, and that at the expense of one's fellow men."²⁵⁸ But for the most part, the care of the self takes precedence over care of others: "To make oneself a complete *person*, and in all that one does to have in view the *highest good* of this person—that gets us further than those pity-filled agitations of actions for the sake of others."²⁵⁹

The morality of pity is the faith Nietzsche finds in *Parsifal*, with its chaste and foolish hero who, instead of pushing old gods aside, like the equally foolish but distinctly not chaste Siegfried, comes to heal the wound and alleviate the suffering of his predecessor king. There are those who would claim that *Parsifal* cannot be regarded as a Christian work. Cosima herself argued in a letter of February 20, 1878, that "*Parsifal* has nothing in common with any Church or any dogma, since in it blood becomes bread and wine, while in the Eucharist it is the opposite."²⁶⁰ Carl Dahlhaus, in turn, dismissed Nietzsche's accusation that in *Parsifal* Wagner "sank down . . . before the Christian cross":²⁶¹ "That was as perverse, and revealed as great a deficiency in artistic understanding, as the contrary accusation that Wagner was an unscrupulous theatromane who dissipated Christian myths and symbols in order to make theatrical effects. The latter charge springs from a fundamentalist acceptance of Christian dogma and contempt for the theatre, whereas Wagner took a philosopher's view of Christianity and regarded theatre in the spirit of ancient Greece."²⁶² Dahlhaus is right about Nietzsche's contempt for the theater, but surely wrong about his fundamentalism. Nietzsche was as uninterested in the literal truth of Christian myths as he was in arguing the finer points of theological doctrine or attacking established churches. He treated Christianity in the same way Wagner did, the way Dahlhaus correctly characterized when he argued that

> Wagner's faith was philosophical, not religious, a metaphysic of compassion and renunciation, deriving its essential elements from Schopenhauer's *World as Will and Idea* and—via Schopenhauer—from Buddhism. Wagner found these elements also present in Christianity, and to that extent he was a Christian. But the predominant spirit of the nineteenth century had become alien to fundamentalist faith, and he too took a historico-philosophical view of the traditions of the religion as an evolving truth, changing its outer shape throughout history. The myth that was once believed as literal truth had become a metaphor for a metaphysical insight; and the rituals of an earlier age, grown hollow and insubstantial as such, passed over into art, so as to preserve or recover in a symbolic role the meaning and cogency that they had lost in their hieratic function.²⁶³

True enough, but this is precisely what Nietzsche thought, too. What he objects to are the ethical values articulated in *Parsifal*; for him, they are the still-living essence of Christianity, whatever the established churches or theologians might think. He is interested not in the dogma, but in the morality of Christianity: "Christianity *as a dogma* was destroyed by its own morality; in the same way Christianity *as morality* must now perish, too."²⁶⁴ On January 27, 1882, Cosima notes in her *Diary*: "He

[Wagner] says that he recognizes no religion except compassion."²⁶⁵ Nietzsche's understanding of religion is identical, he just evaluates it differently. Thus, *pace* Dahlhaus, there was nothing "perverse," deficient, or mistaken in the philosopher's objection to *Parsifal*. In his final work, Wagner did indeed sink down before the Christian cross.

But is the objection persuasive? Do we have to consider Wagner's turn regrettable? Must we, indeed, choose between love of neighbor and care of self? At his best, Nietzsche himself does not believe that we must. I have already quoted the remark from *The Case of Wagner* that made clear that the two perspectives "are *both* necessary" and equally "immune to reasons and refutations." And so they are. In his weaker moments, Nietzsche forgot that the two perspectives apply in two distinct realms of activity, that one belongs to the duties we have toward others, and the other to the duties we have toward ourselves. We need to care for our suffering neighbors *and* care for our own selves. One might even decide that the self one wants to create will be, among others, charitable. Yes, the two cares may come into conflict, but this is true of most ultimate values by which we live: liberty and equality, freedom and security, justice and mercy, the pursuit of truth and the pursuit of happiness—they cannot all be perfectly harmonized, and in trying to balance them against one another we are forced to make compromises. Nietzsche managed to illuminate Wagner's oeuvre in many invaluable ways, but the centerpiece of his case against the composer, his critique of the ethical values projected in *Parsifal*, fails to persuade. We need both Siegfried and Parsifal, both the late Wagner and the late Nietzsche, both Nietzsche contra Wagner and Wagner contra Nietzsche.

This is one way in which the composer implicitly corrects the philosopher. There is another, related, and even more fundamental one. We have already heard how in *Richard Wagner in Bayreuth* Nietzsche remarked: "And will the *Meistersinger* not speak of the German nature to all future ages—more, will it not constitute one of the ripest fruits of that nature, which always seeks reformation not revolution, and though broadly content with itself has not forgotten that noblest expression of discontent, the innovative deed?"²⁶⁶ The philosopher may have ignored the implications of the opera's final scene, but otherwise he captured its significance to perfection. Whether this is specifically German or not, it is the wisdom of *Die Meistersinger* to understand that individual creativity and social traditions are indissolubly linked, that a tradition gets sterile if not fertilized by innovation, while creativity quickly runs dry if it does not grow on the soil of tradition. This wisdom implicitly challenges Nietzsche's radical project of self-creation *ex nihilo*. The materials from which a self is shaped are provided by the culture and social traditions in which the shaping takes place. This is the indispensable obverse side of the call to authenticity and creativity. Nietzsche seems to have understood this point when he wrote about *Die Meistersinger* in 1876, but chose to ignore it in his maturity. He continued to adhere to the post-political utopia of the *Ring* and to remember Siegfried, this prototype of the self-created overman, with gratitude, and he continued to be overwhelmed by the uncompromising ecstatic nihilism of *Tristan*, but he was unwilling to give Wagner credit for his search for ways out of the impasse the latter work represented, the search for ways forward in a universe after God and beyond Reason. Also here we would benefit from imagining what Wagner might have to say contra Nietzsche and not limit ourselves just to what Nietzsche actually wrote contra Wagner.

On many important issues, not the least the danger of racist nationalism that was beginning to engulf Germany, Nietzsche was prophetically right. On other issues, Wagner offered more attractive alternatives (think of Nietzsche's misogyny, or of his readiness to flirt with violence). But apart from specific preferences of this sort, it was Wagner, not Nietzsche, who in his last two works was groping toward a vision richer and more fertile than that of pure authenticity and self-shaping, who glimpsed the emptiness of the idea that values must be created and proposed instead that, if they are to be values, they need to be found and revitalized. It was in the bourgeois community of imperfect but genuine liberty and justice depicted in much of *Die Meistersinger*, an opera the late Nietzsche appreciated but ultimately underestimated, and in the moral community of reciprocal charity depicted in *Parsifal*, an opera he despised, that we can discern the promise of a self-correcting intersubjective and intergenerational conversation, of a deliberative reason first sketched by Hegel, that might allow us to move forward past the *aporia* of solipsistic creativity conducted in the void beyond Reason.

APPENDIX ONE

Das Rheingold
The Music-Dramatic Plan

Form	Key	Content	Text incipit	Measures	CD.track.time
A. Introduction		How the Rhinegold was stolen			
Prelude	E-flat			1–136	I.1
Scene 1		The bed of the Rhine			
a. Mostly orchestral (with superimposed dialogue)	E-flat	Rhinedaughters frolic,	Weia! Waga! Woge, du Welle	137–81	I.2.0:00–1:11
b. Recitative dialogue		repulse Alberich,	Hehe! Ihr Nicker!	182–420	I.2.1:11–3.4:55
c. **The Rhinedaughters' Song**	E-flat	and mock him.	Wallala! Wallala! Lalaleia, leialalei!	421–47	I.4.0:00–44
Internal interlude			Wie in den Gliedern brünstige Gluth	448–513	I.4.0:44–2:24
d. **The Rhinegold Song**	C	The Rhinegold appears.	Lugt, Schwestern!	514–662	I.5
e. Recitative dialogue	→c	Alberich curses love and robs the gold.	Der Welt Erbe gewänn' ich zu eigen durch dich?	663–715	I.6.0:00–1:43
Interlude	c→D-flat			716–68	I.6.1:43–4:25
B. The main story		How Valhalla was paid for			
Scene 2		A mountain summit near the Rhine			
a. **Valhalla** Orchestral (with superimposed voices)	D-flat			769–826	I.7.0:00–3:51
b. Recitative dialogue		Fricka asks Wotan how he plans to pay for Valhalla.	Nur Wonne schafft dir	826–983	I.7.3:51–10:53
c. Recitative dialogue		Giants demand the promised payment.	Sanft schloß Schlaf dein Aug'	984–1183	I.8–9
d. Recitative dialogue with embedded *Loge's Monologue*		Loge narrates how Alberich stole the gold and fashioned the Ring; the giants demand Alberich's treasure in payment and take Freia hostage.	Endlich Loge! Jetzt hör, Störrischer! Halte Stich!	1184–667 1316–425	I.10–13 I.10.3:32–11.4:11
e. Recitative dialogue		Wotan decides to rob Alberich.	Was sinnt nun Wotan so wild?	1668–803	I.14.0:00–15.1:18
Interlude				1803–93	I.15.1:18–3:45

Scene 3		Nibelheim				
a. Recitative dialogue			Alberich tests the Tarnhelm.	Hehe! Hehe! Hieher! Hieher!	1894–2013	I.15.3:45–II.1
b. Recitative dialogue with embedded			Mime complains about the Nibelungs' enslavement.	Nibelheim hier	2014–319	II.2.0:00–3.2:21
Mime's Monologue				Sorglose Schmiede	2084–206	II.2.2:05–5:02
c. Recitative dialogue with embedded			Wotan captures Alberich.	Was wollt ihr hier?	2320–744	II.3.2:21–5.3:05
Alberich's Warning				Die in linder Lüfte Weh'n	2424–519	II.3.5:10–7:33
Interlude					2745–857	II.5.3:05–6:30
Scene 4		A mountain summit near the Rhine				
a. Recitative dialogue with embedded			Alberich yields to Wotan the hoard, Tarnhelm, and Ring; he curses the Ring.	Da, Vetter, sitze du fest!	2858–3207	II.6–8
Alberich's Curse	b			Bin ich nun frei?	3117–202	II.8
b. Recitative dialogue with embedded			Wotan yields to the giants the hoard, Tarnhelm, and, warned by Erda, the Ring; Fafner kills Fasolt.	Fasolt und Fafner nahen von fern	3208–666	II.9–12
Erda's Warning	c-sharp			Weiche, Wotan! Weiche!	3456–528	II.11
c. ***Gods' Entry into Valhalla*** Orchestral, except for an ensemble song (with superimposed voices)	D-flat				3666–897	II.13–15

The sections of closed-form music are in bold; the open-form but non-dialogical sections are in bold italics.

APPENDIX TWO

Die Walküre
The Music-Dramatic Plan

Form	Key	Content	Text incipit	Measures	CD.track time
Act 1					
Scene 1		Hunding's dwelling			
a. *Prelude* with orchestrally accompanied pantomime and brief recitative at the end	d	Siegmund, in flight from enemies,		1–156	I.1.0:00–2.1:30
b. Recitative dialogue with sections of orchestrally accompanied pantomime		encounters Sieglinde.	Ein fremder Mann? Ihn muß ich fragen	157–380	I.2.1:30–3.9:35
Scene 2					
a. Recitative dialogue with sections of orchestrally accompanied pantomime		Hunding returns.	Müd' am Herd fand ich den Mann	381–475	I.4
b. *Siegmund's monologue*	g-a-c	Siegmund introduces himself.	Friedmund darf ich nicht heißen	476–674	I.5–6
c. Recitative with a section of orchestrally accompanied pantomime	c	Hunding challenges the unarmed Siegmund to a fight tomorrow.	Ich weiß ein wildes Geschlecht	674–789	I.7
Scene 3: *Love Duet*					
a. Recitative arioso, **Siegmund's quasi-cantabile,**	C	Siegmund meditates on the sword his father had promised he would find when in need.	Ein Schwert verhieß mir der Vater	790–879	I.8.0:00–4:11
			Nächtiges Dunkel deckte mein Aug'	880–925	I.8.4:11–6:10
Recitative dialogue,			Schläfst du Gast?	926–54	I.9.0:00–0.52
Sieglinde's quasi-cantabile (monologue),	e-E	Sieglinde tells him of a sword buried by a stranger in the stem of the ash tree.	Der Männer Sippe saß hier im Saal	955–1025	I.9.0:52–4:33
Duet quasi-cabaletta	G	They hope the sword is destined for Siegmund.	O fänd ich ihn hier und heut'	1026–87	I.9.4:33–6:19

b. Recitative dialogue, **Siegmund's** and	Love mutually avowed.	B-flat	1087–98	Ha, wer ging? Wer kam herein?		I.9.6:19–6:47
			1099–1167	Winterstürme wichen dem Wonnemond		I.10
Sieglinde's cantabiles, *Tempo di mezzo* dialogue, **Duet cabaletta**		G	1167–220	Du bist der Lenz		I.11.0:00–1:56
	They discover that they are siblings. Siegmund possesses both the sword and Sieglinde.		1221–378	O süßeste Wonne! Seligstes Weib!		I.11.1:56–12.1:21
			1378–523	Siegmund heiß' ich		I.12.1:21–5:05
Act 2						
A. Wotan						
Scene 1						
a. *Prelude*	A wild craggy mountain landscape	a	1–73		II.1	
b. Recitative dialogue twice punctuated by the **Call of the Valkyrie**	Wotan orders Brünnhilde to assist Siegmund in his impending fight with Hunding.	d	74–153	Nun zäume dein Roß	II.2	
			94–112	Hojotoho!		II.2.0:30–1:12
			131–48			II.2.1:58–2:36
c. Recitative dialogue punctuated by **Fricka's three ariosos**	Fricka demands that Wotan punish Siegmund; Wotan assents.	g-sharp	154–588	Der alte Sturm, die alte Müh'!	II.3–6	
			281–344	O was klag' ich um Ehe und Eid		II.4.0:54–2:58
			441–78	Mit Unfreien streitet kein Edler		II.5.3:57–5:15
		E-flat	542–88	Deiner ew'gen Gattin heilige Ehre		II.6.2:57–6:17
Scene 2						
a. Recitative dialogue	Wotan is desperate.		589–687	Schlimm, fürcht' ich, schloß der Streit		II.7.0:00–8.1:12
b. ***Wotan's monologue***	He explains his despair to Brünnhilde and orders her to assist Hunding.		688–989	Als junger Liebe Lust mir verblich		II.8.1:12–9.10:29
c. Recitative dialogue			989–1107	O sag! Künde, was soll nun dein Kind?		II.10.0:00–3:41
d. Recitative	She is heavy-hearted.		1107–58	So sah ich Siegvater nie		II.10.3:41–7:03
B. Brünnhilde						
Scene 3						
a. Recitative dialogue	Siegmund and Sieglinde in flight.		1159–461	Raste nun hier; gönne dir Ruh'!		II.11.0:00–12.7:06
						(continued)

Form	Key	Content	Text incipit	Measures	CD.track.time
Scene 4					
a. **Duet of Brünnhilde and Siegmund:**					
Cantabile	f-sharp	Brünnhilde appears to Siegmund announcing his impending death, but confronted with Siegmund's love for Sieglinde,	Siegmund! Sieh auf mich	1462–619	II.12.7:06– III.2.2:24
Tempo di mezzo	f-sharp		Du sahst der Walküre sehrenden Blick	1618–716	III.2.2:22–3.0:48
Cabaletta with final	f-sharp	changes her mind.	So jung und schön erschimmerst du mir	1716–849	III.3.0:48–5:06
			Halt' ein! Wälsung!	1776–817	III.3.3:03–4:09
Stretto and orchestral Postlude				1818–49	III.3.4:09–5:06
Scene 5					
a. Recitative dialogue with orchestrally accompanied pantomime	d	Brünnhilde assists Siegmund in his combat, but Wotan intervenes and Siegmund falls; Brünnhilde escapes with Sieglinde, pursued by Wotan.	Zauberfest bezähmt ein Schlaf	1849–2065	III.4.0:00–5.6:12
Act 3					
A. The Valkyries					
Scene 1		Brünnhilde's rock			
a. **The Ride of the Valkyries**	b-B	A gathering of the Valkyries.		1–266	IV.1
b. Recitative dialogue		Brünnhilde tells Sieglinde that she is pregnant with Siegfried.	Schützt mich, und helft in höchster Not!	267–602	IV.2–4
Scene 2					
a. Recitative dialogue		Wotan casts Brünnhilde out of the race of the gods; she will be bound in sleep, a future slave to the first man who shall find and awaken her.	Wo ist Brünnhild, wo die Verbrecherin?	602–979	IV.5–7

B. Wotan and Brünnhilde

Scene 3

a. Recitative dialogue		Brünnilde begs Wotan to surround her rock with fire, so that only a fearless hero, Siegfried, may find her there.	War es so schmählich	980–1488	IV.8–11
b. **Wotan's Farewell:**					
Sehr bewegt	e-E	Wotan consents.	Leb wohl, du kühnes, herrliches Kind!	1488–556	IV.12.0:00–13.0:41
Postlude	E			1556–79	IV.13.0:41–2:39
Langsam	e		Der Augen leuchtendes Paar	1580–624	IV.13.2:40–7:21
Postlude	E			1625–44	IV.13.7:21–9:58
Mäßig bewegt	E		Loge, hör! Lausche hieher!	1645–732	IV.14

The sections of closed-form music are in bold; the open-form but non-dialogical sections are in bold italics.

APPENDIX THREE

Siegfried
The Music-Dramatic Plan

Form	Key	Content	Text incipit	Measures	CD.track.time
Act 1					
Scene 1		A cave in the forest			
a. **Prelude** continuous with a recitative over an orchestral development	b-flat	Mime broods over his inability to restore Nothung.		1–250	I.1–2
b. Recitative dialogue with short embedded songs:		Siegfried learns who his parents were and orders Mime to restore the Sword.	Hoiho! Hoiho! Hau ein! hau ein!	250–1291	I.3–9
Siegfried's arietta 1	g		Da hast du die Stücken	342–417	I.4.0:00–0:50
Mime's arietta	f		Als zulendes Kind zog ich dich auf	512–89	I.5
Siegfried's arietta 2	D		Es sangen die Vöglein so selig im Lenz	773–829	I.6.3:54–5:46
Siegfried's arietta 3	B-flat		Aus dem Wald fort in die Welt ziehn	1190–254	I.8.0:44–9.0:26
Scene 2					
a. Recitative dialogue with a refrain	C	Wotan tells Mime that "only he who never knew fear will forge the sword anew."		1289–903	I.10–13
Scene 3					
a. Recitative dialogue		Siegfried decides to forge the Sword himself.	Was flammt dort die Luft?	1904–2430	I.14–II.3
b. **Siegfried's Aria:** Cantabile 1: Smelting Song	d/D	While Siegfried restores Nothung, Mime brews a sleeping potion.	Nothung! Nothung! Neidliches Schwert!	2430–627	II.4.0:00–6:43
Recitative dialogue interlude	d/(D)		Was schafft der Tölpel dort mit dem Topf?	2627–92	II.4.6:43–8:27
Cantabile 2: Forging Song	F		Hoho! Hoho!Hohei!	2692–2781	II.5.0:00–3:03
Cabaletta	d/D		Den der Bruder schuf, den schimmernden Reif	2782–2983	II.5.3:03–5:43
Act 2					
A. Wotan and Alberich		In the depths of the forest			

Scene 1					
a. **Prelude** continuous with a recitative dialogue over an orchestral development of the Prelude's music	f	Wotan warns Alberich of Mime's plans.	In Wald und Nacht	1–103 104–529	II.6 II.7–11
B. Siegfried's education	E				
Scene 2: The Fafner cycle					
a. Recitative dialogue		Mime brings Siegfried to Fafner's cave.	Wir sind zur Stelle	530–714	II.12
b. Recitative embedded with refrains of the **Forest Murmurs**	E	Siegfried communes with nature.	Daß der mein Vater nicht ist	714–960 714–49 764–85 831–71 894–900 923–934	II.13–III.2 II.13.0:00–1:20 III.1.0:00–1:00 III.2.0:51–2:31 III.2.3:10–3:27 III.2.4:25–4:53
c. Recitative dialogue		Siegfried kills Fafner.	Haha! Da hätte mein Lied mir 'was liebes erblasen!	961–1169	III.3–4
d. Recitative embedded with the refrain of the **Forest Murmurs**	E	The Woodbird tells Siegfried of the Tarnhelm and Ring.	Zur Kunde taugt kein Toter	1170–223 1179–223	III.5 III.5.0:18–2:14
Scene 3: The Mime cycle					
a. Recitative dialogue		Mime and Alberich quarrel over who should get Fafner's treasure.	Wohin schleichst du eilig und schlau	1224–352	III.6
b. Recitative embedded with the refrain of the **Forest Murmurs**	E	The Woodbird warns Siegfried of Mime.	Was ihr mir nützt	1352–412 1376–412	III.7 III.7.1:10–2:54
c. Recitative dialogue		Siegfried kills Mime.	Willkommen, Siegfried!	1412–701	III.8.0:00–9.1:20
d. Recitative embedded with refrains of the **Forest Murmurs**	E	The Woodbird tells Siegfried of Brünnhilde.	Heiß ward mir von der harten Last!	1702–910 1793–809 1823–37 1855–61	III.9.1:20–8:53 III.9.4:40–5:21 III.9.5:50–6:23 III.9.7:03–7:21

(continued)

Form	Key	Content	Text incipit	Measures	CD.track.time
Act 3					
Scene 1					
a. **Prelude** continuous with a recitative dialogue over an orchestral development of the Prelude's music	g	At the foot of Brünnhilde's rock Unable to learn from Erda how to prevent the end of the gods' rule, Wotan embraces the inevitable and wills that his inheritance passes on to Siegfried and Brünnhilde.	Wache! Wala! Wala! Erwach'!	1–59 60–439	III.10.0:00–1:50 III.10.1:50–IV.1.3:55
Scene 2					
a. Recitative dialogue		Siegfried destroys Wotan's Spear with his Sword.	Dort seh' ich Siegfried nahn	440–769	IV.1.3:55–5.0:45
Interlude		Siegfried ascends to the top of Brünnhilde's rock.		770–830	IV.5.0:45–6.0:34
Scene 3: Love Duet:	(E/e)/C	On top of Brünnhilde's rock			
a. Recitative monologue	E/e	Siegfried discovers and kisses Brünnhilde.	Selige Öde auf woniger Höh'!	831–1066	IV.6.0:34–7.7:06
b. **Tempo d'attacco**	C	Brünnhilde greets the earth as she returns to consciousness, but is reluctant to succumb to Siegfried,	Heil dir, Sonne! Heil dir, Licht!	1067–161	IV.8.0:00–9.0:54
c. Recitative dialogue			O wüßtest du, Lust der Welt	1161–477	IV.9.0:54–10.8.04
d. **Brünnhilde's cantabile**	E	still clinging to the dream of her past divinity.	Ewig war ich, ewig bin ich	1478–560	IV.11.0:00–4:08
e. **Tempo di mezzo**		Siegfried manages fully to awaken Brünnhilde	Dich – lieb' ich: o liebtest mich du!	1560–712	IV.11.4:08–9:04
f. **Cabaletta**	C	and they embrace.	Lachend muß ich dich lieben	1713–89	IV.11.9:04–11:17

The sections of closed-form music are in bold; the open-form but non-dialogical sections are in italics.

APPENDIX FOUR

Götterdämmerung
The Music-Dramatic Plan

Form	Key	Content	Text incipit	Measures	CD.track.time
Prologue					
a. **The Norns Scene**	e-flat→	On the Valkyrie rock The three Norns tell the story of Wotan's original sin and predict the twilight of the gods.	Welch Licht leuchtet dort?	1–304	I.1–3
b. **Brünnhilde-Siegfried Duet**	E-flat	Brünnhilde sends Siegfried into the world in search of new adventures.	Zu neuen Taten, teurer Helde	305–669	I.4–6
Orchestral prelude				305–54	I.4:0:00–3:15
Brünnhilde's cantabile	E-flat		Zu neuen Taten, teurer Helde	354–417	I.4:3:15–5:43
Tempo di mezzo (recitative dialogue)			Mehr gabst du Wunderfrau, als ich zu wahren weiß	417–593	I.4:5:43–5.5:30
Duet cabaletta	E-flat		Oh! heilige Götter! Hehre Geschlechter!	593–634	I.5.5:30–6.1:16
Orchestral postlude				635–69	I.6.1:16–2:27
Interlude		Siegfried's Rhine Journey		670–892	I.7
Act 1					
Part 1 (Scenes 1–2)		The Hall of the Gibichungs			
a. Recitative dialogue		Hagen plots to marry Gunther to Brünnhilde and Gutrune to Siegfried.	Nun hör', Hagen; sage mir, Held	1–345	I.8–10
b. Recitative dialogue with embedded		Siegfried is entrapped by means of a potion.	Wer ist Gibichs Sohn?	346–869	I.11–II.3
Siegfried-Gunther Duettino and	B-flat		Begrüße froh, o Held, die Halle meines Vaters	388–424	I.12.0:00–1:52
Siegfried-Gunther Oath Duet	B-flat		Blühenden Lebens labendes Blut	637–738	II.2.0:00–2:55
c. **Hagen's Watch**	e-flat	Hagen broods.	Hier sitz' ich zur Wacht	870–966	II.4:0:00–7:24
Interlude				967–76	
Part 2 (Scene 3)		The Valkyrie's rock			
a. Recitative dialogue with embedded		Brünnhilde refuses Waltraute's request that she return the Ring to the Rhinedaughters.	Altgewohntes Geräusch raunt meinem Ohr die Ferne	977–1546	II.4.8:12–7.6:25
Waltraute's narrative			Höre mit Sinn, was ich dir sage!	1218–368	II.6

Section	Key	Description	Opening text	Measures	Timing
b. Recitative dialogue		Siegfried compels Brünnhilde to marry Gunther.	Abendlich Dämmern deckt den Himmel	1547–844	II.7.6:25–9.9:05
Act 2					
Part 1 (Introduction: Prelude and Scene 1)		The shore in front of the Gibichung Hall			
a. **Hagen's Dream**	b-flat/B-flat	Hagen broods further.		1–202	III.1.1–2
Interlude				203–35	III.3.0:00–1:40
Part 2 (Scenes 2–4)					
a. Recitative dialogue	G	Siegfried tells Gutrune and Hagen how he won Brünnhilde for Gunther.	Hoiho! Hagen! Müder Mann!	236–383	III.3.1:40–4.3:51
b. Recitative dialogue with embedded		Hagen assembles the vassals to greet Gunther and Brünnhilde.	Hoiho! Hoihohoho! Ihr Gibichs-Mannen	384–745	III.5
Song of the Vassals with a	C		Groß Glück und Heil lacht nun dem Rhein	636–87	III.5.6:14–7:32
Coda	→			719–45	III.5.8:16–8:59
c. Recitative dialogue with embedded		Brünnhilde accuses Siegfried of having violated her, he denies the charge, and they both swear oaths on Hagen's spear.	Heil dir, Gunther! Heil dir, und deiner Braut!	746–1286	III.6.0:00–11.2:17
Song of the Vassals with Gunther and	B-flat		Heil dir, Gunther! Heil dir, und deiner Braut!	746–87	III.6.0:00–3:30
Siegfried's and Brünnhilde's Oaths Duet	E-flat		Helle Wehr, heilige Waffe: hilf meinem ewigen Eide!	1128–213	III.10.0:00–2:43
Interlude				1286–333	III.11.2:17–12.1:23
Part 3 (Scene 5)					
a. Recitative dialogue with culminating		Hagen convinces Brünnhilde and Gunther that only Siegfried's death would atone for his betrayal of their trust and learns that Siegfried's back is his vulnerable spot.	Welches Unholds List liegt hier verhohlen?	1334–704	III.12.1:23–14.8:19
Trio	c/(C)		So soll es sein! Siegfried falle!	1617–704	III.14.5:39–8:19

(continued)

Form	Key	Content	Text incipit	Measures	CD.track.time
Act 3					
Part 1 (Scenes 1–2)					
a. **Prelude** followed by	F	A wild, wooded, and rocky valley along the Rhine The Rhinedaughters unsuccessfully plead with Siegfried for the Ring.		1–50	IV.1.0:00–2:0:19
The Rhinedaughters' Song with embedded Recitative dialogue			Frau Sonne sendet lichte Strahlen	51–493	IV.2.0:19–5.7:02
b. Recitative dialogue followed by ***Siegfried's Monologue*** followed by **Peroration**	c	Siegfried tells his life story and is killed by Hagen. Siegfried's Funeral March	Ich höre sein Horn. Der Helde naht Hoiho! Hoiho! Mime hieß ein mürrischer Zwerg	150–444 494–652 653–912 913–88	IV.2.4:18–5.5:13 IV.5.7:02–7.2:24 IV.8.0:00–10.4:09 IV.10.4:09–11.6:34
Part 2 (Scene 3)					
a. Recitative dialogue followed by		Hagen, followed by Gunther and the Gibichungs, brings Gutrune Siegfried's body and kills Gunther in a fight over the Ring.	War das sein Horn?	989–1231	IV.12–15
Brünnhilde's Monologue followed by		Brünnhilde claims the Ring as her inheritance, bequeaths it to the Rhinedaughters, and immolates herself with Siegfried.	Starke Scheite schichtet mir dort	1232–501	IV.16.0:00–18.3:40
Peroration	→D-flat	The Rhinedaughters recover the Ring and drown Hagen; Valhalla burns down.		1502–600	IV.18.3:40–8:43

The sections of closed-form music are in bold print; the open-form but non-dialogical sections are in bold italics.

APPENDIX FIVE

Tristan und Isolde
The Music-Dramatic Plan

Form	Key	Content	Text incipit	Measures	CD.track:time
Act 1					
Introduction with	a	Tristan's ship		1–111	I.1
REFRAIN				1–21	I.1.0:00–2:12
Part 1.					
		Prehistory			
		Protagonists:			
Song of a Young Sailor,		Isolde with Brangäne	Westwärts schweift der Blick	112–35	I.2.0:00–1:09
Recitative dialogue			Wer wagt mich zu höhnen?	135–295	I.2.1:09–6:29
Song of a Young Sailor,		Tristan with Kurwenal	Frisch weht der Wind	296–310	I.3.0:00–0:49
Recitative dialogue,			Mir erkoren, mir verloren	310–510	I.3.0:49–4.5:02
Kurwenal's Song			Herr Morold zog zu Meere her	510–37	I.4.5:02–5:50
2.					
Recitative dialogue,		Prehistory narrated	Weh, ach weh! dies zu dulden!	537–602	I.4.5:50–5.1:59
Isolde's Monologue:					
Section 1:					
Prelude			Wie lachend sie mir Lieder singen	602–8	I.6.0:00–0:14
Narrative with embedded			Von einem Kahn, der klein und arm	609–88	I.6.0:14–7.2:10
REFRAIN			er sah mir in die Augen	666–78	I.7.0:30–1:37
Interlude			O Wunder! Wo hatt' ich die Augen?	688–702	I.7.2:10–2:41
Section 2:					
Prelude			Er schwur mit tausend Eiden	703–17	I.7.2:41–3:05
Narrative			Den als Tantris unerkannt ich entlassen	717–66	I.7.3:05–4:49
Interlude		Falling in love	Da Friede, Sühn' und Freundschaft	767–80	I.7.4:49–5:17
Section 3:					
Prelude			O blinde Augen! Blöde Herzen!	780–90	I.8.0:00–0:13
Narrative			Wie anders prahlte Tristan aus	791–840	I.8.0:13–1:48
Coda			Fluch dir, Verruchter!	840–62	I.8.1:48–2:25
Recitative,			O Süße! Traute! Teure! Holde!	862–82	I.8.2:25–9.0:17

Brangäne's Song:					
	Stanza 1			883–917	I.9.0:17–1:26
	Interlude			917–20	I.9.1:26–1:33
	Stanza 2			920–58	I.9.1:33–2:51
	Interlude			959–83	I.9.2:51–3:46
	Stanza 3			984–1036	I.9.3:46–5:08
3.	Recitative dialogue		Welcher Wahn! Welch eitles Zürnen!		
	The two potions		Und warb er Marke dir zum Gemahl		
	The story begins		Ungeminnt den hehrsten Mann		
			Wo lebte der Mann		
Part 2					
4.	Recitative dialogue		Kennst du der Mutter Künste nicht?	1036–318	I.9.5:08–13.4:16
	Tristan decides to drink the potion.		Begehrt, Herrin, was ihr wüscht	1318–753	I.14–II.3.1:15
5.	REFRAIN,	a	Ich trink' sie dir!	1754–97	II.3.1:15–4.2:04
	Recitative dialogue,			1798–802	II.4.204–2:14
	Interruption,			1803–21	II.4.2:14–2:46
	Recitative dialogue with an aborted duet,			1822–79	II.4.2:46–4:30
	Interruption–ensemble coda			1879–948	II.5
Act 2					
Part 1					
1.	Recitative dialogue with embedded		A garden at King Mark's castle Day as the past to be abandoned Isolde awaits Tristan.	1–496	II.6–9
	Isolde's Song				
Part 2			Dein Werk? O tör'ge Magd!	370–471	II.9.1:02–4:32
2.			Night as the lovers' present and future		
			Transition from Day to Night		
	a. Recitative dialogue with embedded		Isolde! Tristan! Geliebte/r!	497–682	II.10.0:00–4:33

(*continued*)

Form	Key	Content	Text incipit	Measures	CD.track.time
Duettino	A-flat/B		O Wonne der Seele	587–634	II.10.2:07–3:15
b. Recitative dialogue	A-flat		Dem Tage! Dem Tage!	682–1116	II.10.4:33–11.9:24
3. **Love Duet:**		Night of love			
Cantabile 1 (Liebesnacht)	A-flat/B		O sink hernieder, Nacht der Liebe	1117–210	II.12
Postlude (Brangäne's Warning)	F-sharp [G-flat]		Einsam wachend in der Nacht	1210–57	II.13
Interlude (recitative dialogue)	G-flat→A-flat		Lausch, Geliebter! Laß mich sterben!	1258–376	II.14–III.1
Cantabile 2 (Liebestod)	A-flat		So starben wir, um ungetrennt	1377–424	III.2.0:00–2:06
Postlude (Brangäne's Warning)	G		Habet acht! Habet acht!	1424–35	III.2.2:06–2:52
Interlude (recitative dialogue)	G→G-sharp [A-flat]		Soll ich lauschen? Laß mich sterben!	1436–80	III.2.2:52–4:53
Cabaletta 1 (derived from Cantabile 1)	→V of B		O ew'ge Nacht, süße Nacht!	1481–529	III.3.0:00–1:07
Cabaletta 2 (derived from Cantabile 2)	B		Wie sie fassen, wie sie lassen	1530–631	III.3.1:07–3:46
Part 3		Return of Day			
4.					
a. Recitative dialogue		Marke interrupts the Night.	Rette dich, Tristan!	1631–89	III.4
b. *Marke's Monologue*			Tatest du's wirklich?	1689–890	III.5–6
c. REFRAIN with	a	Tristan's answer	O König, das kann ich dir nicht sagen	1891–913	III.7.0:00–1:47
Duet Postlude	A-flat	The lovers promise themselves to complete their journey into the Night.	Wohin nun Tristan scheidet	1914–97	III.7.1:53–7:39
d. Recitative dialogue		Tristan is wounded. The garden of Tristan's castle	Verräter! Ha! Zur Rache, König!	1998–2051	III.8
Act 3					
Part 1					
1.		Tristan's auto-analysis			
Tristan's Monologue:					
Series 1:					
Orchestral exposition				1–163	III.9.0:00–11.0:41
Interlude 1			Ha! diese Stimme! Seine Stimme!	164–276	III.11.0:41–12.4:41

Monologue 1			Dünkt dich das? Ich weiß es anders	277–440	III.12.4:41–14.3:19
Interlude 2			Der einst ich trotzt', aus Treu' zu dir	441–516	III.14.3:19–IV.1.2:20
Monologue 2			Isolde kommt! Isolde naht!	516–625	IV.1.2:20–5:42
Series 2:					
Orchestral development with			Noch ist kein Schiff zu sehn!	626–840	IV.2–3
Monologue 3					
Interlude 3		Isolde arrives.	Mein Herre! Tristan!	840–66	IV.4.0:00–1:25
Monologue 4			Bist du nun tot? Lebst du noch?	866–999	IV.4.1:25–5.5:58
Interlude 4			O Wonne! Freude! Ha! Das Schiff!	999–1208	IV.6
Monologue 5 with			O diese Sonne! Ha! dieser Tag!	1209–324	IV.7
REFRAIN	a	Tristan's death		1301–24	IV.7.2:18–3:50
Part 2					
2.					
a. Recitative		Isolde's complaint	Ich bin's, ich bin's, süßester Freund!	1325–428	IV.8
b. Orchestral pantomime		Marke arrives.	Kurwenal! Hör! Ein zweites Schiff	1429–551	IV.9–10.1:02
c. Recitative		Marke's complaint	Tot den alles! Alles tot!	1552–620	IV.10.1:02–6:20
3.					
Transfiguration:	A-flat /B	Isolde's peroration,			
Repetition of Cantabile 2	A-flat		Mild und leise wie er lächelt	1621–31	IV.11.0:00–1:09
Repetition of Cabaletta 2	B		Seht ihr's nicht?	1632–80	IV.11.1:09–4:55
Tonic resolution with	B		Welt Athems wehendem All	1681–99	IV.11.4:55–7:07
REFRAIN		death, and transfiguration		1695–99	IV.11.6:15–7:07

The sections of closed-form music are in bold; the open-form but non-dialogical sections are in bold italics; the refrain is in bold capital letters.

APPENDIX SIX

Die Meistersinger von Nürnberg
The Music-Dramatic Plan

Form	Key	Content	Text incipit	Measures	CD.track.time
Prelude	C			1–222	I.1
Act 1					
1.					
a. **Chorale** with orchestral pantomime	C	St. Catherine's Church	Da zu dir der Heiland kam	222–85	I.2.0:00–3:14
b1. Recitative dialogue	C	Eva and Walther exchange mute gestures and glances.	Verweilt! Ein Wort – Ein einzig' Wort!	285–377	I.2.3:14–3.2:38
b2. Recitative dialogue	C	He asks her if she is betrothed,	Nein! Erst dies Wort!	377–524	I.3.2:38–4.2:03
c. Arioso,	C	learns about the singing contest,	Seh' ich euch wieder?	524–65	I.4.2:03–4:07
Terzetto	C	and decides to become a mastersinger.	Für euch Gut und Blut	545–65	I.4.3:07–4:07
2.	D/G				
a1. Recitative dialogue,	D	David explains to Walther the rules of the mastersinger art	David! Was stehst?	566–76	I.5.0:00–0:21
Ensemble of the Apprentices,			Was der sich dünkt!	576–88	I.5.0:21–0:48
Recitative dialogue,			Fanget an! Was soll's?	589–619	I.5.0:48–2:02
David's Monologue:					
Cantabile Part 1	D		Mein Herr! Der Singer Meisterschlag	619–701	I.5.2:02–6.2:25
Interruption			Hilf Gott! Will ich denn Schuster sein?	701–10	I.6.2:25–2:53
Cantabile Part 2	d		Der Meister Tön' und Weisen	710–810	I.7.0:00–4:58
Cantabile Coda	D		David! Wer ist nun 'Dichter?'	810–62	I.7.4:58–8.1:15
a2. Recitative,	G		Was macht ihr denn da?	862–79	I.8.1:15–1:40
Ensembles of the Apprentices,			Aller End' ist doch David	880–901	I.9.0:00–0:31
David's Cabaletta,		and warns him of the marker.	Ja, lacht nur zu!	902–62	I.9.0:31–2:39
Ensembles of the Apprentices,			Das Blumenkränzlein aus Seiden fein	963–75	I.9.2:39–3:05
Orchestral postlude				975–82	I.9.3:05–3:19
3.					
Part 1	F	Pogner's plan			
a. Recitative dialogue	F	Walther tells Pogner of his wish to become a mastersinger.	Seid meiner Treue wohl versehen	983–1150	I.10.0:00–11.2:26

b. Recitative dialogue, **Pogner's Aria**:	F	Pogner tells the masters of his plan to offer his wealth and his daughter's, Eva's, hand to the winner of tomorrow's singing contest.	Beliebt's, wir schreiten zur Merkerwahl?	1151–66	I.11.2:26–3:05
A	F		Das schöne Fest, Johannistag	1167–217	I.12.0:00–2:18
B	→		In deutschen Landen viel gereist	1218–48	I.12.2:18–3:40
A'	F		Dem Singer, der im Kunstgesang	1248–65	I.12.3:40–4:27
c. Recitative dialogue		The masters approve of the plan.	Das heisst ein Wort	1265–426	I.12.4:27–13.5:21
Part 2.1					
a. Recitative dialogue	(B-flat)/D	Walther admitted to the trial			
	B-flat	Pogner presents Walther as a candidate for admission.	Dacht' ich mir's doch!	1427–78	I.14
b. **Walther's Admission Aria**:		Walther tells the masters who were his teachers of poetry and singing.			
A	D		Am stillen Herd in Winterszeit	1478–500	I.15.0:00–1:17
Recitative dialogue	D		Ein guter Meister!	1501–9	I.15.1:17–1:38
A	D		Wann dann die Flur vom Frost befreit	1510–26	I.15.1:38–2:21
Recitative dialogue	D		Oho! Von Finken und Meisen	1527–56	I.15.2:21–3:29
B	D		Was Winternacht, was Waldespracht	1557–82	I.15.3:29–4:45
Recitative dialogue			Entnahm ihr was	1582–90	I.15.4:45–5:06
Part 2.2					
a. Recitative dialogue	(B-flat)/(C)/F	Walther's trial			
	→B-flat	Beckmesser takes his place in the marker's booth.	Nun, Meister! Wenn's gefällt	1590–640	I.16.0:00–2:42
b. Recitative, **Kothner's Arietta**,	C	Kothner reads the rules of the *Tabulatur*.	Was euch zum Liede Richt' und Schnur	1641–46	I.16.2:42–2:58
			'Ein' jedes Meistergesanges Bar'	1646–85	I.16.2:58–5:11
Recitative dialogue			Nun setzt euch in dem Singestuhl!	1685–98	I.16.5:11–5:55
c. **Walther's Trial Song** with **Ensemble Finale**:	F	Walther fails the trial.			
A1	F		'Fanget an!' So rief der Lenz in den Wald	1699–739	II.1.0:11–1:33
A2			In einer Dornenhecken	1739–57	II.1.1:33–2:09
A1	F		Doch: fanget an!	1758–95	II.1.2:09–3:27
Interruption			Seid ihr nun fertig?	1795–2082	II.2.0:00–3.6:33
A2			Aus finst'rer Dornenhecken	2010–28	II.3.4:26–4:57
B	F		Auf da steigt, mit goldnem Flügelpaar	2029–82	II.3.4:57–6:33
Orchestral coda				2082–119	II.3.6:33–7:42

(continued)

Form	Key	Content	Text incipit	Measures	CD.track.time
Act 2		In the street in front of the houses of Pogner and Sachs			
1.					
a. **Song of the Apprentices**	(G)/F		Johannistag! Johannistag!	1–99	II.4.0:00–3:24
b. Recitative dialogue with embedded	G		Was giebt's?	100–273	II.4.3:24–6:0:50
Pogner's Arietta	B-flat		Will einer Selt'nes wagen	141–98	II.5.0:37–3:56
c. **Sachs's [Elder] Monologue:**	(G)/F	Sachs meditates on the Trial Song.			
Introduction	G		Was duftet doch der Flieder	274–92	II.7.0:00–1:09
Recitative transition			Was gilt's, was ich dir sagen kann?	293–302	II.7.1:09–1:38
Orchestral pantomime	F			302–14	II.7.1:38–2:08
Monologue	F		Und doch, 's will halt nicht gehn	315–71	II.7.2:08–5:28
2.	B-flat				
a1. Recitative dialogue		Eva learns of the failed trial	Gut'n Abend, Meister!	372–593	II.8.0:00–8:16
a2. Recitative dialogue		and decides to elope with Walther.	Das dacht' ich wohl	593–647	II.8.8:16–9.1:45
b. Recitative dialogue with embedded			Da ist er!	647–877	II.10–13
REFRAIN	B		Geliebter, spare den Zorn	773–810	II.10.3:59–12:0:05
c. **Sachs's [Cobbler] Song**	B-flat	Sachs postpones Beckmesser's Serenade and the elopement.			
Stanza 1			Jerum! Jerum! Hallahallohe!	878–913	II.14.0:00–1:19
Dialogue interruption			Wie? Meister! Auf?	914–23	II.14.1:19–1:43
Stanza 2			Jerum! Hallahallohe!	923–58	II.14.1:43–3:03
Dialogue interruption			Gleich höret auf!	959–75	II.14.3:03–3:44
Stanza 3			Jerum! Jerum! Hallahallohe!	976–1012	II.14.3:44–5:19
Dialogue postlude			Das Fenster geht auf!	1012–23	II.15.0:00–0:26
3.	G/(E)				
a. Recitative dialogue, with		Sachs agrees to serve as Beckmesser's marker.	Freund Sachs!	1023–217	II.15.0:26–7:46
REFRAIN	B		Welch toller Spuck!	1202–17	II.15.7:01–7:46
b. **Beckmesser's Serenade:**	G	Beckmesser's singing			
False start			'Den Tag seh' ich erscheinen'	1217–29	II.16.0:00–0:51
Interruption			Treibt ihr hier Scherz?	1230–41	II.16.0:51–1:33

Stanza 1:					
A			'Den Tag seh' ich erscheinen'	1242–50	II.16.1:33–2:17
A			'Warum wohl aller Tage'	1251–58	II.16.2:17–2:52
B			'Wer sich getrau''	1259–69	II.16.2:52–3:33
Interruption			Sachs! Seht, ihr bringt mich um!	1269–76	II.16.3:33–3:57
Stanza 2:					
A			'Will heut' mir das Herz hüpfen'	1276–84	II.16.3:57–4:23
A			'Der Zunft ein bied'rer Meister'	1285–92	II.16.4:23–4:48
B			'Nun gilt es Kunst'	1293–303	II.16.4:48–5:18
Interruption			Seid ihr nun fertig?	1303–13	II.16.5:18–17.0:11
Stanza 3:					
A			'Darf ich mich Meister nennen'	1313–26	II.17.0:11–0:30
A			'Wohl kenn' ich alle Regeln'	1326–39	II.17.0:30–0:50
B			'Ein Junggesell''	1340–57	II.17.0:50–1:16
Ensemble Finale,		G	Zum Teufel mit dir	1357–439	II.17.1:16–3:09
Coda = REFRAIN		E	He! Lene! Wo bist du?	1439–85	II.17.3:09–5:45
			provokes general mayhem, but the riot calms down with the appearance of the Night-Watchman and the elopement is thwarted by Sachs.		
Act 3					
Part 1					
1.					
a. *[Prelude]*		(G)/C		1–64	III.1.0:00–6:28
b. Recitative dialogue with embedded		g/G	Sachs's workshop Sachs's silent meditation Hans Sachs identified with Saint John the Baptist Gleich, Meister! Hier!	65–300	III.1.6:28–3.3:05
David's Little Verse		D	'Am Jordan Sankt Johannes stand'	201–28	III.3.0:00–0:58
c. **Sachs's** *[Folly]* **Monologue:**		→C	Sachs resolves to manipulate folly to bring about a desirable outcome.		
Part 1		a	Wahn! Wahn! Überall Wahn!	301–35	III.3.3:05–4.2:01
Part 2		F→	Wie friedsam treuer Sitten	336–83	III.4.2:01–4:00
Part 3		B→C	Ein Kobold half wohl da	384–407	III.4.4:00–5:08
Part 4		C	Jetzt schaun wir, wie Hans Sachs es macht	407–37	III.4.5:08–6:30

(continued)

Form	Key	Content	Text incipit	Measures	CD.track.time
2.					
a. Recitative dialogue with embedded **Sachs's Arietta**	B-flat	Sachs gives Walther a lesson in poetics.	Grüss' Gott, mein Junker!	438–650	III.5–6
b. **Walther's Dream Song** begins	C	Sachs writes down Walther's poem.	Mein Freund, in holder Jugendzeit	545–611	III.6.0:00–3:02
Stanza 1:					
A			'Morgenlich leuchtend in rosigem Schein'	651–67	III.7.0:00–0:56
Interruption			Das war ein 'Stollen'	668–74	III.7.0:56–1:18
A			'Wonnig entragend dem seligen Raum'	675–86	III.7.1:18–1:52
Interruption			Ihr schlosset nicht im gleichen Ton	687–701	III.7.1:52–2:46
B			'Sei euch vertraut'	702–26	III.7.2:46–3:46
Reaction			Das nenn' ich mir einen Abgesang!	726–43	III.7.3:46–4:47
Stanza 2:					
A			'Abendlich glühend in himmlischer Pracht'	744–57	III.7.4:47–5:29
A			'Nächlich umdämmert, der Blick mir sich bricht'	758–69	III.7.5:29–6:03
B			'Lieblich ein Quell'	770–92	III.7.6:03–7:01
Reaction			Freund, euer Traumbild wies euch wahr	792–801	III.7.7:01–7:47
Stanza 3:					
A			'Weilten die Sterne im lieblichen Tanz?'	1431–46	III.10.3:44–4:27
A			'Wunder ob Wunder nun bieten sich dar'	1447–58	III.10.4:27–5:01
B			'Huldreichstes Bild'	1459–81	III.10.5:01–5:57
Reaction				1481–94	III.11.0:00–0:28
c. Recitative dialogue		The lesson continued	Wo fänd' ich die?	802–61	III.7.7:47–10:27
3.					
a. Recitative dialogue with embedded **Beckmesser's Arietta**	d	Beckmesser steals Walther's poem.		862–1358	III.7.10:27–10.0:08
			Die ich mir auserkoren	1007–48	III. 8.4:54–6:16

4.	a1. Recitative dialogue	C	Eva and Walther meet again.	Grüss' Gott, mein Evchen!	1358–431	III.10.0:08–3:44
	a2. **Walther's Dream Song** ends		Eva hears Walther's Song.	'Weilten die Sterne im lieblichen Tanz?'	1431–94	III.10.3:44–11.0:28
	a3. **Sachs's Arietta**		Sachs's mixed feelings	Hat man mit dem Schuhwerk nicht seine Not!	1495–544	III.11.0:28–2:01
	a4. **Eva's Arietta**		Eva's mixed feelings	O Sachs! Mein Freund!	1545–97	III.11.2:01–4:32
	a5. Recitative		Sachs will not be another King Mark.	Mein Kind, von Tristan und Isolde	1597–610	III.11.4:32–5:24
	b1. Recitative with		Sachs baptizes Walther's song.	Aha! Da streicht die Lene	1610–90	III.11.5:24–IV.1.1:04
	Sachs's Baptism Speech	(D)/(a)/C				
	b2. **Quintet,** Recitative	G-flat	Eva pronounces the baptismal verse.	Ein Kind ward hier geboren	1624–90	III.12.0:00–IV.1.1:04
Part 2				Selig, wie die Sonne	1691–730	IV.1.1:04–5:33
5.			An open meadow on the Pegnitz Introduction: the whole Nuremberg assembles.	Jetzt All' am Fleck'!	1730–32	IV.1.5:33–5:46
	a. Orchestral transformation				1733–78	IV.1.5:46–7:57
	b. **Marches and Choruses of the Guilds**	F/C		Sankt Krispin, lobet ihn!	1779–876	IV.2.0:00–3:42
	c. **Dance of the Apprentices**	B-flat			1876–2058	IV.2.3:42–3.2:39
	d. **March of the Mastersingers**	C		Herr Je! Herr Je!	2059–146	IV.3.2:39–4.0:22
	e. Choral introduction, with **Reformation Hymn, Acclamation of Sachs**	G C	Sachs acclaimed	Ha! Sachs! 's ist Sachs! 'Wach auf! es nahet gen den Tag' Heil! Heil! Heil!	2146–87 2154–70 2171–87	IV.4.0:22–3:23 IV.4.0:42–2:39 IV.4.2:39–3:23
6.	a. **Sachs's Harangue I**	G	The contest: the apotheosis of Sachs Sachs introduces the contest and asks that it be open to all.	Euch macht ihr's leicht	2188–280	IV.5.0:00–4:11
	b1. Recitative dialogue		Beckmesser prepares to sing	O Sachs, mein Freund!	2281–378	IV.5.4:11–6.1:51

(*continued*)

Form	Key	Content	Text incipit	Measures	CD.track.time
b2. **Beckmesser's Prize Song**	e/G	and fails.	'Morgen ich leuchte in rosigem Schein'	2379–454	IV.6.1:51–5:49
b3. Recitative dialogue		Beckmesser accuses Sachs, who introduces his defense witness, Walther,	Verdammter Schuster, das dank' ich dir!	2454–609	IV.6.5:49–7.4:41
b4. **Walther's Prize Song:**	C	who succeeds.			
A			'Morgenlich leuchtend im rosigen Schein'	2610–37	IV.8.0:00–1:34
Interruption			Ja wohl, ich merk'	2637–44	IV.8.1:34–1:58
A			'Abendlich dämmernd umschloß mich die Nacht'	2645–67	IV.8.1:58–3:05
			's ist kühn und seltsam	2667–75	IV.8.3:05–3:26
Interruption			'Huldreichster Tag'	2675–706	IV.8.3:26–4:46
B			Ja, holder Sänger	2706–32	IV.8.4:46–6:02
Postlude					
b5. Recitative dialogue		Walther refuses to join the guild.	Den Zeugen, denk' es, wähl' ich gut	2732–70	IV.8.6:02–8:04
c. ***Sachs's Harangue II***,	C	Sachs explains the meaning of it all	Verachtet mir die Meister nicht	2771–897	IV.9.0:00–5:48
Acclamation of Sachs	C	and is acclaimed again.	Heil! Sachs!	2897–910	IV.9.5:48–6:30

The sections of closed-form music are in bold; the open-form but non-dialogical sections are in bold italics; the refrain is in bold capital letters.

APPENDIX SEVEN

Parsifal
The Music-Dramatic Plan

Form	Key	Content	Text incipit	Measures	CD.track.time
Act 1					
Prelude	A-flat	Forest and castle of the Grail		1–113	I.1
continued with superimposed voices		Forest		114–46	I.2.0:00–2:32
A.					
1.					
a. Recitative dialogue		Gurnemanz and Kundry introduced	Jetzt auf, ihr Knaben!	147–238	I.2.2:32–3.1:54
b. Recitative dialogue with embedded		Amfortas introduced	Er naht, sie bringen ihn getragen	239–372	I.3.1:54–5.0:46
FOOL REFRAIN			'durch Mitleid wissend'	320–26	I.4.3:50–4:18
2. Gurnemanz's Monologue:					
a. Part 1		Amfortas's past: Kundry	He! Du da! Was liegst du wie ein wildes Tier?	373–559	I.5.0:46–6.4:08
b. Part 2		Amfortas's past: Klingsor	Doch, Väterchen, sag' und lehr' uns fein	560–704	I.6.4:08–7.8:35
c. Coda with		Amfortas's future: the redeemer	Vor Allem nun, der Speer kehr' uns zurück!	704–41	I.7.8:35–11:19
FOOL REFRAIN			'Durch Mitleid wissend'	729–41	I.7.10:15–11:19
3.					
a. Arioso with recitative dialogue		Parsifal and the wounded swan	Weh! Weh! Ho-ho! Auf!	742–932	I.8
b. Recitative dialogue		Parsifal's past	Nun sag: nichts weißt du was ich dich frage	933–1072	I.9
B. Communion Sequence I		Castle			
1.					
a. **Transformation**	→C	Parsifal enters the castle	Vom Bade kehrt der König heim	1073–167	II.1.0:00–3.1:23
b. **Processional**	C→ e-flat/ (E-flat)→ A-flat		Zum letzten Liebesmahle	1168–244	II.3.1:23–7:01
2.					
c. Recitative dialogue, **Amfortas's Monologue,**			Mein Sohn Amfortas, bist du am Amt? Wehvolles Erbe, dem ich verfallen	1245–96 1297–404	II.4 II.5.0:00–7:27

	FOOL REFRAIN with Recitative				
d.	**Communion**	A-flat	'Durch Mitleid wissend'	1405–21	II.5.7:27–6:0:22
			'Nehmet hin meinen Leib'	1422–574	II.6.0:22–7.4:46
e.	**Recessional**, Recitative dialogue with embedded FOOL REFRAIN	→E-flat→C	Parsifal driven away Was stehst du noch da? 'Durch Mitleid wissend'	1575–634 1635–66 1655–58	II.8.0:00–4:19 II.8.4:19–6:40 II.8.5:31–5:50
Act 2					
1.			Klingsor's magic castle	1–426	II.9.0:00–12.0:17
2.	a. Recitative dialogue		Klingsor subjugates Kundry Parsifal among the Flowermaidens		
	a. Frame		Hier! Hier war das Tosen!	427–566	II.12.0:17–4:55
	b. **Choral dance**	A-flat	Komm'! Komm'! Holder Knabe!	567–702	III.1.0:00–4:23
	c. Frame		Was zankest du?	703–39	III.1.4:23–5:36
	d. Arioso		Parsifal! Weile!	739–70	III.2.0:00–2:10
	e. Coda		Dich zu lassen! Dich zu meiden!	771–81	III.2.2:10–3:01
3.	**Parsifal-Kundry Confrontation**				
	a. Prelude (arioso)		Parsifal! Weile!	739–70	III.2.0:00–2:10
	b. Recitative dialogue		Dies Alles hab' ich nun geträumt?	781–823	III.3
	c. **Kundry's Narrative Aria**	G	Ich sah das Kind an seiner Mutter Brust	824–915	III.4
	d. Recitative dialogue		Wehe! Wehe! Was tat ich?	916–83	III.5.0:00–4:41
	e. **Parsifal's Monologue**		Amfortas! . . . . Die Wunde!	983–1126	III.5.4:41–6.7:45
	f. **Kundry's Monologue**		Grausamer! Fühlst du im Herzen	1126–275	III.7.0:00–6:26
	g. Recitative dialogue		Auf Ewigkeit wär'st du verdammt	1275–486	III.7.6:26–8.1:39
	h. Postlude (orchestral with superimposed voices)		Halt da! Dich bann' ich mit der rechten Wehr!	1486–539	III.8.1:39–4:06
Act 3					
[*Prelude*]			The domain of the Grail		
A.			Spring flower-meadow at the edge of the forest	1–44	III.9

(continued)

1. The first monologue complex					
a. Recitative dialogue and orchestral pantomime with embedded ***Parsifal's Monologue*** and ***Gurnemanz's Monologue I***		Parsifal's return	Von dorther kam das Stöhnen	45–509	III.10.0:00–IV.5.3:06
			Der Irrnis und der Leiden Pfade	285–332	IV.2.0:52–3.1:58
			Oh Gnade! Höchstes Heil!	332–419	IV.3.1:58–4.5:10
2.					
a. Orchestral pantomime with superimposed recitative dialogue		Parsifal anointed, Kundry baptized	Du wuschest mir die Füße	510–626	IV.5.3:06–7.0:44
3. The second monologue complex					
a. **Good Friday Spell:** **Parsifal's Prologue**	(B)/D B	Gurnemanz's sermon	Wie dünkt mich doch die Aue heut' so schön!	626–63	IV.7.0:44–2:26
Transition			Das ist – Karfreitags Zauber, Herr	663–74	IV.7.2:46–3:37
Gurnemanz's Monologue 2	D		Du siehst, das ist nich so	675–770	IV.8.0:00–4:50
Parsifal's Epilogue Elegy	D		Ich sah' sie welken	770–99	IV.8.4:50–9:0:18
B. Communion Sequence II		Castle			
1.					
a. **Transformation**	→e	Parsifal enters the castle	Mittag: die Stund' ist da	800–856	IV.9.0:18–4:30
b. **Processional**	b-flat →e		Geleiten wir im bergenden Schrein	857–920	IV.9.4:30–10.4:07
2.					
c. ***Amfortas's Monologue***	d→		Ja – Wehe! Wehe! Weh' über mich!	921–1029	IV.10.4:07–11.7:06
d. ***Parsifal's Monologue***			Nur eine Waffe taugt	1029–88	IV.11.7:06–12.3:44
e. **Communion**	A-flat	Parsifal succeeds Amfortas, Kundry dies		1088–141	IV.12.3:44–13.4:09

The sections of closed-form music are in bold; the open-form but non-dialogical sections are in bold italics; the refrain is in bold capital letters.

ACKNOWLEDGMENTS

Several of my friends, in particular Laurence Dreyfus, Thomas Grey, and Laurenz Lütteken, have been good enough to read the manuscript in full or in part and to send me their reactions. Their suggestions and corrections have much improved the book and I am tremendously grateful to them all. Very special thanks are due to Christopher Reynolds, whose detailed reading of the whole manuscript resulted in revisions large and small on virtually every page; I am in awe of his extraordinary scholarly generosity. My wife, Anna Maria Busse Berger, has been yet again my most patient and encouraging reader—remarkably so, given her initial resistance to the Wagnerian magic. I dedicate this book to her and our children with love and gratitude.

I have been fortunate to receive generous support for this project from a number of institutions. I acknowledge with gratitude a yearlong EURIAS Fellowship sponsored by the Institute for Human Sciences in Vienna and the European Commission Seventh Framework Programme—COFUND Action. The hospitality and comfortable working conditions at the Viennese Institute for Human Sciences as well as the warm support of the institute's late rector and Nietzsche expert, Krzysztof Michalski, allowed me to make decisive progress in 2011–12. I am similarly grateful to the Alexander von Humboldt Foundation for the Humboldt Research Award that made it possible for me to finish writing this book in 2015–16 at the Musicological Institute of Humboldt University in Berlin, where I have been fortunate to be hosted by two expert Wagnerian scholars and friends, Hermann Danuser and Arne Stollberg. Last but certainly not least, I would like yet again to express my gratitude to my own home institution, Stanford University, not only for the generosity with leave time, research funds, and publication subsidy, but also for providing an environment exceptionally conducive to creative work and for remaining what a university should be—a site of learning and pleasure in learning.

While working on this book, I have frequently had opportunities to present preliminary results in lecture form and have benefited from my listeners' reactions. I could not possibly acknowledge all of those individually here, but I would like to assure all of them of my gratitude. I would also like to thank all those who gave me such opportunities by organizing the lectures: Kofi Agawu, Scott Burnham, Hermann Danuser, Andreas Dorschel, Laurence Dreyfus, Katharine Ellis, Werner Gephart, Anselm Gerhard, Hans Ulrich Gumbrecht, Hans-Joachim Hinrichsen, John Howland, Steffen Huck, Helmut Loos, Laurenz Lütteken, Krzysztof Michalski, Vera Micznik, Matteo Nanni, Andrzej Nowak, Dana Prescott, Ivana Rentsch, Annette Richards, Valentina Sandu-Dediu, Matthias Schmidt, Julia Simon, Arne Stollberg, Cristina Urchueguia, Joshua Walden, Melanie Wald-Fuhrmann, and David Yearsley. Thanks to them I could present material from the prologue at Stanford University (March 15–17, 2012), Jagiellonian University, Kraków (April 17, 2012), University of Zürich (October 12–14, 2012); from chapter 1 at the State Institute for Musicology, Berlin (June 12, 2008); from chapter 2 at the University of Basel (April 23–24, 2013), University of Leipzig (May 19–25, 2013), the Käte Hamburger Center for Advanced Study in the Humanities "Law as Culture," Bonn (May 28, 2014); from chapter 3 at a Waynflete Lecture at Magdalen College, University of Oxford (June 7, 2008), University of British Columbia (January 15, 2009), John Coffin Lecture in the History of Ideas, Institute of Musical Research, School of Advanced Study, University of London (March 20, 2009), Institute for Human Sciences, Vienna (December 7, 2011); from chapter 4 at the University of Bern (November 6–10, 2012), Institute for Music Aesthetics, the University of Music and Performing Arts, Graz (June 18, 2014), Cornell University (February 19, 2015), Princeton University (April 27, 2015), University of Bern (September 29, 2015), Norwegian University of Science and Technology, Trondheim (April 8, 2016); from chapter 5 at Merton College, University of Oxford (March 26–28, 2010), University College London (July 6–7, 2010), University of Bern (November 21, 2011), Hindemith Lecture 2011, Swiss Musicological Society, Music Division of the Central Library, Zurich (November 22, 2011), Institute for Human Sciences, Vienna (February 21, 2012), University of California, Davis (May 8, 2013); and from the epilogue at the EURIAS Annual Meeting, Collegium Helveticum, Zurich (April 20–21, 2012), Civitella Ranieri Center, Umbertide (July 16, 2012), Humboldt University, Berlin (February 11, 2016), New Europe College, Bucharest (May 25, 2016). The input of my Stanford University students, both undergraduate and graduate, during my numerous seminars devoted to Wagner's individual music dramas has been invaluable.

Earlier versions of some of the sections of the present book have appeared in the following publications:

"Love in the Time of Bismarck," review essay of Roger Scruton, *Death-Devoted Heart: Sex and the Sacred in Wagner's "Tristan and Isolde*," Cambridge Opera Journal 18 (2006): 118–23.

"A Note on Tristan's Death Wish," in *Richard Wagner and His World*, ed. Thomas S. Grey (Princeton, NJ: Princeton University Press, 2009), 123–32.

"Carl Dahlhaus' Konzeption von Wagners Dramaturgie nach 1848," in *Carl Dahlhaus und die Musikwissenschaft: Werk, Wirkung, Aktualität*, ed. Hermann Danuser, Peter Gülke, and Norbert Miller (Schliengen, Germany: Edition Argus, 2011), 52–63.

"*Der Dichter spricht*: Self-Representation in *Parsifal*," in *Representation and Meaning in Western Music*, ed. Joshua S. Walden (Cambridge, England: Cambridge University Press, 2013), 182–202; German trans.: "'Der Dichter spricht': der Karfreitagszauber und die Performanz der Interpretation," in *Ereignis und Exegese. Musikalische Interpretation, Interpretation der Musik. Festschrift für Hermann Danuser zum 65. Geburtstag*, ed. Camilla Bork, Tobias Robert Klein, Burkhard Meischein, Andreas Meyer, and Tobias Plebuch (Schliengen: Edition Argus, 2011), 479–91.

"Tristan und Isolde. Handlung in drei Aufzügen WWV 90," in *Wagner-Handbuch*, ed. Laurenz Lütteken (Kassel and Stuttgart: Bärenreiter and Metzler, 2012), 371–80.

"*Parsifal* und die Regenerationsfrage," *Hundertsiebenundneunzigstes Neujahrsblatt der Allgemeinen Musikgesellschaft Zürich Auf das Jahr 2013* (Winterthur: Amadeus, 2012).

"Wie man wird, was man ist. *Die Walküre*, Erster Aufzug," in *Richard Wagner. Persönlichkeit, Werk und Wirkung*, ed. Helmut Loos, Leipziger Beiträge zur Wagner-Forschung, Richard-Wagner-Verband Leipzig, Sonderband (Markkleeberg, Germany: Sax-Verlag, 2013), 77–83.

"The Uncanny Grace: Kleist between Rossini and Schubert," in *Schubert: Interpretationen*, ed. Ivana Rentsch and Klaus Pietschmann, Schubert: Perspektiven—Studien 3 (Stuttgart: Franz Steiner Verlag, 2014), 155–64; German trans.: "Die unheimliche Grazie: Eine Bemerkung über Kleists Marionetten," in *Kleist Revisited*, ed. Hans Ulrich Gumbrecht and Friedericke Knüpling (Munich: Wilhelm Fink, 2014), 111–22.

"Must One Be Silent About That Whereof One Cannot Speak? Remarks on the First Scene of *Die Walküre*," in *Das Bildliche und das Unbildliche. Nietzsche, Wagner und das Musikdrama*, ed. Matthias Schmidt and Arne Stollberg (Munich: Wilhelm Fink, 2015), 43–56.

"How Holy Is German Art? On the Last Scene of *Die Meistersinger von Nürnberg*," in *Gefühlskraftwerke für Patrioten? Wagner und das Musiktheater zwischen Nationalismus und Globalisierung*, ed. Arne Stollberg, Ivana Rentsch, and Anselm Gerhard (Würzburg, Germany: Königshausen and Neumann, 2015), 137–55.

ABBREVIATIONS USED IN NOTES

AC   Friedrich Nietzsche, *The Antichrist*, trans. Walter Kaufmann, in *The Portable Nietzsche* (New York: Viking Press, 1968), 565–656.

BSNW   Dieter Borchmeyer and Jörg Salaquarda, eds., *Nietzsche und Wagner. Stationen einer epochalen Begegnung*, 2 vols. (Frankfurt am Main and Leipzig: Insel Verlag, 1994).

CT   Cosima Wagner, *Diaries*, ed. Martin Gregor-Dellin and Dietrich Mack, trans. Geoffrey Skelton, 2 vols. (New York and London: Harcourt Brace Jovanovich, 1978–80).

DS   Friedrich Nietzsche, "David Strauss, the Confessor and the Writer," in *Untimely Meditations*, ed. Daniel Breazeale, trans. R. J. Hollingdale (Cambridge, England: Cambridge University Press, 1997), 1–55.

EH   Friedrich Nietzsche, *Ecce Homo: How One Becomes What One Is*, trans. Walter Kaufmann, in *Basic Writings of Nietzsche* (New York: Modern Library, 1968), 671–800.

FW   Friedrich Nietzsche, *The Gay Science*, trans. Josefine Nauckhoff (Cambridge, England: Cambridge University Press, 2001).

GD   Friedrich Nietzsche, *Twilight of the Idols or, How One Philosophizes with a Hammer*, trans. Walter Kaufmann, in *The Portable Nietzsche* (New York: Viking Press, 1968), 463–563.

GM   Friedrich Nietzsche, *On the Genealogy of Morals*, trans. Walter Kaufmann, in *Basic Writings of Nietzsche* (New York: Modern Library, 1968), 449–599.

GS   Richard Wagner, *Gesammelte Schriften und Dichtungen*, 10 vols. (Leipzig: E. W. Fritzsch, 1871–83).

GT   Friedrich Nietzsche, *The Birth of Tragedy*, trans. Walter Kaufmann, in *Basic Writings of Nietzsche* (New York: Modern Library, 1968), 15–144.

454 ABBREVIATIONS USED IN NOTES

HL Friedrich Nietzsche, "On the Uses and Disadvantages of History for Life," in *Untimely Meditations*, ed. Daniel Breazeale, trans. R. J. Hollingdale (Cambridge, England: Cambridge University Press, 1997), 57–123.

JGB Friedrich Nietzsche, *Beyond Good and Evil*, ed. and trans. Walter Kaufmann, in *Basic Writings of Nietzsche* (New York: Modern Library, 1968), 192–435.

KSA Friedrich Nietzsche, *Sämtliche Werke: Kritische Studienausgabe*, ed. Giorgio Colli and Mazzino Montinari, 15 vols., 2nd ed. (Munich and Berlin: Deutscher Taschenbuch Verlag and de Gruyter, 1988).

KSB Friedrich Nietzsche, *Sämtliche Briefe: Kritische Studienausgabe in 8 Bänden*, ed. Giorgio Colli and Mazzino Montinari (Berlin and Munich: Walter de Gruyter and Deutscher Taschenbuch Verlag, 1986).

M Friedrich Nietzsche, *Daybreak: Thoughts on the Prejudices of Morality*, trans. R. J. Hollingdale (Cambridge, England: Cambridge University Press, 1997).

MA Friedrich Nietzsche, *Human, All Too Human*, trans. R. J. Hollingdale (Cambridge, England: Cambridge University Press, 1996).

ML Richard Wagner, *My Life*, trans. Andrew Gray (Cambridge, England: Cambridge University Press, 1983).

PW Richard Wagner, *Prose Works*, ed. and trans. William Ashton Ellis, 8 vols. (New York: Broude Bros., 1966).

SB Richard Wagner, *Sämtliche Briefe*, ed. Gertrud Strobel, Werner Breig, and others (Leipzig: Deutscher Verlag für Musik, 1967–ongoing).

SE Friedrich Nietzsche, "Schopenhauer as Educator," in *Untimely Meditations*, ed. Daniel Breazeale, trans. R. J. Hollingdale (Cambridge, England: Cambridge University Press, 1997), 125–94.

SLN Friedrich Nietzsche, *Selected Letters*, ed. and trans. Christopher Middleton (Chicago: University of Chicago Press, 1969).

SLW Richard Wagner, *Selected Letters*, ed. and trans. Stewart Spencer and Barry Millington (New York: Norton, 1988).

SW Richard Wagner, *Sämtliche Werke*, ed. C. Dahlhaus, E. Voss, and others (Mainz: B. Schott's Söhne, 1970–ongoing).

WA Friedrich Nietzsche, *The Case of Wagner: A Musician's Problem*, trans. Walter Kaufmann, in *Basic Writings of Nietzsche* (New York: Modern Library, 1968), 609–48.

WB Friedrich Nietzsche, "Richard Wagner in Bayreuth," in *Untimely Meditations*, ed. Daniel Breazeale, trans. R. J. Hollingdale (Cambridge, England: Cambridge University Press, 1997), 195–254.

WWV Arthur Schopenhauer, *The World as Will and Representation*, trans. E. F. J. Payne, 2 vols. (New York: Dover Publications, 1969).

Za Friedrich Nietzsche, *Thus Spoke Zarathustra*, in *The Portable Nietzsche*, ed. and trans. Walter Kaufmann (New York: Viking Press, 1954), 112–439.

NOTES

PREFACE

1. WA 7, 627.
2. Alfred Lorenz, *Das Geheimnis der Form bei Richard Wagner*, 4 vols. (Berlin: M. Hesse, 1924–33).
3. Hans Rudolf Vaget, "'Du warst mein Feind von je': The Beckmesser Controversy Revisited," in *Wagner's Meistersinger: Performance, History, Representation*, ed. Nicholas Vazsonyi (Rochester, NY: University of Rochester Press, 2002), 191.
4. Thomas Mann, "The Sorrows and Grandeur of Richard Wagner," in Thomas Mann, *Pro and contra Wagner*, trans. Allan Blunden (Chicago: University of Chicago Press, 1985), 92.

PROLOGUE

1. "il piano e il forte," Edwin M. Good, "What Did Cristofori Call His Invention?," *Early Music* 33, no. 1 (2005): 95–97.
2. Heinrich von Kleist, "Über das Marionettentheater," in Kleist, *Sämtliche Werke und Briefe*, ed. Ilse-Marie Barth, Klaus Müller-Salget, Stefan Ormanns, and Hinrich C. Seeba, vol. 3 (Frankfurt am Main: Deutscher Klassiker Verlag, 1990), 555–63. In what follows, I quote from this edition. Throughout this book, all translations are mine unless indicated otherwise.
3. Ibid., 556.
4. Ibid.
5. Ibid.
6. Ibid.
7. Ibid., 557.

8. Ibid.
9. Ibid.
10. Heinrich von Kleist, "Von der Überlegung. Eine Paradoxe," in *Sämtliche Werke und Briefe*, vol. 3, 554–55.
11. Kleist, "Über das Marionettentheater," 559–60.
12. Ibid., 563.
13. Ibid., 560.
14. Ibid.
15. Ibid., 559.
16. Ibid., 563.
17. Ibid., Kommentar, 1137.
18. Alessandro Baricco, "Morire dal ridere. Saggio sul carattere trascendentale del teatro comico rossiniano," in Baricco, *Il genio in fuga. Due saggi sul teatro musicale di Gioachino Rossini* (Genoa: il melangolo, 1988), 13–47. I would like to thank Michał Bristiger for this reference.
19. Ibid., 33.
20. Ibid., 34.
21. Ibid., 38, 40–41.
22. Ibid., 42.
23. Ibid., 46.
24. Ibid., 33.
25. Richard Wagner, *Oper und Drama*, ed. Klaus Kropfinger (Stuttgart: Philipp Reclam jun., 1984), 40–48.
26. Stendhal, *De l'amour* (1822) (Paris: Garnier, 1959), chapter 17, n. 1.
27. GT 15, 95, 98.
28. The summary in the following four paragraphs is based on my *Bach's Cycle, Mozart's Arrow: An Essay on the Origins of Musical Modernity* (Berkeley and Los Angeles: University of California Press, 2007), 131–76.
29. Leszek Kołakowski, *Religion: If There Is No God . . . On God, the Devil, Sin and Other Worries of the So-Called Philosophy of Religion* (South Bend, IN: St. Augustine's Press, 2001), 27.
30. Immanuel Kant, "What Is Enlightenment?," in *On History*, ed. Lewis White Beck (Indianapolis: Bobbs-Merrill, 1963), 3.
31. See for example Allen W. Wood, *Kant's Ethical Thought* (Cambridge, England: Cambridge University Press, 1999), 97–110.
32. Ibid., 130–31.
33. Immanuel Kant, "Idea for a Universal History from a Cosmopolitan Point of View," in *On History*, 21.
34. Ibid., 16.
35. Ibid., 20.
36. Ibid., 17–18.
37. Immanuel Kant, "An Old Question Raised Again: Is the Human Race Constantly Progressing?," in *On History*, 147.
38. Kant, "Idea for a Universal History from a Cosmopolitan Point of View," 13.
39. Kant, "What Is Enlightenment?," 4.

40. G. W. F. Hegel, *Elements of the Philosophy of Right*, ed. Allen W. Wood, trans. H. B. Nisbet (Cambridge, England: Cambridge University Press, 1991), section 135, p. 162.

41. Ibid., 162–63.

42. The original inspiration for Hegel's "holism" was likely to have come from his friend Friedrich Hölderlin. See Dieter Henrich, "Hölderlin on Judgment and Being: A Study in the History of the Origins of Idealism," in Henrich, *The Course of Remembrance and Other Essays on Hölderlin*, ed. Eckart Förster (Stanford, CA: Stanford University Press, 1997), 71–89.

43. Georg Wilhelm Friedrich Hegel, *Lectures on the Philosophy of World History. Introduction: Reason in History*, trans. H. B. Nisbet (Cambridge, England: Cambridge University Press, 1975), 54. For a recent version of the early portion of this story see Larry Siedentop, *Inventing the Individual: The Origins of Western Liberalism* (London: Allen Lane, 2013).

44. "The nature of spirit can best be understood if we contrast it with its direct opposite, which is matter. Just as gravity is the substance of matter, so also can it be said that freedom is the substance of spirit." Hegel, *Lectures on the Philosophy of World History. Introduction: Reason in History*, 47.

45. Ibid., 64.

46. Ibid., 28.

47. Hegel, *Elements of the Philosophy of Right*, 21–22.

48. Jürgen Habermas, *The Philosophical Discourse of Modernity: Twelve Lectures*, trans. Frederick Lawrence (Cambridge, MA: MIT Press, 1987), 294–326.

49. On the notion of the Counter-Enlightenment see Isaiah Berlin, "The Counter-Enlightenment," in *The Proper Study of Mankind: An Anthology of Essays*, ed. Henry Hardy and Roger Hausheer (New York: Farrar, Straus and Giroux, 1998), 243–68. It is curious to find this notion used by Nietzsche in a private note made in the period between the summer of 1876 and the end of 1879: "There are shorter and longer arches in the development of culture. To the height of the Enlightenment there corresponds the height of the Counter-Enlightenment [*Gegen-Aufklärung*] in Schopenhauer and Wagner." KSA 8, 382.

50. The understanding of Marx's position presented below is heavily indebted to Leszek Kołakowski, *Main Currents of Marxism: Its Rise, Growth, and Dissolution*, vol. 1 (Oxford: Clarendon Press, 1978).

51. Friedrich Engels, *Ludwig Feuerbach und der Ausgang der klassischen deutschen Philosophie* (Stuttgart: J. H. W. Dietz, 1888), 12–13.

52. Max Horkheimer and Theodor W. Adorno, *Dialectic of Enlightenment: Philosophical Fragments*, trans. Edmund Jephcott (Stanford, CA: Stanford University Press, 2002); see also Habermas, *The Philosophical Discourse of Modernity*.

53. See Hegel, "Part One: Abstract Right," in *Elements of the Philosophy of Right*, 65–132.

54. Kant, "Idea for a Universal History from a Cosmopolitan Point of View," 12.

55. "For my introduction to the philosophy of Hegel I chose his *Philosophy of History*." ML 429–30.

56. Hegel, *Lectures on the Philosophy of World History. Introduction: Reason in History*, 29.

57. The classic studies of nationalism on which the following summary is based include Hans Kohn, *The Idea of Nationalism: A Study in its Origins and Background* (New York: Macmillan, 1946); Elie Kedourie, *Nationalism* (New York: Praeger, 1960); Ernest Gellner, *Nations and Nationalisms* (Oxford: Blackwell, 1983); Benedict Anderson, *Imagined*

Communities: Reflections on the Origin and Spread of Nationalism (London: Verso, 1983); Eric J. Hobsbawm, *Nations and Nationalism since 1780: Programme, Myth, Reality* (Cambridge, England: Cambridge University Press, 1990). I have also benefited from Joep Leersen, *National Thought in Europe: A Cultural History* (Amsterdam: Amsterdam University Press, 2006).

58. On Herder, see in particular Isaiah Berlin, "Herder and the Enlightenment," in *The Proper Study of Mankind: An Anthology of Essays*, ed. Henry Hardy and Roger Hausheer (New York: Farrar, Straus and Giroux, 1998), 359–435. (Berlin's essay originally appeared in 1976.)

59. On the notion of the public sphere see Jürgen Habermas, *The Structural Transformation of the Public Sphere: An Inquiry into a Category of Bourgeois Society* (Cambridge, MA: MIT Press, 1989).

60. Johann Gottlieb Fichte, *Addresses to the German Nation*, ed. Gregory Moore, Cambridge Texts in the History of Political Thought (Cambridge, England: Cambridge University Press, 2008), 103–4.

61. Leersen, *National Thought in Europe*, 113.

62. Fichte, *Addresses to the German Nation*, 111.

63. Ibid.

64. Ibid., 112.

65. Gregory Moore, "Introduction," in Fichte, *Addresses to the German Nation*, xxxiii–xxxiv.

66. On the origins and development of the Aryan-Semitic dualism see Suzanne L. Marchand, *German Orientalism in the Age of Empire: Religion, Race, and Scholarship* (Cambridge, England: Cambridge University Press, 2009), 124–30, 292–332.

67. Fichte, *Addresses to the German Nation*, 48.

68. Ibid., 49.

69. Ibid., 57–58.

70. See ibid., 58; for Heidegger see "'Only a God Can Save Us': *Der Spiegel*'s Interview with Martin Heidegger," in *The Heidegger Controversy: A Critical Reader*, ed. Richard Wolin (Cambridge, MA: MIT Press, 1993), 113.

71. Fichte, *Addresses to the German Nation*, 59.

72. Ibid., 96–97.

73. Ibid., 103.

74. Johann Gottfried von Herder, *Ideas for a Philosophy of the History of Mankind*, book VII, chapter 1, in *J.G. Herder on Social and Political Culture*, ed. and trans. F.M. Barnard (Cambridge, England: Cambridge University Press, 1969), 283–84.

75. Fichte, *Addresses to the German Nation*, 97.

76. Ibid., 103.

77. Leersen, *National Thought in Europe*, 210.

78. Ibid., 207.

79. The classic study of European racism and its intertwining with nationalism is Léon Poliakov, *Le mythe aryen: Essai sur les sources du racisme et des nationalismes*, new ed. (Brussels: Complexe, 1987). See also George L. Mosse, *Towards the Final Solution: A History of European Racism* (New York: Howard Fertig, 1978); Francisco Bethencourt, *Racisms: From the Crusades to the Twentieth Century* (Princeton, NJ: Princeton University Press, 2013).

80. Reinhold Brinkmann, "Wagners Aktualität für den Nationalsozialismus. Fragmente einer Bestandsaufnahme," in *Richard Wagner im Dritten Reich. Ein Schloss Elmau-Symposion*, ed. Saul Friedländer and Jörn Rüsen (Munich: Verlag C. H. Beck, 2000), 124.

81. Saul Friedländer, "Hitler und Wagner," in *Richard Wagner im Dritten Reich*, 170.

82. On the notion of the "bloodlands" see Timothy Snyder, *Bloodlands: Europe between Hitler and Stalin* (New York: Basic Books, 2010).

83. WWV I, xviii, xxi, xxiv.
84. WWV I, paragraph 1, 4.
85. WWV I, paragraph 27, 140.
86. WWV I, paragraph 3, 6.
87. WWV I, paragraph 16, 85.
88. WWV I, paragraph 49, 234.
89. WWV I, paragraph 7, 31.
90. WWV I, paragraph 18, 100.
91. WWV I, paragraph 19, 103.
92. WWV I, paragraph 19, 105.
93. WWV I, paragraph 21, 110.
94. WWV I, paragraph 27, 148.
95. WWV I, paragraph 27, 146–47.
96. WWV I, paragraph 27, 149.
97. WWV I, paragraph 29, 164.
98. WWV I, paragraph 56, 309.
99. WWV I, paragraph 38, 196.
100. WWV I, paragraph 57, 312.
101. WWV I, paragraph 59, 326.
102. WWV I, paragraph 27, 152.
103. WWV I, paragraph 34, 178.
104. WWV I, paragraph 34, 178.
105. WWV I, paragraph 34, 179.
106. WWV I, paragraph 36, 184–85.
107. WWV I, paragraph 38, 197.
108. WWV I, paragraph 38, 196.
109. WWV I, paragraph 51, 252–53.
110. WWV I, paragraph 51, 254.
111. KSA 13, 500.
112. WWV II, chapter 37, 433–34.
113. Karol Berger, *A Theory of Art* (New York: Oxford University Press, 2000), 135–36.
114. WWV I, paragraph 52, 256.
115. WWV I, paragraph 52, 256.
116. WWV I, paragraph 52, 257.
117. WWV I, paragraph 52, 257.
118. WWV I, paragraph 52, 257.
119. WWV I, paragraph 52, 260.

120. Carl Dahlhaus, *Esthetics of Music*, trans. William Austin (Cambridge, England: Cambridge University Press, 1982), 43.

121. WWV I, paragraph 52, 267.
122. WWV I, paragraph 27, 152.
123. WWV I, paragraph 69, 398.
124. WWV I, paragraph 56, 310.
125. WWV I, paragraph 66, 372.
126. WWV I, paragraph 66, 372.
127. WWV I, paragraph 66, 374.
128. See David E. Wellbery, *Schopenhauers Bedeutung für die moderne Literatur* (Munich: Siemens Stiftung, 1998).
129. WWV II, chapter 41, 482.
130. WWV II, chapter 18, 198.
131. WWV II, chapter 19, 205.
132. WWV II, chapter 46, 581.
133. WWV I, paragraph 54, 276.
134. WWV II, chapter 28, 351.
135. CT I, 505.
136. CT I, 506.
137. CT I, 594.
138. See for instance Martin Heidegger, "The Word of Nietzsche: 'God Is Dead,'" in *The Question Concerning Technology and Other Essays*, trans. William Lovitt (New York: Harper and Row, 1977), 53–112.
139. Ibid., 65.

1. THE SECRET OF MUSIC-DRAMATIC FORM

1. Alfred Lorenz, *Das Geheimnis der Form bei Richard Wagner*, 4 vols. (Berlin: M. Hesse, 1924–33).
2. Carl Dahlhaus, *Wagners Konzeption des musikalischen Dramas* (Regensburg: G. Bosse, 1971); reprinted in Dahlhaus, *Gesammelte Schriften*, ed. Hermann Danuser, vol. 7 (Laaber: Laaber-Verlag, 2004), 11–140.
3. Carl Dahlhaus, *Richard Wagner's Music Dramas*, trans. Mary Whittall (Cambridge, England: Cambridge University Press, 1979); "The Dramaturgy of Italian Opera," in *Opera in Theory and Practice, Image and Myth*, ed. Lorenzo Bianconi and Giorgio Pestelli (*The History of Italian Opera*, vol. 6, part II, "Systems") (Chicago: University of Chicago Press, 2003), 73–150; "What Is a Musical Drama?," *Cambridge Opera Journal* 1 (1989): 95–111.
4. Dahlhaus, "What Is a Musical Drama?," 95.
5. Ibid., 96.
6. Peter Szondi, *Theory of Modern Drama: A Critical Edition*, trans. Michael Hays (Minneapolis: University of Minnesota Press, 1986).
7. Dahlhaus, *Wagners Konzeption des musikalischen Dramas, Gesammelte Schriften*, vol. 7, 40.
8. Dahlhaus, *Richard Wagner's Music Dramas*, 16.
9. Dahlhaus, "The Dramaturgy of Italian Opera," 75.
10. Dahlhaus, *Wagners Konzeption des musikalischen Dramas, Gesammelte Schriften*, vol. 7, 15.

11. Dahlhaus, "What Is a Musical Drama?," 95.
12. Ibid., 96.
13. Dahlhaus, *Wagners Konzeption des musikalischen Dramas, Gesammelte Schriften*, vol. 7, 48.
14. Dahlhaus, "The Dramaturgy of Italian Opera," 103.
15. Dahlhaus, "What Is a Musical Drama?," 102.
16. Dahlhaus, *Wagners Konzeption des musikalischen Dramas, Gesammelte Schriften*, vol. 7, 11–12.
17. Ibid., vol. 7, 41–42.
18. CT I, 583.
19. Dahlhaus, *Richard Wagner's Music Dramas*, 34.
20. Dahlhaus, "What Is a Musical Drama?," 104.
21. Ibid., 103–4.
22. See for example Carl Dahlhaus, "Tonalität und Form in Wagners *Ring des Nibelungen*" (originally published in *Archiv für Musikwissenschaft* 40 [1983]: 165–73]), in *Gesammelte Schriften*, vol. 7, 81.
23. Dahlhaus, *Wagners Konzeption des musikalischen Dramas, Gesammelte Schriften*, vol. 7, 59.
24. Ibid.
25. Dahlhaus, "What Is a Musical Drama?," 105.
26. Dahlhaus, *Wagners Konzeption des musikalischen Dramas, Gesammelte Schriften*, vol. 7, 76–77.
27. Carl Dahlhaus, *Nineteenth-Century Music*, trans. J. Bradford Robinson (Berkeley: University of California Press, 1989), 255.
28. Dahlhaus, *Wagners Konzeption des musikalischen Dramas, Gesammelte Schriften*, vol. 7, 28.
29. Carl Dahlhaus, "Entfremdung und Erinnerung. Zu Wagners *Götterdämmerung*," (originally published in C. H. Mahling and S. Wiesmann, eds., *Kongreßbericht Bayreuth 1981* [Kassel: Bärenreiter, 1984], 416–20), in *Gesammelte Schriften*, vol. 7, 490.
30. The concept of the "poetic-musical period" was formulated by Wagner in *Oper und Drama* (Leipzig, 1852), 98–104. Its analytical potential was explored by Alfred Lorenz in the four volumes of his *Das Geheimnis der Form bei Richard Wagner*. For Dahlhaus's understanding of the "poetic-musical period," see in particular his "Wagners Begriff der 'dichterisch-musikalischen Periode,'" in *Beiträge zur Geschichte der Musikanschauung im 19. Jahrhundert*, ed. Walter Salmen (Regensburg: G. Bosse, 1965), 179–87, reprinted in *Gesammelte Schriften*, vol. 7, 274–83; see also Dahlhaus, *Wagners Konzeption des musikalischen Dramas, Gesammelte Schriften*, vol. 7, 88–92. Subsequently the concept was discussed in Peter Petersen, "Die dichterisch-musikalische Periode: Ein verkannter Begriff Richard Wagners," *Hamburger Jahrbuch für Musikwissenschaft* 2 (1977): 105–24; Thomas S. Grey, *Wagner's Musical Prose: Texts and Contexts* (Cambridge, England: Cambridge University Press, 1995), 181–241; Werner Breig, "Wagners Begriff der 'dichterisch-musikalischen Periode,'" in *"Schlagen Sie die Kraft der Reflexion nicht zu gering an." Beiträge zu Richard Wagners Denken, Werk und Wirken*, ed. Klaus Döge (Mainz: Schott, 2002), 158–72; Rainer Kleinertz, "Richard Wagners Begriff der 'dichterisch-musikalischen Periode,'" *Die Musikforschung* 67 (2014): 26–47.

31. Dahlhaus, *Wagners Konzeption des musikalischen Dramas, Gesammelte Schriften*, vol. 7, 97.

32. Ibid., 96–97.

33. See in particular Anthony Newcomb, "The Birth of Music Out of the Spirit of Drama: An Essay in Wagnerian Formal Analysis," *19th-Century Music* 5 (1981–82): 38–66; Anthony Newcomb, "Those Images That Yet Fresh Images Beget," *Journal of Musicology* 2 (1983): 227–45; Anthony Newcomb, "Ritornello Ritornato: A Variety of Wagnerian Refrain Form," in *Analyzing Opera: Verdi and Wagner*, ed. Carolyn Abbate and Roger Parker (Berkeley: University of California Press, 1989), 202–21; Carolyn Abbate, "Opera as Symphony, a Wagnerian Myth," in *Analyzing Opera: Verdi and Wagner*, 92–124; Carolyn Abbate, "Wagner, 'On Modulation,' and *Tristan*," *Cambridge Opera Journal* 1 (1989): 33–58; Carolyn Abbate, "Immortal Voices, Mortal Forms," in *Analytical Strategies and Musical Interpretation: Essays on Nineteenth- and Twentieth-Century Music*, ed. Craig Ayrey (Cambridge, England: Cambridge University Press, 1996). A rare but important exception to this rule is Robert Bailey, "The Structure of the *Ring* and Its Evolution," *19th-Century Music* 1 (1977–78): 48–61. See also William Kinderman, "Dramatic Recapitulation in Wagner's *Götterdämmerung*," *19th-Century Music* 4 (1980–81): 101–12; Patrick McCresless, *Wagner's "Siegfried": Its Drama, History, and Music* (Ann Arbor: University of Michigan Research Press, 1982); William Kinderman, "Wagner's *Parsifal*: Musical Form and the Drama of Redemption," *Journal of Musicology* 4 (1985): 431–46; Warren Darcy, *Wagner's Das Rheingold* (New York: Oxford University Press, 1993); William Kinderman, "Dramatic Recapitulation and Tonal Pairing in Wagner's *Tristan und Isolde* and *Parsifal*," in *The Second Practice of Nineteenth-Century Tonality*, ed. William Kinderman and Harald Krebs (Lincoln: University of Nebraska Press, 1996), 178–214; Werner Breig, "Zur musikalischen Struktur von Wagners 'Ring des Nibelungen,'" in *In den Trümmern der eignen Welt. Richard Wagners "Der Ring des Nibelungen*," ed. Udo Bermbach (Berlin: D. Reimer, 1989), 39–62; Eric Chafe, *The Tragic and the Ecstatic: The Musical Revolution of Wagner's Tristan und Isolde* (New York: Oxford University Press, 2005); Warren Darcy, "In Search of C Major: Tonal Structure and Formal Design in Act III of *Die Meistersinger*," in *Richard Wagner for the New Millennium: Essays in Music and Culture*, ed. Matthew Bribitzer-Stull et al. (New York: Palgrave, 2007), 111–28; William Kinderman, *Wagner's Parsifal* (New York: Oxford University Press, 2013).

34. Dahlhaus, *Richard Wagner's Music Dramas*, 122.

35. Ibid., 124.

36. PW, 5, 305.

37. SLW, 474–75.

38. Hans von Wolzogen, *Thematischer Leitfaden durch die Musik zu Richard Wagners Festspiel "Der Ring des Nibelungen"* (Leipzig: E. Schloemp, 1876); Hans von Wolzogen, *Thematischer Leitfaden durch die Musik zu R. Wagners "Tristan und Isolde"* (Leipzig: F. Reinboth, 1880); Hans von Wolzogen, *Thematischer Leitfaden durch die Musik zu R. Wagners "Parsifal"* (Leipzig: Gebrüder Senf, 1882).

39. For a recent example, see Melanie Wald and Wolfgang Fuhrmann, *Ahnung und Erinnerung. Die Dramaturgie der Leitmotive bei Richard Wagner* (Kassel and Leipzig: Bärenreiter and Henschel, 2013). The most substantial recent discussions of the concept include Thomas S. Grey, *Wagner's Musical Prose: Texts and Contexts* (Cambridge, England: Cambridge University Press, 1995); Thomas S. Grey, "'... wie ein rother Faden': On the Origins of 'Leitmotif' as Critical Construct and Musical Practice," in *Music Theory in the Age of*

Romanticism, ed. Ian Bent (Cambridge, England: Cambridge University Press, 1996), 187–210; Thomas S. Grey, "Leading Motives and Narrative Threads: Notes on the 'Leitfaden' Metaphor and the Critical Pre-History of the Wagnerian 'Leitmotiv,'" in *Musik als Text*, ed. Hermann Danuser and Tobias Plebuch (Kassel: Bärenreiter, 1998), 352–58; Christian Thorau, *Semantisierte Sinnlichkeit. Studien zu Rezeption und Zeichenstruktur der Leitmotivtechnik Richard Wagners* (Stuttgart: Steiner, 2003).

40. On the *solita forma* see Abramo Basevi, *The Operas of Giuseppe Verdi*, trans. Edward Schneider with Stefano Castelvecchi (Chicago and London: University of Chicago Press, 2013) and in particular the editor's exemplary glossary, pp. xxv–xxxvi. The controversy regarding the concept can be followed in Harold S. Powers, "'La solita forma' and 'The Uses of Convention,'" *Acta Musicologica* 59 (1987): 65–90; Roger Parker, "'Insolite forme,' or Basevi's Garden Path," in Roger Parker, *Leonora's Last Act: Essays in Verdian Discourse* (Princeton, NJ: Princeton University Press, 1997), 42–60; Anselm Gerhard, "Konventionen der musikalischen Gestaltung," in *Verdi Handbuch*, ed. Anselm Gerhard and Uwe Schweikert (Stuttgart: Metzler, 2001), 182–97.

41. Theodor W. Adorno, "Wagner's Relevance for Today," in *Essays on Music*, ed. R. D. Leppert (Berkeley: University of California Press, 2002), 588.

42. Ibid., 593.

2. DER RING DES NIBELUNGEN

1. CT I, 965.
2. CT I, 127.
3. "Der Welt Erbe gewänne zu eigen, wer aus dem Rheingold schüfe den Ring, der maßlose Macht ihm verlieh," 600–604. All translations of the *Ring* texts are by Stewart Spencer and come from Stewart Spencer and Barry Millington, eds., *Wagner's Ring of the Nibelung: A Companion* (New York: Thames and Hudson, 1993). The numbers after the original German indicate the measures where the words are found.
4. "Nur wer der Minne Macht versagt, nur wer der Liebe Lust verjagt, nur der erzielt sich den Zauber, zum Reif zu zwingen das Gold," 617–24.
5. "ewige Macht," 796–97.
6. "Wie von einem großen Gedanken ergriffen . . ."
7. "Bang' und Grau'n," 3783–84.
8. "Angst," 3767.
9. "Ihrem Ende eilen sie zu, die so stark im Bestehen sich wähnen," 3807–9.
10. "sie aufzuzehren, . . . statt mit den Blinden blöd zu vergehn . . . Nicht dumm dünkte mich das!," 3816–20.
11. "Traulich und treu ist's nur in der Tiefe: falsch und feig ist, was dort oben sich freut!," 3866–73.
12. "Zwang uns allen schüfe der Zwerg, würd' ihm der Reif nicht entrissen"; "Den Ring muß ich haben!," 1526–27.
13. "die ganze Welt gewinn' ich mit ihm mir zu eigen!," 2411–14.
14. "Die in linder Lüfte Weh'n da oben ihr lebt, lacht und liebt: mit goldner Faust euch Göttliche fang' ich mir alle! Wie ich der Liebe abgesagt, alles, was lebt, soll ihr entsagen! Mit Golde gekirrt, nach Gold nur sollt ihr noch gieren!," 2424–68.

15. "den Schwarzalben verachtet ihr," 2482–83.
16. "dient ihr Männer erst meiner Macht, eure schmucken Frau'n, die mein Frei'n verschmäht, sie zwingt zur Lust sich der Zwerg," 2490–94.
17. "Die dein Speer birgt, sind sie dir Spiel, des berat'nen Bundes Runen?," 1034–37.
18. "Was du bist, bist du nur durch Verträge," 1047–49.
19. "Halt, du Wilder! Nichts durch Gewalt! Verträge schützt meines Speeres Schaft: Spar deines Hammers Heft!," 1164–75.
20. "Eilt mit dem Werk: widerlich ist mir's!," 3317–19.
21. "Tief in der Brust brennt mir die Schmach!," 3345–47.
22. "Noch blitzt ihr Blick zu mir her . . . Seh' ich dies wonnige Auge, von dem Weibe lass' ich nicht ab!," 3398–407.
23. "nun zeug' sein Zauber Tod dem, der ihn trägt!," 3134–36.
24. "Wer ihn besitzt, den sehre die Sorge, und wer ihn nicht hat, den nage der Neid! Jeder giere nach seinem Gut, doch keiner genieße mit Nutzen sein!," 3142–51.
25. "Weiche, Wotan! Weiche! Flieh des Ringes Fluch!," 3461–64.
26. "Alles, was ist, endet! Ein düstrer Tag dämmert den Göttern," 3499–504.
27. "Friedmund darf ich nicht heißen; Frohwalt möcht' ich wohl sein: doch Wehwalt muß ich mich nennen," I.482–89.
28. PW I, 91.
29. This allusion was proposed by Curt Mey, *Die Musik als tönende Weltidee. Versuch einer Metaphysik der Musik. Pt. 1: Die metaphysischen Urgesetze der Melodik* (Leipzig: Herman Seemann Nachfolger, 1901), 223–24. I owe this reference to Christopher Reynolds.
30. "Sie neigt sich zu ihm hinab und lauscht," stage direction at I.170.
31. "haftet sein Blick mit steigender Teilnahme an ihren Mienen," stage direction at I.204.
32. "indem er den Blick mit wachsender Wärme auf sie heftet," stage direction at I.290.
33. "So bleibe hier! Nicht bringst du Unheil dahin, wo Unheil im Hause wohnt," I.343–49.
34. ML 510.
35. Carl Dahlhaus, *Wagners Konzeption des musikalischen Dramas, Gesammelte Schriften*, ed. Hermann Danuser, vol. 7 (Laaber: Laaber-Verlag, 2004), 133–40. See also Carl Dahlhaus, "The Twofold Truth in Wagner's Aesthetics: Nietzsche's Fragment 'On Music and Words,'" in *Between Romanticism and Modernism: Four Studies in the Music of the Later Nineteenth Century*, trans. Mary Whittall and Arnold Whittall (Berkeley and Los Angeles: University of California Press, 1980), 19–39.
36. "dem sollte der Stahl geziemen, wer aus dem Stamm es zög'," I.999–1002.
37. "Da wußt' ich, wer der war, der mich Gramvolle gegrüsst; ich weiß auch, wem allein im Stamm das Schwert er bestimmt," I.1013–22.
38. "der Freund, dem Waffe und Weib bestimmt," I.1058–61.
39. "das so sich plötzlich in voller Deutlichkeit wahrnehmen kann," stage direction at I.1089.
40. "bräutliche Schwester," I.1156.
41. Throughout this book, I shall have a number of occasions to note moments where Wagner anticipates Freud. The composer's "intuitive affinity" with the psychoanalyst has been noted by Thomas Mann in his great 1933 essay "The Sorrows and Grandeur of Richard

Wagner," in Mann, *Pro and contra Wagner*, trans. Allan Blunden (Chicago: University of Chicago Press, 1985), 98–99.

42. "Du bist der Lenz, nach dem ich verlangte in frostigen Winters Frist," I.1170–76.
43. "Wonne," I.1222.
44. "An dem Blick erkannt' ihn sein Kind," I.1336–38.
45. "Nenne mich du, wie du liebst, daß ich heiße: den Namen nehm' ich von dir," I.1354–59.
46. "außer sich," stage direction at I.1368.
47. "Lebhafter," tempo indication at I.1368.
48. "Siegmund heiß' ich und Siegmund bin ich!," I.1380–83.
49. "Sehr schnell," tempo indication at I.1378.
50. "Er zieht mit einem gewaltigen Zuck das Schwert aus dem Stamme und zeigt es der vor Staunen und Entzücken erfaßten Sieglinde," I.1437–43.
51. "Heiligster Minne höchste Not, . . . brennt mir hell in der Brust, drängt zu Tat und Tod: Nothung! . . . so nenn' ich dich Schwert," I.1400–22.
52. "Er zieht sie mit wütender Glut an sich. Der Vorhang fällt schnell," I.1498.
53. Cf. the discussion of some of Wagner's pronouncements to this effect in Christopher A. Reynolds, *Wagner, Schumann, and the Lessons of Beethoven's Ninth* (Berkeley: University of California Press, 2015), 163–67.
54. SW 29/1, 103.
55. SW 29/1, 112.
56. "wütet in Waffen die Welt," II.1682–83.
57. "wo kühn Kräfte sich regen, da rat' ich offen zum Krieg," II.212–16.
58. "Stets Gewohntes nur magst du verstehn: doch was noch nie sich traf, danach trachtet mein Sinn," II.351–56.
59. "Not tut ein Held, der ledig göttlichen Schutzes, sich löse vom Göttergesetz; so nur taugt er zu wirken die Tat, die, wie Not sie den Göttern, dem Gott doch zu wirken verwehrt," II.359–72.
60. "denn selbst muß der Freie sich schaffen," II.862–65.
61. "Nur eines will ich noch: das Ende . . . !," II.938–46.
62. "Sehr feierlich und gemessen."
63. "Sehr lebhaft."
64. The resemblance has also been noted in Deryck Cooke, "Wagner's Musical Language," in *The Wagner Companion*, ed. P. Burbidge and R. Sutton (Cambridge, England: Cambridge University Press, 1979), 227–28. Wagner's involvement with Beethoven's music—included, but not limited to, the late string quartets—is the subject of Klaus Kropfinger, *Wagner and Beethoven* (Cambridge, England: Cambridge University Press, 1991).
65. "zu ihnen folg' ich dir nicht!," II.1617–19.
66. "Ha, Schande ihm, der das Schwert mir schuf . . . ! Muß ich denn fallen, nicht fahr' ich nach Walhall: Hella halte mich fest!," II.1691–701.
67. "erschüttert," II.1706.
68. "ewige Wonne," II.1708–9.
69. "das arme Weib, das müd' und harmvoll matt auf dem Schoße dir hängt," II.1710–14.
70. "kalt und hart," II.1721.
71. "Im heftigsten Sturme des Mitgefühles," stage direction at II.1776.

72. "Sieglinde lebe, und Siegmund lebe mit ihr!," II.1782–89.
73. "Ich sehe die Not, die das Herz dir zernagt; ich fühle des Helden heiligen Harm!," II.1738–42.
74. "Knie vor Frikka!," II.2025–26.
75. "den hehrsten Helden der Welt hegst du, o Weib, im schirmenden Schoß!," III.496–503.
76. "der neu gefügt das Schwert einst schwingt, den Namen nehm' er von mir: Siegfried erfreu' sich des Siegs!," III.518–31.
77. CT I, 515.
78. "Der diese Liebe mir ins Herz gelegt, dem Willen, der dem Wälsung mich gesellt, ihm innig vertraut, trotzt' ich deinem Gebot," III.1185–202.
79. "Du folgtest selig der Liebe Macht; folge nun dem, den du lieben mußt!," III.1324–32.
80. "kühnes, herrliches Kind," III.1499–501.
81. "ein bräutliches Feuer," III.1534–35.
82. "freier als ich, der Gott!," III.1554–56.
83. "Die Schlafende schütze mit scheuchenden Schrekken, daß nur ein furchtlos freiester Held hier auf dem Felsen einst mich fänd'!," III.1437–45.
84. "Dem glücklichern Manne glänze sein Stern," III.1602–4.
85. "Wer meines Speeres Spitze fürchtet, durchschreite das Feuer nie!," III.1693–700.
86. For the possible allusion here to Schumann, *Kinderscenen*, "Kind im Einschlummern," see Carl Van Vechten, "Notes on Gluck's Armide," *Musical Quarterly* 3 (1917): 539.
87. "Er blickt schmerzlich auf Brünnhilde zurück," stage direction at III.1708.
88. Cf. *Opera and Drama*, PW II, 224–25. On the possible influence of Rousseau, see Thomas S. Grey, *Wagner's Musical Prose: Texts and Contexts* (Cambridge, England: Cambridge University Press, 1995), 259–62.
89. "Schwarz-Alberich," I.1440–41.
90. "Licht-Alberich," I.1535.
91. "Nur wer das Fürchten nie erfuhr, schmiedet Nothung neu," I.1880–85.
92. "der das Fürchten nicht gelernt," I.1894–96.
93. "Kräftig, doch nicht zu schnell."
94. "Schwer und kräftig, nicht zu schnell."
95. "Belebt."
96. "immer bewegter," I.2816.
97. "Sehr schnell und noch mehr beschleunigend," I.2941.
98. "So schnell wie möglich," I.2953.
99. "düster brütend."
100. "Zu schauen kam ich, nicht zu schaffen," II.191–95.
101. "Helden nur können mir frommen," II.354–57.
102. "Tand," II.380.
103. "Ich lieg' und besitz':—laßt mich schlafen!," II.440–48.
104. "Daß ich nun Kunde gewänne," III.180–82.
105. "wie zu hemmen ein rollendes Rad?," III.214–16.
106. "wie besiegt die Sorge der Gott?," III.331–34.
107. "Um der Götter Ende grämt mich die Angst nicht, seit mein Wunsch es will," III.360–65.
108. "froh und freudig," III.371–72.

109. "wirkt ... erlösende Weltentat," III.410–16.
110. "Was Jene auch wirken, dem ewig Jungen weicht in Wonne der Gott," III.423–28.
111. "O Heil der Mutter, die mich/dich gebar! Heil der Erde, die mich/dich genährt!"
112. "Selige Öde auf wonniger Höh'!," III.857–60.
113. "Das ist kein Mann!," III.926.
114. "Brennender Zauber," III.930–31.
115. "feurige Angst," III.932–33.
116. "Sehrendes Sehnen zehrt meine Sinne," III.972–75.
117. "Im Schlafe liegt eine Frau,—die hat ihn das Fürchten gelehrt," III.988–97.
118. CT I, 137.
119. "Sonne," "Licht," "leuchtender Tag."
120. "Lang war mein schlaf," III.1102–3.
121. "Götter," "Welt," "prangende Erde."
122. "Heil der Erde, die mich/dich genährt!," III.1135–37.
123. "Du selbst bin ich, wenn du mich ... liebst," III.1189–93.
124. "O Weib! Jetzt lösche den Brand!," III.1352–54.
125. "ohne Trutz ein trauriges Weib!," III.1335–37.
126. "maidlichen Leibe ... die Wehr!," III.1328–30.
127. "ein scharfes Schwert schnitt ... entzwei," III.1326–28.
128. "Wehe der Schmach, der schmählichen Not!," III.1373–75.
129. "Noch bist du mir die träumende Maid; Brünnhildes Schlaf brach ich noch nicht," III.1390–97.
130. "Ewig war ich, ewig bin ich," III.1486–89 (I have modified the translation here).
131. "So berühre mich nicht," III.1533–34.
132. "Sie umfaßt ihn heftig," stage direction at III.1685.
133. "in freudigem Schreck," stage direction at III.1686.
134. "kehrt mir zurück mein kühner Mut; und das Fürchten, ... das ich nie gelernt, ... ich ... vergaß es nun ganz," III.1693–704.
135. "lachend laß uns verderben," III.1717.
136. "leuchtende Liebe, lachender Tod!," III.1761–77.
137. George Bernard Shaw, *The Perfect Wagnerite: a Commentary on the Niblung's Ring*, 4th ed. (London: Constable, 1923).
138. "Wollen wir spinnen und singen, woran spannst du das Seil?," 38–42.
139. "So gut und schlimm es geh', schling' ich das Seil, und singe," 43–47.
140. "Wisset ihr noch? So windet von Neuem das Seil; von Norden wieder werf' ich's dir nach. Spinne, Schwester, und singe!," 182–92.
141. "Wollt ihr wissen wann das wird? Schwinget, Schwestern, das Seil!," 250–57.
142. "Singe, Schwester, dir werf' ich's zu: weißt du wie das wird?," 105–9 and 147–51.
143. "Weißt du, was aus ihm ward?," 204–6.
144. "Weißt du was aus ihm wird?," 235–37.
145. "weißt du was aus ihm wird?," 270–71.
146. "Weißt du was daraus wird?," 280–81.
147. "Mein Schlaf ist Träumen, mein Träumen Sinnen, mein Sinnen Walten des Wissens. Doch, wenn ich schlafe, wachen die Nornen: sie weben das Seil, und spinnen fromm, was ich weiß," *Siegfried*, III.190–204.

148. "der ewigen Götter Ende," 176–78.
149. "Tagesgrauen," "Sonnenaufgang," and "Voller Tag."
150. "Hehre Geschlechter."
151. "heilige Götter."
152. "teurer Helde," 364–65.
153. "Wunderfrau," 420–21.
154. "Was Götter mich wiesen," 380–82.
155. "Zu neuen Taten," 362–63.
156. "Weidet eu'r Aug' an dem weihvollen Paar," 602–5.
157. "dünkt er euch niedrig, ihr dient ihm doch, des Niblungen Sohn," I.917–23.
158. CT I, 466.
159. "des tiefen Rheines Töchtern gäbe den Ring sie wieder zurück, von des Fluches Last erlöst wär' Gott und Welt!," I.1331–43.
160. "Siegfrieds Liebespfand," I.1412–14.
161. "mehr als der Ewigen Ruhm," I.1441–43.
162. "die Liebe ließe ich nie," I.1482–85.
163. *Das Rheingold*, 617–24.
164. *Die Walküre*, I.1400–1408.
165. "An dem furchtlosen Helden erlahmt selbst mein Fluch: denn nicht kennt er des Ringes Wert, zu nichts nützt er die neidlichste Macht," II.119–23.
166. Richard Wagner, "A Retrospect of the Stage-Festivals of 1876," PW 6, 106.
167. "Schläfst du, Hagen, mein Sohn?," II.43–44.
168. "Schwörst du mir's, Hagen, mein Sohn?," II.161–63.
169. "Schwörst du mir's, Hagen, mein Held?," II.167–68.
170. "sitzt schlafend," II.30.
171. "immer fort zu schlafen scheint, obwohl er die Augen starr offen hat," II.49.
172. "Von hier an bedeckt ein immer finsterer werdender Schatten wieder Alberich. Zugleich beginnt das erste Tagesgrauen," II.163.
173. "Wie mit dem Folgenden Alberichs Gestalt immer mehr dem Blicke entschwindet, wird auch seine Stimme immer unvernehmbarer," stage direction at II.169.
174. "Ich—und du!," II.106.
175. "des Niblungen Sohn," I.920–23.
176. "Lachend, in liebender Brunst, brennt er lebend dahin," II.123–26.
177. "Ein weises Weib," II.137–38.
178. "verloren ging' mir das Gold, keine List erlangte es je," II.143–46.
179. "Dieser war es, der mir den Ring entriß: Siegfried, der trugvolle Dieb!," II.909–14.
180. "Er zwang mir Lust und Liebe ab," II.1034–39.
181. "klagte das Weib dort wahr," II.1171–73.
182. "denn . . . schwur Meineid jetzt dieser Mann," II.1207–13.
183. "Meineid rächt' ich!," III.855–56.
184. "Eid, und Meineid, müssige Acht!," II.1410–12.
185. "Wer bietet mir nun das Schwert, mit dem ich die Bande zerschnitt?," II.1383–88.
186. "Und dort trifft ihn mein Speer!," II.1460–62.
187. "dir hilft nur Siegfrieds Tod!," II.1515–17.
188. "Uns allen frommt sein Tod," II.1582–84.

189. "wie hell du einsten strahltes," III.90-93; "wie froh du dann strahltest," III.139-42.
190. CT I, 653.
191. "in des Urgesetzes Seil!," III.360-63.
192. "Der Welt Erbe gewänne mir ein Ring: für der Minne Gunst miss' ich ihn gern," III.384-88.
193. "so werf' ich sie weit von mir!," III.400-402.
194. "dem Toren," III.405.
195. "stößt seinen Speer in Siegfried's Rücken," stage direction at III.842.
196. "Süßes Vergehen,—seliges Grauen! Brünnhild' bietet mir Gruß! –," III.907-12.
197. CT II, 417-18.
198. CT I, 458.
199. On Brünnhilde's laughter, see Carolyn Abbate, *Unsung Voices: Opera and Musical Narrative in the Nineteenth Century* (Princeton, NJ: Princeton University Press, 1991), 206-49.
200. "redlichen Rat," III.1390-91.
201. "Männer und Frauen, mit Lichtern und Feuerbränden," stage direction at III.1052.
202. "hebt sich drohend empor," stage direction at III.1157.
203. "mit feierlicher Erhabenheit," stage direction at III.1223.
204. "Ihre Mienen nehmen eine immer sanftere Verklärung an," stage direction at III.1267.
205. "der Reinste," III.1274-75.
206. "trog keiner wie er! –," III.1300-1302.
207. "Wißt ihr, wie das ward? –," III.1305-7.
208. "Oh, ihr, der Eide ewige Hütter! . . . erschaut eure ewige Schuld!," III.1309-19.
209. "Durch seine tapferste Tat, dir so tauglich erwünscht, weihest du den, der sie gewirkt, dem Fluche dem du verfielest," III.1324-32.
210. "mich mußte der Reinste verraten, daß wissend würde ein Weib! –," III.1333-37.
211. "Weiß ich nun, was dir frommt? –," III.1339-40.
212. "Alles, Alles, Alles weiß ich,—Alles ward mir nun frei!," III.1342-46.
213. "Ruhe, ruhe, du Gott!," III.1359-63.
214. "Das Feuer, das mich verbrennt, rein'ge vom Fluche den Ring! Ihr in der Flut, löset ihn auf," III.1398-405.
215. "So werf' ich den Brand in Walhall's prangende Burg," III.1443-48.
216. "Siegfried! Siegfried! Sieh! Selig grüßt dich dein Weib," III.1495-99.
217. PW I, 57-58.
218. PW I, 58.
219. The relevant documents for the 1848-53 period are edited in Gabriele E. Meyer, ed., *Texte zum Bühnenfestspiel "Der Ring des Nibelungen" 1 (1848-1853)*, SW 29, II A (Mainz: Schott, 2012); for *Die Nibelungensage (Mÿthus)* see pp. 19-29.
220. The stages of November-December 1848 are presented in ibid., 50-112.
221. "Freue dich des freiesten Helden," ibid., 110; trans. Spencer p. 361.
222. "What relation bear republican endeavours to the kingship?," PW IV, 137.
223. PW IV, 137.
224. PW IV, 141, 142.
225. PW IV, 138.

226. PW IV, 139.
227. SLW, 140–41.
228. "Machtlos scheidet, die die Schuld nun meidet." Meyer, ed., *Texte zum Bühnenfestspiel "Der Ring des Nibelungen"* 1 *(1848–1853)*, 110; Spencer and Millington, eds., *Wagner's Ring of the Nibelung: A Companion*, 361–62.
229. "The Revolution," PW VIII, 235–36, 237–38.
230. ML 373.
231. Meyer, ed., *Texte zum Bühnenfestspiel "Der Ring des Nibelungen"* 1 *(1848–1853)*, 131–209.
232. "ohne Walter die Welt." Ibid., 208; Spencer and Millington, eds., *Wagner's Ring of the Nibelung: A Companion*, 362.
233. "Nicht Gut, nicht Gold, noch göttliche Pracht; . . . nicht trüber Verträge trügende Bund, noch heuchelnder Sitte hartes Gesetz; selig in Lust und Leid läßt—die Liebe nur sein! –." Meyer, ed., *Texte zum Bühnenfestspiel "Der Ring des Nibelungen"* 1 *(1848–1853)*, 208; Spencer and Millington, eds., *Wagner's Ring of the Nibelung: A Companion*, 362–63.
234. This stage is reflected upon in Wagner's letter of August 23, 1856, to August Röckel; see SLW 357–58.
235. "nach dem wunsch- und wahnlos heiligstem Wahlland, . . . zieht nun die Wissende hin"; "Trauernder Liebe tiefstes Leiden schloß die Augen mir auf: enden sah ich die Welt. –." Meyer, ed., *Texte zum Bühnenfestspiel "Der Ring des Nibelungen"* 1 *(1848–1853)*, 208; Spencer and Millington, eds., *Wagner's Ring of the Nibelung: A Companion*, 363.
236. Quoted from Breig and Fladt, eds., *Dokumente zur Entstehungsgeschichte des Bühnenfestspiels Der Ring des Nibelungen*, SW 29/1, 114; translation mine.
237. SLW 357–58.
238. CT I, 842.
239. SLW 281.
240. CT I, 515.
241. CT I, 515.
242. On the significance of Db in the cycle, see Alfred Lorenz, *Das Geheimnis der Form bei Richard Wagner*, vol. 1 (Berlin: M. Hesse, 1924), 47; and Robert Bailey, "The Structure of the *Ring* and Its Evolution," *19th-Century Music* 1 (1977–78): 54.
243. Karl Marx and Friedrich Engels, *Manifesto of the Communist Party*, trans. Samuel Moore (Chicago: Charles H. Kerr, 1910), 16.
244. Ibid., 29.
245. Ibid., 15.
246. Ibid., 16.
247. Ibid., 42.
248. Ibid., 31.
249. Ibid., 41.
250. Ibid., 42.
251. Ibid., 41.
252. Ibid., 33.
253. Ibid., 42.
254. See Udo Bermbach, *Der Wahn des Gesamtkustwerks. Richard Wagners politisch-ästhetische Utopie*, 2nd ed. (Stuttgart and Weimar: J. B. Metzler, 2004), 28 and 277. Bermbach's book is the most thorough recent analysis of Wagner's political-aesthetic outlook. The question of whether Wagner ever read Marx, or heard of his ideas, is also discussed in Martin Gregor-Dellin, *Richard Wagner: His Life, His Work, His Century*, trans. J. Maxwell

Brownjohn (New York: Harcourt Brace Jovanovich, 1983), 189–90. On Wagner's relationship to the whole spectrum of communist ideas see Eckart Kröplin, *Richard Wagner und der Kommunismus. Studie zu einem verdrängten Thema*, Wagner in der Discussion, vol. 9 (Würzburg: Königshausen and Neumann, 2013).

255. PW IV, 139.
256. PW I, 27–28.
257. Quoted from Breig and Fladt, eds., *Dokumente zur Entstehungsgeschichte des Bühnenfestspiels Der Ring des Nibelungen*, SW 29/1, 30.
258. ML 386.
259. Lewis Namier, *1848: The Revolution of the Intellectuals* (Garden City, NY: Doubleday, 1964).
260. PW I, 41.
261. PW I, 42.
262. PW I, 53.
263. PW I, 54.
264. "mit blendendem Leuchten eine Regenbogen-Brücke"; "die jetzt im Glanze der Abendsonne strahlt," stage direction at 3711.
265. Joachim Bergfeld, ed., *The Diary of Richard Wagner 1865–1882: The Brown Book*, trans. George Bird (Cambridge, England: Cambridge University Press, 1980), 97.
266. SB 3, 424ff.
267. Quoted from Breig and Fladt, eds., *Dokumente zur Entstehungsgeschichte des Bühnenfestspiels Der Ring des Nibelungen*, SW 29/1, 95.
268. SLW 219.
269. CT I, 258.
270. Quoted from Breig and Fladt, eds., *Dokumente zur Entstehungsgeschichte des Bühnenfestspiels Der Ring des Nibelungen*, SW 29/1, 54.
271. SLW 233–34.
272. GS 6, 230.
273. Joep Leersen, *National Thought in Europe: A Cultural History* (Amsterdam: Amsterdam University Press, 2006), 198–99.
274. Friedrich Theodor Vischer, "Vorschlag zu einer Oper," quoted from Breig and Fladt, eds., *Dokumente zur Entstehungsgeschichte des Bühnenfestspiels Der Ring des Nibelungen*, SW 29/1, 20. On the question of whether Wagner knew Vischer's text see Ernest H. Newman, *The Life of Richard Wagner* (Cambridge, England: Cambridge University Press, 1946), vol. 2, 158, 170, 231.
275. Quoted from Breig and Fladt, eds., *Dokumente zur Entstehungsgeschichte des Bühnenfestspiels Der Ring des Nibelungen*, SW 29/1, 113.
276. PW I, 53–54.
277. ML 210.
278. CT I, 861.
279. CT II, 753.
280. Alain Badiou, *Five Lessons on Wagner*, trans. Susan Spitzer (London: Verso, 2010), xii, 6.
281. Quoted from Breig and Fladt, eds., *Dokumente zur Entstehungsgeschichte des Bühnenfestspiels Der Ring des Nibelungen*, SW 29/1, 114.

282. Ibid., 141.
283. SLW 216–17; SB 3, 424ff.

3. TRISTAN UND ISOLDE

1. SB IX, 209.
2. SB VIII, 153.
3. CT II, 286.
4. For the Day motif, see for instance Ernest Newman, *The Wagner Operas* (New York: Alfred A. Knopf, 1949), 241.
5. "Herz an Herz dir, Mund an Mund," II.1174–84.
6. "Nacht der Liebe," II.1125–29.
7. "sink hernieder," II.1123–27.
8. "gieb Vergessen, daß ich lebe," II.1128–33.
9. "löse von der Welt mich los!," II.1136–38.
10. "selbst . . . bin ich die Welt," II.1188–93.
11. "Niewiedererwachens . . . Wunsch," II.1202–10.
12. CT II, 206.
13. "Laß mich sterben!," II.1271–72.
14. "Laß den Tag dem Tode weichen!," II.1284–87.
15. "Tag und Tod, mit gleichen Streichen, sollten unsre Lieb' erreichen?," II.1288–94.
16. "Unsre Liebe? . . . Welches Todes Streichen könnte je sie weichen?," II.1295–304.
17. "wie könnte die Liebe . . . , die ewig lebende mit mir enden?," II.1316–21.
18. "Doch, stürbe nie seine Liebe, wie stürbe dann Tristan seiner Liebe?," II.1322–32.
19. "der Liebe Bund," II.1352–53.
20. "Dies süße Wörtlein: und," II.1345–49.
21. "Was stürbe dem Tod, als was uns stört, was Tristan wehrt, Isolde immer zu lieben . . . ?," II.1358–63.
22. "wie anders als mit Isoldes eignem Leben wär' Tristan der Tod gegeben?," II.1368–72.
23. "So starben/stürben wir, um ungetrennt, ewig einig ohne End', ohn' Erwachen, ohn' Erbangen, namenlos in Lieb' umfangen, ganz uns selbst gegeben, der Liebe nur zu leben!," II.1376–424.
24. "Der öde Tag zum letzten Mal!," II.1673–76.
25. The traditional name of this section, "Isolde's *Liebestod*," is of course equally appropriate and seems to have been used by Wagner, too. See the note in Cosima's diary for September 14, 1882: "When there is mention on the train of the Wagnerites' preference for *T. und I.* even over *Parsifal*, R. says: 'Oh, what do they know? One might say that Kundry already experienced Isolde's *Liebestod* a hundred times in her various reincarnations,'" CT II, 910.
26. "daraus die Mutter mich entsandt," II.1934–36.
27. "ihr Liebesberge," II.1945–46.
28. "wie flöh' ich wohl das Land, das alle Welt umspannt?," II.1978–81.
29. The documentation is collected in Gabriele E. Meyer and Egon Voss, eds., *Dokumente und Texte zu "Tristan und Isolde,"* SW 27 (Mainz: Schott, 2008).
30. SB 11, 120.

31. SB 11, 161.
32. SB 11, 168.
33. "Mild und leise," III.1621.
34. "In dem wogenden Schwall, in dem tönenden Schall, in des Welt-Atems wehendem All-, ertrinken, versinken-, unbewußt-, höchste Lust!," III.1677-91.
35. WWV II, chapter 48, 611.
36. WWV I, paragraph 39, 205.
37. See for example the letter to Karl Eckert, October 4, 1875, and especially the letter to Franz Betz, October 5, 1875, both in Meyer and Voss, eds., *Dokumente und Texte zu "Tristan und Isolde,"* SW 27, 189.
38. "Tagsgespenster! Morgenträume!- täuschend und wüst-! Entschwebt! Entweicht!," II.1723-27.
39. CT II, 767.
40. "Dies wundervolle Weib," II.1810-11.
41. "wer [durft'] mit Stolze sein es nennen, ohne selig sich zu preisen?," II.1815-19.
42. "Der mein Wille nie zu nahen wagte, der mein Wunsch ehrfurchtscheu entsagte," II.1819-23.
43. "der treu'ste aller Treuen," II.1698-700.
44. "der freundlichste der Freunde," II.1702-4.
45. "entsandt, dem König die Braut zu frein," II.1803-5.
46. "Wie lachend sie mir Lieder singen, wohl könnt' auch ich erwidern!," I.604-8.
47. "Fluch dir, Verruchter! Fluch deinem Haupt! Rache! Tod! Tod uns beiden!," I.844-62.
48. "Von seinem Lager blickt' er her, nicht auf das Schwert, nicht auf die Hand,- er sah mir in die Augen. Seines Elendes jammerte mich;- das Schwert—ich ließ es fallen! Die Morold schlug, die Wunde, sie heilt' ich, daß er gesunde und heim nach Hause kehre -, mit dem Blick mich nicht mehr beschwere!," I.658-88.
49. GT 126-27.
50. SLW 452.
51. ML 588-89. The passage concerns the period of April through June 1859 in Lucerne.
52. "Öd' und leer das Meer!"
53. "die alte Weise," III.159-60.
54. "wo ich von je gewesen, wohin auf je ich geh'," III.306-10.
55. "weiten Reich der Weltennacht," III.311-14.
56. "göttlich ew'ges Urvergessen," III.319-22.
57. "in der einzig zu vergehen, zu entschwinden," III.388-91.
58. "Verfluchter Tag mit deinem Schein!," III.405-9.
59. "Noch ist kein Schiff zu sehn!," III.632-34.
60. WB 232.
61. "Durch Abendwehen drang sie bang, als einst dem Kind des Vaters Tod verkündet," III.653-60.
62. See Carolyn Abbate, *Unsung Voices: Opera and Musical Narrative in the Nineteenth Century* (Princeton, NJ: Princeton University Press, 1991), 131-34.
63. "Klage Klang," III.649-50.
64. "sehnsuchtbang," III.676-77.

65. "zu welchem Los erkoren, ich damals wohl geboren?," III.683–87.
66. "Die alte Weise sagt mir's wieder:—mich sehnen—und sterben!," III.691–98.
67. "Nein! Ach nein! So heißt sie nicht!," III.700–702.
68. "Im Sterben mich zu sehnen, vor Sehnsucht nicht zu sterben!," III.706–13.
69. "Die nie erstirbt, sehnend nun ruft um Sterbens Ruh' sie der fernen Ärztin zu," III.719–27.
70. "Sehnsucht klagend," III.736–37.
71. "Die Wunde, die sie heilend schloß, riß mit dem Schwert sie wieder los," III.747–51.
72. "Gifttrank," III.755.
73. "daß nie ich sollte sterben, mich ew'ger Qual vererben!," III.761–66.
74. "Kein Heil nun kann, kein süßer Tod je mich befrein von der Sehnsucht Not," III.775–80.
75. "Sühneeid," I.1721.
76. "Ew'ger Trauer einz'ger Trost: Vergessens güt'ger Trank,- dich trink' ich sonder Wank!," I.1740–49.
77. "Den furchtbaren Trank . . . ich selbst . . . , ich hab' ihn gebraut!," III.805–11.
78. "Aus Vaters Not und Mutter-Weh,—aus Liebestränen eh und je,—aus Lachen und Weinen, Wonnen und Wunden hab' ich des Trankes Gifte gefunden!," III.813–25.
79. "Den ich gebraut,—. . . den Wonne schlürfend je ich genossen,—verflucht sei, furchtbarer Trank! Verflucht, wer dich gebraut!," III.826–40.
80. Za II, "On redemption," 251; Za III, "On old and new tablets," 310.
81. "Das Schiff?—Siehst du's noch nicht?," III.883–87.
82. "Sehr ruhig und nicht schleppend."
83. "Sie lächelt mir Trost und süße Ruh', sie führt mir letzte Labung zu," III.939–49.
84. "Du mußt es sehen!," III.989–90.
85. "Sehr lebhaft."
86. Cf. Joseph Kerman, "*Tristan und Isolde*: The Prelude and the Play," in *Write All These Down: Essays on Music* (Berkeley: University of California Press, 1994), 335–49.
87. "Ich trink' sie dir!," I.1754–56.
88. "Tristan! Isolde! Treuloser Holder!," I.1794–97.
89. "Beide . . . blicken sich mit höchster Aufregung, doch mit starrer Haltung, unverwandt in die Augen, in deren Ausdruck der Todestrotz bald der Liebesglut weicht," I.1761–74.
90. According to Thomas Grey, the "desire" and "glance" motives of the Introduction have been distinguished, though perhaps not so named, by *Tristan* analysts and commentators right from the beginning, already in the 1860 series of articles in the *Neue Zeitschrift für Music* by a Wagner disciple, Wendelin Weissheimer, "presumably . . . the first *Tristan* 'analysis' of any kind." Thomas Grey, "Magnificent Obsession: *Tristan und Isolde* as the Object of Musical Analysis," in *Music, Theatre and Politics in Germany 1848 to the Third Reich*, ed. Nikolaus Bacht (Aldershot, England: Ashgate, 2006), 54ff.
91. "den unerforschlich tief geheimnisvollen Grund."
92. "O König, . . . was du frägst, das kannst du nie erfahren."
93. CT I, 592.
94. John Deathridge, Martin Geck, and Egon Voss, eds., *Wagner Werk-Verzeichnis (WWV): Verzeichnis der musikalischen Werke Richard Wagners und ihrer Quellen* (Mainz: Schott, 1986), 427, 445.

95. Letter to Wendelin Weißheimer, SLW 547ff. See also the letter to Cosima von Bülow, February 2, 1863, SB 15, 72.
96. Meyer and Voss, eds., *Dokumente und Texte zu "Tristan und Isolde,"* SW 27, 145.
97. "Isolde sinkt, wie verklärt, . . . sanft auf Tristans Leiche."
98. "Marke segnet die Leichen."
99. See in particular Carl Dahlhaus, "Entfremdung und Erinnerung. Zu Wagners *Götterdämmerung,"* in *Kongreßbericht Bayreuth 1981*, ed. C. H. Mahling and S. Wiesmann (Kassel: Bärenreiter, 1984), 416–20; reprinted in Dahlhaus, *Gesammelte Schriften*, ed. Hermann Danuser, vol. 7 (Laaber: Laaber-Verlag, 2004), 486–92.
100. See Saint Augustine, *Confessions*, trans. William Watts (Cambridge, MA: Harvard University Press, 1963), vol. 2, book 11, chapter 28, 276–79; WWV, paragraph 52, I, 255–67; Edmund Husserl, *Vorlesungen zur Phänomenologie des inneren Zeitbewußtseins*, ed. Martin Heidegger, *Gesammelte Werke*, vol. 10 (The Hague: Nijhoff, 1966), chapter 2.
101. WWV II, chapter 42, 513–14.
102. Cf. George L. Mosse, *The Fascist Revolution: Toward a General Theory of Fascism* (New York: Howard Fertig, 1999).
103. "jauchzenden Eil'," III.1278–79.
104. "Heia, mein Blut! Lustig nun fließe!," III.1267–70.
105. SLW 323. It is in the same letter that he tells Liszt of his recent discovery of Schopenhauer's philosophy.
106. CT I, 208.
107. "des Weltwerdens Walterin," II.386–88.
108. "Leben und Tod sind untertan ihr, die sie webt aus Lust und Leid," II.389–97.
109. "O König, . . . was du frägst, das kannst du nie erfahren," II.1893–904.
110. "Laß die Frage: du kannst's doch nie erfahren," III.128–31.
111. ML 510.
112. See Richard Wagner, letter to Breitkopf and Härtel, November 26, 1858, SB 10, 157.
113. Cf. Arthur Schopenhauer, *Der handschriftliche Nachlaß*, vol. 5, ed. Arthur Hübscher (Frankfurt: W. Kramer, 1968), 437.
114. SLW 432.
115. "Ungeminnt den hehrsten Mann stets mir nah zu sehen -!," I.961–73.
116. Joseph Kerman, "Opera as Symphonic Poem," in *Opera as Drama* (Berkeley and Los Angeles: University of California Press, 1988), 158–77.
117. Michael Tanner, "The Passion of Passion," in *Wagner* (Princeton, NJ: Princeton University Press, 1996), 140–55; Roger Scruton, *Death-Devoted Heart: Sex and the Sacred in Wagner's Tristan and Isolde* (New York: Oxford University Press, 2004).
118. Deathridge, Geck, and Voss, eds., *Wagner Werk-Verzeichnis (WWV)*, 426. Since *drama* comes from the Greek for "doing" or "action," it would make sense in this context to translate *Handlung* as "drama."
119. CT I, 676.
120. Kerman, "Opera as Symphonic Poem," 160.
121. Ibid., 161.
122. Ibid., 160.
123. Ibid.

124. Ibid., 161.
125. Ibid., 166.
126. Ibid., 168.
127. Ibid.
128. CT II, 855.
129. CT II, 861.
130. Kerman, "Opera as Symphonic Poem," 161.
131. Scruton, *Death-Devoted Heart*, 4.
132. Ibid., 3.
133. Ibid., 3, 14.
134. Ibid., 122.
135. Ibid., 120.
136. Ibid., 121.
137. Marcel Proust, *À la recherche du temps perdu*, vol. 1 (Paris: Gallimard, 1954), 230.
138. Scruton, *Death-Devoted Heart*, 144.
139. Ibid., 147.
140. Ibid., 150.
141. Ibid., 152.
142. Ibid., 179.
143. Ibid., 182.
144. Ibid., 183.
145. Ibid.
146. Ibid., 193.
147. Ibid., 177.

4. DIE MEISTERSINGER VON NÜRNBERG

1. "Mehr als anderswo in der Welt war in Deutschland die Auffassung daheim, dass der Künstler eine geringere gesellschaftliche Verantwortung trage als andere Menschen, ja dass er sozusagen auserhalb der politischen, sozialen, und ökonomischen Ordnung ein Eigenleben führe, dessen Boden und Firmament eben die überzeitliche Welt der Künste sei, die Ewigkeit, das Universum, ein Traumreich, das nicht einmal einer religiösen Autorität, nur der vom Künstler selbst erfühlten Gottheit, unterstehe." Carl Zuckmayer, *Geheimreport* [*Secret Report* (written in 1943-44 for the US Office of Strategic Studies)], ed. Gunther Nickel and Johanna Schrön (Göttingen: Wallstein Verlag, 2002), 9.
2. "Ein Meistersinger muß er sein, nur wen ihr krönt, den soll sie frein," I.1310-13.
3. "des Heils Gebot," I.242-44.
4. "Schumacherei und Poeterei," I.639-40.
5. "Hilf Gott! Will ich denn Schuster sein?," I.702-3.
6. "Singkunst," I.704.
7. "Der Meister Tön' und Weisen," I.713-15.
8. "Dichter," I.813.
9. "der Dichter, der aus eignem Fleiße, zu Wort' und Reimen, die er erfand, aus Tönen auch fügt eine neue Weise: der wird als Meistersinger erkannt!," I.840-54.
10. "der Merker," I.931-32.

11. "ein altes Buch," I.1492–93.
12. "Buch und Hain," I.1559.
13. "Zwei art'ge Stollen faßt' er da ein," I.1530–32.
14. "Fanget an!," I.1697.
15. "der Städte Gruft," I.2050–51.
16. "zum heim'schen Hügel," I.2052–54.
17. "zur grünen Vogelweid'," I.2055–56.
18. "Kein Absatz wo, kein' Koloratur, von Melodei auch nicht eine Spur!," I.1862–66.
19. "neu, doch nicht verwirrt," I.1885–86.
20. "den Stümpern," I.1899–900.
21. Alfred Lorenz, *Der musikalische Aufbau von Richard Wagners "Die Meistersinger von Nürnberg"* (Berlin: M. Hesse, 1931), 10.
22. "ich fühl's und kann's nicht verstehn; kann's nicht behalten, doch auch nicht vergessen," II.320–23.
23. "Doch wie wollt' ich auch messen, was unermeßlich mir schien," II.325–28.
24. "Kein' Regel wollte da passen, und war doch kein Fehler drin," II.329–32.
25. "Es klang so alt, und war doch so neu," II.333–35.
26. "Lenzes Gebot, die süße Not, die legt' es ihm in die Brust: nun sang er, wie er mußt'; und wie er mußt', so konnt' er's," II.344–56.
27. "Mich schmerzt das Lied, ich weiß nicht wie! . . . O, bester Mann! Daß ich so Not dir machen kann!," II.1013–15 and 1021–23.
28. "Wohl kenn' ich alle Regeln, halte gut Maß und Zahl," II.1326–29.
29. "Mich dünkt, sollt' passen Ton und Wort?," II.1235–36.
30. "Gut' Lied will Takt," II.1328–29.
31. "Dieser Reimgesetze Leimen und Kleister," II. 718–21.
32. "Fort, in die Freiheit! Dahin gehör' ich, dort, wo ich Meister im Haus! Soll ich dich frein heut', dich nun beschwör' ich, komm und folg mir hinaus!," II.726–42.
33. "Überall Meister, wie böse Geister, seh' ich sich rotten, mich zu verspotten," II.745–47.
34. "daß Niemand kein Schad' geschicht," II.803–5.
35. "Welch toller Spuck! Mich dünkt's ein Traum . . . ," II.1203–5.
36. "Die Schläf' umwebt mir's wie ein Wahn . . . ," II.1207–9.
37. "bewahrt euch vor Gespenstern und Spuk, das kein böser Geist eu'r Seel' beruck'!," II.1459–63.
38. "in Deutschlands Mitten," III.345–46.
39. Egon Voss, ed., *Dokumente und Texte zu "Die Meistersinger von Nürnberg,"* SW 28, 93.
40. "ohn' den nichts mag geschehen," III.327–28.
41. "ein edler Werk," III.413–15.
42. "nie ohn' ein'gen Wahn gelingen," III.427–34.
43. CT I, 767.
44. "mit freudiger Begeisterung," stage direction at III.350.
45. "Ein Kobold," III.387.
46. "Jetzt schaun wir, wie Hans Sachs es macht, daß er den Wahn fein lenken kann, ein edler Werk zu tun," III.409–16.

47. CT I, 624.
48. "gerührt," III.728.
49. "sehr gerührt," III.794.
50. CT II, 762.
51. Theodor Adorno, *In Search of Wagner*, trans. R. Livingstone (London: Verso, 2005), 56.
52. "wie bezaubert," III.1481ff.
53. "bricht jetzt in heftiges Weinen aus," III.1481ff.
54. "hatte ich die Wahl, nur dich erwählt' ich mir," III.1575–77.
55. "Doch nun hat's mich gewählt zu nie gekannter Qual; und werd' ich heut vermählt, so war's ohn' alle Wahl," III.1582–90.
56. "ein traurig' Stück," III.1601–2.
57. "Herrn Markes Glück," III.1605–6.
58. Quoted from Anthony Kenny, *Philosophy in the Modern World: A New History of Western Philosophy*, vol. 4 (Oxford: Clarendon Press, 2007), 16.
59. WWV I, 383.
60. "Traumbild," III.795.
61. "des Traumes Deutung," III.800.
62. "einen wunderschönen Traum," III.453–55.
63. "Das grad' ist Dichters Werk, daß er sein Träumen deut' und merk," III.466–69.
64. "Glaubt mir, des Menschen wahrster Wahn wird ihm im Traume aufgetan: all' Dichtkunst und Poeterei ist nichts, als Wahrtraumdeuterei," III.469–79.
65. "statt eure Flucht zu hindern, wär' ich selbst mit euch fortgelaufen!," III.497–99.
66. "mit solchem Dicht' und Liebesfeuer verführt man wohl Töchter zum Abenteuer; doch für liebseligen Ehestand man andre Wort' und Weise fand," III.516–23.
67. "Ein schönes Lied, ein Meisterlied," III.536–38.
68. "Die Meisterregeln lernt bei Zeiten, daß sie getreulich euch geleiten und helfen, wohl bewahren, was in der Jugend Jahren mit holdem Triebe Lenz und Liebe euch unbewußt ins Herz gelegt, daß ihr das unverloren hegt!," III.576–90.
69. "ein Bildnis," III.601.
70. "Jugendliebe," III.603.
71. "drum möcht' ich, als bedürft'ger Mann, will ich die Regeln euch lehren, sollt ihr sie mir neu erklären," III.614–19.
72. "aus ihren Augen Wonne saugen," III.751–53.
73. "ein Sternenkranz," III.1444–45.
74. The tradition of the contemplative ensemble to which the quintet belongs has been traced in Carl Dahlhaus, "Über das 'kontemplative Ensemble,'" in *Opern Studien. Anna Amalie Abert zum 65. Geburtstag*, ed. Klaus Hortschansky (Tutzing: Schneider, 1975), 189–95; reprinted in Dahlhaus, *Gesammelte Schriften*, ed. Hermann Danuser, vol. 2 (Laaber: Laaber-Verlag, 2001), 405–11.
75. "Die 'selige Morgentraum Deutweise,'" III.1675–77.
76. "Wach auf!," III.2154.
77. ML 690. Cf. CT I, 747. See also Egon Voss, "*Es klang so alt,—und war doch so neu,—Oder ist es umgekehrt? Zur Rolle des Überlieferten in den Meistersingern von*

Nürnberg," in *"Wagner und kein Ende." Betrachtungen und Studien* (Zurich: Atlantis, 1996), 153-54, who convincingly shows that Wagner invented the melody before he found the text for it.

78. "Bei seinem Anblick stößt sich alles an; Hüte und Mützen werden abgezogen," stage direction at III.2142.

79. "Das Volk nimmt wieder eine jubelnd bewegte Haltung an," stage direction at III.2170.

80. "unbeweglich," stage direction at III.2188.

81. "über die Volksmenge hinweggeblickt hatte," stage direction at III.2188.

82. See my *A Theory of Art* (New York: Oxford University Press, 2000), 95-98.

83. "der Frauen Sinn, gar unbelehrt, dünkt mich dem Sinn des Volks gleich wert. Wollt ihr nun vor dem Volke zeigen, wie hoch die Kunst ihr ehrt, und laßt ihr dem Kind die Wahl zu eigen, wollt nicht, daß dem Spruch es wehrt, so laßt das Volk auch Richter sein: mit dem Kinde sicher stimmt's überein," I.1320-32.

84. "Doch einmal im Jahre fänd' ich's weise, daß man die Regeln selbst probier', ob in der Gewohnheit trägem Gleise ihr Kraft und Leben nicht sich verlier'. Und ob ihr der Natur noch seid auf rechter Spur, das sagt euch nur, wer nichts weiß von der Tabulatur," I.1342-53.

85. "Daß Volk und Kunst gleich blüh' und wachs'," I.1365-67.

86. Quoted from Voss, ed., *Dokumente und Texte zu "Die Meistersinger von Nürnberg,"* SW 28, 72.

87. "Liebestraum," III.2629.

88. "Das gilt uns weltlich," I.1604-5.

89. "die Werbung steh' dem Dichter frei," III.2243-45.

90. "Ei, Sachs, ihr seid gar fein! Doch mag es heut geschehen sein," III.2576-80.

91. "Der Regel Güte daraus man erwägt, daß sie auch mal 'ne Ausnahm' verträgt," III.2580-83.

92. MA I.402, 152.

93. "Ein gutter Zeuge," III.2584-85.

94. "Meister und Volk sind gewillt zu vernehmen, was mein Zeuge gilt," III.2588-92.

95. Carl Schmitt, *Political Theology: Four Chapters on the Concept of Sovereignty*, trans. George Schwab (Cambridge, MA: MIT Press, 1985), 5; *Politische Theologie. Vier Kapitel zur Lehre von der Souveränität*, 5th ed. (Berlin: Duncker and Humblot, 1990), 11.

96. Edmond and Jules de Goncourt, *Journal*, vol. 2: *1858-60*, ed. Jean-Louis Cabanés (Paris: Honoré Champion Éditeur, 2008), 262.

97. "Nicht Meister! Nein! Will ohne Meister selig sein!," III.2764-67.

98. "Verachtet mir die Meister nicht, und ehrt mir ihre Kunst!," III.2773-77.

99. "deutsch und wahr," III.2817-18.

100. "Habt acht! Uns dräuen üble Streich'," III.2826-29.

101. "welschen Dunst mit welschem Tand," III.2837-38.

102. "was deutsch und echt, wüßt' keiner mehr, lebt's nicht in deutscher Meister Ehr'," III.2840-44.

103. "ehrt eure deutschen Meister! . . . zerging' in Dunst das heil'ge röm'sche Reich, uns bliebe gleich die heil'ge deutsche Kunst!," III.2847-48, 2857-65.

104. "als auf ihr Haupt," stage direction at III.2865.

105. Voss, ed., *Dokumente und Texte zu "Die Meistersinger von Nürnberg,"* SW 28, 125, facs. 373.

106. See Voss, ed., *Dokumente und Texte zu "Die Meistersinger von Nürnberg,"* SW 28, 146, 149.

107. PW IV, 41–42, 58.

108. KSA 8, 12[29], 267.

109. Voss, ed., *Dokumente und Texte zu "Die Meistersinger von Nürnberg,"* SW 28, 72–73.

110. CT I, 68–69.

111. CT II, 211.

112. Voss, ed., *Dokumente und Texte zu "Die Meistersinger von Nürnberg,"* SW 28, 57.

113. CT II, 401.

114. Voss, ed., *Dokumente und Texte zu "Die Meistersinger von Nürnberg,"* SW 28, 57.

115. Jörg Linnenbrügger, *Richard Wagners "Die Meistersinger von Nürnberg." Studien und Materialien zur Entstehungsgeschichte des ersten Aufzugs (1861–1866)*, vol. 1 (Göttingen: Vandenhoeck and Ruprecht, 2001), 48ff.

116. PW IV, 356.

117. Voss, ed., *Dokumente und Texte zu "Die Meistersinger von Nürnberg,"* SW 28, 58.

118. WB 206.

119. "zerging' in Dunst das heil'ge römsche Reich, uns bliebe gleich die heil'ge deutsche Kunst!," III.2857–65 and 2876–97.

120. PW IV, 161.

121. Carl Dahlhaus, *Richard Wagner's Music Dramas*, trans. Mary Whittall (Cambridge, England: Cambridge University Press, 1979), 68.

122. On the debt of *Die Meistersinger* to *A Midsummer Night's Dream*, see Yvonne Nilges, *Richard Wagners Shakespeare* (Würzburg: Königshausen and Neumann, 2007), 138ff. See also Egon Voss, "*Meistersinger* und *Sommernachtstraum*. Eine Miszelle," *wagnerspectrum* 10, no. 2 (2014): 285–93, who intriguingly argues that the *Wahn* motive echoes Mendelssohn's incidental music to the play, the music that Wagner conducted when the play was performed in Dresden in 1844.

123. Quoted from Voss, ed., *Dokumente und Texte zu "Die Meistersinger von Nürnberg,"* SW 28, 26.

124. CT I, 609.

125. See my *A Theory of Art*, 95–98.

126. Patrick Carnegy, "Stage History," in John Warrack, *Richard Wagner, Die Meistersinger von Nürnberg* (Cambridge, England: Cambridge University Press, 1994), 140.

127. Ibid., 141.

128. See Udo Bermbach, *Richard Wagner in Deutschland. Rezeption—Verfälschungen* (Stuttgart-Weimar: Metzler, 2011), 419–35.

129. Letter to Friedrich Engels, August 19, 1876, in *The Letters of Karl Marx*, ed. Saul K. Padover (Englewood Cliffs, NJ: Prentice-Hall, 1979), 308.

130. EH, "Why I Am So Clever" 5, 704.

131. "A Retrospect of the Stage-Festivals of 1876," PW VI, 101.

132. Kurt Wölfel, ed., *Richard Wagner und König Ludwig II. Von Bayern. Briefwechsel* (Stuttgart: Gerd Hatje, 1993), 136.

133. PW IV, 154–55.

134. PW IV, 164.

135. Thomas Mann, "The Sorrows and Grandeur of Richard Wagner," in Mann, *Pro and contra Wagner*, trans. Allan Blunden (Chicago: University of Chicago Press, 1985), 141.

136. See in particular Dieter Borchmeyer, *Drama and the World of Richard Wagner*, trans. Daphne Ellis (Princeton, NJ: Princeton University Press, 2003), 180–211; Udo Bermbach, *"Blühendes Leid." Politik und Gesellschaft in Richard Wagners Musikdramen* (Stuttgart and Weimar: J. B. Metzler, 2003), 247–80.

137. Borchmeyer, *Drama and the World of Richard Wagner*, 191–92.

138. Ibid., 194.

139. Bermbach, *"Blühendes Leid,"* 256.

140. Ibid., 257.

141. Ibid., 277.

142. See Bermbach, *Richard Wagner in Deutschland*, 447–48.

143. Thomas Mann, "Bruder Hitler," in *Achtung, Europa! Essays 1933–1938*, ed. Hermann Kurzke and Stephan Stachorski (Frankfurt am Main: Fischer, 1995), 305–12.

144. Thomas Mann, *Reflections of a Non-Political Man* (1918), quoted from Mann, *Pro and Contra Wagner*, 63.

145. Mann, *Pro and Contra Wagner*, 201.

146. Johann Gottlieb Fichte, *Addresses to the German Nation*, ed. Gregory Moore, Cambridge Texts in the History of Political Thought (Cambridge, England: Cambridge University Press, 2008), 82–83.

147. Ibid., 83–84.

148. "Epilogue to the 'Nibelung's Ring,'" PW III, 268.

149. PW I, 343–44.

150. "Nie sollst du mich befragen, noch Wissens Sorge tragen, woher ich kam der Fahrt, noch wie mein Nam' und Art," I.777–84.

151. "Du Ärmste kannst wohl nie ermessen, wie zweifellos mein Herze liebt? Du hast wohl nie das Glück besessen, das sich uns nur durch Glauben gibt?," II.779–88.

152. "So rein und edel ist sein Wesen, so tugendreich der hehre Mann, daß nie des Unheils soll genesen, wer seiner Sendung zweifeln kann!," II.1551–67.

153. "Seht da den Herzog von Brabant, zum Führer sei er euch ernannt," III.1655–69.

154. Bermbach, *Richard Wagner in Deutschland*, 442.

155. "Für deutsches Land das deutsche Schwert! So sei des Reiches Kraft bewährt!," III.1014–31.

156. "Nach Deutschland sollen noch in fernsten Tagen des Ostens Horden siegreich nimmer ziehn," III.1458–63.

157. PW III, 281–82.

158. Cf. Hans Rudolf Vaget, "The 'Metapolitics' of *Die Meistersinger*: Wagner's Nuremberg as Imagined Community," in *Searching for Common Ground: Diskurse zur deutschen Identität 1750–1871*, ed. Nicholas Vazsonyi (Cologne and Weimar: Böhlau, 2000), 269–82.

159. Walter Benjamin, "The Work of Art in the Age of Mechanical Reproduction," in *Illuminations* (New York: Schocken, 1969), 241–42.

160. Cf. for example Joachim Köhler, *Wagner's Hitler: The Prophet and His Disciple* (Cambridge, MA: Polity Press, 2000).

161. SLW 705.
162. CT II, 826.

5. PARSIFAL

1. "Langsam und feierlich."
2. "Stimmen aus der Höhe."
3. "Sehr langsam."
4. "aus der Höhe."
5. "dringt ein blendender Lichtstrahl von oben auf die Kristallschale herab; diese erglüht sodann immer starker in leuchtender Purpurfarbe, alles sanft bestrahlend," stage direction at I.1469.
6. WA, 11, 636.
7. So far as the compositional process is concerned, the reverse is the case: as one might have guessed, "Wagner's point of departure in composing the first act was the Grail scene, which preceded his work on the prelude." William Kinderman, "The Genesis of the Music," in *A Companion to Wagner's Parsifal*, ed. William Kinderman and Katherine R. Syer (Rochester, NY: Camden House, 2005), 167.
8. CT II, 368–69.
9. Martin Geck and Egon Voss, eds., *Dokumente zur Entstehung und ersten Aufführung des Bühnenweihfestspiels Parsifal*, SW 30, no. 165, 45–46.
10. "wer guter Tat sich freut, / ihm wird das Mahl erneut," I.1184–90.
11. "nur dem Reinen vergönnt ist sich zu einen den Brüdern," I.614–16.
12. "einz'ger Sünder unter Allen," I.1306–8.
13. "aus tiefster Seele Heilesbuße / zu Ihm muß ich gelangen," I.1333–39.
14. "des heiligsten Blutes Quell / fühl' ich sich gießen in mein Herz: / des eig'nen sündigen Blutes Gewell', / . . . / muß mir zurück dann fließen, / in die Welt der Sündensucht / mit wilder Scheu sich ergießen; / von Neuem sprengt es das Tor, / daraus es nun strömt hervor, / hier durch die Wunde, der seinen gleich, / . . . / und aus der nun mir, . . . / . . . / das heiße Sündenblut entquillt, / ewig erneut aus des Sehnens Quelle, / das, ach! keine Büßung je mir stillt!," I.1353–88.
15. "durch Mitleid wissend / der reine Tor, / harre sein', / den ich erkor," I.728–35.
16. The fate of the promise music in act 1 and beyond is traced and interpreted in Hermann Danuser, *Weltanschauungsmusik* (Schliengen: Edition Argus, 2009), 217–50.
17. "Mich dünkt, daß ich dich recht erkannt: / kein Weg führt zu ihm durch das Land, / und Niemand könnte ihn beschreiben, / den er nicht selber möcht' geleiten," I.1092–99.
18. "bist du rein, wird nun der Gral dich tränken und speisen," I.1079–83.
19. "Nun achte wohl, und laß mich seh'n: / bist du ein Tor und rein, / welch' Wissen dir auch mag beschieden sein," I.1156–60.
20. "Parsifal hatte . . . eine heftige Bewegung nach dem Herzen gemacht, welches er krampfhaft eine Zeitlang gefasst hielt," I.1631.
21. "durch Mitleid wissend der reine Tor" and "Höchsten Heiles Wunder!," III.1106–9.
22. "Erlösung dem Erlöser!," III.1109–19.
23. For a recent discussion of this much-analyzed progression, see Danuser, *Weltanschauungsmusik*, 243–50. For an early prefiguration of the progression in Wagner's first

opera, see Arne Stolberg, "Im Quintenzirkel zur Erlösung. Kunstreligion und 'musikalischer Mystizismus' in Wagners *Die Feen*," in *Richard Wagner: Persönlichkeit, Werk und Wirkung*, ed. Helmut Loos (Markkleeberg: Sax-Verlag, 2013), 39–48.

24. A rich historical context for this progression is provided in Richard Cohn, "Uncanny Resemblances: Tonal Signification in the Freudian Age," *Journal of the American Musicological Society* 57 (2004): 285–324.

25. "zum letzten Mal!," III.907–18.

26. "tötet den Sünder mit seiner Qual, / von selbst dann leuchtet euch wohl der Gral!"; III.1024–29.

27. "Nur eine Waffe taugt: / die Wunde schließt / der Speer nur, der sie schlug," III.1030–35.

28. "Patmos," trans. Michael Hamburger in Friedrich Hölderlin, in *Poems and Fragments* (Ann Arbor: University of Michigan Press, 1966), 462–63. Cf. Martin Heidegger, "The Question Concerning Technology," in *The Question Concerning Technology and Other Essays*, trans. William Lovitt (New York: Harper and Row, 1977), 3–35.

29. "Sei heil, entsündigt und gesühnt!," III.1038–41.

30. "Denn ich verwalte nun dein Amt," III.1042–45.

31. "Gesegnet sei dein Leiden, / das Mitleids höchste Kraft / und reinsten Wissens Macht / dem zagen Toren gab!," III.1046–56.

32. CT II, 177.

33. See my *Bach's Cycle, Mozart's Arrow: An Essay on the Origins of Musical Modernity* (Berkeley and Los Angeles: University of California Press, 2007), 280–91.

34. SLW 897.

35. Otto Strobel, ed., *König Ludwig II. und Richard Wagner. Briefwechsel*, vol. 3 (Karlsruhe: G. Braun, 1936–39), 158–59.

36. SLW 903.

37. PW VI, 213.

38. CT II, 339.

39. P.: "Ich schreite kaum, / doch wähn' ich mich schon weit." G.: "Du sieh'st, mein Sohn, / zum Raum wird hier die Zeit," I.1099–105.

40. "wilde," I.197, and again I.215.

41. "stürzt hastig, fast taumelnd herein."

42. "wilde Kleidung."

43. "He! Du da! Was liegst du dort wie ein wildes Tier?," I.382–83.

44. "Sind die Tiere hier nicht heilig?," I.384–85.

45. "eine Verwünschte," I.430–31.

46. "Schuld aus früh'rem Leben," I.437–39.

47. "ein furchtbar schönes Weib," I.521–23.

48. "unkund blieb mir, was dorten er gesündigt," I.635–37.

49. "üpp'ges Heidenland," I.633.

50. "Ohnmächtig, in sich selbst die Sünde zu ertöten, / an sich legt' er die Frevlerhand, / die nun, dem Grale zugewandt, / verachtungsvoll dess' Hüter von sich stieß," I.642–49.

51. "Wonnegarten," I.663.

52. "teuflich holde Frauen," I.664–65.
53. "zu böser Lust," I.668.
54. "schon Viele hat er uns verdorben," I. 672–75.
55. WA, 9, 632.
56. "Dienen,—dienen," III.136–37.
57. "Der Irrnis und der Leiden Pfade," III.285–87.
58. "in pfadlosen Irren," III.310–11.
59. "bleich und elend wankt umher / die Mut- und Führerlose Ritterschaft," III.400–405.
60. SLW 885.
61. "zum letzten Male," III.906–8.
62. CT II, 181.
63. As Kinderman pointed out, in "the numerous sketches for the Good Friday music in act 3, . . . the vocal lines and words are hardly ever notated." Kinderman, "The Genesis of the Music," 156.
64. Carl Friedrich Glasenapp, *Das Leben Richard Wagners in sechs Büchern*, vol. 6 (Leipzig: Breitkopf und Härtel, 1911), 183.
65. "heil'ge Quelle," III.463.
66. "senkt das Haupt tief zur Erde; sie scheint heftig zu weinen."
67. "Parsifal wendet sich um, und blickt mit sanfter Entzückung auf Wald und Wiese, welche jetzt im Vormittagslichte leuchten."
68. "Auf! Kundry! Auf! / Der Winter floh, und Lenz ist da!," III.71–74.
69. "Wie dünkt mich doch die Aue heut' so schön!," III.639–41.
70. "Das ist—Karfreitags Zauber, Herr," III.663–67.
71. Cf. Carl Dahlhaus, *Richard Wagner's Music Dramas*, trans. Mary Whittall (Cambridge, England: Cambridge University Press, 1979), 151: "In greatly simplified terms, the use of musical motives in *Parsifal* is governed and conditioned by the contrast of chromaticism and diatonicism: the chromaticism that conveys the deceptions of Klingsor's kingdom also expresses the anguish of Amfortas, while the expressive range of diatonicism reaches from the naïve simplicity of Parsifal's motive to the sublimity of the Grail themes."
72. "der fühlt sich frei von Sündenlast und Grauen," III.713–16.
73. "Ihn selbst am Kreuze kann sie nicht erschauen," III.705–9.
74. "da blickt sie zum erlös'ten Menschen auf," III.710–12.
75. "Des Sünders Reuetränen . . . / . . . mit heil'gem Tau / beträufet Flur und Au: / der ließ sie so gedeihen," III.684–94.
76. "freu't sich alle Kreatur," III.695–96.
77. "Das merkt nun Halm und Blume auf den Auen, / daß heut' des Menschen Fuß sie nicht zertritt, / doch wohl—wie Gott mit himmlischer Geduld / sich sein' erbarmt' und für ihn litt—/ der Mensch auch heut' in frommer Huld / sie schont mit sanftem Schritt," III.722–40.
78. "was all' da blüht und bald erstirbt," III.745–47.
79. "entsündigte," III.748–49.
80. "Unschuldstag," III.752–54.
81. "Höllenrose," II.112.
82. "heut' sie nach Erlösung schmachten," III.775–77.

83. "Segenstaue," III.781–82.
84. "du weinest,—sieh', es lacht die Aue!," III.783–88.
85. See in particular Carl Dahlhaus, "Entfremdung und Erinnerung. Zu Wagners *Götterdämmerung*," in *Kongreßbericht Bayreuth 1981*, ed. C. H. Mahling and S. Wiesmann (Kassel: Bärenreiter, 1984), 416–20; reprinted in Carl Dahlhaus, *Gesammelte Schriften*, ed. Hermann Danuser, vol. 7 (Laaber: Laaber-Verlag, 2004), 486–92.
86. "meinem Fluche mit mir Alle verfallen," II.280–83.
87. "Wer dir trotzte, lös'te dich frei," II.290–93.
88. "Weil einzig an mir deine Macht nichts vermag," II.221–23.
89. "Ungebändigten Sehnens Pein, schrecklichster Triebe Höllendrang, . . . ich zum Todesschweigen mir zwang," II.241–47.
90. "ihn schirmt der Torheit Schild," II.207–9.
91. "schönen Geteufels," II.332–33.
92. "teuflisch holde Frauen," I.664–65.
93. "Ihr schönen Kinder," II.491–93.
94. "wie in anmutigem Kinderspiele," before II.567.
95. "Ihr kindischen Buhlen," II.758–59.
96. "früh welkende Blumen," II.761–63.
97. "ein jugendliches Weib von höchster Schönheit . . . auf einem Blumenlager, in . . . phantastischer Kleidung—annähernd arabischen Stiles," at II.781.
98. CT II, 590.
99. "Entblüh'test du auch diesem Blumenhaine?," II.810–11.
100. "Ich hatte viele, doch weiß ich ihrer keinen mehr," I.906–9.
101. "Riefest du mich Namenlosen?," II.786–87.
102. "Parsifal? . . . So nannte träumend mich einst die Mutter," II.745–49.
103. "Dich nannt' ich, tör'ger Reiner: 'Falparsi'—dich reinen Toren: 'Parsifal,'" II.788–94.
104. SLW 877.
105. Willi Schuh, ed., *Die Briefe Richard Wagners an Judith Gautier* (Erlenbach-Zürich and Leipzig: Rotapfel-Verlag, 1936), 74–75.
106. "O Tor! Blöder, taumelnder Tor! Wo irrtest du hin, ihrer vergessend, deiner, deiner vergessend?," II.926–33.
107. "Ha! Was Alles vergaß ich wohl noch?," II.952–53.
108. "Die Leib und Leben / einst dir gegeben, / . . . / sie beut dir heut' / als Mutter-Segens letzten Gruß / der Liebe ersten Kuß," II.972–83.
109. "heftet nun ihre Lippen zu einem langen Kusse auf seinen Mund," stage direction at II.983.
110. Martin Heidegger, *Being and Time*, trans. John Macquarrie and Edward Robinson (New York: Harper and Row, 1962), 80, paragraph 12.
111. "Amfortas! . . . Die Wunde!," II.994–99.
112. "Die Wunde sah' ich bluten, nun blutet sie in mir!," II.1017–20.
113. "Nein! Nein! Nicht die Wunde ist es. / . . . / Das Sehnen, das furchtbare Sehnen, / das alle Sinne mir faßt und zwingt! / Oh! Qual der Liebe! / Wie Alles schauert, bebt und zuckt—/ in sündigem Verlangen!," II.1025–44.
114. SLW 664.

115. "Des Heilands Klage," II.1062–63.

116. "'Erlöse, rette mich aus schuldbefleckten Händen!,'" II.1067–72.

117. "Verderberin," II.1120–21.

118. But see the more cautious opinion of Thomas Grey in his admirably judicious treatment of the subject of Wagner's anti-Semitism: "Kundry, as a female manifestation of the Wandering Jew of medieval legend, is a possible, partial exception [to the rule that there are no overtly Jewish characters in Wagner's operas], suggested by Klingsor's reference to one of her past lives in the person of Herodias. But the issue is left ambiguous." Thomas S. Grey, "The Jewish Question," in *The Cambridge Companion to Wagner*, ed. Thomas S. Grey (Cambridge, England: Cambridge University Press, 2008), 212.

119. "da traf mich . . . sein Blick!," II.1186–88.

120. See Lucy Beckett, *Richard Wagner: Parsifal*, Cambridge Opera Handbook (Cambridge, England: Cambridge University Press, 1981), 12, where Schopenhauer's words are quoted.

121. "Nun such' ich ihn von Welt zu Welt, / ihm wieder zu begegnen," II.1198–204.

122. "Seit Ewigkeiten," II.1146–48.

123. "nur eine Stunde mich dir vereinen, / . . . / in dir entsündigt sein, und erlös't!," II.1263–75.

124. "Bist du Erlöser, / was bannt dich, Böser, / nicht mir auch zum Heil dich zu einen?," II.1135–42.

125. "kehrt mir das verfluchte Lachen wieder: / ein Sünder sinkt mir in die Arme!," II.1223–28.

126. "Irre! Irre!," II.1476–78.

127. "Auch dir bin ich zum Heil gesandt, / bleibst du dem Sehnen abgewandt. / Die Labung, die dein Leiden endet, / beut nicht der Quell aus dem es fließt; / das Heil wird nimmer dir gespendet, / eh' jener Quell sich dir nicht schließt," II.1287–305.

128. CT I, 977.

129. ML 547.

130. Geck and Voss, eds., *Dokumente zur Entstehung und ersten Aufführung des Bühnenweihfestspiels Parsifal*, 13.

131. CT II, 295.

132. ML 511.

133. Gabriele E. Meyer and Egon Voss, eds., *Dokumente und Texte zu "Tristan und Isolde,"* SW 27, p. 28.

134. Geck and Voss, eds., *Dokumente zur Entstehung und ersten Aufführung des Bühnenweihfestspiels Parsifal*, nos. 6–7, 9, pp. 12–14.

135. Geck and Voss, eds., *Dokumente zur Entstehung und ersten Aufführung des Bühnenweihfestspiels Parsifal*, nos. 9–13, pp. 13–17.

136. SLW 456–57.

137. SLW 458.

138. CT II, 720.

139. Meyer and Voss, eds., *Dokumente und Texte zu "Tristan und Isolde,"* 154.

140. CT II, 696.

141. CT II, 764–65.

142. WWV I, paragraph 67, 376.

143. See for example WWV I, paragraph 66, 372–73.

144. WWV I, paragraph 66, 372.

145. "Against Vivisection" (an open letter to Herr Ernst von Weber, author of *The Torture-Chambers of Science*), PW VI, 210.

146. Ibid., 199.

147. ML 75.

148. CT II, 797.

149. SLW 423–24. Such thoughts occur to Wagner even earlier: see the letter of May 10–12, 1855, to Jacob Sulzer in SLW 338.

150. Leszek Kołakowski, *Religion. If There Is No God . . . On God, the Devil, Sin and Other Worries of the So-Called Philosophy of Religion* (South Bend, IN: St. Augustine's Press, 2001), 51.

151. Wolfgang Golther, ed., *Richard Wagner an Mathilde Wesendonk: Tagebuch blätter und Briefe 1853–1871* (Berlin: A. Duncker, 1904), 110.

152. SLW 359.

153. CT II, 923.

154. *A Communication to My Friends*, PW I, 329.

155. CT II, 773.

156. Cf. Ulrike Kienzle, "*Parsifal* and Religion: A Christian Music Drama?," in *A Companion to Wagner's Parsifal*, 91: "With the [original] conception of *Parzival* [in the 1850s], Wagner intended to create a synthesis of Christian and Indian religions on the basis of Schopenhauer's philosophy. This synthesis remained a constant element of the project until its completion." Kienzle concludes, "Is *Parsifal* a Christian music drama? We need to answer 'no' to this question if we wish to regard Wagner's last work as reinforcing the dogmas of the church, whether Protestant or Catholic. However, we can answer 'yes' if we take the interwoven paths of medieval and modern mysticism seriously as components of the Christian tradition. Wagner's mysticism derives in part from the philosophy of Schopenhauer and in this respect is a mysticism without God. *Parsifal* thus seems to ask whether it is possible to have any kind of a religion in an irreligious age" (130). Cf. also Carl Dahlhaus, *Richard Wagner's Music Dramas*, 143: "Wagner's faith was philosophical, not religious, a metaphysic of compassion and renunciation, deriving its essential elements from Schopenhauer's *World as Will and Idea* and—via Schopenhauer—from Buddhism. Wagner found these elements also present in Christianity, and to that extent he was a Christian. But the predominant spirit of the nineteenth century had become alien to fundamentalist faith, and he too took a historico-philosophical view of the traditions of the religion as an evolving truth, changing its outer shape throughout history. The myth that was once believed as literal truth had become a metaphor for a metaphysical insight; and the rituals of an earlier age, grown hollow and insubstantial as such, passed over into art, so as to preserve or recover in a symbolic role the meaning and cogency that they had lost in their hieratic function."

157. Beckett, *Richard Wagner: Parsifal*, 139.

158. Cf. Dahlhaus, *Richard Wagner's Music Dramas*, 144: "*Parsifal* is therefore undeniably a document of the nineteenth-century 'religion of art.' This does not mean that art should be venerated as religion . . . , but that religion—or its truth—has passed from the form of myth into the forms of art."

159. CT I, 851.

160. CT II, 269–70.
161. WWV II, chapter 48, 604.
162. "Religion and Art," PW VI, 211–52; "'What Boots This Knowledge?' A Supplement to 'Religion and Art,'" PW VI, 253–63; "'Know Thyself'" and "Hero-dom and Christendom," PW VI, 264–74 and 275–84.
163. WWV II, chapter 46, 581.
164. "Religion and Art," PW VI, 225.
165. Ibid., 213.
166. Ibid., 217.
167. Ibid., 231.
168. Ibid.
169. Ibid., 217.
170. Ibid., 233.
171. Ibid.
172. WWV II, 488.
173. WWV I, 232.
174. WWV I, 383.
175. WWV I, 387–88.
176. SLW 346–47.
177. Ernst Theodor Amadeus Hoffmann, "Old and New Church Music," in *E. T. A. Hoffmann's Musical Writings:* Kreisleriana, The Poet and the Composer, *Music Criticism,* ed. David Charlton, trans. Martyn Clarke (Cambridge, England: Cambridge University Press, 1989), 351–76.
178. "Religion and Art," PW VI, 213.
179. Ibid., 251.
180. "'Know Thyself,'" PW VI, 274.
181. Carl Dahlhaus, "Erlösung dem Erlöser. Warum Richard Wagners '*Parsifal*' nicht Mittel zum Zweck der Ideologie ist," in *Richard Wagner, Parsifal. Texte, Materialien, Kommentare,* ed. Attila Csampai and Dietmar Holland (Reinbeck bei Hamburg: Rowohlt, 1984), 265–66. See also Jens Malte Fischer, ed., *Richard Wagners "Das Judentum in der Musik": Eine kritische Dokumentation* (Frankfurt am Main and Leipzig: Insel Verlag, 2000), 84–87.
182. Saul Friedländer, "Hitler und Wagner," in *Richard Wagner im Dritten Reich. Ein Schloss Elmau-Symposion,* ed. Saul Friedländer and Jörn Rüsen (Munich: Verlag C. H. Beck, 2000), 168. It should be noted, however, that at least one contemporary, Johann Christian Lobe, did read the ending of Wagner's pamphlet literally as a call for physical annihilation of the Jews already in 1851. Cf. Fischer, ed., *Richard Wagners "Das Judentum in der Musik,"* 222–27. It should also be noted that in the second edition of his tract Wagner does raise the possibility of "violent expulsion": "I would not wish to judge whether the decline of our culture might be stopped by a violent expulsion of the disintegrating alien element." Ibid., 196. For Fischer's commentary, see ibid., 107–11. For a reading of the closing sentences of the pamphlet that brings Wagner's views close to those of Marx, see Udo Bermbach, *"Blühendes Leid." Politik und Gesellschaft in Richard Wagners Musikdramen* (Stuttgart and Weimar: J. B. Metzler, 2003), 326ff.
183. CT II, 551–52. For the earlier meeting, see the entry for November 30, 1876: [In Rome] "Made the pleasant acquaintance of Count Gobineau, the French ambassador in

Sweden." CT I, 935. On Wagner's relationship to Gobineau, see in particular Udo Bermbach, "Wagner und Gobineau. Zur Geschichte eines Missverständnisses," *wagnerspectrum* 9, no. 1 (2013): 243–58.

184. CT II, 642 and 670.
185. CT II, 613 and 633.
186. CT II, 1108 (editorial note).
187. Cf. Udo Bermbach, *Der Wahn des Gesamtkunstwerks. Richard Wagners politisch-ästhetische Utopie*, 2nd ed. (Stuttgart and Weimar: J. B. Metzler, 2004), 276ff.
188. On the central role played by resentment and envy in the constitution of anti-Semitism in modern Germany, see Götz Aly, *Why the Germans? Why the Jews?: Envy, Race Hatred, and the Prehistory of the Holocaust* (Carlton, Australia: Melbourne University Press, 2014).
189. Thomas S. Grey makes his case in "Masters and Their Critics: Wagner, Hanslick, Beckmesser, and *Die Meistersinger*," in *Wagner's Meistersinger: Performance, History, Representation*, ed. Nicholas Vazsonyi (Rochester, NY: University of Rochester Press, 2002), 165–89.
190. Cf. Fischer, ed., *Richard Wagners "Das Judentum in der Musik*," 122 and 131–32. Throughout, Fischer stresses the particular importance of the second edition; see for example ibid., 14–17.
191. "Hero-dom and Christendom," PW VI, 275.
192. Ibid., 276.
193. Ibid., 280.
194. Ibid.
195. Ibid., 278.
196. Ibid., 284.
197. Ibid., 276–77.
198. Ibid., 280.
199. Ibid., 282.
200. Ibid., 282–83.
201. Ibid., 283.
202. CT II, 647.
203. WWV II, chapter 42, 513–14.
204. Robert W. Gutman, *Richard Wagner: The Man, His Mind, and His Music* (London: Secker and Warburg, 1968), chapters 15 and 16.
205. Ibid., 394.
206. Ibid., 419.
207. Ibid., 420.
208. Ibid., 422.
209. Ibid.
210. Ibid., 423.
211. Ibid., 427.
212. Ibid.
213. Ibid., 428.
214. Ibid., 429.
215. Ibid., 430.

216. WWV I, paragraph 68, 380.

217. Hartmut Zelinsky, "Rettung ins Ungenaue. Zu Martin Gregor-Dellins Wagner-Biographie," in *Richard Wagner: Parsifal, Musik-Konzepte* 25, ed. Heinz-Klaus Metzger and Rainer Riehn (Munich: Edition Text + Kritik, 1982), 74–115; the quoted sentence is on p. 104. See also Hartmut Zelinsky, "Die 'Feuerkur' des Richard Wagners oder die 'neue Religion' der 'Erlösung' durch 'Vernichtung,'" in *Richard Wagner: Wie antisemitisch darf ein Künstler sein?, Musik-Konzepte* 5, ed. Heinz-Klaus Metzger and Rainer Riehn (Munich: Edition Text + Kritik, 1978), 79–112. For further development of Gutman's claims, see Paul Lawrence Rose, *Wagner: Race and Revolution* (New Haven, CT, and London: Yale University Press, 1992), chapter 9; Marc Weiner, *Richard Wagner and the Anti-Semitic Imagination* (Lincoln and London: University of Nebraska Press, 1995), 183–93, 228–59. See also John Deathridge, "Strange Love, or, How We Learned to Stop Worrying and Love *Parsifal*," in *Wagner Beyond Good and Evil* (Berkeley and Los Angeles: University of California Press, 2008), 159–77.

218. For a refutation of Zelinsky's claims, see Carl Dahlhaus, "Erlösung dem Erlöser. Warum Richard Wagners '*Parsifal*' nicht Mittel zum Zweck der Ideologie ist," in *Richard Wagner, Parsifal. Texte, Materialien, Kommentare*, 262–69. A judicious general verdict on Zelinsky's contribution to the debate can be found in Fischer, ed., *Richard Wagners "Das Judentum in der Musik,"* 359, n. 2. For more general objections to the claims of Gutman and his followers, see also Laurence Dreyfus, "Hermann Levi's Shame and *Parsifal*'s Guilt: A Critique of Essentialism in Biography and Criticism," *Cambridge Opera Journal* 6 (1994): 125–45.

219. This, however, is not the conclusion reached by John Deathridge: "But Gobineau's ideas about a racial law of decay fired Wagner's enthusiasm to such an extent that they cannot be entirely airbrushed out of the picture we would like to have of *Parsifal* now, particularly as he had already come to his own conclusions about racial conflict since the dawn of humanity well before he had even heard of Gobineau's *Essai* [namely in *Die Wibelungen*, a pamphlet Wagner wrote in 1848 and published a year later]." Deathridge, "Strange Love," 176. Earlier on, Deathridge writes: "The overblown scenario of *Die Wibelungen* could not be more different from the smooth elegance of the *Essai*. Yet both writers are at one in their view that race, rather than specific cultural factors, can best explain the trajectory of history; and both give primacy to the undermining of racial origin as the root cause of civilization's impending disaster" (167). But if Wagner was a Gobineau *avant la lettre*, if he embraced a racial explanation of history already in the late 1840s, why did he forget this explanation so thoroughly in the earlier regeneration essays as to offer meat eating instead of miscegenation as the cause of degeneration? And if he forgot it when writing "Religion and Art," did he remember it when writing the *Parsifal* poem? In any case, how central was racism to Wagner's explanation of history, if he could forget it when writing the essays? It is only fair to add that *Die Wibelungen* contains no trace of those theories that would make it relevant to a racist interpretation of *Parsifal*, namely, that the degeneration of humanity has been caused by miscegenation, and that any future regeneration is dependent on racial purification.

220. Grey, "The Jewish Question," 211.

221. Ibid., 212.

222. Theodor Adorno, *In Search of Wagner*, trans. Rodney Livingstone, 2nd ed. (London: Verso, 2005), 13.

223. Ibid., 12–13. On the Beckmesser case, see in particular Barry Millington, "Nuremberg Trial: Is There Anti-Semitism in *Die Meistersinger*?," *Cambridge Opera Journal* 3 (1991): 247–60; Rose, *Wagner: Race and Revolution*, chapters 5 and 7; Weiner, *Richard Wagner and the Anti-Semitic Imagination*, chapter 2; Hans Rudolf Vaget, "Der Jude im Dorn oder: wie antisemitisch sind *Die Meistersinger von Nürnberg*?," *Deutsche Vierteljahrschrift für Literaturwissenschaft und Geistesgeschichte* 69 (1995): 271–99; Hans Rudolf Vaget, "Sixtus Beckmesser: A 'Jew in the Brambles'?," *Opera Quarterly* 12 (1995): 34–45; Hans Rudolf Vaget, "The 'Metapolitics' of *Die Meistersinger:* Wagner's Nuremberg as Imagined Community," in *Searching for Common Ground: Diskurse zur deutschen Identität 1750–1871*, ed. Nicholas Vazsonyi (Cologne and Weimar: Böhlau, 2000), 269–82; Hermann Danuser, "Universalität oder Partikularität? Zur Frage 'jüdischer' Charakterzeichnung in Wagners Werk," in *Richard Wagner und die Juden*, ed. Dieter Borchmeyer, Aami Mayaani, and Susanne Vill (Stuttgart and Weimar: J. B. Metzler, 2000), 79–100; Hans Rudolf Vaget, "'Du warst mein Feind von je': The Beckmesser Controversy Revisited," in *Wagner's Meistersinger: Performance, History, Representation*, 190–208; Dieter Borchmeyer, *Drama and the World of Richard Wagner*, trans. Daphne Ellis (Princeton, NJ: Princeton University Press, 2003), 196–211. The most persuasive case for the possibility of interpreting Beckmesser as a caricature of Hanslick and by extension both a Jewish critic and a Jewish composer has been made in Grey, "Masters and Their Critics," 165–89. Grey concludes that Wagner probably did identify Beckmesser "with traits he attributed to his Jewish musical as well as critical adversaries," but did not attempt "to make these associations manifest to his audience." It was, rather, "a vehicle for a kind of semiprivate revenge against . . . Hanslick" (188–89). See also Timothy MacFarland, "The Humiliation of Beckmesser: 'Der Jude im Dorn' and the Authority of Jacob Grimm in Wagner's *Die Meistersinger von Nürnberg*," *Oxford German Studies* 41, no. 2 (2012): 197–212; and Thomas S. Grey and Kirsten Paige, "The Owl, the Nightingale, and the Jew in the Thorn-Bush: Reconsidering Anti-Semitism in *Die Meistersinger*," *Cambridge Opera Journal* 28, no. 1 (2016): 1–34; I would like to thank the authors for making this text available to me prior to its publication. On anti-Semitism in Wagner's operas in general, see in particular Bermbach, *"Blühendes Leid." Politik und Gesellschaft in Richard Wagners Musikdramen*, 313–49.

224. Theodor W. Adorno, "What National Socialism Has Done to the Arts," in *Essays on Music*, ed. R. D. Leppert, trans. S. H. Gillespie et al. (Berkeley: University of California Press, 2002), 375.

225. See, however, William Kinderman, "Wagners Parsifal als Kunst und Ideologie," in *Richard Wagner. Persönlichkeit, Werk und Wirkung*, ed. Helmut Loos (Markkleeberg: Sax-Verlag, 2013), 109–17. Some information on the Wagner reception in Nazi Germany can be found in Friedländer and Rüsen, eds., *Richard Wagner im Dritten Reich*. For the Bayreuth circle see Mary Cicora, *"Parsifal" Reception in the "Bayreuther Blätter"* (New York: Peter Lang, 1987); Annette Hein, *"Es ist viel Hitler in Wagner." Rassismus und antisemitische Deutschtumsideologie in den "Bayreuther Blättern" (1878–1938)* (Tübingen: Niemeyer, 1996). For the Wagner reception in Germany in general, see Udo Bermbach, *Richard Wagner in Deutschland. Rezeption—Verfälschungen* (Stuttgart-Weimar: Metzler, 2011).

226. Jens Malte Fischer, "Wagner-Interpretation im Dritten Reich. Musik und Szene zwischen Politisierung und 'Kunstanspruch," in *Richard Wagner im Dritten Reich*, 162–63.

227. Saul Friedländer, "Hitler und Wagner," in *Richard Wagner im Dritten Reich*, 166.
228. See in particular Robert O. Paxton, *The Anatomy of Fascism* (New York: Knopf, 2004).
229. For the incompatibility of the opera with Nazi ideology, see Robert R. Gibson, "Problematic Propaganda: 'Parsifal' as Forbidden Opera," *Wagner* 20, no. 2 (1999): 78–87.
230. For the information in this and the following paragraphs, I rely mainly on Katherine R. Syer, "*Parsifal* on Stage," in *A Companion to Wagner's Parsifal*, 277–338, and on Bermbach, *Richard Wagner in Deutschland. Rezeption—Verfälschungen*, 437–70. See also Udo Bermbach, "Liturgietransfer. Über einem Aspekt des Zusammenhangs von Richard Wagner mit Hitler und dem Dritten Reich," in *Richard Wagner im Dritten Reich*, 40–65; Friedländer, "Hitler und Wagner," 165–78; Frederic Spotts, *Hitler and the Power of Aesthetics* (Woodstock, NY, and New York: Overlook, 2002).
231. See Dina Porat, "'Zum Raum wird hier die Zeit.' Richard Wagners Bedutung für die nationalsozialistische Führung," in *Richard Wagner und die Juden*, 207–20; Saul Friedländer, "Bayreuth und der Erlösungsantisemitismus," in ibid., 8–18; Friedländer, "Hitler und Wagner," 165–78. But cf. Fischer, *Richard Wagners "Das Judentum in der Musik*," 130–31, who demonstrates that Hitler knew Wagner's "Das Judentum in der Musik" and used its arguments in a speech of 1929.
232. Hans Frank, *Im Angesicht des Galgens* (Munich: Alfred Beck, 1953), 213.
233. Bermbach, *Richard Wagner in Deutschland. Rezeption—Verfälschungen*, 451–52.
234. Hermann Rauschning, *Hitler Speaks: A Series of Political Conversations with Adolf Hitler on His Real Aims* (London: Thornton Butterworth Ltd., 1939), 227.
235. A congruence between Gutman's interpretation and the readings proposed by Nazi critics (in this case by Alfred Lorenz) is pointed out in William Kinderman, *Wagner's Parsifal* (New York: Oxford University Press, 2013), 36.
236. Bermbach, *Richard Wagner in Deutschland. Rezeption—Verfälschungen*, 471–96.

EPILOGUE

1. Marcel Proust, *Remembrance of Things Past*, trans. C. K. Scott Moncrieff and Terence Kilmartin, vol. 3 (New York: Random House, 1981), 155–56.
2. Thomas Mann, "The Sorrows and Grandeur of Richard Wagner," in *Pro and contra Wagner*, trans. Allan Blunden (Chicago: University of Chicago Press, 1985), 93ff.
3. The best summary of the relationship is the "Chronik der Beziehungen Nietzsches zu Richard Wagner," in BSNW II, 1221–54. The book as a whole usefully collects most of the texts and documents relevant to the Nietzsche-Wagner encounter.
4. EH 705–6.
5. SLN 33.
6. SLN 39.
7. BSNW I, 316.
8. BSNW I, 365.
9. BSNW I, 326.
10. CT I, 382.
11. BSNW I, 88.
12. CT I, 368.

13. CT I, 399; cf. also the still earlier entry of May 11, 1871, CT I, 364–65.
14. See in particular Dieter Borchmeyer, "Choral Tragedy and Symphonic Drama: Wagner's Contribution to Nietzsche's *Die Geburt der Tragödie*," in Dieter Borchmeyer, *Richard Wagner: Theory and Theatre*, trans. Stewart Spencer (Oxford: Clarendon Press, 1991), 160–77.
15. CT I, 447.
16. SL 787–88.
17. BSNW I, 157.
18. BSNW I, 157.
19. SLN 92.
20. BSNW I, 161.
21. SLW 809.
22. BSNW I, 374.
23. BSNW I, 397.
24. Cf. especially the documents collected in BSNW I, 482–508.
25. BSNW I, 288–89.
26. BSNW I, 293.
27. BSNW I, 296.
28. SLN 166.
29. MA I.3, 13.
30. MA I.220, 102.
31. SLN 167.
32. See the entry of June 24, 1878, in CT II, 100.
33. KSA 15, 83–84.
34. PW VI, 77.
35. BSNW II, 1239.
36. BSNW II, 733.
37. SLN 167–68.
38. CT II, 144.
39. CT II, 281.
40. CT II, 992.
41. CT II, 1003.
42. CT II, 1004.
43. KSA 11, 506–7.
44. BSNW II, 963–64.
45. SLN 341.
46. EH 706.
47. SLN 260.
48. BSNW II, 830–31.
49. BSNW II, 849.
50. BSNW II, 741.
51. SLN 212.
52. SLN 223.
53. BSNW I, 301–2.
54. SLW 815.

55. CT I, 162.
56. KSA 15, 84.
57. BSNW I, 331.
58. BSNW I, 417.
59. SLN 91.
60. SLN 127.
61. On October 24, 1870, Cosima notes in her *Diary*: "He [Nietzsche] voices his fears that in the coming days militarism, and above all pietism, will make their pressure felt everywhere." CT I, 287. Cf. also for example Cosima Wagner's letter of October 30, 1870, to Nietzsche from which one can infer that the latter must have expressed worries about "the period of bigotry that awaits us." BSNW I, 104. (We are reduced to making such inferences, since Cosima ordered the destruction of Nietzsche's letters to her.) On November 7, 1870, Nietzsche writes to von Gersdorff: "I consider the Prussia of today a most dangerous power for culture." KSB 3, 155. See also Cosima's letter of November 17, 1870, to Nietzsche, BSNW I, 108. On November 24, 1870, Cosima notes: "In the evening a letter from Prof. N., who . . . is terribly pessimistic with regard to Germany." CT I, 299. On April 20, 1874, Cosima writes Nietzsche: "Do you find then that we have really become so especially dumb since the victory?" BSNW I, 247.
62. See Dieter Borchmeyer, "Liszt und Wagner. Allianz in Goethes und Schillers Spuren," *wagnerspectrum* 7, no. 1 (2011): 69–82; Dieter Borchmeyer, *Richard Wagner. Werk—Leben—Zeit* (Stuttgart: Reclam, 2013), 133–48.
63. KSA 8, 522.
64. EH 704.
65. WA "Postscript," 638.
66. KSA 8, 500.
67. Thomas Mann, *Pro and Contra Wagner*, 200.
68. For the consistently conservative, nationalist, right-wing slant that Bayreuth gave to the Wagner reception, see in particular Udo Bermbach, *Richard Wagner in Deutschland. Rezeption—Verfälschungen* (Stuttgart-Weimar: Metzler, 2011).
69. The tradition inaugurated by Nietzsche of insisting on distinguishing Wagner himself from his Bayreuth interpreters continues to this day. See in particular Udo Bermbach, *Der Wahn des Gesamtkunstwerks. Richard Wagners politisch-ästhetische Utopie*, 2nd ed. (Stuttgart and Weimar: J. B. Metzler, 2004).
70. WWV II, chapter 47, 605.
71. WWV II, chapter 17, 170.
72. WWV II, chapter 48, 623.
73. WWV II, chapter 38, 444.
74. See EH 693.
75. GT 24.
76. Friedrich Nietzsche, "On Music and Words," trans. W. Kaufmann, in Carl Dahlhaus, in *Between Romanticism and Modernism: Four Studies in the Music of the Later Nineteenth Century* (Berkeley: University of California Press, 1980), 107–8.
77. Ibid., 108.
78. Ibid.
79. Ibid., 109.
80. Ibid., 108.

81. Ibid., 110–11.
82. Ibid., 116.
83. GT, "Preface to Richard Wagner," 31–32.
84. GT 1, 33.
85. GT 1, 34.
86. GT 1, 35.
87. GT 2, 40.
88. GT 1, 36.
89. GT 4, 46.
90. GT 5, 52.
91. GT 7, 59.
92. GT 7, 59.
93. GT 7, 60.
94. GT 13, 88.
95. GT 14, 92.
96. PW I, 35.
97. GT 15, 97.
98. GT 18, 111.
99. GT 15, 97.
100. GT 18, 112.
101. GT 15, 98.
102. CT I, 191.
103. DS 30–31.
104. DS 30.
105. HL, 112.
106. MA I, paragraph 16, 20.
107. Za II, 198–99.
108. GD 481.
109. GD 486.
110. EH 729.
111. Friedrich Nietzsche, "On Truth and Lie in an Extra-Moral Sense," in *The Portable Nietzsche*, trans. W. Kaufmann (New York: Viking Press, 1954), 46–47.
112. JGB paragraph 14, 211.
113. FW V paragraph 354, 214.
114. GM III, paragraph 12, 555.
115. WWV IV, paragraph 54, 275.
116. Za II, "On Self-Overcoming," 226.
117. JGB paragraph 13, 211.
118. JGB paragraph 36, 238.
119. JGB paragraph 259, 393.
120. FW V, paragraph 349, 208.
121. GM III, paragraph 7, 543.
122. See in particular Martin Heidegger, "The Word of Nietzsche: 'God Is Dead,'" in Martin Heidegger, *The Question Concerning Technology and Other Essays*, trans. William Lovitt (New York: Harper and Row, 1977), 53–112.

123. FW V, 219–20.
124. GD, "The Problem of Socrates," paragraph 2, 474.
125. JGB, paragraph 191, 294.
126. HL, 97.
127. JGB, paragraph 208, 320.
128. HL, 59.
129. JGB, paragraph 4, 201.
130. AC, paragraph 6, 572.
131. JGB, paragraph 259, 393.
132. Za II, 199.
133. Za III, 318.
134. JGB, paragraph 211, 326.
135. See letter to Overbeck of February 23, 1887, SLN 260ff.
136. Za I, "Zarathustra's Prologue," 124.
137. Karl Jaspers, *The Origin and Goal of History*, trans. Michael Bullock (London: Routledge and Keegan Paul, 1953).
138. GD, "'Reason' in Philosophy," paragraph 5, 482–83.
139. Cf. Heidegger, "The Word of Nietzsche: 'God Is Dead.'" For Heidegger, the saying announces the end of all metaphysics, the advent of nihilism.
140. Friedrich Nietzsche, "Notes (1873)," in *The Portable Nietzsche*, trans. W. Kaufmann (New York: Viking Press, 1954), 40.
141. Za I, 171.
142. Za I, 190.
143. Za II, 284.
144. Za III, 307.
145. HL, 111.
146. SE III, 180–81.
147. Za I, 129–30.
148. Za I, 135.
149. Za I, 139.
150. Za I, 156.
151. Za I, 163.
152. Za II, 280.
153. Za II, 281.
154. Za II, 282.
155. Za III, 324.
156. FW IV, 290, 163–64.
157. JGB, paragraph 225, 344.
158. EH 765.
159. SLW 177.
160. EH 714.
161. EH 751.
162. EH 762.
163. EH 764.
164. JGB, paragraph 204, 312.

165. JGB, paragraph 260, 396.
166. GM I, paragraph 11, 476–77.
167. EH 746.
168. EH 686.
169. Za I, 124.
170. Za I, 163.
171. Za II, 280.
172. JGB 307.
173. FW V, 480.
174. FW V, 241.
175. Za II, 213.
176. EH 681.
177. FW V, 242.
178. EH, "Human, All-Too-Human" 2, 740–41.
179. EH, "The Case of Wagner" 2, 777.
180. EH, "Why I Am So Clever" 5, 704.
181. SLW 826.
182. SLW 845.
183. SLW 858.
184. Bermbach, *Richard Wagner in Deutschland. Rezeption—Verfälschungen.*
185. EH, "Why I Am So Clever" 5, 704.
186. WA 7, 626.
187. Paul Bourget, *Essais de psychologie contemporaine* (Paris: A. Lemerre, 1883), 25. The discovery of Nietzsche's use of Bourget was made by Wilhelm Weigand in 1893; see KSA 14, 405.
188. KSA 10, 24 [6], 646.
189. WA, 7, 626–27.
190. WA, preface, 611.
191. WA, 7, 628.
192. SLW 460.
193. SLN 39.
194. KSA 7, 756.
195. KSA 7, 759.
196. KSA 7, 760.
197. WA 8, 628–29.
198. WA 12, 636.
199. SLW 210.
200. SLW 646.
201. CT II, 154.
202. "Opera and Drama," PW II, 95.
203. MA II, "Assorted Opinions and Maxims" 134, 244.
204. WA, epilogue, 646.
205. MA II, "The Wanderer and His Shadow" 217, 366.
206. Immanuel Kant, *The Critique of Judgment*, trans. James Creed Meredith (Oxford: Oxford University Press, 1952), 244, p. 90.

207. WA 6, 623.
208. WA epilogue, 646.
209. WA epilogue, 646.
210. WA epilogue, 648, Nietzsche's note.
211. WA epilogue, 647-48.
212. WA preface, 611.
213. See Nietzsche's letter to H. Köselitz of November 28, 1881, KSB 6, 144.
214. "That I tie up my 'conversion' to Carmen is naturally . . . one more malice on my part." Nietzsche, letter of November 19, 1888, to C. Spitteler, KSB 8, 481. Even less ambiguous is the following passage from Nietzsche's letter of December 27, 1888, to C. Fuchs: "You should not take seriously what I say about Bizet; as I am, Bizet does not come for me at all into consideration. But it has a strong effect as an ironic antithesis against Wagner." KSB 8, 554.
215. WA, 1, 614.
216. WA 5, 622.
217. WA 5, 622.
218. Kant, *The Critique of Judgment*, 244-45, p. 91.
219. Theodor W. Adorno, "On the Fetish-Character in Music and the Regression of Listening," in *Essays on Music*, ed. Richard Leppert (Berkeley and Los Angeles: University of California Press, 2002), 288-317.
220. Walter Benjamin, "The Work of Art in the Age of Mechanical Reproduction," *Illuminations* (New York: Schocken, 1969), 217-51.
221. Adorno, "On the Fetish-Character in Music and the Regression of Listening," 288.
222. Ibid., 314.
223. WA 3, 616.
224. WA 6, 625.
225. EH, "Why I Am So Clever" 10, 714.
226. EH, "Human, All-Too-Human" 5, 744.
227. SLN 188.
228. See the December 25, 1869 entry in Cosima's *Diary*, CT I, 176.
229. BSNW II, 1295, 1317-19.
230. BSNW I, 294.
231. WA 4, 619.
232. WA 4, 620.
233. EH, "Why I Am So Clever" 6, 706.
234. JGB 240, 364.
235. JGB 256, 388.
236. GM III.3, 536.
237. KSA 15, 139.
238. KSA 15, 139-40.
239. KSA 15, 140-41.
240. KSA 15, 187.
241. KSA 15, 190.
242. See the draft of a letter to Brandes from early December 1888 in KSA 15, 193.
243. MA I.45, 37.

244. JGB 260, 394.
245. JGB 260, 397.
246. JGB 46, 251.
247. JGB preface, 193.
248. JGB 202, 306.
249. JGB 195, 298.
250. GM I.6, 469.
251. GM I.16, 488.
252. EH, "Why I Am a Destiny" 9, 791.
253. Cf. GM III.12, 555.
254. WA epilogue, 647.
255. GM III.14, 560.
256. AC 7, 572–73.
257. Cf. M 135, 135; FW 4.338, 191ff.
258. MA I, 50, 38–39.
259. MA I, 95, 50–51.
260. KSA 15, 80.
261. MA II, preface 3, 210–11.
262. Carl Dahlhaus, *Richard Wagner's Music Dramas*, trans. Mary Whittall (Cambridge, England: Cambridge University Press, 1979), 143.
263. Ibid., 143.
264. GM III.27, 597.
265. CT II, 797.
266. WB 3, 206.

WORKS CONSULTED

Abbate, Carolyn. *Unsung Voices: Opera and Musical Narrative in the Nineteenth Century*. Princeton, NJ: Princeton University Press, 1991.
———. "Wagner, 'On Modulation,' and *Tristan*." *Cambridge Opera Journal* 1 (1989): 33–58.
Abbate, Carolyn, and Roger Parker, eds. *Analyzing Opera: Verdi and Wagner*. Berkeley and Los Angeles: University of California Press, 1989.
Adorno, Theodor W. *In Search of Wagner*. Translated by Rodney Livingstone. 2nd ed. London: Verso, 2005.
———. "On the Fetish-Character in Music and the Regression of Listening." In *Essays on Music*, 288–317. Edited by Richard Leppert. Berkeley and Los Angeles: University of California Press, 2002.
———. "Wagner's Relevance Today." In *Essays on Music*, 584–601. Edited by Richard Leppert. Berkeley and Los Angeles: University of California Press, 2002.
———. "Wagner und Bayreuth." In vol. 3 of *Musikalische Schriften*, 210–25. Edited by Rolf Tiedemann and Klaus Schultz. Frankfurt: Suhrkamp, 1984.
———. "What National Socialism Has Done to the Arts." In *Essays on Music*, 373–90. Edited by Richard Leppert. Berkeley and Los Angeles: University of California Press, 2002.
———. "Zur Partitur des 'Parsifal.'" In *Moments musicaux*, 52–57. Frankfurt: Suhrkamp, 1964.
Aly, Götz. *Why the Germans? Why the Jews?: Envy, Race Hatred, and the Prehistory of the Holocaust*. Carlton, Australia: Melbourne University Press, 2014.
Anderson, Benedict. *Imagined Communities: Reflections on the Origin and Spread of Nationalism*. London: Verso, 1983.
Augustine, Saint. *Confessions*. Translated by William Watts. 2 vols. Cambridge, MA: Harvard University Press, 1963.
Badiou, Alain. *Five Lessons on Wagner*. Translated by Susan Spitzer. London: Verso, 2010.

Bailey, Robert. "The Genesis of *Tristan und Isolde* and a Study of Wagner's Sketches and Drafts for the First Act." PhD diss., Princeton University, 1969.

———. "The Structure of the *Ring* and Its Evolution." *19th-Century Music* 1 (1977–78): 48–61.

———. "Wagner's Musical Sketches for *Siegfrieds Tod*." In *Studies in Music History: Essays for Oliver Strunk*, 459–94. Edited by H. S. Powers. Princeton, NJ: Princeton University Press, 1968.

Barber, Richard. *The Holy Grail: Imagination and Belief*. Cambridge, MA: Harvard University Press, 2004.

Baricco, Alessandro. *Il genio in fuga. Due saggi sul teatro musicale di Gioachino Rossini*. Genoa: il melangolo, 1988.

Barnard, F. M., trans. and ed. *J. G. Herder on Social and Political Culture*. Cambridge, England: Cambridge University Press, 1969.

Bartels, Ulrich. *Studien zu Wagners Tristan und Isolde anhand der Kompositionsskizze des zweiten und dritten Aktes*. 3 vols. Cologne: Schewe, 1991.

Barzun, Jacques. *Darwin, Marx, Wagner*. Rev. 2nd ed. Garden City, NY: Doubleday, 1958.

Basevi, Abramo. *The Operas of Giuseppe Verdi*. Translated by Edward Schneider with Stefano Castelvecchi. Chicago and London: University of Chicago Press, 2013.

Baudelaire, Charles. "Richard Wagner and *Tannhäuser* in Paris." In *The Painter of Modern Life and Other Essays*, 111–46. Translated by Jonathan Mayne. London: Phaidon, 1995.

Bauer, Hans-Joachim. *Wagners "Parsifal." Kriterien der Kompositionstechnik*. Munich: Katzbichler, 1977.

Beckett, Lucy. *Richard Wagner: Parsifal*. Cambridge Opera Handbook. Cambridge, England: Cambridge University Press, 1981.

Bekker, Paul. *Richard Wagner: His Life in His Works*. Translated by M. M. Bozmen. New York: Norton, 1931.

Benjamin, Walter. "The Work of Art in the Age of Mechanical Reproduction." In *Illuminations*, 217–51. New York: Schocken, 1969.

Benz, Bernhard. *Zeitstrukturen in Richard Wagners "Ring" Tetralogie*. Frankfurt am Main: Peter Lang, 1994.

Berger, Karol. *Bach's Cycle, Mozart's Arrow: An Essay on the Origins of Musical Modernity*. Berkeley and Los Angeles: University of California Press, 2007.

———. *A Theory of Art*. New York: Oxford University Press, 2000.

Bergfeld, Joachim, ed. *The Diary of Richard Wagner 1865–1882: The Brown Book*. Translated by George Bird. Cambridge, England: Cambridge University Press, 1980.

Berlin, Isaiah. *The Proper Study of Mankind: An Anthology of Essays*. Edited by Henry Hardy and Roger Hausheer. New York: Farrar, Straus and Giroux, 1998.

Bermbach, Udo. *"Blühendes Leid." Politik und Gesellschaft in Richard Wagners Musikdramen*. Stuttgart and Weimar: J. B. Metzler, 2003.

———. *Der Wahn des Gesamtkustwerks. Richard Wagners politisch-ästhetische Utopie*. 2nd ed. Stuttgart and Weimar: J. B. Metzler, 2004.

———. *Houston Stewart Chamberlain. Wagners Schwiegersohn—Hitlers Vordenker*. Stuttgart and Weimar: J. B. Metzler, 2015.

———. *Richard Wagner in Deutschland. Rezeption—Verfälschungen*. Stuttgart and Weimar: J. B. Metzler, 2011.

———. "Wagner und Gobineau. Zur Geschichte eines Missverständnisses." *wagnerspectrum* 9, no. 1 (2013): 243-58.
Bermbach, Udo, and Dieter Borchmeyer, eds. *Richard Wagner—"Der Ring des Nibelungen." Ansichten des Mythos.* Stuttgart and Weimar: J. B. Mezler, 1995.
Berry, Mark. *Treacherous Bonds and Laughing Fire: Politics and Religion in Wagner's Ring.* Aldershot, England: Ashgate, 2006.
Bethencourt, Francisco. *Racisms: From the Crusades to the Twentieth Century.* Princeton, NJ: Princeton University Press, 2013.
Borchmeyer, Dieter. *Drama and the World of Richard Wagner.* Translated by Daphne Ellis. Princeton, NJ: Princeton University Press, 2003.
———. "Liszt und Wagner. Allianz in Goethes und Schillers Spuren." *wagnerspectrum* 7, no. 1 (2011): 69-82.
———. *Richard Wagner: Theory and Theatre.* Translated by Stewart Spencer. Oxford: Clarendon Press, 1991.
———. *Richard Wagner. Werk—Leben—Zeit.* Stuttgart: Reclam, 2013.
———. "'. . . sehnsüchtig blicke ich oft nach dem Land Nirwana . . .' Richard Wagners buddhistisches Christentum." *wagnerspectrum* 3, no. 2 (2007): 15-34.
Borchmeyer, Dieter, Ami Maayani, and Susanne Vill, eds. *Richard Wagner und die Juden.* Stuttgart and Weimar: J. B. Metzler, 2000.
Breig, Werner. "Wagners Begriff der 'dichterisch-musikalischen Periode.'" In *"Schlagen Sie die Kraft der Reflexion nicht zu gering an." Beiträge zu Richard Wagners Denken, Werk und Wirken,* 158-72. Edited by Klaus Döge. Mainz: Schott, 2002.
———. "Zur musikalischen Struktur von Wagners 'Ring des Nibelungen.'" In *In den Trümmern der eignen Welt. Richard Wagners "Der Ring des Nibelungen,"* 39-62. Edited by Udo Bermbach. Berlin: D. Reimer, 1989.
Breig, Werner, and Hartmut Fladt, eds. *Dokumente zur Entstehungsgeschichte des Bühnenfestspiels Der Ring des Nibelungen.* In Richard Wagner. Vol. 29, no. 1, of *Sämtliche Werke.* Edited by Carl Dahlhaus. Mainz: B. Schott's Söhne, 1976.
Brinkmann, Reinhold. "'Drei der Fragen stell' ich mir frei.' Zur Wanderer-Szene im 1. Akt von Wagners 'Siegfried.'" *Jahrbuch des Staatlichen Instituts für Musikforschung Preußischer Kulturbesitz* (1972): 120-62.
———. "'. . . einen Schluß machen!' Über externe Schlüße bei Wagner." In *Festschrift Heinz Becker zum 60. Geburtstag,* 179-90. Edited by Jürgen Schläder and Reinhold Quandt. Laaber: Laaber-Verlag, 1982.
———. "Mythos—Geschichte—Natur: Zeitkonstellationen im 'Ring.'" In *Richard Wagner: von der Oper zum Musikdrama,* 61-77. Edited by S. Kunze. Bern and Munich: Francke, 1978.
———. "Szenische Epik. Marginalien zur Dramenkonzeption im 'Ring des Nibelungen.'" In *Richard Wagner. Werk und Wirkung,* 85-96. Edited by Carl Dahlhaus. Regensburg: G. Bosse, 1971.
Brockmann, Stephen. *Nuremberg: The Imaginary Capital.* Rochester, NY: Camden House, 2006.
Burbidge, Peter, and Richard Sutton, eds. *The Wagner Companion.* Cambridge, England: Cambridge University Press, 1979.
Carnegy, Patrick. *Wagner and the Art of the Theater: The Operas in Stage Performance.* New Haven, CT: Yale University Press, 2006.

Chafe, Eric. *The Tragic and the Ecstatic: The Musical Revolution of Wagner's Tristan und Isolde.* New York: Oxford University Press, 2005.

Cicora, Mary. *"Parsifal" Reception in the "Bayreuther Blätter."* New York: Peter Lang, 1987.

Cohn, Richard. "Hexatonic Poles and the Uncanny in *Parsifal.*" *Opera Quarterly* 22, no. 2 (2006): 230–48.

———. "Uncanny Resemblances: Tonal Signification in the Freudian Age." *Journal of the American Musicological Society* 57 (2004): 285–324.

Csampai, Attila, and Dietmar Holland, eds. *Die Meistersinger von Nürnberg: Texte-Materialien-Kommentare.* Reinbek: Rowohlt, 1981.

———. *Parsifal: Texte-Materialien-Kommentare.* Reinbek: Rowohlt, 1984.

———. *Tristan und Isolde: Texte-Materialien-Kommentare.* Reinbek: Rowohlt, 1983.

Dahlhaus, Carl. *Between Romanticism and Modernism: Four Studies in the Music of the Later Nineteenth Century.* Translated by Mary Whittall and Arnold Whittall. Berkeley and Los Angeles: University of California Press, 1980.

———. "The Dramaturgy of Italian Opera." In *Opera in Theory and Practice, Image and Myth* (*The History of Italian Opera*, vol. 6, part II, "Systems"), 73–150. Edited by Lorenzo Bianconi and Giorgio Pestelli. Chicago: University of Chicago Press, 2003.

———. "Entfremdung und Erinnerung. Zu Wagners *Götterdämmerung.*" In *Kongreßbericht Bayreuth 1981*, 416–20. Edited by C. H. Mahling and S. Wiesmann. Kassel: Bärenreiter, 1984. Reprinted in Carl Dahlhaus. Vol. 7 of *Gesammelte Schriften*, 486–92. Edited by Hermann Danuser. Laaber: Laaber-Verlag, 2004.

———. *Esthetics of Music.* Translated by William Austin. Cambridge, England: Cambridge University Press, 1982.

———. *Gesammelte Schriften.* Edited by Hermann Danuser. 10 vols. Laaber: Laaber-Verlag, 2000–2007.

———. *Nineteenth-Century Music.* Translated by J. Bradford Robinson. Berkeley: University of California Press, 1989.

———. "Richard Wagners 'Bühnenfestspiel.' Revolutionfest und Kunstreligion." In *Das Fest, Poetik und Hermeneutik 14*, 592–609. Edited by Walter Haug and Rainer Warning. Munich: Fink, 1989. Reprinted in Carl Dahlhaus. Vol. 7 of *Gesammelte Schriften*, 544–62. Edited by Hermann Danuser. Laaber: Laaber-Verlag, 2004.

———. *Richard Wagner's Music Dramas.* Translated by Mary Whittall. Cambridge, England: Cambridge University Press, 1979.

———. "Über das 'kontemplative Ensemble.'" In *Opern Studien. Anna Amalie Abert zum 65. Geburtstag*, 189–95. Edited by Klaus Hortschansky. Tutzing: Schneider, 1975. Reprinted in Carl Dahlhaus. Vol. 2 of *Gesammelte Schriften*, 405–11. Edited by Hermann Danuser. Laaber: Laaber-Verlag, 2001.

———. "Über den Schluss der 'Götterdämmerung.'" In *Richard Wagner. Werk und Wirkung*, 97–115. Edited by Dahlhaus. Regensburg: G. Bosse, 1971.

———. "Wagners Begriff der 'dichterisch-musikalischen Periode.'" In *Beiträge zur Geschichte der Musikanschauung im 19. Jahrhundert*, 179–87. Edited by Walter Salmen. Regensburg: G. Bosse, 1965.

———. *Wagners Konzeption des musikalischen Dramas.* Regensburg: G. Bosse, 1971.

———. "What Is a Musical Drama?" *Cambridge Opera Journal* 1 (1989): 95–111.

Danuser, Hermann. "Musical Manifestations of the End in Wagner and Post-Wagnerian *Weltanschauungsmusik.*" *19th-Century Music* 18, no. 1 (1992): 64–82.
———. "Universalität oder Partikularität? Zur Frage 'jüdischer' Charakterzeichnung in Wagners Werk." In *Richard Wagner und die Juden*, 79–100. Edited by Dieter Borchmeyer, Aami Mayaani, and Susanne Vill. Stuttgart and Weimar: J. B. Metzler, 2000.
———. "Verheißung und Erlösung. Zur Dramaturgie des 'Torenspruchs' in *Parsifal.*" *wagnerspectrum* 4, no. 1 (2008): 9–39.
———. *Weltanschauungsmusik*. Schliengen: Edition Argus, 2009.
Danuser, Hermann, and Herfried Münkler, eds. *Deutsche Meister—böse Geister? Nationale Selbstfindung in der Musik*. Schliengen: Edition Argus, 2001.
———. *Zukunftsbilder. Richard Wagners Revolution und ihre Folgen in Kunst und Politik*. Schliengen: Edition Argus, 2002.
Darcy, Warren. "In Search of C Major: Tonal Structure and Formal Design in Act III of *Die Meistersinger.*" In *Richard Wagner for the New Millennium: Essays in Music and Culture*, 111–28. Edited by Matthew Bribitzer-Stull et al. New York: Palgrave, 2007.
———. "The Metaphysics of Annihilation: Wagner, Schopenhauer, and the Ending of the *Ring.*" *Music Theory Spectrum* 16 (1994): 1–40.
———. *Wagner's Das Rheingold*. New York: Oxford University Press, 1993.
Daverio, John. *Nineteenth-Century Music and the German Romantic Ideology*. New York: Oxford University Press, 1993.
Deathridge, John. *Wagner Beyond Good and Evil*. Berkeley and Los Angeles: University of California Press, 2008.
Deathridge, John, Martin Geck, and Egon Voss, eds. *Wagner Werk-Verzeichnis (WWV): Verzeichnis der musikalischen Werke Richard Wagners und ihrer Quellen*. Mainz: Schott, 1986.
Dorschel, Andreas. "Die Idee der 'Einswerdung' in Wagners *Tristan.*" In *Richard Wagner: Tristan und Isolde, Musik-Konzepte* 57–58, pp. 3–45. Edited by Heinz-Klaus Metzger and Rainer Riehn. Munich: Edition Text + Kritik, 1987.
Dreyfus, Laurence. "Hermann Levi's Shame and *Parsifal*'s Guilt: A Critique of Essentialism in Biography and Criticism." *Cambridge Opera Journal* 6 (1994): 125–45.
———. *Wagner and the Erotic Impulse*. Cambridge, MA: Harvard University Press, 2010.
Emslie, Barry. *Richard Wagner and the Centrality of Love*. Woodbridge, England: Boydell, 2010.
Engels, Friedrich. *Ludwig Feuerbach und der Ausgang der klassischen deutschen Philosophie*. Stuttgart: J. H. W. Dietz, 1888.
Fichte, Johann Gottlieb. *Addresses to the German Nation*. Edited by Gregory Moore. Cambridge Texts in the History of Political Thought. Cambridge, England: Cambridge University Press, 2008.
Fischer, Jens Malte. "'Erlösung dem Erlöser.' Richard Wagners letztes Wort." In *Jahrhundertdämmerung. Ansichten eines anderen Fin de sciècle*, 177–89. Vienna: Paul Zsolnay, 2000.
———. *Richard Wagner und seine Wirkung*. Vienna: Zsolnay, 2012.
Fischer, Jens Malte, ed. *Richard Wagners "Das Judentum in der Musik": Eine kritische Dokumentation*. Frankfurt am Main and Leipzig: Insel, 2000.
Foster, Daniel H. *Wagner's "Ring" Cycle and the Greeks*. Cambridge, England: Cambridge University Press, 2010.

Frank, Hans. *Im Angesicht des Galgens*. Munich: Alfred Beck, 1953.
Frank, Manfred. *Mythendämmerung. Richard Wagner im frühromantischen Kontext*. Munich: Wilhelm Fink, 2008.
Friedländer, Saul, and Jörn Rüsen, eds. *Richard Wagner im Dritten Reich. Ein Schloss Elmau-Symposion*. Munich: Verlag C. H. Beck, 2000.
Friedrich, Sven. *Das auratische Kunstwerk. Zur Ästhetik von Richard Wagners Musiktheater-Utopie*. Tübingen: Max Niemeyer, 1996.
———. "Der Gral unter dem Hakenkreuz. Zur Bedeutung und Funktion des Gralssymbols für die NS-Ideolgie." In *"Wer ist der Gral?" Geschichte und Wirkung eines Mythos*, 27–38. Edited by Richard-Wagner-Museum Bayreuth. Munich and Berlin: Deutscher Kunstverlag, 2008.
———. *Richard Wagner. Deutung und Wirkung*. Würzburg: Königshausen and Neumann, 2004.
Geck, Martin. *Richard Wagner: A Life in Music*. Translated by Stewart Spencer. Chicago: University of Chicago Press, 2013.
Geck, Martin, and Egon Voss, eds. *Dokumente zur Entstehung und ersten Aufführung des Bühnenweihfestspiels Parsifal*. In Richard Wagner. Vol. 30 of *Sämtliche Werke*. Mainz: B. Schott's Söhne, 1970.
Gellner, Ernest. *Nations and Nationalisms*. Oxford: Blackwell, 1983.
Gerhard, Anselm. "Konventionen der musikalischen Gestaltung." In *Verdi Handbuch*, 182–97. Edited by Gerhard and Uwe Schweikert. Stuttgart: J. B. Metzler, 2001.
Gibson, Robert R. "Problematic Propaganda: 'Parsifal' as Forbidden Opera." *Wagner* 20, no. 2 (1999): 78–87.
Gilman, Sander L. "Nietzsche, Bizet, and Wagner: Illness, Health, and Race in the Nineteenth Century." *Opera Quarterly* 23 (2007): 247–64.
Glasenapp, Carl Friedrich. *Das Leben Richard Wagners in sechs Büchern*. Leipzig: Breitkopf and Härtel, 1894–1911.
Glass, Frank W. *The Fertilizing Seed*. Ann Arbor, MI: UMI Research Press, 1983.
Golther, Wolfgang, ed. *Richard Wagner an Mathilde Wesendonk: Tagebuchblätter und Briefe 1853–1871*. Berlin: A. Duncker, 1904.
de Goncourt, Edmond and Jules. *Journal, vol. 2: 1858–1860*. Edited by Jean-Louis Cabanés. Paris: Honoré Champion Éditeur, 2008.
Good, Edwin M. "What Did Cristofori Call His Invention?" *Early Music* 33, no. 1 (2005): 95–97.
Gregor-Dellin, Martin. *Richard Wagner: His Life, His Work, His Century*. Translated by J. Maxwell Brownjohn. New York: Harcourt Brace Jovanovich, 1983.
Grey, Thomas S. "Leading Motives and Narrative Threads: Notes on the 'Leitfaden' Metaphor and the Critical Pre-History of the Wagnerian 'Leitmotiv.'" In *Musik als Text*, 352–58. Edited by Hermann Danuser and Tobias Plebuch. Kassel: Bärenreiter, 1998.
———. "Magnificent Obsession: *Tristan und Isolde* as the Object of Musical Analysis." In *Music, Theatre and Politics in Germany 1848 to the Third Reich*, 51–78. Edited by Nikolaus Bacht. Aldershot, England: Ashgate, 2006.
———. "Masters and Their Critics: Wagner, Hanslick, Beckmesser, and *Die Meistersinger*." In *Wagner's Meistersinger: Performance, History, Representation*, 165–89. Edited by Nicholas Vazsonyi. Rochester, NY: University of Rochester Press, 2002.

———. "Wagner's *Die Meistersinger* as National Opera (1868–1945)." In *Music and German National Identity*, 78–104. Edited by Celia Applegate and Pamela Potter. Chicago: University of Chicago Press, 2002.

———. *Wagner's Musical Prose: Texts and Contexts*. Cambridge, England: Cambridge University Press, 1995.

———. "Wagner the Degenerate: Fin-de-Siècle Cultural 'Pathology' and the Anxiety of Modernism." *19th-Century Studies* 16 (2002): 73–92.

———. "'. . . wie ein rother Faden': On the Origins of 'Leitmotif' as Critical Construct and Musical Practice." In *Music Theory in the Age of Romanticism*, 187–210. Edited by Ian Bent. Cambridge, England: Cambridge University Press, 1996.

Grey, Thomas S., ed. *The Cambridge Companion to Wagner*. Cambridge, England: Cambridge University Press, 2008.

Grey, Thomas S., and Kirsten Paige. "The Owl, the Nightingale, and the Jew in the Thorn-Bush: Reconsidering Anti-Semitism in *Die Meistersinger*." *Cambridge Opera Journal* 28, no. 1 (2016): 1–34.

Groos, Arthur. "Constructing Nuremberg: Typological and Proleptic Communities in *Die Meistersinger*." *19th-Century Music* 16 (1992): 18–34.

Groos, Arthur, ed. *Richard Wagner: Tristan und Isolde*. Cambridge Opera Handbook. Cambridge, England: Cambridge University Press, 2011.

Grosse, Helmut, and Norbert Götz, eds. *Die Meistersinger und Richard Wagner. Die Rezeptionsgeschichte einer Oper von 1868 bis heute*. Nuremberg: Das Nationalmuseum, 1981.

Großmann-Vendrey, Susanna. *Bayreuth in der deutschen Presse: Beiträge zur Rezeptionsgeschichte Richard Wagners und seiner Festspiele*. 2 vols. Regensburg: G. Bosse, 1977, 1983.

Gutman, Robert W. *Richard Wagner: The Man, His Mind, and His Music*. London: Secker and Warburg, 1968.

Habermas, Jürgen. *The Philosophical Discourse of Modernity: Twelve Lectures*. Translated by Frederick Lawrence. Cambridge, MA: MIT Press, 1987.

———. *The Structural Transformation of the Public Sphere: An Inquiry into a Category of Bourgeois Society*. Cambridge, MA: MIT Press, 1989.

Hamann, Brigitte. *Winifred Wagner: A Life at the Heart of Hitler's Bayreuth*. London: Granta, 2005.

Hartwich, Wolf-Daniel. "Religion und Kunst beim spätem Wagner. Zum Verhältnis von Ästhetik, Theologie und Anthropologie in den 'Regenerationsschriften.'" *Jahrbuch der deutschen Schiller-Gesellschaft* 40 (1996): 297–323.

Hegel, Georg Wilhelm Friedrich. *Elements of the Philosophy of Right*. Edited by Allen W. Wood. Translated by H. B. Nisbet. Cambridge, England: Cambridge University Press, 1991.

———. *Lectures on the Philosophy of World History. Introduction: Reason in History*. Translated by H. B. Nisbet. Cambridge, England: Cambridge University Press, 1975.

Heidegger, Martin. *Being and Time*. Translated by John Macquarrie and Edward Robinson. New York: Harper and Row, 1962.

———. *Nietzsche*. Translated by David F. Krell. 4 vols. New York: Harper and Row, 1979–86.

———. *The Question Concerning Technology and Other Essays*. Translated by William Lovitt. New York: Harper and Row, 1977.

Hein, Annette. *"Es ist viel Hitler in Wagner." Rassismus und antisemitische Deutschtumsideologie in den "Bayreuther Blättern" (1878–1938)*. Tübingen: M. Niemeyer, 1996.
Henrich, Dieter. "Hölderlin on Judgment and Being: A Study in the History of the Origins of Idealism." In *The Course of Remembrance and Other Essays on Hölderlin*, 71–89. Edited by Eckart Förster. Stanford, CA: Stanford University Press, 1997.
Hobsbawm, Eric J. *Nations and Nationalism since 1780: Programme, Myth, Reality*. Cambridge, England: Cambridge University Press, 1990.
Hoffmann, Ernst Theodor Amadeus. *Musical Writings: Kreisleriana, The Poet and the Composer, Music Criticism*. Edited by David Charlton. Translated by Martyn Clarke. Cambridge, England: Cambridge University Press, 1989.
Hölderlin, Friedrich. *Poems and Fragments*. Translated by Michael Hamburger. Ann Arbor: University of Michigan Press, 1966.
Hollingdale, R. J. *Nietzsche: The Man and his Philosophy*. 2nd ed. Cambridge, England: Cambridge University Press, 1999.
Hollinrake, Roger. *Nietzsche, Wagner, and the Philosophy of Pessimism*. London: George Allen and Unwin, 1982.
Horkheimer, Max, and Theodor W. Adorno. *Dialectic of Enlightenment: Philosophical Fragments*. Translated by Edmund Jephcott. Stanford, CA: Stanford University Press, 2002.
Husserl, Edmund. *Vorlesungen zur Phänomenologie des inneren Zeitbewußtseins*. Edited by Martin Heidegger. Vol. 10 of *Gesammelte Werke*. The Hague: Nijhoff, 1966.
Jacobs, Heiko. *Die Dramaturgische Konstrunktion des Parsifal von Richard Wagner. Von der Architektur der Partitur zur Architektur auf der Bühne*. Frankfurt am Main: Peter Lang, 2002.
Janz, Carl Paul. *Friedrich Nietzsche Biographie*. 3 vols. Munich: Hanser, 1979.
Janz, Tobias. *Klangdramaturgie. Studien zur theatralen Orchesterkomposition in Wagners "Ring des Nibelungen."* Würzburg: Königshausen and Neumann, 2006.
Janz, Tobias, ed. *Wagners Siegfried und die (post-)heroische Moderne*. Würzburg: Königshausen and Neumann, 2011.
Jaspers, Karl. *The Origin and Goal of History*. Translated by Michael Bullock. London: Routledge and Keegan Paul, 1953.
Jeßulat, Ariane. *Erinnerte Musik. Der "Ring des Nibelungen" als musikalisches Gedächtnistheater*. Vol. 8 of *Wagner in der Diskussion*. Würzburg: Königshausen and Neumann, 2013.
Kant, Immanuel. *The Critique of Judgment*. Translated by James Creed Meredith. Oxford: Oxford University Press, 1952.
———. "Idea for a Universal History from a Cosmopolitan Point of View." In *On History*, 11–26. Edited by Lewis White Beck. Indianapolis: Bobbs-Merrill, 1963.
———. "An Old Question Raised Again: Is the Human Race Constantly Progressing?" In *On History*, 137–54. Edited by Lewis White Beck. Indianapolis: Bobbs-Merrill, 1963.
———. "What Is Enlightenment?" In *On History*, 3–10. Edited by Lewis White Beck. Indianapolis: Bobbs-Merrill, 1963.
Karbaum, Michael. *Studien zur Geschichte der Bayreuther Festspiele (1876–1976)*. Regensburg: Bosse, 1976.
Katz, Jacob. *The Darker Side of Genius: Richard Wagner's Anti-Semitism*. Hanover, NH: University Press of New England, 1986.

Kaufmann, Walter. *Nietzsche: Philosopher, Psychologist, Antichrist*. Princeton, NJ: Princeton University Press, 1950.
Kedourie, Elie. *Nationalism*. New York: Praeger, 1960.
Kenny, Anthony. *Philosophy in the Modern World*. Vol. 4 of *A New History of Western Philosophy*. Oxford: Clarendon Press, 2007.
Kerman, Joseph. "Opera as Symphonic Poem." In *Opera as Drama*, 158–77. Rev. ed. Berkeley and Los Angeles: University of California Press, 1988.
———. "*Tristan und Isolde*: The Prelude and the Play." In *Write All These Down: Essays on Music*, 335–49. Berkeley and Los Angeles: University of California Press, 1994.
Kiem, Eckehard, and Ludwig Holtmeier, eds. *Richard Wagner und seine Zeit*. Laaber: Laaber-Verlag, 2003.
Kienzle, Ulrike. "'. . . das freiwillige Leiden der Wahrhaftigkeit.' Zu den philosophischen Hintergründen des Bruchs zwischen Wagner und Nietzsche: Eine Rekonstruktion ihres Dialogs über den Pessimismus Schopenhauers." In *"Der Fall Wagner." Ursprünge und Folgen von Nietzsches Wagner-Kritik*. Edited by Thomas Steiert. Laaber: Laaber, 1991.
———. "*. . . daß wissend würde die Welt!*" *Religion und Philosophie in Richard Wagner Musikdramen*. Vol. 1 of *Wagner in der Diskussion*. Würzburg: Königshausen and Neumann, 2005.
———. *Das Weltüberwindungswerk. Wagners "Parsifal," ein szenisch-musikalisches Gleichnis der Philosophie Schopenhauers*. Laaber: Laaber, 1992.
———. "Tönendes Nirvana. Von der musikalischen Aufhebung der Zeit in Wagners *Tristan* und *Parsifal*." *wagnerspectrum* 3, no. 2 (2007): 35–53.
Kinderman, William. "Die Entstehung der 'Parsifal'-Musik." *Archiv für Musikwissenschaft* 52 (1995): 66–97, 145–65.
———. "Dramatic Recapitulation and Tonal Pairing in Wagner's *Tristan und Isolde* and *Parsifal*." In *The Second Practice of Nineteenth-Century Tonality*, 178–214. Edited by William Kinderman and Harald Krebs. Lincoln: University of Nebraska Press, 1996.
———. "Dramatic Recapitulation in Wagner's *Götterdämmerung*." *19th-Century Music* 4 (1980–81): 101–12.
———. "The Third-Act Prelude of Wagner's *Parsifal*: Genesis, Form, and Dramatic Meaning." *19th-Century Music* 29 (2005): 161–84.
———. *Wagner's Parsifal*. New York: Oxford University Press, 2013.
———. "Wagners *Parsifal* als Kunst und Ideologie." In *Richard Wagner. Persönlichkeit, Werk und Wirkung*, 109–17. Edited by Helmut Loos. Markkleeberg: Sax-Verlag, 2013.
———. "Wagner's *Parsifal*: Musical Form and the Drama of Redemption." *Journal of Musicology* 4 (1985): 431–46.
Kinderman, William, and Katherine R. Syer, eds. *A Companion to Wagner's Parsifal*. Rochester, NY: Camden House, 2005.
Kitcher, Philip, and Richard Schacht. *Finding an Ending: Reflections on Wagner's Ring*. New York: Oxford University Press, 2004.
Klein, Richard, ed. *Narben des Gesamtkunstwerks. Wagners "Ring des Nibelungen."* Munich: Wilhelm Fink, 2001.
Kleinertz, Reiner. "Liszt, Wagner, and Unfolding Form: *Orpheus* and the Genesis of *Tristan und Isolde*." In *Franz Liszt and His World*, 231–54. Edited by Christopher H. Gibbs and Dana Gooley. Princeton, NJ: Princeton University Press, 2006.

———. "Richard Wagners Begriff der 'dichterisch-musikalischen Periode.'" *Die Musikforschung* 67 (2014): 26–47.

———. "'zu ihnen folg' ich dir nicht!' Die Todesverkundingungsszene als Peripetie des *Rings*." In *Richard Wagners Ring des Nibelungen. Musikalische Dramaturgie—Kulturelle Kontextualität—Primär-Rezeption*, 191–212. Edited by Klaus Hortschansky. Schneverdingen: Wagner, 2004.

von Kleist, Heinrich. "Über das Marionettentheater." In vol. 3 of *Sämtliche Werke und Briefe*, 555–63. Edited by Ilse-Marie Barth, Klaus Müller-Salget, Stefan Ormanns, and Hinrich C. Seeba. Frankfurt am Main: Deutscher Klassiker Verlag, 1990.

———. "Von der Überlegung. Eine Paradoxe." In vol. 3 of *Sämtliche Werke und Briefe*, 554–55. Edited by Ilse-Marie Barth, Klaus Müller-Salget, Stefan Ormanns, and Hinrich C. Seeba. Frankfurt am Main: Deutscher Klassiker Verlag, 1990.

Köhler, Joachim. *Wagner's Hitler: The Prophet and His Disciple*. Cambridge, England: Polity, 2000.

Kohn, Hans. *The Idea of Nationalism: A Study in Its Origins and Background*. New York: Macmillan, 1946.

Kołakowski, Leszek. *Main Currents of Marxism: Its Rise, Growth, and Dissolution*. Vol. 1. Oxford: Clarendon Press, 1978.

———. *Religion: If There Is No God . . . On God, the Devil, Sin and Other Worries of the So-Called Philosophy of Religion*. South Bend, IN: St. Augustine's Press, 2001.

Konrad, Ulrich, and Egon Voss, eds. *Der "Komponist" Richard Wagner im Blick der aktuellen Musikwissenschaft*. Wiesbaden: Breitkopf and Härtel, 2003.

Kreuder, Friedemann. "Deutsche Kunst und deutsche Politik. Richard Wagners 'Die Meistersinger von Nürnberg' (1867) in der Zeit einer riskanten Moderne." In *Angst vor der Zerstörung. Der Meister Künste zwischen Archiv und Erneuerung*, 112–24. Edited by Robert Sollich et al. Berlin: Theater der Zeit, 2008.

Kropfinger, Klaus. *Wagner and Beethoven*. Cambridge, England: Cambridge University Press, 1991.

Kröplin, Eckart. *Richard Wagner und der Kommunismus. Studie zu einem verdrängten Thema*. Vol. 9 of *Wagner in der Diskussion*. Würzburg: Königshausen and Neumann, 2013.

Küng, Hans. *Musik und Religion. Mozart—Wagner—Bruckner*. Munich and Zurich: Piper, 2006.

Kunze, Stefan, ed. *Richard Wagner: von der Oper zum Musikdrama*. Bern and Munich: Francke, 1978.

Kurth, Ernst. *Romantische Harmonik und ihre Krise in Wagners "Tristan."* Berlin: M. Hesse, 1920.

Lacoue-Labarthe, Philippe. *Musica Ficta: Figures of Wagner*. Translated by Felicia McCarren. Stanford, CA: Stanford University Press, 1994.

Large, David C., and William Weber, eds. *Wagnerism in European Culture and Politics*. Ithaca, NY: Cornell University Press, 1984.

Leersen, Joep. *National Thought in Europe: A Cultural History*. Amsterdam: Amsterdam University Press, 2006.

Levin, David. "Reading a Staging / Staging a Reading." *Cambridge Opera Journal* 9 (1997): 47–71.

———. "Reading Beckmesser Reading: Antisemitism and Aesthetic Practice in *The Mastersingers of Nuremberg.*" *New German Critique* 69 (1996): 127–46.

———. *Richard Wagner, Fritz Lang, and the Nibelungen: The Dramaturgy of Disavowal.* Princeton, NJ: Princeton University Press, 1998.

Lewin, David. "Amfortas's Prayer to Titurel and the Role of D in *Parsifal*: The Tonal Spaces of the Drama and the Enharmonic C flat/B." *19th-Century Music* 7 (1984): 336–49.

———. "Some Notes on Analyzing Wagner: The *Ring* and *Parsifal.*" *19th-Century Music* 16 (1992): 49–57.

Liebert, Georges. *Nietzsche and Music.* Translated by David Pellauer and Graham Parkes. Chicago: University of Chicago Press, 2004.

Linnenbrügger, Jörg. *Richard Wagners "Die Meistersinger von Nürnberg." Studien und Materialien zur Entstehungsgeschichte des ersten Aufzugs (1861–1866).* 2 vols. Göttingen: Vandenhoeck and Ruprecht, 2001.

Loos, Helmut, ed. *Richard Wagner: Persönlichkeit, Werk und Wirkung.* Markkleeberg: Sax-Verlag, 2013.

Lorenz, Alfred. *Das Geheimnis der Form bei Richard Wagner.* 4 vols. Berlin: M. Hesse, 1924–33.

Love, Frederick R. *Young Nietzsche and the Wagnerian Experience.* Chapel Hill: University of North Carolina Press, 1963.

Lütteken, Laurenz. "'Was noch nie sich traf, danach trachtet mein Sinn.' Mythisches Erzählen und musikalische Wirklichkeit im ersten Akt der 'Walküre.'" *Musiktheorie* 22 (2007): 101–10.

Lütteken, Laurenz, ed. *Wagner Handbuch.* Kassel, Stuttgart, and Weimar: Bärenreiter and Metzler, 2012.

MacFarland, Timothy. "The Humiliation of Beckmesser: 'Der Jude im Dorn' and the Authority of Jacob Grimm in Wagner's *Die Meistersinger von Nürnberg.*" *Oxford German Studies* 41, no. 2 (2012): 197–212.

Magee, Bryan. *Wagner and Philosophy.* London: Allen Lane, 2000.

Magee, Elizabeth. *Richard Wagner and the Nibelungs.* New York: Oxford University Press, 1990.

Mahnkopf, Claus-Steffen, ed. *Richard Wagner. Konstrukteur der Moderne.* Stuttgart: Klett-Cotta, 1999.

Mann, Thomas. *Achtung, Europa! Essays 1933–1938.* Edited by Hermann Kurzke and Stephan Stachorski. Frankfurt am Main: Fischer, 1995.

———. *Pro and contra Wagner.* Translated by Allan Blunden. Chicago: University of Chicago Press, 1985.

Marchand, Suzanne L. *German Orientalism in the Age of Empire: Religion, Race, and Scholarship.* Cambridge, England: Cambridge University Press, 2009.

Marx, Karl and Friedrich Engels. *Manifesto of the Communist Party.* Translated by Samuel Moore. Chicago: Charles H. Kerr, 1910.

Mayer, Hans. *Anmerkungen zu Richard Wagner.* Frankfurt am Main: Suhrkamp, 1966.

McClatchie, Stephen. *Analyzing Wagner's Operas: Alfred Lorenz and German Nationalist Ideology.* Rochester, NY: University of Rochester Press, 1998.

McCreless, Patrick. "Motive and Magic: A Referential Dyad in *Parsifal.*" *Music Analysis* 9 (1990): 227–65.

———. *Wagner's Siegfried: Its Drama, History, and Music.* Ann Arbor, MI: UMI Research Press, 1982.

Metzger, Heinz-Klaus, and Rainer Riehn, eds. *Richard Wagner: Parsifal. Musik-Konzepte 25.* Munich: Edition Text + Kritik, 1982.

———. *Richard Wagner: Wie antisemitisch darf ein Künstler sein? Musik-Konzepte 5.* Munich: Edition Text + Kritik, 1978.

Meyer, Gabriele E., ed. *Texte zum Bühnenfestspiel "Der Ring des Nibelungen" 1 (1848–1853).* In Richard Wagner. Vol 29, II A of *Sämtliche Werke.* Mainz: Schott, 2012.

Meyer, Gabriele E., and Egon Voss, eds. *Dokumente und Texte zu "Tristan und Isolde."* In Richard Wagner. Vol. 27 of *Sämtliche Werke.* Mainz: Schott, 2008.

Millington, Barry. "Nuremberg Trial: Is There Anti-Semitism in *Die Meistersinger?*" *Cambridge Opera Journal* 3 (1991): 247–60.

———. *The Sorcerer of Bayreuth: Richard Wagner, His Work, and His World.* New York: Oxford University Press, 2012.

———. *Wagner.* Rev. ed. Princeton, NJ: Princeton University Press, 1992.

———. "Wagner Washes Whiter." *Musical Times* 137 (December 1996): 5–8.

Minor, Ryan. "Wagner's Last Chorus: Consecrating Space and Spectatorship in *Parsifal.*" *Cambridge Opera Journal* 17 (2005): 1–36.

Mösch, Stephan. *Weihe, Werkstatt, Wirklichkeit. "Parsifal" in Bayreuth 1882–1933.* Kassel, Stuttgart, and Weimar: Bärenreiter and Metzler, 2009.

Mosse, George L. *The Fascist Revolution: Toward a General Theory of Fascism.* New York: Howard Fertig, 1999.

———. *Towards the Final Solution: A History of European Racism.* New York: Howard Fertig, 1978.

Müller, Ulrich, and Oswald Panagl. *Ring und Gral: Texte, Kommentare und Interpretationen zu Richard Wagners "Der Ring des Nibelungen," "Tristan und Isolde," "Die Meistersinger von Nürnberg," und "Parsifal."* Würzburg: Köngshausen and Neumann, 2002.

Müller, Ulrich, and Peter Wapnewski, eds. *The Wagner Companion.* Cambridge, MA: Harvard University Press, 1992.

Namier, Lewis. *1848: The Revolution of the Intellectuals.* Garden City, NY: Doubleday, 1964.

Nattiez, Jean-Jacques. *Wagner Androgyne: A Study in Interpretation.* Princeton, NJ: Princeton University Press, 1990.

Nehamas, Alexander. *Nietzsche: Life as Literature.* Cambridge, MA: Harvard University Press, 1987.

Newcomb, Anthony. "The Birth of Music Out of the Spirit of Drama: An Essay in Wagnerian Formal Analysis." *19th-Century Music* 5 (1981–82): 38–66.

———. "Ritornello Ritornato: A Variety of Wagnerian Refrain Form." In *Analyzing Opera: Verdi and Wagner,* 202–21. Edited by Carolyn Abbate and Roger Parker. Berkeley: University of California Press, 1989.

———. "Those Images That Yet Fresh Images Beget." *Journal of Musicology* 2 (1983): 227–45.

Newman, Ernest. *The Wagner Operas.* New York: Alfred A. Knopf, 1949.

Newman, Ernest H. *The Life of Richard Wagner.* 4 vols. Cambridge, England: Cambridge University Press, 1933–46.

Nietzsche, Friedrich. "On Music and Words." Translated by W. Kaufmann. In Carl Dahlhaus. *Between Romanticism and Modernism. Four Studies in the Music of the Later Nineteenth Century*, 103–19. Berkeley: University of California Press, 1980.
———. "On Truth and Lie in an Extra-Moral Sense." In *The Portable Nietzsche*, 42–47. Translated by W. Kaufmann. New York: Viking Press, 1954.
Nilges, Yvonne. *Richard Wagners Shakespeare*. Würzburg: Königshausen and Neumann, 2007.
Nowak, Adolf. "Wagners *Parsifal* und die Idee der Kunstreligion." In *Richard Wagner: Werk und Wirkung*, 161–75. Edited by Carl Dahlhaus. Regensburg: Bosse, 1971.
Osthoff, Wolfgang. "Richard Wagners Buddha-Projekt 'Die Sieger': Seine ideellen und strukturellen Spuren in 'Ring' und 'Parsifal.'" *Archiv für Musikwissenschaft* 40 (1983): 189–211.
Padover, Saul K., ed. *The Letters of Karl Marx*. Englewood Cliffs, NJ: Prentice-Hall, 1979.
Parker, Roger. "'Insolite forme,' or Basevi's Garden Path." In *Leonora's Last Act: Essays in Verdian Discourse*, 42–60. Princeton, NJ: Princeton University Press, 1997.
Paxton, Robert O. *The Anatomy of Fascism*. New York: Knopf, 2004.
Petersen, Peter. "Die dichterisch-musikalische Periode: Ein verkannter Begriff Richard Wagners." *Hamburger Jahruch für Musikwissenschaft* 2 (1977): 105–24.
Poliakov, Léon. *Le mythe aryen: Essai sur les sources du racisme et des nationalismes*. Brussels: Complexe, 1987.
Porat, Dina. "'Zum Raum wird hier die Zeit.' Richard Wagners Bedutung für die nationalsozialistische Führung." In *Richard Wagner und die Juden*, 207–20. Edited by Dieter Borchmeyer, Ami Maayani, and Susanne Vill. Stuttgart and Weimar: Metzler, 2000.
Powers, Harold S. "'La solita forma' and 'The Uses of Convention.'" *Acta Musicologica* 59 (1987): 65–90.
Rauschning, Hermann. *Hitler Speaks: A Series of Political Conversations with Adolf Hitler on His Real Aims*. London: Thornton Butterworth Ltd., 1939.
Rawitzer, Andreas. *Die Enstehung von Wagners Götterdämmerung. Werkanalytische Untersuchungen anhand der vollständig edierten Kompositionsskizze des Vorspiels, des ersten und des zwieten Aufzugs*. 2 vols. Marburg: Tectum Verlag, 2012.
Reynolds, Christopher A. *Wagner, Schumann, and the Lessons of Beethoven's Ninth*. Berkeley: University of California Press, 2015.
Rose, Paul Lawrence. *Wagner: Race and Revolution*. New Haven, CT, and London: Yale University Press, 1992.
de Rougemont, Denis. *Love in the Western World*. Princeton, NJ: Princeton University Press, 1983.
Salmi, Hannu. *Imagined Germany: Richard Wagner's National Utopia*. New York: P. Lang, 1999.
Sans, Edouard. *Richard Wagner et la pensée Schopenhauerienne*. Paris: Klinksieck, 1969.
Schmidt, Jochen. *Kommentar zu Nietzsches Die geburt der Tragödie*. Vol. 1, no. 1, of *Historischer und kritischer Kommentar zu Friedrich Nietzsches Werken*. Berlin: de Gruyter, 2012.
Schmitt, Carl. *Political Theology: Four Chapters on the Concept of Sovereignty*. Translated by George Schwab. Cambridge, MA: MIT Press, 1985.
Schopenhauer, Arthur. *Der handschriftliche Nachlaß*. Edited by Arthur Hübscher. 5 vols. Frankfurt: W. Kramer, 1966–75.

Schuh, Willi, ed. *Die Briefe Richard Wagners an Judith Gautier.* Erlenbach-Zürich and Leipzig: Rotapfel-Verlag, 1936.

Schüler, Winfried. *Der Bayreuther Kreis von seiner Entstehung bis zum Ausgang der wilhelminischen Ära: Wagnerkult und Kulturreform im Geiste völkischer Weltanschauung.* Münster: Aschendorff, 1971.

Scruton, Roger. *Death-Devoted Heart: Sex and the Sacred in Wagner's Tristan and Isolde.* New York: Oxford University Press, 2004.

———. "A First Shot at *The Ring.*" In *Understanding Music: Philosophy and Interpretation,* 132–62. London and New York: Continuum, 2009.

Shaw, George Bernard. *The Perfect Wagnerite: A Commentary on the Niblung's Ring.* 4th ed. London: Constable, 1923.

Siedentop, Larry. *Inventing the Individual: The Origins of Western Liberalism.* London: Allen Lane, 2013.

Simmel, Georg. *Schopenhauer and Nietzsche.* Translated by Helmut Loiskandle, Deena Weinstein, and Michael Weinstein. Urbana and Chicago: University of Illinois Press, 1997.

Snyder, Timothy. *Bloodlands: Europe Between Hitler and Stalin.* New York: Basic Books, 2010.

Sorgner, Stefan Lorenz, H. James Birx, and Nikolaus Knoepffler, eds. *Wagner und Nietzsche. Kultur—Werk—Wirkung. Ein Handbuch.* Reinbeck bei Hamburg: Rowohlt, 2008.

Spencer, Stewart, and Barry Millington, eds. *Wagner's Ring of the Nibelung: A Companion.* New York: Thames and Hudson, 1993.

Spotts, Frederic. *Bayreuth: A History of the Wagner Festival.* New Haven, CT: Yale University Press, 1994.

———. *Hitler and the Power of Aesthetics.* Woodstock, NY, and New York: Overlook, 2002.

Stein, Jack M. *Richard Wagner and the Synthesis of the Arts.* Detroit: Wayne University, 1960.

Stein, Leon. *The Racial Thinking of Richard Wagner.* New York: Philosophical Library, 1950.

Steinbeck, Wolfram. "Die Idee des Symphonischen bei Richard Wagner: zur Leitmotivtechnik in 'Tristan und Isolde.'" In *Bericht über den internationalen musikwissenschaftlichen Kongress Bayreuth 1981,* 424–36. Edited by Siegrid Wiesman and Christoph Mahling. Kassel: Bärenreiter, 1984.

———. "Zur Formfrage in Wagners *Ring des Nibelungen.*" In *Richard Wagners "Ring des Nibelungen." Musikalische Dramaturgie—Kulturelle Kontextualität—Primär-Rezeption,* 279–97. Edited by Klaus Hortschansky. Schneverdingen: Wagner, 2004.

Stendhal. *De l'amour.* Paris: Garnier, 1959.

Stephan, Rudolf. "Gibt es ein Geheimnis der Form bei Richard Wagner?" In *Das Drama Richard Wagners als musikalisches Kunstwerk,* 9–16. Edited by Carl Dahlhaus. Regensburg: Bosse, 1970.

Stollberg, Arne. "Im Quintenzirkel zur Erlösung. Kunstreligion und 'musikalischer Mystizismus' in Wagners *Die Feen.*" In *Richard Wagner: Persönlichkeit, Werk und Wirkung,* 39–48. Edited by Helmut Loos. Markkleeberg: Sax-Verlag, 2013.

Strobel, Otto, ed. *König Ludwig II. und Richard Wagner. Briefwechsel.* 5 vols. Karlsruhe: G. Braun, 1936–39.

Szondi, Peter. *Theory of Modern Drama: A Critical Edition.* Translated by Michael Hays. Minneapolis: University of Minnesota Press, 1986.

Tanner, Michael. *Nietzsche.* Oxford: Oxford University Press, 1995.
———. *Wagner.* Princeton, NJ: Princeton University Press, 1996.
Thorau, Christian. *Semantisierte Sinnlichkeit. Studien zu Rezeption und Zeichenstruktur der Leitmotivtechnik Richard Wagners.* Stuttgart: Steiner, 2003.
Tietz, John. *Redemption or Annihilation?: Love Versus Power in Wagner's Ring.* New York: Peter Lang, 1999.
Treadwell, James. *Interpreting Wagner.* New Haven, CT: Yale University Press, 2003.
Trippett, David. *Wagner's Melodies: Aesthetics and Materialism in German Musical Identity.* Cambridge, England: Cambridge University Press, 2013.
Vaget, Hans Rudolf. "*Der Jude im Dorn* oder: wie antisemitisch sind *Die Meistersinger von Nürnberg?*" *Deutsche Vierteljahrsschrift für Literaturwissenschaft und Geistesgeschichte* 69 (1995): 271–99.
———. "'Du warst mein Feind von je': The Beckmesser Controversy Revisited." In *Wagner's Meistersinger: Performance, History, Representation,* 190–208. Edited by Nicholas Vazsonyi. Rochester, NY: University of Rochester Press, 2003.
———. "Hitler's Wagner: Musical Discourse as Cultural Space." In *Music and Nazism: Art Under Tyranny, 1933–1945,* 15–31. Edited by Michael H. Kater and Albrecht Riethmüller. Laaber: Laaber Verlag, 2003.
———. "The 'Metapolitics' of *Die Meistersinger*: Wagner's Nuremberg as Imagined Community." In *Searching for Common Ground: Diskurse zur deutschen Identität 1750–1871,* 269–82. Edited by Nicholas Vazsonyi. Cologne and Weimar: Böhlau, 2000.
———. "Sixtus Beckmesser: A 'Jew in the Brambles'?" *Opera Quarterly* 12 (1995): 34–45.
Vazsonyi, Nicholas, ed. *The Cambridge Wagner Encyclopedia.* Cambridge, England: Cambridge University Press, 2013.
———. *Wagner's Meistersinger: Performance, History, Representation.* Rochester, NY: University of Rochester Press, 2003.
Viereck, Peter. *Metapolitics: From the Romantics to Hitler.* New York: Knopf, 1941.
Voss, Egon. "Die 'schwarze und die weiße Flagge.' Zur Entstehung von Wagners 'Tristan.'" *Archiv für Musikwissenschaft* 54 (1997): 210–27.
———. "*Meistersinger* und *Sommernachtstraum.* Eine Miszelle." *wagnerspectrum* 10, no. 2 (2014): 285–93.
———. "Once Again: The Secret of Form in Wagner's Works." Translated by Stewart Spencer. *Wagner* 4 (1983): 66–79.
———. "*Wagner und kein Ende.*" *Betrachtungen und Studien.* Zurich: Atlantis, 1996.
Voss, Egon, ed. *Dokumente und Texte zu "Die Meistersinger von Nürnberg."* In *Richard Wagner.* Vol. 28 of *Sämtliche Werke.* Mainz: Schott, 2013.
Wagner, Richard. *Oper und Drama.* Edited by Klaus Kropfinger. Stuttgart: Philipp Reclam jun., 1984.
Wald, Melanie, and Wolfgang Fuhrmann. *Ahnung und Erinnerung. Die Dramaturgie der Leitmotive bei Richard Wagner.* Kassel and Leipzig: Bärenreiter and Henschel, 2013.
Wapnewski, Peter. *Der traurige Gott: Richard Wagner in seinen Helden.* Rev. ed. Berlin: Berlin Verlag, 2001.
———. *Tristan der Held Richard Wagners.* Rev. ed. Berlin: Berlin Verlag, 2001.
Warrack, John. *Richard Wagner, Die Meistersinger von Nürnberg.* Cambridge Opera Handbook. Cambridge, England: Cambridge University Press, 1994.

Weiner, Marc. *Richard Wagner and the Anti-Semitic Imagination*. Lincoln and London: University of Nebraska Press, 1995.
Wellbery, David E. *Schopenhauers Bedeutung für die modern Literatur*. Munich: Siemens Stiftung, 1998.
Williams, Bernard. *On Opera*. New Haven, CT, and London: Yale University Press, 2006.
Williams, Simon. *Wagner and the Romantic Hero*. New York: Cambridge, 2004.
Winterbourne, Anthony. *A Pagan Spoiled: Sex and Character in Wagner's Parsifal*. Madison, WI: Fairleigh Dickinson University Press, 2003.
Wölfel, Kurt, ed. *Richard Wagner und König Ludwig II. Von Bayern. Briefwechsel*. Stuttgart: Gerd Hatje, 1993.
Wolin, Richard, ed. *The Heidegger Controversy: A Critical Reader*. Cambridge, MA: MIT Press, 1993.
von Wolzogen, Hans. *Thematischer Leitfaden durch die Musik zu Richard Wagners Festspiel "Der Ring des Nibelungen."* Leipzig: E. Schloemp, 1876.
———. *Thematischer Leitfaden durch die Musik zu R. Wagners "Parsifal."* 20th ed. Leipzig: Gebrüder Senf, 1882.
———. *Thematischer Leitfaden durch die Musik zu R. Wagners "Tristan und Isolde."* Leipzig: F. Reinboth, 1880.
Wood, Allen W. *Kant's Ethical Thought*. Cambridge, England: Cambridge University Press, 1999.
Zelinsky, Hartmut. "Die 'Feuerkur' des Richard Wagners oder die 'neue Religion' der 'Erlösung' durch 'Vernichtung.'" In *Richard Wagner: Wie antisemitisch darf ein Künstler sein?, Musik-Konzepte* 5, pp. 79–112. Edited by Heinz-Klaus Metzger and Rainer Riehn. Munich: Edition Text + Kritik, 1978.
———. "Rettung ins Ungenaue. Zu Martin Gregor-Dellins Wagner-Biographie." In *Richard Wagner: Parsifal, Musik-Konzepte* 25, pp. 74–115. Edited by Heinz-Klaus Metzger and Rainer Riehn. Munich: Edition Text + Kritik, 1982.
———. *Richard Wagner: Ein deutsches Thema—Eine Dokumentation zur Wirkungsgeschichte Richard Wagners, 1876–1976*. Frankfurt: Zweitausendeins, 1976.
Žižek, Slavoj, and Mladen Dolar. *Opera's Second Death*. New York and London: Routledge, 2002.
Zuckerman, Eliott. *The First Hundred Years of Tristan*. New York: Columbia University Press, 1964.

INDEX

Abgesang: in *Götterdämmerung*, 141, 154, 159–160; in *Die Meistersinger von Nürnberg*, 247, 248, 249, 257, 271, 279
"About Conducting" (Wagner, 1870), 275
Addresses to the German Nation (Fichte, 1808), 28, 32, 286–87
Adorno, Theodor, xvi, 23, 263, 355, 397; "On the Fetish-Character in Music and the Regression of Listening" (1938), 403; *In Search of Wagner* (1952), 402, 403; "Wagner's Relevance for Today" (1963), 61
Alberich, 63, 98, 114, 118, 141, 334; capitalist economy of, 145, 181, 182; Curse of, 101, 126, 154, 166, 169, 171; in Hagen's Dream, 158–59; history-initiating fall of, 67; Nibelungs and, 70, 74, 122, 184; Rhinedaughters and, 66–67; seen as possible Jewish caricature, 334, 354–55; Tarnhelm as weapon of, 74–75, 156; theft of the Rhine gold, 73, 145; Warning of, 74. *See also* Wotan–Alberich conflict
alienation, 22, 23, 24
American Revolution, 45
Amfortas, 294, 296–98, 300, 305, 309, 484n71; contradictory desires of, 324; fall of, 304, 306, 310; miscegenation and, 353; redemption of, 355; Tristan identified with, 339, 340; war against evil Klingsor, 310
anarchism, xiii, 155, 180, 186, 193
Antichrist, The (Nietzsche, 1888), 406

anti-Semitism, xvi, 33, 347, 348, 356, 359, 486n118; implied by caricatures, 334, 354–55, 395, 491n223; modern racist form of, 349; Nietzsche's opposition to, 368, 374, 392, 393
apocalypse, 17, 177
arias, 51–52, 56, 58
ariosos, 54, 58–59
aristocracy, 33, 63, 174, 178, 182
Aristotle, 50, 398
Art and Revolution (Wagner, 1850), 172–73, 180, 182–83, 188, 379
"Art-Work of the Future, The" (Wagner, 1850), 84
Aryans, 33, 350, 351, 354
atheism, 383
Auden, W. H., 62
Augustine, Saint, 11, 17, 186, 225, 232, 343
automata, music-playing, 6
autonomy, 6, 10, 11, 40, 239; Enlightenment and, 10; failed revolutions of mid-nineteenth century and, 240; history and, 20; human dignity and, 12, 237; invention of, 9; Marx's historical materialism and, 24; moral norms and, 16; radical critiques of, 46; subjective, 7

Bach, Johann Sebastian, 194, 245
Badiou, Alain, 188
Bakunin, Mikhail, xiii, 180, 181, 290, 360
Baricco, Alessandro, 6, 7
Basevi, Abramo, 60
Baudelaire, Charles, 395

518 INDEX

Bayreuth circle and Festival, 33–34, 60, 187, 189, 248, 268, 337, 356; anti-Semitic German nationalism and, 375, 393, 394; as artistic/cultural utopia, 373; Nazi Germany and, 284, 349; Nietzsche and, 364, 365, 366, 367, 369, 372–75, 393; *Parsifal* and, 307–8, 357; reopened festival after World War II, 357
Bayreuther Blätter (newspaper), 345, 357, 368, 372
Bayreuther Programmheften, 358
Beckett, Lucy, 344
Beckett, Samuel, 42
Beckmesser, 248–254, 256, 257, 259, 260, 262, 272, 273; as failed artist, 285; public humiliation of, 278–79; seen as possible Jewish caricature, 284, 334, 354, 355, 491n223; singing contest and, 276, 281; Socratic values and, 378; Walther's poem stolen by, 268, 270, 271
Beethoven (Wagner, 1870), 91, 365, 378
Beethoven, Ludwig van, 61, 194, 396, 465n64; Ninth Symphony, 365; String Quartet in F major, Op. 135, 105
Benjamin, Walter, 289, 403
Berlioz, Hector, 395
Bermbach, Udo, 285, 357, 394
Bernhard, Thomas, 42
Betrachtungen eines Unpolitischen [Reflections of a Nonpolitical Man] (Mann, 1918), 30
Beyond Good and Evil (Nietzsche, 1886), 381, 384, 385, 405, 406
Birth of Tragedy, The (Nietzsche, 1872), 89, 209, 365, 375, 380, 384; Adorno's revision of, 403; on Apollonian-Dionysian opposition, 401; early move toward independence from Schopenhauer, 376–77; rejection of Socratic rationalism, 385
Bismarck, Otto von, 269, 283, 284, 361, 380
Bizet, Georges, 401, 404, 498n214
Borchmeyer, Dieter, 285, 404
Bourget, Paul, 395–96, 399, 497n187
Brahms, Johannes, 399
Brangäne, 195, 196, 206, 207, 208, 215
Breitkopf and Härtel (publisher), 187, 189, 201
Brinkmann, Reinhold, 33
Brockhaus, Clara, 183
Brünnhilde, 63, 77, 99, 113, 114, 118, 135, 362; Apotheosis of, 171, 177; awakening of, 130, 136, 138–39, 144, 168; cabaletta and, 109, 111–12; death of, 140; Feuerbach ending to *Götterdämmerung* and, 174–75; monologue of, 169–173; in *Die Nibelungensage (Mÿthus)*, 173; as revolutionary, 184; Rhinedaughters and, 169, 170, 173; Ride of the Valkyries and, 113; the Ring and, 155–56, 160; Schopenhauer ending to *Götterdämmerung* and, 175, 176; Siegfried's betrothal to Gutrune and, 161–62; Siegfried's union with, 131, 141; world-historical role of, 144, 145
Buddhism, xiv, 176, 343, 410; melded with Christianity, 346, 347, 361, 487n156; negation of the will in, 378; pessimism of, 376
Bülow, Hans von, 360, 363, 365
Burke, Edmund, 185

capitalism, 73, 145, 349, 403
Captive, The (Proust, 1923), 359
Carmen (Bizet opera, 1875), 401, 498n214
Case of Wagner, The (Nietzsche, 1888), 366, 371, 374, 376, 393, 411; critique of Christianity in, 408; on "decadence," 395–97, 400–401; on the *Ring*, 405; on Wagner as actor, 398; on Wagner's opera of redemption, 404
Catholicism, Roman, 11, 30, 306, 487n156
causality, 14, 35, 36
Celestial Mechanics (Laplace, 1799–1825), 9
Chamberlain, Houston Stewart, 33, 344, 375
Chéreau, Patrice, 67
Christianity, xiv, 20, 21, 186, 249, 308, 326, 335; agape, 186, 238, 300, 339–345, 405; drama of redemption, 305, 306; erotic love condemned by, 339; German intellectuals and, 238; Hitler's relation to, 357; human moral responsibility and, 10; independent of churches, 359; Nietzsche's opposition to, 387, 406, 407; pessimism of, 376; race and degeneration of, 349–350, 351; Schopenhauer's philosophy and, 345, 487n156; vegetarianism and, 346
classicism, 29, 400
clavichord, 2
"Communication to My Friends, A" (Wagner, 1851), 184, 287–88
communism, 180, 184, 188, 289
Communist Manifesto (Marx and Engels, 1848), 22, 178–182, 185, 186
community, 19, 20, 21
composition, closed system of, 55, 56, 59, 194
composition, open system of, 55, 56, 59, 60, 80, 194
Cornelius, Peter, 360
Counter-Enlightenment, xiv, 10, 22, 45, 362, 457n49; Herder and, 27; several strands of, 44
Cristofori, Bartolomeo, 2
Critique of Political Economy, A (Marx, 1859), 22

Critiques (Kant), 12, 17; first, 14; second, 14; third, 37, 400
Curse motive, 167

Dahlhaus, Carl, 39, 49, 57, 344; on dialogue in drama, 50–51; "The Dramaturgy of Italian Opera" (1988), 50; on leitmotifs, 224, 327; on *Die Meistersinger von Nürnberg*, 283, 285; on music drama, 53–54, 226; on Nietzsche's view of *Parsifal*, 410, 411; on opera versus drama, 52–53; *Richard Wagners Musikdramen* (1971), 49–50, 58–59; on Wagner's anti-Semitism, 348; on Wagner's early reception of Schopenhauer, 91; *Wagners Konzeption des musikalischen Dramas* (1971), 49; "What Is Musical Drama?" (1989), 50
dance/dancing, 4–5, 6
Da Ponte, Lorenzo, 7
Darwin, Charles, 42–44, 45–46, 232, 339, 380
Day motive, 195, 196
Day–Night opposition: in *Die Meistersinger von Nürnberg*, 245; in *Tristan und Isolde*, 195, 198, 230, 235
Death Lamentation motive, 104
Deathridge, John, 490n219
Debussy, Claude, 3
decadence, 384, 390, 400, 405; aesthetics of, 400–401; of Grecian tragedy, 379; Jewishness associated with, 394; Nietzsche's diagnosis of Wagnerian decadence, 395–97; sensuality as, 324
declamation, 51, 54, 56, 76, 104, 105, 117, 194
Delacroix, Eugène, 395
democracy, 286, 292, 391–92
Derrida, Jacques, 228
"Désordre" (Ligeti, 1985), 3
Deussen, Paul, 407
Deutsche Mythologie (Grimm, 1835), 32
Deutsches Theater (Göttingen), 50
Devrient, Eduard, 181
Dewey, John, 228
dialectic, 18, 22, 23
dialogue, dramatic, 50–51, 52, 54, 56–57
Diary, of Cosima Wagner, 54, 65, 154, 274, 354, 410–11; on Darwin, 43–44; on *Götterdämmerung*, 165, 168, 176, 177; on *Die Meistersinger von Nürnberg*, 260, 261, 283; on national works of art, 188; on Nietzsche, 364–65, 369, 372, 379, 494n61; on *Parsifal*, 263, 296, 312, 337, 338, 340, 345, 399; on relation of Tristan to Parsifal, 344; on *Der Ring des Nibelungen*, 62–63; on *Siegfried*, 136; on *Tristan und Isolde*, 194, 197, 205, 220, 228, 234–35, 472n25; on vivisection, 342; on Wagner and Gobineau, 348; on *Die Walküre*, 114
diatonicism, 324, 484n71
discourse, musical, 55, 217
Discourses (Rousseau, 1750, 1755), 5
Don Giovanni (Mozart opera, 1787), 6, 200
Dostoevsky, Fyodor, 343, 359, 385, 386
dramaturgy, 49–50, 89, 91, 128, 204
"Dramaturgy of Italian Opera, The" (Dahlhaus, 1988), 50
Dresden Amen, 295
Drumont, Édouard, 395

Ecce Homo (Nietzsche, 1888, 1908), 363, 370, 374, 381, 384, 392; on *amor fati*, 389; on German nationalism, 393; on *Parsifal*, 404; on self-formation, 388–89; on Wagner and French romantics, 395
egoism, 180, 185
Elements of the Philosophy of Right (Hegel, 1821), 17
Engels, Friedrich, 22, 178
Enlightenment, xiv, 6–7, 20, 26, 367; challenge to, 22; Kantian, 27; notion of autonomy and, 10; Reason and, 21, 41, 362; religion and, 44; univeralism of, 27
ensembles, 56, 61
Erda (earth goddess), 64, 71, 129–130, 131; Norns as daughters of, 144; Valkyries as daughters of, 100; Warning of, 76
"Erlkonig" (Schubert-Goethe, 1815), 84–85
"Éscalier du diable, L'" (Ligeti, 1985), 3
Essay on the Inequality of the Human Races (Gobineau, 1853–55), 33, 348, 490n219
Essay on the Origin of Languages (Rousseau, 1754–61), 26
Essence of Christianity, The (Feuerbach, 1841), 23
Études (Ligeti, 1985–2001), 3
Eulenberg study scores, xiv
Eumenides, The (Aeschylus, 458 BCE), 187

Fafner, 72–73, 76, 102, 121, 126–27, 147; as dragon, 114, 120; killing of, 125, 127; Nibelung treasure and, 126; Ring guarded by, 101
Faith motive, 299, 300
Fascism, 227, 289, 356
Fate motive, 104–105, 106, 143
Fatherland Association (Dresden), 173, 180, 288
Fergusson, Francis, 235
Festival Theater (Bayreuth), 29

Feuerbach, Ludwig, xiii, 180, 181, 185, 360; erotic love and, 186; Marx influenced by, 23; optimism of, 290
Feustel, Friedrich, 360
Fichte, Johann Gottlieb, xiv, 28–34, 44, 286–87
Fischer, Jens Malte, 356
Fliegende Holländer, Der, xi
Flowermaidens, 327, 329–331, 333, 342
Foundations of the Nineteenth Century, The (Chamberlain, 1899), 33
France, 28, 30
Franco-Prussian war, 183, 394
Frantz, Constantin, 289
freedom, 16–17, 24, 32, 35, 95, 390, 411; "bourgeois," 23, 179, 180, 186; history and, 20; human dignity and, 237; instinct for, 11; love and, 118, 238; moral law and, 14–15; security versus, 29; transcendental, 240–41
French Revolution, 17, 20, 45, 391; feudal society destroyed by, 178; nation born of, 28; popular sovereignty and, 25
Freud, Sigmund, 6, 135, 266
Fricka, 100, 101, 102, 115, 362
Friedländer, Saul, 33–34, 348, 356
Friedrich, Caspar David, 9
Fuchs, Carl, 370, 498n214
Furtwängler, Wilhelm, xv, 284, 356

Gautier, Judith, 259, 263, 331, 360
Gay Science, The (Nietzsche, 1882, 1887), 369, 381, 382, 383–84, 392–93
Geheimreport (Zuckmayer, 1943–44, 2002), 242
"German Art and German Policy" (Wagner, 1867), 274
German language, 31, 283
Germany, 242, 260, 268, 356; failed revolutions of mid-nineteenth century, 188, 240, 359; German Empire (from 1871), 273, 284, 361, 373, 393–94; Germanic tribes, 30–31, 350; postwar liberal democratic, 358; as realm of *Kultur* (cultural nation), 30, 284, 290; as true nation, 31–32
Gersdorff, Carl von, 364, 366, 369, 372, 494n61
Gibichungs, 147, 154, 157, 158, 161, 169; addressed in Brünnhilde's monologue, 170; Feuerbach ending and, 175
Gobineau, Arthur de, 33, 348, 350, 351, 360, 488n183, 490n219
God, 9, 10–12, 27, 29, 34, 40; abolished, 44; human autonomy and, 237; of Judeo-Christian tradition, 362; sovereign authority and, 25; as transcendence, 39

Goethe, Johann Wolfgang von, 28, 29, 373, 397
Goncourt, brothers, 272
Götterdämmerung, 64, 103. See also *Ring des Nibelungen, Der* (*Ring* tetralogy)
Götterdämmerung, Prologue, 140–47; Duet of Brünnhilde and Siegfried, 146; Norns scene, 141–45, 160, 362; Siegfried's Rhine Journey interlude, 147
Götterdämmerung, Act 1, 147–157; Hagen's Watch, 148, 149–153, 157, 159, 160, 362; Oath Duet, 154
Götterdämmerung, Act 2, 157–163; Hagen's Dream, 157–161; Oaths Duet, 157, 162–63; Songs of the Vassals, 157; Trio, 157, 163; Vengeance Alliance complex, 163
Götterdämmerung, Act 3, 163–178, 363; Brünnhilde's monologue, 169–173, 177; Feuerbach ending, 174–75, 176; fiery ending of, 183; Funeral March for Siegfried, 168, 177; narrator's peroration, 172, 177–78; Prelude, 164; Rhinedaughters' Song, 164–65; Schopenhauer ending, 175–76, 405; Siegfried's monologue, 167
gramophone, 1
Greece, ancient, 30, 101, 365, 373, 410
Grey, Thomas, 349, 354, 474n90, 486n118, 491n223
Grimm, Jacob, 32, 33, 187
Grimm, Wilhelm, 187
Groundwork for the Metaphysics of Morals (Kant, 1785), 14–15
Grunsky, Hans, 358
Gunther, 147, 155, 156, 161, 169
Gurnemanz, 294, 297, 299, 300, 304, 307, 328; Flowermaidens and, 330; monologue in *Parsifal*, Act 1, 308–11, 312
Gutman, Robert, 352–53, 354, 357
Gutrune, 154, 161, 163, 166, 168

Habermas, Jürgen, 21
Hagen, 147, 148, 156–57, 162, 167, 355; as Alberich's stand-in, 176; death of, 177; struggle with Gunther for the Ring, 169
Hagen, Friedrich Heinrich von der, 187
Handschin, Jacques, 55
Hanslick, Eduard, 349, 355, 491n223
Hegel, Georg Wilhelm Friedrich, 12, 22, 24, 229, 232, 241, 386, 412, 457n42; on autonomy as rule of reason, 387; "communicative" Reason of, 46; *Elements of the Philosophy of Right* (1821), 17; on historical nature of values, 390; on history, 20–21; Kant critiqued by, 15–16,

17–20; lectures on art, 344–45; *Lectures on the Philosophy of History* (1837), 17–18, 24; *Phenomenology of Spirit* (1807), 17; on property and freedom, 23; on rationality, 21–22; Schopenhauer as academic rival of, 34, 41, 383; on *Sittlichkeit* (uprightness), 257
Hegelianism, left, 100, 175, 177, 181, 290
Heidegger, Martin, 30, 44, 225, 228, 305, 496n139; lectures on art, 344–45; on self and the world, 332–33
Herder, Johann Gottfried von, 25–30, 33
Herheim, Stefan, 285
"Hero-dom and Christendom" (Wagner, 1881), 345, 348, 349, 352, 353, 354
Herwegh, Georg, 41, 360
Himmler, Heinrich, 357
Hinduism (Brahmanism), 346, 347, 376
history, xiv, 24, 34, 45, 390, 490n219; civilization and, 67; destructiveness of, 378; as force beyond reason, 362; Hegel's view of, 20; liberation from burdens of, 63; linear time of, 308; Marx's view of, 24, 44; meaning of, 16; myth as substitution for, xvi; universal history, 16–17
Hitler, Adolf, xvi, 188, 240, 272, 286, 492n231; Bayreuth circle/festival and, 284, 394; "Führer" title from *Lohengrin,* 288; Nuremberg Nazi Party Congress and, 269; on *Parsifal,* 356–57; popular dictatorship of, 289; Wagner seen by, 349
Hoffmann, E.T.A., 6, 39, 348
Hölderlin, Friedrich, 305, 457n42
Holy Roman Empire, 28, 187, 273, 282, 283
Hope motive, 295, 299, 300
Horkheimer, Max, 23
Human, All Too Human (Nietzsche, 1878–80), 367, 372, 374, 380, 399–400, 407
Husserl, Edmund, 225

Ibsen, Henrik, 204
"Idea for a Universal History from a Cosmopolitan Point of View" (Kant, 1784), 16–17
Ideas for the Philosophy of History of Humanity (Herder, 1784–91), 25
individualism, 20, 180, 390
Indo-European languages, 32
In Search of Wagner (Adorno, 1952), 402, 403
Islam, 376
Isolde, 194, 205, 229; death and Transfiguration of, 200–201, 202, 217, 219, 220, 225, 232; *Liebestod* (love-death) and, 198–99, 215; monologue of, 206, 207–208

Jaquet-Droz female organist, 6
Jaspers, Karl, 385
Jesus, 22, 186, 245, 304, 335, 386; Aryan, 352; compassion of, 341; *imitatio Christi,* 306, 307, 334; Schopenhauer's philosophy and, 344
Jesus von Nazareth (planned Wagner opera), 186
"Jewishness in Music" (Wagner, 1850, 1869), 348, 349, 355, 488n181, 492n231
Jews, 30, 39, 307; materialism associated with, 33; "redemption" of, 348; Wandering Jew legend, 334, 486n118
Jones, Sir William, 32
Joukowsky, Paul von, 360
Judaism, 342, 346–47, 376

Kafka, Franz, 193
Kant, Immanuel, 9, 12–17, 35, 41, 232, 240, 241, 377; on autonomy as rule of reason, 387; on the beautiful and the sublime, 402; "categorical imperative," 15, 16, 18; *Critiques,* 12, 14, 17, 37, 400; *Groundwork for the Metaphysics of Morals* (1785), 15; on history, 24; "Idea for a Universal History from a Cosmopolitan Point of View" (1784), 16–17; judgment of beauty, 37–38; Laplace and, 44; Nietzsche's turn against, 392; "transcendental idealism" of, 14; "What Is Enlightenment?" (1784), 12
Karajan, Herbert von, xv
Keats, John, 9
Kerman, Joseph, 234, 235, 237, 291
Kienzle, Ulrike, 487n156
Kierkegaard, Søren, 6, 155
Kietz, Ernst Benedikt, 189, 360
Kleist, Heinrich von, 3–10
Klingsor, 309, 310–11, 334, 355, 484n71; contradictory desires of, 324; enchanted garden of, 293, 310, 311, 318, 327, 329
knowledge, 5, 38, 39, 129, 271, 299, 406; art and, 37; Christian love and, 300; compassion and, 305, 333; of good and evil, 10; Hegel's theory of, 19, 20; instinct versus, 384; Kant on empirical knowledge, 13, 14; limits of, 367; mystical ecstasy as negation of, 202; representation and, 35, 36; self-knowledge, 156; suffering and, 305, 376, 378; universal, 144; will and, 36, 37
"Know Thyself" (Wagner, 1881), 345, 348
Kołakowski, Leszek, 62, 343
Köselitz, Heinrich, 368, 370, 371, 405
Kraft, Zdenko von, 358
Kundry, 300, 304, 311, 315, 340; confrontation with Parsifal, 329; contradictory desires of,

Kundry *(continued)*
324; female animality represented by, 309; Jewishness of, 334, 342, 353, 355, 486n118; kiss of, 329, 332; monologue of, 334–35; as personification of metaphysical will, 355; as racial inferior, 353
Kurwenal, 206, 210, 211–12, 216, 231

labor, division of, 23, 24
language, 50, 54, 309, 398; culture and, 26; ethnicity and, 32; Germanic and Romance, 30; pre-forming logic of, 7; relationship to music, 89, 120
Laplace, Pierre-Simon, 9, 44
Laussot, Jessie, 360
Lectures on the Philosophy of History (Hegel, 1837), 17–18, 24, 457n44
Leersen, Joep, 33
Lehrs, Samuel, 360
leitmotifs, 55, 60, 218, 224, 327, 398; interconnectedness of, 56; as "orchestral melody," 57
Leitmotivtechnik, 54, 57
Lessing, Gotthold Ephraim, 29
Levi, Hermann, 360
liberal democracy, 45, 63
liberalism, xvi, 185, 237, 240, 272
Liebesverbot, Das, 183
Ligeti, György, 3
Liszt, Franz, 99, 176, 227, 347, 360, 398; alliance with Wagner, 373; Cosima Wagner as daughter of, 364; spirit of Counter-Reformation and, 367
Lobe, Johann Christian, 488n182
Lohengrin, xi, 174, 200, 201, 273; Liszt as producer of, 373; musical syntax of, 56; orchestral Prelude to, 340; politics idealized in, 287–89, 291
Lorenz, Alfred, xi, xii, 49, 57, 59, 249
love: animal sexual drive and, 238; Day–Night distinction and, 227; death and, 198–99, 214–15, 222, 228, 239; from eros to agape, 186, 238, 339–345; *fin'amour* courtly conventions, 205, 214; freedom and, 118, 238; free love, 183, 185, 293
Love motive, 294–95, 299
Ludwig II of Bavaria, King, 289, 290, 292, 360, 371–72; Cosima Wagner's letter to, 270–71, 274; *Parsifal* performed for, 296; Richard Wagner's letters to, 307, 312, 333, 340, 394, 398–99
Lueger, Karl, 395
Luther, Martin, 11, 186, 232

Lüttichau, Baron August von, 174
lyrical mode, 194, 195, 197

madness, 7, 260
Magic Flute, The (Mozart, 1791), 307, 356
Maier, Mathilde, 360, 368
Mandeville, Bernard, 185
Mann, Thomas, xvi, 30, 285, 359, 464n41; on Hitler as apolitical artist, 286; speculation on Wagner as Jew, 374
Marke, King, 204–205, 208, 211, 218, 231, 264
Marx, Karl, 23–24, 27, 44, 74, 178; *Communist Manifesto* (1848), 22, 178–182; historical materialism of, 24; "On the Jewish Question" (1844), 180, 349; power of privately owned capital opposed by, 63; Rousseau's influence and, 22, 186, 237; Wagner compared with, 22, 180–81, 182, 184–86; Wagner mocked by, 284
Marxism, 180, 186
mass societies, 34, 392
Measure for Measure (Shakespeare, 1604), 37
Meistersinger von Nürnberg, Die, xi, 8, 64, 157, 174, 187, 189, 205; ambiguity of, xii–xiii, 362; as comedy, 245, 264; examination of love in light of Day, 227; as Feuerbachian erotic utopia, 242; Herderian nationalism and, 28, 29–30; Karajan recording, xv; King David theme, in Prelude, 275; motif of singing contest, 344; Munich premiere of, 371; music used in *Triumph des Willens*, 269; myth of nation and, 279–292; nationalism and, 395; Nazi ideology and, 356; Nietzsche and, 364, 370, 405, 411–12; Prelude, 275–76, 280, 363; social-political optimism and, 361; utopian post-political politics of, xvi; *Wahn* motive, 263, 272, 480n122
Meistersinger von Nürnberg, Die, Act 1, 242–49; Admission Aria, 244; Chorale, 243; closed forms in, 242–46; David's Cabaletta, 243; David's Monologue, 242, 243, 245–46; Ensemble Finale, 243, 250, 279, 280; Ensembles of the Apprentices, 242, 243; Kothner's Arietta, 243, 244, 246; Pogner's Aria, 242, 246, 260–61, 269; Terzetto, 242, 243, 245; Walther's Admission Aria, 242, 243, 247; Walther's Trial Song, 242, 243, 246, 248–49, 250, 251, 279, 280
Meistersinger von Nürnberg, Die, Act 2, 249–257; Beckmesser's Serenade, 249–250, 253, 264, 279, 280; Coda, 250, 254, 280; Ensemble Finale, 249–250, 253, 254, 256, 279, 280; Night

INDEX 523

Music Refrain, 254, 255, 256, 257, 260, 279; Night-Watchman's Cow Horn, 254, 255, 256, 257, 267; Pogner's Arietta, 250, 251; Sachs's [Cobbler] Song, 250, 251, 252, 263; Sachs's [Elder] Monologue, 250, 251, 252, 363; Song of the Apprentices, 250, 251
Meistersinger von Nürnberg, Die, Act 3, Part 1, 257–267; Beckmesser's Arietta, 258; closed forms in, 258, 266–67; David's Little Verse, 258, 261; Eva's Arietta, 258, 263; Prelude, 258, 259, 260, 261; Quintet, 258, 259, 262, 266, 267, 291, 363; Sachs's [Folly] Monologue, 258, 259–261, 272; Sachs's Arietta, 258, 263, 264; Sachs's Baptism Speech, 258, 266, 267; Walther's Dream Song, 258, 259, 262, 263, 264–67, 272, 280
Meistersinger von Nürnberg, Die, Act 3, Part 2, 267–279; Acclamation of Sachs, 258, 273, 277, 278, 280, 281; Beckmesser's Prize Song, 258, 270, 279, 280, 399; closed forms in, 258; Dance of the Apprentices, 258, 268; Marches and Choruses of the Guilds, 258, 268; March of the Mastersingers, 258, 268, 275, 276, 277, 280; Postlude, 272; recapitulation of the Prelude, 275–79; Reformation Hymn, 258, 261, 268, 278; Sachs's Harangue I, 258, 275, 280; Sachs's Harangue II, 258, 272, 274, 277, 280; Walther's Prize Song, 245, 254, 256, 262, 270, 272, 276–79, 280
melody, 51, 56, 127–28; consciousness and, 224–25; endless, 58, 59; open and closed forms of vocal melody, 54
Melot, 210, 213, 214
Mendel, Gregor, 42
Mendelssohn, Felix, 349, 480n122
Meyerbeer, Giacomo, 183, 349, 399
Meysenbug, Malwida von, 360, 366, 370, 371, 373, 406
Millington, Barry, 463n3
Mime, 73, 119, 124, 125, 128, 147, 334; in Hagen's Dream, 158; killing of, 125, 127; monologue of, 72; Nothung and, 120, 121, 122, 124; seen as possible Jewish caricature, 334, 354, 355
Minnesänger, 198, 344
modernism, musical, 396
monism, 230
Monteverdi, Claudio, 233
moral law, 14–15, 35
Morold, 207, 212
Mozart, Wolfgang Amadeus, 2, 7, 194, 263; *Don Giovanni*, 6, 200; *The Magic Flute*, 307, 356; *Le Nozze di Figaro*, 6

Müller, Franz, 175
multiculturalism, 25, 28
music drama, 53–54, 64, 79, 116, 360–61; Beethoven and, 365, 396; large-scale form in, 57; as opera, 61; of *Parsifal*, 335–38; recitative dialogue and, 59; of *Siegfried*, 124; of *Tristan und Isolde*, 220–26; of *Die Walküre*, 92, 98, 99, 103, 113
Musikgeschichte im Überblick (Handschin, 1948), 55
My Life (Wagner, 1865–80), 188, 209, 231, 268, 342
myth, 236, 357, 358, 487n156

Nachlaß (Nietzsche), 374
Namier, Lewis, 181
Nancarrow, Conlon, 3, 4
Napoleon I, 9, 28, 29, 272, 393
Napoleon III (Louis-Napoleon), 272
nation, xiv, 25–34, 45, 390; as family writ large, 29; as force beyond reason, 362; myth of, xiii, 279, 281–292
nationalism, xiv, xvi, 273–74, 283, 286–87; civic, 24; cultural, 32; ethnic, 24; Nazi ideology and, 356; Nietzsche's opposition to, 368, 392, 393; racism and, 33, 34
natural selection, 42–43, 353
nature, 22, 24, 38, 41, 378, 400; alienation from, 181; Christian transcendence of, 340–41, 343; culture in opposition to, 26; Darwin's view of, 42; state of nature, 5; violence against, 310–11; "wild," 310, 311, 318, 327, 339
Nazis/Nazi ideology, xvi, 33, 269, 284, 402; Bayreuth and ex-Nazis, 358; Nietzsche appropriated by, 392; *Parsifal* and, 355, 356–57
Newton, Isaac, 4
Nibelungenlied, 187
Nibelungensage (Mÿthus), Die (Wagner, 1848), 173
Nibelungs, 62, 65, 74, 75, 103; in Hagen's Dream, 158; hammering of, 124; in *Die Nibelungensage (Mÿthus)*, 173; repetitive motive of, 119–120
Nietzsche, Friedrich, xii, 1, 44, 206, 216, 226; on Apollonian-Dionysian opposition, 377–78, 400, 401; on art and truth, 39; correspondence with Cosima Wagner, 262, 366–67, 371, 404, 494n61; on the Counter-Enlightenment, 457n49; on desire for transcendence, 228–29; emancipation from Schopenhauer, 89, 91, 366–67, 375, 380, 383; emancipation from

Nietzsche, Friedrich *(continued)*
Wagner, 89, 366–69, 375, 380; on the exception, 272; on limits of logic, 10; on master morality and slave morality, 401, 407, 408, 409; on *Die Meistersinger von Nürnberg*, 274, 282, 405, 411–12; mental collapse of, 45; Nazi appropriation of, 392; on *Parsifal*, 310, 404, 410–11; post-Enlightenment paradigm and, 45; Schopenhauer's early influence on, 89, 363, 373, 376–78; self-becoming of, 376–393; on *Tristan und Isolde*, 209, 212; on Wagner as miniaturist, xi–xii, 396; on Wagner as possibly Jewish, 374, 394; on Wagner as *reichsdeutsch*, 284, 374, 393–94; Wagner's anticipation of, 138, 140, 233; on Wagner's nationalism, 284. *See also* Wagner–Nietzsche relationship

Nietzsche, Friedrich, works of: *The Antichrist* (1888), 406; *Beyond Good and Evil* (1886), 381, 384, 385, 405; *The Case of Wagner* (1888), 366, 371, 374, 376, 393, 395–97, 398; *The Gay Science* (1882, 1887), 369, 381, 382, 383–84, 392–93; *On the Genealogy of Morals* (1887), 381–82, 383, 408; *Human, All Too Human* (1878–80), 367, 372, 374, 380, 399–400, 407; "On Music and Words" (1871), 377; *Nachlaß*, 374; *Nietzsche contra Wagner* (1888), 376, 406; *Richard Wagner in Bayreuth* (1876), 274, 282, 366, 397, 411; *Thus Spoke Zarathustra* (1883–85), 380, 382, 385, 407; "On Truth and Lie in an Extra-Moral Sense" (1873), 381; *The Twilight of the Idols* (1889), 381, 386; *Untimely Meditations* (1873–76), 380, 384, 386, 387–88. *See also Birth of Tragedy, The; Ecce Homo*

Nietzsche contra Wagner (Nietzsche, 1888), 371, 376, 406

Night motive, 195

nihilism, xiv, 232, 393, 412, 496n139

Notes from the Underground (Dostoevsky, 1864), 385

noumenal, Kantian, 10, 42, 43, 222, 229; freedom and, 35; sexual desire and, 352; transcendental idealism and, 14; will and, 225, 352, 361, 379

Nozze di Figaro, Le (Mozart, 1786), 6

"Old and New Church Music" (Hoffmann, 1814), 348

Ollivier, Blandine, 193

"On Music and Words" (Nietzsche, 1871), 377

"On Reflection" (Kleist, 1810), 4–5

"On the Fetish-Character in Music and the Regression of Listening" (Adorno, 1938), 403

On the Genealogy of Morals (Nietzsche, 1887), 381–82, 383, 408

"On the Jewish Question" (Marx, 1844), 180, 349

"On the Marionette Theater" (Kleist, 1810), 3–6

"On Truth and Lie in an Extra-Moral Sense" (Nietzsche, 1873), 381

opera, 60, 194, 226; dialogue in, 54; drama versus, 52–53; *opera buffa*, 6, 254; opera houses, xi; *opera seria*, 6; *solita forma*, 60–61, 194–95

Opera and Drama (Wagner, 1851), xii, 8, 65, 91, 365, 398

orchestra, operatic, 84, 328

Oresteia (Aeschylus, 458 BCE), 283

Orfeo, L' (Monteverdi, 1607), 233

original sin, 39

Origin of Species, The (Darwin, 1859), 42, 44

Overbeck, Franz, 370, 371, 406

overman, 118, 184, 391, 412

paganism, Greco-Roman, 376, 406

Parsifal, 118, 184, 273, 309; as Christ-like Redeemer, 306, 315, 334; as officiator at Communion, 305; sexual innocence of, 330

Parsifal, xi, xii, 64, 147, 186, 189, 263; anti-Semitism and, 354–56; Bayreuth Festival and, 307–8, 357; Christianity and, 308, 335, 339, 341–42, 344, 357, 362, 410, 487n156; chromaticism and diatonicism in, 324, 484n71; degeneration of community in, 351–52; eros and agape in, 339–345; ethical vision of, xiv, xvi; German national community and, 283; king as artist in, 288, 289; Knappertsbusch recording, xv; music-dramatic form of, 335–38; myth of redemption in, 351–58; Nietzsche and, 370–71, 404, 405–406, 410–11, 412; religion of art and, 344, 487n158; Schopenhauer and, 380; suspicion of hidden racist agenda in, 352–54; Wolzogen's "thematic guidebook" to, 60

Parsifal, Act 1: Amfortas's Monologue, 296–97, 311, 336, 363; Communion sequence, 294–99, 305–306, 336, 482n7; Faith motive, 299; Gurnemanz's Monologue, 308–11, 312, 318, 327, 336, 363; Hope motive, 295; Love motive, 294–95; Prelude, 295, 296, 307, 336, 370; Processional of the Knights, 294, 296, 336; Recessional, 296, 336; Redeemer motive, 298; Redeemer Refrain, 298, 299; Transformation, 308, 336

Parsifal, Act 2, 329–335; Choral Dance, 336; Kundry's Monologue, 334–35, 336; Kundry's Narrative Aria, 330, 332, 336; Parsifal–Kundry

confrontation, 329, 331, 336, 337, 363; Parsifal's Monologue, 333, 336
Parsifal, Act 3: Amfortas's Monologue, 336; Communion sequence, 299–300, *301–303*, 304–306, 336; Faith motive, 299, 300; Good Friday Spell, 314–15, *316–18*, 318, 327, 328, 336, 337–38, 363, 484n63; Gurnemanz's Good Friday sermon, 318, *319–324*, 324, 341; Gurnemanz's Monologue I, 311–12, *313–14*, 314–15; Gurnemanz's Monologue II, 312; Hope motive, 299, 300; Love motive, 299, 300; Parsifal's Epilogue Elegy, 314, *325–26*; Parsifal's Monologue, 304, 312, 336, 363; Parsifal's Prologue, 314, 315, 324; Processional, 299, 305, 336; Transformation, 305, 311, 324, 336
Parsifal poem (Wagner, 1877), 354, 367, 490n219
Paul, Saint, 11, 22, 186, 232
Pelagianism, 11
Phenomenology of Spirit (Hegel, 1807), 17
philology, 32–33, 364
piano, 1–2
Plato, 22, 40, 228, 286, 407
player piano, 2–3, 4, 6
poetic-musical period, 57–58, 461n30
poetics, 50, 55, 57, 265
Poetics (Aristotle), 398
polyphony, 2, 223, 324
Postillon de Longjumeau (Adam, 1836), 359, 401
Praise of Existence motive, 131, 138
Principles of the Philosophy of the Future (Feuerbach, 1843), 23
private sphere, 193, 227
progress, 5, 10, 17, 21, 24
"Prologue to a Reading of the 'Götterdämmerung' before a Select Audience in Berlin" (Wagner, 1873), 59
property, 18, 24; communist view of private property, 179, 180; freedom and, 23; political rights and, 63
Prophète, Le (Meyerbeer, 1849), 183
Protestantism, 20, 28–29, 30, 306, 487n156
Proudhon, Pierre-Joseph, xiii, 174, 180, 360
Proust, Marcel, 42, 238, 359, 401
psychoanalysis, 213
"Public and Popularity" (Wagner, 1878), 368
public sphere, 29, 187
Pusinelli, Anton, 99

Question (Questioning Fate) motive, 105, 109, 143, 144, 170, 171

race, 241, 349–350, 353–54
Racine, Jean, 51
racism, 33, 42, 350, 351, 352–53
Rauschning, Hermann, 357
Reason, 10–22, 24, 27, 34; death of, 386; forces beyond, 362, 390; freedom and essence of, 21; future of humanity and, 241; God as, 12; Hegel's view of, 17–22; inconsequentiality of, 40; instinct and, 384; Kantian view of, 13; perceived insufficiency of, 1; universal history and, 17
recitative dialogue, 51, 52, 54, 56, 194, 203; aria in distinction to, 58; duet and, 54; in *Götterdämmerung*, 147–48, 164; in *Die Meistersinger von Nürnberg*, 254, 256, 261; open system of composition and, 59; in *Parsifal*, 293, 308; in *Das Rheingold*, 66, 68, 78; in *Siegfried*, 119, 121; in *Die Walküre*, 79, 84, 85, 89, 92, 105, 112
record player, 2
Redeemer motive, 298
redemption, 237–38, 239, 240, 304, 305, 306, 326; decadence and, 404; myth of, 345–358
Rée, Paul, 366, 368, 372
Reflections on the Revolution in France (Burke, 1790), 185
regeneration essays, 189, 342, 345, 352; racism and, 349, 351, 354; relationship of music and religion in, 348
religion, 19, 44, 348, 376
"Religion and Art" (Wagner, 1880), 308, 345, 347–48, 350, 404, 490n219
Renaissance, 20, 51
renunciation, 237, 344, 351, 361, 487n156
Republic (Plato), 286
ressentiment, 374, 391, 405
revolution, myth of, xiii, 178–189
"Revolution as a Beautiful Illness" (Kołakowski, 1979), 62
Rheingold, Das, 64, 65–77, *75*, 97–98, 114, 124, 145, 177–78; allegorical natural and divine powers in, 91; ending of, 92, 100, 101; fiery ending of, 183; Interlude, 66, 67, 131; as introduction in *Ring* cycle, 125; Nibelheim (abode of the Nibelungs), 63, 65, 72, 120; plot summary, 69; Prelude, 65, 66, 127; recitative dialogue in, 78; Rheingold Song, 71; Ring motive, 68, 70; Song of the Rhinedaughters, 66, 116; Sword motive, 70, 71; Valhalla motive (scenes 2–4), 67–70, 68, 69, 84, 104. See also *Ring des Nibelungen, Der* (*Ring* tetralogy)

Rhinedaughters, 64, 65, 66–67, 71, 97–98, 114, 120; Brünnhilde and, 169, 170, 173; the Ring and, 155, 160, 165–66, 172, 177; Song in *Götterdämmerung*, 164–65; Song in *Das Rheingold*, 66, 116

Richard Wagner in Bayreuth (Nietzsche, 1876), 274, 282, 366, 397, 411

Richard Wagners Musikdramen (Dahlhaus, 1971), 49–50, 58–59

Richter, Hans, 360

Riefenstahl, Leni, 269

Ring des Nibelungen, Der (*Ring* tetralogy), xi, xiii, 22, 57, 62–64, 130–31, 224; Adorno's view of, 355; anarchist utopia of, 193; as celebration of revolutionary destruction, 187–88; Chéreau-Peduzzi-Boulez interpretation (1976), 357–58; Christian roots of, 186; *Communist Manifesto* compared to, 181–82; compositional technique of, 56; German national community and, 283; German national opera and, 187; musical syntax of, 56; music-dramatic form of, 64; as myth, 78, 287; Nietzsche and, 366; revolutionary optimism of, xiii, xiv, 289, 361, 395; Solti recording, xv; translations of texts, 463n3; Wagner's self-reinvention and, 360; Wolzogen's "thematic guidebook" to, 60. See also *Götterdämmerung; Rheingold, Das; Siegfried; Walküre, Die*

Ritter, Julie, 360

Röckel, August, 174, 175, 180, 343, 360

Rohde, Erwin, 364, 365, 372, 373, 397

Roman Empire, 30

Romanticism, 10, 26, 185, 395; decadence and, 400; Fascist cult of death and, 227

Rorty, Richard, 228

Rosenkavalier, Der (Strauss, 1910), 262

Rossini, Gioachino, 6–9, 254

Rousseau, Jean-Jacques, 5, 9, 12, 20, 118, 120, 232; on autonomy as rule of reason, 387; *Essay on the Origin of Languages* (1754–61), 26; on language, 26; Marx and, 22, 186, 237; on men of nature, 184; nation and, 28; Nietzsche compared with, 386; popular sovereignty concept of, 25; power of privately owned capital opposed by, 63; *The Social Contract* (1762), 25

Royal Saxon Court Opera (Dresden), xi

Rubinstein, Joseph, 360

Saint John's Day (*Johannistag*), 244, 260, 267, 269, 283

Salaquarda, Jörg, 404

Salomé, Lou, 404

"Sandman, The" (Hoffmann, 1816), 6

scena, operatic: in *Siegfried*, 119; in *Die Walküre*, 78, 92, 98

Schiller, Friedrich, 29, 373, 397

Schleinitz, Marie von, 368

Schmeitzner, Ernst, 368

Schmitt, Carl, 272

Schnorr von Carolsfeld, Ludwig, 189

Schoenberg, Arnold, 55

Schöne Müllerin, Die (Schubert, 1823), 8

Schopenhauer, Arthur, xiii, 34–46, 206, 225, 231, 241, 264, 359; Apollonian-Dionysian opposition and, 378; autonomy undermined by, 42; Christianity and, 345, 347; Darwin and, 42–44; on eros and agape, 341; on erotic desire, 225; Hegel as rival of, 34, 41, 383; influence on Nietzsche, 45, 89, 363, 373, 376–78; on life as suffering, 40, 41, 346, 376; on meaninglessness of existence, 383–84; metaphysics of, 42, 242, 261, 339, 351, 367, 376, 377, 380; on mystical ecstasy, 202; Nietzsche's distancing and break from, 366–67; pessimism of, 41, 100, 175, 232, 360–61, 376, 379, 405; on salvation, 345; on *Schadenfreude*, 334; on self-overcoming of the will, 353; on sexual desire, 352; theory of music, 39, 89, 91; on truth, 38–39; on the will to live, 382; *The World as Will and Representation* (1819), 34–35, 345, 410, 487n156

Schott, Franz, 283

Schott *Sämtliche Werke*, xiv

Schubert, Franz, 8–9, 84–85

Schuré, Édouard, 360

science, 379, 380, 384; determinism of, 14; racism and, 33, 42; truth and, 382

Scruton, Roger, 234, 237–240

Semper, Gottfried, 360

sexual desire, 271, 310, 329; as evil necessity, 333; renunciation of, 231, 353; willed suppression of, 335

Seydlitz, Reinhart von, 367

Shakespeare, William, 37, 51

Shaw, George Bernard, 141

Siegfried, 63, 117, 136, 139–140, 240, 273; Aria of, 122, 123, 124; betrothal to Gutrune, 161–62; death of, 147, 162, 163, 167–68, 171; as prototype of the overman, 412; quest to kill Fafner, 122, 124, 126; as revolutionary, 184; Rhinedaughters and, 164–66; Sword as weapon of, 119–121, 124, 130, 139, 141, 156; world-historical role of, 144, 145; Wotan's encounter with, 130–31

Siegfried, 64, 118–19, 121. See also *Ring des Nibelungen, Der* (*Ring* tetralogy)
Siegfried, Act 1, 119–124; Cabaletta, 122, 123, 124; Forging Song, 122, 123, 124; Prelude, 119; Smelting Song, 122, 123
Siegfried, Act 2, 124–28, 148; Forest Murmurs, 127–28; Prelude, 125, 126
Siegfried, Act 3, 129–140, 167; Interlude, 131; Love Duet, 131, *132–34*, 135–36, *137*, 138–140, 144
Siegfrieds Tod (Wagner), 181, 183, 189
Sieglinde, 78, 85, 92, 112, 114, 168, 362; Brünnhilde's Apotheosis and, 171; monologue, 93
Siegmund, 78, 79–80, 115, 168, 362; Cabaletta and, 109, 111–12; pantomime passages and, 84–85, 87, 92; Sword and, 112–13; Valhalla motive and, 105
Slavic peoples, 30
Smith, Adam, 63, 185
Social Contract, The (Rousseau, 1762), 25
socialism, 174, 184
Socrates, 22, 378–79, 386
solita forma, 60–61, 194–95
Solti, Georg, xv
sopranos, 78
"Sorrows and Grandeur of Richard Wagner, The" (Mann, 1933), 464n41
Spencer, Stewart, 463n3
Spinning motive, 143–44
Spinoza, Baruch, 229
Spiritualism, 3
Stendhal, 7–8
Stoecker, Adolf, 395
Stollen: in *Götterdämmerung*, 141, 148; in *Die Meistersinger von Nürnberg*, 247–48, 249, 257, 271, 279
Strauss, Richard, 262
Strobel, Otto, 358
Sulzer, Johann Jakob, 360
Sword motive, 70, 71, 93, 97, 98, 168
symphony, 56, 61, 396, 399
Symposium (Plato), 228
syntax, musical, 56
Szondi, Peter, 50

Tanner, Michael, 234, 344
Tannhäuser, xi, 343, 344, 373, 395
Tatum, Art, 3
Tausig, Carl, 360
tenors, 78
Theorie des modernen Dramas (Szondi, 1956), 50
Thomas Aquinas, 12

Thus Spoke Zarathustra (Nietzsche, 1883–85), 380, 382, 385, 407
"To Die of Laughter" (Baricco, 1988), 6
Tolstoy, Leo, 359
tonality, 55, 400
totalitarianism, xvi, 34
tragedy, 39, 245, 378
transcendence, 6, 155, 226, 229–230; erotic desire and, 228, 229, 231; eternity of, 139; Judeo-Christian God as, 39; nation and, 29; Nietzsche's rejection of, 381, 386; vertical authority of, 7
Tristan: love-death and, 215; meeting with Isolde in Ireland, 213–14; Monologues of, 209–13, 215–17; poisoned potion and, 215; Public Repudiation of Day, 223; Tristan's Delirium, 208, 235
Tristan chord, 202, 223
Tristan und Isolde, xi, xiii, 60, 64, 157, 175, 189; composition of the *Ring* interrupted by, 361; Furtwängler recording, xv; metaphysical radicalism of, 193; as monument of high modernism, 204; music-dramatic form of, 220–26; myth of will and, 226–234; narrative axis of, 203–17; Nietzsche and, 363, 365, 370; nihilism of, 395, 412; orchestral strand of, 217–220; pantomime in, 84, 217; pessimism of, xiv, 362; premiere of, 398; quotation from, in *Die Meistersinger*, 281–82; redemptive solution to erotic torment, 343; as religious drama, 234–241, 291, 344; Schopenhauer and, 380; as tragedy, 236; Wolzogen's "thematic guidebook" to, 60
Tristan und Isolde, Act 1: Avowal of Love, 217, 218, 219, 221, 223, 225; Brangäne's Song, 206, 207, 208; "desire" and "glance" motives, 218, 474n90; Falling in Love, 217, 218, 221, 223, 225; Introduction, 217, 218; Isolde's Monologue, 204, 206–7; Kurwenal's Song, 206; Sailor's Song, 206
Tristan und Isolde, Act 2: Brangäne's Warning, 195, 196, 197, 211; Day motive, 195, 196; interludes, 197; Marke's Monologue, 204, 205, 218, 221; Night motive, 195; Tristan's Answer, 217, 218, 225
Tristan und Isolde, Act 2, Love Duet, 194, 195, 197, 209, 233, 236, 327, 363; as the opera's lyrical axis, 202; *Liebestod*, 199, 201, 202, 235, 340, 472n25; lyrical portion, 196, 197; music-dramatic form of, 221, 225; postlude (Promise Duet), 200, 216, 218; recitative-dialogue interludes, 216

Tristan und Isolde, Act 3: Isolde's Death and Transfiguration, 200–202, 209, 219–221, 225, 236, 327, 363; Tristan's Death, 218, 221, 225; Tristan's Monologues (Tristan's Delirium), 204, 209–10, 212–13, 218–19, 236, 237, 340, 363
Triumph des Willens (Riefenstahl film, 1935), 269
troubadours, 198
truth, 38–39, 229, 345, 381–82, 411
Twilight of the Idols, The (Nietzsche, 1889), 381, 386

Uhlig, Theodor, 183, 184, 189, 360, 389
"Uncanny, The" (Freud, 1919), 6
Untimely Meditations (Nietzsche, 1873–76), 380, 384, 386, 387–88

Vaget, Hans Rudolf, xvi
Valhalla motive, 84, 94, 96, 105
Valkyries: Brünnhilde and, 100, 102, 105, 113–14, 115, 119, 139; Ride of the Valkyries music, 113, 114, 170
Vaucanson, Jacques de, 6
vegetarianism, 341, 346, 349, 351, 352, 359
Vengeance Alliance complex, 163
Verdi, Giuseppe, 60, 61, 263
"Vertige" (Ligeti, 1985), 3
Viereck, Peter, xvi
Vischer, Friedrich Theodor, 187
vocal scores, xv, 363, 370
Volk (people), 25, 29, 32, 269–270; as cultural collectivity, 28; Leader–People symbiosis, 272, 290
Voltaire, 283, 367

Wagenseil, Johann Christoph, 275
Wagner, Cosima von Bülow, 33, 262, 264, 351, 410; letter to Ludwig II of Bavaria, 270–71, 274; marriage to Wagner, 364; Nietzsche's correspondence with, 262, 366–67, 371, 404, 494n61. See also *Diary,* of Cosima Wagner
Wagner, Minna Planer, 360
Wagner, Richard, xii, 1, 73, 237, 286–87, 337; anarchist period, xiii, 186, 360; anticapitalist beliefs of, 181, 182; anti-Semitism of, xvi, 33, 348, 349, 354–56, 374, 394, 486n118; "art of transition," 98; Beethoven and, 91, 105, 396, 465n64; Christianity and, 327, 346–47, 370, 487n156; Darwin and, 43–44, 339; in Dresden/Saxony uprising (1849), xi, 180, 183, 359; Freud anticipated by, 95, 135, 331, 464n41; German Empire and, 394; German national identity and, 274, 283–292; Gobineau and, 348–49, 351, 354, 488n183, 490n219; on *Götterdämmerung,* 175–76; Greek (Attic) tragedy and, 103; Hitler's relation to, 289–290; marriage to Cosima, 364; Marx and, 22, 180–81, 182, 184–86; on *Die Meistersinger von Nürnberg,* 259; operatic dramaturgy of, 49, 51, 53; on *Parsifal,* 331–32, 339–340, 343, 351, 397; political views, 173–74, 189; post-1848 reform of, 56, 59, 78; post-Enlightenment paradigm and, 45; postwar reception of Wagner's oeuvre, 357–58; on Schopenhauer, 91; on suffering of animals, 342–43; in Swiss exile, xi, 41; on *Tristan und Isolde,* 193, 201, 227, 231, 343; vegetarianism advocated by, 341, 346, 349, 351, 352; vivisection opposed by, 341–42; on *Die Walküre,* 99
Wagner, Richard, writings of: "About Conducting" (1870), 275; *Annals,* 183; *Art and Revolution* (1850), 172–73, 180, 182–83, 188, 379; "The Art-Work of the Future" (1850), 84; *Beethoven* (1870), 91, 365, 378; "A Communication to My Friends" (1851), 184, 287–88; "German Art and German Policy" (1867), 274; "Hero-dom and Christendom" (1881), 345, 348, 349, 352, 353, 354; "Jewishness in Music" (1850, 1869), 348, 349, 355, 488n181; "Know Thyself" (1881), 345, 348; *My Life* (1865–80), 188, 209, 231, 268; *Die Nibelungensage (Mÿthus)* (1848), 173; *Opera and Drama* (1851), xii, 8, 65, 91, 365, 398; *Parsifal* poem (1877), 354, 367, 490n219; "Prologue to a Reading of the 'Götterdämmerung' before a Select Audience in Berlin" (1873), 59; "Public and Popularity" (1878), 368; "Religion and Art" (1880), 308, 345, 347–48, 350, 404, 490n219; *Siegfrieds Tod* (1848–52), 181, 183, 189; "What Boots This Knowledge?" (1880), 345; "What Is German?" (1865), 282, 284–85; *Die Wiebelungen* (1849), 490n219. See also regeneration essays; Zurich reform essays
Wagner, Siegfried, 349, 364, 372, 375
Wagner, Wieland, 284, 357, 358, 375
Wagner, Winifred, 349, 375
Wagner, Wolfgang, 357, 375
Wagner–Nietzsche relationship, xiii, xiv, 46, 363; history of, 363–376; Nietzsche's diagnosis of Wagnerian decadence, 395–97
Wagners Konzeption des musikalischen Dramas (Dahlhaus, 1971), 49
"Wagner's Relevance for Today" (Adorno, 1963), 61
Wahn motive, 263, 272, 480n122

Walküre, Die, xiii, 64, 66, 77, 189; human protagonists of, 91, 168; image of flight in, 119. See also *Ring des Nibelungen, Der* (*Ring* tetralogy)

Walküre, Die, Act 1, 78–99, 119, 124, 128, 160, 331; Love Duet, 92–98, 104, 135; pantomime passages, 84–85, *86–87*, 87, *88–89*, *90*, 92; Prelude, 79, 84–85; recitative dialogue, 79, 84, 85, 89, 92; Sieglinde's monologue, 93; Siegmund's monologue, 79–80, *80*, *81–83*, 83–84, 85, 92, 94; Sword motive, 93, 97, 98; Valhalla motive, 84, 94, 96

Walküre, Die, Act 2, 99–113, 136, 147; Cabaletta, 106, *107–9*, 109, *110–11*, 111–12; Death Lamentation motive, 104; Duet of Brünnhilde and Siegmund, 103–106, *104*, 112; Fate motive, 104–105, 106, 143; pantomime passages, 112; Postlude, 100; Prelude, 99, 112; recitative dialogue, 99, 105, 112; Valhalla motive, 105; Wotan's monologue, 102, 103, 129, 130, 142

Walküre, Die, Act 3, 113–18, 120, 138, 170–71; fiery ending of, 183; Postlude, 116; Ride of the Valkyries, 113–14; Wotan's Farewell, 113, 115–17, 139, 362

Wälsungs, 80, 98, 100, 115, 116, 128, 172; Funeral March of Siegfried and, 168; tragedy of, 117; as Wotan's favored race, 122

Weigand, Wilhelm, 497n187

Weissheimer, Wendelin, 474n90

Wesendonck, Mathilde, 60, 209, 231, 339, 342, 343, 360, 397

Wesendonck Lieder, 195

Westernhagen, Curt von, 358

"What Boots This Knowledge?" (Wagner, 1880), 345

"What Is Enlightenment?" (Kant, 1784), 12

"What Is German?" (Wagner, 1865), 282, 284–85

"What Is Musical Drama?" (Dahlhaus, 1989), 50

Wiebelungen, Die (Wagner, 1849), 490n219

will, xiv, 34–44, 45, 231–32; as force beyond reason, 362; of the *Führer*, 393; music and, 91; negation of, 378; rational self-determination of the, 11; Schopenhauer's metaphysics of, 261; self-cancellation of, 351; sexual desire and, 225, 335, 352; as ultimate authority, 390; will to live, 382

Wille, Eliza, 360

will to power, 177, 352, 387; of the artist, 291; Christianity and, 346; future of humanity and, 241; will to live as, 382–85

Winckelmann, Johann Joachim, 101

Winterreise (Schubert, 1827), 8, 9

Woe motive, 148, 154

Wolzogen, Hans von, 60, 357

"Work of Art in the Age of Mechanical Reproduction, The" (Benjamin, 1936), 403

World as Will and Representation, The (Schopenhauer, 1819, 1844), 34–35, 345, 410, 487n156

World History motive, 130

World War, First, 30, 34, 63, 182, 188, 395

Wotan, 62, 63, 73, 92, 99, 114–15, 118, 163; addressed in Brünnhilde's monologue, 170, 171; comparison with Zeus, 101; discouragement of, 101; Farewell of, 113, 115–17, 139; final destiny of the Ring and, 172; "grandiose idea" from ending of *Das Rheingold*, 93, 101; humanity of the future and, 181; in *Die Nibelungensage (Mythus)*, 173; original sin of, 67, 145–46; Spear as weapon of, 75, 117, 130, 131, 141, 145, 165, 167; Sword and, 70, 71, 77, 130; tragedy of, 117–18; as Wanderer, 121, 122, 124, 126; wheel of history and, 129–130

Wotan–Alberich conflict, 64, 100, 102, 112, 125, 138; as hopeless stalemate, 124, 126; Siegfried's murderous acts and, 127

Young Hegelians, 23, 41, 67

"Zauberlehrling, Der" (Ligeti, 1985), 3

Zelinsky, Hartmut, 354

Zimmern, Helen, 407

Žižek, Slavoj, 188

Zuckmayer, Carl, 242

Zurich reform essays, 84, 172, 182, 379

www.ingramcontent.com/pod-product-compliance
Lightning Source LLC
Chambersburg PA
CBHW021413300426
44114CB00010B/482